"In this rapidly changing era, the study of China's relation with the Middle East and North Africa is determined to attract significant attention from scholars, decision makers, and arguably the general public. In reality, comprehensive and good quality research in this field since the 1970s is in extremely short supply. The current edited volume is a much-needed contribution to this deprived field. The editor has done a remarkable job by gathering an impressive group of scholars, with expertise covering subjects from IR to social anthropology, from cultural diplomacy to public policy, and from international political economy to geopolitics. The academic ambition of this volume is also manifested in its astonishingly comprehensive geographic breadth. Papers in this volume have nearly covered all the countries in the MENA region which are involved in the Chinese Belt and Road Initiative. For anyone interested in the growing Chinese entanglement with the MENA region and its implication to the shaping of the future global order, this volume is a must read."

Zhiguang Yin, *Distinguished Professor at the School of International Relations and Public Affairs, Fudan University, China*

"Edited by Yahia H. Zoubir and contributed by noted scholars in the emerging fields, *Routledge Companion to China and the Middle East and North Africa* is an authoritative and handy volume on China's bilateral and multilateral engagement in these important regimes of the world. Strongly recommended."

Suisheng Zhao, *Professor of International Studies, University of Denver and Editor, Journal of Contemporary China, United States*

"This is a book of breathtaking scope and ambition, and it is a rewarding one. It is brimming with insights that cast light not only on the recent past, but also on the future we will all share."

Jon Alterman, *Center for Strategic and International Studies (CSIS), United States*

To my beloved grandchildren Haizam, Tilelli, Amala, and Isaiah, and to the memory of my mother.

ROUTLEDGE COMPANION TO CHINA AND THE MIDDLE EAST AND NORTH AFRICA

Focusing on China's relations with the Middle East and North Africa (MENA), this Companion provides essential analysis of a complex region which threatens to become the battleground for rival powers in the future.

The *Routledge Companion to China and the Middle East and North Africa* brings together China scholars from around the world, including from China, the MENA region, the United States, Asia, and Europe. The contributors, experts in their respective areas—which range from politics, military and nuclear power to economics, energy, and tourism—use different methodologies to understand China's policies in the MENA. Topics analyzed include Chinese investment in infrastructure, the COVID-19 pandemic and the Belt and Road Initiative. Divided into three Parts, the book addresses China's multidimensional presence in the MENA and its impact on the region while also explicating the MENA's relations with its traditional Western allies. Bilateral relations and people-to-people interactions are also explored and provide in-depth context to the areas of cooperation that are part of China's dealings with its partners in the region.

Combining contemporary analysis with accessible prose, the book will be of interest to students, scholars, and policy-makers active in international relations, security studies, and economics, as well to general audiences interested in the MENA region.

Yahia H. Zoubir is Professor of International Studies and Director of Research in Geopolitics at KEDGE Business School, France, as well as Non-Resident Senior Fellow, Middle East Council on Global Affairs (Doha, Qatar). He has published dozens of scholarly works, including books, articles in leading academic journals, entries in encyclopedias, and chapters on international politics, foreign policy, governance, and security issues. He has served as consultant for governments and companies worldwide.

ROUTLEDGE COMPANION TO CHINA AND THE MIDDLE EAST AND NORTH AFRICA

Edited by Yahia H. Zoubir

LONDON AND NEW YORK

Designed cover image: © WANG ZHAO/AFP via Getty Images.

First published 2023
by Routledge
4 Park Square, Milton Park, Abingdon, Oxon OX14 4RN

and by Routledge
605 Third Avenue, New York, NY 10158

Routledge is an imprint of the Taylor & Francis Group, an informa business

© 2023 selection and editorial matter, Yahia H. Zoubir; individual chapters, the contributors

The right of Yahia H. Zoubir to be identified as the author of the editorial material, and of the authors for their individual chapters, has been asserted in accordance with sections 77 and 78 of the Copyright, Designs and Patents Act 1988.

All rights reserved. No part of this book may be reprinted or reproduced or utilised in any form or by any electronic, mechanical, or other means, now known or hereafter invented, including photocopying and recording, or in any information storage or retrieval system, without permission in writing from the publishers.

Trademark notice: Product or corporate names may be trademarks or registered trademarks, and are used only for identification and explanation without intent to infringe.

British Library Cataloguing-in-Publication Data
A catalogue record for this book is available from the British Library

ISBN: 978-0-367-49983-9 (hbk)
ISBN: 978-0-367-49986-0 (pbk)
ISBN: 978-1-003-04840-4 (ebk)

DOI: 10.4324/9781003048404

Typeset in Times New Roman
by Newgen Publishing UK

CONTENTS

List of Figures	*xi*
List of Tables	*xiii*
Notes on Contributors	*xiv*
Acknowledgments	*xxii*

Introduction   1
Yahia H. Zoubir

PART I
China and the MENA   7

1   China and the Middle East: An Overview   9
   Muhamad S. Olimat

2   China's Energy Diplomacy towards the Middle East in the
   BRI Era: Energy Security Versus Geopolitics   25
   Janet Xuanli Liao

3   China's Infrastructure Construction in the Middle East   40
   Chuchu Zhang

4   Market-Driven Industrialization: Production Capacity Cooperation
   Between China and the Middle East Countries   52
   Jiuzhou Duan and Shiyu Hao

5   The Belt and Road Initiative and China's Expanding Ties with
   West Asia and North Africa   64
   Manochehr Dorraj

Contents

6 China as a Geo-Economic and Security Actor in the
   MENA Region   80
   Lisa Watanabe

7 US-China Rivalry in the MENA Region   89
   Zeno Leoni

8 China and US Policy in the Persian Gulf: Is a New Security
   Architecture Evolving?   102
   Lars Erslev Andersen

9 US-China Nuclear Exports Rivalry in the MENA Region   115
   Çiğdem Pekar

10 China and Regional Stability in the Middle East: Economics,
   Engagement, and Great Power Rivalry   125
   Robert Mason

11 The Asian Infrastructure Investment Bank (AIIB) in the
   Middle East   140
   *Muhammad Zulfikar Rakhmat, M. Habib Pashya, and
   Gufron Gozali*

12 China's Maritime Silk Route and the MENA Region   155
   Geoffrey F. Gresh

13 China's Rise and Its Security Presence in the Middle East and
   North Africa   168
   Andrea Ghiselli

14 Building an "Outer Space Silk Road": China's Beidou Navigation
   Satellite System in the Arab World   179
   Degang Sun, Yuyou Zhang, and Luzhou Lin

15 China and the Gulf: Necessary Partners   192
   Karen E. Young

16 China-Maghreb Relations: South-South Cooperation or
   Authoritarian Advancement?   205
   Julia Gurol

17 China and Conflict Management in the Middle East   217
   Guy Burton

Contents

18 The Uyghur Issue in Sino-MENA Relations: The Case of Turkey   228
Thierry Kellner and Vanessa Frangville

19 China's "Health Silk Road" Diplomacy in the MENA   240
Yahia H. Zoubir and Emilie Tran

PART II
Bilateral Relations   **255**

20 The Sino-Algerian Relationship: Strengthening the Comprehensive
Strategic Partnership   257
Siham Matallah

21 China-Egypt Relations: A Model for Comprehensive Strategic
Partnership   273
Bassem Elmaghraby

22 The Sino-Iranian Relationship: Preserving the Status Quo in the
Region?   292
Kambiz Zare

23 China-Israel: Trilateral Dimensions of Bilateral Relations   305
Yitzhak Shichor

24 Unofficial Diplomacy: The Paradox of Israel-Taiwan Relations   317
Yitzhak Shichor

25 Saudi Arabia's Relations with China   333
Sean Foley

26 China and Sudan   360
Daniel Large

27 Railway Cooperation between Türkiye and China within the Belt
and Road Initiative   373
Umut Ergunsü

28 Pragmatic Partners: China-UAE Relations   385
Zhen Yu

PART III
China-MENA People-to-People Interactions   **399**

29 Overseas Chinese in the Middle East and North Africa:
Proposing a Research Agenda   401
Yuting Wang

30 China's Tourism in the Middle East and North Africa:
Trends and Outlook   413
April A. Herlevi

31 Middle Eastern Students in China: Motivations and Implications   426
Roie Yellinek

32 China's Soft Power and Cultural Diplomacy in the MENA   435
Sophie Zinser, Dhahi Li, and Adel Hamaizia

Appendix: China Medical Aid to the MENA States in the
First Months of 2020   *448*
Index   *457*

FIGURES

1.1	China's petroleum and other liquids' production and consumption, 1993–2019	13
1.2	China's crude oil imports by source, 2019	16
1.3	China's natural gas imports by source, 2019	17
2.1	Proportion of Middle East oil in China's total imports, 1996–2020 (%)	27
2.2	China's key oil suppliers from the Middle East, 1996–2021 (mts)	28
3.1	The space- time cube of China's participation in large and medium-sized infrastructure construction projects in the Middle East from 2005 to 2019	43
3.2	The hot spot analysis of China's participation in large and medium-sized infrastructure construction projects in the Middle East from 2005 to 2019	44
15.1	Total Chinese capital investments in the GCC (2003–2020)	195
15.2	Total jobs created by Chinese companies in the GCC (2003–2020)	196
15.3	Jobs created by Chinese companies in the GCC (2003–2020)	196
15.4	Chinese capital investments in the GCC (2003–2020)	197
21.1	Foreign direct investment, net inflows (balance of payments, current US$): Egypt	276
21.2	Foreign direct investment, net inflows (balance of payments, current US$): China	277
21.3	Foreign direct investment, net inflows (balance of payments, current US$): Egypt vs China, 1995–2019	277
21.4	GDP (current US$): Egypt	278
21.5	GDP (current US$): China	278
21.6	GDP (current US$): Egypt vs China, 1995–2019	279
21.7	GDP (current US$): Egypt vs China, 1995–2019	280

21.8	Egyptian imports from China	280
21.9	Egyptian exports to China	281
21.10	Egypt's trade in goods with China, 1995–2020	281
21.11	Top ten Egyptian exports of goods to China in 2020	282
21.12	Top ten Egyptian imports of goods from China in 2020	282
21.13	Bilateral trade between Egypt and China, 1995–2020	283
22.1	The westward direction of the BRI project emanating from China. The proposed economic corridors: in black (Land Silk Road), and in gray (Maritime Silk Road)	295
28.1	China and UAE customs import and export of goods (1997–2011)	387
28.2	China and UAE customs import and export of goods (2012–2019)	388
30.1	North Africa, Chinese tourist arrivals, 1995–2018	417
30.2	Middle East and Gulf States, Chinese tourist arrivals, 1995–2018	418
30.3	Chinese tourist arrivals to Oman, 2007–2015	419
32.1	Do you agree that China contributes positively to the economy of your country?	442
32.2	Which of the following countries would you like your country to have the strongest ties with?	443
32.3	Would you consider sending your child(ren) to a Chinese university for their studies?	444
32.4	Do you agree that Chinese technology has improved significantly over the past decade?	444
32.5	Do you trust Chinese technology (from mobile phones to 5G and critical national infrastructure)?	445

TABLES

1.1	China's growth rates, oil production, oil consumption, net imports, and oil imports from the Middle East, 1993–2019	15
1.2	China-Greater Middle East trade volume, 2001–2019 ($ million)	18
1.3	Confucius Institutes and classrooms in the Greater Middle East	21
2.1	Chinese energy-related investments in Iran, 2004–2021	34
11.1	The Middle East countries that are members of the AIIB	143
11.2	List of AIIB projects in the Middle East	145
14.1	Timeline of cooperation on space systems between China and the Arab states	181
20.1	China-Algeria trade, 1992–2019 ($ million)	261
20.2	Algeria's trade with France, Italy and the USA, 1992–2019 ($ million)	262
20.3	EU-Algeria trade, 2000–2020 ($ million)	263
20.4	Chinese FDI flows to Algeria, 2003–2019 ($ million)	264
20.5	French, Italian, and US FDI flows to Algeria, 2005–2019 ($ million)	265
20.6	Chinese FDI flows to Morocco and Tunisia, 2003–2019 ($ million)	266
22.1	The main products exported from Iran to China in 2020	296
22.2	Sources of China's import of crude petroleum in 2020 (total of $150 billion)	297
22.3	Foreign direct investment, net inflows (% of GDP) in 2020 for Iran standing at 0.6% of GDP	299
26.1	Chinese FDI flows to Sudan, South Sudan and African countries, 2003–2019 (US$ million, unadjusted)	365
29.1	Chinese population in major countries in the MENA region	406
30.1	MENA countries with Approved Destination Status agreements with China	416
30.2	Tourism receipts as a percentage of exports, select MENA countries	420

CONTRIBUTORS

Lars Erslev Andersen is Senior Researcher at the Danish Institute for International Studies (DIIS) and the Center for Modern Middle East Studies at the University of Southern Denmark (SDU). He was Director of the Center for Modern Middle East Studies at SDU and later Research Coordinator for Middle East Studies at DIIS. He has degrees in the History of Ideas and Middle East Studies. His work focuses on the Middle East in international relations and US-China relations in the MENA. He has published in Scandinavia and internationally. His recent book is on the situation in the Arab Middle East after the Arab Springs (in Danish).

Guy Burton is Adjunct Professor at the Brussels School of Governance and a Fellow on the Sectarianism, Proxies and De-sectarianisation Project at Lancaster University, UK. He has previously held research and teaching appointments in Dubai, Malaysia, the Kurdish region of Iraq and Palestine. He is the author of *China and Middle East Conflicts* (2020) and *Rising Powers and the Arab-Israeli Conflict since 1947* (2018).

Manochehr Dorraj received his PhD from the University of Texas at Austin, USA. He has been the recipient of several awards for his research, teaching and mentoring at TCU. He is the author, co-author, editor, or co-editor of seven books and more than 80 refereed articles and book chapters. He has published extensively on Iran-China and China-Middle East relations since 2008. presented his scholarship in national and international symposiums, including those in UCLA, Johns Hopkins, Yale, and Harvard, Beijing University, Fudan University, Shanghai University and Shanghai International Studies University. During 2017–2018 academic year he was a Visiting Scholar at Fudan University Development Institute in Shanghai, China.

Jiuzhou Duan is an Assistant Professor of Political Science at the Institute for International and Area Studies of Tsinghua University, China. His visiting fellowships include the American University in Cairo (2017–2018), and Harvard Kennedy School (2015–2016). He is currently an Adjunct Assistant Professor at Üsküdar University in Istanbul, Turkey. His research is focused on the field of Middle East politics and society in general, with a special concentration on state-society relations, informal and patronage politics, and the political economy of development.

Bassem Elmaghraby is a Lecturer in Political Science at Suez Canal University, Egypt. He holds an MA from Peking University and a PhD from Jilin University. He is the author of more than 15 articles and co-author of three books. His academic interests include international organizations, the Middle East, Peace Studies, theory of IR, and contemporary IR issues. He has received numerous awards, including two "Top Paper" awards for research presented at professional conferences (2017 and 2019); the National Youth Leadership Excellence Award (2017); the Excellent Student Leader Award, 2019–2020; the Outstanding International Student of Chinese Government Scholarship in 2019; and the Outstanding Academic Achievement Award, 2019.

Umut Ergunsü, is a Faculty Member in the School of Economics and Management, Guangxi University of Science and Technology, China, and a Research Fellow, Center for International Political Economy, Peking University, China. He has a multidisciplinary academic background. He received his B.S. in Industrial Engineering from Bilkent University, Turkey and his Master's and PhD degrees from School of International Studies of Peking University, China. His academic interests include industrial economics, international political economy, development economics, Belt and Road Initiative, and Middle Corridor Initiative.

Sean Foley is Professor of Middle East and Islamic History at Middle Tennessee State University, USA. Dr Foley specializes in the contemporary history and politics of the Middle East and the wider Islamic world. and his work focuses on the Middle East, Southeast Asia, and religious and political trends in the broader Islamic world. Previously, he taught at Georgetown University, USA, where he earned an MA in Arab Studies in 2000 and a PhD in History in 2005. He has published widely. He has also held Fulbright Fellowships in Syria, Turkey, and Malaysia. In addition, he has lived and traveled extensively in Saudi Arabia.

Vanessa Frangville is Senior Lecturer and Chair Holder in China Studies at the Université libre de Bruxelles (ULB), Belgium, and Director of EASt, ULB's research centre on East Asia. She is also the Co-director of Routledge's 'Contemporary East Asian Societies' series. Her research deals with discourses on ethnicity and nation-building in modern and contemporary China, with a special focus on cinema and "ethnic minority" film. Her current project looks at cultural and artistic expressions of trauma and nostalgia in the Uyghur diaspora since 2018, with a focus on performative and audio-visual arts.

Andrea Ghiselli is Assistant Professor at the School of International Relations and Public Affairs of Fudan University in Shanghai, PRC. He is also the Head of Research of the TOChina Hub's ChinaMed Project. Professor Ghiselli's research on Chinese foreign policy and Sino-Middle Eastern relations has appeared in peer-reviewed journals, such as the *China Quarterly*, the *Journal of Strategic Studies*, *Armed Forces & Society*, the *Journal of Contemporary China*, *The International Spectator*, and *The RUSI Journal*. He is also the author of the book *Protecting China's Interests Overseas: Securitization and Foreign Policy* (Oxford University Press, 2021).

Gufron Gozali is a recent graduate majoring in International Relations from Universitas Islam Indonesia.

Geoffrey F. Gresh is Professor of International Relations at the College of International Security Affairs (CISA), National Defense University in Washington, D.C. He has served previously as the Department Head of International Security Studies and CISA's Director of the South and Central Asia Security Studies Program. He is the author of *Gulf Security and the U.S. Military*, the editor of *Eurasia's Maritime Rise and Global Security*, and co-editor of *U.S. Foreign Policy in the Middle East*. His most recent book is *To Rule Eurasia's Waves: The New Great Power Competition at Sea* (Yale University Press, 2020). He received a PhD in International Relations and MALD from the Fletcher School of Law and Diplomacy at Tufts University, USA.

Julia Gurol is a postdoctoral researcher and Lecturer at the Chair for International Relations at Freiburg University, Germany, and an Associate Researcher at the Center for Applied Research in Partnership with the Orient (CARPO). She obtained her PhD from Freiburg University. Her research interests are China's international relations and international political economy, transregional authoritarian power, infrastructure, and connectivity, with a regional focus on the Global South. Her articles have been published in the *Journal of Common Market Studies*, the *Chinese Journal of Middle Eastern and Islamic Studies*, and the *Journal of Contemporary China*. Her monograph, *The EU-China Security Paradox: Cooperation Against All Odds?* appeared in 2022 (Bristol University Press).

Adel Hamaizia is currently a visiting fellow at the Center for Middle Eastern Studies, Harvard University. He is also a researcher at the University of Oxford where he focuses on the political economy of Algeria and the broader Maghreb, and where he previously taught Middle East Politics. Adel is the Managing Director at Highbridge Advisory, a strategic boutique advisory focused on information advantage, risk mitigation, policy development and implementation for companies and governments working in the Middle East, the Balkans, and Africa (MEBA). He is also an associate at Global Partners Governance, and an associate fellow at the Chatham House MENA programme.

Shiyu Hao is Lecturer at the Institute for China-Arab Studies, Ningxia University, China. Her main research interests are in the culture of Arab society and China-Arab relations, primarily focusing on the Coptic issue and Egyptian Studies. She received a Master's degree from Loughborough University, UK, and a PhD from Ningxia University. In 2016, she was a Visiting Fellow at Peking University and in 2017 she conducted field research in Egypt. In recent years, her publications have included 'Copts in Abdel Fatah-Sisi's Egypt: Policy and Its Challenges' and 'Egypt's Africa Policy since the Presidency of Sisi', published in top Chinese academic journals.

April A. Herlevi currently serves as Senior Research Scientist at the Center for Naval Analyses (CNA), a nonprofit research organization, based in Arlington, Virginia, USA, and is a Nonresident Fellow for the National Bureau of Asian Research (NBR). Dr. Herlevi is an expert on China's foreign policy, economic statecraft, and the increasing role of China's commercial, economic, and military actors globally. She earned a PhD in international relations and comparative politics from the University of Virginia, a Master of Public Policy from George Mason University, and a Bachelor of Arts in political science and economics from North Carolina State University. She studied Mandarin at Tsinghua University (Beijing) and the Zhejiang University of Technology (Hangzhou). Dr. Herlevi has recently published on China's Maritime Silk Road, the People's Liberation Army's (PLA) views on Oceania, and the artificial intelligence ecosystem in the People's Republic of China.

Thierry Kellner is Lecturer in the Department of Political Science at the Université libre de Bruxelles (ULB), Belgium, where he teaches Chinese foreign policy. He is associated with several ULB research centres (REPI, EASt, OMAM, CECID, IEE) and the Group for Research and Information on Peace and Security (GRIP, Brussels). He has a PhD in International Relations from the Graduate Institute of International Studies in Geneva. He has published numerous books, chapters in edited books, research reports, and review articles on Chinese foreign policy, Xinjiang/East Turkestan, energy issues, Iran's Asian policy and Central Asia.

Daniel Large is an Associate Professor at Central European University, Vienna, Austria, and a Fellow of the Rift Valley Institute, with whom he served as founding director of the digital Sudan Open Archive (www.sudanarchive.net) from 2005. He co-edited, with Luke Patey, *Sudan Looks East: China, India and the Politics of Asian Alternatives* (James Currey, 2011) and, with Chris Alden, *New Directions in Africa-China Studies* (Routledge, 2019). His most recent book is *China and Africa: The New Era* (Polity, 2021).

Zeno Leoni is Lecturer in War Studies at the Defence Studies Department of King's College London, in the Defence Academy of the United Kingdom. He is affiliated to the Lau China Institute of King's College London, where he is co-convener of the policy brief series *China in the World*. Since the academic year 2020/2021, he has been a Visiting Scholar at Nebrija University, in Madrid. In 2021, he published a monograph, *American Grand Strategy from Obama to Trump: Imperialism After Bush and China's Hegemonic Challenge* (Palgrave Macmillan). Dr. Leoni has acted as a consultant for the Italian and British governments, and he is the Executive Director of the International Team for the Study of Security, Verona.

Dhahi Li The pen name of a scholar based in China.

Janet Xuanli Liao is Reader in Energy and Climate Diplomacy and PhD Lead at the Centre for Energy, Petroleum and Mineral Law and Policy (CEPMLP), within the Division of Energy, Environment and Society, School of Humanity, Social Sciences and Law, University of Dundee, UK. She holds a PhD in International Relations from the University of Hong Kong, an MA in International Relations from the International University of Japan, and a BA and an MA in History from Peking University, China. Her research interests include Chinese think tanks and China's foreign policy-making, Sino-Japanese political/energy relations, China's energy diplomacy and the "Belt and Road Initiative". She has published widely on these subjects and is an Editorial Board Member for the Routledge Series on Belt and Road Initiative.

Luzhou Lin is a post-doctoral research fellow at the College of Economics, Peking University, Beijing, China. His research interest focuses on China's Beidou Navigation Satellite System and China's international cooperation in telecommunications.

Robert Mason is a Non-Resident Fellow at the Arab Gulf States Institute in Washington, DC, and a Fellow with the Sectarianism, Proxies and De-sectarianisation project at Lancaster University, UK. Previously, he was an Associate Professor and Director of the Middle East Studies Center at the American University in Cairo. He was also a visiting scholar in the Department of Near Eastern Studies at Princeton University, a Visiting Research Fellow at the University of Oxford, and a Visiting Research Fellow at the King Faisal Center for Research and Islamic Studies in Riyadh. He specializes in Gulf politics and the international relations of the Middle East.

Siham Matallah is Associate Professor of Economics at the University of Oran 2 in Algeria. She received her MA and PhD in economics from the University of Tlemcen in 2013, and 2017 respectively. Her main research interests are institutional economics, development economics, macroeconomics, and theoretical and applied econometrics. She has authored many peer-reviewed articles and has participated in several international conferences and workshops organized by ERF, ESCWA, GDN, Doha Institute for Graduate Studies, Chatham House and The Hillary Clinton Center for Women's Empowerment. She won the Global Development Network (GDN) Essay Competition in 2015.

Muhamad S. Olimat is Professor of International Relations and Middle East Politics at the Emirates Diplomatic Academy. His areas of expertise include Middle East Studies, the US foreign policy toward the Middle East and North Africa (MENA) and Sino-Greater Middle Eastern relations. He is the author of five books, several book chapters, and articles on Middle East politics, the political economy of the Middle East, political development of the Middle East and Sino-Middle Eastern and Sino-Central Asian relations.

M. Habib Pashya is a recent graduate majoring in International Relations from Universitas Islam Indonesia. He has been involved in various research projects and is a researcher at the Center of Indonesia-China Studies (CICS), the first student-run Indonesian think tank. Habib has also been a research assistant at several institutions, including Universitas Gadjah Mada, Universitas Islam Indonesia, and the Center for Economics and Law Studies (CELIOS).

Çiğdem Pekar is Assistant Professor at Çanakkale Onsekiz Mart University, Faculty of Political Science, Department of International Relations, Turkey. Çiğdem Pekar holds an MA degree on European Studies from the University of Exeter, UK, and a PhD from Çanakkale Onsekiz Mart University, Turkey. Her research includes nuclear non-proliferation regimes, Turkey's nuclear and renewable energy policies and nuclear history. She is a member of the International Young/Student Pugwash Group, Women in International Security (WIIS), Women in Nuclear (WIN) and the International Nuclear Law Association (INLA). She serves as the Institution Representative for the IAEA International Nuclear Security Education Network (INSEN).

Muhammad Zulfikar Rakhmat is a Research Professor at Busan University of Foreign Studies, South Korea. His research focuses on the political economy of international cooperation in the context of China-Indonesia-Middle East relations. He holds a BA in International Affairs from Qatar University, an MA in International Politics, and a PhD in Politics from the University of Manchester, UK. Zulfikar is also affiliated with the

London School of Economics and Political Science and the Middle East Institute at the National University of Singapore. In addition, he has been a visiting professor at various universities in Indonesia.

Yitzhak Shichor is Professor Emeritus of Political Science and Asian Studies at the University of Haifa, and Chair Professor Emeritus, the Hebrew University of Jerusalem. He received his PhD from the London School of Economics. His main research interests are: China's Middle East policy, Uyghur politics, Xinjiang, arms transactions and defense conversion, energy relations, and labor exports. His recent publications, include "China and the Middle East" in Jonathan Fulton (Ed.), *Routledge Handbook of China-Middle East Relations*; "Betar China: The Impact of a Remote Jewish Youth Movement, 1929–1949," *Jewish Political Studies Review*; "Separation of State and Religion: The East Asian Model and the Middle East," *Asian Journal of Middle Eastern and Islamic Studies* (2021).

Degang Sun is Director of the Center for Middle Eastern Studies and Professor at the Institute of International Studies, Fudan University in Shanghai, China. His research interests are Middle Eastern politics and international relations, and China and the Middle East. He has published widely on Sino-MENA relations. Prior to joining Fudan, he was Professor and Deputy Director of the Middle East Studies Institute of Shanghai International Studies University. He was a visiting scholar at many universities, including the Center for Middle Eastern Studies, Harvard University (September 2018–September 2019), a Senior Associate Member at St. Antony's College, Oxford University, and an Academic Visitor to Oxford Centre for Islamic Studies (2012–2013).

Emilie Tran is Assistant Professor in the Department of Social Sciences, Hong Kong Metropolitan University, Hong Kong. She obtained her PhD from the Ecole des hautes études en sciences sociales, Paris, France. Driven by international and multidisciplinary collaborations, her scholarship addresses world problems facing political leaders, policy-makers, and the global community. She investigates global China, whose rising power is one of the most important features of twenty-first-century global politics. Her research themes are framed in terms of politics and international relations (China's engagement in global public health; health diplomacy; digital diplomacy; the external relations of the EU, France, the Middle East and Africa), public policy, administration, and management (training of civil servants and the political elite; the smart city; public-private partnerships) and public governance (China's transnational governance of its diaspora, re-creating an extra-territorial space). She has published in the *Journal of Contemporary China*; *Mediterranean Politics*; *China Perspectives*; *China: An International Journal*; and *International Migration*.

Yuting Wang is Professor of Sociology at the American University of Sharjah (UAE) and a Non-resident Research Fellow at the Center on Religion and the Global East at Purdue University, USA. She has been visiting scholar at Northwestern University, Purdue University, University of California-Berkeley, and the London School of Economics and Political Science. She has a PhD in Sociology from the University of Notre Dame. She has published widely on Islam and Muslims in China, transnational religious networks, the Chinese expatriate community in the UAE, and Sino-UAE relations. Her publications include *Between Islam and the American Dream* (Routledge, 2014) and *Chinese in Dubai: Money, Pride, and Soul-Searching* (Brill, 2020).

Roie Yellinek is Associate Researcher at the Begin-Sadat Center for Strategic Studies, a Nonresident scholar at the Middle East Institute, and an Adjunct Researcher at the Dado Center, which is affiliated with the Israeli Defense Forces. He received his PhD from Bar-Ilan University in Ramat Gan, Israel. He specializes in studying the growing relationships between China and the countries of the Middle East, especially regarding Chinese diplomacy and soft power. He has written extensively on Chinese diplomacy in the Middle East and is a frequent commentator in local and international media outlets.

Karen E. Young is Senior Research Scholar in the Center on Global Energy Policy at Columbia University, USA. She was Senior Fellow and founding Director of the Program on Economics and Energy at the Middle East Institute, a Resident Scholar at the American Enterprise Institute and a Senior Resident Scholar at the Arab Gulf States Institute. She was a Research Fellow at the London School of Economics and has taught at George Washington University, Johns Hopkins SAIS and was Assistant Professor of Political Science at the American University of Sharjah. Her books include: *The Political Economy of Energy, Finance and Security in the UAE* (Palgrave, 2014) and *The Economic Statecraft of the Gulf States* (Bloomsbury/IB Tauris, 2023).

Zhen Yu is Associate Professor of Political Science at Xiangtan University, China, and the founding Executive Director of the Gulf Research Centre at Xiangtan University. She received her doctorate in International Relations from Shanghai International Studies University, China. She has been a council member of the Council of China National Association for International Studies since October 2021. She was a visiting scholar at St. Antony's College, Oxford University (October 2019–August 2020). Her research interests include International Relations of the Middle East, Gulf Studies and international aid.

Kambiz Zare is Professor of International Relations and International Business at KEDGE Business School, France. Prior to joining KEDGE Business School, he was Lecturer and Researcher at the European Center for Advanced International Studies and American Graduate School, School of Business and Economics, in Paris. His book, *The Gulf Cooperation Council* was published in 2016. He holds a PhD in International Relations and Diplomacy from the Centre d'Etudes Diplomatiques et Stratégiques (Paris) and two MS in Finance and Financial Risk Management. He also holds degrees from the City University of New York and Università degli Studi di Parma in Italy.

Chuchu Zhang is Associate Professor at the School of International Relations and Public Affairs, and Deputy Director of the Center for Middle Eastern Studies Fudan University, China. She received her PhD in Politics and International Studies from the University of Cambridge, UK. Her research focuses on Middle Eastern Politics, and China-Middle Eastern relations. She is the author of *Islamist Party Mobilization: Tunisia's Ennahda and Algeria's HMS Compared, 1989–2014* (Palgrave, 2020). She has published in several top peer-reviewed journals, including *Mediterranean Politics*, *Eurasian Geography and Economics*, *Middle East Policy*, *Environment and Planning: Economy and Space*, *Globalizations*, and *Pacific Focus*.

Contributors

Yuyou Zhang is an Associate Professor at the Institute of Middle Eastern Studies, Northwest University, Xi'an, China. His research interests are Morocco and North African politics.

Sophie Zinser is Academic Associate, Middle East North Africa Program and Asia-Pacific Program, Chatham House. She provides analysis on China's role in the Middle East and South and Central Asia, with a particular focus on the US's role in the burgeoning China-Middle East relationship. She also works on forced labor and migration issues in the Middle East and Asia. A former Fulbright Scholar in Amman, Jordan and Schwarzman Scholar with a Masters in Global Affairs from Tsinghua University, Sophie has worked for five years on policy across the Middle East and Asia with both United Nations and grassroots organizations.

Yahia H. Zoubir is Professor of International Studies and Director of Research in Geopolitics at KEDGE Business School in France and Non-Resident Senior Fellow, Middle East Council on Global Affairs, Doha, Qatar. He is the author of numerous books and articles on politics, society, and the international relations of North Africa. He co-edited with Gregory White *North African Politics Change and Continuity* (Routledge 2016). In 2014, he co-edited with Sun Degang, *Building a New Silk Road: China and the Middle East in the 21st Century* (Beijing: World Affairs Press). In 2020, he published an edited book, *The Politics of Algeria* (Routledge). He has published dozens of articles in the *Journal of Contemporary China, Global Policy, Middle East Policy, Third World Quarterly, Mediterranean Politics, International Affairs, Africa Spectrum, Journal of North African Studies, Democratization Encyclaopedia of Nationalism,* the *Oxford Dictionary of World Politics,* the *Oxford Research Encyclopaedia of Religion & Politics,* and the *Oxford Encyclopaedia of International Studies.*

ACKNOWLEDGMENTS

I would like to thank first and foremost James "Joe" Whiting, who solicited me and trusted me to undertake this project; though I initially hesitated to undertake such a challenging gigantic task, I am grateful to him for having entrusted me to carry it out as I learned immensely from the contributions of my colleagues. Miss Titanilla 'Ella' Panczel, former Senior Editorial Assistant at Routledge, was of great support. Before she left her position, she was most efficient and supportive of the book.

I would also like to thank profusely her replacement Euan Rice-Coates, the new Editorial Assistant, for ensuring a smooth transition. I owe him an immense debt of gratitude for his dedication to the project, ensuring that before going to production the book fulfilled all the requirements, including minute details. I know that all the contributors concur with my assessments. I would also like to express my utmost gratitude to Susan Dunsmore, the copy-editor of the *Routledge Companion to China and the Middle East and North Africa* for Taylor & Francis. She accomplished this difficult task during the end-of-year holidays and in the most efficient manner. I wish to thank Ms. Jayashree from the Newgen's Production team who has been most helpful with the project, ensuring that deadlines were carefully observed.

I would like to express my gratitude to the contributors for living up to their commitment to participate in this project. I would like to thank the anonymous reviewers, including contributors to this volume, who provided useful comments. Every time I have completed an edited volume, I thought that it would be the last one because of the many difficulties in ensuring the timely return of the chapters. The undertaking of this *Routledge Companion to China and the Middle East and North Africa*, during the COVID-19 pandemic, has been more demanding and exhausting than previous ones because some of the contributors contracted COVID-19 and were weakened for a time by the virus. Yet, they lived up to their commitment. I cannot thank them enough for their dedication. As has happened with other volumes, some authors who had committed to contributing chapters, like the one on China-Morocco, never delivered them. They lost a good opportunity to share their research!

I would also like to thank the management of the Middle East Center for Global Affairs (MEGCA) in Doha, Qatar, where I serve as Non-Resident Senior Fellow, for providing me with the necessary support to carry out this project and for allocating dedicated

Acknowledgments

interns who assisted me in the early stages of the project, namely, Yijia Shannon Chen, Emma Smith, Muhammed Kebbeh, and, later, Anjali Singh and Sisi Han my former Master's degree student at KEDGE Business School. Many thanks to my colleagues and friends at MECGA, Tarik Yousef, Adel Abdel-Ghafar, Nader Kabbani, Nejla Benmimoun, Françoise Freifer, Kais Sharif, Hassan Zwayne, Suzanne Houssari, Nadine Masri, Ghadeer Abu Ali, Omar Rahman, Tsedenya Girmay, Larbi Sadiki, Tanner Manley Ranj Alaaldin, Hana Elshehaby, Nora Abul Dahab, and Galip Dalay.

I extend my special thanks to three scholars at Fudan University in Shanghai. My greatest gratitude goes to Degang Sun, my old-time colleague and co-author, for his unreserved support and close friendship. Collaborating and publishing with Chuchu Zhang has been a real pleasure; she has also been supportive whenever I called on her for assistance. I would also like to thank Andrea Ghiselli for his constructive advice whenever I needed it. Emilie Tran, my co-author and friend, has been most supportive on all the projects I have undertaken, with her or alone. My sincere appreciation and esteem go to Robert Mason, who has never failed to respond without hesitation to my numerous requests on every occasion.

This project would have been impossible without the unconditional support of my family, wherever they are. My greatest gratitude goes to my wife Cynthia, who endured seeing me constantly glued to a chair in front of a computer, including most weekends. I cannot express enough the immense gratitude I owe her.

INTRODUCTION

Yahia H. Zoubir

In the last decade, China's relations with the Middle East and North Africa (MENA) have grown exponentially. While political and security relations are growing at a slower place, trade relations have increased at an incredibly fast pace in the last decade. Although the pandemic has slowed those exchanges, they are still quite significant. Infrastructure works are evident throughout the entire region. Because of its continued modernization, China's imports about 50 per cent of its energy needs from the MENA, especially the Gulf region, with Saudi Arabia as the main supplier.

Since the 2010s, China has intensified its relations with most MENA states both bilaterally (Olimat, 2014) and within multilateral organizations, such as the Forum on China Africa Cooperation (FOCAC), founded in 2000, and the China-Arab States Cooperation Forum (CASCF), established in 2004. After the launch in 2013 of the One Belt, One Road (OBOR), renamed the Belt and Road Initiative (BRI) in 2015, Sino-MENA ties witnessed an extraordinary acceleration which demonstrated, if need be, the importance of the MENA to China. From the onset of the BRI, China aimed to integrate the MENA region into this mammoth project that aims to create connectivity between various parts of the globe. In 2014, President Xi complained about the limited level of trade between China and the MENA arguing that this, in fact, offered opportunities for China and the MENA region (Xi, 2014). He stated:

> In 2013, China's imports from Arab nations amounted to $140 billion, accounting for a mere 7 per cent of its annual import value over the next five years; its outward foreign direct investment in Arab nations totalled $2.2 billion … The gap signals potential and opportunities. China is prepared to support Arab states in increasing employment, advancing industrialization, and pushing economic development.

Therefore, President Xi proposed the launch of a novel approach to the MENA, under the label of the '1+2+3' cooperation model, whereby the '1' stands for the main path of further collaboration, which involves closer cooperation in the energy sector. The '2' in this pattern concerns two branches of cooperation – infrastructure-building and

DOI: 10.4324/9781003048404-1

trade and investment – to deepen China's relations with the Arab governments through partnership in development plans focused on improving the quality of life there. This step also comprises the founding of institutions to boost bilateral trade and investment in numerous sectors, encompassing energy, petrochemicals, agriculture, manufacturing and services. The aim was to increase Sino-MENA trade from $240 billion in 2013 to $600 billion for the following ten years (Xi, 2014); though the trade size has not met Xi's expectation, the trade volume reached $244.3 billion by 2018, jumping 28 per cent year-on-year (*China Daily*, 2019, 6 September). Additionally, according to the 1+2+3 approach, Beijing would increase its non-financial investment stock in the Arab states from $10 billion in 2013 to over $60 billion by 2023 (Embassy of China in Iraq, 2014). In 2018, China committed an additional $23 billion in Foreign Direct Investment in the Middle East alone, that is not counting North Africa. The '3' in Xi's initiative represents the three high-technology fields of nuclear energy, space satellites, and renewable energy. One of the most interesting points relates to cooperation in technology to assist the region in developing nuclear power for civilian use, and in duplicating the Beidou Navigation Satellite System in the MENA. One of the BRI's objectives is to make these transfers of technology possible.

In 2016, to confirm the importance of the MENA to China, Beijing published the *Arab Policy Paper*. The Arab Policy Paper emphasized China's readiness to foster ties with the MENA states through 'strategic cooperative relations of comprehensive cooperation and common development', while advocating China's time-honoured Five Principles of Peaceful Coexistence: mutual respect for sovereignty and territorial integrity; mutual non-aggression; non-interference in each other's internal affairs; equality and mutual benefit; and peaceful coexistence. The Arab Policy Paper suggests many areas of cooperation that include, *inter alia*, political, legal, economic, energy, healthcare, education, science and technology, environmental, and cultural cooperation (Ministry of Foreign Affairs of the People's Republic of China, 2016).

Countries in the MENA did not figure among China's leading trade partners; nevertheless, China soon became the principal one of many of them such as Algeria, Egypt, Iran, Mauritania, Oman, and Saudi Arabia (Sun and Zoubir, 2015). Although initially commercial, these progressively strong relations with the MENA (Fulton, 2019), have been worrisome for the traditional, dominant powers in the region, primarily the US and the European Union. China's role in the MENA during the pandemic exacerbated those concerns when China deployed its health diplomacy as part of the Health Silk Road (HSR) (Zoubir and Tran, 2022). The HSR has become part and parcel of the BRI; its deployment provoked hostile reactions in both the USA and the EU (Tran and Zoubir, 2023). Undoubtedly, those reactions revealed the already intensifying 'systemic rivalry' between the People's Republic of China and the Western world prior to the pandemic (Leoni, 2021).

China's interest in the MENA has gone beyond trade, the import of oil, or the important infrastructure works. Cooperation with the MENA states has expanded to virtually all sectors, including the military, weapons, vaccines, automobile industry, and telecommunications (e.g., the Beidou navigation system whose implementation is critical for the BRI), to name but a few. However, China has avoided taking sides in regional rivalries between its major partners (Iran and Saudi Arabia, for instance) preferring to keep difficult neutrality based on its 'zero-enemy' policy. In some regional conflicts, China has resorted to quasi-mediation diplomacy to assist in resolving conflicts (Sun and Zoubir, 2018). In other conflicts, in which outside small, middle, or big powers have intervened directly as in Libya (Zoubir, 2020), Syria (Patey, 2016), or Yemen (Salisbury, 2020), China has supported strong multilateralism. However, because of its assets in the region (large corporations, investments), as Professor Sun (2018) put it, 'China regards the Middle East as a "market" rather than a "battlefield"'; it is the largest investor in the Middle East and therefore a stakeholder of its security. China is cooperating with some states in the region to combat terrorism (Zoubir, 2022). It lost billions of dollars during the Libyan uprising in 2011 (Zhang and Wei, 2012) and is now cognizant of the necessity to protect its assets in foreign lands. In other protracted conflicts, such as the illegally Moroccan-occupied Western Sahara, China has abstained from any involvement, limiting itself to generic statements at the UN Security Council. Although close to Algeria, which supports self-determination of Sahrawis based on UN resolutions, China has kept at times a questionable neutrality because of its interests in Morocco (Han, 2018; Zoubir, 2022, forthcoming). In the recent conflict between Egypt, one of its major partners in the region, and Sudan, also a major partner, China has pursued a neutral policy on the conflict over the Grand Ethiopian Renaissance Dam (GERD) to avoid alienating either Egypt or Ethiopia, encouraging instead the resolution of the dispute over the GERD through negotiations (Hosny, 2022). China's heavy investment in the GERD and in Ethiopia in general partly explains the choice of this 'neutral' position. Both Egypt and Ethiopia are important partners; China is Egypt's and Ethiopia's main trading partner even if the volume of Sino-Egyptian trade is nearly three times that of Sino-Ethiopian trade.

Concerning China's attitude towards conflicts in the region, Sun captured its underpinnings, stating:

> although China adheres to a 'zero-enemy' policy with regards to the Middle East, it has engaged with the Middle Eastern security affairs to seek their support on Taiwan, Tibet, Xinjiang, human rights and on South China Sea issues, and more importantly to safeguard its legitimate overseas interests in the Middle East.
>
> *(Sun, unpublished paper, 2018)*

This is becoming all the more important since the Sino-US crisis provoked by Nancy Pelosi's trip to Taiwan in August 2022.

Unlike Western powers, mainly the United States, China's deployment of troops in the region is insignificant. There are about 1,000 forces in its dual logistics-military base in Djibouti, inaugurated in 2017 (Sun and Zoubir, 2021). Beijing dispatches military troops mostly on an impermanent basis to evacuate Chinese citizens from Middle Eastern areas of risk (civil wars, uprisings, riots, and terrorism). Thus, from 2008 to 2018, China evacuated 50,000 Chinese employees overseas from conflict zones in the MENA, including those from Libya, which boasted close to 40,000 Chinese citizens. Regarding terrorism, China has provided some military and financial aid to the MENA states or sold appropriate counterterrorism equipment to them.

China has also deployed soft power in the MENA not only through the BRI, but also in 'Assisting other nations through development, economic growth and connectivity' as 'a way of wielding soft power in the interest of advancing China's global standing' (Chaziza, 2019). China has promoted tourism, academic exchanges, and health diplomacy to apply soft power in the region. However, compared to Western countries' soft power, China's soft power in the region has not been nearly as successful. Nevertheless, China's image in the region has been quite positive in recent years (Robbins, 2020). Chinese communities (companies, construction workers) cohabit peacefully in most MENA states, despite minor occasional incidents due mostly to cultural misunderstandings. The interviews of the Editor of this volume with Chinese managers suggest that the local populations in general appreciate China's contribution to their countries' development. But the presence of Chinese workers, though insignificant, generates some resentment in a region suffering from high unemployment.

The major question is what consequences the US-China rivalry will have on Sino-MENA relations. Hitherto, the MENA states have avoided taking sides, preferring to adopt neutral positions; it remains to be seen whether other regional and international geopolitical issues will preserve that neutrality or force some alignments.

The short introduction to this *Routledge Companion to China and the Middle East and North Africa* has provided only a brief synopsis of some of the many issues that the contributors to this 32-chapter volume have addressed in their respective chapters. Although some contributors reneged on their commitment (some at the last minute), the Editor of this volume did his best to find replacements (successfully in most cases) or asked the other contributors to include some of the salient points that should have been covered in this collection. Thus, the chapters in this *Routledge Companion to China and the Middle East and North Africa* investigate the wide-ranging issues in China-MENA relations.

References

Chaziza, M. (2019) China's Outbound Tourism as a Soft Power Tool in the Middle East. Middle East Institute, 12 November. Available at: www.mei.edu/publications/chinas-outbound-tourism-soft-power-tool-middle-east#

China Daily (2019) China, Arab States See Enhanced Production Capacity Cooperation: Report, 6 September. Available at: www.chinadaily.com.cn/a/201909/06/WS5d72e134a310cf3e3556a374.htl

Embassy of China in Iraq (2014) Xi Jinping Attends Opening Ceremony of Sixth Ministerial Conference of China-Arab States Cooperation Forum and Delivers Important Speech Stressing Promotion of Silk Road Spirit and Deepening China-Arab Cooperation. Available at: http://iq.chineseembassy.org/eng/zygx/t1164662.htm (accessed 20 January 2020)

Fulton, J. (2019) China Is Becoming a Major Player in the Middle East. *BRINK News*, 19 September. Available at: www.brinknews.com/china-is-becoming-a-major-player-in-the-middle-east/

Hang, Z. (2018) China's Balancing Act in the Western Sahara Conflict. *Africana Studia*, 29: 145–156.

Hosny, H. (2022) Xi Reaffirms 'Comprehensive Strategic Partnership' in Meeting with Sisi. *Al-Monitor*, 12 February. Available at: www.al-monitor.com/originals/2022/02/xi-reaffirms-comprehensive-strategic-partnership-meeting-sisi#ixzz7KlfigO6O

Leoni, Z. (2021) *American Grand Strategy from Obama to Trump: Imperialism After Bush and China's Hegemonic Challenge*. London: Palgrave Macmillan.

Ministry of Foreign Affairs of the People's Republic of China (2016) China's Arab Policy Paper. Available at: www.fmprc.gov.cn/mfa_eng/zxxx_662805/t1331683.shtml

Olimat, M.S. (2014) *China and the Middle East Since World War II: A Bilateral Approach*. New York: Lexington Books.

Patey, P. (2016) China, the Syrian Conflict, and the Threat of Terrorism. Policy Brief. Danish Institute of International Studies (DIIS). Available at: www.jstor.org/stable/pdf/resrep13114.pdf?refreqid=excelsior%3Afaff143684ec13e9b9d5e3191d7bc29b&ab_segments=&origin=

Robbins, R. (2020) Is This China's Moment in MENA? Arab Barometer. Available at: www.arabbarometer.org/2020/07/is-this-chinas-moment-in-mena/

Salisbury, P. (2020) The International Approach to the Yemen War: Time for a Change? Yemen Policy Center. October. Available at: www.yemenpolicy.org/the-international-approach-to-the-yemen-war-time-for-a-change/

Sun, D. (2018) The Security in the Middle East from China's Point of View. Unpublished paper.

Sun, D. and Zoubir, Y.H. (2015) China's Economic Diplomacy towards the Arab Countries: Challenges Ahead? *Journal of Contemporary China*, 24(95): 903–921.

Sun, D. and Zoubir, Y.H. (2018) China's Participation in Conflict Resolution in the Middle East and North Africa: A Case of Quasi-mediation Diplomacy? *Journal of Contemporary China*, 27(110): 224–243.

Sun, D. and Zoubir, Y.H. (2021) Securing China's Latent Power: The Dragon's Anchorage in Djibouti, *Journal of Contemporary China*, 30(130): 677–692.Xi, J. (2014) Promoting the Silk Road Spirit and Deepening China-Arab Cooperation, speech at the opening ceremony of the 6th Ministerial Meeting of the China–Arab States Cooperation Forum. Available at: www.china.org.cn/report/2014-07/14/content_32941818/

Zhang, J. and Wei, W.X. (2012) Managing Political Risks of Chinese Contracted Projects in Libya. *Project Management Journal*, 43(4): 42–51.

Zoubir, Y.H. (2020) The Protracted Civil War in Libya: The Role of Outside Powers. *Insight Turkey*, 22(4): 11–27.

Zoubir, Y.H. (2022) Algeria and China: Shifts in Political and Military Relations. *Global Policy*. DOI: 10.1111/1758-5899.13115

Zoubir, Y.H. (forthcoming) China in the Southern Mediterranean: Integrating the Greater Maghreb in the New Silk Road. *Mediterranean Politics*. DOI: 10.1080/13629395.2022.2035137

Zoubir, Y.H and Tran, E. (2022) China's Health Silk Road in the MENA amidst COVID-19 and a Shifting World Order. *Journal of Contemporary China*. 31(135): 335–350.

PART I

China and the MENA

1
CHINA AND THE MIDDLE EAST
An Overview

Muhamad S. Olimat

Introduction

The earliest contacts recorded between China and the so-called "Western Region" date back to 138 BC, when Chang'an sent an expedition led by Zhang Qian, a skilled diplomat and warrior, to explore potential military alliances with the Ferghana Valley kingdoms. The aim was to deter raids by the Xiongnu alliance that posed a security threat to the Xian territory. Subsequently, China sent other missions to extend its contacts as far as the shores of ancient Arabia. These expeditions took may months to reach their destination, and Chinese explorers and their large contingents traded with people along the way their most precious commodity—silk—in exchange for goods and services. Thus, the route became known as the Silk Road, a vital framework of security, trade, and culture, the lifeline of China's ties with the people of the Western Regions. Eventually the road became a symbol, particularly in modern times, of political and diplomatic partnerships and energy cooperation between China and the Middle East. This chapter provides a comprehensive survey of the five major points of interaction between China and the Greater Middle East that includes Central Asia, the traditional Middle East, and North Africa. These major points, viewed with a five-dimensional approach, take into consideration: (1) political relations; (2) trade ties; (3) energy relations; (4) cultural ties; and (5) security partnerships with the region.

Sino-Greater Middle Eastern Relations

The Qian expedition carried out in the year 138 BC was the first recorded point of contact between China and its neighbors to the west. The resulting Silk Road over time strengthened the security, trade, and cultural ties between the two regions. The second most important turning point in the history of bilateral ties between the two regions was the advent of Islam in the seventh century. It reached China in the lifetime of the prophet (PBUH) through Silk Road merchants. (Reichelt, 1951: 155). The Prophet Mohamed (PBUH) is reported to have said, "seek knowledge as far as China" (*Living Islam*, 2021), in reference to China as a source of enlightenment.

DOI: 10.4324/9781003048404-3

The Arab conquest of Persia began in 637 and concluded in 654, but in 651, Xian became aware of the rising power of Islam in the region through its contact with the Persian Empire, and China and the Islamic Caliphate State exchanged diplomatic missions. In the year 714, the Muslim army, estimated at 200,000 soldiers and led by Commander Kutaiba Ibn Muslim, marched through Central Asia into Kashgar, the capital of East Turkistan, but halted its advance after reaching a peace agreement with Emperor Gaozong. In 751 AD Chinese armies marched to the west to regain control of East Turkistan (Xinjiang) and the Ferghana Valley. The two armies met in a decisive battle at Talas, in what is currently Kyrgyzstan. Ibn Al Atheer, the Arab historian, in his book *Al Kamil*, reported that each army had roughly 100,000 solders. The Muslim armies ripped through Chinese defenses, splitting, and decisively destroying the army, with an estimated 50,000 killed, 20,000 captured, and the remaining 30,000 fleeing back to China. (Ibn Al Athir, 1160–1233; 1231: 664). The Chinese army and its allies were defeated. Within the context of the face-offs between China and the Islamic Empire, several key events need to be noted, given that they have had an enduring impact on Sino-Islamic relations ever since:

1. The Persian defeat in the Al Qadesya Battle in 637 AD prompted the Persians to alert the Chinese to the rising threat from the West. The Persian Crown Prince moved to China with a military contingent that continued to harass the Muslim armies.
2. Between 656 and 751 AD, the Islamic grip on the Western Region, or Central Asia, weakened due to infighting among the Islamic army's leadership.
3. The Islamic Empire preferred a reconciliation with China rather than a military approach, due to the status that the Prophet Mohamed (PBUH) ascribed to China.
4. At Talas, the Chinese army was led by Korean General Gao Xianzhi, described as re-engaged.
5. The Talas Battle was a decisive victory for the Islamic Empire; however, the decision was taken not to pursue the fleeing army or pursue an all-out war with China. The preference was for peace and trade rather than war.
6. Islam spread in China quickly through trade and political influence.

The post-Talas Battle era was promising in terms of bilateral ties between the Islamic and the Chinese empires. The Silk Road became the main instrument for cultural, religious, and commercial contacts, and the Muslim community, of Arab and Persian origins, prospered in China. Chinese emperors were impressed by its hard work, ingenuity, management, and scientific skills. But this success created jealousy among the Han majority that eventually led to massacres in 878 AD (Hassan, 2010: 2). The Muslim community's presence decreased until the Mongol invasion in the thirteenth century. Both the Chinese and Arab empires were subjected to destruction by the Mongols. However, the Mongols established the Yuan Dynasty in northern China and relied heavily on Muslims, Persians, and even some Han elements to manage the empire as they lacked the necessary administrative skills to manage an empire. Upon the defeat of the Mongols, the conditions of Muslims in China continued to deteriorate for the following century, leading to the annexation of East Turkistan, Xinjiang in 1884.

The political developments in China toward the turn of the twentieth century influenced Sino-Islamic relations and the conditions of Muslims in the country. Chinese Muslims were split in their support of nationalist and communist forces. Primarily,

Muslims supported the Republic of China (ROC), and some were influential in the ROC government. The triumph of communism in mainland China was a fundamental challenge to Muslims in the country. The official annexation of East Turkistan in 1952 was a major blow to the hopes of its independence. Within China itself, Islam was challenged: mosques were destroyed, and the practice of Islam was banned.

The status of Muslims in China was a major foreign policy issue in Sino-Arab and Islamic relations. In fact, in his first meeting with the Chinese Premier Chu En- Lai, the Saudi Foreign Affairs Minister, Prince Faisal (later King Faisal) made it clear that the PRC would not be granted recognition without improving the conditions of Muslims in the country. The Chinese premier pledged to ease the tensions with Muslims and allow the pilgrimage, which occurred from 1955–1966, until the Cultural Revolution.

The political engagement between China and the Arab and Islamic countries was a priority for the revolutionary leaders of China, Enlai, Mao, and Lin Piao. These revolutionary leaders were aware of the Middle East's geostrategic location, in particular during World War II (WWII). They feared a German-Japanese victory might lead to the encirclement of China. In fact, Mao developed his own theory of strategic "zones" and their impact on China's national security. The Middle East lay in the "intermediate zone," the control of which not only would precipitate a third world war, but also "seriously endanger the survival of the PRC" (Shichor, 1979: 35). The defeat of Germany and Japan was a relief to China, but fear of "encirclement" remained a fundamental aspect of China's foreign policy. At a later stage, this perspective developed into a fear of containment, a well-developed framework utilized by the West to suffocate the former Soviet Union within its borders from 1947 to 1991.

In post-WWII, and post-establishment of the PRC, the Middle East was a priority on China's foreign policy agenda. Chu Enlai actively engaged with Asia and Africa in particular. His goal was diplomatic recognition, solidarity against imperial powers, support of national liberation movements, and Third World development. At the Bandung Conference in 1955, Enlai met with every single delegation. In his meetings with delegations representing the newly independent countries of the Middle East, he learned the depth of the Arab Israeli conflict, the Palestinian plight, and met leading figures such as Jamal Abdul Nasser, Egypt's president. Enlai pledged to support the Palestinian cause, underlined the importance of resolving the Arab-Israeli conflict peacefully, free of superpowers' interventions. China simultaneously supported Arab nationalist and communist forces battling imperialism across the Middle East, and stood by the Arab people in major confrontations with the West, as in the cases of the 1956 Tripartite War, known as the Suez Canal Crisis, the 1967 War, the Ramadan War of 1973 and the invasion of Lebanon in 1983. China intervened heavily in the civil wars in Jordan, Oman, and Yemen as well, on the side of leftist forces against monarchies and the so-called "reactionary regimes." Beijing's support of leftist forces and national liberation movements remained a major pillar of its foreign policy until the demise of the revolutionary leaders by 1976. Deng Xiaoping revised such policy in favor of dealing with the status quo, and promoting bilateral and multilateral trade relations rather than revolutionary change in the region.

One of the main developments that occurred in this period was the PRC assuming the Chinese permanent seat on the United Nation's Security Council, in September 1971. Additionally, the American rapprochement of China, a process begun in the mid-1960s that aimed to incorporate China once again into the international system, had a fundamental impact on international relations. The Security Council's membership provided Beijing with the necessary tools to impact developments on the global scene.

In the Middle East, China continued to support Palestinian and Arab causes, national liberation causes, and anti-imperialist policies, but PRC representatives also began to examine alternative tactics for its foreign policy worldwide. By the end of the 1970s, the PRC had totally altered its foreign policy goals. It became a status quo-oriented country, much less revolutionary, and much less into supporting national liberation movements in favor of government-to-government relations. Its aim was incorporation into the international economy, technology transfer, economic reform at home, development, stability, and unity within the PRC itself after the demise of its revolutionary leadership, and its first generational leadership transformation.

Sino-Middle Eastern relations in the Economic Reform Era highlighted the PRC's priorities, namely economic transformation, trade, and energy. China disentangled itself from the Civil War in Oman (1955–1975), Jordan (1969–1973), and Yemen (1962–1970). In fact, Sino-Omani relations developed so rapidly that Oman became the first Gulf country to supply the PRC with shipments of oil as early as 1983 (Olimat, 2016: 146). Beijing pursued an all-out policy to establish diplomatic relations with Arab countries, a process that intensified in the early 1970s. Jordan, Lebanon, Qatar, Iran, the UAE, and other countries recognized China in the 1970s–1980s. Beijing was accepted as a capital that promotes the status quo rather than supporting Maoist movements aimed at destabilizing the Middle East. Additionally, the PRC took major stands on the security challenges confronted by the Middle East. It condemned the Israeli invasion of Lebanon in 1982, the eviction of the Palestinian Liberation Organization (PLO), the massacres of innocent Palestinian refugees in Sabra and Shatila camps, called for a peaceful resolution to the Arab-Israeli conflict, and supported the peace negotiations brokered by the USA and supported by the United Nations.

During the Gulf War (1980–1988), Beijing sold weapons to both Iran and Iraq to ensure a stalemate in the war. This was the aim set forth by the leading superpowers, the USA and the former USSR. Beijing also viewed the Soviet invasion of Afghanistan as a trap to weaken the Soviet Union, a view shared by the United States and its allies in the Middle East. This was an event that had an unprecedented impact on world politics. Beijing was one of the early external powers to provide weapons to the Mujahideen to combat Soviet forces in Afghanistan, as well as the USA, Pakistan, Saudi Arabia, and many other countries. The decade-long war of attrition in Afghanistan proved to be catastrophic by all standards. It contributed to the demise of the Soviet Union, the spread of terrorism, and has produced continued instability in Afghanistan ever since.

The collapse of the Soviet Union brought about fundamental security challenges to China, such as the demise of communist governments, and the aspiration to freedom across the communist world. A freedom wave struck the PRC itself, leading to the Tiananmen Square Massacre in the summer of 1989 where Chinese students demanded similar changes in the country. Beijing was subject to international sanctions, but Middle Eastern countries sided with China, and assisted it in overcoming some economic, diplomatic, and political sanctions imposed by the USA, the European Community, and other international organizations. Middle Eastern governments also supported China's membership in the World Trade Organization. By the end of the 1990s, China had erased the consequences of the massacre.

The demise of the Soviet Union, the end of the Iraqi occupation of Kuwait, the US triumph in the so-called Second Gulf War all brought optimism regarding resolving the

Arab-Israeli conflict, a process that began in the early 1990s, supported by China, that culminated in the establishment of the Palestinian National Authority.

The early twenty-first century brought about catastrophic effects on the global scene. It began with political turbulence in the United States due to the inconclusive results of the 2000 elections, and then the September 11th attacks. China portrayed itself as a victim of international terrorism and demanded that the USA classify the Islamic Movement of Xinjiang a terrorist organization, a demand that was granted. However, China made no objection when the USA invaded Afghanistan, though it called for a war on terror led by the United Nations. Instead, Beijing showed some symbolic "resistance" against the US invasion of Iraq in 2003, and any "regime-change policy" associated with it. Beijing opposed the so-called "Arab Spring," a wave of revolutions that struck the Middle East toward the end of 2010, viewing it as a security threat to its own national interest and national security. Beijing sided with the existing governments, exercised its veto power in the Security Council in support of its allies, especially Syria, and coordinated closely with Moscow in this regard, casting what is called a "Double Veto," where the two countries protected the Syrian regimes from international sanctions, or a UN-led military intervention.

Sino-Middle Eastern Energy Cooperation

China reached energy self-sufficiency in 1963. Three decades later it became a net oil-importing country. The decline of its domestic production was associated with its economic transformation, industrialization, and an increasing demand for energy. In order to meet such increasing demands for oil, China pursued an all-out oil diplomacy "with explicit involvement of the central government aiming to secure foreign oil and gas resources" (Shaofeng, 2008: 80). The US Energy Information Administration (EIA) demonstrated that this trend of increasing imports and declining domestic production in China was the main force behind China's relentless search for energy resources worldwide. Figure 1.1 illustrates the difference between the increasing consumption and production. The EIA maintains:

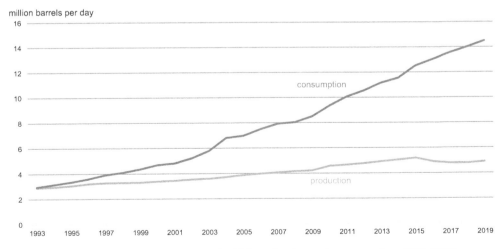

Figure 1.1 China's petroleum and other liquids' production and consumption, 1993–2019
Source: Energy Information Administration, at: www.eia.gov/international/analysis/country/CHN

China had the largest decline in domestic petroleum and other liquids production among non-OPEC countries in 2016 ... it had the second-largest decline in 2017. The total liquids production in China averaged 4.8 million b/d in 2017, a year-over-year decline of 0.1 million b/d (2%) from 2016, and further declines in both 2018 and 2019 are forecasted.

(EIA, 2017)

China approached its Middle Eastern partners and began to import crude oil from Oman in 1983. Since then, Beijing has become increasingly reliant on importing oil and gas from the Middle East, to the extent that energy has become the centerpiece of its engagement with the Middle East. Table 1.1 illustrates China's oil imports from the region, from 1993 to 2019, in terms of economic growth rates, oil production, consumption, net-imports and import-percentage from the Middle East.

The most recent comprehensive report by the EIA on China's energy outlook in 2019 (Figure 1.2) highlighted China's main oil destinations. Obviously, the Greater Middle Easter countries provide China with more than 50 percent of its energy needs, including its Central Asian partners.

In order to meet such a demand, China has launched a global energy project, a massive operation that extends across the globe, from Australia to Latin America. For that end, it has also established three major international oil corporations. These are: (1) the China National Petroleum Corporation (CNPC); (2) the China Petroleum & Chemical Corporation (Sinopec); and (3) the National Offshore Oil Corporation (CNOOC), each of which has its own role and mandate in meeting China's increasing demand for energy. Additionally, China has built a network of international pipelines to ensure the flow of oil and natural gas from its producing partners to the end consumer: China. The Central Asia-China Oil and Gas pipeline is the most important of all China's network of pipelines. China is also increasingly becoming reliant on the Greater Middle East for natural gas, namely on Turkmenistan, Uzbekistan, Kazakhstan, and Qatar. The region provides China with 46 percent of its imports worldwide. Figure 1.3 illustrates this trend.

This trend of increasing reliance on the Greater Middle East as a major supplier of crude oil and natural gas is expected to strengthen in the foreseeable future. The Sino-Central Asia and Middle Eastern economic integration, strategic partnership, and Comprehensive Strategic Partnership with major producers, such as Kazakhstan, Saudi Arabia, Iran, Kuwait, Turkmenistan, and Iraq will only support this trend. On March 27, 2021, China signed a 25-year oil agreement with Iran, worth $400 billion. This is a replica of a 2014 agreement Beijing signed with Moscow, and it will most certainly sign a similar agreement with Saudi Arabia soon.

Sino-Middle Eastern Trade Relations

The third most important pillar of China's ties with the Middle East is trade relations. These were subordinate to the PRC foreign policy goals from 1949 to 1978. Beijing's interests were primarily political, transformed later into abstract "economic" goals in the Economic Reform Era, 1978 to the present. China's involvement in trade with the Middle East encompasses every imaginable sector of the economy, with an ambitious goal of reaching $600 billion by 2025, upon signing the Free Trade Agreement with the Gulf Cooperation Council (GCC). In so doing, China is building on the glorious history

Table 1.1 China's growth rates, oil production, oil consumption, net imports, and oil imports from the Middle East, 1993–2019

Year	Growth rate (%)	Oil production mb/d	Oil consumption mb/d	Net imports mb/d	Oil imports from the Middle East (%)
1993	13.40	2,903,463.00	2,959,491.00	56,028.00	34.70
1994	11.80	2,957,310.00	3,160,605.00	203,290.00	39.70
1995	10.30	3,059,620.00	3,363,155.00	303,530.00	45.50
1996	9.70	3,211,280.00	3,610,085.00	398,780.00	52.90
1997	8.80	3,284,550.00	3,916,270.00	631,720.00	47.30
1998	7.80	3,301,740.00	4,105,835.00	804,090.00	61.00
1999	7.00	3,317,028.00	4,363,601.00	1,046,573.00	46.20
2000	8.00	3,377,527.00	4,795,715.00	1,418,188.00	53.60
2001	7.30	3,434,535.00	4,917,882.00	1,483,347.00	56.20
2002	8.00	3,529,761.00	5,160,714.00	1,630,953.00	49.60
2003	9.10	3,559,006.00	5,578,111.00	2,019,105.00	50.90
2004	9.10	3,657,452.00	6,437,484.00	2,780,031.00	45.40
2005	9.90	3,781,760.00	6,720,000.00	2,939,240.00	47.20
2006	10.50	3,844,870.00	7,201,278.00	3,356,404.00	40.22
2007	11.40	3,900,958.00	7,817,000.00	3,677,000.00	39.95
2008	9.60	3,725,000.00	7,937,000.00	4,212,000.00	46.00
2009	9.20	3,995.620.00	8,537.860.00	4,210.000.00	52.00
2010	10.3	4,071, 000.00	9,057,000.00	4,986,000.00	47.00
2011	9.20	4,100,000.00	9,510,000.00	5,410, 000.00	46.00
2012	8.10	4,300,000.00	9,963,000.00	5, 663,000.00	45.10
2013	7.70	4, 215,000.00	10, 190,000.00	5,975,000.00	51.00
2014	7.50	4,444,000.00	11,209,000.00	5,916,000.00	51.00
2015	6.90	4,309,000.00	11,986,000.00	7,677,000.00	52.00
2016	6.70	3,999.000.00	12,381,000.00	8,382,000.00	49.00
2017	6.90	3,860,000.00	12,799.000.00	8,939,000.00	52.00
2018	6.60	3,790,000.00	13,525.000.00	9,735,000.00	49.00
2019	6.10	3,980,650.00	13.980,650.00	10,100.000.00	48.00

This table is compiled from different sources: Candace Dunn; US Department of Energy (n.d.); Facts Global Energy, 2008, 2010; National Bureau of China Statistics (various years); BP (2022); EIA (2018), and author's calculations and forecasts.

of the Silk Road, and most recently on the Belt and Road Initiative, a massive framework of China's involvement in global trade, launched in 2013.

Table 1.2 illustrates the volume of trade relations between China and its partners in the Greater Middle East from 2001 to 2020. Its trade portfolio is massive and comprehensive; it includes the sectors of construction, industry, manufacturing, consumption, services, aviation, telecommunication, tourism, and energy. China's bilateral trade volume with the region exceeded $370 billion in 2019.

China and its partners in the Middle East have used the Belt and Road Initiative (BRI) as a mechanism for boosting their trade relations, including land and sea trade routes. In fact, countries in the region are competing to become part of the BRI. For

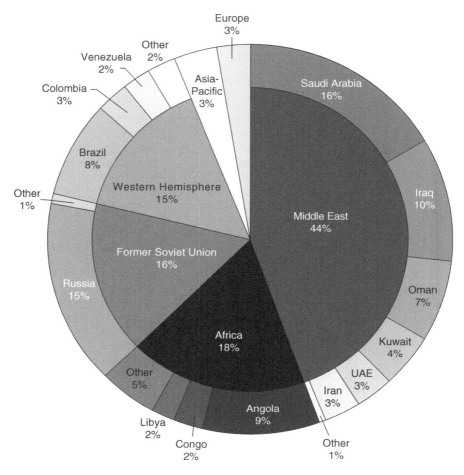

Figure 1.2 China's crude oil imports by source, 2019

Source: Energy Information Administration, available at: www.eia.gov/international/analysis/country/CHN (accessed June 22, 2021).

example, the UAE hosts the largest Chinese business complex outside China, the Dragon Mart, a 175,000 m² complex of Chinese merchandise. Kuwait established Madinat Al Hareer (City of Silk), devoting $110 billion to the project, while Oman embarked upon an ambitious process of reviving the role of its ancient Silk Road ports such as Salalah, Suhar, and Sour. Saudi Arabia touts the role of its Red Sea ports such as Yanbu, as centers of energy and trade cooperation with China. China has extended the railroad network across Central Asia to connect with its partners in the Middle East, Eurasia, Europe, and Africa. Moreover, China has established several economic forums, councils, and organization to strengthen its trade ties with the region, such as the China-GCC Cooperation Forum, the China-Central Asia-West Asia Economic Corridor, the China-Arab States Technology Transfer Center, the China-Turkey Economic Cooperation Forum, the Iran-China Economic Commission, and many other entities and institutions.

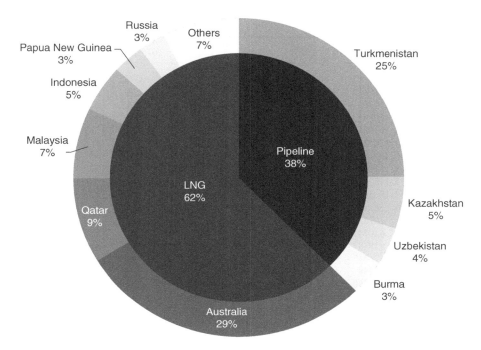

Figure 1.3 China's natural gas imports by source, 2019

Source: Energy Information Administration, available at:www.eia.gov/international/analysis/country/CHN (accessed June 22, 2021).

Sino-Middle Eastern Security Relations

Security threats and opportunities originating in the Western Region were at the core of China's interests in the region. Such interests promoted sending expeditions to the West to explore the possibility of building military alliances with the Ferghana Kingdoms, to deter the threat of the Xinguno alliance as early as 214 AD. The expedition approach governed China's Western Alliances with the rising empires in the region, especially the Persian Empire, an alliance built to deter the influence of the Roman Empire. Within the same approach, the Sino-Persian alliance aimed at deterring the threat of the Arab Empire in the seventh century. Clearly, the Silk Road was primarily a "strategic road, a security, a military road," rather than a trade route in the beginning. However, while military expeditions and explorers embarked on their missions, they began to trade silk, their most precious commodity at the time, with the people they came across along the road. Eventually, the route became known as the Silk Road.

The Arab conquest of Persia in the mid-seventh century alarmed China as they feared the rising power of the Abbasid Caliphate in the Western region. Islamic forces stood at the border of China in 751 AD, preferring a peaceful engagement with the country rather than an all-out conquest, even though China's defeat in the Talas Battle (751 AD) has echoed in Sino-Islamic relations ever since.

China's security was also threatened by the rise of the Mongol Empire, while the Ottoman Empire stood at the border of East Turkistan (Xinjiang). The Chinese expansion into Xinjiang in the eighteenth century well into the present has been a major

Table 1.2 China-Greater Middle East trade volume, 2001–2019 ($ million)

Country	2019	2018	2017	2016	2015	2014	2013	2012	2011
Afghanistan	62908	69167	54463	43583	37359	40193	33785	46924	23441
Algeria	808303	910416	72307	798000	8,350.71	7,395.18	8,188.4	7,728.56	6,432.4
Bahrain	167948	128565	102647	85452	1,123.39	1,415.75	1,544.1	1,550.81	1,205.8
Egypt	1320142	1382973	1082758	1099049	12,876.42	11,620.03	10,214.2	9,544.73	8,801.5
Iraq	3338866	3039860	2214453	1821145	20,583.86	28,505.08	24,878.8	17,567.59	14,268.2
Iran	2303562	3504201	3713851	3124585	33,827.33	51,842.08	39,426.5	34,65.8	45,103.4
Israel	1476915	1391557	1312470	1135396	11,417.98	10,879.74	10,826.6	9,901.45	9,778.5
Jordan	411198	318367	308279	316599	3,711.92	3,627.74	3,604.3	3,225.74	2,769.4
Kazakhstan	2200277	1987814	1794313	1309767	14,290.19	22,451.67	2859596	2568157	2496123
Kuwait	1728379	1865651	1204772	937207	11,269.74	13,433.69	12,262.1	12,556.99	11,303.6
Kyrgyzstan	634656	561112	542386	567669	4,340.69	5,297.94	513770	516232	497645
Lebanon	170561	201827	203365	211839	2,302.85	2,630.25	2,536.4	1,712.27	1,483.3
Libya	726809	620741	239063	153038	2,843.57	2,883.98	4,873.6	8,760.36	2,783.9
Morocco	466789	438781	382682	363264	3,418.71	3,481.50	3,803.07	3,690.84	3,519.3
Oman	2267100	2176312	1569973	1418911	17,163.81	25,861.24	22,941.4	18,787.02	15,874.6
Palestine	8228	7381	6918	5962	696.9	755.9	908.63	410.01	488.6
Qatar	1112279	1162880	808260	5522874	6,890.01	10,590.74	10,174.2	8,483.20	5,893.0
KSA	7807244	6328242	5013688	4228130	51,633.98	69,083.27	72,190.5	73,314.22	64,317.2
Syria	131522	127364	110415	91861	10,261.60	9,865.00	6,9485.7	1,200.36	2,446.4
Tajikistan	167469	150593	134811	175634	1,847.42	2,515.94	195812	185670	206901
Tunisia	782240	160968	152615	388294	1,421.23	1,447.70	1,439.8	1,568.90	1,332.0
Turkmenistan	911688	843630	694324	590177	8,643.13	10,470.44	1003090	1037250	547734
Turkey	2082052	2154546	2190494	1947493	21,551.48	23,010.85	22,233.2	19,095.57	18,737.3
UAE	4874963	4588902	4103512	4006689	48,534.20	54,797.86	46,234.8	40,420.29	35,119.2
Yemen	368565	259454	230300	185844	2,328.11	5,134.17	5,200.1	5,559.15	4,239.9
Uzbekistan	721287	626919	422087	361461	3,495.83	4,276.12	455145	287519	216661

Source: This table is constructed from data provided by the China Statistics Yearbook, volumes from 2001 to 2020, published by the National Bureau of China Statistics (various years).

factor in Islamo-Chinese relations over the past two millennia, an element of constant challenges to both sides.

The security threats and opportunities associated with WWII only highlighted China's traditional anxieties about the Western Region (Middle East-Central Asia), and the impact of military developments in these regions on China's national security and national interests. While China was embroiled in a civil war in the early to mid-twentieth century due to the fierce conflict between the republican and the communist forces, on the minds of Chinese revolutionary leaders were the Japanese occupation and the massacre in Manchuria, a partial European occupation of some of its territories, and fears of military developments in the Middle East. WWII was a defining event in history, and, for Beijing, the defeat of Japan, Germany, and their allies brought some solace because China feared encirclement by its foes from the Middle East.

In the post-WWII era, China made the Middle East central to its foreign policy, ensuring that no security threats would undermine its own national security. Chu Enlai launched a massive campaign to mobilize support for the communist regime in Beijing, supporting anti-imperialism forces and national liberation movements, securing diplomatic recognitions, and signing treaties with the newly independent countries in the Middle East. (Behbehani, 1981: 21). In addition to neutralizing security threats in the region, Beijing was an active participant in

Country	2010	2009	2008	2007	2006	2005	2004	2003	2002	2001
Afghanistan	21489	15432	17181	10067	5272	3452	524	62076607	1742	2529
Algeria	5177.32	5127.46	4601.13	3866.41	20906.4	1768.15	1239.6	745.15	433.81	292.34
Bahrain	1051.42	686.5	786.39	487.15	3487.3	255.94	212.97	135.28	109.68	129.77
Egypt	6958.9	5845.02	6303.2	4672.53	31922.7	2145.18	1576.37	1089.58	944.77	953.21
Iraq	9864.96	5147.95	2652.83	1453.18	144474.1	823.79	469.8	56.38	517.06	469.99
Iran	29391.08	21219.09	27757.62	20589.65	11444.3	10083.27	7045.46	5622.52	3739.57	3312.89
Israel	7644.44	5178.07	6049.82	5309.94	38757.2	3027.88	2484.85	1831.3	1417.09	1315.91
Jordan	2053.61	2070.65	1949.31	1181.36	10309.8	910.68	710.76	524.81	358.03	274.29
Kazakhstan	1412913	1755234	1387777	835775	680611	11250	21269	195475	128837	155696
Kuwait	8556.95	5043.54	6790.12	3629.26	27853.1	1648.97	1248.11	1188.24	727.33	642.49
Kyrgyzstan	533028	933338	377923	222570	97220	12488	10376	20188	11886	17761
Lebanon	1346.73	1065.84	1096.72	717.34	5080.4	476.23	493.56	370.1	280.27	238.24
Libya	6576.92	5178.66	4229.44	2410.07	23980.5	1302.22	671.74	215.68	112.75	95.18
Morocco	2937.5	2504.84	2809.98	2586.11	19289.3	1483.88	1157.56	856.76	573.41	384.23
Oman	10723.72	6158.73	12421.36	7270.29	64690.2	4329.9	4389.51	2067.72	1506.65	1676.32
Palestine	26.37	24.32	41.03	37.65	280.7	23.83	9.92	6.93	4.48	4.95
Qatar	3311.28	2253.87	2385.79	1208.88	9987.9	676.39	437.78	354.88	223.55	408.61
Saudi	43195.49	32548.39	41846.17	25366.97	201403.7	16070.14	10298.1	7319.12	5106.89	4075.19
Syria	2483.26	2220.59	2303.22	1876.74	14062.1	906.37	720.67	506.28	371.08	223.19
Tajikistan	140669	149993	52405	32378	15794	1331	646	1239	1076	1717
Tunisia	1119.8	818.66	787.17	512.23	4080.8	339.63	279.22	200.89	182.41	109.37
Turkmenistan	95744	83038	35268	17858	10996	5980	7297	8752	3271	1616
Turkey	15110.58	10094.75	12569.25	11768.02	80692.4	4875.47	3412.67	2597.81	1377.83	905.02
UAE	25686.89	21226.88	28256.94	20035.65	142015.3	10775.44	8145.61	5810.46	3896.26	2824.99
Yemen	4002.94	2405.95	4394.46	2708.34	30348.1	3214.79	1916.25	1899.23	731.1	661.05
Uzbekistan	192087	160670	112819	97209	68056	4582	6079	13177	5830	5146

security developments in the Middle East on several fronts. First, it was unwavering in its support of national liberation movements battling imperialism in Yemen, Jordan, Oman, Syria, and Lebanon.[1] Second, it supported anti-conservative regime forces by assisting revolutionary forces combatting the so-called "reactionary" regimes in the Middle East, especially in Oman, Yemen and Jordan, and the Arab Gulf region (ibid.: 141). Third, it supported the PLO battling Israel for the independence of Palestine. Fourth, it supported Arab countries in their war against Israel, while simultaneously backing the peaceful settlement of the Arab Israeli conflict, according to the UN resolutions. Fifth, it was an active participant in Great Power conflict over the Middle East. Sixth, it was an active player in responding to major wars and conflicts in the Middle East, such as the Arab-Israeli wars, the Gulf War (Iran-Iraq), the Iraqi Invasion of Kuwait, the US invasion of Iraq and Afghanistan, the Arab Spring wars and conflicts and their aftermath. China opposed the US-European policy of "regime change in the region," and abstained or vetoed some UN resolutions aimed at providing an international cover for Western intervention in the Middle East within the framework of the Arab Spring (Noueihed and Warren, 2012: 183). Currently, China's security interests in the Middle East revolve around combatting the so-called terrorism originating in the Middle East and Central Asia. Primarily, China needs backing to stop the Islamic Movement of East Turkistan, an organization battling for the independence of Xinjiang.

China is also accustomed to marketing its military hardware, such as jetfighters (J21), tanks, drones, and ammunition to the Middle East and Central Asia. In fact, the remarkable growth of its military industry has attracted the attention of major consumers, such as Saudi Arabia, the UAE, and Iran. Additionally, China has constructed defense partnerships with major defense industry producers, such as Israel and Turkey. Israel alone has over 200 large, medium, and small defense industries producing state-of-the-art military hardware. China is interested in joint-defense projects, purchasing Israeli drones, and securing access to American military hardware.

Finally, China is interested in nuclear cooperation with the countries of the Middle East, especially Saudi Arabia, the UAE, Iran, Turkey, Egypt, Algeria, and other countries. The international community and the countries in the region have called repeatedly on China to play a major role in resolving Middle East conflicts, especially the Arab-Israeli conflict, the civil war in Syria, Iraq, Libya, and Yemen. While China seems to be reluctant to assume such a role, it has demonstrated growing interest in resolving such conflicts, sending special envoys, and supporting efforts at the level of the United Nations.

Sino-Middle Eastern Cultural Relations

Under the leadership of Chu Enlai, the PRC made culture an effective instrument of foreign policy; "an instrument of political and economic cooperation between China and the outside world" (Xinhua, 2010). In so doing, China was building on the rich tradition of the Silk Road, a cultural, economic, and security trade route that had connected China with its partners in the West for over two millennia. The underlining theme of China's cultural engagement with the world was "people-people relations." Chu Enlai invested heavily in the Middle East and Africa in particular, an investment that paid a productive dividend at a later stage. Beijing launched the first Health Diplomacy Program in 1962, toward Algeria, at a time when the country needed urgent healthcare due to the departure of most specialists in the post-independence era. Moreover, it exchanged sports delegations, organized music concerts, and regularly celebrated its partners' national days in Africa, Asia, and Middle Eastern countries. In fact, from 1949 to 1978, sports diplomacy, healthcare diplomacy, ping-pong diplomacy, and concluding cultural agreements with countries around the world were dominant themes in the PRC's foreign policy. Regardless of political differences, Beijing made sure to conclude protocols, conventions, and cultural agreements with every single Middle Eastern country. Additionally, it made sure to participate in sports tournaments on the Asian, African, and Middle Eastern scenes (Behbehani, 1981: 230).

Currently, China's cultural engagement with the Middle East is driven by its economic and political interests. It has established several institutions, notably the Confucius Institute (CI), to serve its wide range of cultural goals. The institute is a cultural entity that provides Mandarin instruction, celebrates cultural events, national days, weeks, years, organizes business workshops, etc. It is comparable in its mandate and activities to the American Amideast, the German Goethe Institute, or the Italian Dante Institute. The Greater Middle Eastern countries are competing to host the institute. Families are also keen on teaching their children Mandarin to prepare them for careers with Chinese corporations, or to pursue higher education in China. Table 1.3 illustrates the number and host counties of the CI in the Middle East.

Chinese higher education institutions are keen on teaching Middle Eastern languages like Arabic, Persian, Turkish, Kurdish and Hebrew, and conversely, they have become a major destination for university students from the Middle East, North Africa, and

Table 1.3 Confucius Institutes and classrooms in the Greater Middle East

Country	Number of Confucius Institutes and classrooms	Institution
Afghanistan	1	Kabul University, Faculty of Languages and Literature, Chinese Department
Bahrain	1	University of Bahrain
Egypt	5	Cairo University
		Suze Canal University
		Ain Shams University
		Neil Thematic Channel
		Luxor University
Iran	2	University of Tehran
		University of Mazandaran
Israel	2	Tel Aviv University
		Hebrew University of Jerusalem
Jordan	2	Talal Abu Ghazaleh Organization- Amman
		Philadelphia University
Lebanon	1	Saint-Joseph University
Morocco	3	Mohammed V University
		Hassan II University
		Abdemalek Essaadi University
Palestine	1	Al-Quds University
Saudi Arabia	1	Jeddah University
Sudan	1	University of Khartoum
Tunisia	2	University of Carthage
		Classroom at CRI in Sfax
Turkey	4	Bogazici University
		Middle East Technical University
		Okan University
		Yeditepe University
UAE	2	University of Dubai
		Zayed University
Kazakhstan	4	Eurasian University
		Aktobe State Pedagogical Institute
		National Technical University of Karaganda of Kazakhstan
		Kazakh National University
Kyrgyzstan	4	Bishkek State University
		Kyrgyz National University
		Osh State University
		Jalal-Abad University
Tajikistan	2	Confucius Institute at Tajik National University
		Confucius Institute at Mining-Metallurgical Institute of Tajikistan
Uzbekistan	2	Tashkent State Institute of Oriental Studies
		Samarkand State Institute of Foreign Languages
Total	40	Insufficient demand for more centers

This table is constructed from data provided by the Confucius Institute's website at: www.digm andarin.com/confucius-institutes-around-the-world.html

Central Asia. In fact, the decision to pursue higher education in China is no longer marred by previous ideological reservations, i.e., fear of "communist indoctrination."

Another major aspect of bilateral Chinese-Middle Eastern cultural engagement is tourism. Prior to the coronavirus crisis, hundreds of thousands of Chinese tourists visited ancient sites in Egypt, Jordan, Iran, etc. It is expected that the recovery from the pandemic will most certainly strengthen cultural contacts between China and its partners in the Greater Middle East. Pre-Corona figures estimated that

> Chinese outbound tourists grew by double digits as a percentage each year from 2002 to 2013. In 2016, there were 135 million Chinese outbound travelers, a 6% increase from 2015. In 2012, China became the world's top spender in international tourism and has remained so ever since. Tourism expenditures from China went from $24 billion in 2006 (3% of the world's total) to $261 billion in 2016 (21%) of the world's international tourism spending.
>
> *(UNWTO, 2018)*

Two major cultural events have taken place in China in the past two decades, and they give us an indication of participation in future Chinese world cultural events: the 2008 Olympic Games, and the 2010 Shanghai International Expo. In 2008, China was accused of courting its Sudanese partner, supplying political and diplomatic support to avoid world sanctions over the Darfur Genocide. Some 150 human rights organizations launched a global campaign to boycott the games, but despite such efforts Beijing managed to organize a successful event. The credit goes to the support it received from its partners in the Middle East, Africa, Central Asia, and other Asian partners. The second event was the 2010 Shanghai Exhibition that was described as one of the most successful world exhibitions, due to the wide participation of countries in the event, the level of organization, and the technology used.

Currently, China is accused of committing major human rights violations against the Uyghur-Muslim minority in Xinjiang, and incarcerating over a million Uyghur in concentration camps. However, the majority of Arab and Islamic countries are unwilling to criticize China over its treatment to the Uyghur, due to economic interests.

Finally, the outbreak of the corona pandemic in the winter of 2020, originating in the Chinese city of Wuhan, was alarming to the international community. China worked closely with its partners in the Middle East, especially the UAE, to develop and disseminate the Sinopharm vaccine.

Conclusion

China has made huge inroads into the Middle East. Beijing managed to build massive political engagement with the region during the Revolutionary Period, and well into the Economic Reform Era. Its diplomacy and political engagement are conducted at the highest levels; presidents have made visiting the Middle East and meeting its heads of state a major event in their presidencies. Similarly, monarchs and heads of state from the region frequently exchange visits and meet collectively with their Chinese counterparts.

In terms of energy cooperation, the Middle East provides China with over half of its consumption needs. It is expected that Chinese reliance on the region will increase in both crude oil and natural gas imports. Sino-Middle Eastern trade relations have also witnessed a remarkable growth. Bilateral volume of trade is estimated at $370 billion, heading steadily toward $600 billion by 2025. China wants to deal in free trade agreements with the region, individually and collectively. The conclusion of the GCC-China Free Trade Agreement will most certainly strengthen bilateral trade to unprecedented levels. As for Sino-Middle Eastern security cooperation, the Middle East provides both threats and opportunities for China. Beijing's aim is to neutralize terrorism threats, and market its military hardware to major consumers in the region, especially Saudi Arabia, the UAE, Iran, Iraq, and Libya. Beijing is also interested in close military cooperation with some defense industry producers, such as Israel and Turkey. Ultimately, China is also willing to provide nuclear energy to its partners in the region. Finally, Sino-Middle Eastern cultural cooperation represents a cornerstone of bilateral engagement. The two sides are keen on joint cultural activities, such as sports, concerts, providing scholars for higher education, and hosting the Confucius Institute across the region. In all categories, China is making its presence noticeable in the Middle East. This massive engagement is alarming to European and US interests in the region. It has intensified rivalry in several sectors, especially in the energy sector.

Note

1 Behbehani (1981: 53).

References

Behbehani, Hisham S. H., 1981. *China's Foreign Policy in the Arab World: 1955–1975*, London: KPI.

BP (British Petroleum), 2022. *BP Statistical Review for World Energy*. Available at: www.bp.com/statisticalreview

Chen, Shaofeng, 2008. Motivations behind China's Foreign Oil Quest: A Perspective from the Chinese Government and the Oil Companies, *Journal of Chinese Political Science*, 13(1), 79–104.

EIA (Energy Information Administration), 2017. *China Annual Report*. Available at: www.eia.gov/todayinenergy/detail.php?id=34812

EIA (Energy Information Administration), 2018. *China Energy Report*. Available at: www.eia.gov/todayinenergy/detail.php?id=34812

Hassan, Ahmed, 2010. Islam Came to Southeast Asia from China: Evidence from Chinese Roof Design in Kampung Laut's Old Mosque in Malaysia, *Canadian Social Science*, 6(5): 2–15.

Ibn Al Athir, 1160–1233. *Al Kamil: The Complete History*, Amman, Jordan: International Ideas Home.

Living Islam, 2021. Seek Knowledge as Far as China, June 21. Available at: www.livingislam.org/n/skx_e.html

National Bureau of China Statistics, various years. *China Statistical Yearbook*. Available at: www.stats.gov.cn/tjsj/ndsj/2020/indexeh.htm

Noueihed, Lin and Alex Warren, 2012. *The Battle for the Arab Spring: Revolution, Counter-Revolution and the Making of a New Era*, Newhaven, CT: Yale University Press.

Olimat, Muhamad S. 2016. *China and the Gulf Cooperation Council Countries: Strategic Partnership in a Changing World*, Lanham, MD: Lexington Books.

Reichelt, Karl Ludvig, 1951. *Religion in Chinese Garments*, Cambridge: James Clarke & Company Co.

Shichor, Yitzhak, 1979. *The Middle East in China's Foreign Policy, 1949–1977*, Cambridge: Cambridge University Press.

UNWTO (United Nations World Tourism Organization), 2018. Chinese Outbound Tourism Market. Available at: www2.unwto.org/event/unwto-workshop-chinese-outbound-tourism-market

U.S. Department of Energy, n.d. China's Crude Oil Imports by Source, 2006 and 2007. Available at: www.energy.gov/oil

Xinhua, 2010. Chinese Cultural Events in Turkey Boost Mutual Understanding, Says Ambassador, October 14. Available at: http://news.xinhuanet.com/english2010/china/2010-10/14/c_13557 877.htm

2

CHINA'S ENERGY DIPLOMACY TOWARDS THE MIDDLE EAST IN THE BRI ERA

Energy Security Versus Geopolitics

Janet Xuanli Liao

1 Introduction

China's energy diplomacy towards the Middle East began in the mid-1990s, after the country became a net oil importer in 1993. Driven by worries about the security of oil supply, Beijing's strategy towards the region was to avoid taking sides in the complex power struggles, but to rely on the United States to ensure regional stability (Andrews-Speed et al., 2002). Following China's growing potential and the launch of the "Belt and Road Initiative" (BRI) since 2013, however, its engagements with the Middle East have shown notable changes over the past decade. Coupled with the policy changes of the United States and the major powers in the region, such as Saudi Arabia and Iran, China's energy diplomacy has become more sophisticated and impactful.

The questions to be addressed by this chapter are two-fold: what has changed in China's energy diplomacy towards the Middle East in the BRI era? And, what are the likely implications of Beijing's new strategy on the balance of power and the regional stability of the Middle East? Two regional powers – Saudi Arabia and Iran – will be taken as case studies to show China's changing position over the past decade. The selection of the cases was partially based on their significance in China's energy diplomacy in the region, and it was also due to the delicate relationships between the two powers and their complex dealings with the United States. In Garlick and Havlová's (2020: 4) words, Beijing "aims to establish and maintain ties with Iran, but not at the expense of damaging its relations with US-backed Saudi Arabia". This strategy seems to have succeeded so far, yet how long it can be sustained may not be determined by China alone, but will also be affected by the US-China relations and the US strategy in the Gulf region.

The discussion below is comprised of four sections. Section 2 reviews China's energy diplomacy towards the Middle East over the past decade, to present the context of the analysis. It aims to show the remaining significance of the Middle East oil in China's

DOI: 10.4324/9781003048404-4

25

energy security agenda but will also portray China's growing political influence associated with the BRI. The two sections that follow will investigate, respectively, China's energy diplomacy towards Saudi Arabia (Section 3) and Iran (Section 4), in the BRI era, to show the changing features in Beijing's new approach towards the Gulf region. Section 5 is the conclusion.

2 The Middle East and China's Oil Supply: From the 1990s to the BRI Era

Compared with the other regions China sought for oil supplies from the mid-1990s, such as Southeast Asia, Russia and Central Asia, the Middle East was distant geographically and strange in cultural and religious terms, and therefore, had long been peripheral to China's overall map of interests. In the early 1970s, China formed diplomatic ties with a few Middle Eastern countries, including Iran, Kuwait, Lebanon, Jordan and Turkey, but it was not until the beginning of 1992 that China established diplomatic relations with all the Middle Eastern countries. Underpinned by the strategy to "get along with everyone", China's dealings with the region at the initial stage were focused on economic and energy cooperation, while the United States was expected to take responsibility for regional order and stability (Zhang, 1999; Chen, 2018: 18–19; Guzansky and Lavi, 2020). But China's growing economic strength since the early 1990s made its energy engagements with the Middle East alarming to many, over its likelihood of challenging the US position as the "principal external security guarantor of the region" (Andrews-Speed et al., 2002: 65, 90), long before it stretched political mussels.

Following the launch of the Belt and Road Initiative (BRI) in 2013 – the Silk Road Economic Belt and the 21st Century Maritime Silk Road – China's potential to contest US dominance in the Middle East seems to have become more a reality than a theoretical hypothesis. As China's most ambitious foreign policy scheme, the BRI was aimed to link China to Central and South Asia and onward to Europe via land and maritime connections, respectively. It was estimated that over $1 trillion of investment would be made via BRI on hundreds of infrastructure projects in more than 60 countries (Chatzky and McBride, 2020). Sitting at the juncture of Asia, Africa, and Europe, the Middle East occupies an unique position at the intersection of the BRI, especially with some vital maritime chokepoints, such as the Strait of Hormuz, the Strait of Bab al-Mandeb, and the Suez Canal. To facilitate the success of the BRI and further ensure its oil supply, Beijing has paid greater attention to the Middle East going beyond energy supply. Between 2013 and 2019, China made investments totalling $93.3 billion in the region, mostly in the energy sector ($52.8 billion), followed by transport ($18.6 billion), real estate ($18.4 billion), and utilities ($3.5 billion) (Chaziza, 2020a). To date, China has surpassed the United States as the top trading partner in the Middle East, and is also the largest external source of direct foreign investment (Ghasseminejad, 2021).

For China, the Middle East remains a vital player in oil provision: it was Beijing's top oil supplier in 1996 and has remained so 25 years later. During this period, China's GDP has grown 18 times from $863.75 billion in 1996 to $15.42 trillion in 2020 (*Trading Economics* 2021; Xinhua, 2021), while its oil imports have increased nearly 24 times, from 22.62 million tonnes (mts) to 540 mts (Tian, 1997: 8; V boshi619, 2022). Holding 48 per cent of the world's proven oil reserves and 32 per cent of the total oil output, the Middle East has supplied around 50 per cent of China's total crude imports and the highest amount reached over 60 per cent, as indicated in Figure 2.1.

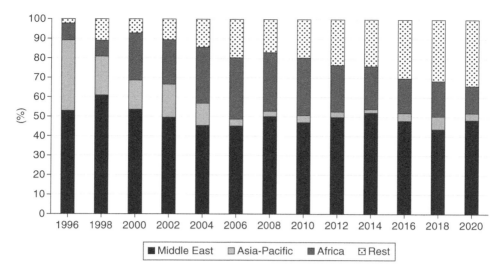

Figure 2.1 Proportion of Middle East oil in China's total imports, 1996–2020 (%)
Sources: The figures for 1996–2016 were adapted from Tian (1997) and Tian's other reports in 2001, 2007, 2013 and 2018); those for 2018–2021 were from Kunlun Consultancy (2019), V boshi619 (2022) and Yuhoucaihong 8453 (2022), respectively.

The key suppliers from the region varied to a certain extent, as shown in Figure 2.2. Saudi Arabia, for instance, supplied little crude oil to China initially but became its top supplier from 2002 and has remained so ever since. Oman used to be China's top supplier but lost such a position to Saudi Arabia pretty soon, and stayed as secondary supplier, together with Iran and, more recently, Iraq. In the old days, Beijing aimed to separate politics and business for the security of the oil supply, so the significance of the Gulf states was largely based on their capacity of oil supplies. Since the BRI era, Beijing has more often combined energy and politics in its dealings with the Middle East countries, but has still tried to work with all the countries without taking sides to avoid heavy involvement in regional disputes (Sun and Wang, 2020). Beijing has also chosen two regional giants Saudi Arabia and Iran, as strategic partners, despite the differences in their capacity of oil provision and political ambitions.

On 19–23 January 2016, Chinese President Xi Jinping paid his first state visit to Saudi Arabia, Egypt and Iran. Xi emphasized the need to further strengthen Sino-Arab relations and signed a comprehensive strategic partnership with the two regional rivalries, Saudi Arabia and Iran, in the same week (Perlez, 2016; Fulton, 2020). Prior to President Xi's departure, the Chinese government issued its first "Arab Policy Paper", on 13 January, outlining Beijing's broad policy goals towards the region. These goals included the so-called "1+2+3" formula, centring around (1) energy cooperation as the core; (2) infrastructure, trade, and investment; and (3) high-tech fields, such as clean energy and aerospace. Other initiatives include concluding a free trade agreement with the Gulf Cooperation Council and Chinese efforts to combat terrorism (Wille, 2016). In July 2018, President Xi again visited the United Arab Emirates (UAE), when the two sides signed 13 agreements and MoU relating to financial, business and trade issues, including an approval for the first Chinese state-owned financial services firm to set up in Abu Dhabi

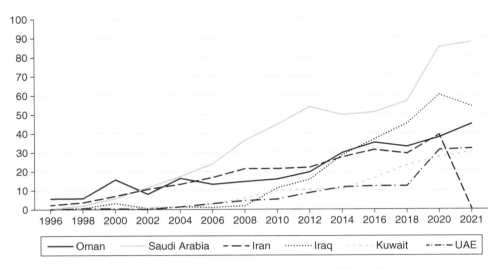

Figure 2.2 China's key oil suppliers from the Middle East, 1996–2021 (mts)

Global Market, a financial centre. The Abu Dhabi National Oil Company and the China National Petroleum Corporation (CNPC) also agreed to explore joint business opportunities within the country (Carvalho, 2018).

Following the COVID-19 pandemic, Beijing stepped up vaccine diplomacy to its Middle East partners. On 9 December 2020, the UAE became the first country in the world to approve a vaccine developed by the China National Pharmaceutical Group Corporation (Sinopharm). Bahrain followed suit and approved the vaccine on 13 December. In May 2020, Dubai and Huawei announced an initiative to expand cooperation in artificial intelligence and digital transformation (Fulton, 2020). China has also endorsed the low-carbon initiatives of the Gulf countries, such as Saudi Arabia's "2030 vision", though its investment in the renewable sector is still limited.

3 China's Energy Diplomacy Towards Saudi Arabia

3.1 Oil Trade Involving Little Politics: the 1990s–2014

Saudi Arabia has the world's second largest oil reserves and is also a strong economic and politic power in the Persian Gulf, but China did not establish diplomatic relationship with the Kingdom until July 1990. Prior to that, Saudi Arabia was a strong opponent of communism and kept diplomatic relations with Taiwan, though unofficial ties remained after China's "Open Door" policy in 1979 (Al-Tamimi, 2012: 4). Since China turned into a net oil importer in 1993, a more concrete relationship started to take shape bilaterally, though their oil trade did not progress as well as expected initially, as China had constrained refinery capacity in handing Saudi's "sour" crude. Thanks to the "strategic oil partnership" proposed by Chinese President Jiang Zemin, in his first state visit to Saudi Arabia in October 1999, the two sides signed a "Strategic Oil Cooperation Agreement" and agreed to open domestic refinery sectors for each other's investment. As a result, three joint-venture refineries were built and became operational, between 2008 and 2014, in China's Qingdao (Sinopec and Aramco) and Fujian (Sinopec, Aramco and ExxonMobil), and in Saudi Yanbu (Sinopec and Aramco) (Liao, 2015: 96–98). In the meantime, the "Look East" policy adopted by the Saudi government in the post-9/11 era also helped fortify the Sino-Saudi partnership, making Saudi Arabia China's No. 1 crude supplier from 2002 (Al-Tamimi, 2012: 3, 5).

Bilateral energy cooperation was further enhanced by official visits of top leaders from both countries. In January 2006, King Abdullah bin Abdulaziz al-Saud visited China, the first foreign visit since his succession and the first visit by a Saudi monarch to the People's Republic since their diplomatic establishment in 1990. During his two-day visit, King Abdullah was well received by Chinese President Hu Jintao and other high-ranking leaders, and the two sides signed a series of agreements on economic, technical and energy cooperation, including a $1.7 billion investment by the state-controlled Saudi Basic Industries Corp (SABIC) in an ethylene complex owned by the China Petroleum & Chemical Corp. (Sinopec) in Tianjin (Xinhua, 2006a; Reuters, 2008). Three months later, in April 2006, Chinese President Hu Jintao paid a three-day state visit to Riyadh on his five-nation tour. Hu was happy to see the smooth development of the bilateral ties, especially that Saudi Arabia had already become China's largest trading partner in the Middle East (Xinhua, 2006b).

In June 2008, coinciding with Chinese Vice-President Xi Jinping's first official visit to Saudi Arabia, SABIC and Sinopec signed a deal in Riyadh to expand the earlier agreed investment from $1.7 billion to $4 billion, making SABIC's first major investment in China more sophisticated, to cover the whole production of ethylene and all downstream products, instead of a partial involvement. This also helped release Sinopec's refining losses due to the Chinese government's cap of domestic fuel prices, which did not match the rapid increase in international crude prices, from $80 per barrel in 2006 to above $130 per barrel in 2008. According to Zhang Xiaodong, a Middle East expert at the China Academy of Social Sciences, "Having both oil trade ties and investment in oil-related businesses like this will be a solid partnership" (Reuters, 2008). On 14 January 2012, Saudi Aramco and Sinopec established a joint venture called Yanbu Aramco Sinopec Refinery (Yasref), holding a 62.5 per cent and a 37.5 per cent share, respectively. Involving an investment of $10 billion, Yasref was Sinopec's first international downstream invest-ment. The project had a designed capacity to process 400,000 barrels per day (bpd) of Arabian Heavy crude oil and produce high-quality transportation fuels (*Hydrocarbon Processing*, 2016; Valori, 2016).

3.2 *China and Saudi Arabia in the BRI Era*

China's dealing with Saudi Arabia since the BRI era has involved more political elem-ents, though oil trade still is the centre of the bilateral relationship. After the United States decreased its oil imports following the shale revolution, Saudi Arabia became increasingly reliant on trade with China to compensate for the loss and to maintain its market share. In 2014, Saudi was already China's largest oil supplier, whose crude demand accounted for 16 per cent of China's oil imports. The record low oil prices in late 2014 deepened Saudi reliance on the Chinese market even further, as it led the Kingdom to a deficit of over 360 billion riyals in 2015 (Wille, 2016). When Saudi King Salman bin Abdulaziz Al Saud assumed power in January 2015, he decided to reform the Saudi economy by cooperating with non-OPEC countries via the OPEC+ mechanism, listing Saudi Aramco on international stock markets, and developing renewable energy. He also focused on developing relations with the "key minority" countries globally and building semi-alliance regionally to contain Iran (Chen, 2020).

Against such a background, Chinese President Xi Jinping's tour visit to Saudi Arabia, Egypt and Iran, on 19–23 January 2016, was viewed as being of strategic significance to those powers and for China's "Belt and Road Initiative". During Xi's visit, Beijing upgraded its ties with both Saudi Arabia and Iran to "comprehensive strategic partnership", despite their rivalries since the 1979 Iranian Revolution. As a matter of fact, the Saudi-Iran tensions escalated on 2 January 2016, when Iranian protesters stormed the Saudi embassy in Tehran over the execution of a Shiite cleric on terrorism charges, which had broken the bilateral diplomatic relations. As President Xi stuck to his agenda of the visit, many wondered whether Beijing would mediate the Saudi-Iranian tensions. In contrast to its previous position of staying out of regional politics, the Chinese Ambassador to Tehran, Pang Sen, explicitly stated that China would be willing to play a role in helping restore peace and stability in the Middle East. According to Gordon Kwan, head of oil and gas research at Nomura, "China wants some reassurance that tensions in the Middle East will not continue to escalate, especially between Saudi Arabia and Iran" (*Tehran Times*, 2016; Wille, 2016). King Salman and President Xi also agreed that the two countries should cooperate under the BRI framework, and jointly inaugurated the new Yasref refinery. President Xi defined Yanbu as the regional point of arrival of the Silk Road and the axis of the new Saudi industrialization (Valori, 2016). Equally keen to help the Saudi regime move away from an oil-centred economy, the China Nuclear Engineering Group Corp. (CNEC) agreed to conduct research on high-temperature gas-cooled (HTGR) nuclear reactor technology with the Saudi government, which would allow CNEC to export its HTGR nuclear technology to Saudi, and 16 nuclear power plants were expected to be constructed by 2032 (Lim, 2016).

On 15–18 March 2017, King Salman paid a state visit to China at President Xi's invitation, after his tour to Malaysia, Indonesia and Japan. Faced with the post-Joint Comprehensive Plan of Action (JCPOA) Iran that now held a more robust regional role, on one hand, and with President Trump's vague policy towards the Middle East, on the other, Saudi Arabia had worries on both strategic and economic grounds. King Salman's unprecedented long trip indicated how eager he was to build ties with new friends in order to rely less on Washington, yet building ties with Japan side by side with China also showed his intention to avoid over-reliance on Beijing (Malik, 2017). Still, Saudi Arabia made political efforts to please China, by backing China's policy of handling the Muslim minority Uighurs in Xinjiang on the international stage. In July 2019, Saudi Arabia was among the 37 countries that sent the United Nations a letter of support for China and praised Beijing's policy as "remarkable achievements in the field of human rights" (Guzansky and Lavi, 2020). The Kingdom continued to expand its investment in the Chinese market as well. When Crown Prince Mohammed bin Salman visited Beijing in February 2019, for instance, a joint venture was signed between the Saudi Aramco and North Industries Group Corp. (Norinco) and Panjin Sincen to develop a fully integrated refining and petrochemical complex in China's Liaojing Province, the Huajin Aramco Petrochemical Co.. The project was the largest Sino-foreign joint venture to date that involved a $10 billion investment, including a 300,000-b/d refinery, a 1.5mts/yr ethylene cracker, and a 1.3mts/yr paraxylene unit. The Saudi Aramco was to supply up to 70 per cent of the crude required and held 35 per cent of the stakes, with Norinco and Panjin holding 36 per cent and 29 per cent stakes, respectively (*OGJ*, 2019). Before long, however, the Saudi Aramco suspended the planned project in August 2020, due to the uncertain market prospect caused by the COVID-19 pandemic (Bloomberg, 2020).

The unfortunate incident did not seem to harm much of the Sino-Saudi collaboration, though. In late 2020, the Saudi Telecom decided to build a partnership with China's Alibaba Cloud to help the Kingdom build its cloud computing infrastructure (Guzansky and Lavi, 2020; Kantor, 2021). In April 2021 again, Saudi Arabia announced the sale of 1 per cent of Aramco's stake (around $19 billion) and a pipeline of 160 projects across 16 sectors, with the aim of raising $55 billion funding over the next four years, to increase revenue and reduce the government budget deficit. This was a part of the privatization programme launched by the Saudi Council of Economic and Development Affairs to achieve the Vision 2030 objectives. Unsurprisingly, some major Chinese investors, including the sovereign wealth fund, the China Investment Corporation (CIC), were reportedly in talks with the Saudis to buy a stake (CNBC, 2021), which should not be purely for business purposes, but this attracted little attention from the outside world. What did spark more international concerns was the development in Saudi-China collaboration on civilian nuclear technology.

Saudi Arabia's nuclear energy plan was first initiated in 2006, together with the other members of the Gulf Cooperation Council. But it was soon changed to be a nuclear power programme on its own, as suggested by a royal decree in April 2010, "to meet the Kingdom's growing requirements for energy to generate electricity, produce desalinated water and reduce reliance on depleting hydrocarbon resources." In 2011, Riyadh declared its plan to construct 16 nuclear power reactors within 20 years at a cost of $80 billion, to generate 20 per cent of the Saudi electricity (WNA, 2022). The Saudis then signed contracts with Japan's GE Hitachi Nuclear Energy and Toshiba/ Westinghouse in September 2013, with South Korea's Atomic Energy Research Institute in March 2015, and agreed with China on nuclear energy cooperation. In August 2017, two MoUs were signed between the China National Nuclear Corp. (CNNC) and the Saudi Geological Survey (SGS), and by the Saudi Technology Development and Investment Corp. with China Nuclear Engineering Group Corp., on developing nuclear technologies for civilian purposes (Reuters, 2017; WNA, 2022). Riyadh also sought assistance from the Trump administration for its civilian nuclear programme, but the effort did not succeed as the Saudis refused to sign on to the standard International Atomic Energy Agency (IAEA) requirements. Therefore, when Saudi Arabia asked China to build a facility for extracting uranium yellowcake from uranium ore, a *Wall Street Journal* report, on 4 August 2020, claimed that the considerable shift in Riyadh's civilian nuclear programme had caused concerns in the US Congress, where a bipartisan group of lawmakers expressed alarm about Saudi nuclear energy plans and the intentions behind them (Chaziza, 2020b). Despite the Saudi Energy Ministry denying "categorically" having built a uranium ore facility, China's growing presence in the Middle East, together with its BRI scheme, seemed unbearable by Washington. In May 2021, the US Senate advanced legislation designed to counter China's growing global influence, including in the Middle East. The legislation included $300 million for a "Countering Chinese Influence" fund, and $100 million in funding for journalists and media companies to "raise awareness of and increase transparency regarding the negative impact of activities related to the Belt and Road Initiative" (*Wall Street Journal*, 2020; Farooq, 2021).

To be sure, Riyadh has no intention of seeing its relationship with Beijing damaging its ties with Washington, as there is no substitute for the US presence in the Gulf to halt the Iranian expansion. In terms of China, although it has become more confident and assertive in the Gulf region and may wish to strengthen its relations with Riyad at the expense of the United States, it has neither the capacity nor the intention of displacing the USA as a strategic guarantor of the security of the region (Guzansky and Lavi, 2020). Saudi Arabia perhaps also wishes to use its relations with China for leverage on Washington, but the Biden administration has already shown its resolve to maintain strong ties with Riyadh to prevent the "autocracy" regimes, including China, from playing an upper hand in the Persian Gulf. Therefore, although Biden's visit to Saudi Arabia in July 2022 was criticized by some as compromising the US value-based foreign policy, senior officials in the White House believed that the realist turn in Biden's approach towards the Middle East was "a necessary corrective" (Heydemann, 2022).

4 China's Energy Diplomacy Towards Iran

China's energy diplomacy towards Iran since the 1990s has triggered numerous controversies and suspicions, probably more than any other oil suppliers, especially after Iran's nuclear programme was discovered. There are two main factors responsible for this situation: one was China's dealing with the Iranian nuclear crisis, and the other was the Sino-Iranian "Comprehensive Strategic Partnership" that came into being in early 2021. If Beijing's dealings with Tehran in the early years could be said to be a choice that it was compelled to make, then the latest development of the bilateral relationship is certainly a preference taken by China.

4.1 China's Dealing with Iran Prior to the 2015 JCPOA: Playing a Dual Game?

Iran was one of the first Middle Eastern countries to establish diplomatic relations with China in August 1971, and it also supported China's entry to the United Nations in October the same year to replace the Nationalist government in Taiwan (Liao, 2015: 100). Yet the cordial relationship did not last long, due to Ayatollah Khomeini's policy on "Neither East, nor West – but the Islamic Republic" after the Iranian Revolution in 1979 (Therme, 2019). When China was looking for oil supplies from the Middle East in the 1990s, Iran soon became an important supplier due not so much to politics but rather to Iran's status as the fourth largest oil reserves in the world. Between 1993 and 2000, oil supplies from Iran grew ten-fold in China's crude imports, from 67,900 tonnes to 7mts, and the two sides also signed a series of treaties on trade promotion and petroleum cooperation around the time (Liao, 2015: 100). Washington was unhappy to see Beijing's dealing with Iran, which was listed by President G.W. Bush as a part of the "Axis of Evil" in 2002, but China's polite attitude at the time seemed to help the two powers avoid further tensions.

In August 2002, Iran's secret nuclear programme was revealed, which caused concerns from the international community about Iran's likelihood in violation of the Non-Proliferation Treaty (NPT), which Iran signed in July 1968 and ratified in February 1970, a month before it came into force (United States Institute of Peace, 2020). Between February 2003 and November 2004, the International Atomic Energy Agency (IAEA) made several inspections of Iran's nuclear sites and reported the discovery of highly enriched uranium. Soon after, the EU3+3 (Britain, France and Germany, the USA, Russia and China) held a series of meetings with Iran asking it to suspend all nuclear related activities, and the United Nations Security Council also passed a number of Resolutions, between 2006 and 2009, demanding Iran suspend its uranium enrichment, plus introducing sanctions against Iran's noncompliance (Security Council Report, 2020). Yet, the process seemed to have little effect, in which Beijing aligned with the other powers politically, to prevent Iran from obtaining nuclear weapons, as it never blocked the UN Security Council efforts against Tehran.

In the meantime, China resisted the US pressure to isolate Iran and continued its energy trade and cooperation with Iran to secure its own energy interest. Since 2004, the state-owned China National Petroleum Corp. (CNPC) has been operating in Iran's oil and gas sectors, together with the China Petroleum & Chemical Corp. (Sinopec), and the China National Offshore Oil Corporation (CNOOC). As shown in Table 2.1, Beijing committed nearly $130 billion in investment in Iran's oil and gas sector between 2004 and 2011, partially due to the forced withdrawal of Western oil majors, such as Japan's Inpex and French oil major Total. Taking Inpex as an example, which invested 75 per cent of a $2 billion plan to Iran's Azadegan, in 2004, one of the largest oil fields in the world. But after being listed by the US as one of the 41 firms dealing with Iran's oil and gas sectors, Inpex reduced its stake to 10 per cent in 2006 and withdrew from Iran completely in 2010 (UANI, 2021). This enabled the CNPC to sign two deals with the National Iranian Oil Co. (NIOC) in 2009 and 2011, respectively, on developing the North and South Azadegan oilfields to increase oil outputs, plus a technical service contract on oil field upgrading. According to Leverett and Leverett (2011), Beijing's move was part of the US-China tacit compromise whereby China would agree to the US-led multilateral sanctions against Iran, while America would agree to refrain from applying unilateral sanctions against major Chinese corporations.

Therefore, despite an MoU reached between the CNOOC and the NIOC on developing the North Pars gas field, in late 2006, the CNOOC decided in February 2008 to cancel the signing of the $16 billion contract at the last minute (AGOC, 2008), due to Iran's non-compliance with two UN Security Council Resolutions (Res. 1737 and Res. 1747). After the IAEA report, on 8 November 2011, with "credible" details showing that Iran already had obtained some of the expertise needed to build nuclear weapons, "should it decide to do so", the EU decided in January 2012 to ban oil imports from Iran, starting 1 July as part of the measures to ratchet up the pressure on Iran's nuclear programme. Beijing followed suit immediately and nearly halved its oil imports from Tehran in 2012, and CNPC as well as pulling out of the South Pars Phase 11 (SP11) in July 2012 (ACA, 2011; Bloomberg, 2012a, 2012b). China might be playing a dual game in Iran (Garver, 2010), but it was largely aimed at securing its energy supply while preventing Iran from violating its NPT obligations, rather than pursuing geopolitical advantages, as some assumed.

4.2 China and Iran in the BRI Era: "No East, No West but China?"

After a decade of negotiations between the P5+1 and Iran, the JCPOA was finally reached on 14 July 2015, under which Iran agreed to limit its sensitive nuclear activities and allow in international inspectors, in return for the lifting of sanctions imposed previously that had cost the country more than $160 billion in oil revenue from 2012 to 2016 alone. The deal would also allow Iran to gain access to more than $100 billion in assets frozen overseas and to resume selling oil on international markets and using the global financial system for trade (BBC, 2019). On 16 January 2016, the IAEA submitted a report

Janet Xuanli Liao

Table 2.1 Chinese energy-related investments in Iran, 2004–2021

Year	Company	Investment amount (US$ billion)	Content of the Agreements
2004	Zhuhai Zhenrong	20	Importing 110 mts of LNG over 25 years;
2004	Sinopec & NIOC	70	Sinopec helps develop Yadavaran oilfields &and buy 150k bpd of oil/yr for 25 yrs and 250mts of LNG for 30 yrs
2007	Sinopec & NIOC	2	Develop Phase 2: North Yadavaran oil field
2007	CNOOC & NIOC	16	Agreement reached for CNOOC to help develop North Pars field but the contract was not signed due to US pressure
2009	CNPC & NIOC	1.76	Help increase North Azadegan oil fields' outputs to 115k bpd within 6 yrs
2009	CNPC & NIOC	4.7	Help develop Phase 11 of South Pars but pulled out in 2012 without much progress made
2009	Chinese Consortium	2-3	Help develop capacities of Abadan & Persian Gulf Star refineries
2011	CNPC & NIOC	2.5	Help develop the South Azadegan oilfields' output from 55k bpd to 600k bpd
2017	Total, CNPC & Petropars (Iran)	4.8	Help develop Phase 11 of South Pars gas field, but Total had to pull out in Aug. 2018, selling its 50.1% stake to CNPC in Nov. 2018. Yet CNPC also pulled out in June 2019 to avoid US sanctions.
2021	Governments deal	400	The deal was agreed in 2019 but was signed in 2021. Of the total, $280 bn would be invested in Iran's oil, gas and petrochemicals sectors. The rest would be invested in dozens of fields, e.g. banking, telecom, ports, railways, health care & info technology, over 25 years, in exchange for Iranian discounted oil supply.

Sources: adapted from various sources, including *China Daily*, 2004; *Tehran Times*, 2011; Liao, 2015; *New York Times*, 2021.

to the UN Security Council confirming that Iran had taken the steps required under the JCPOA for nuclear-related sanctions to be lifted (Security Council Report, 2020).

As Iran's largest crude market since 2007 (receiving 40 per cent of Iran's crude exports), China was happy to see Iran returning to the international oil market, although this meant that China had to face more competitions from international oil majors (Perlez, 2016). More importantly, with the "Belt and Road" scheme in operation, China has placed more emphasis on Iran politically, due not only to its important geopolitical position, but also to the shared antipathy by the two countries towards Western domination of the world order (Wille, 2016). Therefore, a week after the lifting of international sanctions, on 22–23 January, Chinese President Xi Jinping visited Tehran as the last stop of his tour in the Middle East. During Xi's visit, the two sides signed 17 agreements for cooperation in areas of energy, trade and industry, etc., and also agreed to increase bilateral trade by tenfold in the next decade to $600 billion. Prior to this, China was already Iran's top trading partner, with bilateral trade surpassing $50 billion in 2014 (CNBC, 2016).

China also resumed its energy activities with Iran soon afterwards. In November 2016, the CNPC joined an agreement signed by French oil major Total on the SP11 project, the first Western energy investment in Iran since the lifting of international sanctions earlier in the year. The SP11 project has a production capacity of 1.8 bcfd and would be pursued in two phases with an estimated investment at $4.8 billion. Total would hold a 50.1 per cent interest, with the CNPC taking 30 per cent interest and Iran's Petropars holding the rest (Dittrick, 2016). The NIOC also planned to begin supplying its domestic market in 2021 with the country's first-ever international petroleum contract (IPC), which would be applicable to SP11, to "prompt other IOCs to re-enter the country's upstream sector" (Dunnahoe, 2017). Before long, US President Donald Trump abandoned the JCPOA deal in May 2018 unilaterally and reinstated sanctions, targeting Iran in August. Consequently, Total decided to withdraw in August 2018 and sold its 50.1 per cent stake to the CNPC in November. The CNPC also had to pull out in June 2019 to avoid likely sanctions (UANI, 2021).

Following a visit by Iranian Foreign Minister Javad Zarif to Beijing, in August 2019, China announced that it planned to incorporate Iran into the BRI with a pledged $400 billion of investment in 17 different projects, covering several fields of nuclear energy, port, trade and transport. Of this, $280 billion would be invested in Iran's oil, gas and petrochemicals sectors, where Chinese firms would be given the first refusal to bid on any and all petrochemical projects in Iran. The remaining $120 billion would be used to upgrade Iran's transport and manufacturing infrastructure. In return, Iran was to provide China with heavily discounted oil that its huge economy required (South Front, 2019; Talwar, 2020). The deal was confirmed on Chinese Foreign Minister Wang Yi's visit to Tehran, on 26 March 2021, when he signed an agreement with his Iranian counterpart Javad Zarif, according to the *New York Times* (2021).

Interestingly, both Tehran and Beijing maintained a low profile on the agreement. Monshipouri and Heiran-Nia (2020: 159–160), for instance, argued that Iran's "Look East" policy was forced upon it by Tramp's "maximum pressure", as the Rouhani government would prefer a balanced relationship with both the West and East. They also saw the deal benefiting more Tehran's ruling elites rather than the Iranian population. China did not officially confirm that it was on the verge of an agreement with Iran either, trying to maintain a balance between Riyadh and Tehran. Just days before word of the China-Iran agreement leaked, Chinese and Arab League foreign ministers adopted the Amman Declaration, with Arab states endorsing China's central foreign policy concept of "a community with a shared future for mankind". Indeed, China's combined trade with Saudi Arabia, the UAE and Israel in 2018 was 3.5 times greater than its trade with Iran ($123 billion vs $35 billion) (Vakil, 2021). While China remains Iran's top oil importer, Chinese firms have not increased investment, imports or exports at the exponential levels pledged in 2016. In fact, Chinese investment has decreased substantially since then, and there was no record of oil imports from Iran either in 2021, as shown in Figure 2.2. Some concluded that the Sino-Iranian deal would not mean a massive shift in China's international policy, and the deal was unlikely to fundamentally threaten the balance of power in the Middle East as well (Figueroa, 2021).

5 Conclusion

China's energy diplomacy towards the Middle East has a history of nearly 30 years by now. Employing a strategy of getting along with everyone in the region, China has made the Middle East not only the most important source of its oil and gas supply, but also a crucial front line for its BRI strategy. China has managed to develop a comprehensive strategic partnership with two regional rivals – Saudi Arabia and Iran – who are competing for both regional leadership and oil markets, their dealing with the United States also vary greatly. China has attempted to build solid trade and energy relationship with both powers, while maintaining a balance between them. Beijing has also learnt from this process that it is not always possible to stay out of regional politics, especially with its growing influence and the fading US interest in the Middle East.

As its growing presence in the Middle East has been viewed as achieved at the cost of American national security interests (Farooq, 2021), China has tried to pursue a strategically hedged approach to build up an economic and political presence without challenging the US dominance in the region, in particular, in the security domain (Fulton, 2020). In the BRI era, energy supply may still be a crucial pillar in China's diplomacy in the Middle East, but it is no longer dominant. Regardless whether the BRI ambition could succeed in the end, the controversies triggered so far by China's presence in the Middle East have gone far beyond oil and gas supplies, and will have geopolitical implications for the region and even the whole world.

Finally, despite the more than 15 months of talks in Vienna between Iran and P5+1, on resuming the 2015 JCPOA that was abandoned by President Trump in 2018, there has been no deal reached when the meetings ended on 8 August 2022 (Bloomberg, 2022). Although Tehran insisted that its nuclear programme is entirely peaceful, the IAEA Director General Rafael Grossi warned in early August 2022 that, Iran's nuclear programme was "growing in ambition and capacity", and the US Special Envoy for Iran, Robert Malley, also said Tehran has enough highly enriched uranium on hand to make a bomb and could do so in a matter of weeks (Voice of America, 2022). If Iran decided to go nuclear in the foreseeable future, Beijing might need to re-think its dealings with Tehran, or to play on its potential to push Iran into behaving itself. This would not only allow Iran to have better energy cooperation with a wider world, but could also enhance China's geopolitical significance in the Middle East and ultimately serve the purposes of its BRI ambition.

References

ACA (Arms Control Association) (2011). "The IAEA's Iran report: Assessment and implications", 8 November. Available at: www.armscontrol.org/issue-briefs/2011-11/iaeas-iran-report-assessment-implications

AGOC (Alexander's Gas & Oil Connections) (2008). "CNOOC and NIOC agree on development plan for North Pars gas field", 12 November. Available at: www.gasandoil.com/news/ middle_east/ 60640cbb2f6b96c196a0f7cf47b8ae0b

Al-Tamimi, N. (2012). "China-Saudi Arabia relations: Economic partnership or strategic alliance?" Available at: www.academia.edu/4101698/China_Saudi_Arabia_Relations_Economic _Partnership_or_Strategic_Alliance_Durham_University_UK_

Andrews-Speed, P., Liao, X. and Dannreuther, R. (2002). "The Strategic Implications of China's Energy Needs", Adelphi Paper No. 346, New York: Oxford University Press.

BBC (2019). "Iran nuclear deal: Key details", 11 June. Available at: www.bbc.co.uk/news/world-middle-east-33521655

Bloomberg (2012a). "EU agrees to ban Iran oil imports to target nuclear program", 23 January. Available at: www.bloomberg.com/news/articles/2012-01-22/european-union-likely-to-agree-on-iranian-oil-ban

Bloomberg (2012b). "Iran crude supplies to China fall for fourth month in March", 23 April. Available at: www.bloomberg.com/news/articles/2012-04-23/china-crude-oil-imports-from-iran-drop-54-on-year-customs-says

Bloomberg (2020). "Saudi Aramco suspends $10 billion china oil refinery venture", 21 August. Available at: www.bloomberg.com/news/articles/2020-08-21/saudi-aramco-suspends-10-billion-china-oil-refinery-venture

Bloomberg (2022). "US, Iran face deadline as nuclear talks end without a deal", 8 August. Available at: https://uk.news.yahoo.com/us-iran-face-deadline-nuclear-143047117.html

Carvalho, S. (2018). "Xi's visit to UAE highlights China's rising interest in Middle East", 20 July. Available at: www.reuters.com/article/us-emirates-china-idUSKBN1KA26k

Chatzky, A. and McBride, J. (2020). "China's massive Belt and Road Initiative", 28 January. Available at: www.cfr.org/backgrounder/chinas-massive-belt-and-road-initiative

Chaziza, M. (2020a). "China's New Silk Road strategy and the Middle East", 8 March. Available at: https://besacenter.org/china-silk-road-middle-east/

Chaziza, M. (2020b). "Saudi Arabia's nuclear program and China", 18 August. www.mei.edu/publications/saudi-arabias-nuclear-program-and-china

Chen, J. (2020). "Saudi Arabia's diplomatic transformation under King Salman: Ambition, policy and means", *Arab World Studies*, 1: 62–82.

Chen, X. (2018). "China in the post-hegemonic Middle East: A wary dragon?" Available at: www.e-ir.info/2018/11/22/china-in-the-post-hegemonic-middle-east-a-wary-dragon/

China Daily (2004). "China, Iran sign biggest oil & gas deal", 31 October. Available at: www.chinadaily.com.cn/english/doc/2004-10/31/content_387140.htm

CNBC (2016). "China tilts to Iran as Xi caps visit with 17 accords", 25 January. Available at: www.cnbc.com/2016/01/25/china-tilts-to-iran-as-xi-caps-visit-with-17-accords.html

CNBC (2021). "Major Chinese investors are reportedly in talks to buy Saudi Aramco stake**",** 28 April, Available at: www.cnbc.com/2021/04/29/major-chinese-investors-reportedly-in-talks-to-buy-saudi-aramco-stake.htm

Dittrick, P. (2016). "Total signs deal to help develop Iran's South Pars gas field", 8 November. Available at: www.ogj.com/drilling-production/article/17249971/total-signs-deal-to-help-develop-irans-south-pars-gas-field

Dunnahoe, T. (2017). "Total, NIOC to develop Phase 11 of South Pars gas field", 3 July. Available at: www.ogj.com/articles/2017/07/total-nioc-to-develop-phase-11-of-south-pars-gas-field.html

Farooq, U. A. (2021). "US Senate attempts to curb China's Middle East influence", 28 May. Available at: www.middleeasteye.net/news/china-middle-east-us-bill-seeks-counter-growing-influence

Figueroa, M. (2021). "China-Iran relations: The myth of massive investment", 6 April. Available at: https://thediplomat.com/2021/04/china-iran-relations-the-myth-of-massive-investment/

Fulton, J. (2020). "China's making inroads in the Middle East. The Trump administration isn't happy", 3 June. *The Washington Post*. Available at: www.washingtonpost.com/politics/2020/06/03/chinas-making-inroads-middle-east-trump-administration-isnt-happy/

Garlick, J. and Havlová, R (2020). "The dragon dithers: Assessing the cautious implementation of China's Belt and Road Initiative in Iran", *Eurasian Geography and Economics*. https://doi.org/10.1080/15387216.2020.1822197

Garver, J. W. (2010). "Is China playing a dual game in Iran?" *The Washington Quarterly*, 34(1): 75–88.

Ghasseminejad, S. (2021). "Biden's Persian Gulf policy benefits China", 23 March. Available at: https://thefrontierpost.com/bidens-persian-gulf-policy-benefits-china/

Guzansky, Y. and Lavi G. (2020). "Saudi Arabia-China relations: A brave friendship or useful leverage?" *Policy Analysis*, 23(2): 108–114.

Heydemann, S. (2022). "Rights as realism in the Middle East", 25 July. Available at: www.brookings.edu/blog/order-from-chaos/2022/07/25/rights-as-realism-in-the-middle-east/

Hydrocarbon Processing (2016). "Aramco, Sinopec inaugurate YASREF refinery, pledge more cooperation", 22 January. Available at: www.hydrocarbonprocessing.com/news/2016/01/aramco-sinopec-inaugurate-yasref-refinery-pledge-more-cooperation

Kantor, A. (2021). "Cloud becomes new front line between China and the West", 18 May. Available at: www.ft.com/content/ddc4d6ff-13dc-449d-a4ca-9ad3d1d6a184

Kunlun Consultancy (2019). "Sources and amount of China's oil imports in 2018", 8 June. Available at: www.sohu.com/a/319212399_6533764 (in Chinese).

Leverett, F. and Leverett, H. M. (2011). "U.S. sanctions and China's Iran policy", 30 July. Available at: www.campaigniran.org/casmii/index.php?q=node/11576

Liao, X. (2015). "China's energy diplomacy towards the Middle East: A blessing or curse for the world?" in A. Ehteshami and Y. Miyagi (eds), *The Emerging Middle East–East Asia Nexus*. London: Routledge, pp. 94–109.

Lim, A. C. (2016). "Middle East and China's 'Belt and Road': Xi Jinping's 2016 state visits to Saudi Arabia, Egypt and Iran: Analysis", 30 January. Available at: www.eurasiareview.com/ 30012016-middle-east-and-chinas-belt-and-road-xi-jinpings-2016-state-visits-to-saudi-arabia-egypt-and-iran-analysis

Malik, S. (2017). "King Salman's visit to China", 15 March. Available at: www.china.org.cn/opin ion/ 2017-03/15/content_40455690.htm

Monshipouri, M. and Heiran-Nia, J. (2020). "China's Iran Strategy: What Is at Stake?" *Middle East Policy*, 27(4): 157–172.

New York Times (2021). "China, with $400 billion Iran deal, could deepen influence in Mideast", 27 March. Available at: www.nytimes.com/2021/03/27/world/middleeast/china-iran-deal.html

OGJ (*Oil & Gas Journal*) (2019). "Aramco forms combine for $10-billion Chinese refining complex", 22 February. Available at: www.ogj.com/refining-processing/refining/optimization/ art-icle/17279636/aramco-forms-combine-for-10billion-chinese-refining-complex

Perlez, J. (2016). "President Xi Jinping of China is all business in Middle East visit", *New York Times*, 30 January. Available at: www.nytimes.com/2016/01/31/world/asia/xi-jinping-visits-saudi-iran.html

Reuters (2008). "UPDATE 1-Saudi SABIC to expand China petchem JV: source", 18 June. Available at: www.reuters.com/article/sabic-sinopec-idUSPEK4672020080618

Reuters (2017). "Saudi Arabia signs cooperation deals with China on nuclear energy", 25 August. Available at: www.reuters.com/article/saudi-china-nuclear-idUSL8N1LB1CE

Security Council Report (2020). "Chronology of events: Iran". 2 September. Available at: www.securitycouncilreport.org/chronology/iran.php

South Front (2019). "Iran and China to start 25-year strategic partnership with 400 billion in investments". 18 September. Available at: https://southfront.org/iran-and-china-to-start-25-year-strategic-partnership-with-400-billion-in-investments/

Sun, D. and Wang, Y. (2020) "Overall integration: On China-Saudi comprehensive strategic partnership: abstract", *Arab World Studies*, 4: 28–54 (in Chinese).

Talwar, P. (2020). "China is getting mired in the Middle East", 17 August. Available at: https://foreig npolicy.com/2020/08/17/china-is-getting-mired-in-the-middle-east/

Tehran Times (2011). "China to invest $2.5b in Iran's Azadegan oilfield", 17 March. Available at: www.tehrantimes.com/news/237748/China-to-invest-2-5b-in-Iran-s-Azadegan-oilfield/

Tehran Times (2016). "Xi Jinping's Iran visit is of 'historic significance': ambassador", 20 January. Available at: www.tehrantimes.com/news/252338/Xi-Jinping-s-Iran-visit-is-of-historic-significa nce-ambassador

Therme, C. (2019). "Iran's 'Neither East Nor West' slogan today", 8 February. Available at: www.ispionline.it/sites/default/files/pubblicazioni/commentary_therme_08.02.2018.pdf

Tian, C. (1997) "An analysis of China's oil imports and exports", *International Petroleum Economics*, 3 (in Chinese).

Trading Economics (2021). "China GDP annual growth rate, 1996–2021". Available at: https://tradi ngeconomics.com/china/gdp-growth-annual

UANI (United Against Nuclear Iran) (2021). "Inpex", 16 February. Available at: www.unitedaga instnucleariran.com/company/inpex

United States Institute of Peace (2020). "Iran and the NPT", 22 January. Available at: https://ira nprimer.usip.org/index.php/blog/2020/jan/22/iran-and-npt

Vakil, S. (2021). "Stability in the Middle East requires more than a deal with Iran", *Foreign Affairs*, 22 February. Available at: www.foreignaffairs.com/articles/middle-east/2021- 02-22/ stability-middle-east-requires-more-deal-iran

Valori, G. E. (2016). "President Xi Jinping's travel to the Middle East", 12 February. Available at: https://moderndiplomacy.eu/2016/02/12/president-xi-jinping-s-travel-to-the-middle-east/

V boshi619 (2022). "Sources and amount of China's oil imports in 2020", 21 May. Available at: (in Chinese). Available at: https://zhuanlan.zhihu.com/p/483085292 (revised 18 March 2022).

Voice of America (2022). "IAEA Chief: Iran's nuclear program growing", 2 August. Available at: www.voanews.com/a/good-words-not-enough-iaea-hopes-for-transparency-from-iran-/6684109.html

Wall Street Journal (2020). "Saudi Arabia, with China's help, expands its nuclear program", 4 August. Available at: www.wsj.com/articles/saudi-arabia-with-chinas-help-expands-its-nuclear-program-11596575671

Wille, D. (2016). "Xi Jinping's visit to the Middle East: What's in store for Saudi Arabia, Egypt, and Iran?" 27 January. https://globalriskinsights.com/2016/01/xi-jinpings-visit-to-the-middle-east-whats-in-store-for-saudi-arabia-egypt-and-iran/

WNA (World Nuclear Association) (2022). "Nuclear power in Saudi Arabia", Available at: www.world-nuclear.org/information-library/country-profiles/countries-o-s/saudi-arabia.aspx Updated in April.

Xinhua (2006a). "Ambassador underlines significance of Saudi King's visit", 23 January. Available at: www.china.org.cn/english/2006/Jan/156090.htm

Xinhua (2006b). "President Hu arrives in Saudi Arabia for state visit", 22 April. Available at: www.chinadaily.com.cn/china/2006-04/22/content_574220.htm

Xinhua (2021). "China's GDP expands 2.3% in 2020", 18 January. Available at: www.china.org.cn/business/2021-01/18/content_77127004.htm

Yuhoucaihong8453 (2022). "Statistics of China's oil imports in 2021", 21 April. Available at: www.aisoutu.com/a/2536924 (in Chinese).

Zhang, X. (1999). "China's interests in the Middle East: Present and future". Available at: https://mepc.org/journal/chinas-interests-middle-east-present-and-future

3

CHINA'S INFRASTRUCTURE CONSTRUCTION IN THE MIDDLE EAST

Chuchu Zhang

1 Introduction

As a country with an ancient civilization and a large population, China has long been concerned with large-scale public infrastructure projects critical to the country's economy and people's livelihood, such as water conservation facilities. As early as in the Qin Dynasty, large-scale projects such as Dujiangyan, Lingqu Canal, and the Great Wall of Qin Dynasty were already pioneering in the world and became architectural wonders. Entering the modern era, despite being a latecomer to the field of infrastructure construction, compared to Western developed countries, China has risen as the largest global manufacturing base of engineering machinery and a global infrastructure power in four decades following the reform and opening-up. Infrastructure construction has not only served as the principal engine driving China's national economy, but has also constituted a significant component of economic diplomacy with Chinese characteristics. China's collaboration with other countries in the construction of ports, high-speed railways, highways, and other infrastructure projects contributes significantly to the "going global" process of China's infrastructure construction and its international image building (Shi and Wu, 2017: 138–139; Sun, 2018: 30–31).

Involvement in overseas infrastructure construction represents a key component of advancing China's "going global" strategy in the new era, and is a core sector of the grand Belt and Road Initiative. In 2017, China participated in more than 1,000 overseas construction projects, across six continents and representing 16 percent of the total number of global infrastructure projects (Haiwai Net, 2017). In 2019, as emphasized by Chinese President Xi Jinping at the opening ceremony of the Second Belt and Road Forum for International Cooperation

> Building high-quality infrastructure that is sustainable, resilient, inclusive, accessible and reasonably priced could help countries give full play to their advantages in resources and better integrate into the global supply, industrial and value chains for interconnected development. China will work with all

parties to establish ... a connectivity network composed of railroads, ports, pipeline networks, etc.

(China Daily, 2019)

In 2020, at the Fifth Plenary Session of the 19th Central Committee of the Communist Party of China (CPC), the CPC Central Committee's proposals for formulating the 14th Five-Year Plan (2021–2025) for National Economic and Social Development and the Long-Range Objectives through the Year 2035 were adopted. In particular, the strategic deployment of "persisting in the enforcement of opening up to the outside world on a larger scale, in a wider field and at a deeper level" was proposed, with an emphasis on "advancing infrastructure connectivity" and "building a mutually beneficial and win-win collaboration system between industrial chain and supply chain" (*People's Daily Net*, 2020).

Serving as the third largest infrastructure market worldwide only after Asia, Oceania and Europe, the Middle East is also one of the major focuses of China's international infrastructure collaboration. Following decades of exploration and practice, Chinese infrastructure enterprises have accumulated a wealth of international cooperation experience in Middle Eastern countries. Large-scale flagship projects undertaken by China in the region so far include the Ankara-Istanbul high-speed railway project, the Algerian East-West Highway Project, the New Doha Project, etc. Notably, the infrastructure density per capita in Middle Eastern countries not only falls below many developed countries, but even below many developing countries with much weaker economic strength. Therefore, the region possesses great development potential and constitutes a crucial infrastructure market needing to be deeply explored by China in the future to facilitate "the Belt and Road Initiative" international cooperation. In this context, the study of the evolving patterns, achievements and challenges concerning China's infrastructure cooperation with the Middle Eastern countries is of both academic value and practical relevance.

2 China's Infrastructure Diplomacy: Spatial and Temporal Characteristics and Evolving Stages

2.1 Data Source

The primary data source for this chapter is the China Global Investment Tracker (2021) database. Developed by the American Enterprise Institute, it represents the only integrated public data set available on China's global investment and construction, which documents Chinese enterprises' global investment and infrastructure construction activities from 2005 to 2019, covering investment and infrastructure projects worth more than $100 million. The database is composed of three sub-databases: (1) China's Overseas Investment Database; (2) China's Overseas Infrastructure Construction Database; and (3) Database of Canceled or Suspended Projects. This chapter mainly adopts China's Overseas Infrastructure Construction Database, and ignores the projects that were canceled or suspended. By relating the database with relevant media reports, I have identified each project's contract value, project type, year of agreement signing, as well as the spatial information such as the latitude and longitude of each project.

Meanwhile, this research investigates and analyzes China's infrastructure collaboration with Middle Eastern countries based upon China's Policy Documents on Arab Countries, Chinese leaders' speeches on relations between China and Middle Eastern countries, the Country Reports on Contract Engineering Markets released by the Ministry of Commerce of the PRC, and Middle Eastern countries' reports on China. The chapter mainly focuses on six types of infrastructure projects, namely: (1) agricultural infrastructure, such as farmland irrigation facilities, agricultural products distribution facilities; (2) architectural projects, such as residences, shopping malls, office buildings, hotels, schools, hospitals, steel plants, cement plants, etc.; (3) transportation projects, such as railroads, highways, aviation, bridges, ports, tunnels, etc.; (4) energy power projects related to oil, coal, natural gas, electric power, new energy, etc.; (5) communication projects, such as telecommunications, information networks, etc.; and (6) environmental protection and water conservation projects, such as dams, reservoirs, sea water desalination plants, sewage treatment, air purification, etc.. As the China Global Investment Tracker database only includes infrastructure construction projects which have a contract value of more than $100 million, this research primarily addresses large and medium-sized infrastructure construction projects.

2.2 Research Methods

In order to elucidate the spatial and temporal characteristics and evolving patterns concerning China's involvement in overseas infrastructure construction, this research employs descriptive statistical analysis, space-time cube, and emerging space-time hot spot analysis in conjunction with a qualitative research approach. Both space-time cube and emerging space-time hot spot analysis represent key spatial analysis methods in geography. The space-time cube utilizes two-dimensional coordinate axes to indicate planar locations, while adopting height coordinates to illustrate changes in geographic location over time. The square cube is thus created with two-dimensional geographic coordinates x and y as the base and the time of event occurrence as the height axis z. The space-time cube approach places spatial-temporal data in three-dimensional space for visualization.

The emerging space-time hot spot analysis functions primarily to identify spatial clustering of high values (hot spots) with statistical significance. The so-called statistically significant hot spot means not only that an element should be of high value, but also that the element should be enclosed by other high value elements. Emerging space-time hot spot analysis can be performed to discern significant hot spot trends of cubic data in spatial distribution as it evolves over time (Liu et al., 2017).

In this research, a descriptive statistical analysis is first conducted based upon the data collected from the China Global Investment Tracker database and press reports, to evaluate the quantitative changes, project types, main construction bodies, and financing patterns of China's participation in medium and large infrastructure construction projects in Middle Eastern countries. Subsequently, the space-time cube is generated by using ArcGIS software according to the spatial and temporal geographic information of each infrastructure construction project collated by the author. In this way, we can visualize the temporal and spatial distribution of China's engagement in medium and large infrastructure construction projects in the Middle Eastern countries. Next, we employ the contract values as a weighted term to conduct an emerging space-time hot spot analysis on the previously derived space-time cube. The hot spot trends are then recognized to facilitate the analysis of the spatial and temporal characteristics and evolving patterns of China's participation in large and medium-sized infrastructure construction projects in Middle Eastern countries. Ultimately, with the foregoing research methods coupled with qualitative analysis, this chapter draws conclusions on the features and trends of China's infrastructure collaborations with Middle Eastern countries.

2.3 Results Analysis

Based upon data analysis, this research classifies China's overseas infrastructure construction participation course into four stages: (1) Gentle Growth Period (2005–2009); (2) Dramatic Fluctuation Period (2010–2012); (3) Rapid Surge Period (2013–2016); and (4) Steady Rise Period (2017–2019). Such a classification has taken into consideration the quantitative increase of the number of large and medium-sized projects, the spatial distribution of the projects, as well as their main construction bodies and financing methods.

2.3.1 Phase I: Gentle Growth Period (2005–2009)

With respect to quantitative changes, the number of medium and large-scale infrastructure construction projects undertaken by China in the Middle East during this period generally exhibited a gradual incremental trend, as shown in Figure 3.1. Over a four-year span, the number of projects progressively doubled from 10 in 2005 to 21. Regarding spatial distribution, there was a significant expansion in the distribution scope of China's participation in medium-sized and large-scale infrastructure construction projects in Middle Eastern countries during this period, with China's markets for medium-sized and

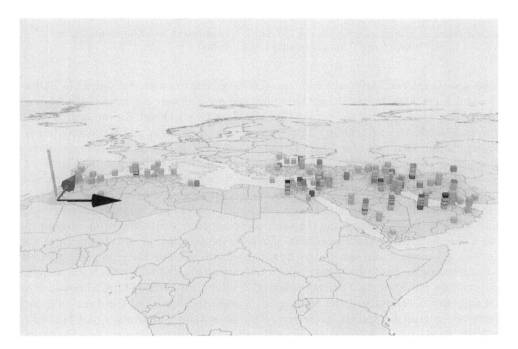

Figure 3.1 The space-time cube of China's participation in large and medium-sized infrastructure construction projects in the Middle East from 2005 to 2019

Source: Based on spatial statistical analysis of data collected from China Global Investment Tracker. https:// www.aei.org/china-global-investment-tracker/

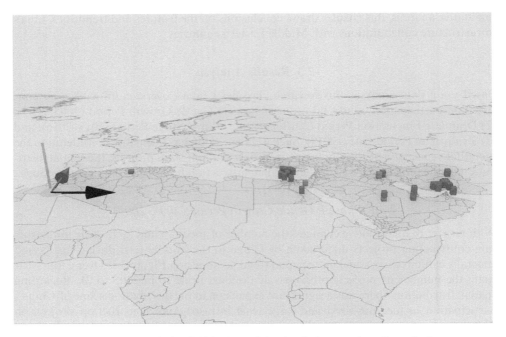

Figure 3.2 The hot spot analysis of China's participation in large and medium-sized infrastructure construction projects in the Middle East from 2005 to 2019

Source: Based on spatial statistical analysis of data collected from China Global Investment Tracker. https:// www.aei.org/china-global-investment-tracker/.

large-scale infrastructure construction projects increasing from seven countries in 2005 to 13 countries in 2008. In this phase, the majority of projects were clustered in the Arabian Peninsula (including Saudi Arabia, the UAE, Bahrain, Qatar, Oman, Kuwait, and Yemen), Iran and North Africa (including Egypt, Libya, Tunisia, Algeria, and Morocco). In particular, the hot spot areas for China to embark on large and medium-sized engineering contracting projects were Saudi Arabia, Iran, and the UAE, as indicated in Figure 3.2. As for the project types, China's large and medium-sized infrastructure construction projects in the Middle Eastern countries at this stage were dominated by residential and transportation projects, representing 39 percent and 30 percent of the total project number, respectively. Concerning the main construction bodies, the central government and Chinese state-owned enterprises (SOEs) were the principal actors. At this stage, the Chinese government allowed greater powers to the SOEs, introduced market-oriented transformation in the electric power industry, transportation and other fields, encouraged autonomous operation, and promoted liberal development among SOEs. Subsequent to the complete decoupling of the Ministry of Communications and the direct affiliated waterway enterprises, and the demerger of the State Grid Corporation of China (directly affiliated with the Ministry of Water Resources and Electric Power) into 11 entities, including State Grid and China Southern Power Grid Co., Ltd., various SOEs have successively instituted modern enterprise systems. In 2006, the China Communications Construction Company (CCCC) was reconstituted, restructured, and founded as a joint stock corporation. These restructured Chinese infrastructure SOEs enjoy greater scope and freedom in pursuing overseas investments. In 2007, SINOMACH and China

Nonferrous Metal Industry's Foreign Engineering and Construction Co., Ltd. (CNMC) made a nearly $4 billion investment in aluminum ore facilities near the Red Sea in Saudi Arabia, making it then the largest Chinese capital investment project in the Middle East. In terms of financing, the dominant financiers of medium-sized and large infrastructure projects invested in by China in Middle Eastern countries consisted of state-owned financial institutions, such as the China Development Bank and Chinese construction giants.

2.3.2 Phase II: Dramatic Fluctuation Period (2010–2012)

Regarding quantitative changes from 2010 to 2012, there was a drastic fluctuation in the quantity of medium-sized and large infrastructure construction projects engaged in by China in the Middle East, which was largely caused by the "Arab Spring." As for the spatial distribution, the project numbers plummeted in Middle Eastern countries, such as Yemen, Tunisia, Libya, and Syria, which suffered regime transitions and were embroiled in wars during the revolutionary surge of the "Arab Spring." In contrast, countries that suffered less from the impact of the political upheavals, such as Algeria, emerged as main infrastructure construction markets. Meanwhile, there was an expansion of the infrastructure construction market in the Fertile Crescent (including Iraq, Syria, Lebanon, Jordan, and Israel) during this period, with significant project increases occurring in Iraq and Israel. Throughout these three years, hot spot areas for Chinese infrastructure construction projects in the Middle East included Saudi Arabia, Iran, and Algeria. With regard to project types, China maintained its strength in the building infrastructure market, while it also achieved considerable breakthroughs in the energy power and agricultural infrastructure sectors. At this stage, the numbers of construction and energy power projects in Middle Eastern countries undertaken by China represented 50 percent and 27 percent respectively of the total number of medium-sized and large infrastructure construction projects. During this period, as the central Chinese government further strengthened decentralization, the Chinese SOEs commenced direct investment in infrastructure construction projects in Middle Eastern countries. In 2013, the Power Construction Corporation of China invested in Jordan's first oil shale power project under the Building-Owning-Operation (BOO) model, signifying the transformation of Chinese SOEs from being contractors to being investment operators in the Middle East market. As for financing approaches, there was a significant increase in joint venture investment in infrastructure construction projects between China and host countries. For example, in 2011, Yanbu Aramco Sinopec Refining Company (YASREF) jointly invested in by Sinopec Group and Saudi Arabian Oil Company (Saudi Aramco), represented the first joint venture refinery founded by a Chinese oil corporation in the Middle East.

2.3.3 Phase III: Rapid Surge Period (2013–2016)

With respect to quantitative changes since 2013, against the background of "the Belt and Road Initiative." China's engagement in Middle East infrastructure construction grew rapidly. Moreover, thanks to President Xi Jinping's choice of three Middle Eastern countries as the destinations of his first overseas trip in 2016, which indicated the importance that Beijing attaches to the region, China's involvement in Middle East infrastructure construction peaked in that year. From 2013 to 2016, a total of 138 new medium-sized and large infrastructure construction projects were undertaken by China in the Middle East. In terms of spatial distribution, China's collaboration with its traditional infrastructure construction markets in the region (e.g., Saudi Arabia and Algeria) continued to deepen during this period. Over these four years, due to the political stabilization in Egypt after 2014, coupled with the blueprint development plans introduced by the new President Abdel Fattah al Sisi to revitalize the economy through major infrastructure construction projects, including the development of the Suez Canal corridor and the construction of the new administrative capital in Egypt, there was a remarkable rebound in infrastructure construction projects in Egypt undertaken by China. Also, China's presence in the infrastructure markets of the UAE, Qatar, and Kuwait strengthened. Saudi Arabia, the UAE, and Algeria were the hot spot areas for China's participation in Middle East infrastructure construction at this stage. Concerning project types, given the constant decline in international oil prices since 2014, Middle Eastern oil-producing countries such as Saudi Arabia, the UAE, Qatar, and Kuwait adopted an energy diversification strategy, leading to a swift demand growth for energy-powered infrastructure construction represented by new energy sources. Consequently, cooperation between China and oil-producing countries in the Middle East continuously deepened. An important change during this period is that energy power projects became the most predominant medium-sized and large infrastructure construction projects undertaken by China in the Middle East, accounting for 34 percent of the total project number. Concurrently, there was a decrease in the proportion of construction and transportation projects, accounting for 32 percent and 21 percent of the total project number. As for the main construction bodies, in addition to the central government and Chinese SOEs, which remained the promoters of infrastructure construction projects in the Middle East, private enterprises' engagement in Middle Eastern infrastructure construction rose significantly, emerging as a new essential player. Following the proposal of the BRI, more efforts were devoted by the Chinese government to offering policy support to private enterprises, particularly small and medium-sized private enterprises (SMEs), which were regarded as the new backbones of the BRI. In 2017, the Ministry of Industry and Information Technology and the China Council for the Promotion of International Trade (CCPIT) announced the *Notice on Special Actions to Support SMEs' Involvement in the BRI Construction*. Measures were proposed on perfecting foreign-related legal services and establishing a comprehensive commercial service platform, etc. Under the framework of the BRI, a growing number of Chinese private enterprises have joined hands with SOEs to develop consortia and undertaken infrastructure construction projects in the Middle East. In 2013, Yingli Solar made its first entry into the North African infrastructure market, and undertook a photovoltaic power plant project in Algeria by setting up a consortium with Sinohydro Corporation. In 2016, Beijing Su Power Technology Co., Ltd. ventured deep into the Iranian market and contracted the Tehran-Mashhad railroad electrification project amounting to $2.1 billion jointly with China National Machinery Import and Export Corporation. With respect to financing methods, the forms of Chinese investment in Middle East infrastructure construction became more diverse. In particular, there was a remarkable increase in individual funding by Chinese financial institutions or enterprises, group funding by Chinese banks, and Sino-foreign joint ventures. When establishing Sino-foreign joint ventures, in addition to investing jointly with host countries, China also actively co-financed with Singapore, Germany and other developed countries to enhance the transparency and capital market efficiency of engineering projects.

2.3.4 Phase IV: Steady Rise Period (2017–2019)

As for quantitative changes, after a slight decline in 2017, China's participation in large and medium-sized infrastructure construction projects in the Middle East has rebounded steadily since 2018 and approached the peak level of 2016 in 2019. In terms of spatial distribution, efforts were made to further deepen China's infrastructure construction market in the UAE, Saudi Arabia, and Egypt during this period. All these three countries served as hot spot areas for China's involvement in infrastructure construction projects in the Middle East, constituting 58 percent of China's medium-sized and large infrastructure construction projects in the region. As a result of the widespread protests and political upheavals in Algeria in 2019, there was a significant decline in China's participation in infrastructure construction projects in Algeria. As for project types, China maintained its strong presence in the energy power market in the Middle East following the introduction of "2030 Vision" by Saudi Arabia, which focused on breaking away from a single oil economy, the proposal of the "2050 UAE Energy Strategy" by the UAE, and the announcement of similar strategies by other Gulf countries. The proportion of such projects climbed rapidly to 45 percent. As for the main construction bodies, joint efforts were initiated by the central government, Chinese SOEs, and private firms to explore the Middle Eastern infrastructure construction market collectively. In this regard, there was further enhancement of the participation and competitiveness of Chinese private enterprises, some of which commenced to solely assume the contracting and investment of infrastructure construction projects in Middle Eastern countries.

For instance, since 2018, ZPEC has concluded multiple contracts with British Petroleum (BP), Weatherford Oilfield Services Ltd., and other companies for large and medium-sized oilfield drilling projects in Iraq, totaling over $100 million in contract amount. Concerning financing methods, ever since the implementation of the BRI, China has incorporated new multilateral financial institutions such as the Silk Road Fund and the Asian Infrastructure Investment Bank (AIIB) to diversify the financing platforms for developing countries to develop their infrastructure. Such multinational financial institutions have been supporting the infrastructure construction in Middle Eastern countries with substantial funding since 2017. Additionally, they have collaborated extensively with international financial institutions, thereby contributing to the diversification of infrastructure financing channels in Middle Eastern countries. In September 2017, a joint loan was granted by the AIIB and the International Finance Corporation (IFC) to 11 solar projects in Egypt. In August 2018, the Silk Road Fund, the Harbin Electric Corporation, and investment institutions in the UAE co-invested in the Hassyan Clean Coal Power Plant, representing the first investment of the Silk Road Fund in the Middle East.

In short, China has engaged in a broad range of infrastructure construction projects in the Middle East since 2005, encompassing nearly all Middle Eastern countries. The hot spot areas for large and medium-sized infrastructure construction projects have spread across every corner of the Middle East, and have been continuously varying in line with the market laws. Furthermore, diversified ways have been adopted for China's participation in infrastructure construction and financing in the Middle East, gradually shaping into an infrastructure construction system in which the Chinese government, Chinese SOEs, and Chinese private enterprises serve as the principal actors, with multiple financial sources such as Chinese financial institutions, financial institutions in host countries and developed countries, and China-led multilateral financial entities.

3 Achievements of China's Infrastructure Construction in the Middle East

China's cooperation with Middle Eastern countries over the past decades in infrastructure construction has achieved preliminary success. In an interview with Al Arabiya in

March 2021, the State Councilor and Chinese Foreign Minister Wang Yi stated, "China-Arab relations are full of vitality and have become a model of South-South cooperation" (Xinhua Net, 2021).

The achievements were first reflected in the signing of multiple infrastructure cooperation agreements between China and the Middle Eastern countries. In 2012, a Memorandum of Understanding (MOU) was concluded between the Ministry of Transport of the PRC and the Ministry of Transport and Road Safety of Israel. In 2015, the Ministry of Transport of the PRC and the Ministry of Transport of Turkey signed the Draft Agreement on International Road Transport. In 2017, an MOU on Cooperation in Welfare Housing Infrastructure was concluded between the Ministry of Commerce of the PRC and the Public Authority for Housing Welfare of Kuwait. On top of that, the BRI cooperation documents agreed between China and Middle Eastern countries also include a lot of infrastructure cooperation.

Second, the cooperation between China and the Middle Eastern countries in various infrastructure fields has progressed in an orderly manner, as demonstrated by a batch of iconic achievements. The Tel Aviv Light Rail Red Line, carried out by China Railway Engineering Group Ltd. (REC), and the Egyptian Light-Rail Project, performed by REC and AVIC International Holding Corporation (AVIC International), have proceeded smoothly with no extensive postponements brought about by the Covid epidemic outbreak. The other landmark achievements include the Algerian Grand Mosque, constructed by the CSCEC, the Al Mutlaa Residential City Project, undertaken by the CGGC, and the Algerian Central Port Project which is under construction by the CCCC.

Third, the capacity of China in infrastructure construction has been converted into a vital productivity for numerous Middle Eastern countries. According to the Global Competitiveness Index 2019, released by the World Economic Forum, there is a generally positive correlation between the economic competitiveness of Middle Eastern countries and their infrastructure competitiveness (World Economic Forum, 2019). Nevertheless, quite a number of countries are suffering from funding gaps, whereas Chinese investments have made a great contribution to filling the infrastructure gap in the region and boosting its economic competitiveness. As revealed in a report published by the Arab Investment & Export Credit Guarantee Corporation, China emerged as the largest investor in the Middle East in 2016, accounting for approximately one-third of direct investments from extra-territorial countries, for which a considerable amount of investment was directed to the infrastructure construction sector (*Middle East Monitor*, 2017). After years of effort, China's investment and involvement in construction, transportation and power projects in the Middle East have dramatically upgraded the working, residential, and recreational environments of local populations. Domestic and foreign enterprises have been attracted to settle and invest in the region, accelerating the flow of factor resources in various regions of the host countries. For example, the Algerian North-South Highway constructed by the CSCEC has connected the country's north-south traffic arteries, which has fulfilled its dream of transporting cargoes from the north to the south in recent times, contributing to narrowing the development gap between northern and southern Algeria.

4 Challenges of China's Infrastructure Construction in the Middle East

Nonetheless, compared to China's infrastructure construction in other regions, and the share of the Middle Eastern infrastructure market held by other global powers, China-Middle Eastern infrastructure cooperation has not reached its heyday, as one might expect. Today, China's expansion in the region's infrastructure market is still confronted with a number of challenges.

The first one concerns political risks. On the one hand, many Middle Eastern countries suffer from poor political stability as compared to other regions (Zhang et al., 2019). Countries, such as Syria, Libya, and Yemen, have been deeply plagued by external interventions and internal conflicts, engulfed in perennial wars and serious turmoil. Tunisia, Egypt, and Algeria have struggled with tough transition and political reconstruction, resulting from regime change and political transformations. Countries such as Turkey and Iran have experienced economic slumps and increased social conflicts, triggering heightened tensions and protests. The instability of many Middle Eastern countries has imposed relatively substantial macro-political risks on the region. Therefore, China's engagement in infrastructure construction in the region is vulnerable to interruptions and schedule delays caused by wars or riots, which may result in extra expenditures such as equipment preservation fees, personnel costs, and overdue liquidated damages. On the other hand, there are also challenges associated with weak government effectiveness, low administrative levels, rampant government corruption and bureaucracy, even in countries with relatively stable political situations, such as Saudi Arabia and Egypt. Consequently, the high level of micro-political risks in most Middle Eastern countries has exposed Chinese infrastructure enterprises to high institutional costs for investment and construction in these countries.

The second issue involves security risks. The Middle Eastern region has not only suffered from traditional security challenges in the form of regional conflicts, but also non-traditional security challenges, such as attacks by religious extremist groups and transnational crime. An estimated total of 32,346 terrorist attacks have taken place in the Middle East from 2010 to 2018, as documented by the Global Terrorism Database (2021). Security risks have imposed enormous threats to Chinese enterprises' overseas interests, and personal safety of overseas Chinese employees.

The third one is legal risks. Due to the imperfect legal systems and the lack of uniform standards for engineering procedures and regulations in some Middle Eastern countries, Chinese enterprises are likely to face a variety of legal risks, such as contract text risk and labor employment risk. In countries like Qatar, overseas investors are legally mandated to establish joint ventures with local capital, and the former's shareholding should not exceed 49 percent. As the leading party of infrastructure construction projects, the Chinese capital will suffer losses in case of quotation adjustment or schedule delay of the other party's capital. Also, the complicated visa and employment procedures in Algeria, Saudi Arabia, and other countries make it extremely difficult to export labor from China, while the employment of local laborers presents another challenge of having to deal with local labor laws regarding vacations, work injuries, and working hours different from those of China.

The fourth issue concerns the risk of damaging public opinion. China's infrastructure collaboration with Middle Eastern countries is affected by the overseas public opinion environment. As most of the Middle Eastern countries were former colonies or protectorates of Western powers, Western powers have a deep-rooted influence on the media of many countries in the region. Following the proliferation of statements such as "geopolitical expansionism" and "Chinese monopoly," the image of Chinese enterprises in some Middle Eastern countries has been seriously undermined. As shown by the survey conducted in 2018 by the Arab Barometer (2018), in Algeria and Egypt, China's two largest infrastructure construction markets in the Middle East, only 36.3 percent and

30.3 percent of respondents expressed a favorable perception toward China. Against this backdrop, many Chinese strategists worry that trade protectionism in Middle Eastern countries may further resurface, while some large-scale infrastructure construction projects may be politicized and thus face contract breaches.

5 Conclusion

Over several decades of reform and opening up, China has achieved remarkable success in infrastructure construction. Nowadays, China's engagement in overseas infrastructure construction plays an essential role in its "going global" strategy and the BRI proposal. In the Middle Eastern infrastructure markets, in spite of achieving remarkable accomplishments, China has also been confronted with challenges and suffered from huge losses in the region. For instance, the Mecca Light Railway Project in 2009, won by CRCC, caused a substantial loss of over $500 million during the project execution process (*People's Daily* Net, 2013); in 2011, most infrastructure construction projects were forced to halt upon the outbreak of the Libya war, resulting in a contract loss of at least $18 billion (Yicai Net, 2011). In this context, it is imperative for China to fully unleash the cooperation potential with the Middle East, strengthen the competitiveness and comparative advantage of its infrastructure construction, improve risk awareness of Chinese enterprises, and enhance its public and cultural diplomacy in the region in order to strengthen mutual trust between Beijing and the Middle Eastern countries.

References

Arab Barometer. (2018). Survey data. Available at: www.arabbarometer.org/survey-data/data-analysis-tool/

China Daily. (2019). Xi's full remarks at the leaders' roundtable meeting of the Second Belt and Road Forum for International Cooperation, April 27. Available at: www.chinadaily.com.cn/a/201904/27/WS5d9c5982a310cf3e3556f389.html

China Global Investment Tracker. (2021). China. Available at: www.aei.org/china-global-investment-tracker/Global Terrorism Database. (2021). Available at: https://start.umd.edu/data-tools/global-terrorism-database-gtd

Haiwai Net. (2017). China leads global infrastructure investment, accounting for 31% of global investment, September 22. Available at: http://m.haiwainet.cn/middle/3542291/2017/0922/content_31129261_1.html

Liu, H., et al. (2017). Pattern evolution and its contributory factor of cold spots and hot spots of economic development in Beijing-Tianjin-Hebei region, *Geographical Research*, no. 1, pp. 97–108.

Middle East Monitor. (2017). China is largest foreign investor in Middle East, July 24. Available at: www.middleeastmonitor.com/20170724-china-is-largest-foreign-investor-in-middleeast

People's Daily Net. (2013). Huge loss of 1.3 billion for China Railway Construction Corporation in Saudi Arabia, November 19. Available at: http://finance.people.com.cn/stock/n/2013/1119/c67815-23583996.html

People's Daily Net. (2020). Suggestions of the CPC Central Committee on formulating the 14th Five-Year Plan for national economic and social development and the long-term goals for the year 2035, November 4. Available at: http://cpc.people.com.cn/n1/2020/1104/c64094-31917780.htmlShi, Z., and Wu, Y. (2017). Characteristics and practice of China's high speed rail diplomacy, *Contemporary Asia-Pacific Studies*, no. 5, pp. 133–155.

Sun, D. (2018). China's seaport diplomacy: Theory and practice. *World Economics and Politics*, no. 5, pp. 4–32.

World Economic Forum. (2019). The Global Competitiveness Report 2019, September 10. Available at: www3.weforum.org/docs/WEF_TheGlobalCompetitivenessReport2019.pdf

Xinhua Net. (2021). State Councilor and Chinese Foreign Minister Wang Yi accepted an interview with Arabiya TV, March 26. Available at: www.xinhuanet.com/world/2021-03/26/c_1127260 452.htm

Yicai Net. (2011). China's projects in Libya suffers from huge loss of more than 100 billion yuan, May 24. Available at: www.yicai.com/news/811327.html

Zhang, C., et al. (2019). Spatial Big Data analysis of political risks along the Belt and Road, *Sustainability*, no. 11, p. 2216.

4

MARKET-DRIVEN INDUSTRIALIZATION

Production Capacity Cooperation Between China and the Middle East Countries

Jiuzhou Duan and Shiyu Hao

Due to the differences in the factors of production, levels of development, geographical locations and industrial policies, international production capacity cooperation aims to optimize the international allocation of resources, create new comparative advantages and extend existing or form new global value chains through transnational industrial transfer, along with exchanges of capital and products. International capacity relocation and production capacity cooperation are closely related to factors, such as specific industrial fields, locations and policy differences. The basis of international production capacity cooperation lies not only in the product life cycle, the investment development cycle and the internal demand for industry relocation and expansion and technological innovation, but also includes comparative advantages, industrial agglomeration and expansion or innovation of the value chain brought about by resources, location and policies (Li, 2019).

As a trans-Eurasian region and an important emerging market, the Middle East is a crucial hub and commodity distribution center which connects the Eurasian continent and the surrounding regions. It is an important emerging investment market and consumer market in the world, with unique advantages in attracting foreign investment. In the twenty-first century, China and the Middle East countries have been developing closer ties in political and economic cooperation through frequent high-level exchanges of visits. In particular, the proposal and rapid implementation of the "Belt and Road Initiative" (BRI) have brought new opportunities for production capacity cooperation between China and the Middle East countries. The internal motivations behind the production capacity cooperation between China and the Middle East countries originate from both the demand of international relocation and extension of industry, products and technology, and the differences in location, policy and markets. In addition, market size, market growth potential and investment stimulus policies of the Middle East countries are also important influencing factors.

DOI: 10.4324/9781003048404-6

Market-Driven Industrialization

1 Motivation behind the China-Middle East Production Capacity Cooperation

In recent years, many of China's manufacturing sectors that used to have strong international competitiveness have lost their comparative advantages so that they need to transfer large-scale high-quality over-capacity to the overseas market. On the other hand, many Middle East countries hope to take this opportunity to drive their own industrialization process, which provides a political guarantee for the China-Middle East production capacity cooperation. Compared to China, the Middle East countries have potential comparative advantages in areas including rich oil and gas resources, labor reserves, and an extremely favorable trading environment (Office of the United States Trade Representative, 2017).

First, China and the Middle East countries are committed to carrying out production capacity cooperation. Having experienced the rapid development of the national economy and increasing productivity in manufacturing industry in the past decade, China now faces serious overcapacity in many industrial and manufacturing sectors. Additionally, the rapid rise in labor costs in many manufacturing sectors have led to a sharp decline in profit margins, which requires China to transfer surplus production capacity abroad. Moreover, while China has become "the world's factory," it has also become the country that suffers the most trade frictions in the world (Feng, 2017: 12). In particular, the products that are subject to the most anti-dumping investigations in China are also mainly in industries with severe domestic overcapacity. In 2016, half of the trade dispute cases against China were in the steel industry. The petrochemical and photovoltaic industries also suffer many trade frictions. Facing these challenges in the development of the industrial manufacturing industry, the Chinese government encourages enterprises to make more direct foreign investments to solve domestic overcapacity and facilitate the upgrading of the export structure.

As for the Middle East, under the pressure of low oil prices and the unemployment problem, in recent years, many regional countries have adopted the development of industrial manufacturing as the main way to diversify and improve their national economy. With the formulation of specific goals and plans for developing industrial manufacturing in each country, a new round of industrialization has become popular in the Middle East countries. Because China has made remarkable achievements in the development of manufacturing industry, many Middle East countries have high expectations of the BRI. They hope to take advantage of China's transfer of its industries to overseas markets to develop their own manufacturing industry (Yang, 2016: 44). Moreover, many Middle East countries have promoted the development of their own manufacturing industries through the BRI. According to the "National (Regional) Guidelines on Foreign Investment and Cooperation" issued by the Ministry of Commerce of China in 2016, Egypt, the United Arab Emirates, Saudi Arabia, and other countries have signed framework agreements on international production capacity cooperation with China. Egypt has established the Suez Economic and Trade Cooperation Zone, while Oman, Saudi Arabia, Djibouti, Morocco, and other countries in the region also have launched industrial parks jointly with China.

Second, the Middle East countries have an outstanding advantage in oil and gas resources. The ultimate goal of production capacity cooperation between China and the Middle East countries is to promote the industrialization process and achieve sustainable development of industrial manufacturing. To exert their comparative advantages, both parties need to cultivate industrial clusters based on the available resources. The characteristic of production capacity cooperation between China and the Middle East is the transfer of industrial manufacture capacity from industrially developed countries to developing countries. This type of international production capacity cooperation also matches the key areas that can be promoted by enterprises' direct investment, as prescribed in the "Guidelines on Promoting International Production Capacity Cooperation and Equipment Manufacturing," issued by the State Council of China, including steel, non-ferrous metals, cement, plate glass and other building materials, petrochemicals, chemical fertilizers, pesticides, tires, coal, the chemical industry and other heavy chemical industry, cotton spinning, chemical fibers, household appliances, food processing and other light textile industry (Chinese Government, 2015). The extremely rich oil and gas resources ensure the energy supply of many Middle East countries, so they have strong potential comparative advantages in undertaking and developing heavy industry and the chemical industry which require substantial energy inputs (OAPEC, 2020).

Third, Middle East countries have abundant labor resources and low-price labor costs. In terms of the composition of the industrial transfer from China to the Middle East countries, the industries include not only the heavy chemical industry with high energy consumption, but also the labor-intensive manufacturing industry. Therefore, the status of labor resources in the host country is an important factor in the effectiveness of bilateral production capacity cooperation. Besides, the Middle East countries have a large labor pool and young people form a large proportion of the population of the countries in the region. According to the World Bank, in 2015, 62.4 percent of the population in the Middle East countries is aged from 15–65, slightly lower than the world average of 65.6 percent. Moreover, the population of those under 14 accounts for 33.2 percent in the Middle East countries, higher than the global average of 26.1 percent (World Bank, 2016). Therefore, the relatively young age structure of the population means that the Middle East countries have sufficient labor resources to ensure the development of labor-intensive industrial manufacturing.

2 Characteristics of the China-Middle East Production Capacity Cooperation

2.1 Traditional Energy Industry as the Basis for Production Capacity Cooperation

China and the Middle East countries are naturally complementary in energy-intensive production capacity cooperation and also the hydrocarbon energy sector has been the focus of the two sides' cooperation. China is the world's largest oil importer and energy consumer market while the Middle East countries have huge oil reserves that can meet China's energy demands. Since the 1990s, China has been cooperating with the Middle East countries on energy production capacity in the oil industry. With the gap between China's oil production and energy consumption gradually widening, the Chinese market can no longer be ignored by the Middle East countries, and cooperation between the two sides in the energy field has been deepening and expanding.

Cooperation between China and the Middle East countries in the upstream oil and gas energy industry started in the 1990s, when China's economic development needed a stable energy supply and oil exploration technology from the Middle East countries. Large Chinese oil and gas enterprises, represented by the China National Petroleum

Corporation (CNPC) and the China Petroleum & Chemical Corporation (Sinopec), began to enter the upstream oil field in the Middle East countries. Chinese companies have been authorized to explore oil and gas in Tunisia, Sudan, Algeria and other countries through cross-border mergers and acquisitions, and have focused on developing upstream energy production capacity cooperation between the two sides (Wei, 2016: 9). For example, in September 1995, CNPC signed a contract with the Sudanese government to acquire oil mining rights in Block 6 of the Muglad Basin, and in October 1996, CNPC led a joint venture with several other international oil companies to form the Greater Nile Petroleum Operating Company (GNPOC), which won the bid for oil exploitation in Sudan's Block 1/2/4 (CNPC Sudan Project Coordination Leadership Bureau, 1999). In the twenty-first century, Chinese oil companies have advanced their energy cooperation with Middle Eastern countries, especially before 2010, when Sinopec, CNPC and the China National Offshore Oil Corporation (CNOOC) were building oil and gas cooperation throughout all the major Middle Eastern oil-producing countries. In October 2000, Sinopec signed a contract with Algeria for a project to improve the recovery rate of the Zarzaitine oil field; and, in 2003, CNPC signed a risk exploration project for blocks 102a/112 and 350. In November 2008, CNOOC signed a service contract with Iraq for the development of the Aghadeb oil field, and in June 2009, CNOOC signed a service contract with the Turkish State Oil Company for the development of the Missan oil and gas field complex in Iraq (Liu, 2019: 17).

In addition, in recent years, the Gulf countries, represented by Saudi Arabia and the United Arab Emirates (UAE), have gradually opened up their oil exploration and exploitation rights, breaking the long-time monopolization of the upstream industry chain by local and Western companies, which also provided new impetus for energy production capacity cooperation between China and the Middle East countries. In 2018, CNPC signed cooperation agreements with the UAE for the development of the Umm Shaif-Nasr oil field and the Lower Zakum oil field development project cooperation agreements (China Petroleum News Center, 2018). Chinese oil companies have successfully pursued the right to develop the upstream fields of the high-quality oil industry in the Middle East oil-producing countries and undoubtedly have consolidated the existing energy production capacity cooperation between China and the Middle East countries, especially considering the soaring domestic demand for energy in China.

Despite the slowdown in upstream energy development after 2010, the cooperation in downstream energy industries between China and the Middle East countries is still relatively strong. The mode of energy production capacity cooperation between the two sides has shifted from "China one-way input" to both sides jointly seeking the downstream extension of the energy industry chain, thus promoting integration of the upstream and downstream industry chains. In 2000, the CNPC and other enterprises invested in the construction of the Khartoum refinery and chemical plant in Sudan, which is the first attempt at petrochemical production capacity cooperation between China and the Middle East countries (Zhi, 2016: 253–256). In 2003, the CNPC and the Algerian National Oil Company jointly built the Algerian SORALCHIN upstream and downstream integration project; in 2014, Sinopec took a stake in Saudi Aramco's Saudi Yanbu Red Sea Refinery Project. All these are representative of large-scale petrochemical projects invested in and built by Chinese enterprises in Arab countries.

At the same time, in order to meet China's crude oil demands and stabilize the energy trade cooperation between China and the Middle East countries, the Arab energy powers, represented by the Gulf Cooperation Council (GCC) are also extremely keen on investing and building large petrochemical projects in China. For example, in 2007, Saudi Aramco joined hands with ExxonMobil and China's Fujian Refining and Chemical to build the Fujian Quanzhou Refining and Chemical Integration Project; in 2009, Sinopec and Saudi Basic Industries funded the Tianjin Refining and Chemical Integration Project; and Sinopec and Kuwait National Petroleum Company joined hands to build the Zhanjiang Refining and Chemical Integration Project. In addition, in terms of petroleum engineering technology services, Chinese multinational companies keep improving their technology and management, and providing materials, engineering technology services in drilling, logging, recording and other oil and gas field, and petroleum engineering construction services to oil companies in the Middle East countries and to international oil companies, such as BP, Total and Shell. For example, in 2002, CNPC constructed the 1,050 km western oil pipeline project in Libya, which was the largest oil and gas pipeline project under construction in the world up to that time (Xinhua News Agency, 2004). This shows that the downstream energy industry cooperation between China and Middle East countries has moved into a mature stage and received global recognition.

2.2 Automobile Manufacturing as a Market-Oriented Feature in Production Capacity Cooperation

The automotive industry has became one of the few industrial sectors that have reached the capacity of exporting and establishing joint ventures for industrial transfer between China and the Middle East countries. The technology, quality, price and after-sales service of Chery, Lifan, BYD and other Chinese auto brands precisely meet the auto market demand in Iran and Egypt, and have gained a certain influence and brand reputation in the region. In addition, the production capacity cooperation between China and the Gulf countries in the field of automobile industry is mainly based on downstream product sales, which accounts for a small market share and has not yet entered the upstream and midstream industry chain.

The Middle East has traditionally been one of the most important export destinations for Chinese automobiles, as China FAW Jiefang Auto, Foton Motor, Dongfeng Motor and other cargo vehicle manufacturers all set up their own business in the region. In 2003, the China First Automobile Group established a joint venture located in Isfahan with Sam Motor, the third largest automotive group in Iran. Since then Chinese companies have made direct investments in Iran, Egypt and Algeria to establish joint ventures and have built production capacity cooperation in the form of technology transfer and components supply packages. In 2014, Liberty Auto-mobiles in the UAE announced that it would sell a full range of Foton heavy, medium and light trucks and special purpose vehicles locally. China's Beiqi Foton's truck products has signed agreements with local dealers in the UAE to enter the country's auto market. Haima Motor has chosen local dealers to represent itself in the UAE and other Middle East and North Africa (MENA) countries to enter the Middle East market. In 2016, China exported more than 200,000 vehicles to the Middle East countries, amounting to more than $1.5 billion, accounting for 15 percent of China's total vehicle exports (China Economic Web, 2017). In 2017, China's Foton Motor Group signed a cooperation agreement with Algeria's KIV Group, planning to invest in a plant in its eastern city of Annaba. The total investment in the project reaches $50 million, and the mass production is estimated to reach 50,000 units after completion (*People's Daily*, 2017).

At present, Chery, Brilliance, BYD, Geely, Lifan, Changan and other auto brands have founded joint business (or businesses) in production and sales operations in the Middle East countries, and have built up sales networks throughout the region. More than 10 Chinese vehicle manufacturers have entered the Iranian market, and some brands (Huachen, BYD, Geely) have been leading the industry in the local market (Fang, 2017: 32). In order to achieve capacity transfer, the Chinese auto industry aims to base its business in the Middle East, expanding to the African and European markets. On October 30, 2019, a celebration was held in Cairo in Egypt for the delivery of 50 pure electric buses by Foton to the Egyptian government and the launch of the Foton Egypt new energy bus manufacturing cooperation project. The delivery became the largest pure electric bus order in Egypt in 2019, and the Foton Egypt new energy manufacturing project is also the first Sino-Egyptian new energy bus manufacturing cooperation project. As the Egyptian government's Ministry of Military Industry said, the project would bring a new industrial revolution in the technology of electric vehicle manufacturing in Egypt (Bus Information Web, 2019).

2.3 Equipment Manufacturing Highlighted in the Technology Transfer

In the field of equipment manufacturing, China-Middle East production capacity cooperation has witnessed the transformation from the export of products to technology export, from the upstream exploration and design of the industry chain, to the manufacturing of intercity rail vehicles, electric locomotives, rolling stock and high-speed trains and other rail vehicles, and further to the provision of after-sales service for rail vehicle products covering the whole industry chain. China has accomplished the real sense of production capacity cooperation in the Middle East following the path of foreign direct investment (Wei, 2016: 18).

Currently, China's production capacity cooperation with the Middle East countries has shifted gradually from the initial project-driven equipment machinery exports into founding joint ventures to build factories. In recent years, the Middle East countries have been vigorously developing domestic highways, a railroad backbone network and urban metro construction, as the demand for international production capacity cooperation in the field of equipment manufacturing is strongly increasingly. In 2009, Turkey Izmir light rail project marked the entry of Chinese high-end rail transportation equipment into the Middle East market. In 2012, China Railway Construction won the bid for the Ankara-Istanbul high-speed railroad phase II project, which is the first electrified high-speed railway project contracted by Chinese enterprises abroad. In 2014, CSR Group and Turkey's MNG Holding A.S. jointly invested $110 million to establish a joint venture in Turkey, which is mainly engaged in the manufacturing, operation and maintenance of rail transportation equipment. The company plans to produce 200 metro cars per year and will be a rail vehicle manufacturing base and after-sales service center for markets in Europe, Central Asia, West Asia and North Africa. This joint venture has become a model of production capacity cooperation between China and the Middle East countries in the field of rail transportation equipment technology. As a pioneer in the sector, the company achieved the upgrade from exporting products to Europe to exporting technology in the field of rail transportation (Zou, 2017: 135). In the production of basic railroad vehicles, China Vehicle Group exports to the Middle East, including electric locomotives, internal combustion locomotives, passenger cars, subway cars, light rail cars, and the wagons six product series. In Sudan, China's exports of internal combustion locomotives, internal combustion locomotives and wagons have taken more than 80 percent of the local freight and passenger transportation tasks, and the availability of locomotives has reached more than 90 percent (*Yi Cai News*, 2015). In 2009, China Harbor (Egypt) Engineering Co., Ltd. was established, mainly engaged in transportation infrastructure construction, including maritime engineering, dredging and blowing, highways and bridges, rail transportation, aviation hub and the supply and installation of related complete sets of equipment.

Steel manufacturing equipment is also one of the key sectors of cooperation between China and the Middle East countries. In 1996, China's crude steel production exceeded 100 million tonnes for the first time and it became the world's top producer of crude steel. In December 2007, Sinosteel Equipment signed a general contract with Turkey's Tosyalı Group, in which Sinosteel Equipment is responsible for the continuous casting and rolling system of Tosyalı Group's new, 1.1 million tonnes per year, short process steel plant, marking China's largest overseas contracted construction project to that date. In 2008, China became the world's largest steel exporter and the largest net exporter (Sinosteel, 2019). In 2011, Sinosteel completed the 300 square meter sintering project at Iskenderun Steel Plant in Turkey, which was the largest overseas blast furnace project ever constructed by China at that time, with a contract value of $150 million (Chinese Ministry of Commerce, 2011). In 2014, Sinosteel invested $347 million in a steel plant with a capacity of 1 million tonnes per year in southwestern Iran and planed to invest €1.8 billion (about RMB15 billion) in seven local steel projects in Iran (Xinhua News Agency, 2015). In recent years, Turkey has attached great importance to cooperation with Chinese steel enterprises and has imported from China steel metallurgical equipment and related technologies, such as sintering machines, coke ovens, blast furnaces, continuous bar rolling mills, continuous wire rod rolling mills and hot strip rolling mills, and is exploring ways to further develop production capacity cooperation.

2.4 New Energy Industry as an Accelerator for Production Capacity Cooperation

In recent years, most Middle Eastern countries have started the process of energy transition, China's advantages in the field of renewable energy technology are distinct, which can strongly support accelerating energy transitions in regional countries. Besides, the technologies in traditional oil and gas energy, clean energy and renewable energy constitute a new accelerator for energy production capacity cooperation between China and the Middle East countries. China-Middle East energy cooperation has gradually expanded to the field of new and alternative energy, which forms a three-dimensional and multi-dimensional energy industry cooperation model. In June 2014, Chinese President Xi Jinping delivered a speech entitled "Promoting the Silk Road Spirit and Deepening Sino-Arab Cooperation" at the 6th Ministerial Conference of the China-Arab Countries Cooperation Forum, formally proposing the "1+2+3" Sino-Arab cooperation model, in which the three major high-tech fields of nuclear energy, space and satellite, and new energy are the key sectors of Sino-Arab practical cooperation (Xinhua News Agency, 2014).

In fact, China-Middle East new energy production capacity cooperation shows a strong complementarity in the new era. For the sake of energy security and sustainable economic development, most Middle Eastern countries have launched plans to transform and upgrade their energy structures to avoid over-dependence on traditional fossil energy. Take the UAE as an example, according to the UAE "2050 Energy Strategy," by 2050, the proportion of renewable energy in the UAE energy production will increase to 44 percent, and the share of clean energy will rise from 25 percent in 2017 to 50 percent (Kang, 2019: 79). The new energy sector is precisely where China has a lot of technology and surplus capacity. Taking solar power as an example, in the twenty-first century, China has developed into the world's largest producer of solar panels and the solar power market. In 2015, China's solar power generation accounted for 25 percent of the total global solar power generation (Chen, 2017: 102). Meanwhile, China has became the world's largest producer of hydroelectric power, with 1,155.8 TWh of hydroelectric power in 2017, accounting for 28.5 percent of the global hydroelectric power generation of 4,059.9 TWh, according to BP statistics (Huang, 2019).

Due to its enormous potential, the energy infrastructure development will certainly be the focus of future energy production capacity cooperation between China and the Arab countries. Since 2015, China Shandong Electric Construction Group and Spanish enterprises have jointly constructed the second and third phases of the Nouao Power Station project in Morocco with a total investment amount of $2 billion (Wang, 2018: 27). Nouao Power Station is currently the world's largest planned tower-type concentrated solar power plant project, which will lay a solid foundation for China's solar industry investment in North Africa. In 2016, the BYD Company and Abu Dhabi Clean Energy Company in Masdar City jointly promoted the commercialization of clean energy transportation and battery storage systems; China JinkoSolar was involved in the "Abu Dhabi Light," the world's largest solar power project, in which China's JinkoSolar has a 20 percent stake (Cheng, 2018). In 2018, Shanghai Electric signed a turnkey contract with the Saudi International Electricity and Water Company for the Dubai Water and Electricity Authority's Solar Thermal Phase IV 700 MW power plant project, which includes the world's largest and most technologically advanced power station, a landmark development for China's new energy technology export. In addition, in 2018, there were more than a dozen energy cooperation projects between China Energy Construction, Tianjin Electric Power Construction and Arab countries such as Egypt and Sudan (Guo, 2019: 33). It can be seen that the energy transformation cooperation between China and the Middle East countries has become a key area of energy cooperation and production capacity cooperation between the two sides. At this stage, energy security governance is a common concern for both sides, and via strengthening renewable energy development, energy poverty reduction and governance, it can provide a new and stable space for China-Middle East production capacity cooperation.

3 The Difficulties and Challenges of China-Middle East Production Capacity Cooperation

At present, the production capacity cooperation between China and the Middle East countries still faces realistic difficulties, such as high security risks and a poor business environment, due to the regional environment and the status of national economic, political and industrial development.

In terms of security risks, it mainly includes the political risks and financial risks in the Middle East countries. As for the political risks, the Middle East is highly unstable, as it is unsettled while it is reshaping the regional pattern. Since the Arab Spring erupted in 2011, most Middle Eastern countries are still in the transitional period of turbulence and transformation. Some countries are still in the state of civil war, which imposes several security risk challenges, such as internal national conflicts, international external interventions and extremist threats. Some countries have already entered the process of social transformation, but they are still unable to guarantee a safe business environment, because of serious economic problems, slow infrastructure reconstruction, fierce political competition and other prominent social problems. In terms of financial risks, since 2018, some Middle Eastern countries have experienced increasing financial deficits, which reduces their ability to repay foreign debts. Thus, the production capacity cooperation between China and the Middle East countries face serious financial risks. According to Xinhuanet, Saudi Arabia had 298 billion riyals fiscal deficit, that accounts for 12 percent of Saudi Arabia's GDP in 2020, far above the international redline at 3 percent (Xinhuanet, 2020). Moreover, some Middle Eastern countries have heavy foreign debts that far exceed their foreign exchange revenues. Many Chinese overseas investment enterprises, especially the smaller private enterprises, have failed to correctly assess the risks in the Middle East overseas markets and are unable to bear the default risk of repaying foreign debt principal and interest. The increasing risks in production capacity cooperation between China and the Middle East countries will reduce the enthusiasm and hinder further progress in bilateral cooperation.

In terms of the business environment, the inconsistent institutional environment and imperfect regulatory system in the Middle East countries will have a negative impact on the cost control, decision-making and risk prediction of bilateral cooperation, thus impeding the implementation of production capacity cooperation. First, the Middle East countries adopt relatively strict cooperation policies on overseas enterprises, such as laws on foreign investment, permission for employment, regulation of logistics and transportation. Taking Turkey as an example, to protect local employment, the Turkish government strictly controls the import of foreign labor. Hence, the entry procedure and enrollment process of overseas employees are complicated, and the period of processing cycle is relatively long, which will increase the cost of Chinese enterprises in their overseas business. For China, as more and more private enterprises enter the Middle East market, insufficient internationalization of Chinese enterprises and inadequate understanding of the environment of the overseas market institutions are important factors that impede the production capacity cooperation between China and the Middle East countries. According to China Net Television, the index of the world's top 100 multinational corporations in 2019 is 58.07 percent, while the average index of China in the same period is only 15.96 percent (China Network Television, 2019). Chinese enterprises lack knowledge of the local legal environment, accounting system and market environment in the Middle East countries, so it is difficult for them to make accurate investments and operation decisions. Additionally, the Chinese government imposes lots of restrictions on state-owned enterprises in the early stage of overseas investment. In contrast, the regulation system for approved overseas projects has yet to be established. Therefore, it is impossible to grasp the whole picture and make real-time adjustments to enterprise decisions. The insufficient understanding of institutional arrangement in the overseas markets and imperfect regulation system of Chinese enterprises will encourage mistakes in corporate decision-making, and discourage bilateral production capacity cooperation.

Focusing on the process of production capacity cooperation, there are still several obstructions to bilateral cooperation between China and the Middle East countries, such as uneven industrial cooperation, lack of technical standards and lack of market attractiveness. First, the production capacity cooperation is limited to certain areas. The investment of Chinese enterprises in the Middle East market is mainly concentrated in secondary industry, including the energy industry, manufacturing, or technical facilities construction. However, these enterprises are not strong players in the service industry, such as legal services, real estate, tourism, financial services. Second, Chinese enterprises can launch business activities smoothly only after they have established strong local ties in the economic, social, cultural and political fields due to the specific situation of the Middle East countries. This increases the cost of production capacity cooperation for Chinese enterprises (Yao, 2016: 16). Finally, most enterprises in China or the Middle East countries do not consider the other region attractive for trading, because the two regions have relatively separate industrial chains and different industrial environments, which constrain the integration of the resource advantages of the two sides. For instance, Chinese enterprises have less competitiveness in providing semi-finished manufactured goods for the Middle East market. For Middle Eastern enterprises, they tend to cooperate with European and West Asian countries with distinctive industrial capacity and lower transport costs.

In summary, China and the Middle East countries still have several realistic challenges in their production capacity cooperation. On the one hand, Chinese enterprises have to face high risks with regard to security and finance. Additionally, due to the low degree of internationalization and the imperfect regulatory system, Chinese enterprises are unable to predict and take investment risks. On the other hand, because of the inconsistent business systems and market environments, China and the Middle East countries need to adapt policy to prevent making business misjudgments, which will increase the cost of cooperation. Lastly, the bilateral production capacity cooperation is still in limited areas, compared to European and West Asian enterprises, Chinese enterprises need to enhance their business attractiveness to Middle East market.

Therefore, to facilitate production capacity cooperation between China and the Middle East countries, both parties need to expand openness, enhance communications and make mutual beneficial cooperation basis on mutual trust. First of all, China and the Middle East countries should increase the frequency of high-level visits and communications, enhance political mutual trust and improve the regulatory framework, which can provide effective guidance and support for bilateral production capacity cooperation. Furthermore, China and the Middle East countries should promote cultural and educational exchanges, which can cement the foundation of public opinion. In particular, "closer people-to-people ties" can be promoted through non-governmental cultural exchanges and economics cooperation via platforms, such as the China-Arab States Cooperation Forum and the China-Arab States Expo. Finally, to enhance industrial competitiveness and attractiveness, both parties should optimize the cooperation mechanism. Besides the existing investment agreements, it is necessary to sign a comprehensive bilateral agreement covering taxation, shipping, energy and technical standards to guide future enterprise cooperation.

4 Conclusion

Production capacity cooperation between China and the Middle East countries is deeply affected by the world economic growth cycle, the economic development stage and industrial characteristics of the Middle East countries. After the financial crisis in 2008, the world economy has entered a new growth period. International industrial transfer has shown a new trend of "two-way transfer" away from the previous "one-way transfer." As a result, the Middle East has seen its best development ever. During this period, the production capacity cooperation between China and the Middle East countries has expanded its cooperation field from traditional oil industry to infrastructure construction industry, the manufacturing and services field. According to the resources advantage and degree of industrialization in the Middle East, besides the oil and gas energy cooperation, the main form of production capacity cooperation between China and the Middle East countries is international outsourcing projects. Nowadays, Chinese enterprises have already expanded their cooperation field from acting as subcontractors in civil engineering to the high value-added fields such as commercial retail, project financing, design consulting and operation management. In the manufacturing sector, China's production capacity cooperation with Egypt, Turkey, Iran and other Middle Eastern countries has made important breakthroughs in technology transfer and standardized operation management.

References

Bus Information Web (2019) "China-Egypt first new energy bus manufacturing project started," October 31. Available at: https://baijiahao.baidu.com/s?id=1648871206262549719&wfr=spider&for=pc

Chen, Mo (2017) "BRI: Opportunity to strengthen economic cooperation between China and Saudi Arabia," *Ningxia Social Science*, vol. 5, pp. 97–104.

Cheng, Chunhua (2018) "China and UAE jointly build energy Silk Road," China Petro Newspaper, 09–03(008).

China Economic Web (2017) "Joint promoting BRI, Sino-Arab vehicle cooperation has promising prospects," September 12. Available at: http://auto.ce.cn/auto/gundong/201709/12/t20170912_2 5907527.shtml

China Network Television (2019) "The index of China's top 100 multinational corporations in 2019 is 15.96%," September 1. Available at: www.sohu.com/a/337934348_428290

China Petroleum News Center (2018) "China Petroleum and UAE National Petroleum Company signed cooperation contract," March 22. Available at: http://news.cnpc.com.cn/system/2018/03/22/001682039.shtml

Chinese Government (2015) "Guidelines on promoting international production capacity cooperation and equipment manufacturing," May 23. Available at: www.gov.cn/zhengce/content/2015-05/16/content_9771.htm

Chinese Ministry of Commerce (2011) "Consul General Zhang Qingyang visits Sinosteel's largest cooperation project in Turkey," September 23. Available at: http://istanbul.mofcom.gov.cn/aarti cle/jmxw/201109/20110907759237.html

CNPC Sudan Project Coordination Leadership Bureau (1999) "Monument built along Nile River," *China Petroleum and Petrochemical*, vol. 6, pp. 22–23.

Fang, Zheng (2017) "Prospects of China-Iran production capacity cooperation," *China Commercial Journal*, vol. 18, pp. 30–33.

Feng, Jun (2017) "The number of trade remedy cases against China hit a record high in 2016," *China Tendering Weekly*, vol. 3, p. 12.

Guo, Dandan (2019) "Sino-Arab international energy cooperation: current status and future prospect," *International Business Forum*, vol. 5, p. 33.

Huang, Xiaoyong (2019) *World Energy Blue Book: World Energy Development Report (2019)*, Beijing: Social Science Literature Press.

Kang, Yu (2019) "Energy policies of major countries in the world in 2018," *World Petro Economy*, vol. 2, pp. 73–79.

Li, Yiding (2019) "New thinking on capacity cooperation between China and Africa under the 'Belt and Road Initiative,'" *Open Journal of Social Sciences*, vol. 7, pp. 95–106.

Liu, Dong (2019) "China-Arab energy cooperation tends to be three-dimensional," *World Affairs*, vol. 17, pp. 16–17.

OAPEC (2020) *2020 Annual Statistical Report*, Kuwait: OAPEC.

Office of the United States Trade Representative (2017) Free Trade Agreements," May 3. Available at: www.ustr.gov/trade-agreements/free-trade-agreements/bahrain-fta

People's Daily (2017) "Futon Vehicle and Algerian company signed cooperation contract," April 22. Available at: http://world.people.com.cn/n1/2017/0422/c1002-29228432.html

Sinosteel (2019) "China strengthens cooperation with Turkey in steel construction: Note on Sinosteel Equipment Co.," December 10. Available at: http://news.sinosteel.com/magazine/html/63/582/content/2912.shtml

Wang, Jing (2018) "China-Maghreb production capacity cooperation," *Arab Studies*, vol. 2, pp. 21–36.

Wei, Min (2016) "The theory and policy analysis of China-Middle East international production capacity cooperation," *Arab World Studies*, vol. 6, pp. 3–20.

World Bank (2016) "WDI Database," August 1. Available at: http://databank.worldbank.org/data/reports. aspx?source=world-development-indicators

Xinhua News Agency (2004) "The world's largest oil and gas pipeline project under construction contracted by China is completed in Libya," June 2..Available at: http://news.cri.cn/gb/1827/2004/06/02/405@181835.htm

Xinhua News Agency (2014) "Xi Jinping: Make best of top design, build "1+2+3" Sino-Arab cooperation framework," June 5. Available at: www.xinhuanet.com/politics/2014-06/05/c_1111000667.htm

Xinhua News Agency (2015) "Chinese enterprises' chances to go abroad," –October 23. Available at: http://news.hexun.com/2012-11-19/148095963.html

Xinhuanet (2020) "Saudi Arabia's fiscal 2021 budget deficit has been significantly reduced," December 16. Available at: https://baijiahao.baidu.com/s?id=1686230482504393802&wfr=spider&for=pc%EF%BC%8C2020%E5%B9%B412%E6%9C%8816

Yang, Guang (2016) "Petroleum rentier economies and the cooperation potential of West-Asia with China," *West Asia and Africa*, vol. 5, pp. 32–51.

Yao, Kuangyi (2016) "Opportunities and challenges of China-Middle East countries' production capacity cooperation," *Journal of Middle Eastern and Islamic Studies (in Asia)*, vol. 10, no. 2, pp. 1–19.

Yi Cai News (2015) "China's South Vehicle exports internal combustion locomotives to Sudan," October 23. Available at: www.yicai.com /news/2693822.html

Zhi, Yuchen (2016) *Chinese State-Owned Enterprises Enter Africa*, Beijing: China Social Science Literature Press.

Zou, Zhiqiang (2017) "China-Turkey international production capacity cooperation under BRI framework," *Northwest Minzu University Journal*, vol. 6, pp. 131–139.

5

THE BELT AND ROAD INITIATIVE AND CHINA'S EXPANDING TIES WITH WEST ASIA AND NORTH AFRICA

Manochehr Dorraj

Introduction

Long before the European encroachment on West Asia and North Africa (WANA) from the eleventh to the twentieth centuries began, China had a history of trade, political and diplomatic ties and cultural exchange with the region through the ancient "Silk Road" that goes back more than 2100 years (Frankopan, 2015). This chapter will focus on the dynamics of the current expansion of economic and political ties between East and West Asia and North Africa regions in the context of China's Belt and Road Initiative (BRI).

"The Asianization" of the "Middle East" (Khanna, 2019), fostered in large part by the expanding energy, trade, investment, immigration, security and political ties between the two regions of East and West Asia, in large part led by China, foretells a political realignment in which Beijing is filling the vacuum created by the diminishing US and European influence. One of the more significant indicators of this trend is China's expanding energy ties with the region, which is complemented by a substantial increase in bilateral trade, investments, security, and political ties.

In 2019, nine countries of the region were responsible for providing China with 44.8 percent of its oil imports (Workman, 2020). In 2020, due to economic slowdown induced by the Covid-19 pandemic, this figure shrank to 38 percent (Rapp and O'Keefe, 2020). For countries such as Saudi Arabia, Iran and Iraq, the three regional energy giants, China is the number one importer of their energy resources, and their number one trading partner in the world. China has become the number one trading partner of the United Arab Emirates (UAE), Egypt, Algeria, Kuwait, Oman, and Bahrain, as well.

In the past decade, the UAE's bilateral trade with China has annually increased by 35 percent. and currently, it ranks as the second largest trading partner for China in the region after Saudi Arabia. The UAE is projected to increase its trade with China by 40 percent in the coming years (Carvalho, 2021). Qatar, the number one producer of liquefied natural gas (LNG) in the world, was the number one exporter of LNG to China in 2014, and provided as much as 34 percent of Chinese total import of 41 percent LNG from the region (Fulton, 2020a). In 2021, the two countries signed a 10-year agreement that will culminate in Qatar exporting 2 trillion tones of LNG to China annually (Watkins, 2021).

China has overtaken France as the major exporter to Algeria. Beijing has created two of the largest sovereign funds in the world and has declared that the Arab world is going to be one of the major destinations for its investments. Trade ties between China and the Arab world have increased by 600 percent in the last decade alone. In 2014, the value of this trade was $230 billion. A 2015 estimate projected the value of bilateral trade with the 22 countries of the Arab world alone to reach $600 billion by 2024 (Sun and Zoubir, 2015). While in light of the onset of Covid-19 and the consequential economic downturn in the global economy in general and China in particular, this projection now seems overly optimistic, once the recovery in the global economy resumes, the current dynamics indicate that China is well positioned to expand its economic presence in the WANA region. Xi Jinping's visit to Saudi Arabia in December of 2022 and the declaration of the expansion of economic ties between the two countries are early indications of this trend.

China has also expanded its military and security ties with the region and is increasingly a major supplier of armaments and advanced weapon systems to the WANA. It has held joint military exercises with Iran (2014, 2016), with Russia (2019), with Turkey (2015), with Pakistan (2021), and with Saudi Arabia (2016). In addition, as the list of the naval exercises above indicate, many countries in the region are attempting to diversify their security partnership by including China in their security architecture through procurement of Chinese weapons and by undertaking joint military exercises. As such, the WANA regions are playing a significant role in China's energy and economic security, becoming indispensable to its economic and national security, lubricating and sustaining China's rise on the global stage as well as providing it with viable markets for its exports.

Lacking a colonial history in the region, through its policy of "respect for sovereignty and win-win economic ties," China has chipped away at US influence, thus redrawing the geostrategic map. In light of China's new ambitious global BRI, in which West-Central Asia and North Africa figure prominently, China's partnership with many countries of this region has been transformed from primarily transactional ties to a hybrid that also includes potentially a strategic dimension.

This chapter will discuss these developments by providing a brief overview of the select countries of the WANA region's expanding economic and security ties with China. The broader geostrategic implications of this shift and their political and economic impact will also be discussed.

The Belt and Road Initiative

Since the ascendance of Xi Jinping to power in 2012, China has embarked on an ambitious global outreach so that its contours have taken it well beyond the confines of its traditional sphere of influence, East Asia. The new initiative, dubbed the "Belt and Road Initiative" (BRI), also known as the "New Silk Road and the new Maritime Silk Road" or "One Belt, One Road" is "an Afro-Eurasian, Pacific-Atlantic, Mediterranean-Arctic vision of a multipolar world and the place of China's soft power in that world"

(Bianchi, 2019). It is designed to connect the four continents of Asia, Europe, Africa, and Latin America, while expanding China's bilateral relations and influence in West Asia, Central Asia, Africa, Europe, and Russia. This initiative has both land and a maritime components, and the magnitude of its estimated investment is projected to surpass the US Marshall Plan investment in Europe after World War II by seven- to ten-fold. This initiative that began with an initial capital investment of $1 trillion is projected to expand to $5–8 trillion by 2030 (Macaes, 2018). As such, it is intended to substantially expand China's trade, commerce and bilateral ties globally. China's new strategic ambition will make an indelible mark on all of these regions for decades to come and will transform the global political economy in unmistakable ways.

Three major factors may explain China's new ambitious global initiative:

1. With China's impressive rate of growth ranging from 6–10 percent in the last three decades enabling it to emerge as a major global manufacturer, this has necessitated an earnest search for new markets for China's goods and services. The BRI has proven to be a very useful instrument for finding new markets for China's excess production capacity, new markets for investment, and injecting new blood into China's economy and expanding its global economic power and political influence.
2. It is a response to the US haphazard soft containment policy under the presidencies of George W. Bush and Barack Obama. Under these two presidents, the USA attempted to forge closer ties with India, the large country in Asia with a history of conflict with China, in order to enlist it as a partner in the containment of China. India, however, has proved adept in playing both sides, simultaneously expanding trade ties with Washington and Beijing and even joining the Chinese-initiated Brazil, Russia, India, China, and South Africa (BRICS) group and the Infrastructure Investment Bank, although as of late, its enthusiasm for joining China's BRI has waned as it entertains its own regional and global ambition. Another example of such an attempt was demonstrated when the Obama administration held joint military exercise with Australia. Seen in this light, the BRI was and continues to be a response to the US containment strategy that has continued with more intensity under the Trump and Biden administrations with even more aggressive attempts to woo India into the US orbit of influence and the escalation of economic conflict and the imposition of tariffs on Chinese goods. Despite the opposition of some of its European allies, the Biden administration has continued the Trump era containment strategy toward China, attempting to mobilize the support of India, Australia, Japan, and other like-minded Asian countries.
3. The BRI is an expression of the Chinese leadership's realization of its expanding global power and the assumption of a more assertive role on the world stage. In other words, the BRI is a clear break from the Deng Xiao Ping era dictum of "biding our time" and not drawing attention to ourselves and keeping a low profile. Xi Jinping's administration's global ambitions demanded a new, more proactive, political posture. By launching the BRICS, and the Bank for Investment in Infrastructure and Development, regarded by many observers as an alternative to the International Monetary Fund, China began building block by block the initial institutional infrastructure of an alternative to the current Western-dominated global financial system. As such, China is also preparing for the possibility of the current attempts at "economic decoupling" becoming more entrenched.

In Beijing's calculations, the area encompassing the BRI "contains 4.4 billion people (63 percent of the world's population) with an aggregate GDP of $2.1 trillion (29 percent of the world's aggregate wealth)" (Leverett, Leverett, and Wu, 2015) . To implement this vision, China has embarked on creating a network of transportation, Internet, broadband and ports to facilitate the expansion of trade, using regional and Chinese currencies, thus bypassing the US dollar.

As originally conceived, the BRI has six routes and one waterway:

- China–Mongolia–Russia Economic Corridor;
- New Eurasia Land Bridge Economic Corridor;
- China–Central Asia–West Asia Economic Corridor;
- China–Pakistan Economic Corridor;
- China–Bangladesh–India–Myanmar Economic Corridor;
- China–Indochina Peninsula Economic Corridor;
- The twenty-first-century Maritime Silk Road connects China's coastal ports to Europe through the North Pacific Ocean, the Indian Ocean, the Arabian Sea, and the Mediterranean by passing in waterways adjacent to the surrounding countries in Asia, the Middle East, Africa, and Europe.

Hundreds of projects are currently underway throughout these corridors. In 2014, China dedicated a fund of $40 billion to provide the initial financing for the BRI. Soon after, this investment expanded to $1 trillion that encompassed 67 countries in three continents. Later, many countries in Latin America, Asia, and Europe were also added to the list and, by 2020, the number had jumped to 124 nations. The initial investment is projected to expand to $5–8 trillion by 2030 (Ferdinand, 2016: 950). In 2015, 900 deals were underway, worth $890 billion. That year, 44 percent of China's engineering projects were in Belt and Road countries. This figure increased to 52 percent in 2016. The inter-BRI trade is anticipated to climb to $2 trillion (*The Economist*, 2016). The China–Pakistan trade corridor, for example, involved an initial investment of $46 billion that is intended to facilitate the flow of trade from Western China to Pakistan and the WANA region. China is building roads and rail systems to connect the Muslim city of Kashgar in the Xinjiang region to Gwadar Port in Pakistan and from there to send goods to West Asia and Europe.

A fast bullet train system, established in 2014, connects Eastern China to the city of Ürümchi in Xinjiang in order to expand the flow of trade and people to Central Asia and from there to Kazan. Another route would link Urumqi to Tehran, Ankara, Moscow, and North and Central Europe.

The China–European Union trade corridor through Central Asia–Iran and Turkey, using a 10,000-miles-long rail line, is intended to expand China's trade with the continent of Europe substantially, using West and South Asia as a land bridge to Europe.

China is building not only the financial vehicles for its BRI, but also a global financial apparatus as an alternative to the ascendant financial institutions dominated by the USA and its European allies. The two more important multinational institutions led by China are: the Asian Infrastructure Investment Bank (AIIB) with 57 founding members, with an initial capital of $100 billion, and the Shanghai-based New Development Bank, with a starting capital of $50 billion (Gabusi, 2017: 23–45). The sheer ambition of BRI-related projects indicates that China is no longer "a rising power": it has risen.

The BRI and the Expanding Trade Ties with West Asia and North Africa region

In 2018, Xi Jinping announced an investment of $60 billion in the Arab world. Trade ties between China and the Arab world have increased by 600 percent in the last decade alone. In 2014, the value of this trade was $230 billion. In 2021, the value of the bilateral trade between China and the Arab world jumped to $330 billion, and this was a one-third increase from 2020. Twenty nations in the WANA region have joined the BRI and 15 have signed a Strategic Partnership agreement with China in the last decade.

A combination of the emergence of China as the number one importer of their energy resources, and the need to diversify their trade partnership, meant, by 2019, for several countries in the WANA region, China was their number one trading partner. This includes Iran, Egypt, Algeria, Saudi Arabia, the United Arab Emirates, Kuwait, and Oman, to name a few (Lons et al., 2019). The United Arab Emirates, for example, hosts more than 4,200 Chinese companies and is poised to receive an additional 1,400 Chinese firms. China-UAE bilateral trade has increased annually by 35 percent in the last decade. In anticipation of the expanding flow of Chinese good to Dubai, Chinese companies have invested heavily, modernizing and expanding their ports.

In April 2015, Qatar, the largest provider of LNG to China, established a clearing bank to facilitate doing transactions in Yuan.

Whereas the value of Saudi-Chinese bilateral trade in 1990 was a meager $417 million, by 2010, it had reached $40 billion, this amount climbed to $73 billion in 2019 (Chaziza, 2013: 167; Fulton, 2020b: 8). On the eve of his visit to Saudi Arabia in January 19–20, 2016, Xi Jinping declared that the two countries should expand their bilateral trade ties and push for further progress in China-GCC Free Trade Agreement Talks. They should also establish the China-Saudi Energy Cooperation Community. He expressed his appreciation at Saudis Arabia's joining the Asian Infrastructure Investment Bank as a founding member in 2015 and hoped to enlist their further support for the BRI (CCTV, 2016).

This was followed by King Salman's trip to China in 2017 and the signing of a $65 billion trade and investment agreement. The two countries also pledged to create synergy between the BRI and the Saudi "Vision 2030." The Saudis hope to attract Chinese investment for the diversification of their economic system. In an attempt to diversify their funding and financial assets, the Saudis have expressed an interest in doing trade in Yuan and putting some of their assets in Renminbi bonds (Al-Arab, 2017). In August 2017, in Riyadh, another $70 billion's worth of deals were signed along with a Memorandum of Understanding (MoU) for a $20 billion joint investment fund (Fulton, 2020b: 1–19).

China has constructed a major railroad in Saudi Arabia, in order to connect the two holy cities of Mecca and Medina, that came online in January 2018 (Kynge, 2017). This was followed by another agreement in 2019 that would enable Chinese companies to improve the transport capacity of the freight railway between Dammam and Riyadh.

During Crown Prince Mohammed bin Salman's visit to China in 2019, several MoUs were signed for downstream investments, "including one between Saudi Aramco and Norinco to build a $10 billion refinery in Liaoning." Saudi Aramco also completed a deal that gave it a 9 percent stake in a Zhoushan refinery as well as the use of crude oil storage facilities for Aramco's other Asian markets. Aramco President and CEO Amin H. Nasser recently described the company's China strategy as "moving beyond a buyer-seller relationship to one where we can make significant investments to contribute to China's economic growth and development." (Fulton, 2020b: 1–19).

In addition to a trade imbalance—nearly $20 billion in 2019—that has tilted in Saudi Arabia's favor, the nature of China-Saudi trade reveals another kind of imbalance. Whereas Chinese exports to Saudi Arabia are diverse and include industrial and construction equipment, services, consumer goods, textiles, electronics, and food; in 2018, 97 percent of Saudi exports to China were fossil fuels and petrochemicals. This is a feature that characterizes the bilateral trade of other major oil-producers of the WANA region with China as well. In light of the looming reality of the post-hydrocarbon age, this trend represents a major long-term vulnerability for Saudi Arabia and other petro-economies of the region (ibid.: 1–19).

The Digital Silk Road (DSR), announced in 2015, sparked the interest of the Saudis as a useful tool for their Vision 2030 initiative and the diversification of their economy. The DSR has a dual aim: (1) it is intended to expand international digital connectivity, with China serving as the epicenter of this network; and (2) it is designed to establish China as a global technological superpower, and an alternative to the US supremacy in the high-tech arena. China intends to use the DSR to mine data, build a digital infrastructure, create 5G networks, fiber-optic cables, and broadband networks to facilitate the expansion of Chinese commerce, communication, and influence throughout the world. The Saudis also hope the DSR will play an instrumental role in the development of Neom mega city, using artificial intelligence, automation, manufacturing, and renewable energy in order to create a new economy and abolish the unsustainable dependence on the fossil fuel and petro-dollar as the engines of economic growth. In this pursuit, the Saudi Telecom Company signed a contract for wireless network modernization and 5G network construction. In 2019, the Saudi-Sino Investment Forum and Huawei signed a MoU with Saudi ministries and companies, focusing on "smart cities, smart campuses, smart logistics, smart education, smart tracts, smart grids, smart security, and smart roads" (ibid. 1–19).

It is important to note that while China has elevated its bilateral ties with both Saudi Arabia and Iran as a comprehensive strategic partnership, due to the imposition of draconian sanctions on Iran, the value of China-Saudi bilateral trade outstrips the bilateral trade between Iran and China. For example, whereas the value of Chinese investment in Saudi Arabia since 2005 has been $41 billion, in contrast, Chinese investment in Iran in the same period was $27 billion. Hence, whereas, in 2019, the value of bilateral trade between China and Saudi Arabia was nearly $73 billion, the value of China-Iran trade was $19 billion (ibid.: 8). Thus, without substantial sanction relief, Iran would continue to lag behind Saudi Arabia and the UAE in terms of value of its bilateral trade with China.

In an attempt to build synergy between China's BRI and the Saudi Vision 2030, in February 2019, Saudi Arabia signed over 30 economic cooperation agreements with China worth a total value of $28 billion. One such contract was between the China Railway Construction Corporation (CRCC) and the Saudi Arabian National Petroleum Corporation (Aramco) for the energy and industrial hub, known as the King Salman Energy Park (Spark). Between 2019 and 2020, Chinese purchases of Saudi oil surged 47 percent and the Saudis became the number one provider of oil to China in the world, a place formerly held by Russia. This was followed by a new MoU between the Saudi Aramco and China's Sinopec, signed in August 2022, to broaden energy cooperation in refining and petrochemical integration, oil field services, upstream and downstream technologies, carbon capture, and hydrogen processes. China also intends to expand its economic ties with Saudi Arabia by constructing a large manufacturing hub in King Salman energy park. To safeguard its investments, China plans to deploy its own security force in the Kingdom (Watkins, 2022).

Due to the Trump administration's imposition of sanctions on Iran and Venezuela that have hampered their ability to export their oil to China, Iraq also became able to expand its oil exports to China by 16.1 percent, reaching 60.12 million tones in 2020, making it China's third largest oil supplier (Aizhu and Xu, 2020).

China is also actively involved in the development of renewable energy in the Kingdom. In May 2020, China's Silk Road Fund bought a 49 percent stake in the renewable energy platform of Saudi Arabia's ACWA Power Renewable Energy Holding Company that has solar and wind assets in the UAE, South Africa, Jordan, Egypt, and Morocco (Chen, 2020). Since Saudi Arabia geographically does not directly lie on one of the proposed BRI land corridors, it has pledged to join the China-Pakistan landline corridor.

In 2012, Sino-Egyptian bilateral trade reached $9.6 billion and more than 1,066 Chinese companies were investing in Egypt. China's imports to Egypt were worth $8.5 billion and Egypt's exports to China in contrast were valued at $1.06 billion. The Egyptian government began to negotiate to change its trade deficit with China. In 2016, China started investing in overhauling and modernizing the Suez Canal. With a population of 85 million, Egypt has become a major destination for Chinese manufactured goods in the region. (Gadallah, 2016: 94–114).

Since the uprising of 2011, however, the Egyptian economy has declined substantially, and Cairo is strapped for cash and aspires to revive its foundering tourism industry. As Magdy Amer, the Egyptian ambassador to China, said in *Al-Ahram*, the state-run daily, on January 18, 2016, upon the impending visit of Xi Jinping, "Beijing will sign a $1bn loan agreement to shore up Cairo's foreign currency reserves and will open a $700m credit line with the National Bank to fund joint projects." He also said, "Negotiations are advanced on various Chinese investments in transport, power and construction, and that the visit will see the launch of a year-long series of cultural events intended to encourage Chinese tourism" (Clover et al., 2016).

By 2017, Egypt had become China's third largest trade partner in Africa. In the same year, the bilateral trade between the two countries reached $10.87 billion, while the value of Egypt's imports from China reached $8 billion, the highest in North Africa. In 2018, the value of bilateral trade between the two countries jumped 28 percent (Abdel Ghafar and Jacobs, 2019). China has also actively participated in the expansion and modernization of the Suez Canal in anticipation of bringing the Suez Canal economic zone project to fruition. Since the launch of the BRI, between 2013 and 2018, Chinese investment in Egypt has increased to $19.298 billion. There are plans underway for Chinese companies to build a new capital city outside Cairo (Molavi, 2019).

Algeria is another country in North Africa that has witnessed expanding trade ties with China. In 2013, China replaced France as its number one trading partner. In 2018, the value of bilateral trade between the two countries reached $7.85 billion. Like Egypt, Algeria's exports to China are insignificant and it has a trade deficit with China. However, its exports to China are rising. From 2000 to 2017, its exports to China have grown by 60-fold (Abdel Ghafar and Jacobs, 2019). Between 2005 and 2018, total Chinese investments in Algeria have reached $23.048 billion. (Molavi, 2019). Chinese construction engineering companies are also building the port of Cherchell in Algeria in anticipation of expanding future trade.

By 2007, the three major East Asian economic powerhouses, namely, China, Japan, and South Korea were respectively, Iran's number one, two, and three trading partners in the world, a position that was previously held by European powers (Garver, 2013: 76–77). In May 2011, China signed a $20 billion agreement to expand the bilateral cooperation in Iran's mining and industrial sectors, and the leadership of both countries announced plans to expand the then annual $30–40 billion bilateral trade to $100 billion by 2016 (Harold and Nader, 2012: 10). The 2011 imposition of the fourth set of sanctions, followed by the sanctions imposed on Iran during the Obama administration prior to the nuclear agreement of 2015, that included Iran's energy and banking sectors, interrupted this plan and this estimate did not come to fruition. The abrogation of the nuclear deal and the imposition of "Maximum Pressure" campaign by the Trump administration in May 2018, that made Iran the most sanctioned nation in the world, had a dual impact on Iran-Chia ties: While immediately, it reduced the volume of bilateral trade between the two countries, substantially, its more enduring impact was to usher in the signing of $400 billion 25-year strategic agreement in 2021, intended to expand the bilateral energy, trade, and security ties substantially (Bloomberg, 2021).

China has become Iran's largest market for its petrochemical exports, especially methanol. According to the head of Iran's Petrochemical Commercial Company, Reza Hamzelou, by 2012, "Iran surpassed Saudi Arabia as the biggest methanol exporter to China and Chinese companies were negotiating the construction of a $5 billion methanol plant in the Iranian city of Mahshahr" (Harold and Nader, 2012: 10–11). In the post-nuclear deal era, Tehran hoped to expand economic and investment ties with Beijing. In an interview, Mr. Majid-Reza Hariri, deputy head of the Iran-China Chamber of Commerce, said, now that many sanctions have been lifted, it is time to expand relations. According to Mr. Hariri, "Iran and China have so far had trade ties but from now on our expectation is to see Chinese investments in our infrastructure projects." Mr. Hariri also asserted, "We need between $30 bn to $50 bn foreign investments annually, a big chunk of which can be secured by China for such sectors like road, rail and air transportation, agriculture and industries such as household, textile and ceramics" (Clover et al., 2016).

During the January 2016 state visit of Xi Jinping to Tehran, he described the Iran-China relations as "natural partners" and the two sides pledged to expand the value of their bilateral trade ties to $600 billion by 2025 (CCTV.com., 2016). Iranian leaders pledged to play an active role in the BRI. In 2016, the first Chinese freight train carrying goods arrived in Tehran (Bozorgmehr, 2016). China is also building several high-speed rail systems connecting Western and Eastern parts of Iran to Central Asia and Turkey, in anticipation of increasing trade flows to Iran as a major transit point for flow of goods from China. A delegation from Iran visited China in 2017 seeking more Chinese investment in Iranian market.

As the BRI unfolds, the strategic geography of Iran looms larger for China's regional and global ambitions. With the largest coastline of any country in the Persian Gulf and as a gateway to the Central-Eurasia, and the Caspian Sea, and through Turkey, a bridge to Europe, Iran plays an important role in the success of the BRI in the larger West Asia region. As one commentator has observed, "for China's global ambitions, Iran is at the center of everything" (Erdbrink, 2017). However, as Washington under the Trump administration intensified its economic and political pressure on the Islamic Republic, to counter this pressure, the Iranian government sought closer ties with Beijing and Moscow. The value of Iran–China trade in 2015, for example, was more than $52 billion. But with Trump's policy of economic warfare with Iran and the threat of secondary sanctions against China, in 2018, the value of bilateral trade between the two countries plummeted below \$30 billion. By 2019, the value of China's trade with Iran had declined by nearly 40 percent, reaching the lowest point in the last decade, according to Radio Farda, on December 1, 2019.

The next major turning point in Iran-China bilateral trade ties came in August 2019 when Iran and China unfurled their 25-year plan for the substantial expansion of bilateral trade. Having seen its ability to sell its oil and gas diminish substantially, and barred from access to the global banking system and the dollar-based economic transactions; and the drying up of foreign investment and the plunge in the value of its currency, the Rial, by 75 percent—all due to Trump's maximum pressure campaign—Iran needed economic relief. The planned \$400 billion 25-year investment in Iran, that would include \$280 billion's worth of Chines investment in Iran's oil, gas, and petrochemical industry followed by another \$120 billion in upgrading Iran's transportation and manufacturing infrastructure, is designed to further integrate Iran into China's BRI and through it to China's orbit of economic and political power (Watkins, 2019).

While much of the specific details of the deal is shrouded in secrecy, from what has been revealed in the Western and the Iranian media so far, it would be safe to conclude it is going to expand China's presence and influence in the Iranian economy and market exponentially. Chinese would receive substantial benefit from this deal. Chinese companies would be given

> the first refusal to bid on any new, stalled or uncompleted oil and gas field developments. Chinese firms will also have the first refusal on opportunities to become involved with any and all petchems project in Iran, including the provision of technology, systems, process ingredients and personnel required to complete such projects. China will also be able to buy any and all oil, gas and petchems products at a minimum guaranteed discount of 12pc to the six-month rolling mean price of comparable benchmark products, plus another 6pc to 8pc of the metric for risk-adjusted compensation.
>
> *(ibid.)*

China would also be granted the right to delay payments for Iranian products up to two years. China would also be allowed to bring to Iran 5,000 of its security forces to safeguard its projects, investments, and the transit of oil and gas and petchems from Iran to China, including through the Persian Gulf.

As the flow of West Asia's trade moves eastward, East Asia, led by China, has become the number one destination of exports and imports for countries like Iran, Iraq, Saudi Arabia, Kuwait, United Arab Emirates, and Qatar. Hence, China's investment in the region has steadily expanded since 2005, and the BRI has accelerated this process.

Politically, Chinese policies of "respect for sovereignty and non-intervention in internal affairs" in much of the region that has bitter memories of colonialism is well received. China refuses to take sides between such antagonists as Iran and Saudi Arabia, Iran and Israel, or the Palestinians and the Israelis. Hence, China's mediation of regional conflict renders it an "impartial broker" in a polarized region. Beijing's constructive role in bringing Iran's 2015 nuclear deal to fruition and its attempt to invite the leaders of Syria and the opposition to Beijing for negotiation, and its welcoming of Iran-Saudi dialogue and diplomatic negotiations in 2021, all serve as examples of its constructive regional diplomacy. These are all indications that the current economic and political realignment of great powers underway in West Asia, which involves a more prominent Chinese role, is bound to expand and become more consequential with unmistakable social and political impact in future.

In large part, because of Chinese prudent non-interventionist political posture discussed above, and its skillful economic diplomacy, by 2008, China overtook the USA as the number one exporter to West Asia and, by 2010; it had outstripped the USA in imports from the region as well (World Trade Organization, 2013). By 2013, Asia, led by China, was overwhelmingly the largest trading partner for the West Asia and North Africa regions (ibid.).

China's Expanding Security Ties with the Region

China is the number five producer of the armament in the world. Between 2005 and 2010, the WANA regions were the recipients of 31 percent of China's global arms sale and ranked number two behind East Asia that received 50 percent of China's global arms sales in the same period (PRC Worldwide Arms Sales, 2011). This trend has since expanded.

China provides the region with long-range missiles and missile technology, drones, and numerous other armaments. During the Iraq-Iran War (1980–1988), Beijing sold arms to both antagonists through third parties. It has also provided countries like Iran and Saudi Arabia with nuclear technology. China played a major role in the early stages of development of Iran's missile system. Since Iran does not possess a viable air force, its missile system functions as its major defense shield and deterrence. Iran is scheduled to become a member of the Shanghai Cooperation Organization in 2023—a collective security pact that includes China, Russia, India, Pakistan, and several Central Asian countries. China also held joint naval exercises with Iran in 2014, 2016, 2019, and 2021 (jointly with Russia) and with Saudi Arabia (in 2016).

China-Saudi security ties began when in 1986 through a secret negotiation the Saudis bought 50 DF-3/CSS-2 ballistic missiles. This was followed by the purchase of 54 PLZ-45 155-millimeter self-propelled guns in 2007. In 2014, the Saudis bought 15 Wing-Loong 1 unmanned aerial vehicles (UAV), followed by the purchase of 5 Ch-4 armed UAVs in the same year (Fulton, 2020b:1–19).

In March 2017, Saudi Arabia's King Abdulaziz City for Science and Technology and China Aerospace Science and Technology Corp signed a deal to produce China's CH-4 UAV, which is similar to the US-made MQ-1 Predator drone. Fearing political instability in Saudi Arabia, the USA refused to build drone factories in Saudi Arabia. Both Saudi Arabia and Iraq have possessed these drones since 2014. This Saudi facility will likely operate as a hub "for manufacturing and servicing for other CH-4 operators in the Middle East, including Egypt, Iraq and Jordan." Likewise, the UAE imported Chinese-made Wing Loong I drones in 2011, and became the first customer of the Wing Loong II drone in 2017 (Ningthoujam, 2021). In 2019, the Saudi Ministry of Defense signed an MoU to cooperate with the Equipment Development Commission of China on the military use of the Beidou Navigation Satellite System (Fulton, 2020b:1–19). In 2021, US intelligence agencies disclosed that Saudi Arabia is now manufacturing its own ballistic missiles with the help of China (Watkins, 2022). But still the total of Saudi arms imports from China pales in contrast to what the Saudis purchase from the USA and Europe.

China and Turkey have signed several defense agreements between their respective defense industries that have culminated in the production of several rockets and missile systems. This includes the production of Kasirga Rockets (1996–1997), Yildirim Missiles (1997–1998) and a number of other medium- and short-range missiles between 1998 and 2011 (Kumar, 2013: 127–134). Turkey received a landing platform dock from China in 2011. The two countries have also had a number of joint training and military exercises, most notably in 2015. Since Turkey is a member of NATO and as such enjoys the NATO Alliance's military protection and receives sophisticated weaponry from them, its military cooperation with China, compared to Iran, remains limited.

Lesser known is the expanding Israeli high-tech arms transfer to China worth $3–4 billion dollars annually despite US government objections. This has led to the expansion of bilateral Israeli-Chinese trade ties. In 2010, these were worth $6.77 billion. In 2013, the bilateral trade climbed to $10 billion and was projected to double by 2020 (Kumarawamy, 2013: 148–158). Chinese companies are engaged in building the new port of Ashod in Israel and they will be operating the port in Haifa, to the dismay of the US government, using Israeli ports as a hub for export to Europe. In 2016, China's investment in Israel surpassed $16.5 billion. By 2017, during Natanyhu's visit to China, the two countries signed a $25 billion trade and business agreement. By 2018, China was responsible for one-third of the high-tech investment in Israel. By 2021, the value of bilateral trade had jumped to $22.8 billion (Zhang, 2022). The Chinese are scheduled to build the "Red Med" railway connecting the Red Sea to the Mediterranean that would go through Israel. In 2022, Israel reduced the allocation of dollars and Euros in its national reserve and added Yuan as a currency to its $206 billion reserve (Avis, 2022).

China's Assets and Challenges

China's rapidly expanding economic influence in the region, in part, reveals the financial and the political windfall of military non-intervention and "respect for sovereignty." Unlike the West and Russia, China lacks a history of war and conflict with WANA regions. The policies of non-intervention in internal affairs of other nations, keeping a low political profile, and accentuating trade have served its diplomacy well so far. China has accumulated a good deal of political capital in the region. How it spends this capital will go a long way to determine the future viability of the BRI (Luft, 2016). If successfully implemented, this initiative is going to change China and the world.

"Win-win" trade ties and investment in building infrastructure have paid dividends for Beijing. Expanding infrastructure often provides jobs and public welfare, and, for the most part, is perceived in a positive light by the public in the host countries. Another benefit of investment in new infrastructure for Beijing is that it embeds China in the economies of the region for the long haul. Thus, a relation of dependency emerges that cannot be easily severed. In addition, the US national debt of $26.70 trillion deficit in 2020 stands in sharp contrast to China's foreign exchange surplus reserves of $ 3.1 trillion. While, in 2013, China's Gross National Saving of 50 percent of GDP ranked number four in the world, by 2014, China ranked number one in purchasing power parity, and was the number two largest economy in the world in term of GDP (Mahbubani, 2020). According to some analysts, by 2060, the US economy is projected to count for 17 percent of global GDP, while China's economy would count for 28 percent of global GDP (Tselichtchev, 2012). Other scholars are also bullish on the future of China and anticipate it will overtake the USA as the largest and the most productive economy in the not too distant future. One such assessment concludes:

Unlike the contest with the Soviet Union, over time China could overtake the United States in terms of GDP. If this happens, with its huge population, China's resulting economic parity likely will metamorphosize into military superiority. If China grows to its full potential, it could become the leading nation in the international system by the mid to the latter part of the twenty-first century.

(Tammen, 2006)

One recent assessment that also takes stock of the impact of Covid-19 on the future prospects for China's economic expansion, concludes:

Chinese influence has grown in both size and reach around the world, reinforcing and contextualizing experts' understanding of this changing international system. From the end of the Cold War to the present, Chinese influence has cut into or supplanted Western countries' sway in every geographic region. More recently, the COVID-19 pandemic has further accelerated the rate of these Chinese gains, with new and existing partners increasing their dependence on China.

(Moyer et al., 2021: 1)

Thus, the fact that China's deep pockets have served its economic diplomacy well so far and as a late-comer to the region, has allowed it to gain much leverage in a relatively short space of time, is not an aberration and must be understood as a part of a global pattern.

The biggest challenge to China. however, is political. It is often the case that where the economy goes, politics follows. As China's economic investment in the region expands, can it afford to continue the policy of "non-intervention," "respect for sovereignty" and "offend no-one"? The fateful question is: can China continue to maintain this policy as its investment in the region expands? Additionally, how long can China remain a friend to all and an ally to none in such polarized regions as West Asia and North Africa?

While many nations aspire to emulate and replicate China's "economic miracle," the same enthusiasm does not appear to exist in copying China's political system. The old orthodox Communist ideology of Marxism-Leninism has faded. Chinese nationalism or "Socialism with Chinese characteristics" are not appealing beyond the borders of China. Hence, while many intellectuals in the WANA region admire China's economic achievements, including lifting some 800 million out of poverty in the last four decades, they don't aspire to emulate its political authoritarianism. But there is an aspect of China's political model that is appealing to authoritarian regimes in the WANA region: the fact that China has fostered one of the fastest rates of economic growth in modern history with a political system that is not a part of Western democratic tradition.

With the rise of nationalism and populism in many parts of the world, China faces the task of effectively meeting the political challenges of management of its fast-rising economic and political power domestically and globally. Currently, in contrast to the large appeal of US pop culture among the youth, as of yet, China also lacks a universally appealing culture to export. While rising fast, it also lacks the global military capability that the USA has. China is dependent on the US navy for the security of the shipping lanes in the Persian Gulf where much of its energy supply pass through. Because of these factors, some scholars like Shambaugh regard China as a "partial power" rather than a comprehensive one, and cast doubt on its ability to replace or seriously challenge US power globally any time soon (Shambaugh, 2013).

Conclusion

The march of history in the WANA region has witnessed the Crusaders, the Spanish, the Dutch, the Ottomans, the Russians, the Anglo-French, and the Americans as the major political players. Whereas the Western powers have had a presence in the region since the eleventh century when the Crusaders invaded Jerusalem, China's ties with WANA go back more than 2,100 years. China has been there before and knows the way. Seen in this larger historical context, the rapid rise of Chinese influence in the region should not be regarded as an anomaly. Rather, it is a clear signal that the era of ascendancy of China and the realignment of global powers in the region have begun. Whereas the history of the WANA nations' encounter with the West is riddled with the examples of colonial conquest, war, and conflict, lacking such a history, China enters the region with a clean slate.

Since the end of the Cold War in 1991, the strategic map of the world has been transformed from a bipolar world to a multipolar one and, with the rise of China and the emergence of the region of East Asia, led by China, as the new engine of economic growth in the past three decades, we have witnessed the dawn of non-polarity in which no single power can dictate the terms of engagement on the global stage (Kupchan, 2013). This new development is manifested in a shared sentiment against US hegemonic policies that many rising powers, including the BRICS group aspire to. The early manifestation of this new development in a multiplex and non-polar world is an attempt by rising powers to reshape their region in order to align it with their own national interest (Ehteshami, 2015: 225). In this pursuit, they seek global partners. China, for example, prefers partnerships primarily based on "win-win economic ties" rather than getting entangled in alliances that would sap its power and oblige it to take sides in regional conflicts, that may induce the loss of market share and political capital. So far, China has been careful not to repeat the example of the imperial overreach and military interventionist policies of the United States.

In the context of this larger shift in the global power transition, deepening relations with the regions encompassing the New Economic Silk Road and the New Maritime Silk Road, including West Asia and North Africa, is a part of Beijing's new strategy. The January 2016 state visit of Xi Jinping to Iran, Saudi Arabia, and Egypt, the three countries for whom China is the number one trading partner in the world, followed by Xi's state visit to Saudi Arabia in December of 2022, in order to expand and solidify the mutually beneficial bilateral ties, is an indication of China's heightened interest in the region. During that trip, Xi Jinping also made it clear that Beijing is not looking to "fill a vacuum." As he put it, "we are not looking for proxies. We are looking for mutually beneficial partnerships" (CCTV.com, 2016). In 2018, China's trade with all the corridors of the BRI declined by about $100 billion, with one exception, the WANA region (Molavi, 2019).

In 2018, China was also a major destination of exports for several countries in the region. This includes Saudi Arabia ($38.398 billion), Iraq ($21.198 billion), Iran ($20.738 billion), Oman ($17,988 billion), the UAE ($15.38 billion), Kuwait ($14.488 billion), Qatar (9.68 billion), Israel ($4.68 billion), and Libya ($3.848 billion). What is transpiring is a transition in favor of China and to the detriment of US economic fortunes in the region. By 2018, some of the key US regional allies like Saudi Arabia were sending 30 percent more exports to China than the to United States. The UAE was sending three times more exports to China than to the United States. For Kuwait, this margin is eight times more. For Qatar, it is nine times more. And Oman exports 28 times more to China than to the United States. In contrast, the North African countries' and Israel's primary targets of exports are respectively Europe and the United States (ibid.).

No doubt, this expanding relationship is deepening the economic integration of the entire Asian continent. The attendant political consequences of this integration are already underway. Based on the current dynamics of expanding trade ties with the region, chronicled in this chapter, it is not too far-fetched to predict that the value of China's bilateral economic ties with the WANA region is going to surpass the amount of $650 billion by 2030. If this projection comes true, then the region is going to surpass the US-China annual trade that has fluctuated between $450 billion and $630 billion in 2017–2022. One of the political ramifications of this new reality is that, in future, the USA may no longer be the indispensable trade partner for China as it has been in the past three decades. Thanks to its BRI, astute economic diplomacy, and aversion to militarism or economic warfare, China now has many more economic partners to sustain its BRI.

In April 2015, Qatar opened up the first Clearing Bank in West Asia to handle financial transactions with China in Yuan. This was followed by the Chinese-led creation of the New Development Investment Bank for Developing Nations and the creation of the BRICS nations in July 2015. Therefore, we may have already witnessed the realization of one of the cornerstones of the BRI: that the trade between the countries comprising "the New Silk Road" and "the New Maritime Road" is going to be done in Chinese and the regional currencies, thus bypassing the US dollar. The Trump administration's escalation of economic warfare against Iran and the trade war with China, that has been continued by Biden's imposition of draconian sanctions on Russia for its war against Ukraine; have prompted all three countries to seek to trade with some of their partners in their own currency or crypto currencies. If this trend becomes more expansive, this may open cracks in the hegemony of the dollar in future. Since the BRI is also an attempt to boost the value of Chinese currency and put it in a better position to compete with the dollar and the Euro, Trump's policies of America first, economic nationalism vs China, that to a large extent have also been adopted by the Biden administration so far, may inadvertently accelerate the rise of the Yuan as an international currency. As such, this would serve as another steppingstone in creating a China-led alternative economic power, thus forging a new reality: one world with two economic systems. If such economic decoupling materializes, several countries in the WANA region are likely to be integrated into the Chinese orbit of global economy.

The signs of the return of the Middle East to its Asian home are unmistakable. The realignment of great powers in the region of West Asia and North Africa has begun, and as its dynamics unfold, it will impact the region and the world profoundly for decades to come. In fact, the emergence of a "post-American Middle East" might be a harbinger of a larger global transition of power.

It remains to be seen if the official Chinese leadership's claim that the BRI provides China with a new opportunity to recast and reconfigure global politics through a new "moral imagination" that does not see the political domain as one of conquest and dominance, but as a "win-win" strategy based on mutual respect and cooperation to usher in an era of co-prosperity (Xinhua News Agency, 2014), will come to fruition. Unlike the West, China's global rise so far has not been accompanied by wars of conquest and political imposition and dominance, some observers are less skeptical about such claims. Should China change its current course of high-profile economics, low-profile politics, it has a unique chance to put international relations on a new trajectory and provide an alternative to the power politics of old that have been accompanied with war and bloodshed. Can China use this opportunity and turn the BRI into a vehicle not only for its own economic gain, but also to remake the world on the basis of a new foundation? Or encumbered by its own authoritarian political impulse, and primarily driven by commercial interest and an aversion to political entanglements, will China prove to be a status quo rather than a transformative power, interested in profiting from the current global capitalist system rather than fundamentally altering it? The next two decades will reveal what role China will assume in the WANA region and the larger world as the full dimensions of the BRI unfold.

References

Abdel Ghafar, L. and Jacobs, A.L. (2019) "Beijing Calling: Assessing China's Growing Footprint in North Africa," Brookings, Doha Center, September 23.

Aizhu, C. and Xu, M. (2020) "Saudi Arabia Pips Russia to China's Biggest Oil Supplier in 2020," Reuters, January 20.

Al-Arab, S. (2017) "Chinese Yuan Rises in Global Oil Markets as Saudi Seeks Funding in RMB," Xinhua News Agency, September 1.

Al–Filali, I.Y. and Gallarotti, G.M. (2012) "Smart Development: Saudi Arabia's Quest for the Knowledge Economy," *International Studies*, 49(3–4): 47–76.

Avis, D. (2022) "Israel Adds Yuan to $206 Billion Reserves in 'Philosophy' Change," Bloomberg, April 20.

Bianchi, R.R. (2019) *China and the Islamic World: How the New Silk Road Is Transforming Global Politics*, Oxford: Oxford University Press.

Bloomberg (2021) "China Signs 25-Year Deal with Iran in Challenge to the US," March 28.

Bozorgmehr, N. (2016) "First Freight Train from China Arrives in Tehran," Financial Times, May 10.

Carvalho, S. (2021) "Gulf News," May 9. Available at: CCTV.com1-18-2016

CCTV.com. (2016) "President Xi Meets Iran's Supreme Leader Khamenei." Available at: http:// english.cntv.cn/2016/01/24/VIDED0GDkzGPj6k7O7kEpDv3160124.shtml (accessed January 26, 2016).

Chaziza, M. (2013) "China's Policy on the Middle East Peace Process after the Cold War," *China Report*, 49(1): 167.

Chen, Y. (2020) "Graphics: How Is BRI Bolstering China-Saudi Arabia Ties?," *CGTN*, 21: 42.

Clover, C., Saleh, H., Bozorgmehr, N., and Kerr, S. (2016) "Xi Faces Diplomatic Test on First Middle East Visit," Financial Times, January 18.

Ehteshami, A. (2015) "Regionalization, Pan-Asian Relations, and the Middle East," *East Asia*, 32: 225.

Erdbrink, T. (2017) "For China's Global Ambitions, 'Iran Is at the Center of Everything'," New York Times, July 25.

Ferdinand, P. (2016) "Westward Ho – The China Dream and 'One Belt, One Road': Chinese Foreign Policy Under Xi Jinping," *International Affairs*, 92(4): 950.

Frankopan, P. (2015) *The Silk Roads: A New History of the World*, London: Bloomsbury.

Fulton, J. (2020a) *China's Relations with the Gulf Monarchies*, New York: Routledge.

Fulton, J. (2020b) "Stranger to Strategic Partners: Thirty Years of Sino-Saudi Relations," The Atlantic Council, August, pp. 1–19.

Gabusi, G. (2017) "Crossing the River by Feeling the Gold: The Asian Infrastructure Investment Bank and the Financial Support to the Belt and Road Initiative," *China and World Economy*, 25: 23–45.

Gadallah, Y.M. (2016) "An Analysis of the Evolution of Sino-Egyptian Economic Relations," in N. Horesh (Ed.), *Toward Well-Oiled Relations: China's Presence in the Middle East Following the Arab Spring*, London: Palgrave-Macmillan, pp. 94–114.

Garver, J. (2013) "China-Iran Relations: Cautious Friendship with America's Nemesis," *China Report*, 49(1): 76–77.

Harold, S. and Nader, A. (2012) "China and Iran: Economic, Political, and Military Relations," Santa Barbara, CA: Rand Corporation, Occasional Paper Series, 10.

Khanna, P. (2019) *The Future Is Asian: Commerce, Conflict and Culture in the 21st Century*, New York: Simon & Schuster.

Kumar, A. (2013) "Sino-Turkish Strategic Partnership: Prudent Hedging or Irreversible Strategic Shift?," *China Report*, 49(1): 127–134.

Kumarawamy, P.R. (2013) "China, Israel and the US: The Problematic Triangle," *China Report*, 49(1): 148–158.

Kupchan, C. (2013) *No One's World: The West, the Rising Rest, and the Coming Global Turn*, Oxford: Oxford University Press.

Kynge, J. (2017) "China's Railways Diplomacy Hits the Buffers," Financial Times, July 17.

Leverett, F., Leverett, H.M., and Wu, B. (2015) "China Looks West: What Is at Stake in Beijing's New Silk Road Project," *World Financial Review*, January 28.

Lons, C., Fulton, J., Sun, D., and Al-Tamimi, N. (2019) "China's Great Game in the Middle East," European Council on Foreign Relations, Policy Brief, 21, October.

Luft, G. (2016) "China's New Grand Strategy for the Middle East," January 26. Available at: http://foreign policy.com/2016/01/26/china's –new-middle –east-grand-strategy-iran-saudi-arabia-oil-xi-jinping

Macaes, B. (2018) *Belt and Road: A Chinese World Order*, London: Hurst.

Mahbubani, K. (2020) *Has China Won?: The Chinese Challenge to American Primacy*, New York: Hachette Book Group.

Molavi, A. (2019) "China's Global Investments Are Declining Everywhere Except for One Region," *Foreign Policy*, May 16.

Moyer, J.D., Meisel, C.J., Matthews, A.S., Bohl, D.K., and Burrows, M.J. (2021) "China-US Competition: Measuring Global Influence," Atlantic Council and Frederick S. Pardee Center for International Studies, 1 .

Ningthoujam, A. (2021) "The Middle East: An Emerging Market for Chinese Arm Exports," *The Diplomat*, June 25.

PRC Worldwide Arms Sales (2011) Available at: www.politicienii.ro/2011/09/03/peoples-liberation-army-of-china-annual-report-2011/

Rapp, N. and O'Keefe, B. (2020) "China Is Guzzling Crude Oil: Where Is It all Coming From?," *Fortune*, January 22.

Shambaugh, D. (2013) *China Goes Global: The Partial Power*, Oxford: Oxford University Press,

Sun, D. and Zoubir, Y. (2015) "China's Economic Diplomacy Towards the Arab Countries: Challenges Ahead?," *Journal of Contemporary China*, 24(95): 903–921.

Tammen, R.L (2006) "The Impact of Asia on World Politics: China and India Options for the United States," *International Studies Review*, 8(4): 571.

The Economist (2016) "Our Bulldozers, Our Rules: China's Foreign Policy Could Reshape a Good Part of the Global Economy," July 2.

Tselichtchev, I. (2012) *China Versus the West: The Global Power Shift of the 21st Century*, New York: John Wiley and Sons.

Watkins, S. (2019) "China and Iran Flesh Out Strategic Partnership: Staggered 25-Year Deal Could Mark Seismic Shift in the Global Hydrocarbons Sector," *Petroleum Economist*, September 3.

Watkins, S. (2021) "The Real Ramifications of China's LNG Deal with Qatar," May 31. Available at: https://Oil Prices.com/

Watkins, S (2022) "China and Saudi Arabia Intensify Energy Cooperation with Critical Deal," August 12. Available at: https://Oil Prices.com/Energy/Energy-General/China-And Saudi-Arabia-Intensify-Energy-Cooperation-With-Critical-Deal.html

Workman, D. (2020) "Top 15 Crude Oil Suppliers to China," *World Top Exports*. Available at: www.WorldTopExports.com/Top-15-Crude-Oil-Suppliers-to-China

World Trade Organization (2013) "Trade with the Middle East, 2013." Available at: www.wto.org

Xinhua News Agency (2014) "Xi Jinping's Address at the Central Conference on Work Relating to Foreign Affairs," Available at: http://News.Xinhuanet.com/politics/2014-11-29/c.1113457 723.htm

Zhang, H. (2022) "China-Israel Economic Cooperation Flourishes in 30 Years of Diplomatic Ties," *Global Times*, January 24.

6

CHINA AS A GEO-ECONOMIC AND SECURITY ACTOR IN THE MENA REGION

Lisa Watanabe

Introduction

China's role in the Middle East and North Africa (MENA) region has significantly increased over the past two decades, especially following the launch of its ambitious Belt and Road Initiative (BRI) in 2013. The principal driver behind this development is China's energy needs. The region is one of China's main crude oil and gas suppliers. Yet energy is not the only reason for China's heightened interest in the region. The latter's strategic location also makes it key for the transportation of Chinese goods to Europe and Africa, and the regional market itself is of commercial interest. Relations with countries in the region have thus been largely focused on energy cooperation, as well as investments aimed at improving sea-borne and land-borne transportation of goods, which has been welcomed by many regional states, both resource-rich and resource-poor alike.

Although China is principally a geo-economic actor in the MENA, with much of its activities focused on ensuring energy security and its investments aimed at facilitating supply chains, China's engagement in the region has become more and more multifaceted as time has gone by. Although Beijing has been reluctant to get too entangled in the politics and security affairs of the region, its diplomatic and security-related activities in the MENA have been growing. This has been partly to foster the image of a responsible power, as well as to protect its energy and economic interests in the region (Rózsa, 2020: 2). Nowhere is this more visible than in the Gulf, where it has a permanent naval presence tied to ensuring the safety of shipping lanes and is developing military cooperation arrangements with a number of states.

Although Beijing's growing security role in the region pales in comparison to that of the USA, it does come at a time when the USA is recalibrating its engagement in the region and is clearly reluctant to get involved in the management of the region's conflicts and any direct military intervention, leaving many doubts about the reliability of Washington as a partner, as well as uncertainties about the durability of the US security umbrella over the longer term. While regional states recognize that China is not seeking to take on the role of the USA in the region and thus are unlikely to see it as a real

DOI: 10.4324/9781003048404-8

alternative in security terms, at least at this stage, many are keen to diversify their partners and are interested in developing security and military ties with Beijing, sometimes even as a source of leverage vis-à-vis Washington.

Uneven US engagement could be a poisoned chalice for Beijing, though. It is likely to exacerbate regional rivalries, potentially making it more difficult for Beijing to remain above regional divisions as it has done fairly successfully so far. The USA is also still very much militarily present in the region and maintains strong security relations with a number of key regional states with which China is seeking to develop ties. As a result, tension between the two powers could intensify in the Middle East, in particular. Washington is likely to wish to prevent its security relations with key allies from being compromised and although it would like other states to take on greater responsibilities for the safety of their own shipping, a greater Chinese naval presence in the region is already making Washington nervous. Regional states could, therefore, find themselves caught up in the broader US-China rivalry that may complicate cooperation with both China and the USA. Similarly, Europe will need to weigh up what China's presence in the MENA region means for the promotion of its interests.

A Burgeoning Interest in the Region

China is a relatively new arrival on the scene in the MENA region. Its engagement with the region has evolved as China has itself undergone transformation. Following the establishment of the People's Republic of China (PRC) in 1949, China's involvement in the region was ideologically driven and thus focused on the non-aligned, Arab republics. With China's economic reform and opening up in the 1980s, engagement with the region was guided by economic considerations. The need to fuel economic growth and the consequent movement away from a revolutionary to a more pragmatic foreign policy meant that relations with the oil-producing regional states, in particular, became increasingly important to what was still a modest engagement with the MENA. China's seat on the UN Security Council (UNSC) also enabled it to establish a stronger diplomatic profile in the region, facilitating greater economic and political cooperation with regional states (Andersen et al., 2020: 11–12; Fulton, 2019a: 256).

During this early phase of expanding relations, China's engagement with the region was characterized by Deng Xiaoping's philosophy of "hide-and-bide," i.e., secure China's position, while maintaining a low profile and avoiding a leadership role. By the second decade of the 2000s, China was taking on a more confident and assertive role under Hu Jintao and thereafter even more so under Xi Jinping. The dictum of "hide-and-bide" was replaced with "seek proactive achievements." The BRI came into being against this backdrop of economic success and a more strident foreign policy (ibid.: 259).

The inauguration of the BRI, in particular, has intensified cooperation with the region. This is an ambitious initiative designed to maintain China's impressive growth rate and, by default, the Chinese Communist Party's legitimacy. Two elements were introduced with its launch in 2013: the Silk Road Economic Belt (SREB), i.e. the land-based component of the BRI; and the Maritime Silk Road Initiative (MSRI), i.e. the maritime dimension of the initiative. The MENA region is particularly significant for the maritime component of the BRI, given Beijing's energy imports from the region. Almost 50 percent of China's crude oil imports come from the Middle East, largely from Saudi Arabia, as well as approximately 10–20 percent of its natural gas needs (Watanabe, 2019: 2). The region's strategic location at the crossroads between Asia, Europe and Africa also add to its importance for the enhanced connectivity that the BRI seeks to achieve.

The significance of the Arab world for Beijing was articulated in China's 2016 Arab Policy Paper that expressed a desire to further expand mutually beneficial, 'win-win' cooperation with the MENA countries, particularly through the SREB and the MSRI, while adhering to the five principles of peaceful co-existence: mutual respect for sovereignty and territorial integrity, mutual non-aggression, non-interference in each other's domestic affairs, and equality and mutual benefit (Rózsa and Peragovics, 2020: 59; Zoubir, 2020: 6). It envisaged developing relations with regional states through the "1+2+3 cooperation pattern," which has energy cooperation as its core, flanked by infrastructure and trade and investment, and supplemented by new areas of cooperation linked to new technologies in the field of nuclear energy, space satellites and renewable energy (Ministry of Foreign Affairs, the People's Republic of China, 2016).

Although the Arab Policy Paper does not mention any specific states, it is understood as largely directed towards the Arab League (AL) states with which China established the China-Arab State Cooperation Forum (CASCF) in 2004, as the result of an AL initiative (Rózsa, 2020: 5). However, the BRI is not focused on Arab states alone. Iran, Israel and Turkey are also important to the Initiative, as well as China's regional engagement more broadly. The lack of a regional approach to the MENA has led to cooperation within a number of fora, such as the CASCF, the Forum on China-Africa Cooperation (FOCAC), established in 2006, and the Gulf Cooperation Council (GCC), with which it established a China-GCC Strategic Dialogue in 2010. Cooperation, nevertheless, tends to take place bilaterally (Andersen et al., 2020: 17–18).

Beijing has been engaging regional states through a series of partnership deals that reflect the scope and importance of China's relations with individual states. The partnerships' hierarchy is not informed by regional divisions, but rather by China's economic and energy interests. The fullest form of partnership is the comprehensive strategic partnership encompassing a full range of cooperation. Only Saudi Arabia, the UAE, Algeria and Egypt have concluded this type of partnership with China, indicative of their significance either for China's energy needs or their strategic location for the distribution of Chinese goods. Iran too recently concluded such a deal with China, which at the time of writing has yet to be ratified by the Iranian parliament. Several other regional states, including Turkey, Iraq, Jordan, Kuwait, Qatar, Oman and Morocco, have strategic partnerships with Beijing, which implies wide-ranging cooperation, including in the military sphere (Fulton, 2019b: 3–4; Yadlin and Heistein, 2020).

Expanding Economic Ties

On the whole, regional states have welcomed intensified relations with Beijing. China's non-colonial background, policy of non-interference and a focus on stability through development without conditionality has made it popular with governments in the region. Beijing is also on good terms with regional rivals, such as Iran and Saudi Arabia, and has thus far avoided being drawn into regional divisions, in contrast to the USA. In general, many governments in the region view China as a welcome source of commercial opportunities and investment, and often see synergies between the BRI and their economic and development goals. For some countries in the region, such as those in the Maghreb, relations with China are also seen as a mean of reducing dependence on the West (Chaziza, 2020: 21; Zoubir, 2020: 3).

Trade relations with the MENA region have grown over the last two decades in particular. China's position as both an importer and exporter has increased. The oil-rich states in the Gulf have seen their commercial relations with China develop the most. Roughly 50 percent of China's regional trade is with the GCC states, with Saudi Arabia and the UAE qualifying as China's top two regional trading partners (Sidło, 2020: 34–35). Trade with Saudi Arabia largely comprises the export of Saudi crude oil and petrochemicals, and the import of Chinese machinery and consumer goods. Much the same is true of the UAE, with Emirati exports to China being largely energy-based, while the UAE imports Chinese textiles, machinery and light industrial products (Watanabe, 2019: 2–3).

The oil-rich states of Iran and Iraq have also seen trade with China increase (Sidło, 2020: 35). Not surprisingly, Chinese imports from Iran are dominated by crude oil, though its exports are more varied and include telephones, parts and accessories for automobiles and orthopedic appliances (Ghasseminejad, 2020). While there is much talk about the upcoming formalization of the Sino-Iranian comprehensive strategic partnership significantly boosting trade between the two countries, this would likely only transpire if US sanctions on Iran are lifted and Chinese companies no longer fear the repercussions of doing business in Iran (Calabrese, 2019).

In North Africa, China's initial trade interests were focused on oil and gas, making Algeria and Egypt primary trade partners for Beijing due to the former's oil resources and the latter's gas reserves, though trade has gradually expanded (AFDB, 2012: 3). China is now the main trading partner of Egypt, while the bulk of Algeria's trade is still with the EU (European Commission, n.d.; China International Import Expo, 2019). Even though Algeria is an oil-rich country, and most of its exports to China are energy-related, it tends to run a trade deficit with China. Most of its imports are Chinese and a larger proportion of its exports are with the EU (Sidło, 2020: 38).

Chinese investments in the region have also been on the rise. Most Chinese foreign direct investment (FDI) is in Saudi Arabia and the UAE. Investments in the former are focused on the energy sector, with investments in petrochemical facilities, as well as the construction of nuclear energy power plants and reactors, the latter being linked to Riyadh's aim of reducing domestic consumption of hydrocarbons and regional security concerns. Chinese companies have also been investing in industrial parks linked to the goal of diversifying the economy. Chinese investments in the UAE are largely related to its role as a logistics hub and include investment in Dubai's port and Abu Dhabi's Port Khalifa (Watanabe, 2019: 2–3) in the Gulf, Iran too has benefited from much-needed investment, though US sanctions have prevented many Chinese companies from investing in the country since 2017 (Sidło, 2020: 45).

Chinese investment in Israel has grown significantly in recent years, particularly advanced technology (Efron et al., 2019: 81, 84). China is also investing in Israel's transport infrastructure to facilitate the transportation of goods to Europe. This has seen proposed investments in the construction of a high-speed railway from Eilat on the Gulf of Aqaba to the Mediterranean, as well as the construction of a new port in Haifa (Watanabe, 2019: 3). and the expansion of the Ashdod port, both ports being on the Mediterranean Sea (Efron et al., 2019: 83). These kinds of infrastructural projects are very much linked to creating an additional route to the Mediterranean to supplement that of the Suez Canal.

Within the North African context, Egypt too has seen increased Chinese investment. Some of Cairo's flagship projects, such as the construction of the new capital city, as well as the redevelopment of the Suez Canal and Port Said in the north, and industrial zones, have benefited from Chinese investment (Watanabe, 2019: 3). Chinese investment in Algeria tends to be in construction, housing and the energy sector (Ghafar and Jacobs, 2019: 4).

Thus, not surprisingly given Beijing's energy interests in the region, the hydrocarbon-rich countries of the region have benefited the most from increased trade and investment relations with China, followed by states that are strategically key for moving goods between Asia and Europe. For many of these states, China is either already or fast becoming their top trade partner (Calabrese, 2019; Ghafar and Jacobs, 2019: 4; Sidło, 2020: 34–35). Non-hydrocarbon-rich states or those that are less well strategically situated have tended to benefit less. These states are more likely to run a trade deficit with China, and are also more susceptible to debt problems as a result of BRI lending (Sidło, 2020: 38, 42).

The coronavirus crisis has dealt a blow to economic relations between China and the region. Gulf States that rely heavily on energy exports to China saw their export revenues tumble, though their sovereign wealth funds can help cushion the impact, they need the Chinese economy to recover rapidly. Disruption to supply chains has also caused delays and increased the costs of BRI projects that some regional states may find difficult to absorb (Chaziza, 2020: 12–13, 20). It is no surprise, therefore, that the pandemic resulted in a mutual show of support, particularly between the Gulf capitals and Beijing, even if Beijing's initial handling of the outbreak of the coronavirus was not without criticism within the region. The fact that China's economy is rebounding is undoubtedly a welcome development.

China's Regional Security Profile

China is not just a geo-economic actor in the MENA region. The security dimension of its presence in the MENA is growing. This is motivated both by a desire to be perceived as a responsible power, as well as the need to safeguard its energy and economic interests in the region. Beijing has been gradually building up its contribution to regional security, starting with peacekeeping and anti-piracy operations, though without seeking to take the lead. Though China's contribution to peacekeeping operations in the region is still modest, Chinese observers are stationed in Lebanon and the Western Sahara (Rózsa and Peragovics, 2020: 66; Sun, 2015). In line with its interest in energy and shipping security in the Gulf, China has also been undertaking UN Security Council-mandated escort missions since 2008 as part of anti-piracy operations in the Gulf of Aden and around the Horn of Africa (Efron et al., 2019: 63).

As part of its broader concern for stability in the Persian Gulf, China has also been undertaking joint naval exercises with its partners in the area. Its first-ever joint naval drill with Iran took place in 2014 and again in 2017. The same year, China also carried out a joint naval exercise with Oman in the Gulf of Aden. Beijing is also trying to reassure and work with Saudi Arabia, as demonstrated following the attack on a Saudi oil tanker near the entrance to the Persian Gulf in 2019, allegedly carried out by Iran, after which China undertook naval exercises with Riyadh as well as Tehran (Efron et al., 2019: 63; Rózsa and Peragovics, 2020: 66; Watanabe, 2019: 3–4).

In line with these commitments, the Chinese navy has an increasing presence in the region. It maintains a number of technical service stops in the Middle East for fuel and material resupply, including in Saudi Arabia and Yemen (Sun, 2015). In 2017, China established its first overseas military base in Djibouti. The military facility itself is located south-west of the main port. However, reports suggest that the Chinese navy will also have its own berth in the port. Officially, the base has been established to support Chinese anti-piracy and peacekeeping operations in the region. However, it is also likely to be used to secure its investments and protect its citizens in the MENA region from Yemen in 2015 (Andersen et al., 2020: 91; Efron et al., 2019: 104).

Beijing is also increasing bilateral military cooperation with regional states. The various partnership agreements that China has with regional states more often than not imply some form of military cooperation. The People's Liberation Army, for example, is providing some training on a very low level to Saudi armed forces and is set soon to do the same with the Emiratis. The Sino-Iranian partnership deal, if ratified, would also formalize the military component of the relationship between Beijing and Tehran. However, China's relationship with Saudi Arabia has thus far limited Beijing's military cooperation with Iran and could continue to place limits on the extent to which it can feasibly develop (Coughlin, 2020; Wuthnow, 2020).

China is also eager to increase sales of weapons and equipment to the MENA region (Ministry of Foreign Affairs, the People's Republic of China, 2016), though it has thus far tended to focus on building up this aspect of relations where its energy and economic stakes are highest, notably in the Gulf. Iran, Saudi Arabia and the UAE are thus far China's largest arms customers in the Middle East. Although China cannot offer technologically superior weapons to regional states (Calabrese, 2019; Rózsa and Peragovics, 2020: 70), Chinese arms are attractive for some regional states that wish to diversify their arms suppliers or are under sanctions that limit access to Western weapons systems and equipment. Nevertheless, the USA is still the major arms supplier to the majority of MENA states (Wezeman et al., 2020: 6). The extent to which many of these states are integrated into Western weapons systems is, moreover, likely to limit the extent to which China can increase its share of the regional arms market. One area where China has managed to carve out a niche for itself in the MENA arms market is Unmanned Aerial Vehicles (UAVs), due in part to Washington's self-restraint in the supply of drones to countries in the region, which created a gap in the market (Calabrese, 2019). The expiry of UN Security Council restrictions on arms transfers to Iran in late 2020 and the commercial opportunities this may offer could also see China increase this dimension of its military relations with Iran (Wuthnow, 2020). Yet, again, this will likely be tempered by Beijing's desire not to antagonize Saudi Arabia and other regional states that have aligned with Riyadh, along with Washington, against Tehran.

Although China has been reluctant to get too involved in the region's conflicts, Beijing has also been increasing its profile in the area of mediation in recent years. In 2017, Beijing put forward a peace proposal to end the Israeli-Palestinian conflict and establish an independent Palestinian state, and even hosted trilateral meetings to kick-start talks between Israelis and Palestinians (Rózsa and Peragovics, 2020: 60). In 2016, Beijing also appointed a special envoy to Syria to help mediate the Syrian conflict, and, in 2017, hosted representatives from the Syrian government and the opposition, as part of its efforts to promote talks between both sides. Although its forays into conflict mediation in the region are tentative at present and have produced few concrete results, mediation activities clearly have the advantage of allowing China to boost its image as an honest broker in the region, while adhering to the principle of non-interference (Chaziza, 2018: 29–30, 35).

Geopolitical Ramifications

While China is becoming more influential in the MENA, it is far from seeking to replace the USA as the dominant external power in the region. From Beijing's perspective, the USA provides an important public good, namely navigation security in the Gulf, as well as contributing to the stability of its main partners in the region (Watanabe, 2020: 3), not least of which is Saudi Arabia. Beijing is thus able it to reap the benefits without taking on the main responsibility for regional peace and security (Rózsa, 2020: 3–4). Even if China wanted to get militarily and diplomatically more involved in the region, it would be unlikely at this point to be perceived as a serious alternative to the USA. Even if Washington has been recalibrating its engagement in the region since the Obama Administration, the US military presence in the MENA region has not altered as significantly as rhetoric about US retrenchment would suggest. Despite radical reductions in troop numbers in Iraq, the recent withdrawal of troops from Syria, and a rotational rather than continuous aircraft carrier presence in the Gulf, the USA maintains tens of thousands of military personnel in 14 MENA countries, and troop deployments even increased following the Iranian missile attacks on US soldiers in Iraq following the US assassination of Qasem Soleimani, a major general in the Iranian Revolutionary Guard Corps in January 2020 (Benaim and Hanna, 2019: 1–2). US weapons and military equipment are, moreover, hard to rival and would take a long time to replace.

Nevertheless, the growth in China's regional role necessarily contributes to multipolarity in the MENA. China's engagement in the region does comes at a time when regional states harbor doubts about Washington's long-term commitment to regional security. The Middle East is no longer as important to the USA as it once was, due to its near complete energy independence as a result of domestic shale gas production and its increased focus on the Asia-Pacific. Since the 2003 War in Iraq, there has also been a growing reticence to intervene militarily in the region's conflicts and to engage in nation building. The drawdown of troops in Iraq, the Obama Administration's reluctance to enforce its redline in Syria, and the Trump Administration's decision to withdraw US troops from Syria, are all indicative of a change in the way the USA engages in the region that has so far been unchanged under the new Biden Administration (Andersen et al., 2020: 90).

A more selectively engaged USA is likely to alter the calculations of regional states, particularly since US economic and political clout in the region is perceived as waning (Rózsa, 2020: 5). China is an appealing partner for many regional governments as it has a strong desire to increase its economic and political engagement with them, without seeking to tie it to the kind of political conditionality that Western states often insist on. For the oil-producing states of the region, China is an important trade partner. As alluded to earlier, the BRI also dovetails with the long-term economic plans of many regional countries that make Chinese investment attractive. As Beijing gradually builds up its regional security profile, many capitals in the region may seek to complement their military and security relations with the USA by deepening cooperation in this area with Beijing. Should the USA become more inward-looking post-pandemic and reduce its diplomatic and military presence further, this tendency could be further reinforced. States in the region may also expect China to contribute more to promoting peace and security in the region as its presence continues to grow, which could also prompt it to step up its involvement in the region's security affairs.

However, the USA cannot realistically retrench completely from the region. Washington still has an interest in maintaining a strategic influence over regional energy resources for the sake of its allies and reassuring its allies in the region, not least Saudi Arabia, Riyadh's GCC allies and Israel, especially with regards to Iran. Moreover, within the context of intensified Sino-American rivalry, concerns about Chinese involvement in the region are growing in Washington (Rózsa, 2020: 3–5) and MENA states cannot afford to antagonize the USA by drawing too close to China, particularly in areas that have security ramifications in Washington's eyes. The USA has already warned some states in the Middle East, including Israel, about their growing relations with Beijing, particularly in relation to Chinese investment in critical infrastructure and technology, including ports and 5G telecommunication networks (Andersen and Lons, 2020: 94), on the basis of security concerns (Samet, 2019). States in the region are, therefore, likely to experience increased pressure from Washington to bolster investment-screening mechanisms (Mitnik, 2020). As long as the USA maintains enough military assets and personnel in the region to enable rapid force mobilization, key US allies are likely to respect Washington's red lines with regards to Chinese investments. Yet, regional governments will have to tread carefully, weighing up their economic and security interests.

For Europe, China's increased presence in the region could make it harder to further its interests. The EU and non-EU states have long-established political, trade, and development relations with many countries in the region. As such, they have political influence in the MENA region, as well as a deep understanding of the Middle East and North Africa. Yet, a continued growth in China's economic cooperation with states in the MENA could make it more difficult for Europeans to promote a normative agenda in the region and may erode some of their influence. In the security realm, Beijing's preference for state stability and non-interference could mean that Beijing and European capitals will often be at odds, particularly in instances of civil unrest and civil conflict, which could again limit Europe's capacity to shape civil-state relations. However, their interests could overlap in other areas, such as security of shipping, which indicates that a selective engagement will be necessary.

Acknowledgments

The views expressed in this chapter are those of the author alone and do not reflect those of the institutions with which she has been or is affiliated. The author would like to express her thanks to Marc Friedli for his assistance with background research.

References

AFDB (2012) "Chinese Investments and Employment Creation in Algeria and Egypt." Available at: www.afdb.org

Andersen, L. E. et al. (2020) "China-MENA Relations in the Context of Chinese Global Strategy," in K. W. Sidło (ed.), *The Role of China in the Middle East and North Africa (MENA: Beyond Economic Interests*, EuroMeSCo Joint Policy Study, No. 16. Available at: www.euromesco.net

Andersen, L. E. and Lons, C. (2020) "The Geopolitical Implications of China's Presence in the MENA Region," in K. W. Sidło (ed.), *The Role of China in the Middle East and North Africa (MENA): Beyond Economic Interests*, EuroMeSCo Joint Policy Study, No. 16. Available at: www.euromesco.net

Benaim, D. and Hanna, M. W. (2019) "The Enduring American Presence in the Middle East: The U.S. Military Footprint Has Hardly Changed Under Trump," *Foreign Affairs*, August 7.

Calabrese, J. (2019) "China-Iraq Relations: Poised for a 'Quantum Leap'?" London: Middle East Institute.

Chaziza, M. (2018) "China's Mediation Efforts in the Middle East and North Africa: Constructive Conflict Management," *Strategic Analysis*, 42(1), 29–41.

Chaziza, M. (2020) "Coronavirus, China, and the Middle East," *Mideast Security and Policy Studies*, No. 174, 171–203.

China International Import Expo (2019) "Egypt, China Share Promising Potentials for Joint Trade, Investment: Experts." Available at: www.ciie.org/zbh/en/news/exhibition/News/20191218/20512.html

Coughlin, C. (2020) "Iran's Military Alliance with China Threatens Middle East Security," Gatestone Institute. Available at: www.gatestoneinstitute.org/16252/iran-china-military-allianceEfron, S. et al. (2019) "The Evolving Israel-China Relationship," Santa Monica, CA: RAND.

European Commission (n.d.) "Algeria." Available at: https://ec.europa.eu/trade/policy/countries-and-regions/countries/algeria/

Fulton, J. (2019a) "China-UAE Relations in the Belt and Road Era," *Journal of Arabian Studies*, 9(2), 253–268.

Fulton, J. (2019b) "China's Changing Role in the Middle East," Washington, DC: Atlantic Council.

Ghafar, A. A. and Jacobs, A. (2019) "Beijing Calling: Assessing China's Growing Footprint in North Africa," Brookings Doha Center, Policy Briefings. Available at: www.brookings.edu/center/brookings-doha-center

Ghasseminejad, S. (2020) "Iran-China Trade Plummets Despite Plans for Strategic Partnership," FDD, Policy Brief. Available at: www.fdd.org/category/analysis/policy-briefs

Ministry of Foreign Affairs, the People's Republic of China (2016) "China's Arab Policy Paper," Beijing: People's Republic of China.

Mitnik, J. (2020) "Why the US Can't Get Israel to Break Up with China," *Foreign Policy*. Available at: https://foreignpolicy.com/2020/06/16/us-israel-china-deals/

Rózsa, E. N. (2020) "Deciphering China in the Middle East," EUISS, Brief No. 14. Available at: www.iss.europa.eu/publications/briefs

Rózsa, E. N. and Peragovics, T. (2020) "China's Political, Military and Cultural Engagement in the MENA Region," in K. W. Sidło (ed.), *The Role of China in the Middle East and North Africa (MENA): Beyond Economic Interests*, EuroMeSCo Joint Policy Study, No. 16. Available at: www.euromesco.net

Samet, D. J. (2019) "China, Not Iran, Is the Power to Watch in Iraq," *The Diplomat*. Available at: https://thediplomat.com/2019/10/china-not-iran-is-the-power-to-watch-in-iraq/

Sidło, K. W. (2020) "China's Economic Engagement in the MENA Region," in K. W. Sidło (ed.), *The Role of China in the Middle East and North Africa (MENA): Beyond Economic Interests*, EuroMeSCo Joint Policy Study, No. 16. Available at: www.euromesco.net

Sun, D. (2015) "China's Soft Military Presence in the Middle East," London: Middle East Institute.

Watanabe, L. (2019) "The Middle East and China's Belt and Road Initiative," *CSS Analyses in Security Policy*, No. 254.

Watanabe, L. (2020) "China and Russia Maneuver in the Middle East," *CSS Analyses in Security Policy*, No. 271.

Wezeman, P. D. et al. (2020) "Trends in International Arms Transfers, 2019," SIPRI, Fact Sheet. Available at: sipri.org/taxonomy/term/297

Wuthrow, J. (2020) "Will China Strengthen Iran's Military Machine in 2020? ," *The National Interest*. Available at: https://nationalinterest.org/blog/middle-east-watch/will-china-strengthen-iran%E2%80%99s-military-machine-2020-

Yadlin, A. and Heistein, A. (2020) "The Prospects of a China-Iran Axis," *War on the Rocks*, August 10.

Zoubir, Y. H. (2020) "Expanding Sino-Maghreb Relations: Morocco and Tunisia," research paper, Middle East and North Africa Programme, London: Chatham House.

7

US-CHINA RIVALRY IN THE MENA REGION

Zeno Leoni

Introduction

Since the early Obama Administration, and even more so in the Donald Trump era, US-China competition has steadily increased. This is not a surprise. The United States has been a quasi-global hegemon for decades, while China 'continues to be omnipresent throughout the globe in all walks of life' (Mascitelli and Chung, 2019: 5). Nonetheless, competition between the two great powers is not reproduced with equal intensity in every geopolitical region of the world. Exploring competition in the Middle East and North Africa (MENA) region adds important evidence to the study of relations between Washington and Beijing. With this objective in mind, this chapter puts forward three interrelated arguments. First, US-China relations have entered a race that can be described as the New Cold War (NCW). Although many differences remain between this and the original Cold War, the two rivals are involved in a confrontation that has ramifications across different geographical regions, industries, and political issues.

Second, the MENA region – and especially the Persian Gulf – is not immune to this New Cold War. Yet, competition here is less confrontational than, for instance, in the Western Pacific. Chinese power in the MENA region is on the rise and it is eroding the US influence, but this is affecting areas where the United States is unable to or uninterested in competing with China anyway. Meanwhile, the United States has not yet abdicated its role of guardian of sea-lanes and global chokepoints such, as the Hormuz Strait or the Suez Canal. Indeed, China is not yet ready to militarily compete on a par with, let alone take over, the power of the United States. Therefore, on a systemic level, both powers appear to have tacitly found a *modus vivendi*.

Third, however, this equilibrium exists in the context of much uncertainty. While the United States remains concerned with the rise of China in the MENA region, it may consider the possibility of cooperating with China to patrol sea-lanes of global importance at a time when Washington is increasingly investing in the Indo-Pacific. Likewise, China, is facing a dilemma between continuing to free-ride on the United States as a security provider or seek a more proactive military role and prevent it from conducting destabilizing activities, such as the killing of Qasem Soleimani, among many others.

DOI: 10.4324/9781003048404-9

These points are discussed as the reader advances through the rest of this chapter. The first section provides an illustration of why the United States and China have been entangled in a New Cold War and what the different regional dynamics in this confrontation are. The second section discusses the US disengagement from the Middle East during the Obama-Trump years against China's strategy for the Arab region. The third section offers a picture of US-China competition, looking at three different areas, such as the regional geostrategic picture, arms sales, and Huawei's investments, in addition to the dilemma between competition and cooperation faced by both powers.

US-China Competition: Explaining the Causes of a New Cold War

Since the end of the Second World War, American power has spread with the logic of a 'global sphere of influence' based on international and free-market rule of law (Leoni, 2021: 74). For decades, this has advantaged Washington because the United States has enjoyed the most competitive and technologically advanced economy in the world. This 'open door' strategy, however, contains a structural flaw. To succeed, the United States must ensure that other countries follow the path of competitive capitalism. This is necessary so that these countries can constantly provide new stimulus to a global economy that faces periodical crises of over-accumulation, bubble bursts, and downturns (Harman, 2009). However, this approach in the long term tends to lead to 'blowbacks' because some countries learn to imitate the United States in an efficient manner (Johnson, 2000). This was the case of Germany and Japan in the 1980s, and of China today. In the 1980s, Germany's and Japan's technology became too competitive and challenged American industries. However, given the lack of geopolitical aspirations of these countries, the United States could reject their economic leadership bid by imposing dollar devaluations and export restraints (Berry et al., 1995). China's rise, however, is a much more formidable historical event. China lies outside of the US network of military alliances; it has revisionist geopolitical aspirations over a highly strategic region such as the Western Pacific; and it enjoys a military power that is incomparable to that of Germany and Japan. In addition, the economic interdependence between the United States and China has led to a situation where they are simultaneously both 'best friend' and 'worst enemy': 'best friends' because the US global sphere of influence cannot function without China acting as the locomotive of the world economy; 'worst enemies' because China has stepped up the value chain, moving from being the world's sweatshop to competing in strategically sensitive industrial sectors (Leoni, 2021: 72–76). Given this contradictory relationship, the two powers have entered a stalemate that bears important similarities with and differences from the Cold War (McFaul, 2020). There are two important differences between this and the first Cold War, such as economic interdependence and multipolarity. Nonetheless, as history evolves, differences will always exist. But what about similarities? As argued above, the risk of mutual (economic) destruction acts as a restraint between the United States and China. Because of this, both players have been unwilling to undertake above-the-threshold military actions. Direct military competition has been displaced onto other battlefields, one of which is represented by influencing American allies. This has led to discursive and material efforts to delegitimize the adversary in the eyes of the rest of the world, from Huawei's 5G technology to Covid-19, from Hong Kong to George Floyd.

Beyond such a global framework, the complex relationship between the United States and China has been developing 'unevenly' in different regions and sub-regions (Shambaugh, 2018: 87). China's military rise worries the Pentagon in the Western Pacific Ocean – within the First Island Chain (Townshend et al., 2019: 9–11). In Eurasia, the United States has not been able to fill the void left by the Soviet Union. If Washington still dominates along the Indo-Pacific rimland, China also. thanks to its relationship with Russia, has a geographical and demographic advantage over the heartland (Mankoff, 2013: 2; Pham, 2006: 57). In Europe, China remains an economic as opposed to a military actor. Yet, the geography of some infrastructures owned or operated by Beijing paints a geostrategic-logistic arc that surrounds the Old Continent from Germany through Israel to Greece and Italy, and that could allow Beijing to influence Euro-Asiatic trade. Competition in the Middle East appears to be at a less advanced stage compared to that in the Western Pacific but, with regard to Europe, it is more multifaceted.

The MENA Region: From US Disengagement to China's Engagement

In an exchange of letters between American and Chinese scholars, Kenneth Lieberthal wrote to Wang Jisi:

> [w]hile the United States will for many years remain the dominant outside military power in this region, it is less likely to get embroiled in a war over oil there than it has been in recent decades. China's position is very different … China will not have the military capacity to shape events in the Persian Gulf by 2020—or for a considerable time thereafter. But China's oil dependency will draw it ever deeper into the politics of the region in a way that Beijing has largely avoided heretofore.
>
> *(Lieberthal and Jisi, 2014: 3)*

At a grand strategic level, this relatively old statement continues to capture with accuracy the state of US-China competition in the MENA region. In 2011, the Obama Administration announced that it intended to make the Asia-Pacific its geopolitical priority (Clinton, 2011). Meanwhile, it wanted to go beyond George W. Bush's military adventurism and War on Terror to recover the relationship with the Muslim world (Obama, 2009). The financial crisis and the wars in Afghanistan and Iraq required Obama to cut the defence budget (Townsend et al., 2019: 28). The rise of a powerful China in the Western Pacific demanded more attention from Washington, which decided to shift from a 50–50 per cent distribution of naval assets between the Atlantic and the Indo-Pacific to a 40–60 per cent one (Alexander, 2012). A changing geopolitical global order and the rise of a middle class of hundreds of millions in the Asia-Pacific have made this region highly appealing, especially to an impoverished Europe and an ever-complex MENA region. Meanwhile, the United States has nearly achieved energy self-sufficiency – its imports have dropped to mid-1980s levels – together with a geographical diversification of suppliers (US EIA, 2018). In addition, Obama believed that there was no 'direct American national-security interest' in the region. The president 'frequently remind[ed] his staff that *terrorism* takes far fewer lives in America than handguns, car accidents and falls in *bathtubs* do'. To him, ISIS was 'a flash in a pan' rather than 'an existential threat to the United States' (Goldberg, 2016). The Trump

Administration confirmed such grand strategic rebalancing away from the Middle East and towards the Asia-Pacific, although with a different tactical approach – for instance, he changed the name 'pivot to Asia' to Free and Open Indo-Pacific, as a way to charm Indian elites (Trump, 2017b). When visiting Saudi Arabia during his very first trip abroad as president of the United States, Trump defined US foreign policy in the region as informed by a 'Principled Realism', a foreign policy that rejected democracy promotion and therefore was less ideological compared to Bush's policy. Trump believed that the United States does not 'tell other people how to live, what to do, who to be, or how to worship' (Trump, 2017a). He stated that the Middle East remains a 'troubled place' and that the United States 'can[not] produce lasting peace and security in the region'. Therefore, its 'fate ... lies in the hands of its own people' (Trump, 2018). The US president added that his country does not necessarily 'have to use' its powerful military capabilities (Trump, 2020). The election of Joe Biden to the White House has not changed this grand strategic approach, since China remains the priority for the USA (The White House, 2021: 8). At this stage, it appears that the foreign policy of Joe Biden will continue that of his last two predecessors. On the one hand, for structural reasons concerning the post-2008, post-American world order, China and the Asia-Pacific will remain the priority for this administration (Leoni, 2021: Chapter 4). On the other hand, Biden appears unable to lead any major shift in US policy towards Iran and Saudi Arabia – the two most influential actors in regional politics – even though he will be more 'institutionally minded and sensitive to human rights violations' (Khan and Saeed, 2021). More to the point, it was argued that his personal political history with the Middle East in the last three decades and some recent decisions demonstrate that the region is not a priority for the US president (Bertrand and Seligman, 2021). As of February 22, 2021:

> [Biden] has made only one call to a head of state in the Middle East ... which ... followed calls to other allies and even adversaries like Russia and China. He announced an end to U.S. support for Saudi-led operations in Yemen in his first two weeks in office, a move preceded by a freeze on some arms sales to the region. And his administration had deliberately taken a back seat in responding to a recent deadly rocket attack in northern Iraq that targeted the U.S.-led coalition,
>
> *(ibid.)*

Regardless, the United States continues to project its influence across the whole globe with its five regional commands, and with CENTCOM and the Fifth Fleet it monitors the flow of oil in the Gulf. However, the Trump Administration clearly signalled that it wanted other countries to carry the burden of sea-lanes security.

While the US commitment to the region is declining, the MENA region is experiencing a geopolitical transition where '[t]he increasing engagement of both powerful external actors and assertive middle-sized regional powers in a setting marked by Saudi-Iranian rivalry bolsters the outlook of competitive multipolarity' (Kausch, 2015: 2; Kamrava, 2018: 599). In this context, China has demonstrated that it is keen to engage more with regional partners at almost all levels. This can be evinced from two key strategic documents such as the *Vision and Actions on Jointly Building Silk Road Economic Belt and 21st-Century Maritime Silk Road* (National Development and Reform

Commission, Ministry of Foreign Affairs, and Ministry of Commerce of the People's Republic of China, 2015) and China's Arab Policy Paper (Ministry of Foreign Affairs of the People's Republic of China, 2016). Contrary to Obama's and Trump's narratives on burden-sharing and rebalancing towards Asia, China's two documents offer a compelling illustration of the extent to which Beijing values the Middle East. Indeed, in the *Vision and Actions* document China stated that it 'should enhance the role of multilateral cooperation mechanisms, make full use of existing mechanisms … [such as] … China-Arab States Cooperation Forum (CASCF), China-Gulf Cooperation Council Strategic Dialogue' among others, and that it should 'continue to encourage the constructive role of the international forums and exhibitions at regional and sub-regional levels hosted by countries along the Belt and Road', among other platforms (National Development and Reform Commission, Ministry of Foreign Affairs, and Ministry of Commerce of the People's Republic of China, 2015). While the United States is questioning the geoeconomics – if not geopolitical – value of the region, China portrays its strategy as a commitment 'to build a community of shared interests, destiny and responsibility featuring mutual political trust, economic integration and cultural inclusiveness' (ibid.). Meanwhile, the *Arab Policy Paper* depicts a comprehensive relationship between China and Arab states that touches only marginally on military affairs but includes agriculture, tourism, and non-traditional security among other things. Signalling a more robust cultural affinity compared to Washington, Beijing stated that 'China and Arab countries are all in an important development stage and have a shared mission of rejuvenating the nation' (Ministry of Foreign Affairs of the People's Republic of China, 2016). Beyond grand strategic narratives, China's engagement with the MENA region is substantial and cautious at the same time. China seeks to 'cultivate and maintain good relations with all of the region's major countries' to manifestly 'avoid challenging US interests in the region', to prop up its military presence but 'from a position offshore, and preferably without attracting unnecessary attention'; and it 'prefers economic leverage to military force as a means of securing influence' (Hiim and Stenslie, 2019: 158–160). In stark contrast to the crisis of American power in the region, however, the Middle East – and the Gulf in particular – appear to be an ideal space for China to further important interests such as securing energy imports but also investing capital and providing industrial and technological know-how to countries that are slowly transitioning to a post-oil economy. There is a 'high degree of convergence … between China and the GCC' (Qian and Fulton, 2018: 14). Geopolitically, since 2014, China and the Gulf Cooperation Council (GCC) members have agreed to a strategic partnership. It was noted that while 'partnerships rather than alliances have been a long-standing Chinese approach to diplomacy', strategic partnerships 'are considered the second highest level in the hierarchy of relationships after comprehensive strategic cooperative partnerships' (ibid.: 17). On the one hand, Chinese partnerships in the region are a concern for the United States to the extent that American power relies on both multilateral security and hub-and-spokes relationships for its global reproduction. If the United States was to lose allies, it would be the end of US hegemony. Conversely, it was noted that Chinese engagement with the Middle East 'makes it hard but not impossible for the two powers to have a constructive relationship', especially since China follows an approach of 'strategic partnership diplomacy and the 1+2+3 cooperation pattern' which 'seem[s] designed to complement rather than challenge US interests in the region' (Fulton et al., 2021). Others, indeed, have noted that 'China aims to dethrone the United States, but not supplant it' (Singh, 2020: 8).

US-China Security-Military Competition in the MENA Region

As alluded to earlier, US-China competition in the MENA region is limited for two reasons: on the one hand, China is expanding its geoeconomics reach in areas where the United States does not want to or cannot compete; on the other hand, while the United States is less committed to the region from an economic, diplomatic, and security viewpoint, China is not yet ready or willing to challenge the US military hegemony. From a security-military perspective, this has led to a temporary *modus vivendi* which is tolerated by the United States – to an extent. The following three sub-sections seek to capture the current non-confrontational geopolitical competition between the two great powers. According to Gangzheng She, Middle Eastern scholars tend to identify 'five major domains wherein China and the United States are competing, or will compete, asymmetrically yet fiercely, across the region', such as ''access to strategically important areas; security system and military sales; trade and investment; high technology for the digital age; and the soft power-related fields' (She, 2021: 305, 317). The rest of this chapter focuses on those areas that are more closely related to defence and security. It also considers the dilemma faced by both the United States and China in providing security to the region.

The Geostrategic Picture: The United States Remains Unchallenged

From a geostrategic viewpoint, the Middle East allows China to bypass containment efforts in East Asia, where there is a 'network of [US] alliances' and where several regional powers are increasingly antagonistic towards Beijing. China's slogan of *xijin* – that is, 'march west' – is based on the belief that 'the U.S. encirclement strategy does not look as strong in Central Asia and beyond' because there are several US allies who 'do not appear as hostile to Beijing as some U.S. allies in East Asia' (Scobell and Nader, 2016: 10; The State Council Information Office of the People's Republic of China, 2019). Nonetheless, China is still militarily unable to play a role in the waters and lands between the Indian Ocean and the Mediterranean.[1] Contrary to the South China Sea, the Northern Indian Ocean and the Mediterranean are distant from China's coasts and a wide-open maritime geography. These areas are crowded by US allies such as India and NATO members, while the United States enjoys several forward bases, such as in Djibouti, Bahrain – where both CENTCOM's naval assets and the 5th Fleet are stationed – in addition to the British Indian Ocean Territory of Diego Garcia. China instead can only count on one state-of-the-art aircraft carrier – the *Fujian* – two additional aircraft carriers – one of which is an old Soviet one, the *Liaoning* – and a recently built military installation in Djibouti (Leoni, 2021: Chapter 4). The lack of a forward base could only be substituted with alliances or partnerships similar to those that NATO provides. While Chinese partnerships in the region have grown increasingly solid, it is still too early to talk of China's relations with Middle Eastern countries in terms of military alliances – for instance, China's neutrality between Iran and Saudi Arabia is evidence of this (Lons et al., 2019: 4). The evolution of the Sino-Iranian relationship, however, deserves to be monitored and this is closely related to whether President Biden will try to overcome the diplomatic crisis provoked by Trump's policy towards Iran or abandon Tehran and give this as a reason for embracing China diplomatically and militarily.[2] Indeed, when the news was shared that China and Iran were about to sign an agreement on energy, investments, and security and military cooperation, the Trump

Administration responded that it would 'continue to impose costs on Chinese companies that aid Iran, the world's largest state sponsor of terrorism' and that China, by doing so 'is undermining its own stated goal of promoting stability and peace' (Fassihi and Myers, 2020). The Sino-Iranian deal was eventually signed soon after the Biden Administration was sworn in. At the same time, the *Wall Street Journal* reported in May 2021 that China, according to the USA, was likely to build a naval military facility in the UAE (Strobel and Youssef, 2021). But recently it confirmed that deal was undermined after successful pressure from the US government on the UAE (Lubold and Strobel, 2021). Yet, as Guy Burton pointed out in an interview, while US actions annoy China, Beijing 'doesn't want to retaliate too strongly. Although important, it [the Middle East] is further down the CCP's hierarchy of priorities (after the homeland, Taiwan, Tibet, and East Asia)' (Kuo, 2020). Therefore, '[f]rom a security perspective, … U.S. fears are overblown' (ibid.).

If from a military logistic perspective, China is still behind, it is instead investing in 'a network of trade hubs and routes' that does concern the United States (Sheineh, 2021: 18). The list of these projects is constantly evolving. The projects involve several countries and at this stage, it is difficult to predict whether China will only be the builder, or the operator as well or, eventually, the long-term owner of every single infrastructure its companies are involved in. Certainly, investments in Israel's ports have drawn the attention of the United States and caused friction between Washington and Tel Aviv. Under particular scrutiny is the Haifa port, where the Shanghai International Port Group (SIPG) is building a harbour that will operate for 25 years and where the US Navy docks are (Sheineh, 2021). According to the former US Chief of Naval Operations Jonathan Greenert and the former Commander of the US 7th Fleet, John Bird, who co-chaired a report on 'countering' Chinese investments in Israel for a US-based Jewish think tank, 'Israel could find itself outside of trusted U.S. military, financial, commercial, and technological networks, unless it acts decisively' (Greenert and Bird, 2021: 13).

Security: Arms Sales and Huawei

In recent years, China's relationship with the MENA region has been characterized by a rise in arms sales, particularly to Iran, Saudi Arabia, and the United Arab Emirates (UAE). In 2018, China's defence industry ranked 'prominently among global defence prime' since 'eight Chinese SOEs ranked in the top 22, three ranked in the top ten, and Aviation Industry Corporation of China (AVIC) ranked in the global top five' (Nouwens, 2020). These are important numbers considering that the Middle East has registered a record spending in defence, with Saudi Arabia becoming the third top country for military expenditures in 2020, while Israel and Iraq ranked, respectively, fourteenth and fifteenth (IISS, 2020). Furthermore, these data are even more important if viewed in the context of Washington's geostrategic shift towards Asia. This has allowed China to cut out a space in the regional market at a time when several countries, especially the Gulf monarchies, are keen to signal their far-reaching relationships with different great powers aside from the United States. Chinese sales have mostly focused on Intelligence, Surveillance and Reconnaissance (ISR) and Unmanned Aerial Vehicles (UAVs): China has sold the *Wing Loong I* drone since 2016 to the UAE and, since early 2018, the deadlier Wing Loong II, which it also sold to Saudi Arabia – they used it in the conflict in Yemen. Saudi Arabia also bought China's *CH-4*, another armed drone, also used by the

UAE, Iraq, and Egypt (Turak, 2019; Milan and Tabrizi, 2020: 734–735). [3] But it has to be pointed out that the US 'pivot' bears only part of the responsibility for China's success. Indeed, it was argued that

> Middle Eastern governments had to face both Israel's and the United States' refusal to provide them with armed drones, they were left with only two viable alternatives: embarking upon ambitious domestic projects for the production and procurement of indigenous UCAV, or, more recently, the purchase of armed platforms from China.
>
> *(Milan and Tabrizi, 2020: 732)*

Ultimately, China's success led to the 'breaking of the US–Israel duopoly in the field of UCAVs in the Middle East' exactly because Beijing imposed 'far fewer restrictions' on buyers since it was not a member of the Missile Technology Control Regime (MTCR) (ibid.:734). This trend led a US official to state that 'China has been selling the hell out of its drones' to Gulf militaries, such as those of the UAE and Saudi Arabia (Turak, 2019). The United States was so concerned by China's success that Trump decided to reverse the US drones sales policy, until then restricted by the MTCR 'to prevent the spread of missiles with the potential to carry weapons of mass destruction' (Cage, 2018). Trump's policy maintained that, in some cases 'drone sales can now go through the direct commercial sales process', a move that has allowed US drones manufacturers to 'export more directly to other countries and bypass the foreign military sales process' (ibid.). According to Laura Cressey, Deputy Director for Regional Security and Arms Transfers of the US Department of State, this was necessary to address growing 'strategic competition' (Cressey, 2018: 8). [4] However, it was noted by John Calabrese that 'Saudi Arabia's – for instance – long-term reliance on Western weapons systems means that new purchases from either China or Russia will not easily integrate with pre-existing systems' (Calabrese, 2019; Leoni and Roberts, 2020).

Furthermore, it was noted that the way MENA countries are balancing their relations with the United States and China 'is further fueled by the fact that China's record of living up to those expectations has been poor' (Dorsey, 2017: 3). Indeed, although the pace of China's trade with the region is growing steadily, this vignette of Saudi Arabia and other countries gives a sense of how the erosion of US hegemony is a process that will take years. Yet, China has also drawn the attention of the United States with Huawei's investments in the 5G network of the Middle East. Indeed, the latter is the second least advanced area in the field of telecommunications. However, it was reported that '[b]y 2025, GCC countries will house much of the world's growing 5G subscribers' and in this scenario Huawei's 5G know-how and the Gulf cash availability appear to be a perfect match (Zinser, 2020). When the UAE announced during a trade conference in Barcelona in February 2019 that Huawei intended to invest in the country, US representatives 'called a hastily arranged news conference to reiterate their concerns' (Satariano, 2019). This was confirmed by the *Financial Times* when reporting on Huawei and citing a Western official who stated: 'there is a sense of you are with us or against us in this cold war' (Kerr, 2020). Although GCC members hoped they would not get caught up in a 'Digital Cold War', the US-designed Clean Network Initiative and the support that this has received from Israel – which rejected Huawei's 5G – has added a new layer to the containment of China. So far, this initiative has been endorsed by 53 US allies. The transition from Trump to

Biden has, however, given the GCC time to avoid making a hard decision about the CNI (Soliman, 2021).

Military Competition or Cooperation? Beijing's and Washington's Dilemmas

China's military endeavours in the MENA region are mainly characterized by participation in UN-led missions and counter-piracy efforts in the Gulf of Aden and off the Somali coasts. Such contributions to international security allow China to appear a responsible great power but also uphold its strategic interests. This is what has been defined as 'soft military footprints', that is, an approach that can include 'international peacekeeping, such as rescuing, combating piracy, safeguarding the security of the marine channel, maintaining maritime rights, and shouldering other military and civilian missions: in other words, providing public goods' (Sun, 2018: 7). But such a 'soft' engagement may in the coming years prove unsatisfactory for both the United States and China. Considering the cost that comes with patrolling international sea-lanes, the United States has implicitly signalled that it would welcome a degree of cooperation from China to share the burden of maritime security. Trump stated that countries having stakes in the Gulf's oil 'should be protecting their own ships on what has always been a dangerous journey' (MEE Staff, 2019). However, there is a fine line between China's supporting (informal) multinational efforts to secure oil and Beijing becoming capable of challenging the US military presence. In fact, General Kenneth McKenzie, commander of the United States Central Command, pointed out that great power competition is not limited to the Asia-Pacific or Eastern Europe, and defined his area of responsibility as the 'Wild West' and a 'newly active area of engagement between us and other great powers' (Woody, 2020). According to him, China would leverage on local partners to pursue its security interests. [5] Meanwhile, Vice Admiral James Malloy, who led CENTCOM's naval forces, was said to be concerned not so much about Beijing's 'combat capability in the near-term, but ... all levers of national power that come into play' – a clear reference to China's investments in a rapidly evolving sphere of all-domains capabilities (ibid.).

On the one hand, to date, China 'seems amenable' to the current 'state of affairs' where the United States carries the burden of regional security (Scobell and Nader, 2016: 75). Although the rivalry with Washington has been evolving fast, Beijing 'desires to maintain an overall climate of cordial and cooperative U.S.-Chinese relations, as well as promote stability in the Middle East' (ibid.: 76). China is acting as a 'wary dragon' that wants to 'stay aloof' and 'let the United States do all the heavy lifting' (ibid.). In addition, following the economic crisis provoked by the Covid-19 pandemic, China should become the 'single largest country-to-country source of funding for the region's many showpiece infrastructure projects that help prop up the legitimacy of many of its ruling elites' (Kamat, 2020). This could give China an upper hand in ensuring consensus and expecting political stability and support in return from local partners (ibid.). The currency of stability could be the pawn that Beijing could offer the United States in exchange for Washington's military efforts. On the other hand, China has demonstrated its concern about the US posture in the region which could lead to instability as in the case of the killing of Qasem Soleimani or, most importantly, the Iraq War in 2003. On this matter, a Chinese foreign ministry spokesman stated that 'major countries outside the region can do more to promote the Middle East region's peace and security, and avoid taking actions that escalate regional tensions' (Reuters Staff, 2020).

As Lyle Goldstein also pointed out, the never-ending turmoil in the region offers an opportunity for 'fruitful ... US-China cooperation. ... Chinese analysts have long considered the Middle East to be "the graveyard of the superpowers," yet Beijing is now also inexorably being drawn into the vortex' (2015: 163).

Conclusion

This chapter provided an illustration of US-China competition in the MENA region through a security and military lens. The ways in which Washington and Beijing interact in this geopolitical area of the world are still evolving and, contrary to the Western Pacific, do not indicate a clear trend. While the objective reality of US-China relations in the region is one of competition, it is still not possible to determine whether the current scenario could spill over from diplomatic into military tensions, or whether the two great powers will be compelled to cooperate in some areas such as patrolling sea-lanes of global value.

Amidst such a scenario, this chapter argued that US-China competition in the Middle East is developing in the context of a global New Cold War at a time when the region is a declining priority for US policy-makers, of growing geoeconomics interest – but not a geostrategic priority – for China, and experiencing a shift towards multipolarity. If indeed this is the current situation, eventually both the United States and China will have to resolve the dilemma of competing in a region which is not a priority for either of them, or cooperating with a fierce rival.

This chapter has not explored US-China competition in relation to the many countries and national issues that characterize the region. However, it is possible that the diversity of interests, alliances, priorities in the MENA region will lead to a patchy competition between Washington and Beijing, at times causing direct diplomatic confrontation and at other times forced cohabitation, if not cooperation. Overall, as a contribution to the broad debate about US-China relations, this chapter has also provided evidence that China's erosion of US hegemony will be uneven in general and relatively slow in the sphere of defence policy. Aside from direct confrontation, this competitive but uncertain relationship is likely to have important implications involving key issues in the region. Although this chapter's author has gathered direct testimonies about pressures that local elites and foreign diplomats in the MENA region are facing, the region, like the rest of the world, is not caged into a bipolar international security structure. This means that countries can still avoid hard choices by constructing diplomatic platforms and developing shared practices with groups of countries in the world that are facing similar pressures, such as ASEAN or the EU, among others.

Notes

1 This is also acknowledged in China's military doctrine with the concept of 'strategic space' that refers to areas where China's national interests lie and where Beijing needs to project influence with its military capabilities but not with combat operations; and by the concept of 'effective control', by which China acknowledges the limits of its military capabilities (Fravel, 2016: 14–17).
2 China has also conducted joint naval drills with Iran and Russia in the Indian Ocean and the Gulf of Oman (Reuters Staff, 2019).
3 Meanwhile, it was reported that the Libyan National Army (LNA) has also deployed the Wing Loong which it received from the United Arab Emirates, even though Chinese officials maintained they were not responsible for this (Cafiero, 2020).

4 For more on the US shift in its drones policy during Trump, see Calabrese (2019).
5 China has also direct concerns with regard to the Middle East being a source of Islamist ideology that seeks to make its way into Xingjang. It was revealed that 'as many as 5,000 ethnic Uyghurs from Xinjiang province have been engaged in the Syrian Civil War in recent years' while others may have received training in Afghanistan (Sidło, 2020: 68).

References

Alexander, D. (2012) U.S. will put more warships in Asia: Panetta. Reuters. June 3. Available at: www.reuters.com/article/us-asia-security/u-s-will-put-more-warships-in-asia-panetta-idUSBRE85100Y20120603

Berry, S., Levinsohn, J., and Pakes, A. (1995) Voluntary export restraints on automobiles: evaluating a strategic trade policy. National Bureau of Economic Research. Working Paper No. 5235. August.

Bertrand, N. and Seligman, L. (2021) Biden deprioritizes the Middle East. *Politico*, February 22. Available at: www.politico.com/news/2021/02/22/biden-middle-east-foreign-policy-470589

Cafiero, G. (2020) The geopolitics of China's Libya foreign policy. *ChinaMED*, August 4. Available at: www.chinamed.it/publications/the-geopolitics-of-chinas-libya-foreign-policy

Cage, M. (2018) A new U.S. policy makes it (somewhat) easier to export drones. The Washington Post. April 20. Available at: www.washingtonpost.com/news/monkey-cage/wp/2018/04/20/a-new-u-s-policy-makes-it-somewhat-easier-to-export-drones/

Calabrese, J. (2019) Intersections: China and the US in the Middle East. Middle East Institute, June 18. www.mei.edu/publications/intersections-china-and-us-middle-east

Clinton, H. R. (2011) America's Pacific century. *Foreign Policy*, October 11. Available at: https://foreignpolicy.com/2011/10/11/americas-pacific-century/

Cressey, L. (2018) U.S. arms transfer policy: shaping the way ahead. Center for Strategic and International Studies. August 8. Available at: https://csis-website-prod.s3.amazonaws.com/s3fs-public/publication/180808_U.S._Arms_Transfer_Policy.pdf

Dorsey, J. M. (2017) China and the Middle East: venturing into the maelstrom. *Asian Journal of Middle Eastern and Islamic Studies*, 11(1): 1–14.

Fassihi, F. and Myers, S. L. (2020) Defying U.S., China and Iran near trade and military partnership. New York Times, July 11. Available at: www.nytimes.com/2020/07/11/world/asia/china-iran-trade-military-deal.html

Fravel, M. T. (2016) China's changing approach to military strategy: the science of military strategy from 2001 and 2013. MIT, Open Access Articles. Available at: https://dspace.mit.edu/bitstream/handle/1721.1/109318/China%27s%20changing%20approach.pdf?sequence=1&isAllowed=y [draft]

Fulton, J., Propper, E. and Fahmy, A. (2021) US, Israel, and GCC perspectives on China-MENA relations. Atlantic Council. Available at: www.atlanticcouncil.org/blogs/menasource/us-israel-and-gcc-perspectives-on-china-mena-relations/

Goldberg, J. (2016) The Obama Doctrine. *The Atlantic*. April. Available at: www.theatlantic.com/magazine/archive/2016/04/the-obama-doctrine/471525/

Goldstein, L. J. (2015) *Meeting China Halfway: How to Defuse the Emerging US-China Rivalry*. Washington, DC: Georgetown University Press.

Greenert, J. W. and Bird, J. M. (2021) Countering Chinese engagement with Israel: A comprehensive and cooperative U.S.-Israeli strategy. Jewish Institute for National Security of America. February. file:///C:/Users/k1466458/Downloads/Countering-Chinese-Engagement-with-Israel.pdf

Harman, C. (2009) *Zombie Capitalism: Global Crisis and the Relevance of Marx*. London: Bookmarks Publications.

Hiim, H. S. and Stenslie, S. (2019) China's realism in the Middle East. *Survival*, 61(6): 153–166.IISS (2020) The military balance 2020. February 14. Available at: www.iiss.org/press/2020/military-balance-2020

Johnson, C. (2000) *Blowback: The Costs and Consequences of American Empire*. New York: Henry Hold and Company.

Kamat, D. (2020) US-China tensions create uncertainty for Middle East. Asia Times, June 4. Available at: https://asiatimes.com/2020/06/us-china-tensions-create-uncertainty-for-middle-east/

Kamrava, M. (2018) 'Multipolarity and instability in the Middle East'. *Orbis*, 62(4): 598–616.

Kausch, K. (2015) Competitive multipolarity in the Middle East. *The International Spectator*, 50(3): 1–15.

Kerr, S. (2020) UAE caught between US and China as powers vie for influence in Gulf. *Financial Times*. June 2. Available at: www.ft.com/content/1ff119ff-50bf-4b00-8519-520b8db2082b

Khan, F. and Saeed, K. (2021) Contours of President Biden's foreign policy towards the Middle East. Blog, LSE Middle East Centre. February 3. Available at: https://blogs.lse.ac.uk/mec/2021/02/03/contours-of-president-bidens-foreign-policy-towards-the-middle-east/

Kuo, M. A. (2020) China and the Middle East: Conflict and cooperation. *The Diplomat*. December 1. Available at: https://thediplomat.com/2020/12/china-and-the-middle-east-conflict-and-coop eration/

Leoni, Z. (2021) *American Grand Strategy from Obama to Trump: Imperialism after Bush and China's Hegemonic Challenge*. Cham: Palgrave Macmillan.

Leoni, Z. and Roberts, D. B. (2020) Could the Gulf become a proxy in the new US-China cold war? *Middle East Eye*. September 3. Available at: www.middleeasteye.net/opinion/could-gulf-become-proxy-new-us-china-cold-war

Lieberthal, K. and Jisi, W. (2014) An overview of the U.S.-China relationship. In N. Hachigian (ed.), *Debating China: The U.S.-China Relationship in Ten Conversations*. Oxford: Oxford University Press, pp. 1–20.

Lons, C. et al. (2019) China's Great Game in the Middle East. European Council on Foreign Relations, Policy Brief. October. Available at: www.ecfr.eu/page/-/china_great_game_middle_e ast.pdf

Lubold, G. and Strobel, W. P. (2021) Secret Chinese port project in Persian Gulf rattles U.S. relations with U.A.E. Wall Street Journal, November 19. Available at: www.wsj.com/articles/us-china-uae-military-11637274224

Mankoff, J. (2013) The United States and Central Asia after 2014. Center for Strategic & International Studies. January. Available at: https://csis-website-prod.s3.amazonaws.com/s3fs-public/legacy_files/files/publication/130122_Mankoff_USCentralAsia_Web.pdf, 2

Mascitelli, B. and Chung, M. (2019) Hue and cry over Huawei: Cold war tensions, security threats or anticompetitive behaviour? *Research in Globalization*, 1(December): 5.

McFaul, M. (2020) Cold War lessons and fallacies for US-China relations today. *The Washington Quarterly*, 43(4): 8–9.

MEE Staff (2019) Trump says countries should protect their own ships in the Gulf amid Iran tensions. *Middle East Eye*, June 24. Available at: www.middleeasteye.net/news/trump-says-countries-should-protect-their-own-ships-gulf-amid-tensions-iran

Milan, F. F. and Tabrizi, A. B. (2020) Armed, unmanned, and in high demand: The drivers behind combat drones proliferation in the Middle East. *Small Wars and Insurgencies*, 31(4): 730–750.

Ministry of Foreign Affairs of the People's Republic of China (2016) China's Arab Policy Paper, January 13. Available at: www.fmprc.gov.cn/mfa_eng/zxxx_662805/t1331683.shtml

National Development and Reform Commission, Ministry of Foreign Affairs, and Ministry of Commerce of the People's Republic of China (2015) Vision and Actions on Jointly Building Silk Road Economic Belt and 21st Century Maritime Silk Road. March. Available at: www.chin ese-embassy.org.uk/eng/zywl/t1251719.htm

Nouwens, M. (2020) China's defence-industry rankings: down but by no means out. *IISS*. August 17. Available at: www.iiss.org/blogs/analysis/2020/08/china-defence-industry-rankings

Obama, B. H. (2009) The president's speech in Cairo: A new beginning. The White House. June 4. Available at: https://obamawhitehouse.archives.gov/issues/foreign-policy/presidents-speech-cairo-a-new-beginning

Pham, J. P. (2006) Beijing's great game: Understanding Chinese strategy in Central Eurasia. *American Foreign Policy Interests*, 28(1): 57.

Qian, X. and Fulton, J. (2018) China-Gulf economic relationship under the "Belt and Road" Initiative. *Asian Journal of Middle Eastern and Islamic Studies*, 11(3): 12–21.

Reuters Staff (2019) Russia, China, Iran start joint naval drills in Indian Ocean. Reuters. December 27. Available at: www.reuters.com/article/us-iran-military-russia-china-idUSKBN1YV0IB

Reuters Staff (2020) China says U.S. use of force aggravating Middle East tension. Reuters. January 6. Available at: www.reuters.com/article/us-iraq-security-iran-china-idUSKBN1Z50MO

Satariano, A. (2019) U.A.E. to use equipment from Huawei despite American pressure. New York Times, February 26. Available at: www.nytimes.com/2019/02/26/technology/huawei-uae-5g-network.html

Scobell, A. and Nader, A. (2016) China in the Middle East: The wary dragon. RAND Corporation. Available at: www.rand.org/content/dam/rand/pubs/research_reports/RR1200/RR1229/RAND_RR1229.pdf

She, G. (2021) Asymmetric competition on a new battleground? Middle Eastern perspectives on Sino-US rivalry. *The Chinese Journal of International Politics*, 14(2): 289–320.

Sheineh, M. A. (2021) Chinese investment in Haifa port could compromise US-Israel intelligence sharing: Report. *Middle East Eye*, February 1. Available at: www.middleeasteye.net/news/israel-us-china-investment-intelligence-compromise-haifa-port

Sidło, K. W. (2020) The role of China in the Middle East and North Africa (MENA): Beyond economic interests? EuroMesco, Joint Policy Study 16, July. Available at: www.euromesco.net/wp-content/uploads/2020/05/JPS_The-Role-of-China-in-the-MENA.pdf

Singh, M. (2020) China and the United States in the Middle East: between dependency and rivalry. The Washington Institute for Near East Policy. September. Available at: file:///C:/Users/k1466458/Downloads/Singh20200909-china-us-chapter-USF.pdf [draft]

Soliman, M. (2021) The coming US-China cold war: the view from the Gulf. Middle East Institute, March 15. Available at: www.mei.edu/publications/coming-us-china-cold-war-view-gulf

State Council Information Office of the People's Republic of China (2019) China and the World in the New Era. White Paper. September. Available at: http://english.www.gov.cn/archive/whitepaper/201909/27/content_WS5d8d80f9c6d0bcf8c4c142ef.html

Strobel, W. P. and Youssef, A. N. (2021) F-35 sale to U.A.E. imperiled over U.S. concerns about ties to China. Wall Street Journal, May 25. Available at: www.wsj.com/articles/f-35-sale-to-u-a-e-imperiled-over-u-s-concerns-about-ties-to-china-11621949050

Sun, D. (2018) China's soft presence in the Middle East. *Dirasat*, 30.

The White House (2021) Interim National Security Strategic Guidance, March. Available at: www.whitehouse.gov/wp-content/uploads/2021/03/NSC-1v2.pdf

Townshend, A., Thomas-Noone, B., and Steward, M. (2019) Averting crisis: US defence spending, deterrence and the Indo-Pacific. United States Studies Centre. August. Available at: www.ussc.edu.au/analysis/averting-crisis-american-strategy-military-spending-and-collective-defence-in-the-indo-pacific

Trump, D. (2017a) President Trump's speech to the Arab Islamic American Summit. The White House. May 21. Available at: www.whitehouse.gov/the-press-office/2017/05/21/president-trumps-speech-arab-islamic-american-summit

Trump, D. (2017b) Remarks by President Trump on his trip to Asia. The White House. November 15. Available at: www.whitehouse.gov/briefings-statements/remarks-president-trump-trip-asia/

Trump, D. (2018) Statement by President Trump on Syria. The White House. April 13. Available at: www.whitehouse.gov/briefings-statements/statement-president-trump-syria/

Trump, D. (2020) Remarks by President Trump on Iran. The White House. January 8. Available at: www.whitehouse.gov/briefings-statements/remarks-president-trump-iran/

Turak, N. (2019) Pentagon is scrambling as China 'sells the hell out of' armed drones to US allies. CNBC. February 21. Available at: www.cnbc.com/2019/02/21/pentagon-is-scrambling-as-china-sells-the-hell-out-of-armed-drones-to-americas-allies.html

US EIA (2018) United States. Available at: www.eia.gov/international/overview/country/USA

US EIA (2020) China. September 30. Available at: www.eia.gov/international/analysis/country/CHN

Woody, C. (2020) 'The US is looking away from the Middle East, but it's keeping a wary eye on what China is doing there'. *Business Insider*, July 24. Available at: www.businessinsider.com/us-officials-worry-about-china-presence-in-the-middle-east-2020-7?r=US&IR=T

Zinser, S. (2020) China's Digital Silk Road grows with 5G in the Middle East. *The Diplomat*, December 16. Available at: https://thediplomat.com/2020/12/chinas-digital-silk-road-grows-with-5g-in-the-middle-east/

8
CHINA AND US POLICY IN THE PERSIAN GULF

Is a New Security Architecture Evolving?

Lars Erslev Andersen

Introduction

Today we are seeing an intensified global rivalry between China and the USA increasing tensions in the South China Sea, and a rapprochement between China and Iran was confirmed in 2020 when Iran leaked a draft agreement between the two states to the *New York Times* (*New York Times*, 2020). That disclosure sparked a discussion on whether China was ready to challenge the US Persian Gulf policy by initiating close cooperation with Iran in all aspects, from economy to security and military affairs, at a time when the USA, with support from the Arab Gulf States and Israel, was imposing sanctions on Iran. The discussion changed with the election of Joe Biden as US president, but it is still very much on the table as this chapter will show.

China waited until March 2021 to sign the agreement with Iran, at a time when the USA and Iran had started negotiations on getting the USA back into the Joint Cooperation Plan of Action (JCPOA) (Xinhua, 2021). Also, in March of the same year, the Chinese Minister of Foreign Affairs Wang Yi met his American counterpart Antony Blinken in Alaska in a meeting that confirmed that the Biden administration would not be soft on China but, on the contrary, intensified the critical rhetoric and conflict with China that had developed during the Donald Trump administration (Yi, 2021).

The message on foreign policy from Joe Biden at his inauguration was that America wants to improve relations with its allies in Europe and NATO, which during the Trump era were marked by conflict and arrogance. There is much to indicate, however, that under the leadership of Biden the US will continue to prioritize the so-called 'Indo-Pacific' strategy and downgrade transatlantic relations as well as its political engagement in the Middle East. What this will mean for the Middle East and China relations and how the unfolding rivalry between China and the USA will impact the Persian Gulf are the focus in this chapter.

From the end of the Second World War until at least the end of the Cold War, geopolitical ideas framed the US strategy in the Persian Gulf, which was seen as a region of the highest importance for US national security interests. Speculations among leaders in the

102

DOI: 10.4324/9781003048404-10

Persian Gulf as well as among commentators have in recent years raised doubts about whether the USA is still willing to provide security to the Arab Gulf States and to militarily guarantee the free sea route through the Strait of Hormuz.

These speculations coincide with an increasing interest and engagement from China in all the states in the Persian Gulf region. Although Chinese economic interest in the region is not new, it is only a little more than a decade since China stepped in as a new global player in the region, signing partnership agreements with all the states in the Persian Gulf and significantly increasing trade and investment both with Iran and with the Arab Gulf states, in particular Saudi Arabia and the United Arab Emirates (UAE). This coincides with the launch of the ambitious Belt and Road Initiative (BRI) that all the Gulf states have engaged in by concluding contracts with China and with the first public outline of a Chinese Middle East policy in the Arab Policy Paper of 2016, published during President Xi Jinping's first visit to the region. Not many expect that China is about to replace the USA as a regional security provider in the Middle East, but with the USA downgrading its policy in the Persian Gulf and China increasingly widening its investment and cooperation in the Middle East where more than one million Chinese are already living, China unavoidably needs to protect its assets and people, thus demanding a Chinese security policy and presence in that region.

The global context for these developments is a rapidly changing world order from the so-called unipolar moment at the end of the Cold War when the USA expected a new world order under American leadership to the current rise of authoritarian states that threatens the leading position of the international economic institutions connected to the US vision of a liberal order. Before turning to a sketch of the USA, and of the Chinese engagements in the Persian Gulf, a brief outline of the changing global order will set the scene for the discussion about the current situation in the Persian Gulf.

The New World Order that Never Was

Despite the enthusiasm that the idea of the new world order was met with when it was announced by George H.W. Bush in the US Congress on 11 September 1990, it was never realized. The enthusiasm was limited to the Western world that translated the idea into a vision of a liberal world order under the unipolar leadership of the USA. The president of the Soviet Union (USSR), Mikhail Gorbachev, had already, in 1988, suggested establishing a rules-based world order, which was later supported by China (Sakwa, 2017). Both powers were critical of a liberal world order and the so-called US unipolarity and argued for multipolarity. They opposed the US attitude that the international institutions were the result of American policy and maintained they were outcomes of multilateral cooperation after the Second World War. Many other states around the world, including in the Middle East, were also opposed to the leadership of the USA and the idea of a liberal world order (Huntington, 1999). Close allies of the USA, such as Saudi Arabia and the UAE, accepted America as their main security provider but did not subscribe to the idea of a liberal order, especially not in domestic and regional affairs, which became very clear during the Arab uprisings in 2011 and since (Steinberg, 2014). Together with Israel they initiated a counter-revolution that effectively put an end to the democratization and reform process in Egypt and elsewhere. The Arab rulers seem to prefer the Chinese model of economic development without political representation to the model of liberal democracy that the West wants to export to the Middle East. The so-called 'rentier state' model of the Arab Gulf states is much more in line with the process of economic reforms started by Deng Xiaoping in China in 1978, authoritarian capitalism, than with Western theories of modernization claiming that the market economy and economic development should be accompanied by political liberalization and democratic reforms (Pomeps, 2019).

Today, 30 years after the George H.W. Bush speech, not many believe in the realization of a liberal world order, even if they still would like it to happen. Distinguished scholars and authors, who in the years after the end of the Cold War wrote books and articles about the coming of a liberal order, today write rather about the coming of an illiberal order and the vanishing of new world order as it was conceptualized 30 years ago (Cooley and Nexon, 2021). Speculations and theories on what went wrong are abundant and many argue that failures in the grand strategy and leadership of the USA are the main reason, together with the wrongdoings of the so-called 'War on Terror' with the wars in Iraq and Afghanistan as perhaps the worst mistakes (Mearsheimer, 2018; Walt, 2018). Others see the changing role of Russia, especially under Vladimir Putin, and interpret the Russian policy as undermining international law. They particularly highlight Russia's interference in and invasion of Ukraine and the annexation of Crimea, and point to the Russian intervention in the Syrian war. Seen from an Atlantic point of view, Russia's intervention in Syria in 2015 with support for the Bashar al-Assad regime and, together with China, the vetoing of Western-sponsored resolutions on Syria in the UN Security Council have undermined a liberal order. The term 'undermined' is of course transatlantic because Russia and China never subscribed to the liberal order in the first place. Both Russia and China are strictly opposed to regime change strategies, which they claim are clear violations of the international order based on rules that respect the sovereignty of states. They argue that only respect for state sovereignty will uphold a legitimate world order based on rules, not values as the West will have it (Walt, 2021). This interpretation of international order and sovereignty, which is in line with the UN Charter, clearly includes China's own sovereignty and territorial integrity, which in the eyes of the People's Republic of China is threatened by the so-called Indo-Pacific strategy initiated by Barack Obama and followed up on by both Donald Trump and Joe Biden. This explains China's hard power projection in East Asia and the Southeast China Sea, where around 40 per cent of its foreign trade passes through and therefore is vital to the Chinese economy (Sun and Zoubir, 2021). It also explains the significant difference in the interpretation of a world order between China and Russia: when Russia invaded Ukraine in 2014, it was a big challenge for China *not* to see it as a violation of its own principle of non-intervention in sovereign states. China does not recognize Russia's annexation of Crimea, has repeatedly stated opposition to violation of sovereignty and territorial integrity in debates about the war in Ukraine in 2022 and at the meeting in the Shanghai Cooperation Organisation (SCO) in September 2022 Xi Jinping expressed "worries" about the war in a dialogue with Vladimir Putin (Andersen, 2022). How the principle of non-intervention is still guiding China's policy in the Persian Gulf will be discussed, following a brief historical overview of US policy in the region.

The USA in the Persian Gulf

Shortly after the end of the Second World War, the USA defined the USSR as a global threat as expressed in the famous 'Long Telegram' written by American diplomat George Kennan. Under the pseudonym 'Mr X', he published a revised edition in 1947 in *Foreign Affairs* and concluded: 'The main element of any United States policy toward the Soviet Union must be that of a long-term, patient but firm and vigilant containment of Russian expansive tendencies' (Kennan, 1947). The key concept in the quote is of course 'containment'. But it was not Kennan, but rather the geopolitical theorist Halford Mackinder who already, 40 years beforehand in his seminal 1904 lecture 'The Geographical Pivot of History', coined the idea and strategy of containment (Mackinder, 2018 [1904]). He identified Russia as the large Eurasian land power, called it 'the heartland', and claimed that it needed to be contained to obstruct it from getting access to the deep-water ports of the Persian Gulf in order to prevent the land power from becoming a hegemonic world power threatening the great sea powers of the UK and the USA. Kennan warned that the USSR would aim for expansion of its power and want to spread the communist ideology globally, and that to avoid this it was necessary to contain the land power and deny it access to the high seas from the Persian Gulf.

America adopted this containment strategy: examples include the Baghdad Pact (later the Central Treaty Organization) and their support for the Islamist opposition groups in Afghanistan to prevent the USSR from entering the Gulf only 400 miles from Afghanistan. While priorities in US-Middle East policy changed in the decades following the Second World War, three areas have consistently been at the top of the US agenda as crucial: (1) the security of Israel; (2) the close cooperation with Saudi Arabia; and (3) control of the straits in the Persian Gulf (Andersen, 2019). Indeed, they have determined not only US policy in the region but also regional balances of power: for instance, Israel's position in the region is based on military strength with US support to give Israel the ability to deter aggression from regional states, especially Iran, which Israel considers its number one existential threat. The importance of the security of the Persian Gulf for the USA is perhaps most clearly expressed in the Carter Doctrine, as formulated in President Jimmy Carter's State of the Union speech in 1980. Here he stated:

> An attempt by any outside force to gain control of the Persian Gulf region will be regarded as an assault on the vital interests of the United States of America, and such an assault will be repelled by any means necessary, including military force.
>
> *(Carter, 1980)*

Although the Arab Gulf States might have their doubts, it still applies to US policy today. It was made manifest in the so-called 'tanker war' between the USA and Iran during the latter's war with Iraq in 1980–1988, the Iraq War in 1990–1991 (the liberation of Kuwait), the Iraq War initiated in 2003 and in the build-up of tensions in the spring of 2019 between the USA and the Arab Gulf states (especially the UAE and Saudi Arabia), on the one hand, and Iran, on the other. Tensions increased substantially when the United States, by order of Donald Trump, withdrew from the JCPOA in 2018 but the USA did not send the same clear signals it had done before (JCPOA, 2015).

This has impacted the third area, the stability of Saudi Arabia. The kingdom's stability has been a high priority in the White House (though often contested in Congress) since the end of the Second World War, when the two states began cooperating over oil extraction. Among the reasons for the West treating Saudi Arabia's stability as a priority are the enormous Saudi Arabian investments in the USA (and general Western) economy, the country's willingness to spend vast sums of money buying US (and other Western) produced weapons, and because Saudi Arabia has the largest swing capability in oil sales and hence the greatest influence over the global oil market. These were explicitly the reasons for the Trump administration desire to maintain close relations with Saudi

Arabia, even when the kingdom was conducting war crimes in Yemen and executing dissidents abroad (Council of Foreign Relations, 2018).

Clearly, these three areas have a significant impact on regional balances of power: the USA will not tolerate Israel becoming a weak military power in the region, nor the collapse of Saudi Arabia, nor that control of the straits in the Persian Gulf falls into the hands of America's adversaries. Based on these three priorities, the USA has inserted a substantial military presence into the region, including a naval base in Bahrain, the al-Udaid Air Base in Qatar, and minor bases in the UAE, Kuwait, and Oman. In 1983, the USA established US Central Command in the Ministry of Defense with its headquarters in Tampa, Florida, tasked with coordinating military policy in the Middle East, the Horn of Africa, and Central Asia. Until 1971, the security responsibility for the Persian Gulf had been shared with the UK, but after the British announced a withdrawal in 1968, with some reluctance the USA became the sole security provider. All states that conduct trade in the Persian Gulf, including imports of liquefied gas and oil, such as Japan and China, have benefitted from the US security of the Strait of Hormuz, which has led to China being accused of being a free-rider and exploiting US security in the Gulf.

America developed its containment strategy by building up alliances and deploying a substantial military presence with the dual purposes of deterring others from challenging US national security interests in the Gulf region and of being prepared if some nevertheless did intervene. Alliances in these defence agreements were targeted at adversaries, which means the containment strategy is a military strategy clearly distinguishing between friendly and hostile states.

The strategic importance of the Gulf to the USA is considered by many to be in flux today, which is forcing the Arab Gulf States to seek alternatives to the USA in a so-called hedging strategy where they increasingly have looked towards China. At the same time as the USA is somewhat downgrading or at least changing its security policy in the Persian Gulf, China is becoming an ever more visible and important player in the region.

China in the Persian Gulf

During the last decade, and especially in the aftermath of the so-called Arab Spring in 2011, coupled with China's more active and assertive foreign policy after Xi Jinping became president in 2013, China has increasingly become involved in the Persian Gulf. The Arab states in the Gulf Cooperation Council (GCC) began looking east during the Arab uprisings, partly because they were annoyed with the support given to the reformers in Egypt by the Obama administration, but also because they were aware of China's increasing need for energy and that China was becoming a vast and fast-growing market and investor, one that was thought to fit the much-needed economic diversification strategy of the GCC states. To maintain good growth rates, China needed a stable supply of energy, which the GCC states could provide (Andersen and Jiang, 2018a). However, so too could Iran: thus, when sanctions were lifted under the JCPOA in 2015, China became the largest buyer of oil from Iran as well as from Saudi Arabia, which are the two long-time rivals competing for regional power in the Middle East. Thereby China showed a very different approach to the Persian Gulf than that of the USA. Iran and the Arab Gulf States, as well as Iraq, including Iraqi Kurdistan, are also very important for President Xi's ambitious BRI and are attractive areas where China can invest funds in large infrastructure projects like the building or expansion of ports, establishing factories, investing in energy sectors, including nuclear energy, and developing cooperation in defence and high-tech projects, including both space capabilities and IT communications, such as the 5G network and AI (Fulton, 2019).

Iran, Iraq and the Gulf are important sites in China's expansion into Eurasia and further on to Europe. Apart from Egypt and Israel, and in the Gulf, Iran, the UAE, and Saudi-Arabia, China's engagement with other MENA countries is more limited. Egypt is of course very important to China because of the Suez Canal and Israel offers competence in high-tech cooperation and allows China port facilities, for example, in Haifa, which is managed by a state-owned company in Shanghai, major infrastructure investments, e.g., the metro in Tel Aviv (Axios, 2021). China is negotiating a free trade agreement with Israel and the two states also cooperate on areas such as AI technology. Interestingly, when President Xi travelled to the Middle East in January 2016, he selected Egypt, Saudi Arabia and (as the first state leader after the adoption of JCPOA) also Iran to visit. Almost all states in the MENA region are looking to China as a promising market and a provider of investment and finance without the political conditionalities on democracy and human rights that Western countries and institutions try to insist on. At the same time the rulers in the Arab Gulf States look to China for inspiration on economic development without political reforms.

Of course, China has been economically active in the Middle East, especially in the Persian Gulf, for more than three decades, but its engagement has recently increased substantially alongside its economic growth and its more assertive position in the global economy and politics. Thus, China is a new and attractive partner for MENA countries. This is confirmed by the 15 partnership agreements China has concluded with Middle Eastern states in the last ten years (except for the one with Egypt, which was settled in 1999). As explained by Dubai-based scholar Jonathan Fulton and Fudan Professor in Middle East Affairs Degang Sun, China has developed sophisticated partnership diplomacy built on three pillars outlined in the Arab Policy Paper: 'Central to this is the "1+2+3 cooperation pattern", with "1" representing energy as core interest; "2" infrastructure construction, as well as trade and investment; and "3" nuclear energy, satellites, and new energy sources' (Lons et al., 2019). China operates with different levels of partnerships, from basic economic cooperation to those including more sensitive matters, such as security, satellite-based surveillance systems, ballistic missile programmes and space weapons, as well as conducting joint naval drills, which China has done with Saudi Arabia and Iran. Depending on how China interprets their strategic importance, the Middle Eastern states are offered partnership on the lowest or the highest level (which is offered to Saudi Arabia, for example). It is important to underline that these partnerships are very different from alliances in the American strategy that China considers to be primarily military cooperation directed against what are defined as common enemies. Even if the highest level of partnerships involves military and security cooperation, they are not targeted at a third party considered an enemy and this gives China the opportunity to have extended cooperation with two rivals, for example, Iran and Saudi Arabia, simultaneously.

During the visit of President Joe Biden to Israel and Saudi Arabia in July 2022, it became clear that none of the Arab states are currently willing to be involved in an alliance against Iran established by the USA and with the potential participation of Israel but are more attracted to the Chinese partnership strategy. They are clearly worried about the threat from Iran and are already coordinating various defence initiatives that also involve Israel but in a manner that compares more to the Chinese multilateral approach than to President Biden's idea of an Arab–Israeli–US alliance. Biden's visit was the outcome of the February 2022 Russian-initiated war in Ukraine that has led to increasing energy prices. One goal of the visit was to strengthen US–Arab relations and assure the Arab Gulf states that America remains committed to the Middle East and will continue to be an active partner in the region. The relationship with Crown Prince Mohammad Bin Salman in Saudi Arabia needed to be repaired as Biden has refused to communicate with him because of his involvement in the murder of dissident journalist Jamal Khashoggi in Istanbul in 2018. After the outbreak of the war in Ukraine, President Biden asked Saudi Arabia to put more oil on the market to bring energy prices down, but the Arab Gulf state declined with reference to quota agreements with Russia. The Arab states refused to condemn Russia and support sanctions as the USA wanted. They have increasingly good relations with both Russia and China and did not change their position in response to Biden's visit (Vakil, 2022). In a way, the overall goal of President Biden's visit, meeting nine Arab leaders from the GCC countries plus Egypt, Iraq, and Jordan, can be defined as a mission to position the USA in the Middle East as a reliable and trustworthy power to counter the growing role of Russia and China. Central to this initiative were plans for infrastructure and connectivity investments that should clearly be seen as intended to counter China's BRI in the region. China is already well established through connectivity, infrastructure investment, and cyber technology. Thus, the meeting was a clear indication of US awareness of the increased role of China (and Russia) in the Persian Gulf and shows that the Arab Gulf states' hedging strategy is working successfully.

China's Global Connectivity Ambitions and the Persian Gulf

Aside from energy, trade, and investment projects, the opportunities that the Persian Gulf offers for connectivity are indeed important for China. With the BRI, China is connecting the Eurasian land power in Central Asia to the oceans via the Persian Gulf in a way that the USSR never succeeded in doing. Interesting in this context is the 'industrial park–port interconnection' announced by Wang Yi at the 8th Ministerial Meeting of the China–Arab States Cooperation Forum in Beijing in 2018, arguing for connecting four industrial parks built by Chinese companies in Abu Dhabi, Duqm in Oman, Jizan in Saudi Arabia, and in Ain Sokhna in Egypt to the four ports in Abu Dhabi, Oman, the Chinese base in Djibouti, and Port Said in Egypt. Together with Gwadar port in Pakistan and Chabahar in Iran, this will strengthen the Maritime Silk Route significantly. But perhaps even more important are the land routes, including pipelines in Iran making it possible to bypass the Strait of Hormuz in oil export, the China–Pakistan Economic Corridor (CPEC), connecting the Arabian Sea via road to west China, and roads and high-speed train connections from Chabahar to Afghanistan and Central Asia.

For Iran, China is of course extremely important but Iran's enemies in the Persian Gulf, especially Saudi Arabia and the Emirates, also look increasingly to China and have concluded a range of agreements and contracts. For them, it is apparently not an issue that China is simultaneously working with Israel and Iran. China provides a stable market for oil and gas export and at the same time the Chinese model of economic development fits the necessary economic diversification strategies of the Arab Gulf states. Egypt is also very important to China because of the Suez Canal and Egypt is inviting China to invest both in infrastructure projects, building the new prestige project of an administrative capital, and in the education sector. The Arab states are eager to develop digital resources and have all concluded contracts with Huawei in developing 5G networks. In other words, with the BRI, China is securing and expanding the Maritime Silk Route and overland from Xinjiang though Pakistan further into Central Asia, making China the possible Eurasian land power of the twenty-first century with round-the-clock access to the oceans.

Investments in development, connectivity, and infrastructure are of course accompanied by security measures. First, China needs to protect its interests in commerce, shipping, development, and other projects. Second, in case of conflict and destabilization China would need plans and facilities making it possible to evacuate Chinese citizens involved in the many projects. Third, in a multilateral approach, China wants to contribute to building stability and security as well as countering threats from piracy, terrorism, and insurgencies (Sun and Zoubir, 2021). To do this, China has increasingly engaged itself in multilateral security cooperation, such as the Shanghai Cooperation Organization (SCO) and in UN Peacekeeping Operations (PKO) where China today is the second-largest contributor after the USA to UN PKO funds (Andersen and Jiang, 2018b; Lanteigne and Hirono, 2012). Clearly, when investing in seaports China has the dual motivation of global economic interests and of security. Security, though, is not as claimed through building a 'String of Pearls' through the Pacific and the Indian Oceans in the form of naval bases disguised as commercial hubs. As Zhexin Zhang (2018) writes:

> From a military perspective, many Western observers worry that China's heavy investment in the building of more than 40 seaports in 34 countries – such as the Port of Piraeus in Greece, the Hambantota Port in Sri Lanka, and the Gwadar Port in Pakistan – will end in its control of these ports due to growing financial dependence of the host countries on China, helping realize its 'String of Pearls' strategy for the Indo-Pacific.

Zhexin Zhang underlines that this worry is unfounded and goes on to say,

> China has indeed used many of those seaports for naval supplies on commercial escort and international peace-keeping missions in the past years. As China's navy continues growing and conducts more overseas exercises, the military significance of those seaports will become more prominent. The long-term security implication of BRI, however, lies in its potential to help strengthen security between China and BRI-covered countries and thus foster new security mechanisms outside of the US dominance.
>
> *(ibid.)*

The wording 'dual-use' indicates some secrecy in investing in seaports, but China is quite open on what has been defined as the development–security nexus, which basically expresses the obvious fact that heavy investments are accompanied by security measures: economic engagement is followed by policy and diplomacy is followed by security policy. This security policy does not have to be in the form of hegemony and military dominance but can be developed in multilateral settings, as China has demonstrated in the SCO and in relation to the management of its only overseas base in Djibouti as well as elsewhere.

China, Iran, and the USA

The question, of course, is how China's increased interest and activity in the Middle East will influence the security situation in the Persian Gulf and what it will mean for US and China relations, both in the region and in the broader global context. To answer these questions, the position of Iran is perhaps the most obvious one to look at. China is Iran's biggest trading partner and main buyer of Iranian oil, and China sees Iran as an important hub in its BRI. Iran comprises a promising market for Chinese investment projects, as well as an important provider of energy. Iranians are generally well educated and thus constitute a good workforce, and China can use Iran as an alternative partner to balance its policy towards the Arab Gulf States and the USA (Alterman, 2019). Added to that is the strategic position of Chabahar port that gives access to the Persian Gulf and the Indian Ocean. After the US withdrawal from the JCPOA and the placing of new sanctions on Iran, the port was exempted from these sanctions. India, which was the main contractor in Chabahar, reduced its activities and investments despite the port's importance for India's connectivity to Afghanistan and Central Asia. Since Joe Biden took over as US president, India has again increased its engagement in the port as well as with the Central Asian states. Meanwhile China has negotiated access to Chabahar with Iran on the condition that China accepts not having exclusive access rights, thereby keeping the door open to India and other nations accessing the 'Gate of Nations' as Iran calls Chabahar (Kazmi, 2021).

The USA views Iran as a sponsor of terrorism through its support of Hamas and Hezbollah, as well as a threat to the stability of the Levant and Israel by exploiting the civil war in Syria to establish its military presence there and open a corridor connecting Lebanon with Iran through Syria and Iraq. Iran is also criticized by the USA, Israel, and the Arab Gulf States for supporting hostile groups and militias in Yemen and Iraq. At the same time, the United States under President Trump had accused Iran of aiming at developing nuclear weapons by deceiving the control regime of the JCPOA. Following these arguments, the USA withdrew from the JCPOA in 2018.

As all the other partners in the deal opposed Trump's decision and declared they would stick to it, China was left with two options. It could ignore the USA's confrontational Iran policy by continuing to invest in Iran and buying Iranian oil, despite the threat from the USA that China would be punished for breaking the unilateral sanctions. Alternatively, China could choose to follow its traditional policy of avoiding challenging the USA and comply with the US sanctions, which would shift the regional balance of power to the benefit of the Arab Gulf states, at least concerning the economy, trade and investments, at only a tiny price for China: only 1 per cent of China's trade is with Iran, and only about 5 per cent of its energy imports come from Iran. In fact, concerning economy, Iran is dependent on China rather than the other way round (Alterman, 2019). However, Iran is geographically an important territory in the architecture of BRI and today China is a stronger international actor than before 2015 and the Chinese are signalling their clear self-confidence in this position. Furthermore, as already mentioned, China can trade off its relationship with Iran against the Arab states. Finally, by giving Iran a lifeline, China can count on Iran as a partner in the future.

However, despite declarations that China was not obliged to follow the US sanctions, China reduced its trade with Iran and put investment projects there on hold. When Iran leaked the Iran–China 25-year programme in July 2020 to the *New York Times* China did not confirm it. Only after Trump had left office and Biden clearly announced his intention of having the USA back in the JCPOA did China confirm the deal that was signed in March 2021 and, later that same year, China confirmed the implementation of the deal. Like Russia and the European Union, China is eager to have the JCPOA restored but will probably continue its cooperation with Iran even if a new agreement is not reached. During 2021, there were indications that revealed policy initiatives by the Gulf Arabs towards Iran were preparing for a situation of no new deal being completed between the USA and Iran. Already in January 2021, Saudi Arabia and the UAE invited Iran to a dialogue and during the year meetings took place in Baghdad. Should such initiatives result in more substantial negotiations it cannot be excluded that China, with its good relations to partners on both sides, could step in as a mediator. China has already performed a role as conflict mediator in Darfur, Palestine, Afghanistan, Syria, and Qatar, which demonstrate China's willingness to play such a role. If that happens, China could conduct its mediation in cooperation with Russia which, in 2019, suggested a 'Collective Security Program in the Persian Gulf' and has since tried to revive at the end of 2021. These thoughts are of course speculation, but they do indicate that a new security architecture could be evolving in the Persian Gulf with a greater role for China but in a multilateral setting rather than the alliance-based US strategy.

China's Latent Power and Mixed US Signals in the Persian Gulf

Looking back on China's conduct of relations to Iran before the JCPOA indicates that China is not interested in challenging the US position in the Persian Gulf and especially not in taking over the role of security provider to the Arab Gulf states, which has been the sole responsibility of the USA since the British left the region in 1971. During the sanction regime up to the JCPOA, China downgraded its engagement and trade with Iran. When the Trump administration withdrew from the JCPOA and imposed new sanctions on Iran, China called them unilateral and said that no states were obliged to follow suit. Nevertheless, China did reduce investments in Iran and did not declare that it would provide Iran a lifeline. It continued to have some economic activity, including buying oil, and found ways to bypass the US sanctions but China clearly acted in a manner that was careful not to challenge the USA in a provocative way. When the Iran–China deal was leaked, China kept a low profile. The deal was agreed on during President Xi's visit in January 2016 and was in no way against US policy as the USA was a member of the JCPOA at the time. As such, the China–Iran deal is much more to be seen as an integrated part of the BRI and China's geoeconomics strategy than as a weapon in the US–China rivalry.

In their illuminating study of China's management of its only overseas naval base in Djibouti, Professors Degang Sun and Yahia H. Zoubir suggest a conceptual distinction between hard power and *latent power*, which is a new concept coined by them (Sun and Zoubir, 2021). When their sovereignty and territorial integrity are threatened China uses traditional hard power, expanding military power aggressively. That is what we see in the South China Sea. But when it comes to geoeconomics interest, which is what it is all about in the Persian Gulf, China uses latent power, as Sun and Zoubir (ibid.) define it:

> States may have three ways to consolidate their latent power: to appease world powers, to accommodate regional powers or to satisfy host states. First, they may exhibit their resolve to protect soft targets without, however, challenging militarily other powers in their sphere of influence (e.g., China in the Middle

East or Latin America); second, a latent power may demonstrate good will in partaking in security cooperation, through what Chinese refer to as military multilateralism (cooperation), for instance, and offering public security goods; third, states may strive to integrate military, political, and economic cooperation with the host country.

This is a very accurate description of what I have shown in this chapter of what China has been doing in the Persian Gulf by building up its geoeconomics interests both with Iran and the Arab Gulf States. China seeks to protect its geopolitical interests and gains, secure civilian targets, and contribute to providing stability and security (e.g., for container ships passing through the Strait of Hormuz) by means of multilateral military cooperation.

At this point, the Arab Gulf states do not see China replacing the USA as a security provider in the region. Rather they see China as a promising alternative to US dominance, one which might temper the US policy, so they welcome China to the region. An indication of that is their approach to the Uighur problem in Xinjiang. There are reports in the UN system and in international media and thinktanks that 1–3 million Uighurs have been illegally detained in camps in Xinjiang and, among other things, forced to suppress their religion. One could expect solidarity with the Muslim Uighurs and criticism from the regimes in the Persian Gulf that China is violating religious rights and Muslims. Maybe one could even expect Arab support to their US ally for its accusation that China is conducting genocide in Xinjiang. While the EU is supportive on this point and sanctioned China with reference to the Uighur problem (BBC, 2021), the Arab and other Muslim states, on the contrary, are supportive of China's policy in Xinjiang (Sheline and Cafiero, 2021).

Where does all that leave the USA in the Gulf? It is important to underline that the USA still is very much a military presence in the region with its naval base in Bahrain, airbase in Qatar, minor bases in Kuwait and the Emirates, special forces in Iraq and Syria, and with a capacity to build up troops and deliver weapon systems very fast to the Persian Gulf. Add to that a very large diplomatic representation in the Middle East, training of Middle Eastern forces and the huge US aid programme. Despite this, there are several reasons for an ongoing discussion about the US position in the Gulf and whether America still adheres to the Carter Doctrine (Brands, Cook and Pollack, 2019) given that the USA withdrew troops from Iraq in December 2011 and from Afghanistan in August 2021 and that during the tensions in the Persian Gulf in 2019, America sent very mixed signals about its willingness to provide security in the region.

Conclusion

All these developments point in the direction of a new security architecture evolving in the Persian Gulf with China in a new and important role. This is *not* as a unilateral security provider but one of seeking stability, based on multilateral cooperation to secure its ambitious BRI by building connectivity with the Gulf region as an important hub. Clearly the regional states are welcoming this new role for China, which certainly does not mean they will abandon the USA but rather exploit the alternative options when it comes to security. Broadly speaking, the visit by President Biden to Saudi Arabia, where he met with leaders from nine Arab states confirmed these points, indicating that a new security architecture is evolving in the Persian Gulf with a greater role for China.

References

Alterman, J. (2019). 'Who Wins When US–Iran Tensions Rise? China', *Defense One*, 15 May. Available at: www.defenseone.com/ideas/2019/05/who-wins-when-us-iran-tensions-rise-china/157050/ (accessed 2 April 2022).

Andersen, L.E (2019). 'China, the Middle East, and the Reshaping of World Order – the Case of Iran', Danish Institute for International Studies, DIIS Working Paper, 2019:14. Available at: www.diis.dk/node/21863

Andersen, L.E. (2022). 'Shanghai Cooperation Council: A Forum Where China Works for Multilateral Order in Central Asia', Danish Institute for International Studies, DIIS Policy Brief, November.

Andersen, L.E. and Jiang, Y. (2018a). 'China in the Persian Gulf: A Delicate Balance in Global Security', University of Nottingham Asia Research Institute, 28. April. Available at: https://theasiadialogue.com/2018/05/01/china-in-the-persian-gulf-a-delicate-balance-in-global-security/

Andersen, L.E. and Jiang, Y. (2018b). 'China's Engagement in Pakistan, Afghanistan, and Xinjiang', Danish Institute for International Studies, DIIS Report. 2018:06. Available at: www.diis.dk/node/21433

Axios (2021). 'CIA Director Raised China Concerns with Israeli Prime Minister'. Available at: www.axios.com/2021/08/18/cia-israel-china-investments

BBC (2021). 'Uighurs: Western Countries Sanction China Over Rights Abuses', 22 March. Available at: www.bbc.com/news/world-europe-56487162

Brands, H., Cook, S.A. and Pollack, K. (2019). 'RIP The Carter Doctrine 1980–2019', American Enterprise Institute, AEI. Available at: www.aei.org/articles/rip-the-carter-doctrine-1980-2019/

Carter, J. (1980). 'Doctrine', Office of the Historian. Available at: https://history.state.gov/historicaldocuments/frus1977-80v18/d45

Cooley, A. and Nexon, D.H. (2021). 'The Illiberal Tide. Why Is the International Order Tilting Towards Autocracy?' *Foreign Affairs*, 26 March. Available at: www.foreignaffairs.com/articles/united-states/2021-03-26/illiberal-tide

Council of Foreign Relations (2018). 'US–Saudi Arabia relations', 7 December. Available at: www.cfr.org/backgrounder/us-saudi-arabia-relations

Fulton, J. (2019). 'China's Changing Role in the Middle East', Rafik Hariri Center for the Middle East, Atlantic Council, June. Available at: https://atlanticcouncil.org/wp-content/uploads/2019/06/Chinas_Changing_Role_in_the_Middle_East.pdf

Huntington, S.P. (1999). 'The Lonely Superpower', *Foreign Affairs*, March/April. Available at: www.foreignaffairs.com/articles/united-states/1999-03-01/lonely-superpower

JCPOA (2015). 'Section 3: Understanding the JCPOA', Arms Control Association. Available at: www.armscontrol.org/2015-08/section-3-understanding-jcpoa

Kazmi, S.H. (2021). 'Who Will Control Iran's Chabahar? India or China?', *Eurasia Review*, 28 April. Available at: www.eurasiareview.com/28042021-who-will-control-irans-chabahar-india-or-china-oped/

Kennan, G. (1947). 'The Sources of Soviet Conduct'. *Foreign Affairs*, July. Available at: www.foreignaffairs.com/articles/russian-federation/1947-07-01/sources-soviet-conduct

Lanteigne, M. and Hirono, M. (eds) (2012). *China's Evolving Approach to Peacekeeping*. London: Routledge.

Lons, C., Fulton, J., Sun, D., and Al-Tamimi, N. (2019). 'China's Great Game in the Middle East'. European Council on Foreign Affairs, policy brief. Available at: https://ecfr.eu/publication/china_great_game_middle_east/

Mackinder, H. (2018 [1904]). 'The Geographical Pivot of History', in H. Mackinder, *Democratic Ideals and Reality: The Geographical Pivot of History*. Singapore. Origami Books, pp. 165–187.

Mearsheimer, J.J. (2018). *The Great Delusion: Liberal Dreams and International Realities*. New Haven, CT: Yale University Press.

New York Times (2020). 'Defying US, China and Iran Near Trade and Military Partnership'. 11 July. Available at: www.nytimes.com/2020/07/11/world/asia/china-iran-trade-military-deal.html

Pomeps (2019). 'The Politics of Rentier States in the Gulf', *Pomeps Studies* 33, January. Available at: https://pomeps.org/pomeps-studies-33-the-politics-of-rentier-states-in-the-gulf

Sakwa, R. (2017). *Russia Against the Rest: The Post-Cold War Crisis of World Order*. Cambridge: Cambridge University Press.

Sheline, A. and Cafiero, G. (2021). 'Muslim Governments Are Giving China a Free Pass on Xinjiang', *World Politics Review*, 19 May. Available at: www.worldpoliticsreview.com/articles/29661/on-abuses-against-uyghurs-in-china-muslim-governments-give-beijing-a-free-pass

State Council, PRC (2016). 'Arab Policy Paper'. Available at: http://english.www.gov.cn/archive/publications/2016/01/13/content_281475271412746.htm

Steinberg, G. (2014). 'Leading the Counter-Revolution. Saudi Arabia and the Arab Spring', SWP Research Paper 7/2014, Berlin: SWP.

Sun, D. and Zoubir, Y.H. (2021). 'Securing China's "Latent Power": the Dragon's Anchorage in Djibouti'. *Journal of Contemporary China* 30(130). DOI: 10.1080/10670564.2020.1852734

Vakil, S. (2022). 'Biden's Middle East Trip Shows the Long Game Is His Aim', London: Chatham House, 19 July. Available at: www.chathamhouse.org/2022/07/bidens-middle-east-trip-shows-long-game-his-aim?utm_source=Chatham%20House&utm_med ium=email&utm_campaign=13356984_CH%20-%20CH%20Newsletter%20-%20Origi nal%20Version%20-%2022.07.2022&utm_content=Biden-CTA&dm_i=1S3M,7YABC,NUS JZM,WI2E6,1Walt, S. (2018). *The Hell of Good Intentions: America's Foreign Policy Elite and the Decline of US Primacy*. New York: Farrar, Straus, and Giroux.

Walt, S. (2021). 'China Wants a "Rules-based International Order", Too', *Foreign Policy*, 31 March. Available at: https://foreignpolicy.com/2021/03/31/china-wants-a-rules-based-internatio nal-order-too/

Xinhua (2021). 'China, Iran Sign Agreement to Map Out Comprehensive Cooperation', 28 March. Available at: www.xinhuanet.com/english/2021-03/28/c_139841044.htm (accessed 2 April 2022).

Yi, W. (2021). 'Interview with al-Arabiya During Visit in the Middle East', March. Available at: www.fmprc.gov.cn/mfa_eng/zxxx_662805/t1864531.shtml

Zhang, Z. (2018). 'The Belt and Road Initiative: China's New Geopolitical Strategy?', *China Quarterly of International Strategic Studies* 4(3): 327–343.

9

US-CHINA NUCLEAR EXPORTS RIVALRY IN THE MENA REGION

Çiğdem Pekar

Introduction

Most of the nuclear newcomer states are countries in the Middle East and North Africa (MENA) that have been showing great interest in the construction of nuclear power plants. Adding nuclear energy to their energy mix has become one of the priorities in their future energy programs. Saudi Arabia is one of the most nuclear energy-demanding Arab states, Iran has a long history of its contested nuclear energy program, Egypt, Jordan, and several other MENA countries offer nuclear markets with important opportunities for the nuclear exporter countries. Most of those MENA countries are either in the negotiation process or already had nuclear cooperation agreements with different nuclear supplier states.

In this regard, private US companies also show an interest in taking part in those nuclear energy markets. Although the United States was a long-standing leader in nuclear energy export, according to the US Department of Energy today, it has lost its "competitive global position as the world leader in nuclear energy to state-owned enterprises" (DOE, 2020: 4). Strong nonproliferation safeguards (namely the "gold standard") which are required by the USA before civil nuclear export agreements are of critical importance for the development of nuclear trade relations with the MENA countries.

On the other hand, China, with its developing indigenous nuclear technology and "going global" nuclear power strategy is actively engaged in international cooperation in the peaceful use of nuclear energy. Under the "Belt and Road Initiative" (BRI), state-owned corporations in China aim to strengthen cooperation in the field of nuclear energy by concluding several cooperation agreements and memorandum of understandings (MoUs). Furthermore, the China National Nuclear Corporation (CNNC) aims to "establish an industry wide supply chain operation, investment and financing platform of CNNC in overseas and global markets, with a view to jointly explore and establish a development model of China's nuclear industry (industry + finance + overseas market)" (IAEA, 2020). The MENA countries are also on the list of Chinese state-owned corporations as potential partners for nuclear export.

DOI: 10.4324/9781003048404-11

This study aims to present an overview of the policies and the current status of the Chinese and American civil nuclear exports to the MENA region. To this end, it first assesses Chinese indigenous nuclear technology and civil nuclear exports policy toward MENA region. Then, it focuses on the civil nuclear cooperation agreements between China and the region countries. Moving from this point, it analyzes American civil nuclear exports policy toward the MENA region with a focus on the status of civil nuclear cooperation among these countries. Finally, the chapter assesses why state-owned companies will dominate civil nuclear exports to the MENA states.

Chinese Indigenous Nuclear Technology and the Civil Nuclear Exports Policy toward the MENA Region

Since the 1980s, nuclear technology has been regarded as a "strategic" export issue by the Chinese central planners. Thus, development of indigenous nuclear technology has been prioritized in the country (Hibbs, 2018: 8). In order to make China a leader in the development of nuclear technology several steps have been taken by the Chinese government. In this regard, in 2015, the "Made in China 2025" (MIC 2025) program was established as a state-led industrial policy. It basically aims to make China dominant in global high-tech manufacturing, including nuclear technology (McBride and Chatzky, 2019). MIC 2025 also foresees Chinese nuclear expansion to the world via China's nuclear power industry. In order to strengthen the status of the Chinese nuclear power industry, China's Nuclear Safety Law entered into force in 2018. In the same year, the State Council's "issuance of guidelines for the standardization of the nuclear system" was also adopted (Hickey, 2018). Both developments can be regarded as significant progress regarding the regulation of China's nuclear industry and the future of the civil nuclear exports to other nations.

Thus, domestic nuclear reactor development with Chinese intellectual property rights is of significant importance for the future of the Chinese nuclear industry and civil nuclear exports. Today, China is producing two types of reactors in nuclear power plants; Generation II and Generation III reactors. While the former is heavily based on the Chinese origin production, for the Generation III reactors, currently China is mostly importing from foreign nuclear suppliers. China also is a significant producer of uranium for the nuclear fuel in Chinese reactors. Almost 70 percent of the uranium for these reactors comes from the mines in China (ITA, 2016).

There is a competitive domestic environment in China with regard to the development of reactors with Chinese intellectual property rights. China's state-owned nuclear company, the China General Nuclear Power Corporation (CGN), was established in 1994 while the State Nuclear Power Technology Corporation (SNPTC) was established in 2007. Both of these companies are the followers of state-owned China National Nuclear Corporation (CNNC). While the CNNC aims to produce reactors with Chinese indigenous technology, the SNPTC was in favor of importing the main technology and upgrading it. In the end, the SNPTC preferred to use the Westinghouse (owned by Japan) AP1000 pressurized water reactor technology as the main basis of the Generation III reactors' local development technology, in the phase of development of a nuclear reactor with a local technology (CAP 1400 reactors) (WNA, 2021a). In May 2016, the CAP1400 design, which may be exported to the ambitious countries, successfully passed the International Atomic Energy Agency's (IAEA) Generic Reactor Safety Review (WNN, 2017).

Furthermore, the Generation III ACP-1000 reactor, as the advanced version of CGN's Generation II reactor CPR 1000 and CNNC's ACP-1000 designs, was developed with a partnership of these two companies with full Chinese intellectual property rights. These two corporations have further worked together on a standardized design of a Generation III reactor as a merged version of the CNNC's ACP1000 and the CGN's ACPR1000. The new Generation III reactor is called Hualong One (HPR1000). In 2020, the reactor design of the Hualong One was certified "as compliant by the European Utility Requirements (EUR) organisation" which is a technical advisory group for European utilities on nuclear power plants (WNN, 2020).

According to the China General Nuclear Power Corporation with its "full proprietary intellectual property rights," the Chinese Generation-III (HPR1000) reactors will be the preferred reactor technology for China's nuclear power industry's "going global" strategy. The Generation III Hualong One (HPR1000) and CAP1400 pressurized water reactors have been selected as the strategic vehicles for this blueprint by the high-level Chinese political decision-makers (Kenderdine, 2019). The Chinese National Development and Reform Commission (NDRC) has a consistent policy to support the export of Hualong One (HPR1000) and CAP1400 reactors "with Chinese intellectual property rights and backed by full fuel cycle capability" (WNA, 2021a).

The Chinese indigenously developed Generation III Hualong One nuclear reactor is regarded as one of China's "business cards" (Warsaw Institute, 2020). Thus, China aims to reach the MENA region's nuclear market mainly through the CNNC. The CNNC declares that it aims "to build as many as 30 'Belt and Road' reactors in developing nations by 2030" (Reuters, 2019). Furthermore, the CNNC's international nuclear project platform, the China Zhongyuan Engineering Corporation (CZEC), has opened offices in several MENA countries, such as Algeria Iran, Egypt, and Saudi Arabia. These initiatives demonstrate "a degree of seriousness about its nuclear export intentions to the MENA states" (Hickey, 2018).

Civil Nuclear Cooperation between China and the MENA Countries

Today China has several civil nuclear cooperation agreements and MOUs with many countries. Today, there are several bilateral agreements for cooperation in the peaceful use of nuclear energy between the Government of China and the European Atomic Energy Community and 26 states.[1] With regard to potential civil nuclear cooperation with the MENA states, the "One Belt, One Road" (OBOR) initiative can be regarded as a significant tool for China. At the high-level policy meetings, the importance of this initiative for mutual gains was frequently emphasized. In the Opening Ceremony of the Ministerial Conference of the China-Arab States Cooperation Forum, the Chinese President Xi Jinping delivered a speech promoting the "Silk Road spirit" and emphasizing the role of OBOR as the path to "mutual benefits" and "win-win results" among China and particularly the Arab states which are members of the MENA regions. According to Xi Jinping:

> The two sides should hold a broader vision and down-to-earth attitude to establish a "1+2+3" cooperation pattern, namely, to take energy cooperation as the core, infrastructure construction and trade and investment facilitation as two wings, and, three, high and new tech fields of nuclear energy, space satellite and new energy as new breakthroughs.
>
> *(FMPRC, 2014)*

Several other high-level policy statements from China have declared the intention to deepen China-Arab cooperation in energy cooperation, including nuclear energy. According to the Chinese Ministry of Foreign Affairs: "China and the Arab states are natural cooperation partners in the joint building of the Belt and Road," where practical cooperation exists between the two sides. Furthermore, the two sides have further strengthened "the '1+2+3' cooperation framework with energy cooperation as the main axis" (FMPRC, 2018).

Although the Sino-Arab "1+2+3" framework focuses on several cooperation areas, it mainly focuses on the "energy cooperation, advancing infrastructure cooperation, trade and investment facilitation and upgrading results-oriented cooperation on three high tech fronts of nuclear energy, space and satellites, and new energy." Under the title of "Cooperation Priorities and Measures," the importance attached to the development of peaceful nuclear energy is emphasized. It is stated that in order to develop energy cooperation which also includes several phases of peaceful use of nuclear energy, such as the design and construction of nuclear power plants, nuclear safety, training on nuclear power technologies "joint efforts will be made to build the Global Energy Interconnection and achieve green development" (CASCF, 2018).

There have also been other attempts to establish cooperation platforms to support the development of nuclear energy among Arab states. The China-Arab States Cooperation Forum (CASCF) was established in 2004 as an important example of a "formal dialogue initiative" between China and the Arab League countries. China clearly emphasizes its intention to support the transfer of nuclear technology to Arab states in a CASCF statement. According to the Forum's statement: "China supports the Arab states in the peaceful use of nuclear energy and transfer of peaceful energy technology to the Arab states" (SISU, 2018). Furthermore, in order to strengthen mutual cooperation in the nuclear energy field, the China-Arab States Technology Transfer Center was established in 2015. It is also stated that studies in order to establish an Arab training center for the peaceful use of nuclear energy is on the agenda between these countries (CASCF, 2018).

Apart from above-mentioned cooperation initiatives, there are also other cooperation agreements between China and several other MENA countries regarding the development of civilian nuclear energy in those states.

Iran

Since the beginning of the 2000s, Iran's nuclear agenda and multilateral negotiations on this issue have been regarded as critical in terms of global nuclear nonproliferation efforts. China has been a strong supporter of the Joint Comprehensive Plan of Action (JCPOA), which is mostly called a "Iran nuclear deal" as a member of the P5+1 countries (the United States, China, France, Russia, and the United Kingdom plus Germany). Following the conclusion of the deal in 2017, the Iran Atomic Energy Organization and the CNNC signed a contract in order to redesign the Iranian Arak reactor. However, there have been some delays in the implementation of the contract mostly due to the US withdrawal from the deal and the re-introduction of US sanctions against Iran. It can be said that this issue has been taken very seriously by the Iranians. The head of Iran's Atomic Energy Organization, Ali Akbar Salehi said: "Ever since the U.S. withdrew from the nuclear deal, China has slowed its cooperation with Iran for redesigning the Arak reactor" (*Tehran Times*, 2020).

There have been other initiatives to deepen Tehran-Beijing ties. In 2021, Iran and China signed a Comprehensive Strategic Partnership agreement which will last 25 years (Reuters, 2021). This agreement has been under discussion since 2016. In their joint statement, the parties declared their intention to develop the relations between the two states in several areas, such as "Political," "Executive Cooperation," "Human and Cultural," "Judiciary, Security and Defense," and "Regional and International" domains. The agreement also placed particular emphasis on the use of nuclear energy for peaceful purposes. According to the agreement: "Both sides express their agreement to enhancing investment and trade exchanges and promote tangible cooperation in the areas of economy, banking, mutual investment, financing, … use of nuclear energy for peaceful purposes and renewable energies" (Office of the President of Islamic Republic of Iran, 2016).

The parties also declared their strong support for the implementation of the JCPOA and put emphasis on the modernization of the Arak heavy-water reactor. The Chinese intention to advance the modernization efforts of the Arak reactor is of significant importance to keep Iranian nuclear program in peaceful limits and for the global nuclear nonproliferation regime as a whole.

Saudi Arabia

Saudi Arabia is an important nuclear newcomer country from the MENA region who intends to develop its own nuclear energy program. In 2016, a Joint Statement between the People's Republic of China and the Kingdom of Saudi Arabia on the Establishment of Comprehensive Strategic Partnership was finalized in Riyadh.

In the same year, the two countries signed an agreement to build a high-temperature reactor (HTR) in the country. In 2017, both agreed on supporting Saudi Arabia's nuclear energy program. Furthermore, the Saudi Geological Survey (SGS) and the CNNC signed a MoU "to pursue further cooperation to explore and assess uranium and thorium resources." The CNNC announced that "it would explore nine potential areas for uranium resources in Saudi Arabia" (WNA, 2021b). The Kingdom also aims to use gas-cooled nuclear reactors in order to develop their own water desalination projects. So other MoUs were signed to this end between the CNEC and the Saudi Technology Development Corporation (Chaziza, 2020).

Other MENA Countries

Egypt is another potential partner of China in nuclear energy cooperation in the region. In 2014, a Comprehensive Strategic Partnership agreement between the two countries was signed. Furthermore, in May 2015, the CNNC and the Egyptian Nuclear Power Plants Authority (NPPA) signed an agreement to enhance nuclear cooperation and to "become an official partner" in the country's nuclear Project (WNA, 2021c).

Algeria is another partner country on China's list for nuclear cooperation. In 2014, a Comprehensive Strategic Partnership agreement between the two countries was signed. The CNNC also concluded a cooperation agreement with the Algerian Atomic Energy Commission in the areas of nuclear energy, research reactors, nuclear safety, nuclear technology, and water desalination in 2015. Similarly, the CNNC signed a cooperation agreement with Tunisia's National Centre of Nuclear Sciences and Technology in 2017.

Sudan also signed a nuclear cooperation agreement with the CNNC to construct 600 MWe nuclear power reactors. Jordan and the CNNC also signed a cooperation agreement covering uranium mining. Furthermore, the Jordan Atomic Energy Commission (JAEC) and the CNNC are in the negotiation phase regarding construction of a 220 MWe HTR-PM high temperature, gas-cooled reactor on Jordan's soil (WNA, 2021d). Kenya, Uganda, Ghana, and Nigeria are the other countries that have concluded MoUs with Chinese state enterprises on cooperation in the peaceful uses of nuclear energy and the development of nuclear energy programs (WNA, 2021e).

American Civil Nuclear Exports Policy toward the MENA Region

It is clear that the US nuclear industry is eager to take part in the MENA countries' nuclear energy programs. However, the state-owned Chinese enterprises are a tough competitor of the US companies. In this regard, the current international status of the US nuclear industry, its nuclear exports, and the economic opportunities it presents are being discussed on several platforms.

The ambitious development of Chinese indigenous nuclear technology also has attracted the attention of the USA. According to the US Department of Commerce: "China aims to become a reactor design exporter and compete alongside established companies for reactor tenders worldwide" (ITA, 2016).

Today the USA currently has 23 nuclear cooperation agreements in force. Just two MENA countries, Egypt (1981) and the United Arab Emirates (2009), have concluded 123 Agreements with the USA until now (Hickey, 2018). Negotiations with two other MENA countries (Jordan and Saudi Arabia) were deadlocked due to the gold standard requirements in the civil nuclear cooperation agreements (123 Agreements). In the eyes of the USA and its allies, the Middle East has been carrying significant nuclear proliferation risks and these concerns have directly affected negotiations regarding the nuclear fuel cycle capability of the importing state (Einhorn, 2018).

According to the US Atomic Energy Act, every civil nuclear cooperation agreement (123 Agreements) with other countries should include a "gold standard." Gold standard means none of the nuclear material supplied by the USA to these countries can be enriched or reprocessed (which are regarded as the two major paths for the production of a nuclear weapon) without the consent of the US government. Other parties to the agreement should request this permission before any such kind of uranium enrichment or plutonium reprocessing act. These two paths for nuclear weapons production are aimed at being blocked by this requirement.

However, according to the US nuclear suppliers, these "strict conditions and time-consuming legal requirements put them at a competitive disadvantage." It is mainly because other major nuclear suppliers do not have such strict nonproliferation safeguards for the conclusion of a nuclear cooperation agreement with the nuclear newcomer states (Kane, 2019).

The US Department of Energy's (DOE) assessment of the US nuclear industry, "Restoring America's Competitive Nuclear Energy Advantage: A Strategy to Assure US National Security," provides a clear picture of the US nuclear industry's current status vis-à-vis other major actors (DOE, 2020). The report emphasizes strong nonproliferation safeguards (namely the "gold standard") required by the USA before any civil nuclear export and focuses on the importance of these safeguards for the US nonproliferation goals and national security. The report also points out that: "America has lost its competitive global position as the world leader in nuclear energy to state-owned enterprises, notably Russia and China" (ibid.: 4).

It also makes a clear assessment regarding the actions of the state-owned nuclear companies of other states, such as Russian and Chinese state-owned enterprises and states that "unfortunately, some foreign exporting nations, like Russia and China, do not hold their trading partners to the same high standards and may even use lower standards as a selling point." This situation enables nuclear-ambitious states to "import nuclear technologies without the same non-proliferation safeguards required by the United States and its allies, further disadvantaging U.S. civil nuclear exports, as well as reducing global efforts for a robust international nuclear safeguards and security regime" (ibid.: 24).

This issue was also studied in a U.S. International Development Finance Corporation (DFC) report in 2020. The report emphasizes the significant importance of the entire nuclear supply chain and focuses on the state-owned actors' efforts to dominate the growing market for civil nuclear technologies in emerging economies. It states that:

> At the same time, countries like Russia and China have increased their focus and deployment of state financing tools for nuclear projects … in emerging economies, as a tool to expanding their geopolitical influence, while not requiring the same high standards for nuclear security, safety and nonproliferation that the United States requires.
>
> *(DFC, 2020: 2)*

According to the same report, those efforts of the state-owned companies (such as Russia and China) have put the US nuclear industry "at a competitive disadvantage" (ibid.: 2).

There are several reasons why state-owned enterprises dominate the civil nuclear export to the MENA states. First and most importantly, many MENA states refuse to sign a nuclear cooperation agreement which includes the US "gold standard" not because they aim to produce nuclear weapons by enriching or reprocessing US nuclear materials, but because they aim to protect their sovereign rights guaranteed to them under Article IV of the Non-Proliferation Treaty (NPT), which came into force in 1970.

According to Article IV of the NPT, "nothing in this Treaty shall be interpreted as affecting the inalienable right of all the Parties to the Treaty to develop research, production and use of nuclear energy for peaceful purposes." It is widely discussed among the state parties to the treaty (especially between nuclear weapon states and non-nuclear weapon states) whether enrichment and reprocessing activities can be regarded as the "inalienable right" or not (United Nations, 2005).

Furthermore, private US companies have particular financial challenges in their competition against state-owned Chinese companies in the region. Chinese companies can offer lower construction costs and attractive financing options to the region countries (Kane, 2019). That gives China a competitive edge over the USA.

In order to tackle the financial challenges and to support its private nuclear industry against state-owned competition on the global nuclear export market, the US International Development Finance Corporation (DFC), which calls itself "America's development bank," has taken an important step and announced a change in its Environmental and Social Policy and Procedures (ESPP) in 2020. This move is aimed at lifting the ban on financing nuclear power projects abroad. Following the change in this policy, DFC CEO Adam Boehler said that this step is a significant one in "US efforts to support the energy needs of allies" and to "accelerate growth in developing economies with limited energy resources" (DFC, 2020). It is also stated on the DFC website regarding the policy change that: "This update recognizes the vast energy needs of developing countries as well as new and advanced technologies such as small modular reactors and microreactors that could be particularly impactful in these markets." To implement this removal of the prohibition on support of nuclear power projects, the Department of Commerce took an important step in 2008 and launched the Civil Nuclear Trade Initiative (CNTI). The CNTI aimed at "strengthen[ing] the competitiveness of the U.S. nuclear industry as it endeavors to rebuild its manufacturing base by capturing opportunities abroad" (DOC, 2016). Furthermore, by identifying the industry's "most pressing trade challenges" and "most promising commercial opportunities," the Initiative coordinates public and private sector efforts to address these issues (ibid.).

The Initiative involves four areas:

1. The Trade Promotion Coordinating Committee's (TPCC) Civil Nuclear Trade Working Group.
2. The Civil Nuclear Trade Advisory Committee (CINTAC).
3. Trade policy and promotion activities,
4. Stakeholder resources.

These steps are of significant importance in order to support American private sector companies in competing with the state-backed companies, such as Chinese ones. According to the experts, without that support the US companies are faced with a "tilted playing field" where China is poised to become the Amazon.com of nuclear commerce in the twenty-first century (Luongo, 2018: 5).

Conclusion

The MENA region with its growing market for civil nuclear technologies is the focus of attention of several nuclear exporter states. The MENA countries constitute an important part of the Chinese state-owned companies' nuclear energy cooperation ambitions. Through their collaboration with other states, Chinese companies have learned Western technology and now "they are developing and building indigenously designed reactors and trying to export them overseas" (DIIS, 2016). Furthermore, civil nuclear cooperation constitutes a significant part of China's OBOR Initiative, and China and the MENA countries have developed several levels of cooperation. According to the US Department of Commerce: "China aims to become a reactor design exporter and compete alongside established companies for reactor tenders worldwide" (ITA, 2016).

It is also known that the USA has lost its competitive global position as the world leader in nuclear energy to state-owned enterprises. The most significant barrier to the private US companies exporting to the MENA region is the region countries' unwillingness to sign a nuclear cooperation agreement which includes the US "gold standard." Another barrier for these companies are the financial challenges in their competition against state-owned Chinese companies which offer lower construction costs and attractive financing options in the region.

It is clear that establishing strategic ties which would last a century (the lifetime of a nuclear power reactor) would enable these states to expand their geopolitical influence in the MENA region. Furthermore by assisting the region's countries with their energy security and development, nuclear exporter states would have a significant influence over the regional and global norms for nuclear safety and nonproliferation. Without a doubt, states' abilities to conclude nuclear cooperation agreements with the MENA countries will also affect their potential influence on several aspects of these civilian nuclear programs, such as safeguards, nonproliferation, security, and safety.

Note

1 These states are the following: Algeria, Argentina, Australia, Bangladesh, Belarus, Belgium, Brazil, Canada, Egypt, France, Germany, Islamic Republic of Iran, Japan, Jordan, Kazakhstan, Republic of Korea, Pakistan, Russian Federation, Saudi Arabia, South Africa, Spain, Switzerland, Turkey, United Kingdom, United States of America, Viet Nam (IAEA, 2020).

References

CASCF (China-Arab States Cooperation Forum). (2018). "Declaration of Action on China-Arab States Cooperation under the Belt and Road Initiative." Available at: www.chinaarabcf.org/chn/lthyjwx/bzjhywj/dbjbzjhy/P020180726404036530409.pdf

CGNPC (China General Nuclear Power Corporation). "HPR 1000." Available at: http://en.cgnpc.com.cn/encgn/c100048/business_tt.shtml

Chaziza, M. (2020). "Saudi Arabia's Nuclear Program and China." Available at: www.mei.edu/publications/saudi-arabias-nuclear-program-and-china

DFC (U.S. International Development Finance Corporation). (2020). "DFC Modernizes Nuclear Energy Policy." Available at: www.dfc.gov/sites/default/files/media/documents/ESPP_Nuclear_Summary_of_Decision_23July2020.pdf

DIIS (Danish Institute for International Studies). "China's Overseas Investment in Critical Infrastructure: Nuclear Power and Telecommunications." DIIS Report. Available at: http://pure.diis.dk/ws/files/727852/DIIS_RP_2016_8_WEB.pdf

DOC (U.S. Department of Commerce) (2016). "Top Markets Report Civil Nuclear a Market Assessment Tool for U.S. Exporters." Available at: http://large.stanford.edu/courses/2017/ph241/morris-s1/docs/ita-may16.pdf

DOE (U.S. Department of Energy). (2020). "Restoring America's Competitive Nuclear Energy Advantage: A Strategy to Assure U.S. National Security." Available at: www.energy.gov/sites/prod/files/2020/04/f74/Restoring%20America%27s%20Competitive%20Nuclear%20Advantage-Blue%20version%5B1%5D.pdf

Einhorn, R. (2018). "US-Saudi Civil Nuclear Negotiations: Finding a Practical Compromise." *Bulletin of the Atomic Scientists.* Available at: https://thebulletin.org/2018/01/us-saudi-civil-nuclear-negotiations-finding-a-practical-compromise/

FMPRC (Ministry of Foreign Affairs, the People's Republic of China). (2014). "Xi Jinping Attends Opening Ceremony of Sixth Ministerial Conference of China-Arab States Cooperation Forum and Delivers Important Speech Stressing to Promote Silk Road Spirit and Deepen China-Arab Cooperation." Available at: www.fmprc.gov.cn/mfa_eng/zxxx_662805/t1163554.shtml

FMPRC (Ministry of Foreign Affairs, the People's Republic of China). (2018). "The Joint Building of the Belt and Road Between China and Arab States in the Middle East Is Rapidly Taking Shape." Available at: www.fmprc.gov.cn/mfa_eng/wjb_663304/zzjg_663340/xybfs_663590/dqzzywt_663826/t1576568.shtml

Hibbs, M. (2018). *The Future of Nuclear Power in China.* Washington, DC: Carnegie Endowment for International Peace.

Hickey, S. (2018). "China's Nuclear Diplomacy in the Middle East." *The Diplomat.* Available at: https://thediplomat.com/2018/10/chinas-nuclear-diplomacy-in-the-middle-east/

IAEA (International Atomic Energy Agency). (2020). "Country Nuclear Power Profiles: China." Available at: https://cnpp.iaea.org/countryprofiles/China/China.htm

ITA (International Trade Administration). (2016). "ITA Civil Nuclear Top Markets Report: China." Available at: https://legacy.trade.gov/topmarkets/pdf/Civil_Nuclear_China.pdf

Kane, C. (2019). "Why Proposals to Sell Nuclear Reactors to Saudi Arabia Raise Red Flags." *The Conversation.* Available at: https://theconversation.com/why-proposals-to-sell-nuclear-reactors-to-saudi-arabia-raise-red-flags-112276

Kenderdine, T. (2019). "Global Ambitions Fuel China's Nuclear Power Strategy." East Asia Forum. Available at: www.eastasiaforum.org/2019/02/21/global-ambitions-fuel-chinas-nuclear-power-strategy/

Luongo, K. N. (2018). "Nuclear Power in a New Era: Four Essential Policy Pillars For Its Future." Partnership for Global Security. Available at: https://partnershipforglobalsecurity.org/wp-content/uploads/2018/12/nuclearpower2018-1.pdf

McBride, J. and Chatzky, A. (2019). "Is 'Made in China 2025' a Threat to Global Trade?" Council on Foreign Relations. www.cfr.org/backgrounder/made-china-2025-threat-global-trade

Office of the President of Islamic Republic of Iran. (2016). "Joint Statement on Comprehensive Strategic Partnership between I.R. Iran, P.R. China." Available at: www.president.ir/EN/91435

Reuters. (2019). "China Could Build 30 'Belt and Road' Nuclear Reactors by 2030: Official." Available at: www.reuters.com/article/us-china-nuclearpower-idUSKCN1TL0HZ

Reuters. (2021). "Iran and China Sign 25-Year Cooperation Agreement." Available at: www.reuters.com/article/us-iran-china/iranand-china-sign-25-year-cooperation-agreement-idUSKBN2BJ0AD

SISU (Shanghai International Studies University). (2018). "Joint Development of the 'Belt and Road', a New Era of Promoting China-Arab Collective Cooperation." Available at: http://mideast.shisu.edu.cn/_upload/article/files/95/d5/159cb85b4c218c71efee7bb400c9/9b738dd6-d9d1-4217-B989-8c48cf8b12e4.Pdf

Tehran Times. (2020). "If Redesign of Arak Reactor Delayed: Iran Will Return to Previous One: Salehi." Available at: www.tehrantimes.com/news/445064/If-redesign-of-Arak-reactor-delayed-Iran-will-return-to-previous

United Nations. (2005). "The Treaty on the Non-Proliferation of Nuclear Weapons (NPT)." Available at: www.un.org/en/conf/npt/2005/npttreaty.html

Warsaw Institute. (2020). "Chinese-Saudi Nuclear Cooperation." Available at: warsawinstitute.org/chinese-saudi-nuclear-cooperation/

WNA (World Nuclear Association). (2021a). "Nuclear Power in China." Available at: www.world-nuclear.org/information-library/country-profiles/countries-a-f/china-nuclear-power.aspx

WNA (World Nuclear Association). (2021b). "Nuclear Power in Saudi Arabia." Available at: world-nuclear.org/information-library/country-profiles/countries-o-s/saudi-arabia.aspx

WNA (World Nuclear Association). (2021c). "Nuclear Power in Egypt." Available at: world-nuclear.org/information-library/country-profiles/countries-a-f/egypt.aspx

WNA (World Nuclear Association). (2021d). "Nuclear Power in Jordan." Available at: www.world-nuclear.org/information-library/country-profiles/countries-g-n/jordan.aspx

WNA (World Nuclear Association). (2021e). "Emerging Nuclear Energy Countries." Available at: world-nuclear.org/information-library/country-profiles/others/emerging-nuclear-energy-countries.aspx

WNN (World Nuclear News). (2017). "CAP1400 Reactor Vessel Passes Pressure Tests." Available at: www.world-nuclear-news.org/NN-CAP1400-reactor-vessel-passes-pressure-tests-2203174.html

WNN (World Nuclear News). (2020) CGN's Hualong One Design Certified for European Use." Available at: world-nuclear-news.org/Articles/CGNs-Hualong-One-design-certified-for-European-use

10

CHINA AND REGIONAL STABILITY IN THE MIDDLE EAST

Economics, Engagement, and Great Power Rivalry

Robert Mason

Introduction

China's contemporary foreign policy is a function of its history and traditions, ideology, leadership, political system, and modernisation (Huwaidin, 2002: 26). A key historic aspect has been the Opium War of 1840–1842 and the "national rejuvenation" which followed to ensure China would no longer be vulnerable to attack (Niblock, 2020: 4). This element was articulated by the National People's Congress of the People's Republic of China as recently as 2012 (National People's Congress of the People's Republic of China, 2012). China's territorial sovereignty, security, and development are paramount in its global strategy. It is notable that the most substantial Chinese military cooperation has so far been confined to North Korea, Pakistan, and members of the Shanghai Cooperation Organisation (SCO), but even these belie the overall focus on the Chinese homeland as articulated in a 2015 White Paper (Scobell, 2018: 21). As will be discussed in the context of China's Belt and Road Initiative (BRI), the Middle East represents an important node of Chinese national interest, especially in terms of energy security, investments, and counterterrorism cooperation. To support the BRI, China seeks to create a global community with a shared future, with emphasis on working with the United Nations (Niblock, 2020: 5).

China's modern engagement with the world has coincided with a period of communist rule from 1949. Since the Bandung Conference of 1955, China has helped to set the objectives of Asian-African cooperation spanning political, economic, and cultural spheres as well as opposition to colonialism or neo-colonialism, which has morphed into broader south-south cooperation. China promotes socialism with Chinese characteristics (the "China Model"), but also respects alternative development models and opposes interference in the internal affairs of other states.

DOI: 10.4324/9781003048404-12

However, China has been accused of deploying sharp power through manipulative diplomatic practices designed to influence or undermine a target country, evident in Australia, Hungary, and Zambia. European states have already started to push back against what they see as predatory trade policies, attempts to dominate key industries, and suppress criticism of its domestic human rights situation (Brands and Sullivan, 2020). China has also been accused of "coercive environmentalism" by causing negative environmental impacts, high emissions development, and sidelining communities (Shepherd, Zhou, and Manson, 2020). While there is evidence of possible overreach in developing countries, accusations of Chinese debt owed in places such as the Sri Lankan port of Hambantota have been rebuffed on the basis that China has restructured loans and never seized an asset from any country (Brautigam and Rithmire, 2021).

China's Middle East policy takes place in the context of chronic regional instability, caused by, among other issues, the unresolved Israel-Palestine conflict; weak, failed, and failing states that have been penetrated by sub-national and trans-national forces, politically motivated violence; human rights abuses; and nuclear proliferation issues. Political contestation, sectarian mobilisation, and external influence have been particularly pronounced in the region since 1979. Saudi Arabia and Iran have vied for influence, often through leveraging local sectarian affiliation and links to non-state actors, notably in Lebanon, Palestine, Bahrain, Iraq, Syria, and Yemen. In the Maghreb, Libya has experienced foreign power intervention led by NATO, and then linked to fresh antagonisms between Turkey, the UAE, and Egypt in the Eastern Mediterranean. Foremost, the Arab uprisings highlighted economic and political conditions as well as social justice as being key to future development of the region. China avoids taking sides and has managed, successfully so far, to balance its affairs with all major parties and has engaged in positive dialogue through the League of Arab States.

It is argued in this chapter that the greatest impact China has on the Middle East region is, first, through Beijing's ability to help meet the region's economic development and diversification needs. Second, how China's non-intervention and security relations influence human security in each state. Third, how China's evolving relations with the USA could significantly impact the region, especially whether and how the "China Model" might usurp the "Washington Consensus". The following sections explore these issues in more detail, with concluding remarks assessing its overall engagement.

China's Developmental Approach Towards the Middle East

The source of China's soft power influence in the Middle East is centuries old and there are suggestions that China-Iran political contacts might date back to the pre-imperial Chinese era. China's developmental approach is partly a consequence of China's integration into global markets from the 1980s and a policy of "going outside" (*Zou Chuqu*) from 1999. In 2001, China acceded to the World Trade Organization (WTO) and at the same time implemented the 10th Five-Year plan (2001–2005) which encouraged Chinese companies to invest abroad. Foreign companies were also attracted to many industries in China through liberalised laws. Trade has thus come before substantial political engagement in the Middle East, which stems from China's mercantilist roots. This has evolved in the 2000s. Wang Shijie was the first Chinese envoy to the Middle East from 2002, and the China-Arab States Cooperation Forum was established in 2004. The forum did not challenge well-established bilateral links with other external actors and is unlikely to until there is a revised or consolidated Middle East and North Africa (MENA) regional order

(Burton, 2020a). Sun Bigan became the second Chinese envoy to the Middle East in 2006, followed by Wu Sike in 2009, Gong Xiaosheng in 2014, and Zhai Jun in 2019. There has been some attempt at mediation with other international powers in conflicts including the Israel-Palestine conflict and the Yemen war (Horesh and Ehteshami, 2018: 5).

The form of Chinese foreign policy changed when Xi Jinping became president in 2013. China has become more assertive through its Striving for Achievement (*fenfayouwei*) policy. The old Silk Road which ran across Asia to Europe has experienced a renaissance and, together with the Maritime Silk Road (MSR), now forms the BRI which is part of China's rebalancing strategy from its previously Asia-centric focus. The BRI was launched by President Xi Jinping in September and October 2013 and has a planned completion date of 2049. It is at the centre of China's re-engagement in the Middle East.

In 2014, Xi Jinping announced a 1 (energy) + 2 (construction and infrastructure, trade and investment) + 3 (nuclear energy, aerospace, and new energy) framework for China Arab cooperation (Qian and Fulton, 2017: 18). He also encouraged economic cooperation be expanded from $240 billion in 2013 to reach $600 billion by 2023 (Jinping, 2014). Policy coordination, connectivity of infrastructure, unimpeded trade, financial integration, and people-to-people bonds became the touchstones of the 2015 Vision and Actions on Jointly Building the Silk Road Economic Belt and the 21st Century Maritime Silk Road. The Arab Policy Paper, launched in 2016, which coincided with President Xi Jinping's trip to the Middle East, was clear on strengthening relations and expanding economic cooperation, but also detailed support for the Middle East Peace Process and the establishment of a Palestinian state with full sovereignty, based on 1967 borders, and with East Jerusalem as its capital (Scobell, 2018: 18).

China-Middle East trade jumped 600 per cent in the decade to 2014 to stand at $230 billion (ibid.: 13–14), and then reached almost $245 billion by 2020 (Elnaggar, 2020). China overtook the USA to become the largest source of foreign investment in the Middle East in 2016. Most projects, 75 per cent, awarded to Chinese contractors between 2000 and 2017, came from Iran, Iraq, Algeria, Saudi Arabia, and the UAE (MEED, 2018). China remains the largest trading partner of 11 MENA states (Lons et al., 2019). The Gulf Cooperation Council (GCC) ranks as China's sixth largest export destination and fifth largest import destination (Qian and Fulton, 2017: 14). Relations are based on securing energy supplies but the GCC states also rely on Chinese trade (especially industrial products, such as machinery and electronics) and investment. To confirm Chinese interest in priority states, it has concluded Comprehensive Strategic Partnerships with Algeria (2014), Egypt (2014), Saudi Arabia (2016), Iran (2016), and the UAE (2018). Commercial activity between China and the GCC states rose from less than $10 billion in 2000 to almost $115 billion in 2016 (Young, 2018). According to the Ministry of Foreign Affairs of the People's Republic of China (2014) and the GCC, the ultimate aim is to build political relations up to the point of concluding a Free Trade Area (FTA), reflecting the lower barriers that already exist among WTO members. The China-GCC Strategic Dialogues were established in 2010 as "conducive to deepening mutual trust, expanding beneficial cooperation, and promoting bilateral consultation and coordination in international organizations" (Qian and Fulton, 2017: 16).

During King Salman's visit to Beijing in 2017, Saudi Arabia and China signed an MoU which could be worth $65 billion in joint ventures. While the USA sees this as problematic, the MENA states point to US policy failures in places such as Egypt, Syria, and Iraq, a lack of dependability following the attacks on Saudi oil installations in 2019, and pressure on human rights and arms control, as good reasons to pursue or deepen relations with China. The UAE has attracted $2.3 billion in Chinese loans between 2016 and 2018, including the expansion of Dubai International Airport and Al Maktoum Airport (Young, 2018). But this belies a much higher figure of $53 billion of trade with the UAE in 2018 (Murphy, 2019), which was expected to have reached $70 billion by 2020 (HSBC, 2022), due to it being an entrepôt for Chinese access to overseas markets. Israel represents a valued commercial relationship in the high-tech sector and government-to-government relations on security and counterterrorism concerns. Yet, China has backed anti-Israeli resolutions at the UN with a view to its Gulf and wider Arab League partnerships. China has invested in Egypt's new capital city and is building a monorail and Egypt's first high-speed railway. The stability of Egypt is vital to the success of the BRI since it controls the Suez Canal, an essential link to Europe. There will also be a railway in the UAE where Huawei is already present. Both China and rentier states such as the UAE seek a stable and prosperous environment in which to develop, reach, and consolidate middle or global power status. Indeed, their close relationship and focus are evident in the Asian Infrastructure Investment Bank (AAIB, 2020) meeting and the Dubai Expo, both held in Dubai in 2021.

Beyond bilateral trade, investment, technology, security, and counterterrorism, the Comprehensive Strategic Partnerships also call for more tourism, part of people-to-people connections. Numbers of Chinese tourists in Egypt rose from 135,000 in 2015 to 450,000 in 2018 (Elnaggar, 2020). China has funded at least 13 Confucius Institutes in the Middle East and the Egyptian Chinese University, while numbers of Arab students studying at Chinese universities increased by 26 per cent from 2014 to 2017 and numbers of Chinese students studying in Arab universities increased by 21 per cent in the same period (Sawahel, 2018). President Trump's Executive Order 13769, which extended a travel ban on people entering the USA from seven Muslim-majority countries, including: Iran, Libya, Somalia, Syria, and Yemen in the Middle East, may have encouraged students to pick China over the USA before the ban was repealed by President Biden in January 2021. The increasing number of education partnerships and Chinese language teaching in the region are also likely to reinforce such linkages.

There were reports in 2020 of increased Chinese investments in Iran expected to amount to $400 billion (Fassihi and Myers, 2020), which, along with military cooperation, such as military exercises carried out with Russia and China in 2021 (Reuters, 2021), suggest that China is building a new ally in the region. More likely, as Alterman (2019) notes, is that Iran represents a distressed asset in the region, and its non-alignment with the USA gives China increased opportunity through trade routes that are more difficult to disrupt. In fact, in March 2020, Iran had only received $115 million in declared oil payments from China (Batmanghelidj, 2020) and bilateral trade was at a ten-year low in 2019 (Figueroa, 2020). However, as global prices rise in 2021, China's purchase of discounted Iranian oil (due to US sanctions) is bouncing back (Bloomberg News, 2021).

There are several reasons why China would want to work more closely with Iran, Pakistan, Turkey, and Azerbaijan in particular. Working with these states helps to isolate India, counterbalance close US defence relations with many major Arab states – the combined populations would be comparable – and these states represent greater levels of economic development and technical training than is generally the case in the Arab world. Like Iran, Pakistan is economically vulnerable and has close ties to China through the China - Pakistan Economic Corridor (CPEC). Turkey has looked East in recent years driven by geopolitical and economic considerations such as stalled EU membership negotiations and tensions with the USA and EU over its purchase of the S-400 surface-to-air defence system (delivery began in July 2019), increasingly authoritarian governance, the rule of law and lack of civil liberties, especially since the July 2016 coup attempt. But Turkey was the only MENA state to criticise Beijing in 2009 over its treatment of the Uyghurs. Security ties were expanded in 2010 when the People's Liberation Army (PLA) participated in "Anatolian Eagle" military exercises and Turkey agreed to buy an air defence system from China in 2013 before pressure from other NATO members led it to cancel that plan in 2015 (Scobell, 2018: 27). Turkish importers paid for Chinese goods in RMB in 2020 and President Erdogan has remained silent on fresh allegations of China's actions against the Uyghurs in 2021 (Jones, 2021).

Beijing has strategic cooperation with Turkey and strategic partnerships with Qatar, Jordan, Iraq, Morocco, Sudan, Djibouti, Oman, and Kuwait which are blossoming in terms of trade and investment. The stakes are perhaps greatest for the Iraqi government whose reconstruction and recovery plan hinges on expanding the oil industry. Revenue has increased to more than $850 billion in the period 2003–2018 (IMF, 2019), and China is Iraq's top trading partner, developing infrastructure projects, such as power plants, cement factories, and water treatment facilities. China's risk-taking in Iraq remains susceptible to many vicissitudes, including domestic and regional insecurity, which could cause Beijing to withdraw from some valued economic activities in an extreme case.

China has not only consumed more than 70 per cent of Oman's total crude exports since 2014, but has also bought a 49 per cent stake in the Oman Electricity Transmission Company via the State Grid Corporation of China in December 2019 (Mogielnicki, 2020). China is not without competitors in Oman. Up to the time of writing, Oman had received more GCC state investment than that from China (Young, 2020). For semi-rentier states such as Oman, which have suffered from declining oil revenues since the 2014 crash, and for non-rentier or semi-rentier states whose tourism or other sectors have been substantially affected by Covid-19, China will remain an important investor.

China's narrative of "peace with development" fits well in the Middle East where autocrats seek to reorganise their strategies of governance in new global, regional, and domestic circumstances that undermine the promotion of democracy (Heydemann, 2007). They seek to diversify international links, control communications technology, and capture the benefits of selective economic reforms. As Kamrava argues, the state-led China model (combining social, economic. and political resources) may be appealing to authoritarian MENA states, but deep structural challenges and incongruities in their political economies will continue to create great uncertainties as to the successful transfer of this approach (Kamrava, 2018: 59–60).

For the MENA states, the BRI will be what they make of it. According to the U.S. Energy Information Administration (2018), China surpassed the USA as the world's largest oil importer in 2017, making it a vital market for the oil-rich Gulf states. China is set to overtake the US economy as the world's largest economy by 2028 (BBC News, 2020), making it more important for trade and investment more generally. It also aims to be carbon-neutral by 2060 (Regan, 2020). This raises the prospect of relatively rapid shifts into renewable energy on which it leads and therefore a limited window of opportunity for some MENA states, notably in the Gulf, to leverage their co-dependent relations with Beijing to attract increased inward investment in to their strategic industries.

The BRI, plus additional humanitarian aid, raises the prospect that China will provide financing to the Middle East beyond the levels of the Marshall Plan aid for Europe in

1948. However, as Mills (2008: 80–83) notes, the lessons learnt from the Marshall Plan include:

- aid given in consultation with the countries receiving it;
- aid is given regionally and not to favoured nations;
- aid is given with long-term interests of the countries receiving it in mind;
- aid is equal to the task;
- aid cannot be open-ended.

The BRI appears to deviate on favouring some nations over others, the amount of aid versus loans and other investments, and possibly on the long-term interests of countries, given the narrow interests of the MENA ruling elite. Although this last point is debatable, it raises the ongoing issue of China engaging with illiberal regimes which often challenge the multifarious aspects of human security.

Restrained Militarisation, Non-Intervention, and Security

Non-intervention has been a hallmark of Chinese foreign policy, and yet this was not always the case. China was active in supporting nationalist movements in Algeria, Palestine, and Eritrea in the 1960s (Burton, 2020b). Beijing had good relations with South Yemen in the early 1970s, but Beijing's interests were subordinated to the USSR and later, Saudi Arabia and the West (Halliday, 1985: 46). By the 1980s, China was arming both sides of the Iran-Iraq War. Ultimately, China was never able to usurp significant geo-strategic space in the Middle East from either the United States or the Soviet Union during the Cold War (Horesh and Ehteshami, 2018: 2–3). Instead, China began to prioritise diplomatic relations. This has been aided by a lack of "historical baggage". For example, China was absent from the British and French attempts to extend influence in the Middle East through such treaties as Sykes-Picot or through the Suez Crisis. US military adventurism in Afghanistan, and particularly the 2003 US-led intervention in Iraq, have done untold damage to US standing in the region and to liberal foreign policy and interventionism more broadly. China learnt early on, from being dragged into conflicts by junior clients North Korea and North Vietnam, the necessity of staying out of conflicts.

Beijing's discourse favours long-term solutions based on its Five Principles of Peaceful Coexistence and it continues to emphasise the links between economic development and reductions in conflict. China has been involved in pragmatic steps to protect civilians in armed conflict under UN Security Council authorisation. This has notably been the case in Mali and South Sudan, where Beijing has generally supported UN Security Council resolutions and introduced combat troops into force contingents, requiring consideration of how they can protect women and children (Foot, 2020: 100). It has been part of UN peacekeeping operations in the Golan Heights since 1990. In 2015, China changed its anti-terror law to allow the People's Liberation Army (PLA) to take part in anti-terror missions abroad, implicitly targeting ISIS as a national and energy security threat, thereby contributing to its international status (Chaziza, 2016: 26). However, proposed Chinese counterterrorism cooperation against ISIS has been used to deflect an enhanced local counterterrorism agenda against the East Turkistan Islamic Movement (ETIM) in Xinjiang, highlighting links between internal and external security. The USA removed the ETIM from its terrorist list in December 2020 (Kashagarian, 2020).

Facing western state agendas for regime change in the UN Security Council, China's behaviour is said to be inconsistent with rationalist arguments which premise its calculations based on material interests. Instead, Fung notes that China's dual status as a great power and member of the Global South means it must negotiate and contest within peer groups, such as the G77 (a coalition of 134 developing countries), the Shanghai Cooperation Organisation (SCO), the BRI, and more recently the UN Human Rights Council, where there may be members who favour humanitarian intervention (Fung, 2019: 6). China now has a much more diversified position on intervention, including Responsibility to Protect (R2P), an emergent international norm that was explicitly decided upon in the World Summit Outcome Document (WSOD) of September 2005, which attracted the largest gathering at UN headquarters of heads of state and government. They agreed that each state has the responsibility to protect populations from genocide, war crimes, ethnic cleansing, and crimes against humanity (the so-called four crimes) (Foot, 2020: 132). China has thus sought to shape rather than reject R2P entirely, an approach that is being replicated in forums of global governance more broadly. Working with other interested state parties, it has added weight behind a more cautious approach to how the norm might be used and is yet to apply the norm to its own territory (Foot, 2001).

Subsequently, China acquiesced to the International Criminal Court's (ICC) referral for Sudan in 2005, supported intervention in Darfur through a Chapter VII authority for a UN peace operation and supported an ICC referral and acquiesced to a no-fly zone in Libya in 2011. But China was outraged by regime change in Libya in October 2011, and consistently condemned the NATO bombing campaign. It has stopped UN-sanctioned intervention in the Syria crisis through repeated vetoes since 2011 (seven times as of September 2019); an extremely unusual move, given it has only used its veto on six occasions between 1971, when it became a UN Security Council member, and 2009 (Foot, 2020: 164). It could be argued that more coordination between western states and China in the UN Security Council may result in a return to a more cooperative era of pre-2011, although the likelihood of further turmoil in the MENA region and the western response to it might preclude this in the short to medium term.

China has been able to mitigate the negative effects of its position on Syria from some Gulf states through an incremental and non-hegemonic regional approach (Mansour, 2019). It has also shown a good citizen approach by promoting the idea of rapid reconstruction in Syria, first, through some small infrastructure projects, in contrast to western state insistence on reconstruction and development being tied to political transition arrangements. China's main short-term interest in Syria is to prevent East Turkestan jihadists fighting there and detect any Uyghur Muslim militants attempting to return to Xinjiang (Yaari, 2019). The UK Foreign, Commonwealth and Development Office (2020) has so far outspent China on humanitarian aid in Syria, standing at £3.2 billion from 2012 to 2020 compared to China's 800 million yuan (about £91 million from June 2019 exchange rates) according to the Syrian Arab News Agency, 2019). However, the UK cut aid by more than half in 2021 to reach £91 million (Loft and Brien, 2022) and Chinese aid does not include a 2017 Chinese pledge to invest $2 billion in Syrian industry and an unknown part of $90 million earmarked for humanitarian aid to Yemen, Lebanon, Jordan, and Syria, part of $23 billion in loans and aid for the Arab region as a whole (Burton, 2018). In October 2018, China delivered 800 electrical power transformers to Lattakia (Syrian Arab News Agency, 2018) and in 2020 Huawei negotiated an agreement to set up a broadband network in Syria (Harris, 2017). China National Petroleum Corporation continues to hold major stakes in the Syrian Petroleum Company and Al Furat Petroleum. The head of Syria's Planning and International Cooperation Commission signed a memorandum of understanding with the Chinese ambassador to Syria in January 2022, formerly bringing Syria into the orbit of China's BRI (COAR, 2022). Nevertheless, there is uncertainty as to whether China will significantly ramp up trade and investments as long as geopolitical instability remains. Changing donor priorities, including shifting engagements across the region and domestic economic imperatives, make calculations surrounding aid and development spending complex and dynamic.

China's engagement in Yemen has similarly integrated aid and development objectives to the benefit of Chinese industry and energy imports. In 2012, the China National Corporation for Overseas Economic Cooperation (CCOEC) signed a deal to build three natural gas-fired power plants in Yemen. In 2013, before Saudi-led coalition air strikes in Yemen, China had been intent on supporting Yemen's electricity, oil, and gas sectors including a $508 million soft loan to expand container ports in Aden and Mocha, which are useful alternatives to dominant ports such as Jebel Ali in the UAE (Chang, 2018). By 2014, Sinopec was producing 20,000 barrels of oil per day before being forced out of the country by the conflict (Rakhmat, 2014). In July 2017, China delivered humanitarian aid to Aden worth $22.5 million, including food and medicine (Ramani, 2017). Support for the Hadi government has been part of China's attempts to stabilise a united Yemen, strengthen security relations with Saudi Arabia (including drone production), secure its military base in Djibouti, and its shipping lanes through Bab el Mandeb to Europe, and advance its mediation prospects and therefore its international status. China has supported regional and international initiatives, including the GCC initiative, the National Dialogue Conference and the UN-led peace talks (Chang, 2018). It has also developed some contact with the Houthis through China's former ambassador to Yemen, Tian Qi, for example (Tekingunduz, 2019). The World Food Programme (n.d.) puts 16 million Yemenis as food-insecure and 24.3 million in need of humanitarian assistance. China sent 1200 metric tonnes of rice to Yemen in March and again in May 2019 (Xinhua, 2019).

China sees the Middle East as a "market" so doesn't yet need military bases to influence governments, although it is interested in protecting its commercial interests (Sun, 2018: 85). China's cooperation agreements also include military, counterterrorism, policing, and non-traditional concerns, such as anti-piracy (Marks, 2020). China has developed a base in Djibouti and is developing a new port area in Gwadar, Pakistan, based on both a security and economic rationale, and is planning to establish a military presence in the port at Duqm, Oman. China has a history of supporting UN peacekeeping operations, counter-piracy operations, participation in UN humanitarian assistance, disaster relief, and delivering aid. It has thus been described by Sun and Zoubir as a "latent power" (Sun and Zoubir, 2020). Since China has not so far been intent on hegemony in the Middle East, it has little need to develop a "string of pearls" to match military bases opened by others, but India fears China's reach will soon extend beyond East Africa. Both states are launching their blue water navies to project force across the deep Indian and Pacific Oceans. There have been drawbacks for China not developing more military bases, as Sun notes, concerning China's search for Malaysian Airlines Flight 370 in 2014 which it had to conduct from home bases. China was forced to evacuate more than 35,000 nationals from Libya in 12 days between February and March 2011, testing its crisis management capacity (Zerba, 2014). It was forced to do the same again in 2014 (Sun, 2018: 84–85).

The lack of overt alliances along with political neutrality have put China in a strong position in the Middle East. The Arab uprisings have underlined this. A return to great power is not necessarily the same thing as hegemony but the question remains whether China will be a benign influence on human security or complicit in repression. For example, Beijing is said to be extending its "Serbia Model" to the Gulf, where artificial intelligence (AI) technology exports could be worth $320 billion by 2030 (Robinson, 2020). The model includes so-called "Safe and Smart Cities" which use extensive tracking and surveillance for counterterrorism and urban safety concerns, in addition to unmanned aerial vehicles, some of which could be armed using AI (ibid.).

China still lags behind the USA, France, Russia, and the UK in terms of arms sales to the Middle East (Congressional Research Service, 2020: 3). Although the Biden administration, as of early 2021, temporarily halted arms sales to Saudi Arabia due to the conflict in Yemen, which could open the way for more Chinese and Russian arms sales. CENTCOM Commander General Kenneth McKenzie said in June 2020 that "We don't want [US partners in the Middle East] turning to China, we don't want them turning to Russia to buy those systems" (ibid.: 3). Beijing would certainly like to sell more missiles, tanks, and fighter jets, and some investments in remote sensing could have military applications.

Unlike Japan, which has only recently relaunched its civil nuclear energy plans, China is actively promoting the development of its peaceful use and could assume global leadership of nuclear technology development, nuclear safety, and non-proliferation by 2030 (Hibbs, 2018: 1). It is working with states such as Saudi Arabia to expand its civil nuclear power industry (Graham-Harrison, Kirchgaessner, and Borger, 2020). But without the same 123 "gold standard" agreement that addressed nuclear proliferation and safety concerns about the new Emirati civil nuclear programme, China could end up inadvertently contributing to the so-called "tipping point" towards nuclear proliferation in the Middle East.

Great Power Rivalry

US-China relations went from cooperation in 2003 in important areas such as counter-terrorism and denuclearisation on the Korean peninsula to more tense bilateral relations from 2009 to 2019. This included 'strategic distrust' from 2009 to 2012, an inability to find a new model to manage great power relations from 2013 to 2016, and the USA defining China as a strategic adversary since 2017 (Jisi and Ran, 2019). This prolonged period of poor relations has led some analysts to predict confrontation in the future. However, scholars such as Horesh and Lim (2018) note that the long-term challenge to American hegemony will not be military, but rather focus on economics or the "China Model".

China's status as a rising power has focused US attention on its foreign policy and raised questions about its motivations, impacts, and possible pathways to global dominance (Brands and Sullivan, 2020). But as Womack (2016) notes, confining analysis along the conceptual lines of the "Thucydides Trap", i.e., the apparent tendency towards war when an emerging power threatens to displace an existing power as the international hegemon, is redundant due to the continuing asymmetry of their respective sources of power. The USA derives much of its power from wealth and technology versus China's which is based more on population and production, and there is a broader diffusion of international power that favours some middle-income countries (ibid.: 1464). The chances of conflict spill-over in the Gulf are limited as China receives 40 per cent of its oil and gas from the Gulf states (Le Miere, 2020) and the USA maintains a formidable military presence there. Furthermore, in the short term at least, a "brittle but bold" China in the MENA region may be less consequential to regional and international security than an assertive China in a polarised MENA state system which Russia, India, and Japan may find harder to accommodate (Ehteshami, 2018: 395).

President Trump's legacy of uneven, divisive, and transactional policies which included escalating tensions with Iran, contributing to a grave humanitarian situation in Yemen, and encouraging the isolation of Qatar, has further undermined US credibility in the region. His support for MENA authoritarian leaders and refusal to overtly champion democratisation, human rights, and the rule of law, have emboldened state repression and human insecurity, undermined allies such as Canada, and left civil society weaker. While political conditionality could favour China, this has not been borne out by the empirical evidence. At the onset of the Biden administration in 2021, rentier states such as Saudi Arabia and the UAE with large and growing economic relations with China were quick to indicate policy U-turns on Qatar and Iran. Thus, the USA continues to shape, including through strategic arms exports and security relationships, the environment in which Middle East-Asia relations develop.

China's hitherto lack of political and military baggage in the region and its attempts to enhance its international image through health diplomacy during the Covid-19 pandemic stood initially in contrast to a lack of global US health diplomacy. China has engaged in giving health advice to Saudi Arabia, donated large amounts of personal protective equipment (PPE), and offered to set up a field hospital in Kuwait (Fulton, 2020). Covid-19 vaccines are important too, especially to states such as Bahrain and the UAE, who are relying on an effective China vaccine to remain open, attract tourists, and support Chinese aspirations to lead in the global rollout of a vaccine (*The Economist*, 2021). Morocco will initially be relying on a Sinopharm vaccine (Media24, 2020). However, there is evidence that the USA will catch up on health diplomacy to stabilise societies and restart economies in places such as Jordan, Tunisia, and Morocco (Ferguson, 2021). Without further support, once Covid-19 is over, these societies still remain susceptible to pressures associated with the Arab uprisings.

Conclusion

China is certainly an important player in the region for a number of reasons:

- it is a leader in the rollout of a global Covid-19 vaccine;
- the BRI is greater in size and geographical breadth than the Marshall Plan;
- Beijing lacks recent political and military baggage and therefore the MENA states' trust is higher.

China has lower arms sales to the Middle East than the USA and some European states but still sells and manufactures some strategic arms. But China has, overall, a rather neutral impact on stability and security, broadly defined, in the Middle East. This is for three main reasons: First, China's rapidly increasing trade and investment relations, encapsulated in the BRI and supplemented by health diplomacy, have the potential to help lift millions out of poverty, improve health conditions, and could address a number of points raised by the Arab uprisings. But this is tempered by uneven engagement, a lack of adaptability of China's development model or the "Beijing Consensus" to local conditions and decision-making, and openness to direction from authoritarian MENA leaders often with elite survival rather than national development in mind. Second, Chinese arms to the Middle East remain relatively low, but this is again tempered by contentious strategic security-related exports and assistance (especially AI-related), and the potential to significantly ramp up exports pending the right geopolitical conditions. Third, NATO's intervention in Libya and China's non-interventionist approach have barred UN Security Council cooperation, notably on Syria and Yemen and possibly on future conflicts, favouring economic reconstruction over political transition, although the potential for cooperation still exists. None of these points are particularly clear-cut, and are made more complex by China's evolving domestic policies, East Asian and Middle Eastern security complexes. They are also challenged by, predominantly, US, Russian, and the emerging group of ten leading democracies, the D-10 (South Korea, India, and Australia, plus the G7 states of the USA, Italy, France, Japan, Germany, Canada, and the UK) or Quad (India, Australia, the USA, and Japan) in the Indian Ocean.

Increasing trade certainly indicates that transformative potential exists with partners in the MENA region, but as this chapter shows, those relations continue to favour rentier states within the confines of China's transition to become carbon-neutral by 2060. Questions remain over how growing trade and investment with China might fuel the "Gulfisation" – projecting ideology and influence – or the growing relative autonomy of some Gulf states as major actors in regional politics, and how non-rentier states might modify their political economies to maximise their exposure to, and benefit from, the BRI.

The onus is on China and other international actors to move past distrust to discover a new *modus vivendi* for constructive diplomatic engagement and more coordinated development outcomes in the Middle East and elsewhere. The agenda should be necessarily broad, including stricter arms control and other regional security mechanisms, as well as an ambitious agreement addressing civil nuclear programmes and safety concerns. China's approach is perhaps less counterproductive than the actions of other members of the international community which have higher aid budgets but also higher arms sales to the region, or who have actively contributed to conflict and thereby undermined critical aid, investment and developmental opportunities.

References

AIIB (Asian Infrastructure Investment Bank). (2020). "AIIB to Hold its First Annual Meeting in the Middle East in the UAE", July 28. Available at: www.aiib.org/en/news-events/news/2020/AIIB-to-Hold-its-First-Annual-Meeting-in-the-Middle-East-in-the-UAE.html

Alterman, J. (2019). "China's Middle East Model", Center for Strategic and International Studies, May 23. Available at: www.csis.org/analysis/chinas-middle-east-model

Batmanghelidj, E. (2020). "Iran Can No Longer Rely on Trade with China", Bloomberg Opinion, April 27. Available at: www.bloomberg.com/opinion/articles/2020-04-27/iran-can-no-lon ger-rely-on-trade-with-china

BBC News. (2018). "China's Xi Allowed to Remain 'President for Life' as Term Limits Removed", March 11. Available at: www.bbc.com/news/world-asia-china-43361276

BBC News. (2020). "Chinese Economy to Overtake US 'by 2028' Due to Covid", December 26. Available at: www.bbc.com/news/world-asia-china-55454146

Bloomberg News. (2021). "China Buying Record Volumes of Iran's Sanction-Discounted Crude", *World Oil*, March 11. Available at: www.worldoil.com/news/2021/3/11/china-buying-record-volumes-of-iran-s-sanction-discounted-crude

Brands, H. and Sullivan, J. (2020). "China Has Two Paths to Global Domination", *Foreign Policy*, May 22. Available at: https://carnegieendowment.org/2020/05/22/china-has-two-paths-to-glo bal-domination-pub-81908

Brautigam, D. and Rithmire, M. (2021). "The Chinese 'Debt Trap' is a Myth", *The Atlantic*, February 6. Available at: www.theatlantic.com/international/archive/2021/02/china-debt-trap-diplomacy/617953/

Burton, G. (2018). "China and the Reconstruction of Syria", *The Diplomat*, July 28. Available at: https://thediplomat.com/2018/07/china-and-the-reconstruction-of-syria/

Burton, G. (2020a). "China and Regionalism in the Middle East" in M. Telo and Y. Feng (eds), *China and the EU in the Era of Regional and Interregional Cooperation*. Bern: Peter Lang.

Burton, G. (2020b). *China and Middle East Conflicts: Responding to War and Rivalry from the Cold War to the Present*. Abingdon: Routledge.

Chang, I-W. (2018). "China and Yemen's Forgotten War", United States Institute of Peace, Peace Brief 241, January 1. Available at: www.jstor.org/stable/resrep20161?seq=1#metadata_info_t ab_contents

Chaziza, M. (2016). "China's Middle East Policy: The ISIS Factor", *Middle East Policy*, 23(1). Available at: https://mepc.org/journal/chinas-middle-east-policy-isis-factor

COAR. (2022). "China in Syria: Aid and Trade Now, Influence and Industry Later", July 11. Available at: https://coar-global.org/2022/07/11/china-in-syria-aid-and-trade-now-influence-and-industry-later/

Congressional Research Service. (2020). "Arms Sales in the Middle East: Trends and Analytical Perspectives for U.S. Policy", CRS Report for Congress, November 23. Available at: https://fas. org/sgp/crs/mideast/R44984.pdf

Ehteshami, A. (2018). "Gold at the End of the Rainbow? The BRI and the Middle East", *Global Policy*, 9(3): 387–397. https://doi.org/10.1111/1758-5899.12552.

Elnaggar, Y. (2020). "China's Growing Role in the Middle East", January 9. Available at: www.mei. edu/publications/chinas-growing-role-middle-east

Fassihi, F. and Myers, S. (2020). "Defying U.S., China and Iran Near Trade and Military Partnership", New York Times, November 30. Available at: www.nytimes.com/2020/07/11/ world/asia/china-iran-trade-military-deal.html

Ferguson, H. (2021). "Biden Can Support Recovery in the Middle East While Building a Foreign Policy for the Middle Class". Wilson Center. July 6. Available at: www.wilsoncenter.org/article/ biden-can-support-recovery-middle-east-while-building-foreign-policy-middle-class

Figueroa, B. (2020). "A '$400 Billion' China-Iran Deal? The View from History". *Jadaliyya*, October 14. Available at: www.jadaliyya.com/Details/41852

Foot, R. (2001). *Rights Beyond Borders: The Global Community and the Struggle over Human Rights in China*. Oxford: Oxford University Press.

Foot, R. (2020). *China, the UN, and Human Protection: Beliefs, Power, Image*. Oxford: Oxford University Press.

Foreign, Commonwealth and Development Office. (2020). "Syria Crisis Response Summary", December 7. Available at: https://assets.publishing.service.gov.uk/government/uploads/system/ uploads/attachment_data/file/944596/UK_Syria_Crisis_Response_Summary__07.12.2020___ FCDO_.pdf

Fulton, J. (2020). "China's Soft Power During the Coronavirus Is Winning Over the Gulf States", Atlantic Council MENA Source, April 16. Available at: www.atlanticcouncil.org/blogs/menasou rce/chinas-soft-power-during-the-coronavirus-is-winning-over-the-gulf-states/

Fung, C. (2019). *China and Intervention at the UN Security Council: Reconciling Status*. Oxford: Oxford University Press.

Graham-Harrison, E., Kirchgaessner, S. and Borger, J. (2020). "Revealed: Saudi Arabia May Have Enough Uranium Ore to Produce Nuclear Fuel", *The Guardian*, September 17. Available at: www.theguardian.com/world/2020/sep/17/revealed-saudi-arabia-may-have-enough-uran ium-ore-to-produce-nuclear-fuel

Halliday, F. (1985). "Aspects of South Yemen's Foreign Policy: 1967–1982", PhD thesis. Available at: https://core.ac.uk/download/pdf/9063236.pdf

Harris, S. (2017). "China Looks at Syria, Sees $$", *Daily Beast*, April 13. Available at: www.thedai lybeast.com/china-looks-at-syria-sees-dollardollardollar

Heydemann, S. (2007). "Upgrading Authoritarianism in the Arab World". The Saban Center for Middle East Policy at the Brookings Institution, Analysis Paper No. 13. Available at: www. brookings.edu/wp-content/uploads/2016/06/10arabworld.pdf

Hibbs, M. (2018). *The Future of Nuclear Power in China*. Washington, DC: Carnegie Endowment for International Peace.

Horesh, N. and Ehteshami, A. (2018). *How China's Rise Is Changing the Middle East*. Abingdon: Routledge.

Horesh, N. and Lim, K. (2018). *An East Asian Challenge to Western Neoliberalism: Critical Perspectives on the 'China Model'*. Abingdon: Routledge.

HSBC. (2022). "China-UAE Trade Corridor: New MoUs and Agreements to Boost Belt and Road Initiative", March 25. Available at: www.business.hsbc.ae/en-gb/ae/article/china-uae-trade-corridor.pdf

Huwaidin, M. (2002). *China's Relations with Arabia and the Gulf, 1949–1999*. Abingdon: Routledge.

IMF (International Monetary Fund). (2019). "Iraq: Selected Issues". IMF Country Report No. 19/249, July 2. Available at: www.imf.org/~/media/Files/Publications/CR/2019/1IRQEA2019 002.ashx

Jinping, X. (2014). "Promote the Silk Road Spirit, Strengthen China-Arab Cooperation", June 5, CPC Central Committee Bimonthly: Qiushi. Available at: http://en.qstheory.cn/2021-02/05/c_587438.htm

Jisi, W. and Ran, H. (2019). "From Cooperative Partnership to Strategic Competition: A Review of China-US Relations 2009–2019", *China International Strategy Review*, 1: 1–10.

Jones, D. (2021). "Turkish Opposition Challenges Erdogan Over Uighur Silence", *VOA News*, January 28. Available at: www.voanews.com/europe/turkish-opposition-challenge-erdogan-over-uighur-silence

Kamrava, M. (2018). "The China Model and the Middle East", in J. Reardon-Anderson (ed.), *The Red Star and the Crescent*. Oxford: Oxford University Press, pp. 59–83.

Kashagarian, A. (2020). "Uighur Diaspora Hails Removal of ETIM from US Terror List", VOA News, December 25. Available at: www.voanews.com/extremism-watch/uighur-diaspora-hails-removal-etim-us-terror-list

Le Miere, C. (2020). "Increasing Mutual Dependence in Sino-Gulf Relations is Changing the Strategic Landscape", Atlantic Council, May 11. Available at: www.atlanticcouncil.org/blogs/energysource/increasing-mutual-dependence-in-sino-gulf-relations-is-changing-the-strategic-landscape/#:~:text=Overall%2C%20the%20Gulf%20supplied%20more,plurality%20of%20China's%20oil%20imports

Loft, P. and Brien, P. (2022). "Reducing the UK's Aid Spend in 2021 and 2022", UK Parliament, December 13. Available at: https://commonslibrary.parliament.uk/research-briefings/cbp-9224/#:~:text=Almost%20all%20countries%20had%20large,%C2%A3156m%20to%20%C2%A396m

Lons, C. Fulton, J. Sun, D. and Al-Tamimi, N. (2019). "China's Great Game in the Middle East", European Council on Foreign Relations, October 21. Available at: https://ecfr.eu/publication/china_great_game_middle_east/

Mansour, I. (2019). "Treading with Caution: China's Multidimensional Interventions in the Gulf Region", *The China Quarterly*, 239: 656–678.

Marks, J. (2020). "China's Pursuit of a 'Strategic Fulcrum' in the Middle East", Middle East Institute, September 15. Available at: www.mei.edu/publications/chinas-pursuit-strategic-fulcrum-middle-east

Media24. (2020). "Le Maroc boucle ses préparatifs et attend l'autorisation du vaccin en Chine", December 3. Available at: www.medias24.com/le-maroc-boucle-ses-preparatifs-et-attend-l-autorisation-du-vaccin-en-chine-14774.html

MEED. (2018). "Report: The Future of Middle East Energy", September 20. Available at: www.meed.com/future-middle-east-energy/

Mills, N. (2008). "A Marshall Plan for the Middle East", *World Policy Journal*, 25(3): 79–83. www.jstor.org/stable/40210146

Ministry of Foreign Affairs of the People's Republic of China. (2014). "Third Round of China-Gulf Cooperation Council Strategic Dialogue Held in Beijing", January 17. Available at: www.fmprc.gov.cn/mfa_eng/zxxx_662805/t1121625.shtml

Mogielnicki, R. (2020). "How China Is Quietly Expanding its Economic Influence in the Gulf", *World Politics Review*, July 21. Available at: www.worldpoliticsreview.com/articles/28924/how-china-is-quietly-expanding-its-economic-influence-in-the-gulf

Murphy, D. (2019). "The UAE Signed a Massive, $3.4 Billion Deal with China – And That Isn't a Surprise", *CNBC*, April 29. Available at: www.cnbc.com/2019/04/29/china-uae-trade-deal-on-belt-and-road-isnt-a-surprise-wef-president.html

National People's Congress of the People's Republic of China (2012). "Achieving Rejuvenation Is the Dream of the Chinese People", November 29. Available at: www.npc.gov.cn/englishnpc/c23934/202006/32191c5bbdb04cbab6df01e5077d1c60.shtml

Niblock, T. (2020). "China and the Middle East: A Global Strategy Where the Middle East Has a Significant but Limited Place", *Asian Journal of Middle Eastern and Islamic Studies*, 14(4): 481–504. https://doi.org/10.1080/25765949.2020.1847855

Qian, X. and Fulton, J. (2017). "China-Gulf Economic Relationship Under the 'Belt and Road' Initiative", *Asian Journal of Middle Eastern and Islamic Studies*, 11(3): 12–21.

Rakhmat, M. (2014). "Why Is China Interested in a Volatile Yemen?", *The Diplomat*, June 4. Available at: https://thediplomat.com/2014/06/why-is-china-interested-in-a-volatile-yemen/

Ramani, S. (2017). "China's Role in the Yemen Crisis", *The Diplomat*, August 11. Available at: https://thediplomat.com/2017/08/chinas-role-in-the-yemen-crisis/

Regan. H. (2020). "China Will Become Carbon Neutral by 2060, Xi Jinping Says". *CNN*, September 23. Available at: https://edition.cnn.com/2020/09/22/china/xi-jinping-carbon-neutral-2060-intl-hnk/index.html

Reuters. (2021). "Russia, China, and Iran to Hold Joint Naval Drills in Indian Ocean Soon", February 8. Available at: www.reuters.com/article/russia-military-iran-china/russia-china-and-iran-to-hold-joint-naval-drills-in-indian-ocean-soon-ria-idUSKBN2A81Q8

Robinson, W. (2020). "The Rise of Chinese AI in the Gulf: A Renewal of China's 'Serbia Model'", Washington Institute for Near East Policy Fikra Forum, October 13. Available at: www.washingtoninstitute.org/policy-analysis/rise-chinese-ai-gulf-renewal-chinas-serbia-model

Sawahel, W. (2018). "Arab Chinese HE Cooperation on the Rise", *University World News*, September 8. Available at: www.universityworldnews.com/post.php?story=2018090806594431

Scobell, A. (2018). "China's Search for Security in the Greater Middle East", in J. Reardon-Anderson (ed.), *The Red Star and the Crescent*. Oxford: Oxford University Press, pp. 13–37.

Shepherd, C., Zhou, E. and Manson, K. (2020). "Climate Change: China's Coal Addiction Clashes with Xi's Bold Promise", Financial Times, November 3. Available at: www.ft.com/content/9656e36c-ba59-43e9-bf1c-c0f105813436

Sun, D. (2018). "China's Military Relations with the Middle East", in J Reardon-Anderson, (ed.). *The Red Star and the Crescent*, Oxford: Oxford University Press, pp. 83–103.

Sun, D. and Zoubir, Y. (2020). "Securing China's 'Latent Power': The Dragon's Anchorage in Djibouti", *Journal of Contemporary China*, November 26. Available at: https://doi.org/10.1080/10670564.2020.1852734

Syrian Arab News Agency. (2018). "800 Electrical Power Transformers Arrived in Lattakia as a Grant from China", October 10. Available at: www.sana.sy/en/?p=148524

Syrian Arab News Agency. (2019). "Foreign and Expatriates Ministry Receives a Chinese Grant", March 7. Available at: https://sana.sy/en/?p=160414

Tekingunduz, A. (2019). "What is China Doing in Yemen?", *TRT World*, December 13. Available at: www.trtworld.com/middle-east/what-is-china-doing-in-yemen-32183

The Economist. (2021). "Bahrain and the UAE Are Relying on a Chinese-Made Vaccine", January 16. Available at: www.economist.com/middle-east-and-africa/2021/01/13/bahrain-and-the-uae-are-relying-on-a-chinese-made-vaccine

U.S. Energy Information Administration. (2018). "China Surpassed the United States as the World's Largest Crude Oil Importer in 2017", December 31. Available at: www.eia.gov/todayinenergy/detail.php?id=37821#:~:text=China%20surpassed%20the%20United%20States%20in%20annual%20gross%20crude%20oil,other%20liquid%20fuels%20in%202013

Womack, B. (2016). "Asymmetric Parity: US-China Relations in a Multinodal World", *International Affairs*, 92(6): 1463–1480.

World Food Programme. (n.d.). "Yemen Emergency". Available at: www.wfp.org/emergencies/yemen-emergency

Xinhua. (2019). "Chinese Envoy Urges Int'l Community to Increase Humanitarian Assistance to Yemen", May 16. Available at: www.xinhuanet.com/english/2019-05/16/c_138061493.htm

Yaari, E. (2019). "China's Middle East Policy: Speak Softly and Wave a Large Purse", Washington Institute for Near East Policy, Policy Watch No. 3139, June 17. Available at: www.washingtoninstitute.org/policy-analysis/chinas-middle-east-policy-speak-softly-and-wave-large-purse

Young, K. (2018). "Master Developers: The New Sino-Arab Gulf Visions of Economic Development", *Lawfare*, December 21. Available at: www.lawfareblog.com/master-developers-new-sino-arab-gulf-visions-economic-development

Young, K. (2020). "China Is Not the Middle East's High Roller", July 2, American Enterprise Institute. Available at: www.aei.org/op-eds/china-is-not-the-middle-easts-high-roller/

Zerba, S. (2014). "China's Libya Evacuation Operation: A New Diplomatic Imperative - Overseas Citizen Protection", *Journal of Contemporary China*, 23(90): 1093–1112. Available at: https://doi.org/10.1080/10670564.2014.898900

11

THE ASIAN INFRASTRUCTURE INVESTMENT BANK (AIIB) IN THE MIDDLE EAST

Muhammad Zulfikar Rakhmat, M. Habib Pashya, and Gufron Gozali

Introduction

In addition to having the most populous population in the world, China is one of the most powerful economies in Asia and second in the world, behind the United States. Since the economic reforms under Deng Xiaoping in 1978, China's economy has boomed (Australian National University, 2018). According to a report by the World Bank, China's Gross Domestic Product (GDP) has almost increased by 10 percent on average and was able to save 800 million people from poverty (World Bank, n.d.). China's economic progress is a great achievement for Asian countries. After the end of World War II, Asian countries, such as Japan, South Korea, Taiwan, and China, tried to improve their economic conditions.

The role of China and its economic development has become increasingly influential in the global economic system since Xi Jinping was inaugurated as President of China (formerly Vice President in the Hu Jintao era) in 2013 through a vote held by the National People's Congress, obtaining 2,952 votes (McDonell, 2018). Under Xi Jinping's rule, China's economy has not only developed but has begun to be oriented into the international system, with the Belt and Road Initiative (BRI) in 2013.

Internationally, since the end of World War II, when the United States became the hegemon of the international economy, the system that came into effect was called the Washington Consensus (Lopes, 2012). As coined by British economist, John Williamson, that concept stressed maintaining fiscal discipline, reordering public spending priorities (from subsidies to health and education expenditures), reforming tax policy, allowing the market to determine interest rates, maintaining a competitive exchange rate, liberalizing trade, permitting inward foreign investment, privatizing state enterprises, deregulating barriers to entry and exit, and securing property rights. Hence, these elements were to create a free market economy as explained by Adam Smith in the eighteenth century.

However, the development of the Washington Consensus has recently faded since China has a strategy to meet national interests known as the Beijing Consensus. In that way, China emphasizes three points:

DOI: 10.4324/9781003048404-13

1. The country's development is based on innovation (Yusuf, n.d.).
2. Economic success is not only measured by the growth of Gross Domestic Product (GDP) per capita, but also by its sustainability and quality level (ibid.).
3. Self-determination for China (ibid.).

As part of China's efforts to sustain its economic growth and to expand its influence, on January 16, 2016, the Chinese government inaugurated the Asian Infrastructure Investment Bank (AIIB), based in Beijing. Since its establishment, some scholars have argued that the AIIB would become a challenger to the monopoly of the World Bank and the International Monetary Fund (IMF) in the global financial system (Tien, 2019). This argument is in line with the opinion put forward by Patrick Bessler who argues that the Beijing government is in competition with the IMF and the World Bank systems (Bessler, n.d.).

The development of the AIIB in the past five years has been quite tremendous, especially in Asian. However, this chapter describes and analyzes the role of the AIIB in the Middle East, which has increased in the past three years when tiny countries, Kuwait and Oman received funds for their infrastructure projects development.

The AIIB

Historically, the Asian Infrastructure Investment Bank (AIIB) was launched by the President of China, Xi Jinping in 2013. In his speech at the Asia-Pacific Economic Cooperation (APEC) CEO Summit in Bali, Indonesia, President Xi Jinping introduced: "[a]n Asian infrastructure investment bank to promote interconnectivity and economic integration in the region." Through his proposal, the AIIB can be interpreted as a multilateral development bank (MDB) based on enhancing infrastructure development, focused on the Asian region.

According to Yuliantoro and Dinarto (2019), in 2014, 24 Asian countries signed a Memorandum of Understanding (MoU) and discussed how the distribution of votes would be decided, after concluding a proposal approved by the founding countries, based on Purchasing Power Parity and GDP, namely by region: Asian or non-Asian. According to the proposal, Asian members hold 75 percent of the total voting power, with non-Asian members holding 25 percent (AIIB, n.d.a).

On 25 December 2015, the Articles of Agreement entered into force and on 16 January 2016, the board of governors of the bank convened its inaugural meeting in Beijing and declared the bank open for business. Jin Liqun was elected as the bank's president for a five-year term (AIIB, n.d.h). However, the development of the AIIB has been rapid. Evidently, within four years, the AIIB has attracted 100 members. According to the official website of the AIIB, the countries involved already represent nearly 79 percent of the global population and 65 percent of the global GDP (ibid.).

In mid-2019, in Luxembourg, when the Board of Governors received its 100th members, namely Benin, Djibouti, and Rwanda, AIIB President, Jin Liqun said: "With the backing of all of our members, we are building a lean, clean, and green institution that can help to support their sustainable development" (AIIB, 2019).

AIIB Vice President and Corporate Secretary, Sir Danny Alexander also argued:

> AIIB was created by 57 founding members as a multilateral institution focused on supporting sustainable development through infrastructure. That another

43 members have joined in the last three years is recognition that AIIB has established itself as part of the rules-based international system, with strong governance and high international standards ... We now have members on every continent, and we welcome the growing interest of African countries in AIIB. We look forward to working with Benin, Djibouti and Rwanda to support their development in the years to come.

(ibid.)

The establishment of the AIIB as a financial institution in Asia has system/model similarity with the World Bank, the European Investment Bank (EIB), the African Development Bank (AfDB), the Development Bank Inter-American (IDB), and the European Bank for Reconstruction and Development (EBRD) (Wang, 2019). The AIIB aims to fund the investment gap in Asia of around $800 million per year. Moreover, based on the Article of Agreement (AoA), the AIIB is built to build connections between member countries.

The AIIB's initial funding at the time of its establishment was $100 billion. Within one year of its founding, the AIIB agreed to fund the first nine projects in Pakistan, Tajikistan, Bangladesh, Indonesia, Myanmar, Oman, and Azerbaijan to develop power, transport, and urban investment. For those project, financial aid reached $1.73 billion. In the period 2017–2018, AIIB has received proposals by financing or co-financing around 20 projects with a total loan amount of up to $3.5 billion.

According to a report by Masahiro Kawai entitled "Asian Infrastructure Investment Bank: China as Responsible Stakeholder?," while many developing and developed countries openly support the AIIB's establishment, the USA and Japan view the instrument with skepticism. The two countries seriously questioned China's motivation for initiating the AIIB. In fact, in Asia, there are already banks that have great potential such as the Asian Development Bank (ADB), which is financially supported by the USA and even Japan. In addition, both the USA and Japan see that the AIIB is a major competitor to the ADB in the region (ibid.).

AIIB's Projects in the Middle East

The AIIB has also expanded into the Middle East. Although the AIIB's coverage in the Middle East is not as much as in the Asian region, the AIIB, especially due to its Asian focus, has attracted the interest of many Middle Eastern countries.

According to the Asian Infrastructure Investment Bank website, several members of the Middle East countries are members of the AIIB (Table 11.1).

In mid-2021, on 27–28 October to be exact, the AIIB Board of Governors held its 6th Annual Meeting in Dubai, in the United Arab Emirates (AIIB, n.d.b). It was the first time the Annual Meeting in the Middle East has taken place at the same time as the Dubai World Expo (ibid.). In addition, the meeting was held to serve as a platform to bring the AIIB closer to its members, partners, businessmen, community organizations, and even researchers.

AIIB Vice and Corporate Secretary, Sir Danny Alexander said :

As a founding member of AIIB, the UAE played an important role in helping to create a 21st-century multilateral development bank committed to promoting sustainable infrastructure development in Asia and beyond ... We look forward

The Asian Infrastructure Investment Bank

Table 11.1 The Middle East countries that are members of the AIIB

No.	Country	Membership commenced
1	Bahrain	August 24, 2018
2	Iran	January 16, 2017
3	Israel	January 15, 2016
4	Jordan	December 25, 2015
5	Oman	June 21, 2016
6	Qatar	June 24, 2016
7	Saudi Arabia	February 19, 2016
8	UAE	January 15, 2016
9	Kuwait (Prospective Founding Member)	–
10	Lebanon (Prospective Member)	–
11	Libya (Prospective Member)	–

Source: (AIIB, n.d.a).

to continuing to work with the UAE and its investment leaders to increase connectivity and strengthen economies in the Middle East, and around the world.

(ibid.)

Responding to this, Dr. Sultan Ahmed Al Jaber, Minister of Industry and Technology of the UAE, also emphasized that:

The UAE has a strong track record that spans five decades in funding development projects that deliver a profound social and economic impact for numerous communities worldwide. We look forward to welcoming AIIB members, development partners, and key stakeholders to share their ideas and best practices in accelerating the development process in Asia. Such efforts will enable the beneficiary countries to maintain a balanced level of economic growth and meet the funding challenges facing development projects in these challenging times.

(ibid.)

The meeting was followed by the AIIB's already existing foothold in the Middle East through funding the largest solar power project in Oman (AIIB, n.d.a). In 2022, the AIIB announced its first overseas office in the UAE. The Bank has funded a number of projects in the Middle East such as the largest solar power project in Oman. The project was proposed by ACWA Power Gulf Investment Corporation and Alternative Energy Project Co. with funds spent around $400 million. This is emphasized by AIIB Vice President, D.J. Pandian:

AIIB's investment will increase the availability of Oman's renewable power generation capacity and contribute to filling the anticipated gap in peak demand … The project will also help the country move toward a more balanced and environmentally sustainable energy mix to ensure long-term energy sustainability.

(ibid.)

This is not the only time since 2017 that Oman has applied for funds for the Information Communication and Technology (ICT) sector by spending $152.1 million (AIIB, n.d.g). Jordan followed these projects. In 2021, the Jordanian government proposed a project called the Inclusive Transparent and Climate Responsive Investment Program for Results which cost $250 million (ibid.). In addition, Islamic Development (IsDB) and the AIIB have also agreed on an MOU regarding the development of Islamic finance-based infrastructure. On October 7, 2021, a virtual meeting took place between IsDB President Muhammad Al Jasser and AIIB President Jin Liqun, to discuss this, as well as developments related to the Multilateral Cooperation Center for Development Finance (MCDF) preparation facilities and capacity projects, led by China and supported by KSA, designed to support cross-border connectivity projects.

In 2018, the AIIB and IsDB formally formed an MOU entitled "Mobilizing Finance for Infrastructure: Innovation & Collaboration." This collaboration is an important step for the AIIB to show that they are serious about being a part of regional development. Jin Liqun stated: "We have complementary skills and expertise. We believe working together on joint investments and initiatives will strengthen our capacity to realize each other's missions and benefit our members."

The IsDB, which has been running for 40 years, involves 57 countries with Muslim-majority populations with an annual transaction value of $10 billion and financing capital of $33 billion (ibid.). This collaboration is not only about increasing the volume of investment but, more than that, the AIIB wants to show that they are ready to integrate for the common good (Table 11.2).

If we reflect on the concept that has been proposed by Canadian scholar, Robert Cox on how institutions help hegemons to co-opt lesser powers and to assimilate opposing interests, the AIIB in the Middle East represents such an institution (Moolakkattu, 2009). The AIIB's most crucial step is to include the Middle East region as part of its "Asia" focus (AIIB, n.d.a). This means that the region, including the Middle East, has a dominant voice in the institution. While in the US-led institutions, such as the IMF and the World Bank, the Middle East countries do not have significant power to make decisions, China, through the AIIB, wants to provide a platform for these countries to voice their interests in a global-level institution.

As previously explained, Asian or regional countries have 75 percent of the votes which are divided into three parts, namely the state capital share, the basic voting rights, and 600 votes for each Founding Member Candidate (PFM) (AIIB, n.d.h). Specifically, the share of capital is calculated according to the weighted average of GDP (60 percent market exchange rate and 40 percent purchasing power parity). The basic voting rights constitute 12 percent of the total voting rights and are divided equally among all member states. Together, the basic and PFM voting rights constitute 15 percent of the total voting rights. As a result of this complex formula, Asian countries, with the exception of China, have a combined 30 percent of the votes in the Bank.

This means that Middle Eastern countries have greater decision-making power than non-regional member countries and are able to hold a majority share of the Bank's capital. This allocation gives more influence to Middle Eastern countries in the AIIB than non-Asian countries which only have 20–25 percent of the votes. So far, countries such as Saudi Arabia, Qatar, the UAE, and Oman are among the founding members of the AIIB, having a large vote (AIIB, n.d.e). The AIIB grants these countries the privilege of being elected as director deputy director (AIIB, n.d.h). As stated in the AoA, the Board

Table 11.2 List of AIIB projects in the Middle East

No	Country	Year	Sector	Project name	Amount (US$ million)	Status
1	Egypt	2017	Energy	Egypt Round II Solar PV Feed-in Tariffs Program	210	Approved
		2018	Water	Sustainable Rural Sanitation Services Program, Phase-2	300	Approved
		2019	Multi-sector	Egypt: National Bank of Egypt On-Lending Facility for Infrastructure	150	Approved
		2021	CRF-Economic Resilience/PBF	Inclusive Growth for Sustainable Recovery DPF Program	360	Approved
		-	Transport	Alexandria – From Sun Metro Ligi	250*	Proposed
2	Jordan	2021	CRF-Economic Resilience/PBF	Inclusive Transparent and Climate Responsive Investments Program for Results (the Program or PforR)	250	Approved
3	Oman	2016	Transport	Duqm Port Commercial Terminal and Operational Zone Development	265	Approved
		2017	Digital Infrastructure and Technology	Oman Broadband Infrastructure	265	Approved
		2020	Energy	Ibri II 500MW Solar PV Independent Power Plant Project	60	Approved
		2021	Digital Infrastructure and Technology	Oman Broadband Company – Tranche 2	46	Terminated / Cancelled
		-	CRF-Public Health	Support to COVID-19 Response	475	Proposed

Note: * = Euros, not dollars.

of Directors consists of representatives elected by the Board of Governors and appointed to handle the day-to-day operations of the AIIB, such as grants and loans.

Unlike the IMF or the World Bank, which have permanent directors based and operating in Washington, DC, the AIIB's Board of Directors consists of non-resident directors who live and operate in their respective home countries. Being a founding member means that Middle Eastern countries are given the right to appoint individuals from their country to become directors and deputy directors. In addition, because constituencies are based on territory, founding members are allowed to hold positions alternately or permanently.

For example, Mohammed Al Jadaan, Saudi Arabia's finance minister, has been appointed as one of the directors on the AIIB Board of Directors (AIIB, n.d.e). Meanwhile, Sultan Al Jaber, the UAE Minister of Industry and Technology, and Wissam Rabadi from Jordan have also been selected to become members of the Council (ibid.). The strategic position is authorized to approve the Bank's plans, the annual plan, and budget to formulate policies; make decisions regarding the Bank operations; establish a supervisory mechanism; and oversee the management and operations of the Bank. Although examples are not available yet, this arrangement within the AIIB's institutional structure can be considered a strategy to attract regional countries into the AIIB policy-making process and to integrate their interests into mainstream policy dialogue. This framework is designed to support the legitimacy of China's interests among Middle Eastern countries.

Another institutional element of the AIIB that helps advance China's interests in the Middle East is the Bank's primary objective, which is to provide loans for infrastructure projects to less-developed countries. In the Middle East, the AIIB's focus on infrastructure lending has turned into a tangible endeavor in recent years. For example, it has agreed on two large loans for construction projects in Oman: one for the development of the Duqm port and the other for the construction of a rail link (AIIB, n.d.c).

In 2016, the AIIB granted Oman a $36 million credit to build a rail project under the guidance of the Oman Rail Direction (Prabhu, 2016). This is one of the new breakthroughs for Oman to develop its infrastructure to become a mineral-exporting center in the Middle East, especially the Gulf (ibid.). The Beijing-based AIIB said that it would encourage Oman to continue realizing the Railway System Project. Therefore, the AIIB has also helped fund 60 percent of the cost of around $60 million (ibid.).

The construction of the Duqm port, which is intended as an economic driver of Oman's economy because it can improve connectivity between regions, shorten shipping times and reduce costs, is assumed to cost $353.33 million. The AIIB played an important role by providing funding of 75 percent, worth $265 million, and the government of Oman gave $88 million. The construction of this port involves not only the government of Oman and the AIIB but also many parties such as the Special Economic Zone Authority in Duqm (SEZAD). SEZAD is a special authority that is responsible for the process of planning, managing, and regulating every economic activity carried out in Duqm. Furthermore, there are logistics companies from Oman, namely ASYAD and the dredging and reclamation company DEME. And, finally, there is the Antwerp Port Consortium (CAP), which is collaborating through a 50:50 joint venture scheme with the government of Oman to build the Duqm port (Port of Duqm, 2021) . The project started in 2017, and by September 2020, phase one of the physical construction of the Duqm port funded by the AIIB is estimated to have reached 99.28 percent (). As for the rail system development project, the AIIB provided financing of $36 million out of the total financing estimated at $60 million. Just like the Duqm port development project, the project is aimed at supporting the process of transforming Oman into a transportation hub in the region.

Deviating from the existing Western principles that involve restricting loan guidelines and terms, which are often a source of criticism from developing countries, including Middle Eastern countries, the AIIB is committed to not applying loan terms and conditions and takes into account the country's actual conditions and needs, with an emphasis on efficiency, simplicity, and transparency of loan procedures.

Such efforts have triggered criticism from the United States and its allies, who claim that China has allowed non-democratic regimes to exist and indirectly provided them with support through loans and funding. A report from AMEinfo, for example, has reaffirmed that "the promise of no-strings-attached infrastructure financing" is one of the reasons why Middle Eastern countries join and support the AIIB (El-Namaki, 2017). Given some of the regional countries' poor human rights records and their authoritarian systems which are often criticised by the West, the Middle East nations' decision to support and join the AIIB is not surprising.

The AIIB and China's interests

At the beginning of the nineteenth century, the Middle East was not a region that had extensive bargaining power in global politics, until the discovery of oil in 1938. Khamis bin Rimthan and American petroleum geologist, Max Steineke discovered Saudi Arabia's first oil well, known as Damman No. 7. At that time, the Arab Kingdom granted the establishment of the first oil company concession in Arabia and collaboration with the US company, namely Standard Oil of California or California-Arab Standard Oil Co. (CASOC). The company grew rapidly until 1950, which was then known as ARAMCO. Crude oil transactions also occurred at that time but did not develop significantly. However, Middle East wealth began to emerge and increase dramatically after the Yom Kippur War of October 1973. According to existing reports, OPEC cut oil exports to the USA and Europe and quadrupled its oil prices resulting in a major energy crisis in the United States and Europe.

The relationship between China and the Middle East runs like an upward-sloping demand curve. China officially established diplomatic relations with countries in the Middle East, such as Egypt and Syria, in 1956. During the Cold War, especially in the 1960s, China did not have close relations with countries in the Middle East, this was because China was still too focused on dealing with its own domestic problems. Recognition of the People's Republic of China as the legitimate government of the Chinese people, replacing Taiwan, opened a new chapter of China's relations with countries in the Middle East, as evidenced by the opening of diplomatic relations with Iran, Lebanon, and Kuwait in 1971 (Scobell and Nader, 2016). Entering the late 1980s under Deng Xiaoping, China began to see the Middle East as a very promising market, although China's presence was still very limited due to the presence of the United States and the Soviet Union. In 1993, driven by rapid economic growth, China turned the Middle East into a supplier for petrochemicals to support China's industry. And this relationship continued to become closer after 1995, until now the Middle East has become the main supplier for China's crude oil needs (ibid.).

China has succeeded in embracing two rivals in the Middle East, namely Saudi Arabia and Iran. In 1999, China formed a Strategic Partnership with Saudi Arabia and continued with Iran in 2000, despite the fact that it has more extensive trading and investment ties with Riyadh. It should be noted that Iran has not good relations with the United States, China was able to take advantage of this opportunity through economic cooperation in the oil sector (ibid.: 13).

China has not only built close ties with Islamic countries in the Middle East but has also embraced a robust cooperation with Israel. China's relationship with Israel has been built since Israel recognized the government of the People's Republic of China (ROC) as the legitimate government in 1950. However, this newly established relationship did not limit China's maneuvers in the Middle East, China condemned the Israeli invasion of Egypt in 1956, which caused the severance of diplomatic relations. Relations between the two countries improved again after the end of the Cold War, as evidenced by China's purchase of Patriot anti-missile prevention technology in 1992 (Smith, 2018). In fact, in 1995, 20 percent of China's weapons needs were supplied by Israel. This proves that China is trying to embrace all parties in the Middle East in order to fulfill its national interests, it can obtain oil and weapons at the same time without having to take sides (ibid.).

The Middle East occupies a very important position for China, as the Middle East is part of the BRI and AIIB projects. Thus, China is able to secure this region through sea and land connections through economic cooperation. First, China built a Maritime Silk Road connecting Iran, Oman, the UAE, Yemen, Saudi Arabia, and Egypt. Then land connections through Iran and Turkey. However, the BRI project cannot accommodate all the needs of all countries in the Middle East. Therefore, the AIIB played an important role in filling the void left by the BRI (Loans et al., 2019).

The image of a region that is very dependent on its natural resources is slowly starting to be changed by countries in the Middle East. The involvement of countries in the Middle East in the AIIB project is a breath of fresh air for reform. Several countries, such as Saudi Arabia, Qatar, and the UAE have publicly stated that they will make changes to their economies through reducing the dependence on oil. They are aware that oil cannot be relied on forever, and therefore there is a need for economic reform.

One of the most ambitious countries in carrying out reforms is Saudi Arabia, through its "Saudi Vision 2030," which was launched in 2016, Saudi Arabia wants to change its socio-economic status by reducing its dependence on oil. Oil accounted for 42 percent of GDP and 90 percent of Saudi Arabia's exports in 2018 (Ghafar, 2018). This is a huge amount and shows how important the role of oil is for the Saudi Arabian economy. Therefore, one of the goals that Saudi Arabia wants to achieve through Vision 2030 is to form a futuristic city called "Neom" as a center of logistics, trade, and investment which is located between Jordan and Egypt (Nereim and El Din, 2021). Not only Saudi Arabia, but Oman is also doing the same thing. Establishing a city and reform system requires substantial funding, therefore cooperation from many parties is needed, one of which is China through the AIIB.

Funding in the form of infrastructure development to create inter-regional connectivity has been planned quite well by Oman and the AIIB through the construction of Duqm port. The port development project in Duqm is funded by the AIIB, and this port has created a transportation and logistics center in Oman. The AIIB approved a $265 million government-backed loan to enable clients to start developing greenfield projects. The loan term of 35 years also provides stable long-term financing that was not previously available in the market. This project will not only have an economic impact on Oman but will also encourage regional cooperation. The AIIB's official website states: "This project reflects the AIIB's focus on its thematic priorities, particularly regional connectivity and cooperation, as well as its commitment to financing Infrastructure for the Future" (AIIB, n.d.e).

It can be seen that the AIIB is a way for China to take advantage of domestic overproduction. China has been pushing for mass production, especially in the industrial sector, such as cement and steel at low prices as a driver of economic growth. However, this abundant production is not accompanied by market needs. This causes the price of goods to fall and economic growth to slow down. Experts see that the BRI and the AIIB projects are one way for China to solve this problem, by allowing a country to join the AIIB, the country's infrastructure projects are financed and the materials come from China (). If the AIIB is really successful, then China should be able to budget $20–60 billion per year to meet construction needs in a sector, such as steel, while project needs include cement to heavy equipment (Dollar, 2015).

As China is very dependent on natural resources from the Middle East, the AIIB is not only a way to overcome the problem of overproduction, but also a way for China to secure energy supplies from the Middle East (Scobell and Nader, 2016).

Not only as a way to overcome the problem of overproduction, the AIIB project is used by China as a way to secure energy supplies from the Middle East. Energy needs are an unavoidable problem for China, its rapid economic growth makes China highly dependent on oil, gas, and coal. Currently, China occupies the first position as the largest energy consumer country in the world. China has been importing crude oil since 1993, this is due to the enormous demand for China's domestic industry. In 2017, China overtook the United States as the world's largest importer of crude oil. Specifically, in 2017, China imported 60 percent of its energy needs from the Middle East. And in the following year China needed 41.2 percent of oil supplies from the Middle East with a total import of $85.6 billion. In fact, China is the largest buyer of oil in the Middle East with a total of 72 percent in 2021.

In short, the AIIB is a way for China to expand its zone of influence, promote economic and social development that emphasizes investment in the infrastructure sector by applying the principles of zero tolerance on corruption and sustainable development in the form of a Green Policy. In his book *The Future Is Asian*, Khanna said that the BRI and the AIIB projects are equivalent to the Marshall Plan, United Nations and World Bank projects, as if these three projects are combined into one, and the important difference is that AIIB operations are focused on Asia and the rest of the world. The Bank's patrons come from countries in Asia (Khanna, 2019).

AIIB officials stated their aim is: "enhancing infrastructure connectivity in Asia by investing in infrastructure and other productive sectors" and by "mobilizing much-needed resources from within and outside Asia." China has shown great commitment to countries in the Middle East through the AIIB. In 2016, in a speech made in Cairo, Xi Jinping stated China intends to disburse $15 billion in special loans to countries in the Middle East, specifically for the infrastructure sector, and $20 billion in soft and commercial loans to increase production. Wang Zemin, who was China's Foreign Minister, in an interview with Al-Jazeera in 2014, made a clear statement about how important development is in overcoming current problems (Ministry of Foreign Affairs of People's Republic of China, 2014).

We believe that development holds the key and becomes the basis for solving all problems. Any solution to hot spots and political issues hinges on economic growth and a better life for people. As far as Arab countries are concerned, the most important task facing them is national development and economic revitalization.

The AIIB is not just about infrastructure development but goes beyond that. The Hegemony theory, put forward by Gramsci, is very suitable to explain how China embraces countries in the Middle East through the AIIB. In this theory, the dominant party tries to try to build a narrative claiming that the interests they have are the same as the interests of their partners. The United States has followed the same pattern in the case of the IMF and the World Bank. (Wade, 2002). In the governance system of the IMF and the World Bank, the country which is the largest donor of funds gets privileges such as having a veto over the policies taken by the IMF and the World Bank. The United States took on this role by being the largest contributor to the $65 billion funds. This makes the role of developing countries limited and the decisions taken by the IMF and the World Bank are closely related to the political interests of the United States. According to Wade, America will intervene in the institutions when there are policies that are not in America's interests (ibid.).

In offering foreign aid, China has consistently applied the principle of "equality and mutual benefit" which has been adhered to since the 1960s. This principle also upsets the assumption that China will not provide aid only as a form of charity. China also did not ask for conditions that would burden the recipient country or, in other words, ask for privileges. The Chinese government applies not only the principle of "equality and mutual benefit" but also the principle of non-conditionality. This principle was reaffirmed by Xi Jinping through the AIIB project:

> When providing foreign aid, China adheres to the principles of not imposing any political conditions, not interfering in the internal affairs of recipient countries and fully respecting their right to independently choose their own path and model of development. The basic principles that China upholds in providing foreign aid are mutual respect, equality, keeping promises, mutual benefit and win-win.
>
> *(State Council, 2014, cited in Karimova, 2016: 27)*

This non-conditionality principle is also applied in the form of a rule that stipulates that any party working for the Bank, from the President to the staff, is not allowed to be involved in political affairs between members. Every decision made must be based on the results of a review of rational economic benefits.

The AIIB project offers many advantages for the recipient countries. The AIIB does not bind member states with political commitments. Not only that, there is no binding political commitment, but AIIB also gives a position on the Board of Directors to the founding countries, and countries that are Asian regional members have 70–75 percent of the votes and countries outside Asia have only 20 percent of the votes. By being part of the Board of Directors and having 70 percent voting rights, of course, countries in the Middle East have the right to form and approve the proposals made (Rakhmat, 2020). The head of the AIIB Economic Unit, Dr. Thia Jang Ping explained that the founding countries not only get privileges in the number of voting rights but also get the authority to manage or regulate the activities of the Bank. This treatment is quite unfair because new members do not get the same rights. This will facilitate the interests of countries in the Middle East and build a sense that they are now an important part of a global institution. China is trying to apply the concept of co-optation to the Middle East through the AIIB, by giving positions in the AIIB to Middle Eastern countries in order to build the feeling that they have the same interests (AIIB, 2017).

Conclusion

The lack of US hegemony and the increasing role of the AIIB make China's presence in the Middle East, especially in the Gulf part of the region, grow. China views the Middle East as a treasure of natural resources. According to David Shinn, a professor at the Elliot School of International Affairs, George Washington University, China reduced oil imports from Africa to 18 percent and adjusted their directions to the Middle East (Manning and Preble, 2021).

The plan for peace talks with the regional members of the AIIB, namely Iran and Saudi Arabia, is a good way for China to increase its presence. Not only that, the AIIB will also become an instrument for China to increase its legitimacy among the regional countries through providing them with loans and incorporating them into the AIIB's institutional frameworks.

The need for oil will always be the main attraction for China in the Middle East. Without a continued supply of oil, China's industry will certainly be disrupted. Therefore, securing supplies especially from the Middle East is very important and crucial for China. While serving as President of China, Xi Jinping has made several trips to the Middle East to visit the two largest oil-producing countries there, namely Saudi Arabia and Iran in 2016 and steadily forming a Strategic Partnership. This proves that China is very dependent on the two countries, bearing in mind that other Gulf countries also play a major role in China's oil needs. In 2019–2020, Saudi Arabia alone accounted for 16 percent of China's oil needs and the Gulf countries as a whole contributed 40 percent (Loans et al., 2019). However, it must be remembered that China also has a commitment to reduce its carbon emissions by 2060, currently China is the country that contributes the most carbon emissions (28 percent). Therefore, through carbon neutrality, China must reduce its oil supply to 60 percent and gas to 45 percent (Yin, 2021).

Apparently, the instability of the Middle East will not be an obstacle for China to grow its presence in the region. In fact, China has consistently continued to build close relations with countries affected by internal and external conflicts such as Myanmar, Afghanistan, and Sudan. This is evidenced in China's economic relations with countries in the Middle East, through energy cooperation and the fact that China has become the largest trading partner of and investor in 11 countries in the Middle East (Cook and Green, 2021).

In an interview with the Brookings Institute in January 2021, Jin Liqun, the President of the AIIB, stated that one of their missions is to carry out cooperation based on climate change prevention (Brookings, 2021).

> AIIB has set an ambitious target to ensure that 50% of our financing approvals by 2025 will be directed towards climate finance. It is important to point out that efforts to strengthen our health systems and tackle climate change can no longer be handled in silence. They are closely related. We need to investigate the

intricate patterns that emerge from the relationship between climate and health outcomes. We must explore new development paradigms that are environmentally smart and smart ecosystems.

This mission will help strengthen China's ties with the Middle Eastern countries as it is in line with Saudi Arabia's "Vision 2030," as well as that of other GCC countries, which is to reduce oil dependence. This can be a very good alternative considering that countries in the Middle East are carrying out social and economic reforms. However, it is important to note that China's huge dependence on oil can make this mission only a sweetener to be able to create an image that the AIIB has the same sense of crisis as the world community.

References

AIIB. 2015. "Jin Liqun Selected President-designate of the Asian Infrastructure Investment Bank – News – AIIB." Available at: www.aiib.org/en/news-events/news/2015/Jin-Liqun-Selected-President-designate-of-the-Asian-Infrastructure-Investment-Bank.html

AIIB. 2016. "Asian Infrastructure Investment Bank Breaks New Ground Approving Two Projects in Oman." Available at: www.aiib.org/en/news-events/news/2016/Asian-Infrastructure-Investment-Bank-breaks-new-ground-approving-two-projects-in-Oman.html

AIIB. 2017. "AIIB Governance." Available at: www.aiib.org/en/about-aiib/governance/board-directors/board-members/index.html

AIIB. 2019. "AIIB Reaches 100-Member Milestone – News – AIIB.". Available at: www.aiib.org/en/news-events/news/2019/AIIB-reaches-100-member-milestone.html

AIIB. 2020a. "AIIB's USD60-M Solar Investment in Oman Supports Diversified Energy Mix – News – AIIB.". Available at: www.aiib.org/en/news-events/news/2020/AIIBs-USD60-M-Solar-Investment-in-Oman-Supports-Diversified-Energy-Mix.html

AIIB. 2020b. "AIIB to Hold its First Annual Meeting in the Middle East in the UAE – News – AIIB.". Available at: www.aiib.org/en/news-events/news/2020/AIIB-to-Hold-its-First-Annual-Meeting-in-the-Middle-East-in-the-UAE.html

AIIB. 2021. "SBF Project Implementation Monitoring Report." Available at: www.aiib.org/en/projects/details/2016/approved/_download/project-implementation-monitoring-report/AIIB-PIMR_SBF_Oman_Duqm-Port-Commercial-Terminal-and-Operational-Zone-Development-Project_11_June-2021_Public-Version.pdf

AIIB. n.d.a "About AIIB – AIIB.". Available at: www.aiib.org/en/about-aiib/index.html (accessed November 12, 2021).

AIIB. n.d.b "AIIB Board of Directors." Available at: www.aiib.org/en/about-aiib/governance/board-directors/board-members/index.html accessed November 12, 2021.

AIIB. n.d.c "Approved Projects Overview – AIIB." Available at: Asian Infrastructure Investment Bank. www.aiib.org/en/projects/approved/index.html (accessed November 12, 2021).

AIIB. n.d.d "Focus Areas – AIIB." Available at: www.aiib.org/en/about-aiib/who-we-are/focus-areas/index.html (accessed November 12, 2021).

AIIB. n.d.e "Members of the Bank – AIIB." Available at: www.aiib.org/en/about-aiib/governance/members-of-bank/index.html (accessed November 12, 2021).

AIIB. n.d.f "Oman: Connecting Commerce and Future-Proofing the Economy." Available at: www.aiib.org/en/news-events/annual-report/2020/our-investments/detail/oman2/index.html (accessed November 12, 2021).

AIIB. n.d.g "Project List – Project – AIIB." Available at: Asian Infrastructure Investment Bank.. www.aiib.org/en/projects/list/index.html (accessed November 12, 2021).

AIIB. n.d.h "Articles of Agreement." Available at: www.aiib.org/en/about-aiib/basic-documents/_download/articles-of-agreement/basic_document_english-bank_articles_of_agreement.pdf

Australian National University. 2018. *China's 40 Years of Reform and Development 1978–2018*. Acton: ANU Press.

Bessler, Patrick. n.d. "China's AIIB: Competition for Bretton Woods or an Opportunity for Asia?". Konrad-Adenauer-Stiftung. Available at: www.kas.de/documents/252038/253252/7_dokument_dok_pdf_43917_2.pdf/5430d52c-14aa-163b-8f91-d54a79a1779d?version=1.0&t=1539651359100 (accessed November 12, 2021).

Brookings. 2021. "How We Rebuild: A Conversation with President Jin Liqun on the Asian Infrastructure Investment Bank's Fifth Anniversary." Available at: www.brookings.edu/events/how-we-rebuild-a-conversation-with-president-jin-liqun-on-the-asian-infrastructure-investment-banks-fifth-anniversary/

Cook, Steven A., and James Green. 2021. "China Isn't Trying to Dominate the Middle East But U.S. Retrenchment Might Allow It To." *Foreign Affairs*. Available at: www.foreignaffairs.com/articles/united-states/2021-08-09/china-isnt-trying-dominate-middle-east#author-info

CSIS China Power. 2021. "How Is China's Energy Footprint Changing?" Available at: https://chinapower.csis.org/energy-footprint/

Dollar, David. 2015. "The AIIB and the 'One Belt, One Road.'" Brookings. Available at: www.brookings.edu/opinions/the-aiib-and-the-one-belt-one-road/

El-Namaki, M. S. S. 2017. "Neoglobalization, China's Silk Road and the Middle East." *AME Info*. Available at: www.ameinfo.com/business/neoglobalization-chinas-silk-road-middle-east/

Ghafar, Adel A. 2018. "A New Kingdom of Saud?" Brookings. Available at: www.brookings.edu/research/a-new-kingdom-of-saud/

Global Times. 2019. "Overproduction Remains Top Risk for Chinese Companies." Available at: www.globaltimes.cn/content/1144876.shtml

IsDB. 2021. "IsDB and AIIB Presidents Eye More Inclusive Collaboration | IsDB." Islamic Development Bank. Available at: www.isdb.org/news/isdb-and-aiib-presidents-eye-more-inclusive-collaboration

Karimova, Tahmina, 2016. *Human Rights and Development in International Law*. New York: Routledge.

Kawai, Masahiro. 2015. "Asian Infrastructure Investment Bank: China as Responsible Stakeholder?" Available at: https://spfusa.org/wp-content/uploads/2015/07/AIIB-Report_4web.pdf

Khanna, Parag. 2019. *The Future Is Asian: Global Order in the Twenty-First Century*. London: Weidenfeld & Nicolson.

Loans, Camille, Jonathan Fulton, Degang Sun, and Naser A. Tamimi. 2019. "China's Great Game in the Middle East." European Council on Foreign Relations. Available at: https://ecfr.eu/publication/china_great_game_middle_east/

Lopes, Carlos. 2012. "Economic Growth and Inequality: The New Post-Washington Consensus." *Open Edition* 4(2): 69–70.

Manning, Robert A., and Christopher Preble. 2021. "Rethinking US Military Policy in the Greater Middle East." Atlantic Council. Available at: www.atlanticcouncil.org/content-series/reality-check/reality-check-8-rethinking-us-military-policy-in-the-greater-middle-east/

McDonell, Stephen. 2018. "China's Xi Allowed to Remain 'President for Life' as Term Limits Removed." BBC. Available at: www.bbc.com/news/world-asia-china-43361276

Ministry of Foreign Affairs of People's Republic of China. 2014. "Wang Yi Gave an Interview to Al Jazeera." Available at: www.fmprc.gov.cn/mfa_eng/wjb_663304/wjbz_663308/2461_663310/t1116509.shtml

Moolakkattu, John S. 2009. "Robert W. Cox and Critical Theory of International Relations." *International Studies* 46(4): 439–456.

Nereim, Vivian, and Yousef G. El Din. 2021. "Saudi Arabia Starts Moving Earth for Its Futuristic Linear City." Bloomberg. Available at: www.bloomberg.com/news/articles/2021-10-31/saudi-arabia-starts-moving-earth-for-its-futuristic-linear-city

Port of Duqm. 2021. "The Port of Duqm.". Available at: www.portofduqm.om/About/Port-of-Duqm

Prabhu, Conrad. 2016. "$36 Million AIIB Loan to Part Finance Oman Railway Preparation Project." *Oman Observer*. Available at: www.omanobserver.om/article/91420/Business/36-million-aiib-loan-to-part-finance-oman-railway-preparation-project

Rakhmat, Muhammad Z. 2020. "How the AIIB Grows China's Interests in the Middle East." *The Diplomat*. Available at: https://thediplomat.com/2020/09/how-the-aiib-grows-chinas-interests-in-the-middle-east/

Scobell, Andrew, and Alireza Nader. 2016. *China in the Middle East: The Wary Dragon*. Santa Monica, CA: RAND Corporation. Available at: www.rand.org/t/RR1229.

Smith, Daniel L. 2018. "China and Israel." *The Jerusalem Post*. Blog. Available at: www.jpost.com/blogs/arabisraeli-conflict/china-and-israel-533321

Tien, Nguyen H. 2019. "AIIB as a Challenger for IMF and WB." AIJBM. Available at: www.aijbm.com/wp-content/uploads/2019/10/G2106268.pdf

Wade, Robert H. 2002. "US Hegemony and the World Bank: The Fight over People and Ideas." *Review of International Political Economy* 9(Summer): 217–219. doi:10.1080/09692290110126092

Wang, Hongying. 2019. "The New Development Bank and the Asian Infrastructure Investment Bank: China's Ambiguous Approach to Global Financial Governance." *Development and Change* 50(1): 221–244.

World Bank. n.d. "The World Bank in China." Available at: www.worldbank.org/en/country/china/overview#1

Yin, Ivy. 2021. "China Must Cut Coal Demand by Over 80%, Oil by 60% by 2060 to Meet Climate Goals: IEA." S&P Global. Available at: www.spglobal.com/platts/en/market-insights/latest-news/energy-transition/092921-china-must-cut-coal-demand-by-over-80-oil-by-60-by-2060-to-meet-climate-goals-iea

Yuliantoro, Nur Rachmat and Dinanto, Dedi. 2019. "Between Revisionist and Status Quo: The Case of China's Leadership in the AIIB." *Jurnal Hubungan Internasional* 7(2), 169–177.

Yusuf, Shahid. n.d. "Beijing Consensus or Washington Consensus: What Explains China's Economic Success?" Open Knowledge Repository. Available at: https://openknowledge.worldbank.org/handle/10986/6098 (accessed November 12, 2021).

12

CHINA'S MARITIME SILK ROUTE AND THE MENA REGION[1]

Geoffrey F. Gresh

Introduction

Across the Middle East and North Africa (MENA) region, geoeconomics and security are two primary drivers motivating China's ever-increasing seaward tilt and further investment in its Maritime Silk Route (MSR). China was recently named the world's largest trading partner, surpassing the United States with about $4 billion in annual trade volume. Some estimates also predict that China will dominate 17 of the world's top 25 global trading avenues between Europe and Asia. Today, more than 90 percent of the world's goods transit the sea, bringing into relief the continued importance of the stability and security of the global commons. As China continues to grow its geoeconomic interests and investments across the MENA region, securing them, along with the sea lanes of communication, will become ever more critical.

The 2013 launch of its "One Belt, One Road" or "Belt and Road" Initiative (BRI) and the "Maritime Silk Route" aligns with this larger dynamic that sees China's geoeconomic and security interests increasingly interwoven due to mounting maritime and global trade. Between 2003 and 2014, for example, Chinese international trade multiplied significantly, growing from $851 billion to more than $4.16 trillion. China also views peace in its peripheral territories and maritime waterways as critical for domestic harmony and thus its future development. This is why China is concerned about preventing or mitigating the undue influence of external powers, especially those trying to undermine or block its BRI projects. The BRI is indeed a risky endeavor because it is an agglomeration of many competing interests that will be hard to manage toward one singular strategic goal, as some critics argue. But even moderate success rates across the BRI and the MSR could bring China significant geoeconomic and geostrategic victories (Humpert, 2013: 8; Yung and Rustici, 2014; China Power Team, 2017; Maçães, 2018: Kindle location 1985–2005; Scobell et al., 2018: xv–xvi, 24–27; Li, 2019).

In addition to growing geoeconomic investments and interlinked security interests across maritime Eurasia, China seeks great power status and more international prestige. For China, this also means challenging the American-dominated world order to suit its respective global interests. Here, the term great power is defined as a country

DOI: 10.4324/9781003048404-14

that demonstrates "global structural power," or has "the ability to shape governance frameworks in the economic, military, and political-diplomatic sectors" (cf. Brady, 2017: 6). But to achieve great power status, a critical component has historically included the build-up and deployment of a blue-water navy that can project power and protect interests and China's BRI and MSR more fluidly in far-flung corners of the world. In the words of the scholars George Modelski and William R. Thompson (1988: 3), "There can be no global system without global reach. Only those disposing of superior navies have, in the modern world, staked out a good claim to world leadership." Developing blue-water navies is therefore seen as an essential vehicle or instrument of national power through which to establish great power status and reshape the world order. China and Russia put their blue-water naval capabilities on display during the Joint Sea 2017 exercises held for the first time ever in the Baltic Sea and Okhotsk Sea on opposite sides of Eurasia. Two years prior, they also held their first joint exercises in the Mediterranean under the umbrella of the same joint maneuvers.

Maritime Geoeconomics and Energy Security

Maritime geoeconomics is a key first category or primary driver behind China's "embrace of its" maritime space and support for the MSR. Geoeconomics is a term that has come back into fashion in recent years as "more states are waging geopolitics with capital, attempting with sovereign checkbooks and other economic tools to achieve strategic objectives that in the past were often the stuff of military coercion or conquest" (Blackwill and Harris, 2016: 4). This is particularly the case for China as it extends its economic arms regionally and throughout the MENA. Stated another way, geoeconomics is the economics of geopolitics or what has also been referred to as economic statecraft. Robert Blackwill and Jennifer Harris provide a good working definition of geoeconomics that is used here: "the use of economic instruments to promote and defend national interests and to produce beneficial geopolitical results; and the effects of other nations' economic actions on a country's geopolitical goals" (ibid.: 5, 9).

But even this definition is broad and needs to be narrowed down further when employing a saltwater perspective. In general, and as noted by Blackwill and Harris, there are seven main geoeconomic instruments that are used by states: trade policy, investment policy, economic sanctions, the cybersphere, aid, monetary policy, and energy and commodity policies. When applying these as a part of this chapter's analytical framework, three of the primary instruments are most applicable to Eurasia's maritime competition: trade policy, investment policy, and energy and commodity policies. The cybersphere is still developing but is of growing importance due to the vulnerabilities posed to the physical cables laid along the oceans' floors and through the MENA region's narrow strategic chokepoints, in addition to other shipping technology innovations tied to cyber security, such as the Automatic Identification System (AIS). Foreign aid is another critical factor of maritime geoeconomics although it is similarly harder to lump into distinct maritime categories. Foreign aid and the cybersphere will therefore not be a main focus. I unpack the three other main geoeconomic tools that are most relevant to the maritime domain here (Luttwak, 1990: 17–23; Miller, 2015; Reiber, 2018: 83–94; see also Baldwin, 1985).

The first two elements are global maritime trade and investment. Many view global trade in a post-Cold War era as more inclined toward cooperation as opposed to conflict due to rising economic interdependence and the complex and international nature of the shipping industry and supply and logistics chains. At the same time, others point toward a darker period during the age of mercantilism and the staunch competition that emerged between the Dutch and British East India companies of the seventeenth and eighteenth centuries. Competition was at the core of this system and drove the national interests of the European powers and their state-run enterprises, and one of the main ways to protect these valued and complex trading systems was to invest in the global maritime trade and port infrastructure (Hochstrasser, 2005: 173; Till, 2013: 11).

The growing trends of maritime trade and investment between China and MENA region countries align with a third critical tool that includes the mounting importance of energy security and the transportation of vital natural resources via the sea. Due to Eurasia's growing and developing population—estimated at 60 percent of the world's population, with China and India accounting for 40 percent of it—India and China in particular are on the hunt for more natural resources to fuel their growing economies. Since the 1990s, 42 percent of the world's expanding energy consumption is directly linked to India and China. On the supply side, Eurasia—mainly the Middle East and Central Asia—accounts for 66 percent of proven oil reserves and an estimated 71 percent of proven natural gas. When broken down further, 40 percent of the world's energy resources are either located in the Indian Ocean region or must traverse it while headed to Asia or Europe. More than 60 percent of the world's oil is shipped via sea, for example, while the Strait of Hormuz alone handles more than 20 percent of it or an estimated 17 million barrels of oil per day. Similarly, approximately 80 percent of China's oil imports transit the Strait of Malacca (Calder, 2012: xxv; Dombrowski and Winner, 2014: 1; Clemente, 2015; Arnold, 2016; 11; Grigas, 2017: 134; U.S. Energy Information Administration, 2017b; Wuthnow, 2017). According to some estimates, the Persian/Arabian Gulf region accounts for approximately 45 percent of the world's gas reserves and about 60 percent of proven crude oil. Additionally, the Indian Ocean is known to have heavy mineral deposits along its coastlines and continental shelf. As for the Suez Canal/SUMED Pipeline specifically, about 9 percent of international oil shipments and approximately 13 percent of the world's natural gas transit the waterway annually. Anything that threatens the closure of such a vital and narrow waterway as the Strait of Hormuz or the Suez Canal can present devastating global economic and political consequences, as was witnessed when the *Ever Given*, a 20,000-TEU container ship, ran aground in the Suez Canal for six days in March 2021 (Shelala, 2014; Albert, 2016; Kalim, 2016: 211; U.S. Energy Information Administration, 2017b; *Deutsche Welle*, 2018; Trickett, 2018; Wingfield, Dodge, and Sam, 2018; Wignaraja and Panditaratne, 2019).

Despite aggressively pursuing supply diversity, as much as 70–80 percent of China's future oil imports could come from the Middle East and North Africa. To meet growing demand, over the past decade China has actively courted Iran and the Gulf Arab monarchies through various economic and political inducements. Moreover, since 2011, it has grown heavily involved in the Middle East as it seeks to reshape the global energy markets through more robust Gulf partnerships. In Iran, for example, China is the top importer of Iranian petroleum, while also being Iran's largest foreign investor, but mainly with regards to land-based geoeconomics investments. On the shipping side, Bandar Abbas currently handles approximately 85 percent of Iran's shipping, but can only handle ships smaller than 100,000 tons, making Iran dependent on its neighbor, the United Arab Emirates (Jaffrelot, 2011; Ramachandran, 2014; *Guardian*, 2016; *SME Times*, 2016; *Gulf News*, 2018; Marlow and Dilawar, 2018; Pant and Mehta, 2018: 666; Pant and Ratna, 2018; Quamar, interview with author, New Delhi, June 12, 2018).

Growing Maritime Focus on the Mediterranean

The Mediterranean may be small by oceanic standards at approximately 2.5 million square kilometers, but it is complex and has been subjected historically to the winds of change between east and west, by forces from both inside and outside the Mediterranean littoral. The Mediterranean's emerging economic importance is indeed noteworthy. About 15 percent of the world's natural gas shipments and approximately 5 percent of oil shipments traverse the Mediterranean either from North Africa or via the Suez Canal. Soon, it is likely that natural gas and oil exploration will become another valuable asset from which both regional states and other Eurasian powers, such as Russia, China, or India, can benefit. At the same time, it is likely to be a point of contention since the exclusive economic zones (EEZs) are still widely disputed between Israel and Lebanon or Greece, Cyprus, and Turkey. The eastern Mediterranean basin, especially near Cyprus, Lebanon, Egypt, and Israel, is forecast to have an estimated 3.45 trillion cubic meters of gas and 267 million tons of oil (Karagiannis, 2016: 1–11; Malysheva, 2016: 92; Gurcan, 2018).

China is increasingly stepping into the arena to take advantage of the region's economics with its massive maritime investment and infrastructure projects, with a focus on ports. Some have referred to it as the "port-industrial park" model. In the past several years, China has invested about $47 billion in an estimated 40 port projects (Ghiselli, 2017; Kuo, 2017). It began a global project that ultimately aspires to rewrite the global economic order, creating a new and independent system moving beyond the reach of traditional leverage by other outside powers. As described by one scholar, the BRI and the MSR attempt

> [to] unbundle different segments of the production chain. It attempts to create a set of political and institutional tools with which China can start to reorganize global value chains and stamp its imprint on the rules governing the global economy.
>
> *(Maçães, 2016)*

Turkey and Israel

To understand China's growing MSR footprint in the MENA, we look first at Turkey and Israel. Though they are not on the same scale as the well-documented case of Piraeus, Greece, they will help to further China's more massive BRI/MSR agenda to build up an east-west trading empire, including control and access to ports and other outlets or transportation corridors, and sea lines of communication (SLOCs). The Suez Canal factors into this but is instead analyzed in the next section on the Red and Arabian Seas.

As a country that straddles both the Black and Mediterranean Seas with the Bosphorus Straits connecting the two, Turkey hopes to attract further Chinese regional maritime investments to build up several of its Mediterranean ports. In 2015, a conglomerate of several Chinese firms—China Merchants Holdings International, China Investment Corporation, and COSCO—raised capital to purchase a 65 percent stake in Istanbul's main port terminal, Kumport, worth about $920 million. Kumport terminal is part of the larger Istanbul Ambarli port and is Turkey's third largest port, processing about 2.7 million TEUs annually. In addition, China is surveying three other prospective ports to expand its foothold in Turkey. The first two ports are located in the Izmir region along the western edge of the country or eastern shores of the Aegean Sea. The first port, Çandarlı, is north of Izmir and has a 4 million TEU annual capacity but it still lacks the requisite land and railroad connections to make it fully operational. The second port, Alsancak, is in Izmir and considered one of the leading export terminals for Turkey. The third port, Mersin, is located closer to Turkey's southeast border near Cyprus (Atli, 2017; *Daily Sabah*, 2017; Ergunsu, 2017; *World Port Source*, 2019; Izmir Development Agency, 2021).

South and east of Turkey lies Israel where China is equally interested in creating an additional node in its larger east-west shipping and trade network; Israel might also someday act as a contingency transportation corridor, albeit on a much smaller and largely uneconomical scale, to the Suez Canal. With China's growing regional interests, it must mitigate the risk that is posed to its east-west trade routes and transportation corridors. Finding alternative ports and routes, therefore, fits in line with its increasing focus on Israel. Israel also benefits since 99 percent of its imports and exports travel via the sea. The Israeli government's bigger objective is to privatize several terminals at two of its largest ports—Haifa and Ashdod—to raise more capital for the government. Additionally, and as examined below, Israel desires to upgrade and expand its terminals to stay competitive with other regional transshipment ports. With these port projects, Israel can showcase greater stability for other foreign direct investment (FDI) projects, especially since Ashdod was the target of a Hamas rocket attack launched from Gaza in the spring of 2014 (Israel Ports and Development Assets Company, 2011; *Container Management*, 2014; Lappin, 2014; Shamah, 2014).

China has made progress on establishing significant footholds at the ports of Ashdod and Haifa. By some accounts, China is investing around $2.9 billion in their port investments, including terminal expansion and other requisite upgrades. The two ports handle around 3 million TEUs collectively per year, or around 1.5 million TEUs at each port. Each port has the capacity to handle around 2.5 million TEUs but with the terminal expansion projects underway, the hope is to double each port's capacity to 5 million TEUs per year or a total of 10 million TEUs. The terminal expansion projects have grown in urgency since 2017 when Israel witnessed a spike in ship waiting times to offload cargo. For container ships, wait times have been anywhere between 13 and 15 hours at either port. In prior years, the waiting time was closer to 4 or 5 hours on average.

In 2014, and after outbidding two Israeli conglomerates, Israel granted Pan-Mediterranean Engineering Ltd., a subsidiary of China Harbour Engineering Company, the right to begin construction on a new $930 million terminal at Ashdod. According to Israelis, they tried to persuade and lobby several US firms at the time to bid on Israel's two main port projects, but the American firms declined to bid. China's competitive bid on Ashdod fits into a broader pattern of constructing its own trading and logistics system by monopolizing regional and global maritime economies, making it harder to leverage or control down the road. Over the next several years, the Chinese subsidiary will construct the new terminal, in addition to other modernization efforts in Ashdod, including an expansion of the deep-water berths, and the construction of new docks, warehouses, and jetties. It will also include a 1,000-meter pier and a 2,800-meter breakwater (Bar-Eli, 2014; Reuters, 2014; Shamah, 2014; Kuo, 2017; Lim, 2017).

To the north in Haifa, Israel awarded the Shanghai International Port Group (SIPG), majority-owned by the China Merchants Group, a 25-year concession in 2015 to manage and operate the new Haifa terminal constructed for about $1 billion by Shapir Engineering and the Ashtrom Group, two Israeli companies. The new bay terminal, which sits next to Haifa airport, was inaugurated in 2021. The SIPG Chairman recently commented: "Investing in Haifa will help strengthen relations between Shanghai port and other ports along the Maritime Silk Road and form a closer trade network between Shanghai port and ports in Europe" (Petersburg, 2015; *Port Finance International*, 2015).

Despite increased pressure from the United States and others, China and Israel continue to strengthen bilateral ties. In 2016, they began the first of several rounds of negotiations regarding the establishment of a China-Israel Free Trade Area. The second round of trade talks resumed in the summer of 2017. According to recent estimates, China is the third largest trading partner with Israel, reaching about $11 billion in trade (People's Republic of China, 2017). If Israel's domestic politics can remain stable, the future looks promising for the geoeconomic relationship between China and Israel. China's influence over Israel's main ports has already been largely fulfilled.

The Maghreb

Libya has proven to be a no-go zone since the fall of Qaddafi in 2011, but toward the western edges of the Mediterranean, Morocco and Algeria are emerging as two additional and important transshipment hubs or ports. The proximity to the Strait of Gibraltar makes Morocco a particularly strategic asset toward constructing a new and increasingly independent supply and logistics chain of maritime transportation networks. Tunisia is a rather small nodal point due to its small economy and population, but it hopes that a new shipping line between its Rades port and China's Qingdao port will help bolster bilateral ties while aiding China's expanding presence on the African continent (*Famagusta Gazette,* 2017).

The Strait of Gibraltar handles about 20 percent of the world's shipping traffic, passing along Morocco's northern tip. This amounts to around 100,000 ships nearing or traversing the strait each year. Recognizing Morocco's geostrategic location, King Mohammed VI launched the $7 billion Tanger Med port project in 2003 that includes a 1,000-hectares port facility and an accompanying 5,000-hectares industrial zone. On a clear day, the Rock of Gibraltar and southern Spain, just 9 miles away, are clearly visible and symbolize the importance of Morocco's emerging transshipment hub. In 2007, Morocco completed the first phase of the project and business has been booming. It currently serves 169 ports and 68 countries around the globe and is inching forward to hopefully reach a top 20 position among the world's ports, especially when the port is at full capacity. It can handle around 3 million TEUs per year—making it one of Africa's largest—but hopes to expand to 9 million TEUs with the 2019 opening of the Tanger Med 2 port which added 1.6 km of docks and an additional 5 million-TEU capacity (Saleh, 2016; Spirk, 2016; *Morocco World News,* 2018; *Global Construction Review,* 2019).

China's economic relationship with Morocco has only become more noticeable in the last several years. In 2015, China was only Morocco's fourth largest trading partner. Bilateral trade, however, increased 195 percent in 2014 while increasing 95 percent the following year. When the king traveled to China in 2016, the two partners signed a bilateral strategic partnership similar to that of Greece. One deal from the visit was an agreement for China to build a $10 billion industrial city next to Tanger Med. Launched in late 2017, 200 Chinese firms will join the industrial zone project with plans to purportedly create up to 100,000 jobs. Tanger Med and Tanger Med 2 are currently run by European port operators but China began paying closer attention to maritime investment opportunities in the country and hopes to transform the Tanger Med into a major BRI hub. At a recent

China-Africa investment forum held in Marrakech, Chinese investment firms promised billions in projects to invest in Tanger Med's industrial zone and other maritime logistic operations (*Daily Mail,* 2017; Hammond, 2017; Omondi, 2017; Xinhua Net, 2017a).

From Morocco, China has turned its vision eastward to Algeria. China's growing interest in Algeria follows a trend of rising bilateral trade between the two nations (Zoubir, 2021). In 2017, China was the largest exporter to Algeria worth approximately $7.3 billion. This amounted to about 19 percent of Algeria's total imports. Some speculate that lower oil and gas prices spurred Algeria's government to think more about diversifying its economic portfolio beyond oil and gas, which accounts for about 94 percent of Algeria's export revenues and an estimated 60 percent of state revenues (*Nusantara Maritime News,* 2016; *Maritime Executive,* 2017).

China commenced construction on a transregional port at El Hamdania, about 50 miles west of the capital Algiers. With the project, Algeria hopes to pull maritime commerce away from Morocco and southern Europe. The 2000-hectare plan is to build up to 23 shipping berths with a projected vision of handling an estimated annual capacity of 6.3 million TEUs and 26 million tons of goods, making it Africa's second largest port after Morocco's Tanger Med. Similar to Israel, the China Harbour Engineering Company, in collaboration with the China State Construction Engineering Corporation, purchased a 49 percent concession in the port. Algeria's Port Authority owns the other 51 percent of the project. The loan agreement for $3.3 billion is being backed by Chinese firms as well as about $900 million from the African Development Bank. Construction of the port "reportedly" began in 2017, and the first berths are supposed to open soon. The full opening is expected in the near future when it will then be transferred to SIPG for the operation and management of the port. According to some reports, COSCO shipping has proposed making El Hamdania its regional hub in the western Mediterranean. Nevertheless, Algeria is optimistic for its future and believes it can be an important hub for regional trade throughout northern and western Africa, especially with upgraded roadways like the Trans-Saharan road that traverses to the southern portion of the country (Zoubir, forthcoming; *Nusantara Maritime News,* 2016; *African Business,* 2017; *Maritime Executive,* 2017; Xinhua Net, 2017b).

Maritime Southwest Asia

One important element factored into the Indian Ocean's prominence and significance is that it is home to some of the world's most vital maritime chokepoints along its western edges, including the Suez Canal, the Bab al-Mandeb, and the Strait of Hormuz. Maritime chokepoints, narrow channels along global sea lanes of communications, transit high volumes of oil and natural gas, essential to global energy security and trade. The Strait of Hormuz—connecting the Persian/Arabian Gulf to the Arabian Sea and Indian Ocean—and the Bab al-Mandeb—linking the Indian Ocean to the Red Sea and the Suez Canal—are two of the world's most strategic maritime chokepoints and certainly the focal points of Southwest Asia. The two chokepoints combined account for an estimated 35 percent of the world's seaborne-traded oil and other liquids (Keay, 1994: 105; Pearson, 2003: 17; U.S. Energy Information Administration, 2017a; 2019),

The maintenance of security at the Arabian Peninsula's two strategic chokepoints is a real concern for China and other international actors who rely on the region's maritime trade. The effects of a small cutoff within either strait could have significant economic and security ramifications for China. Due to the delicacy of the Arabian Peninsula's politics and security situation, President Xi Jinping's desire to secure the BRI will likely strengthen as China seeks to solidify and protect new trade networks at sea and over land. The PLA Navy, for example, placed greater emphasis on the protection of SLOCs, especially those flowing from the Persian/Arabian Gulf, across the Indian Ocean, through the Strait of Malacca and into Pacific Asia. In 2015, a defense strategy paper emphasized China's "far seas" strategy, detailing its desire for greater and more proactive naval projection beyond its near seas, specifically the South China Sea (cf. Holmes and Yoshihara, 2010: Le Mière, 2014; Feng, 2015; Fravel, 2015; Jacobs, 2015; 42–46; Raina, 2015).

The Red Sea and the Suez Canal

In recent years, China, among others, is beginning to home in on the Red Sea's importance. China very much views the Suez Canal as a "front door" into Europe and began investing significantly in the space through its maritime economic initiatives (Brewster, 2018).

In recent years, China has expanded its geoeconomic, diplomatic, and military engagements as part of its larger MSR efforts. During the first of President El-Sisi's two trips to China between 2014 and 2015, the two nations signed a "comprehensive strategic partnership" agreement, signaling Egypt's growing foreign policy posture away from the United States, and China's growing focus on Egypt and its vital maritime chokepoint. China's foreign policy of non-intervention in domestic politics was another strong selling point for El-Sisi following the Arab uprisings of 2011 and the overthrow of then President Hosni Mubarak (Namane, 2017).

On the maritime geoeconomic front, China focused much of its attention and efforts on bolstering trade linked to Egypt and the Suez Canal Zone. Most recently, the Suez Canal has generated nearly $5.6 billion for the Egyptian government, owing to the 18,000 ships that traversed the canal annually. This number of transiting ships peaked at 21,415 in 2008 before the global financial downturn. Currently, the canal generates more foreign capital for Egypt than any other sector of the economy. China has benefitted from Egypt's 2015 Suez Canal expansion project that now decreases the transit time from 18 to 11 hours, permits two-way traffic, and accommodates some of the world's largest container ships to more easily transit to ports in the Mediterranean basin and other destinations in Europe. The follow-on problem, however, is that not all of the European ports are able to handle the largest vessels such as the Triple-E Class ships. That said, this presents an incentive for China to continue buying up ports and expanding them so they can more readily handle these mega-ships, many of which are Chinese-flagged. The Egyptian government also hopes shipping and government revenues from the canal expansion will more than double by 2023, but experts are skeptical of these projections because global trade and shipping would have to increase by approximately 10 percent per year to meet them. The daily number of ships traversing the canal would have to jump from 50 (the current average) to around 97 ships every day. This number is unlikely to be achieved (Shelala, 2014; Prodi, 2015: 1–4; Saleh, 2015; Tasch, 2015; Reuters, 2018; Elhamy and Davison, 2018; Shumake, 2019).

On the investment side, China went from roughly $500 million in investments, as Egypt's 23rd largest investor, to $10 billion, when it increased financing for new projects in 2016. In the near future, China announced its intentions to invest a total of $40 billion in development projects in Egypt—though Egyptian government negotiations with a Chinese firm for a $20 billion deal to construct a new administrative capital east of Cairo recently fell through. In 2015, around 1,200 Chinese firms operated in Egypt, with this number easily expected to grow. President Xi Jinping followed El-Sisi with an official state visit to Cairo in January 2016. During his visit, the two nations signed $17 billion worth of agreements focused on the prior comprehensive strategic partnership agreement and other economic initiatives in technology, communications, and trade. One such project included a $3 billion agreement to construct a central business district in Ismaila about 50 kilometers east of Cairo as part of the larger Suez Canal Zone investments (Namane, 2017; Trickett, 2017; Magdy, 2018; Xinhua Net, 2018).

More investment means growing trade between the two nations. For the past several years, bilateral trade averaged around $11 billion, but this is up almost 96 percent since 2009. COSCO's shipping office in Egypt also expressed a desire to use Egypt as a part of a new series of shipping routes. According to Xie Manding, managing director of China COSCO shipping company in Egypt, COSCO was looking at shipping routes between Egypt-Ukraine-Russia-Turkey, prior to the Russian invasion of Ukraine, in addition to other routes between either Egypt or Morocco with northern Europe. Similar to Russia, China is focused on developing the Suez Canal Zone—it also fits neatly into its Maritime Silk Route as one of the world's most strategic chokepoints. Through China's Tianjin Economic-Technological Development Area (TEDA) Corporation, one of the oldest and largest developers of the Suez Canal Zone, it is focused on building up a 7 square-kilometer area in Ain Sokhna toward the south end of the canal in the Gulf of Suez. In 2013, it signed a 45-year contract for the development project; in 2019, they reportedly signed a second deal initiating phase two of the project. Under Egyptian law, TEDA is only permitted to hold a 49 percent stake in the initial $1.5 billion project. In many respects, this is a prudent law and helps prevent Egypt from a possible Chinese business monopolization should Egypt ever be unable to pay back its debts, as was the case in Sri Lanka. Thus far, 70 Chinese firms have signed up and are interested in further investment, trade, and development projects (Mitchell, 2010; *China Daily*, 2017a; 2017b; Namane, 2017; Al-Aees, 2018; Al-Masry Al-Youm, 2019).

Growing maritime investment and trade also mean a greater need for security. Egypt is surrounded by conflict, whether it is in Libya to the west or Israel and Palestine to the east. But perhaps most pressing is the ongoing conflict and ungoverned territory in large portions of the Sinai peninsula, adjacent to the Suez Canal Zone. China has already learned difficult lessons from Libya and Yemen, and any threats of a Suez Canal shutdown and its other maritime geoeconomic investments could prove devastating for its economy and larger global ambitions. China's PLAN fleet first traversed the Suez Canal and docked in Alexandria in 2002 during its first circumnavigation voyage. Though the relationship still pales in comparison to military cooperation with the USA, the relationship continues to grow. From 1989 to 2008, for example, Egypt was China's largest weapons market in Africa behind Sudan and Zimbabwe. By comparison, the USA and France accounted for 80 percent of Egyptian arms imports, with Germany in third place from 2012 to 2016 (Fleurant, Wezeman, et al., 2017).

Conclusion

China is potentially well positioned to take a larger and more leading regional role as it works toward sustaining its blue-water naval capacity and reach. It is using new maritime geoeconomic investments from the Suez Canal and Red Sea to the Arabian Sea and the Gulf to create and fortify maritime trade and logistics networks that are growing increasingly independent from the global system that has been dominated for so long by the

United States and the West. This system includes a new network of Chinese-dominated ports and infrastructure projects, in addition to a robust telecommunications network aided by submarine cables newly laid across the Mediterranean through the Suez Canal and into the Red Sea and the Indian Ocean. The emergence of this maritime network will ensure greater Chinese resilience in the future should any conflicts break out between China and another great power.

China's maritime geoeconomic interests are giving way to increased investments in its blue-water naval capabilities. China wants to avoid another Libya or Yemen scenario in the future where it had to rescue Chinese foreign nationals. To do so, it will need to take a more proactive security stance to ensure that its growing investments and regional interests are protected. It cannot rely on another power and therefore will need to continue the forward projection of its military and navy. It is unlikely that Chinese bases will start proliferating in rapid succession, but the only way to ensure that its maritime geoeconomic investments are secured from Europe to Pacific Asia is by having a force at the ready.

Note

1 The views expressed here are the author's alone and do not represent the U.S. Government, the Department of Defense, and National Defense University.

References

African Business. (2017) "Algeria: $3.5bn El Hamdania Port to Compete with Tanger Med," February 1.

Al-Aees, S. (2018) "Egypt TEDA Expects to Attract $3bn in Suez Canal Region," *Daily News Egypt*, April 18.

Albert, E. (2016) "Competition in the Indian Ocean," Council on Foreign Relations, Backgrounder, May 19. Available at: www.cfr.org/backgrounder/competition-indian-ocean

Al-Masry Al-Youm. (2019) "China to Invest US$5 billion in Egypt's Suez Canal Economic Zone," *Egypt Independent*, April 28.

Arnold, D.D. (2016) "Six Pressing Issues in Asia and How We're Adapting Our Approach to Address Them," Asia Foundation, September 6. Available at: https://asiafoundation.org/2016/09/06/six-pressing-issues-asia-adapting-approach-address/

Atli, A. (2017) "Turkey seeking its place in the Maritime Silk Road," *Asia Times*, February 26.

Baldwin, D.A. (1985) *Economic Statecraft*, Princeton, NJ: Princeton University Press.

Bar-Eli, A. (2014) "Chinese Firm Wins Tender, Opts to Build $1b Private Port in Ashdod," *Haaretz*, July 24.

Blackwill, R.D. and Harris, J.M. (2016) *War by Other Means: Geoeconomics and Statecraft*, Cambridge, MA: Harvard University Press.

Brady, A-M. (2017) *China as a Polar Great Power*, New York: Cambridge University Press.

Brewster, D. (2018) "Through Quiet Dealmaking, New Delhi Extends Its Influence in the Indian Ocean," *War on the Rocks*, February 16.

Calder, K.E. (2012) *New Continentalism: Energy and Twenty-First-Century Eurasian Geopolitics*, New Haven, CT: Yale University Press.

China Daily. (2017a) "Belt and Road Initiative to boost China-Egypt Trade," May 12.

China Daily. (2017b) "Egypt Launches Largest Trade Fair for Chinese Investors," October 25.

China Power Team. (2017) "How Much Trade Transits the South China Sea?" China Power, August 2 (updated October 27, 2017), Available at: https://chinapower.csis.org/much-trade-trans its-south-china-sea/

Clemente, J. (2015) "How Much Energy Does Russia Have Anyways?," *Forbes*, March 25.

Container Management. (2014) "Israeli Government Set to Private Ashdod and Haifa Container Management," October 10. Available at: https://container-mag.com/2014/10/10/israeli-government-set-privatise-ashdod-haifa/

Daily Mail. (2017) "Morocco's Tangiers to Host Chinese Industrial City," March 20.

Daily Sabah. (2017) "China Plan 'Caravan' Project for Transportation on Silk Road," March 15.

Deutsche Welle. (2018) "Russia and Saudi Arabia Forge Alliance to Engineer Oil Prices," April 20.

Dombrowski, P. and Winner, A.C., Eds. (2014) *The Indian Ocean and U.S. Grand Strategy: Ensuring Access and Promoting Security*, Washington, DC: Georgetown University Press.

Elhamy A. and Davison, J. (2018) "Egypt's Suez Canal Reports Record High $5.585 Billion Annual Revenue," *Reuters*, June 17.

Ergunsu, U. (2017) "Belt and Road Will Make Turkey-China Cooperation A Success," *China Daily*, June 1.

Famagusta Gazette. (2017) "New Tunisia -China Shipping Line to Enhance China's Presence in Africa," December 3.

Feng, C. (2015) "Embracing Interdependence: The Dynamics of China and the Middle East," Brookings Doha Center, Policy Briefing, April 28.

Fleurant, A., Wezeman, P.D., et al. (2017) "Trends in International Arms Transfers, 2016," SIPRI, February.

Fravel, M.T. (2015) "China's New Military Strategy: 'Winning Informationized Local Wars'," *China Brief*, 15(13), June 23.

Ghiselli, A. (2017) "Reflecting on China's Presence in the Mediterranean Region," ChinaMed Project, note no. 41, September.

Global Construction Review. (2019) "Morocco Opens Africa's Largest Port," July 1.

Grigas, A. (2017) *The New Geopolitics of Natural Gas*, Cambridge, MA: Harvard University Press.

Guardian. (2016) "India to Invest $500m in Iranian Port of Chabahar," May 25.

Gulf News. (2018) "India to Get Control of Key Port in Iran for 18 Months," February 18.

Gurcan, M. (2018) "Eastern Mediterranean Starting to Resemble Disputed South China Sea," *Al-Monitor*, March 13.

Hammond, J. (2017) "Morocco: China's Gateway to Africa?," *The Diplomat*, March 1.

Hochstrasser, J.B. (2005) "The Conquest of Spice and the Dutch Colonial Imaginary: Seen and Unseen in the Visual Culture of Trade," in L. Schiebinger, and C. Swan (Eds.), *Colonial Botany: Science, Commerce, and Politics in the Early Modern World*, Philadelphia, PA: University of Pennsylvania Press.

Holmes, J.R. and Yoshihara, T. (2010) "China's Navy: A Turn to Corbett?," *U.S. Naval Institute Proceedings*, 136(12): 42–46.

Humpert, M. (2013) "The Future of Arctic Shipping: A New Silk Road for China?," The Arctic Institute. Available at: www.thearcticinstitute.org/future-arctic-shipping-new -silk-road/

Israel Ports and Development Assets Company. (2011) "Israel's Southern Gateway," PowerPoint presentation (accessed July 8, 2019).

Izmir Development Agency. (2021) "Seaports of Izmir," May 1. Available at: https://izka.org.tr/?lang=en

Jacobs, A. (2015) "China, Updating Military Strategy, Puts Focus on Projecting Naval Power," *New York Times*, May 26.

Jaffrelot, C. (2011) "A Tale of Two Ports," *YaleGlobal Online*, January 7.

Kalim, I. (2016) "Gwadar Port: Serving Strategic Interests of Pakistan," *South Asian Studies*, 31(1): 207–221.

Karagiannis, E. (2016) "Shifting Eastern Mediterranean Alliances," *Middle East Quarterly*, 23(2): 1–11.

Keay, J. (1994) *The Honourable Company: A History of the English East India Company*, New York: Macmillan.

Kuo, M.A. (2017) "The Power of Ports: China's Maritime March," *The Diplomat*, March 8.

Lappin, Y. (2014) "Rocket Fire from Gaza Renews with Two Projectiles Hitting Ashdod, Ashkelon Area," *Jerusalem Post*, March 13.

Le Mière, C. (2014) "Presence Through Partnership? PLAN Improves China's Middle East Links," *Jane's Navy International*, November 19.

Li, M. (2019) "The Belt and Road Initiative: Geo-Economics and Indo–Pacific Security Competition," Draft paper for ISA Asia-Pacific Conference, Singapore, July 4–6.

Lim, K. (2017) "How Israel Can Align Its Strategy with China's Silk Road," *Asia Times*, January 21.

Luttwak, E.N. (1990) "From Geopolitics to Geo-Economics: Logic of Conflict, Grammar of Commerce," *The National Interest*, no. 20: 17–23.

Maçães, B. (2016) "China's Belt and Road: Destination Europe," *Carnegie Europe*, November 9.

Maçães, B. (2018) *Dawn of Eurasia: On the Trail of the New World Order*, New Haven, CT: Yale University Press.

Magdy, M. (2018) "China's $20 Billion New Egypt Capital Project Talks Fall Through," Bloomberg, December 16.

Malysheva, D. (2016) "Russia in the Mediterranean: Geopolitics and Current Interests," *International Affairs*, 62(1): 91–101.

Maritime Executive. (2017) "Algeria to Build New Deepwater Port," February 10.

Marlow, I. and Dilawar, I. (2018) "India's Grip on Vital Chabahar Port Loosens as Iran Looks towards China," *Business Standard*, April 11.

Miller, G. (2015) "Undersea Internet Cables Are Surprisingly Vulnerable," *Wired Magazine*, October 29.

Mitchell, T. (2010) "Egypt Courts China for Suez Special Zone," *Financial Times*, March 2.

Modelski, G. and Thompson, W.R. (1988) *Seapower in Global Politics, 1494–1993*, Seattle, WA: University of Washington Press.

Morocco World News. (2018) "World's Largest Container-Handling Cranes Arrive on Tangier Coast," March 9.

Namane, W. (2017) "China-Egypt Ties in the Age of the New Maritime Silk Road," The Delma Institute, July 20. Available at: http://delma.io

Nusantara Maritime News. (2016) "Algeria and China Sign $3.3 Billion Port Deal," January 25.

Omondi, G. (2017) "Lessons from Morocco in China-Backed Mega Project Plans in Africa," *Business Daily*, December 26.

Pant, H.V. and Mehta, K. (2018) "India in Chabahar: A Regional Imperative," *Asian Survey*, 58(4): 660–678.

Pant, H.V. and Ratna, P. (2018) "Why It Makes Sense for India and China to Cooperate on Iran's Chabahar Project," Observer Research Foundation, May 10. Available at: www.orfonline.org/research/why-it-makes-sense-for-india-and-china-to-cooperate-on-irans-chabahar-project/

Pearson, M. (2003) *The Indian Ocean (Seas in History)*, New York: Routledge.

People's Republic of China. (2017) "The 2nd Round of Negotiation of China-Israel Free Trade Area Held in Beijing," Statement by PRC Ministry of Commerce, July 15.

Petersburg, O. (2015) "Chinese Company Wins Bid to Run New Haifa Port," *Ynetnews*, March 24.

Port Finance International. (2015) "SIPG Signs Haifa Port Deal with Israel," June 3.

Prodi, R. (2015) "A Sea of Opportunities: The EU and China in the Mediterranean," *Mediterranean Quarterly*, 26(1): 1–4.

Raina, H. (2015) "China's Military Strategy White Paper 2015: Far Seas Operations and the Indian Ocean Region," Center for International Maritime Security, July 1.

Ramachandran, S. (2014) "India to Invest in Iran's Chabahar Port," *Central Asia-Caucasus Analyst*, November 26.

Reiber, J. (2018) "The Fastest Way across the Seas: Cyberoperations and Cybersecurity in the Indo-Pacific," in G.F. Gresh (Ed.), *Eurasia's Maritime Rise and Global Security*, New York: Palgrave Macmillan.

Reuters. (2014) "China Harbour Engineering Subsidiary to Build New Port at Ashdod in Israel," June 23.

Reuters. (2018) "Egypt's Suez Canal Revenues Rise to $5.3 Bln in 2017 – Statement," January 4.

Saleh, H. (2015) "Choppy waters for Egypt's Suez Canal Expansion," *Financial Times*, December 22.

Saleh, H. (2016) "Morocco's Tanger-Med Container Port Provides Bridge to Europe," *Financial Times*, March 23.

Scobell, A., Lin, B., Shatz, H.J., et al. (2018) *At the Dawn of Belt and Road China in the Developing World*, Washington, DC: RAND Corporation.

Shamah, D. (2014) "China Firm to Build New Ashdod 'Union Buster' Port," *Times of Israel*, September 23.

Shelala, R.M. (2014) *Maritime Security in the Middle East and North Africa: A Strategic Assessment*, Washington, DC: Center for Strategic and International Studies.

Shumake, J. (2019) "Suez Canal Has Record-Setting 2018," *American Shipper*, February 21.

SME Times. (2016) "Chabahar Port Will Boost India's Connectivity," May 23.

Spirk, D. (2016) "Bigger, but Not Necessarily Better," *U.S. News & World Report*, July 5.

Tasch, B. (2015) "'Build It And They Will Come' Is Not Enough: Egypt's $8 billion Suez Canal expansion sounds dubious," *Business Insider*, August 6.

Till, G. (2013) *Seapower*, 3rd ed., New York: Routledge.

Trickett, N. (2017) "Sino-Russian Shadow Competition Plays Out in Egypt," *The Diplomat*, August 11.

Trickett, N. (2018) "Why Putin's Oil Maneuvers Will Keep Russia in the Middle East," *Washington Post*, April 5.

U.S. Energy Information Administration. (2017a) "Three Important Oil Trade Chokepoints Are Located Around the Arabian Peninsula," August 4.

U.S. Energy Information Administration. (2017b) "World Oil Transit Chokepoints," July 25.

U.S. Energy Information Administration. (2019) "The Strait Of Hormuz Is The World's Most Important Oil Transit Chokepoint," June 20.

Wignaraja, G. and Panditaratne, D. (2019) "Sri Lanka's Quest for a Rules-Based Indian Ocean," *East Asia Forum*, January 31.

Wingfield, B., Dodge, S., and Sam, C. (2018) "OPEC+ Petro-Powers Ignored Oil Cuts Before Reset," Bloomberg, December 14.

World Port Source. (2019) "Port of Ambarli," July 10.

Wuthnow, J. (2017) *Chinese Perspectives on the Belt and Road Initiative: Strategic Rationales, Risks, and Implications*, Chinese Perspectives, no. 12, Washington, DC: NDU Press.

Xinhua Net. (2017a) "Morocco Eyes Mutual Benefit under Belt and Road Initiative," May 8.

Xinhua Net. (2017b) "News Analysis: Sino-Algerian Relations Witness Steady Progress in 59 Years of Diplomatic Ties," December 21.

Xinhua Net. (2018) "Spotlight: Egypt's Ismailia Province Eager to Attract More Chinese Investments," May 1.

Yung, C.D. and Rustici, R. (2014) *"Not an Idea We Have to Shun": Chinese Overseas Basing Requirements in the 21st Century*, China Strategic Perspectives no. 7, Washington, DC: NDU Press.

Zoubir, Y.H. (2021) "China's Relations with Algeria: From Revolutionary Friendship to Comprehensive Strategic Partnership," in A. Abdel-Ghafar (Ed.), *China and North Africa*. London: I.B. Tauris, pp. 126–165.

Zoubir, Y.H. (forthcoming) "China in the Southern Mediterranean: Integrating the Greater Maghreb in the New Silk Road," *Mediterranean Politics*. https://doi.org/10.1080/13629395.2022.2035137

13

CHINA'S RISE AND ITS SECURITY PRESENCE IN THE MIDDLE EAST AND NORTH AFRICA

Andrea Ghiselli

Introduction

Andrew J. Nathan and Andrew Scobell (2012) argued that the Middle East and North Africa (MENA) are important in Chinese diplomacy because of energy, but China has little to do there, especially in military terms. Ten years later, that assessment has not changed significantly, despite the expansion and diversification of Chinese interests and their presence in the region (Scobell and Nader, 2016; Scobell, 2018). Bringing about a change in a country's foreign policy such as China's move to expand its military footprint in the MENA region has not been easy (Ghiselli, 2021). Moreover, as tensions with the United States in Asia continue to rise, the center of China's foreign and defense policy remains in its home region. Nonetheless, this chapter argues that the study of the development of China's limited military presence in the MENA region can offer key insights into that country's rise in international affairs.

After a lengthy analysis of its capability to influence world affairs, David Shambaugh declared that China is a "global actor without, yet, being a true global power" (2013: 8). Because it can wield global influence only in some areas of international politics, China remains what he calls a "partial power." On the one hand, China does not have the global capabilities in certain policy areas. For example, the Chinese armed forces can hardly project substantial offensive power outside Asia. On the other hand, even in those policy areas where Chinese capabilities are sufficient, material resources alone do not automatically buy long-lasting influence; a country needs to develop both soft and smart power to do so (Nye, 2011). Such a social understanding of power, and therefore of the status of great power, means that other countries are not always willing to recognize a rich country as a great power.

In an article on Chinese and Japanese frustration at not being fully recognized as "legitimate" great powers, Suzuki (2008: 45) showed that differences in culture and political systems ultimately generate the fear that an aspiring great power might use its military

DOI: 10.4324/9781003048404-15

power either against other countries or not use it to promote the interests of the international community. In order to show their commitment to the society of states, Suzuki argued, Japan and China started to participate in peacekeeping operations under the aegis of the United Nations (UN). This is part of what Suzuki describes as the "recognition game" that countries play to be recognized as good members of the international society.

This chapter studies the evolution of the Chinese military presence in the MENA region through the lens of Suzuki's work in order to offer a new perspective on the status of China's bid to join the ranks of legitimate great powers and gain an insights into the future of the international system. The argument presented here is twofold. First, following the decline of war as an institution of the international society and the simultaneous rise of nontraditional security in world affairs, China adapted rather successfully to a new logic dominating the mechanism of great power management. Hence, China also managed to strengthen its bid to great power status despite the persistent tensions in Asia and the ongoing rivalry with the United States. Second, China's rise is likely to lead to a world without superpowers, characterized by what Buzan calls *decentered* globalism (Buzan, 2011). That means that vis-à-vis increasingly dangerous nontraditional security threats, from terrorism to climate change, no country will be able to solve them singlehandedly. Rather, it will need to find common ground and cooperate with other great powers.

The underlying assumption of my argument is that military power remains the indicator *par excellence* of great power status. Indeed, even non-military uses of the armed forces, such as search and rescue operations, are often interpreted as demonstrations of strength because countries usually deploy their most advanced hardware to impress their peers (Lin-Greenberg, 2018). Although war as an institution of the international society might have been undermined by its tremendous human and economic costs (Bull, 2002; Buzan and Lawson, 2015), military power still "provides a degree of security that is to order as oxygen is to breathing: little noticed until it begins to become scarce. Once it occurs, its absence dominates all else" (Nye, 2011: 59). Yet, order does not only mean peace among great powers. As convincingly argued by Cui Shunji and Barry Buzan (2016), great power management—the main duty of great powers—has changed from purely guaranteeing order through the prevention of wars to ensuring effective global governance. This shift happened because of the growing importance of nontraditional security since the end of the Cold War.

In order to pinpoint the process of China's evolution into a great power of a future decentered world, the chapter posits an ideal connection between Suzuki's "recognition game," played by frustrated great powers, and the set of strategies envisioned by Mastanduno, Lake, and Ikenberry (1989), in their realist theory of state action. Such a connection is evident when one examines the logic of Suzuki's "recognition game" and that of the pursuit of external validation by a state whose international standing is weak, as described by the other three scholars.

Once the position on the international stage of a state has been strengthened, Mastanduno et al. (1989) argue that state will change its strategy to pursue external extraction. External extraction "refers to state efforts to accumulate resources from outside its borders that can be of use in achieving domestic objectives" and "often requires an ability to influence other nation-states, to get them to do what they would otherwise not do" (ibid.: 469).

In a decentered world, although great powers are likely to focus on their own region, they will still require international government organizations (IGOs), such as the UN, to address transnational problems that pose a substantial threat to their global interests (Buzan, 2011). Therefore, supporting and acting through IGOs is an effective way to do so. In the specific case of military power, this does not simply entail participating in UN-sanctioned missions, but also being able to influence them in ways so that national interests are better served. This means that, for example, while China in the past did participate in peacekeeping missions mostly in order to boost its international reputation, now its main goal is to ensure a stable environment for Chinese businesses to operate in potentially unstable regions. This is a demonstration of great power status, both in material and social terms: China has the capabilities to act and it is recognized by other countries as having the right to enjoy the benefit of a great power's "legalized hegemony" (Simpson, 2004).

This chapter looks at two particular kinds of Military Operations Other Than War (MOOTW)—international peacekeeping and anti-piracy operations—carried out by the Chinese People's Liberation Army (PLA) under the aegis of the UN in recent years in the MENA region. These are the two situations where Chinese MOOTW are more significant and where political instability and terrorism, two typical issues of a decentered world, unfortunately are important phenomena.

In the analysis it is important to understand the main goals that China aimed to achieve through those operations, distinguishing between boosting the country's international standing (recognition game/pursuit of external validation) and promoting international stability in relation to Chinese overseas interests (external extraction). As the term *overseas interests* is a rather vague one in the writings of Chinese scholars and analysts, this chapter looks at the presence of Chinese workers, the value of the engineering projects contracted to Chinese companies, and China's reliance on some countries for its energy supplies.

China's Recognition Game in Sudan and the Gulf of Aden

Until 2011, Chinese behavior can be considered consistent with the logic of the recognition game. Besides the fact that China is a permanent member of the UN Security Council (UNSC), and, therefore, is expected to play a leading role in international security, 2008 was also the year of the Beijing Olympic Games. Naturally, the Chinese government did not want to have such a symbolic event ruined by international criticism.

Although they were all from engineering and medical units, between 2000 and 2011 the number of Chinese peacekeepers deployed abroad every year grew from 100 up to roughly 2,000, mostly in Africa. The westward transition of the center of gravity of Chinese military operations overseas was also caused by the participation of the PLA Navy (PLAN) in the international anti-piracy missions in the Gulf of Aden. Thanks to this development, China started to be a security actor also outside its home region, thereby crucially expanding the geographical reach of its influence in security affairs.

Since the first UNSC resolution on the Darfur crisis, China has tried to water down the criticism against the Sudanese government. However, as the crisis continued to worsen and the year of the Olympic Games came closer, a harsh media campaign that linked the killing in Darfur with the Games was mounted against Beijing. The publication of a 2007 report by Amnesty International (2007) on the failure of the arms embargo against the

Sudanese government added further pressure on Beijing, one of the main arms suppliers to the African government.

In 2005, China started to press the Sudanese government through the missions of the Chinese government's special envoy Liu Guijun in order to allow the deployment of peacekeepers in the country. President Hu Jintao reportedly spoke about the issue personally with al-Bashir (Xinhua, 2007). At the same time, China emphasized many times that there was no reason to link the events in Darfur with the Olympic Games and criticized the international media for doing so. Later, under China's presidency, the UNSC passed Resolution 1769 providing for the African Union/United Nations Hybrid Operation in Darfur (UNAMID). China contributed more than 300 medical and engineering troops and they were among the first to arrive.

China was not only defending its own growing international reputation and learning how to act like a great power, the presence of Chinese workers and companies was an important factor, too. Chinese companies had invested heavily in the Sudanese upstream and downstream oil sector. Between 1996 and 2007, 43 percent of the foreign investments in the Sudanese upstream oil sector were from China. Between 2001 and 2007, an average of 6 percent of Chinese crude oil imports came from Sudan.[1] Moreover, between 2003 and 2007, the number of Chinese contract workers, a term used by Chinese statistics usually referring to state-owned companies' employees, grew from 3,618 to 16,904 (National Bureau of Statistics of China, 2016: 612–614).

Characterized by a mix of innovation and continuity, the diplomatic intervention and the participation in the peacekeeping mission signaled a change in China's bargain with the international community. On the one hand, China was acting in an unprecedentedly proactive way by engaging and mediating between the different parties involved. On the other hand, the concrete military participation was consistent with the general trends of Chinese peacekeeping in those years. Since 2004, China had increased its contribution of troops in a significant way, but, as in past missions, the Chinese peacekeepers in UNAMID still came from engineering and medical units.

China's participation in the international anti-piracy mission off Somali waters since late 2008 shows how China's recognition game was becoming more expensive in terms of level of engagement required by the international community. Indeed, as in the Sudanese case, the decision to join the international mission was mainly determined by the government's necessity to show China's commitment to neutralize a threat, rather than actually eliminate it. The Chinese government wanted to send a strong message to both domestic and international observers (Erickson and Strange, 2015).

After all, as Bull (2002) argued, a great power is not only acknowledged as such by other states, but also by its citizens. According to online polls, more than 86 percent of Chinese "netizens" supported the deployment of warships to protect Chinese cargoes in the Gulf of Aden (Sina.com, 2008). Although these data can hardly be taken as a scientific measurement of the national attitude toward the anti-piracy missions, they are still indicative of the opinion of a section of the Chinese population that is able to exert a growing influence over the policy-making process through the social media.

The Chinese task forces still follow rather conservative rules of engagement in comparison with their Western counterparts (Lin-Greenberg, 2010). Yet, it is clear that the Chinese government was under great pressure to act. Indeed, China removed its most modern ships from their traditional defense duties and sent them into faraway waters, despite the first signs of growing tensions in Asia (Ghiselli, 2021: 203–240). Only after the departure from Qingdao of the eleventh task force did the number of rotations per ship decline. Since then, almost all of the surface combatants deployed participated in only one expedition. In order to avoid the embarrassing problems of the past, such as not being able to repair its own engines at sea without foreign assistance (Collins and Grubb, 2008), and support the leadership's decision to join the international anti-piracy efforts in the Middle East, the PLAN had to remove some of its most modern ships from traditional defense duties. This is a typical example of swaggering.[2]

Once again, there are signs of continuity and discontinuity with the past. On the one hand, China was able to make the best out of a bad situation by taking the chance to start a robust naval diplomacy through port calls and joint exercises with the other navies. On the other hand, the decision to send the best naval hardware far away from home is extremely indicative of the importance that the Chinese government attached to effectively projecting a strong image abroad. Moreover, the importance of the economic interests abroad began to be evident.

Indeed, a key point of the work of Mastanduno et al. (1989) is that the shift toward a more proactive foreign policy is ultimately aimed at achieving domestic goals. Having the support of its citizens, preferably in a consensual way, is the main goal of every government (Kinne, 2005). Guaranteeing their citizens' well-being and preserving the territorial integrity of the country are the two vital pillars upon which the legitimacy of a government rests (Klosko, 2005). Therefore, when the citizens perceive that their assets or their nation's assets abroad are under threat, the necessity for the state to change strategy and participate more actively in international affairs becomes more urgent. Besides, trade and investments abroad naturally make a country richer. The newly acquired wealth can be transformed into material power through, for example, military buildup, the symbol of great power status.

At the same time, the more trade and investments abroad expand, the more a country will be seen by others as rich and powerful, thereby making their expectations grow. The internal demand for great power status will increase, too, as happened in China after the 2008 financial crisis (Shambaugh and Ren, 2012). Within the Chinese International Relations community, Wang Yizhou's concept of "creative intervention" (2008; 2011) is probably the clearest call to change China's approach to its own great power status and understanding of its role in international affairs.

As the first decade of the new century ended, the period of pure recognition game was also almost over. The growing overlap of China's interests and those of the international community was crucial in closing this process. As the next section argues, to contribute to the promotion of international stability was no longer going to be only about convincing the international community, but also about protecting China's own interests as a rich and increasingly globalized economy.

Beyond External Validation, the Importance of Libya

The evacuation of some 36,000 Chinese citizens from Libya in the spring of 2011 radically changed the situation and, consequently, China's behavior. The pressure from public opinion was high, both during and after the crisis. A number of Weibo users, some of whom were trapped in Libya, indeed complained about the inefficient emergency hotline set up by the Ministry of Foreign Affairs (Chin, 2011). The Ministry of Commerce stated that Chinese companies had thus far signed contracts worth $18.8 billion (*Global Times*, 2011).

To avoid the repetition of any similar incident became a new top priority of Chinese foreign policy. The Libyan crisis had deep repercussions on the regional security environment, thereby also affecting the increasingly diversified Chinese interests there. For example, the destabilization of Mali, where in November 2015 three Chinese managers were killed during a terrorist attack, happened also because of the diffusion throughout the Sahel of weapons from the Libyan arsenals. Before moving on to assess how the focus of China's strategy has shifted from obtaining external recognition to pursuing external extraction, it is important to outline the scale of Chinese interests in the neighboring countries of Mali, Sudan, and South Sudan, all countries prey to different degrees of instability and/or civil war.

While in Mali the volume of Chinese investments and the number of Chinese workers are negligible, the failure of the Malian state as a result of civil war might provide unnecessary fertile ground for the growth of terrorist organizations capable of infiltrating into the neighboring countries. Among them, Algeria has hosted the largest number of Chinese contract workers in North Africa since 2002, growing from 14,000 to more than 91,000 in 2016 (Zoubir, 2021). The Algerian market is extremely important for Chinese companies: The total value of the engineering and construction projects awarded to Chinese companies between 2004 and 2017 is around $72 billion. Mali and Algeria should be seen as part of a delicate mosaic, where the other pieces are Morocco and Niger. Those two countries are lucrative markets for Chinese engineering companies worth $9 billion together between 2011 and 2015.

Moving eastward, in Egypt and Ethiopia, separated by Sudan and South Sudan, Chinese companies were contracted for engineering projects from energy to big logistic infrastructures, respectively worth $13 and $30 billion between 2011 and 2017. While in Egypt, the China-Egypt Suez Economic and Trade Cooperation Zone has been developing quickly in recent years, the number of Chinese contract workers in Ethiopia has grown from 5,600 to 10,000 (the peak was in 2014 with more than 14,000 workers). Energy-wise, North Africa is less important than in the past, especially since the imports of Libyan and Sudanese crude oil have significantly decreased because of war. However, the Ethiopian natural gas sector has become the target of Chinese investments recently. The Middle East, which has consistently supplied between 40 and 50 percent of Chinese crude oil and natural gas imports between 2001 and 2018, is the last segment of this *arch of interests* that stretches from Morocco to Iran. Unfortunately, the Middle East is as unstable as it is important. To sum up, it is clear why China is trying to transform its material power into the "legalized hegemony" of a great power to protect its interests.

A first evident sign of change can be found in the quantitative and, especially, the qualitative growth of China's engagement in peacekeeping operations since 2012. That year, a platoon-sized unit of so-called guard troops was deployed in South Sudan to provide exclusive protection to the Chinese peacekeepers already there. They had no other role within the UN Mission in South Sudan (UNMISS) framework and, for this reason, they were not officially considered China's first combat troops operating under the UN aegis. They nonetheless set an important precedent for the ensuing deployments of combat troops. After the first deployment, the PLAN continued to contribute similar troops both to UNMISS and the UN Multidimensional Integrated Stabilization Mission in Mali (MINUSMA). Those troops differ from the standard PLAN infantrymen. Indeed, they boast full body armor, new weapons, drones, and modern armored carriers, which in many ways make them similar to special forces (PRC MOD, 2015).

Reflecting the need to provide better support to its troops and sailors, the Chinese military leadership also decided to bring an end to the discussion about whether, where, and how to establish military bases abroad. In 2013, Zhao Keshi, a member of the powerful Central Military Commission and leader of the former PLA General Logistic Department, wrote an article on this issue that was published in *China Military Science*, the flagship journal of the PLA Academy of Military Science. He argued that it was high time that China established overseas bases/logistic spots to support its expanding military operations, especially peacekeeping and noncombatant evacuations (Zhao, 2013). Such a strong statement from Zhao implicitly confirmed that a decision had already been made.

Like other great powers, China needed military facilities abroad in order to step up the protection of its overseas interests and, at the same time, better contribute to international stability. In late 2015, China finally confirmed that the negotiations with Djibouti were practically over. Although it is not possible to know exactly what kind of operations the facilities in the East African country will support, there is no doubt that they will greatly help to cement Chinese military presence in the region. The PLAN and the PLA Air Force had been waiting for a stable berth and perch (Ghiselli, 2016a). By looking at the presence of Chinese peacekeepers, the facilities in Djibouti, and the naval task forces in the Gulf of Aden, it is possible to see the emergence of Chinese military infrastructure built through growing engagement in the UN. A Chinese scholar put forward the term "soft military presence" to describe the PLA presence in this faraway region (Sun, 2014).

The decision to deploy combat troops and establish overseas facilities reflects a broader reconsideration about the use of force vis-à-vis nontraditional security issues in foreign policy in recent years. In many ways, China's approach to political instability in other countries directly grows out of its experience of promoting economic development in its own western provinces in order to create social harmony. Although this has not changed much, it is possible to see the emergence of a new trend.

In 2013, China voted in favor of UN Resolution 2100, which provided for the deployment of MINUSMA and tasked the peacekeepers to take "all necessary means, within the limits of its capacities and areas of deployment" in order to "stabilize" population centers in northern Mali and to "deter threats and to take active steps to prevent the return of armed elements in those areas" (UN Security Council, 2013: 7). The same year, China was in favor of the creation of an "intervention brigade," with offensive tasks, as part of the UN Organization Stabilization Mission in the Democratic Republic of the Congo (MONUSCO). Finally, after Xi Jinping called for a boost to the international efforts against terrorism in the aftermath of the killing of the Chinese hostages in Syria, the Chinese Ambassador to the UN mentioned that tragic event among the motivations behind China's vote in favor of allowing the use of force against terrorists in Syria and Iraq (UN Security Council, 2015). Considering that China had been opposed to this since 2011, when a similar resolution led to the fall of Gaddafi in Libya, and that the future of Assad in Syria was still uncertain, this fact is quite indicative of the change going on in China's understanding of terrorism and the protection of its overseas interests (Ghiselli, 2016b).

As in a virtuous circle, the qualitative and quantitative growth of China's participation in peacekeeping missions ensures that the country has a stronger voice regarding where, how, and when to launch or extend old and new missions. At the same time, the more the Chinese policy-makers see the benefits derived from acting through the UN, the more they will also be likely to increase their engagement and contribution.

China's Rise and Its Security Presence

An example of this development is the extension of UNMISS in 2014. China's offer to provide 700 more troops to the mission is likely to have had an influence during the debate on how to modify and extend the mandate of the mission in order to protect the oil installations, many of which were operated by Chinese companies. Two years later, after it had already pledged the creation of an 8,000-troops-strong standby force and the contribution of helicopters to the peacekeeping operations, China also reportedly tried to take more direct control of the peacekeeping planning process by proposing to put a Chinese officer in charge of the UN Peacekeeping Department (Lynch, 2016). Although he was arrested by Chinese authorities for corruption in 2018, the appointment of Meng Hongwei, former Vice Minister for Public Security, as the head of Interpol in November 2016 can be seen as a precedent for such an event (Griffiths, 2016).

China's ambition to play an active role in regional security affairs was finally spelled out in the first White Paper on the Middle East, published in January 2016 (PRC State Council, 2016), shortly before President Xi Jinping went there for the first time since he took power in 2013.

To conclude, it is quite clear that in recent years China has been trying to pursue a strategy of external extraction. The importance of being recognized as a great power never disappeared; it was simply upgraded, because the growing overlap between the interests of the international community and China required a more proactive engagement. Thus, while the Chinese contribution to peacekeeping missions is praised internationally, domestic forces keep the pressure on the government high. The concluding section of the chapter will discuss the implications of China's rise as a great power in a decentered world on the international system.

Conclusion

This chapter has offered a new perspective on China's rise by pinpointing the transition from an external validation strategy to an external extraction, as shown by the development of Chinese MOOTW in the MENA region. At the same time, although it might be less eye-catching than the American operations we have grown used to over the years and China has been very careful to keep a low profile, it was also shown that China's military presence in that region should not be ignored, for its evolution reflects the broader changes in China's foreign policy.

The critical factor in China's strategic shift was the growing overlap between the interests of the international community and those of China. As China's status as a great power consolidates, its bargaining power with the international community is also growing. As the attempts to influence the process of planning of the peacekeeping operations shows, it is the other great powers that are likely to pay for this. The UN Peacekeeping Department has traditionally been a French turf for almost 20 years. More broadly, Chinese scholars today also suggest that cooperation between China and other great powers in Africa, especially in security affairs, should happen through the adjustment of those countries' policies to the Chinese policies, rather than the other way around (Zhi, 2016; Zhou, 2016). This is consistent with the emergence of a decentered world, the precondition of which is the diffusion of material capabilities that limits the influence of the traditional great powers and boosts that of the new ones.

In such a context, given their geopolitical and geoeconomic importance, the MENA region will remain a crucial place in which to observe the evolution of China's rise. There are two main reasons for this. First, great powers have the responsibility to promote stability and fight terrorism, and the expectations of China's role in doing so are likely to continue to increase in the future. Second, China's interests in the region are growing and will continue to grow within President Xi Jinping's Belt and Road Initiative (Ghiselli and Morgan, 2021). China must not only find a way to protect its interests there, but it must also find a way to prevent threats from those places, i.e. the so-called "foreign fighters," to return. Hence, China's rise and its engagement with the region will keep going hand-in-hand.

Yet, of course, this does not mean that it will be easy for China to successfully implement its strategy. Three interconnected issues are particularly important in this regard. First, many regimes in the region remain extremely fragile. They, therefore, are easy prey of stronger powers, more inclined to seek external patrons, and less resistant to non-state challenges. Syria and Iraq are two examples of this. This fact, combined with historical rivalries, makes the MENA region extremely difficult to navigate for a country that has little regional experience there. Second, the slow but steady withdrawal of the United States, made worse by the erratic decisions of President Trump during his first and only presidential mandate, has created power vacuums that (over-)ambitious regional powers, such as Saudi Arabia, Turkey, and Israel, as well as external ones such as Russia are trying to fill. This renewed struggle for power puts Chinese diplomacy in a difficult position because the "blinds" and the stakes in this dangerous game are extremely high. Goals that seemed achievable once, might not be so any longer. Third, the rocky relations with the United States might force China to focus all its energy on that, thereby pausing any significant development of its strategy in the MENA region. At this point, we can only wait and see how the situation will continue to evolve.

Notes

1 Elaboration of data from ITC Trade Map, www.trademap.org/Index.aspx
2 Robert J. Art (1980) argued:

> Swaggering almost always involves only the peaceful use of force and is expressed usually in one of two ways: displaying one's military might at military exercises and national demonstrations and buying or building the era's most prestigious weapons. The swagger use of force is the most egoistic: it aims to enhance the national pride of a people or to satisfy the personal ambitions of its ruler. A state or statesman swaggers in order to look and feel more powerful and important, to be taken seriously by others in the councils of international decision-making to enhance the nation's image in the eyes of others.

References

Amnesty International (2007) "Sudan Arms Continuing to Fuel Serious Human Rights Violations in Darfur." Available at www.amnesty.org/download/Documents/60000/afr540192007en.pdf (accessed March 20, 2021).
Art, R. J. (1980) "To What Ends Military Power?" *International Security*, 4(4): 3–35.
Bull, H. (2002) *The Anarchical Society*. New York: Palgrave.
Buzan, B. (2011) "A World Order Without Superpowers: Decentred Globalism," *International Relations*, 25(1): 3–25.
Buzan, B. and Lawson, G. (2015) *The Global Transformation*. Cambridge: Cambridge University Press.
Chin, J. (2011) "China's Other Problem with Protests Abroad," Blog. *The Wall Street Journal*, February 23. Available at: http://blogs.wsj.com/chinarealtime/2011/02/23/chinas-other-problem-with-protests-abroad/ (accessed March 20, 2021).
Collins, G. B. and Grubb, M. C. (2008) "A Comprehensive Survey of China's Dynamic Shipbuilding Industry," *China Maritime Studies*, 1: 1–56.

Cui, S. and Buzan, B. (2016) "Great Power Managment in International Society," *The Chinese Journal of International Politics*, 9(2): 181–210.

Erickson, A. S. and Strange, A. M. (2015) *Six Years at Sea... and Counting: Gulf of Aden Anti-Piracy and China's Maritime Commons Presence*. Washington, DC: Jamestown Foundation.

Ghiselli, A. (2016a) "China's First Overseas Base in Djibouti, An Enabler of its Middle East Policy," *China Brief*, 16(2): 6–9.

Ghiselli, A. (2016b) "Growing Overlap Between Counter-Terrorism and Overseas Interest Protection Acts as New Driver of Chinese Strategy," *China Brief*, 16(9): 15–18.

Ghiselli, A. (2021) *Protecting China's Interests Overseas: Securitization and Foreign Policy*. Oxford: Oxford University Press.

Ghiselli, A. and Morgan, P. (2021) "A Turbulent Silk Road: China's Vulnerable Foreign Policy in the Middle East and North Africa," *China Quarterly*. Available at: https://doi.org/10.1017/S0305741020001216

Global Times (2011) "Chinese Companies Had Contracts Worthy USD 18,8 Billion in Libya: It Is Difficult to Calculate the Losses," March 24. Available at: http://finance.huanqiu.com/roll/2011-03/1584398.html (accessed April 11, 2021).

Griffiths, J. (2016) "Chinese Security Official Elected Interpol Chief," CNN, November 10. Available at: www.cnn.com/2016/11/10/asia/china-interpol-president/ (accessed April 12, 2021).

Kinne, B. J. (2005) "Decision Making in Autocratic Regimes: A Poliheuristic Perspective," *International Studies Perspectives*, 6: 114–128.

Klosko, G. (2005) *Political Oblications*. New York: Oxford University Press.

Lin-Greenberg, E. (2010) "Dragon Boats: Assessing China's Anti-Piracy Operations in the Gulf of Aden," *Defense & Security Analysis*, 26(2): 213–230.

Lin-Greenberg, E. (2018) "Non-Traditional Security Dilemmas: Can Military Operations other than War Intensify Security Competition in Asia?" *Asian Security*, 14(2): 282–302.

Lynch, C. (2016,) "China Eyes Ending Western Grip on Top U.N. Jobs with Greater Control over the Blue Helmets," *Foreign Policy*. October 2. Available at http://foreignpolicy.com/2016/10/02/china-eyes-ending-western-grip-on-top-u-n-jobs-with-greater-control-over-blue-helmets/ (accessed April 25, 2021).

Mastanduno, M., Lake, D. A. and Inkenberry, J. G. (1989) "Toward a Realist Theory of State Action," *International Studies Quarterly*, 33(4): 457–474.

Nathan, A. J. and Scobell, A. (2012) *China's Search for Security*. New York: Columbia University Press.

National Bureau of Statistics of China (2016) *China Trade and External Economic Statistical Yearbook*. Beijing: China Statistics Press.

Nye, J. (2011) *The Future of Power*. New York: Public Affairs.

PRC MOD (2015) "China's Peacekeeping Equipment Questioned," January 4. Available at http://eng.mod.gov.cn/DefenseNews/2015-01/04/content_4561933.htm (accessed March 17, 2021).

PRC State Council. (2016) "China's Arab Policy Paper," January. Available at http://english.gov.cn/archive/publications/2016/01/13/content_281475271412746.htm (accessed March 3, 2021).

Scobell, A. (2018) "Why the Middle East Matters to China," in A. Ehteshami and N. Horesh (Eds.), *China's Presence in the Middle East: The Implications of the One Belt, One Road Initiative*. New York: Routledge, pp. 9–23.

Scobell, A. and Nader, A. (2016) *China in the Middle East: The Wary Dragon* . Santa Monica, CA: RAND Corporation.

Shambaugh, D. (2013) *China Goes Global*. New York: Oxford University Press.

Shambaugh, D. and Ren, X. (2012) "China: The Conflicted Power," in H. R. Nau and D. M. Ollapally (Eds.), *Worldviews of Aspiring Powers*. New York: Oxford University Press, ebook position 767–1459.

Simpson, G. (2004) *Great Powers and Outlaw States: Unequal Sovereigns in the International Legal Order*. Cambridge: Cambridge University Press.

Sina.com (2008) "中国海军远征索马里揭秘：速射炮最适合打海盗" [Uncovering the Secrets of the Chinese Navy's Long-Distance Operations in Somalia: Rapid-Fire Assault Is the Most Suitable Way to Fight Pirates], December 26. Available at http://mil.news.sina.com.cn/2008-12-25/1033536352.html (accessed February 9, 2021).

Sun, D. (2014) "About the New Era of Chinese Soft Military Presence in the Middle East," *World Economics and Politics*, 8: 4–29.

Suzuki, S. (2008) "Seeking 'Legitimate' Great Power Status in Post-Cold War International Society: China's and Japan's Participation in UNPKO," *International Relations*, 22(1): 45–63.

UN Security Council. (2013) "Resolution 2100 (2013)," April 25. Available at www.un.org/en/peace keeping/missions/minusma/documents/mali%20_2100_E_.pdf (accessed April 21, 2021).

UN Security Council. (2015) "Security Council 'Unequivocally' Condemns ISIL Terrorist Attacks, Unanimously Adopting Text that Determines Extremist Group Poses 'Unprecedented' Threat," November 20. Available at: www.un.org/press/en/2015/sc12132.doc.htm (accessed April 21, 2021).

Wang, Y. (2008) *High Land Over China Foreign Affairs*. Beijing: China Social Science Press.

Wang, Y. (2011) *Creative Involvement: A New Direction in China's Diplomacy*. Beijing: Peking University Press.

Xinhua (2007) "Hu Puts Forward Principle on Darfur Issue," February 5. Available at: www.chi nadaily.com.cn/china/2007-02/05/content_801393.htm (accessed April 14, 2021).

Zerba, S. H. (2014) "China's Libya Evacuation Operation: A New Diplomatic Imperative - Overseas Citizens Protection," *Journal of Contemporary China*, 23(90): 1093–1112.

Zhao, K. (2013) "Strategic Thoughts on Accelerating Modernization of PLA Logistics in the New Situation," *China Military Science*, 4: 1–10.

Zhi, Y. (2016) "Evolution of French Military Policy toward Africa and Its Implications for China-French-Africa Trilateral Peace and Security Cooperation," *Global Review*, 6: 73–92.

Zhou, J. (2016) "China-U.K.-Africa Trilateral Peace and Security Cooperation: Prospects and Challenges," *Global Review*, 6: 93–109.

Zoubir, Y. H. (2021) "China's Relations with Algeria: From Revolutionary Friendship to Comprehensive Strategic Partnership," in A. Abdel-Ghafar, (Ed.), *China and North Africa*. London: I.B. Tauris, pp. 126–165.

14

BUILDING AN "OUTER SPACE SILK ROAD"

China's Beidou Navigation Satellite System in the Arab World

Degang Sun, Yuyou Zhang, and Luzhou Lin

China's Beidou Navigation Satellite System in the Arab World: Progress and Development

In ancient China, people used the Big Dipper to navigate. These seven bright stars of the constellation Ursa Major are known in Chinese as "beidou qixing," and China's navigation satellite system is named Beidou, which means "pointing out the right direction." With the advance of China's satellite navigation technology, Beidou has become a tool for China to promote its all-round cooperation with other countries. In June 2014, President Xi Jinping attended the sixth session of the ministerial conference of the China-Arab States Cooperation Forum. During the meeting, Xi put forward the strategic concept of the China-Arab cooperation model of "1+2+3." The "3" here includes nuclear energy, aerospace and satellites, and new energy. President Xi Jinping made it clear that attempts should be made to implement China's Beidou Navigation Satellite System in the Arab world (Xi, 2014). In 2016, the seventh session of the ministerial conference of the China-Arab States Cooperation Forum was held in Doha, Qatar; after consultations, China and the Arab states unanimously decided to hold the first China-Arab Beidou Cooperation Forum and issued a joint declaration to this effect. The implementation of the Beidou system in the Arab world is still at a preliminary stage, but the system is a strategic support and diplomatic resource for China to look westward in the twenty-first century, to carry out the implementation of the Belt and Road Initiative and to build a comprehensive strategic partnership with the Arab League.

The 22 member states of the Arab League have a population of 400 million with diverse national conditions; the Gulf countries such as Saudi Arabia, the United Arab Emirates (UAE), Qatar and Kuwait boast abundant petrodollars; Egypt, Algeria and Morocco, albeit low in per capita GDP, have large population and market potential, which has created good conditions for the promotion of the Beidou system in the Arab world.

From 2007 to 2019, China and the Arab states signed 15 space cooperation documents and carried out 21 cooperation projects. Among them, China and the Gulf countries signed 8 cooperation documents and carried out 12 cooperation projects; China and the

DOI: 10.4324/9781003048404-16

North African Arab states signed 4 cooperation documents and carried out 9 cooperation projects, including 4 satellite communication projects, 10 satellite remote sensing projects and 20 navigation satellite projects (Lin, 2020: 97–121).

China's Navigation Satellite System Office and the Arab Information and Communication Technology Organization (AICTO) have forged close ties in recent years. On January 20, 2014, the two sides signed a memorandum of understanding on cooperation in the field of China-Arab satellite navigation at the headquarters of the Arab League in Cairo, Egypt, establishing a formal cooperation mechanism in the field of satellite navigation. They subsequently held the first and second China-Arab Beidou cooperation meetings in Shanghai and Tunisia, in 2017 and 2019 respectively. In addition:

- the China-Arab Beidou/GNSS center was built in Tunisia;
- the Beidou system test experience activities were jointly held;
- the Beidou system test evaluation results in the Arab region were released;
- the Beidou application demonstration experience activities were carried out;
- several special training activities for Arab states were held;
- Chinese government scholarships for Arab students to come to China were provided;
- China dispatched technicians to Arab states to carry out multiple rounds of navigation technology and application training (Lin and Li, 2018: 68).

In terms of satellite navigation, the rapid launch network of the Beidou system can provide services for Arab states and the two sides have engaged in extensive satellite navigation cooperation. The Beidou Navigation Satellite System had officially provided services to the Asia Pacific region in 2012, and after a high-density network launch, it began to provide positioning, testing, timing and other services to the Arab states in 2018. The test and evaluation results jointly conducted by China and the Arab states show that eight Beidou satellites can be seen over Arab states, with positioning accuracy of better than 10 meters and more than 95 percent availability. The Beidou system can serve the Arab states and regions by providing high-quality satellite navigation services (Chen, 2019: 69). In addition, the Beidou satellite navigation has formed an independent, controllable, complete and mature industrial chain in China. The time and spatial location information provided by the Beidou satellite navigation is widely used in transportation, marine fisheries, surveying and mapping, disaster prevention and mitigation, emergency rescue, finance, power timing and many other core fields related to people's livelihood. The US global positioning system (GPS) is widely used in the Arab states; however, relying on a single system may result in security risks, as was apparent in the fluctuation of the GPS signal strength during the Syrian war. The Arab states can maintain the application security of a national navigation satellite by using Beidou through the common mode of multisystem compatibility and interoperability (Lin and Deng, 2018: 34). The rapid development of China's satellite navigation technology has laid a technical foundation for China and the Arab states to build a Sino-Arab North/GNSS center in the field of satellite navigation, carry out education and training, and promote many different Beidou satellite navigation applications.

China and Saudi Arabia signed a memorandum of understanding on cooperation in the field of satellite navigation in 2016 (Yun, 2016: 85). After that, the two sides successfully held a Beidou/GNSS seminar in Riyadh, Saudi Arabia, on April 18–19, 2017, to carry out cooperation regarding technical exchange and navigation applications. Table 14.1 presents the timeline of cooperation on space systems between China and the Arab states.

Table 14.1 Timeline of cooperation on space systems between China and the Arab states

Dates	Categories	Target countries	Themes	Contents
February 15, 2017	GNSS	Arab states	Arab delegations visiting Beidou	Arab delegations visited Beidou at the invitation of China's Ministry of Foreign Affairs
March 18, 2017	Deep space exploration	Saudi Arabia	Joint lunar exploration	China and Saudi Arabia carry out joint lunar exploration and remote sensing camera cooperation
April 18, 2017	Satellite navigation	Saudi Arabia	China-Saudi Arabia Beidou Seminar	Beidou/GNSS seminar held in Riyadh, Saudi Arabia
May 15, 2017	Satellite remote sensing	Egypt	Egypt Satellite Assembly Integration Test Center	Director General of the National Bureau of Remote Sensing and Space Science of Egypt met with his Chinese counterpart, Wu Yanhua
December 11, 2017	Satellite communication	Algeria	Algeria-1 Communications satellite	Algeria-1 is the first space cooperation project between China and the Arab states in satellite communications.[1]
April 1, 2018	Communications satellite	Algeria	Algeria-1 communications satellite	Algeria-1 was successfully delivered
April 10, 2018	Satellite navigation	Tunisia	China-Arab States Beidou/GNSS Center	The China-Arab States Beidou Center was inaugurated at the headquarters of the Arab Information and Communication Technology Organization in Tunisia, the first overseas center of China's Beidou Navigation Satellite System
April 10, 2018	Satellite navigation	Tunisia	Short-term training	China-Arab Beidou/GNSS held the first short-term training course for satellite navigation
April 12, 2018	Satellite navigation	Arab states	China-Arab Beidou Cooperation Forum	China and Arab states signed a memorandum on holding the second China-Arab Beidou Cooperation Forum in Tunisia
April 12, 2018	Satellite navigation	Arab states	Satellite navigation signal test	China and Arab states jointly launched the Beidou-3 user experience evaluation program

(*continued*)

Table 14.1 (Cont.)

Dates	Categories	Target countries	Themes	Contents
May 6, 2018	Infrastructure	Egypt	Space city of Egypt	Tian Yulong, Secretary General of the National Space Administration of China, and Mahmoud Zaran, President of the National Remote Sensing Space Science Administration of Egypt, signed a cooperation agreement between China and Egypt in Tiancheng
June 14, 2018	Deep space exploration	Saudi Arabia	China and Saudi Arabia moon exploration	China and Saudi Arabia jointly released images of the moon with cameras
July 5, 2018	Remote sensing satellite	Arab states	International training course on application of FY-4A products	FY-4A was officially put into operation to provide meteorological data for Arab states
July 5, 2018	Infrastructure	Egypt	Egyptian Satellite Assembly Integration Test Center	The Fifth Academy of Aerospace Science and Technology won the bid for the construction project of the Egyptian satellite assembly and integration test center
10 July 2018	Satellite navigation	Arab states	China-Arab States Cooperation Forum	President Xi Jinping attended the eighth Ministerial Conference of China-Arab States Cooperation Forum and delivered an important speech [2]
July 2, 2018	Overall design	The UAE	Joint statement by China and the UAE on establishing a comprehensive strategic partnership	Promotion of bilateral cooperation in space and strengthen technical exchanges and personnel exchanges between educational institutions of the two countries.
July 29, 2018	Deep space exploration	Saudi Arabia	Saudi Arabia's moon sighting camera	The second batch of scientific data delivered by China to Saudi Arabia
September 24, 2018	Satellite navigation	Sudan	The first regional smart agriculture forum	Beidou enters Sudan to participate in a series of activities of China-Arab cooperation
September 24, 2018	Satellite navigation	Sudan	Personnel training	The second short-term training course on satellite navigation of China-Arab Beidou/GNSS Center

November 4, 2018	Satellite navigation	Arab states	Joint conference	Arab Information and Communication Organization promotes Beidou Satellite Service
December 7, 2018	Remote sensing satellite	Saudi Arabia	Saudi-5A/5B satellite	Long March-2 launch vehicle successfully launched Saudi satellite
January 21, 2019	Remote sensing satellite	Egypt	Egypt-2 satellite	Han Bing, Minister Commercial Counsellor of the Chinese Embassy in Egypt, and Mahmoud Hussein, Chairman of the National Bureau of Remote Sensing and Space Science of Egypt, signed an agreement on remote sensing satellite
March 11, 2019	Satellite navigation	Tunisia	Beidou precision agriculture	Application of Beidou technology in precision agriculture in Tunisia
March 24, 2019	Satellite navigation	Arab states	Arab journalists visit Beidou	Journalists from 15 Arab states, including Oman, Egypt, and Tunisia, visited relevant Beidou organizations and enterprises
April 2, 2019	Satellite navigation	Arab states	China-Arab Beidou Cooperation Forum	The second China-Arab Beidou Cooperation Forum was successfully held in Tunisia

1 It is also Algeria's first communication satellite.

2 President Xi Jinping advocated promoting China's Beidou navigation system to serve the construction of Arab countries. The action plan of the China Arab Cooperation Forum was released, and China Arab Beidou cooperation has become a new highlight.

Source: "Beidou Navigation Satellite System." www.beidou.gov.cn/

Strategic Opportunities for the Beidou System to Take Root in the Arab World

China's Beidou system is quite young compared to the US GPS system. However, it has great momentum. The promotion of the Beidou Navigation Satellite System in the Arab world is a significant component of the Belt and Road Initiative; it is an important measure to deepen the strategic partnership between China and the Arab world and to realize the mutual connectivity and communication between the two sides. The Beidou system is also an important element of China's "going out" strategy to realize Beijing's global blueprint in the next ten years.

With the consistent expansion of the Beidou system's overseas markets, China's image has evolved from traditional to modern. Chinese culture is no longer confined to traditional elements such as the Chinese knot, Chinese opera, calligraphy, porcelain, paper cutting, and shadow play. The leaps and bounds of China's high-tech industries have added modern features to these traditional ones, in the form of high-speed railways, nuclear power plants, aerospace technology and the Beidou system, among others. China is marching forward from being a backward country to being a great power in the world of science and technology, and this has brought a wealth of resources and content to China's diplomacy. China's diplomacy, in return, has included the promotion of the Beidou system in the Arab world.

First, the Arab world enjoys a vast area and has a great potential market. As an important component of the Organization of Islamic Cooperation, the 22 Arab states cover an area of 14.26 million sq km, accounting for 9.5 percent of the world. The population in the Arab states has grown rapidly and has reached nearly 400 million, making up 5 percent of the total world population, of which the Egyptian population alone is over 100 million. Young people below the age of 30 account for 60–70 percent of the total population of the Arab world; Egypt, Saudi Arabia, Oman, the UAE and Algeria are the most populous countries in the region. They have increasing demands for the Beidou system, particularly in the domains of hydrology, meteorology, agriculture, fishery, infrastructure and transportation.

Second, the Beidou system is of great significance to the development of industries in the Arab world. Arab states have the following features: the main ethnic group is Arab, but individual countries have varied political systems and levels of economic advancement, as well as their own relationships with foreign powers. The majority of these countries are stable, but several countries, such as Yemen, Syria, Iraq, Libya and Somalia are in turmoil, facing severe sectarian disputes and the threat of terrorism. They all support the Palestinian cause and the Arab peace initiative. The Arab world is the point where Europe, Asia and Africa converge and it is pivotal to East-West trade routes. However, while they all have ports, stations, and crucial sea coastlines, inter-Arab trade and investment are insignificant. Moreover, the Arabian Gulf countries, Iraq, Libya and Algeria, have rich oil and gas resources, whose proven oil reserves account for 57.5 percent of the world's total. They are relatively undeveloped in satellite navigation (satnav) and other high-tech areas due to a lack of human resource investment and expertise; but the market demand is huge, which provides an opportunity for Chinese enterprises. In recent years, companies such as Beijing LinkStar, Unicorecomm, Guoteng electronics, Hwa Create and Beidou Tianhui have launched satellite positioning which is compatible with the US GPS, the Russian GLONASS and the European Galileo. These companies provide their own chips for China's navigation satellite market (Anon., 2011: 56), and provide an important launch pad for China to enter the Arab market.

Third, after several years of pro-democracy uprisings and anti-government protests—the so-called "Arab Spring"—Arab countries have now re-focused on domestic economic and social development, which has created conditions for the Beidou system to become established in the Arab world. Since the beginning of the twenty-first century, secular authoritarian Arab regimes have been subject to different degrees of impact, and the challenges include the Greater Middle East Initiative, and the rise of extremism. The result is that these Arab states have become centers of unrest in the Middle East, together with Israel, Iran, and Turkey, the three non-Arab states. The Arab states have been disintegrating due to political alliances with Russia and the West: Syria, Egypt and Iraq maintain a traditional strategic cooperation with Russia whereas the GCC states, Turkey, and Israel retain their long-term security cooperation with the USA.

The Arab Spring did not bring democracy and freedom to the Middle East, but added more unrest, conflict and humanitarian crises. Many Arab countries were in transition and realized the importance of improving the livelihood of their people and the development of their economies, which created favorable conditions for the Beidou system. In recent years, Arab states have shown great interest in the Beidou Navigation Satellite System, responding positively to President Xi Jinping's proposal in June 2014 to launch this system in the Arab world as soon as possible. For example, in October 2014, a delegation of 14 diplomats (including Abdullah Al-Saadi, the head of the Arab Diplomatic Corps in China and Omani Ambassador to China, the Jordanian Ambassador Yahia Qarrally, and other Arab representatives) visited Qinhuangdao "Beidou Digital Valley – Digital City" technology exhibition sites. Their main topic of discussion was the application of the Beidou system in the Arab states.

Fourth, the nature of the relationship between foreign powers and the Arab world creates the conditions for the Beidou system to launch in the Arab world. The US GPS was widely used in the Middle East before the 2011 upheaval. It basically monopolized the Arab world, especially in Saudi Arabia, the UAE, Qatar, Oman, Bahrain, Kuwait, Egypt, Morocco, and other US allies. In the name of providing free public goods, the US occupied more than half the military and civilian satellite navigation market in the Arab states. In addition, the European Galileo system has developed strongly in recent years, despite being a late starter.

The dependence of the Western powers on the Middle East has declined, especially in the field of energy. The Obama administration pulled its major forces out of Iraq and Afghanistan, and the US global strategic focus shifted eastward to the Asia Pacific region. As a result, the Arab states began to pursue a political and economic policy of looking east (Lars and Yang, 2014: 31). On the one hand, they rely on the USA and European powers in areas of national security; on the other hand, they depend on China, India, Japan and South Korea for economic and energy cooperation. There are strong anti-American and anti-Western sentiments in the Arab world, especially after Israel launched an offensive attack in Gaza in 2014 and 2015, which led to thousands of Palestinian casualties. China was expected to be a political force and major investor to balance against Western influence, and this has provided an important opportunity for China's Beidou system to enter the Arab world.

Fifth, under the new leadership of President Xi Jinping, the Belt and Road Initiative has created more favorable conditions for the Beidou system to enter the Arab market. Since the 18th National Congress of the Communist Party of China (CPC), a central collective leadership has changed China's policy of opening to the East, to Western powers and to the Southeast in the past few decades, and instead has implemented a westward development strategy. Since President Xi Jinping proposed the Belt and Road Initiative in 2013, China's westward strategy has become increasingly prominent. The promotion of the Beidou System in the Arab world is an important part of the strategy to open to the West and realize the "mutual connectivity and communication" proposed by the new administration. In January 2016, China announced its first Arab Policy Paper, expressing Beijing's strong desire to expand bilateral and multilateral cooperation. During President Xi Jinping's visit to Saudi Arabia, Egypt and Iran, these host countries all expressed their willingness to become pilot countries for the Beidou Navigation Satellite System in the Arab world. The strategic priority of China and the Arab world is expected to move from the fringe to the center in each other's policy.

Opportunities for China's Beidou System to Enter the Arab World

The Arabs, like the Persians, the Turks, and the Jews, have brilliant ancient civilizations and it is Arab ambition to spearhead their national rejuvenation with an advance in outer-space technology. The promotion of China's Beidou system in the Arab world has clear advantages. First, the satellite navigation systems of world powers form a multi-polar pattern; this creates a strategic advantage for the Beidou system to expand in the new market. At the beginning of the twenty-first century, the Middle East was in a state of multi-polarity. All the major powers were trying to expand their influence in this region— the USA, Europe, Japan, Russia, India, and Brazil—but no one country could or did predominate. Major countries have attached great importance to the upgrading and pro-motion of satellite navigation system technology, and have regarded the market share of their respective satnav systems in international markets as an indication of science and technology power. In March 2013, the Japanese government announced that the number of satellites in their Quasi-Zenith satellite system would be increased from three to four. The Japanese government cooperated with Mitsubishi Electric and scheduled to complete the construction and launch of three satellites by the end of 2017 (*Spaceflight Now*, 2013). In October 2014, India launched the third satellite in India's regional navigation satel-lite system, called the IRNSS-1C satellite. According to New Delhi, India had launched seven such navigation satellites by 2015, and hence became one of the world powers in satnav technology (Anon., 2014). Russia accelerated its promotion of GLONASS. The USA and the European Union have used their own technological advantage in trying to expand the gap between them and other powers in the field of satellite navigation. The internationalization and development of international navigation satellite systems create opportunities for the promotion of Beidou in the Arab world. In March 2016, China's first new-generation Beidou navigation satellite was successfully launched and sent into orbit by the LM-3C rocket, indicating that China's system had expanded from a regional to a global reach (Beidou, 2015).

Second, China shares a similar culture, historical experience, development and national conditions with many Arab states and this provides political advantage for the Beidou system to enter the Arab world. After the establishment of the China-Arab States Cooperation Forum in 2004, bilateral political exchanges have been increasingly frequent. In promoting political multi-polarization, cultural diversification and other aspects, China and the Arab states have reached considerable consensus. Anti-American sentiment in the Arab world is partly due to the US pro-Israel policy and its stance on the Iranian nuclear issue, while China seeks impartiality and non-alignment, which is appreciated by the Arabs. In addition, China and the Arab states share common strategic objectives. Compared with East Asia, Southeast Asia and Europe, Western control of outside powers over the region is weak, providing leeway and opportunity for China to gain traction.

China and the Arab states are all Oriental civilizations; they have similar views on international order, democracy and human rights. For example, their view is that democracy cannot be exported, or imposed by outsiders; democracy must be compatible with national values; it must be either a socialist democracy with Chinese characteristics or an Islamic democracy with Arab characteristics. In recent years, China and the Arab states have jointly explored the road to economic and social development for developing countries. The Arab States, especially the Gulf countries, have put forward the Arab version of "Orientalism" in recent years, stressing the need to carry out positive diplomatic relations with East Asian countries such as China, Japan, South Korea and India, and adhere to "equilibrium among great powers," relying on the West in security issues and depending on Asia for economic ones. In the United Nations Security Council, China has always supported the Palestinian cause, and this has won wide acclaim in the Arab world, creating a sympathetic political environment for the promotion of the Beidou system in the Arab world (Sun and Zoubir, 2014: 87).

Third, the rapid development of economic and trade relations between the Arab states and China in the twenty-first century has created an economic advantage for the Beidou system in the Arab market. In recent years, China has replaced the USA as the second largest trading partner of the Arab League, second only to the European Union. In 2013, the bilateral trade volume amounted to $240 billion, of which the commodities China imported from the Arab states amounted to $140 billion (Xi, 2014). As of 2020, China was the largest trading partner of ten Arab states. China is encouraging Chinese companies to import more non-oil products from Arab states, to optimize the trade structure, and try to increase the bilateral trade volume from $240 billion in 2013 to $600 billion in 2023. China will encourage Chinese enterprises to invest in energy, petrochemicals, agriculture, manufacturing industry and the service sector. The two sides have agreed on the establishment of the China-Arab Center for Technology Transfer, the construction of training centers for the peaceful use of nuclear energy by the Arab states, and research on launching China's Beidou Navigation Satellite System in the Arab states (ibid,).

Fourth, the development of China's satellite navigation technology creates a technical advantage for the Beidou system in the Arab market. At present, in terms of the Beidou system, China has completed one master control station, such as synchronous/injection stations; and 17 monitoring stations for development and construction. At the same time the GPS modernization transformation work is steadily advancing in the USA and the Russian GLONASS is stepping up the implementation of recovery. Since making significant progress in compatibility with the GPS in L1 and L5 signals, the European Galileo system planned to start operation in 2012. In terms of constructing a wide area and local navigation augmentation system (WAAS, an air navigation aid), the USA, the European Union, Russia and China have all made great headway; Japan has also stepped up the pace of constructing QZSS and MSAs; the construction of Indian IRNSS and GAGAN is also in progress (Zhu, Li and Yang, 2011: 1). In the next decade, competition between the foreign powers in the Arab world will further intensify, which has created opportunities for Beijing to open markets in the Middle East for the Beidou system.

Fifth, the aerospace bureau and other institutions established by the Arab world create advantages for the Beidou system to open the Arab market. China has already identified its counterparts in its cooperation with Arab states in the field of satellite navigation. So far, Algeria, Egypt, Morocco and Tunisia have set up a National Aeronautics and Space Administration individually. In 2006, the UAE set up the United Arab Emirates high-tech research institute, and launched two satellites—Dubai I and Dubai II—and launched the independently developed satellite Dubai III in 2017. Even the Bashar al Assad government of Syria, which was still at war, announced the establishment of the Syria Aerospace Bureau in 2014 (Shaykhoun, 2014). Although Arab states were late starters in satellite communication technology, in recent years they have shown greater development potential, laying a foundation for China's Beidou system to use remote sensing technology; identify counterparts; carry out targeted training; open up the Arab agricultural market; mapping; railway and sea transportation; and containerization. Technical training by China in Morocco's Space Technology Research Center and cooperation with the United Arab Emirates Institute of Advanced Technology have both formed important bilateral ventures.

Conclusion

At present, administrative laws and regulations related to China's Beidou Navigation Satellite System in Arab states have been released. These include the "Mid- and long-term development plan for National Navigation Satellite Industry," the Chinese White Paper released in 2013; and 'Opinions on the promotion and application of the Beidou Navigation Satellite System' which was released by the State Bureau of Surveying and Mapping Geographic Information in March 2014. However, a top-level design for the internationalization of the Beidou system is still lacking. The promotion of the Beidou system in the Arab world needs to be based on existing planning, following a gradual and steady path, to facilitate the incremental introduction of the Beidou system in the Arab world.

First, the China-Arab States Cooperation Forum should be a platform to deepen Sino-Arab outer-space cooperation. In promoting the Beidou system in the Arab world, China should incorporate their system into the dual frameworks of multilateral mechanisms of the China-Arab Cooperation Forum, and bilateral strategic cooperative relations between China and the respective Arab states, making it a part of China's technical assistance. China has already established a task-oriented sub-forum on satellite navigation, and may form a working group in the multilateral arena of the China-Arab States Cooperation Forum. Attempts will be made to establish training and education centers in the Arab states for navigation satellite systems to pave the way for Beidou.

Second, attempts should be made to enrich the content of the Beidou system in the Arab world and implement China's current scientific and technological diplomacy. The Beidou system is an important achievement of China's space infrastructure; it is of great significance in promoting the implementation of the "going out" strategy, and in speeding up the construction of a surveying and mapping power. China will treat the Beidou system as an important part of its technological assistance to its Arab counterparts, and offer it as a public good to the Arab world. In the fields of management, public security, police, fishery, hydrology, shipping, transportation, agriculture, forestry, water conservancy, meteorology, land resources, environmental protection, disaster prevention and mitigation, and emergency search and rescue, the Beidou system can play a positive role by providing a quality service to the Arab people.

The ultimate goal of the development of the space industry is for civil purposes, and the Beidou system is a case in point. After China's development of this system, it is necessary to consider how to apply it further to the entire economic structure. This will undoubtedly provide a development opportunity for Beidou, so China needs to improve the quality of its products, manage the space tube in the transport control system, and serve its users well, making it an important part of the infrastructure in Arab states. To do so, China and the Arab states should do the following:

- continue to strengthen the China-Arab States Cooperation Forum in political cooperation, making it a regional organization instead of a loose forum;
- establish a stable relationship in energy cooperation and carry out mutually beneficial economic and trade cooperation;
- support each other politically, for example, China should actively safeguard the legitimate rights of the Arab states at the United Nations, in the Asian Infrastructure Investment Bank, in the Silk Road Fund, in the G20 and in the International Monetary Fund. In return, the Arab states should actively support China's territorial integrity and interests in both the Middle East and the world.
- strengthen military exchanges, including China's training of Arab military officers;
- strengthen high-level visits, and increase the scale of people-to-people and youth exchanges;
- standardize bilateral strategic cooperative relations systematically, and establish a dialogue and cooperation in a comprehensive fashion. The Department of West Asian and North African Affairs and the Ministry of Foreign Affairs should establish closer cooperation with related agencies of the Beidou system to jointly promote the Beidou system in the Middle East countries.

Third, people-to-people exchanges between China and the Arab states should be strengthened to create a favorable atmosphere for the promotion of the Beidou system in the Arab world. China and Arab states decided to set 2014 and 2015 as the Years of China-Arab Friendship and organized a series of events for people-to-people diplomacy. China is also willing to expand the scale of cultural exchanges with Arab states, such as the Arts Festival, to encourage more young students to exchange visits for academic activities, and strengthen cooperation in areas such as tourism, aviation, the media, and publications. In the next ten years, China will organize exchange visits for 10,000 Chinese and Arab artists, promote and support 200 Chinese and Arab cultural institutions in cooperative ventures, and invite and support 500 Arab cultural and artistic practitioners to receive training in China. China is considering the establishment of a publicity, training and demonstration center for the Beidou system in the framework of the Confucius Institutes in Arab states. The center may carry out surveys and field work in the host countries, and pave the way for the promotion of the Beidou system in the Arab world.

Fourth, strengthen China's agenda-setting capability in international organizations related to the Beidou system, and obtain more international certifications. China attaches great importance to the Global Navigation Satellite System (GNSS), the International Maritime Organization (IMO), the International Electrotechnical Commission (IEC/TC80), the International Telecommunication Union (ITU), the International Association of Lighthouse Authorities (IALA), and the Radio Technical Commission for Maritime Services (RTCM). In November 2014, the 94th meeting of IMO Maritime Safety Committee was held in London. The session examined and recognized the Beidou Navigation Satellite System—it passed the Navigation Security Letter for Beidou. This is the third navigation satellite system that the international maritime organization has approved, following GPS and GLONASS. Beidou system standards obtained international certification for the first time, indicating that this system has officially become a component of the global radio navigation system and would foster international judicial status for its maritime applications. In the next decade, global navigation satellite systems will evolve from the monopoly of the USA to the multi-polarity of the USA, Europe, Russia, China, India, and Japan, and this may provide a strategic opportunity for the Beidou system to expand into the Arab market.

Fifth, identify pivotal countries to promote the Beidou system overseas. Arab states face different types and degrees of political, security and social risks, which must be taken into consideration in the application of the Beidou system in the Arab world. This determines that in the twenty-first century, China needs to identify pivotal countries in the region to promote the Beidou system, and select key areas and pilot projects. Saudi Arabia and the UAE in West Asia, together with Egypt, Morocco and Algeria in North Africa, may serve as the priority areas for the Beidou system to establish its business. These countries have a huge demand for the Beidou system. They have relatively large populations and/or sizable economic output, and the industry demand for the Beidou system is strong. Saudi Arabia, the UAE, Egypt, Morocco and Algeria have had relatively stable political situations since 2014; they have favorable conditions for the promotion of the Beidou system. Again, these countries have close political ties with China. These five countries have similar national situations to China in that they all treat economic and social development as the priority of national construction; they retain a long-term friendly policy towards China, and adhere to a "Look East" strategy. The Saudi Minister of Defense and Crown Prince Mohammed bin Salman and the Egyptian President Al-Sisi visited China and both were well received by President Xi Jinping. In 2014, Yu Zhengsheng, Chairman of the Chinese People's Political Consultative Conference (CPPCC), visited Morocco and Algeria; in January 2016, President Xi Jinping visited Saudi Arabia, Egypt and Iran, and signed an MOU on satellite navigation cooperation with Saudi Arabia and the Arab League. President Xi Jinping and Egypt's President Al-Sisi jointly visited the Beidou session of China's high-tech exhibition. China established a comprehensive strategic partnership with Saudi Arabia, Egypt, Algeria and the UAE, and a strategic partnership with Morocco, and has attached great importance to relations with these countries for a long time. As of 2020, China's government agencies had established contact and cooperation with their counterparts in Saudi Arabia, Egypt, Morocco, Algeria and the UAE; the parties are exploring ways of joint research, technological development and market promotion. In the foreseeable future, the Beidou system may serve as an 'outer space Silk Road' connecting the Chinese and Arab peoples in the twenty-first century.

Acknowledgments

An earlier version of this chapter by Degang Sun and Yuyou Zhang was published in 2016 in the *Journal of Middle Eastern and Islamic Studies (in Asia)*. This updated version is by kind permission of the publisher.

References

Anon. (2011). "Beidou navigation satellite system as an escort carrier for national security." Satellite and Network 4, p. 46.

Anon. (2014). "India successfully launched navigation satellite, its regional navigation system is complete." Available at: http://mil.huanqiu.com/world/2014-10/5169578.html (accessed March 28, 2021).

Beidou (2015). "China successfully launched the first new-generation Beidou Navigation Satellite." Available at: www.beidou.gov.cn/2015/04/01/20150401b4b91ddc213a45129a665ea3272b5aed.html (accessed March 28, 2021).

Chen, B. (2019). "The second China-Arab Beidou Cooperation Forum was successfully held in Tunisia." *International Space*, 4, pp. 68–69.

Lin, L. (2020). "China-Arab joint construction of 'Space Silk Road': status, problems and counter measures," *Journal of West Asia and Africa*, 1, pp. 97–121.

Lin, L., and Deng, P. (2018). "Navigation satellite security and the development of Beidou system," *Information Security and Communication Confidentiality*, 11, pp. 33–36.

Lin, L., and Li, Z. (2018). "Opportunities and challenges of China Arab Beidou Cooperation Forum." *Arab World Studies*, 2, pp. 62–75.

Shaykhoun, S. (2014). "Pan-Arab Space Agency: Pipe dream or real possibility?" Available at: www.satellitetoday.com/uncategorized/2014/08/26/pan-arab-space-agency-pipe-dream-or-real-possibility/undefined (accessed March 23, 2021).

Spaceflight Now. (2013). "Japan to build fleet of navigation satellites." Available at: www.spaceflightnow.com/news/n1304/04qzss/ (accessed March 28, 2021).

State Bureau of Surveying and Mapping Geographic Information. (2014). "Opinions on the promotion and application of Beidou Navigation Satellite system." *Navigation Satellite Information*, 1, pp. 36–38.

Sun, D., and Zoubir, Y. (2014). "China-Arab states strategic partnership: Myth or reality?" *Journal of Middle Eastern and Islamic Studies (in Asia)*, 8(3), pp. 70–101.

Sun, D., and Zoubir, Y. (2016). "The five satellites are pushing Beidou Navigation System to the world." Available at: http://scitech.people.com.cn/GB/n1/2016/0202/c1007-28103957.html (accessed March 23, 2021).

Xi, J. (2014). "To carry forward the spirit of the Silk Road and deepen cooperation between China and the Arab states." Speech at the opening ceremony of the Sixth Ministerial Conference of the China-Arab State Cooperation Forum. People's Daily, June 5.

Yun, C. (2016). "Accelerating China's satellite service to Arab countries." *Satellite Applications*, 2, pp. 83–85.

Zhu, X., Li, X., and Yang Y. (2011). "To accelerate the construction of China's Beidou Navigation Satellite system based on the development of international Navigation Satellite system." *Mapping Bulletin*, 8, pp.1–4.

15

CHINA AND THE GULF

Necessary Partners

Karen E. Young

1 Introduction

The oil and gas exporters of the Gulf Cooperation Council (GCC) find themselves in an unenviable position: China seeks their resources but is less interested in providing or replacing the current US security umbrella. China needs the Gulf (both the Arab Gulf states and Iran) but has other sources of hydrocarbons. The Gulf needs China as an export market, but any political partnership with China carries limited benefits. The tension between the United States and China, whether termed great power competition or more simply a growing sense of distrust and economic rivalry between the two states, puts the Arab Gulf states in a difficult security position. The timing is also especially difficult, as the oil exporters of the Gulf face an imminent energy transition in which they seek to expand their national oil companies into full-scale energy firms, with operations in renewable energy production and ownership in both the trading of their products from raw materials into refined products such as petrochemicals and plastics. China will likely need the Gulf states less in 20 years as a source of hydrocarbon resources. And China will also seek to be in some of the same businesses that the Gulf states seek to dominate, specifically in renewable energy, such as solar, but also in contracting or construction businesses for infrastructure development across the Middle East and the Horn of Africa.

There is also substantial variance among the GCC states in their economic linkages with China. Iran's economic ties with China are even more tenuous. Given the restrictions imposed by sanctions over the last decade, more progress has been made in cementing China's economic links to the Arab side of the Gulf. China is neither a monolithic presence across the Middle East, nor an equal partner across the six GCC states. China's leverage as a provider of contracting services and development finance is disparate. And in some cases, even when Beijing has been ready to act as a source of finance, in providing commitments of investment, Gulf states have had second thoughts. Iraq is one example; Iran is another. In 2021, Iraq suspended a potential deal to accept $2 billion for future deliveries of crude oil to China, despite a desperate need for external finance (Al-Ansary, 2021). Likewise, the much-lauded 2021 Iran-China investment memorandum of understanding was large on promises ($400 billion of them over 25 years), but short on specifics, while facing considerable objections in Iranian domestic politics over

192　　　　　　　　　　　　　　　　　　　　DOI: 10.4324/9781003048404-17

concerns of a flood of lower-priced Chinese goods onto the Iranian consumer market (Esfandiary, 2021).

The aim of this chapter is to conceptualize Gulf-China economic and political ties amidst a shifting global power balance and a global energy transition. The chapter proceeds in the following order. First, the chapter asks, what does China imagine as an endgame in the Gulf? What is the longer-term value of political and economic ties to the Gulf states? Second, how do we explain variance in the location and abundance of economic ties with China, from investments and loans to contracting across the Gulf? And what are the various sources of economic ties and what do they tell us about China's ability to partner in the development and economic diversification goals of the Gulf states? From loans to contracting and commitments of foreign investment, how can we measure or compare the depth of China's economic interests in the Gulf? Third and finally, what are the potential roadblocks ahead in Gulf-China ties, specifically on investments in technology and military capability and areas of strategic competition, such as electricity generation from renewable energy? And how might China's own demographic transition fit into a larger picture of declining or plateaued demand for traditional hydrocarbon exports from the Gulf? The chapter asks these questions in an attempt to step back from some of the escalating rhetoric of a great power confrontation in the Gulf, and to more carefully evaluate some of the lofty expectations of China's economic dominance of the Gulf and wider Middle East. It argues that while China-Gulf economic ties are increasing, they also come at a moment of tremendous change and expected reconfigurations of energy markets and consumer demand. This is the reason to see the transactional nature of relationships now in a studied and tempered manner.

2 China's Outward Vision for the Gulf

China, via its ruling party, has made it very clear how the Middle East is just one part of a much larger outward strategy in its foreign policy and economic growth. In January 2021, China's State Council Information Office issued a White Paper entitled "China's International Development Cooperation in the New Era," a detailed policy description of China's approach to international development and how to use its state institutions and private citizens and firms to more firmly establish ties, both economic and political, in developing countries (United Nations Development Programme, 2021). For the Middle East, and for the Gulf Arab states in particular, the Chinese approach to development emphasizes a South-South focus. The rhetoric of a development ideal that is divorced from liberal democratic capitalism and the ideals of the West has a certain attraction to the authoritarian capitalist states of the Gulf. There are no imposed conditions on domestic politics, and there is a welcome role for state-related entities, as well as private sector actors in economic development.

China formalizes relationships through a hierarchy of partnership agreements. Loosely, these are memoranda of understanding which are not legally binding, but rather aspirational in commitments of investment and levels of diplomatic engagement. From "friendly cooperative partnership" at the lowest level to "comprehensive strategic partnership" at the highest, China engages the Middle East and the Gulf in proportion to its own development objectives (Fulton, 2019). For that reason, the countries with the highest level of "partnership" are those that are most valuable to China as a source of energy products, as geographic locations for re-export with good port infrastructure, and those that are open to awarding Chinese contracting firms opportunities. China has a "strategic partnership," the second highest level of engagement, with at least a dozen Middle East states. But its "comprehensive strategic partnerships" are reserved for a few: Iran, Saudi Arabia, the United Arab Emirates (UAE), Egypt, and Algeria.

China and Iran have been slowly socializing a strategic partnership since 2016, also the year China released its "Arab Policy Paper," outlining general areas of trade and cooperation with the Middle East more broadly, making little distinction between Arab and non-Arab regional partnerships. Iran was also the site of a high-level visit by President Xi Jinping in 2016, as was Saudi Arabia (Perlez, 2016). Iran's "comprehensive strategic partnership" with Iran is less a breakthrough about the 25-year, $400 billion investment commitment, which is not binding or real cash on the table now, but about the "sanctions-free" nature of the partnership. China has made an interjection in Gulf regional politics based on economic rationale, but that is highly contentious not just with its Arab state partners, but also with the United States. China needs Iran as a source (but not its only source) of a reliable and inexpensive oil supply. Iran needs China more as a diplomatic wedge against the United States. Iran is afraid of becoming a dumping ground for cheap Chinese goods; the "sanctions-free" nature of the Chinese relationship is what has been necessary to gain Iranian domestic support for the strengthening of bilateral ties.

If US sanctions on Iran's oil exports are lifted or eased as part of a return to the Joint Comprehensive Plan of Action (JCPOA), oil prices may weaken further given a global supply glut (Gordon, 2021). But there is some question of how much impact Iran's exports to China would have on the existing market share supplied by Saudi Arabia and other Gulf Arab states: probably not much, though Saudi Arabia will not welcome the return of Iranian oil to the market, especially if Iran has agreed to sell at steep discounts. China is also not likely to stop buying from its Gulf Arab partners, given the shared co-investments in refineries and petrochemical facilities across the wider region. They all have become connected, willingly or not.

For the United States, China's ability to be an economic and political actor across the Persian Gulf can be threatening. The problem with viewing China as a great power competitor in the Middle East is that China is competing in entirely different mechanisms than the United States. The goal for China is not to be a security umbrella, a regional alliance or solely to gain a market for exports. China is after energy resources and strategic locations for its trade and transport security, which means it has invested in certain choke points in the Middle East, the Horn of Africa, and the Indian Ocean. And China has made relationship-building a priority, as these "comprehensive strategic partnerships" signify.

3 Variance in China-Gulf Economic Ties

Iran is not nearly as attractive to China as an investment destination as the Gulf Arab states can be. There is an energy imperative to China's investments and partnerships in the Gulf, mostly concentrated in Saudi Arabia and the UAE for now. Interestingly, new partnerships and co-investments include areas of potential competition, as the Gulf Arab states develop expertise in renewable energy, especially solar energy production, and as Gulf national oil companies begin a diversification strategy to privatize some pipelines and state port facility assets. Trade and finance come second in importance, though China has steadily increased the presence of its banking sector in the UAE and

China and the Gulf: Necessary Partners

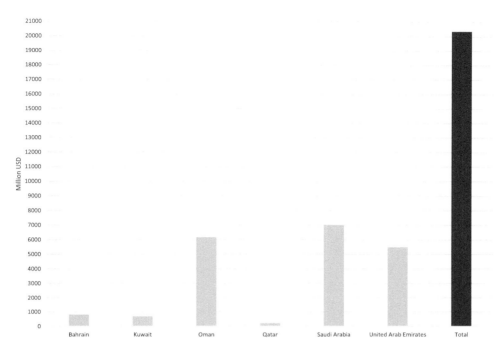

Figure 15.1 Total Chinese capital investments in the GCC (2003–2020)

increased its ability to win contracting awards for its construction companies working in the Gulf Arab states.

In data collected by fDi Markets, a *Financial Times* company, the stand-out recipients of Chinese foreign direct investment from 2003–2020 are three states in the GCC: Oman, Saudi Arabia, and the UA (Figure 15.1).

In terms of job creation, these same three states are the most intense sites of Chinese investment intervention in the GCC, but not necessarily in the creation of jobs for nationals, as low wage foreign workers account for most of the construction sector (Figure 15.2).

In terms of the variability over time in Chinese job creation in the GCC, the sharp increase in job creation after 2016 is most evident, pointing to more contract awards in the construction sector (Figure 15.3).

In terms of Chinese capital investment flows to the GCC between 2003 and 2020, we see at least three periods of spikes or sharp increases, in the period around 2008, 2011, and 2016 (Figure 15.4). The other trend that emerges is the variability in those states most "favored" by China in its economic linkages. The UAE is certainly emergent in that trend now, though competition between Gulf national oil companies in attracting investment partners in partial privatizations means China also has a bit of new leverage.

China's direct economic gains in the wider Middle East relied mostly on winning contracting awards from Gulf governments, including a recent award in Etihad rail in the UAE (Bhatia, 2020). As part of strategic partnerships, there is also equal interest from the Gulf side to become a part of the China One Belt, One Road initiative. The appointment of Chinese contractors to Gulf infrastructure projects is a complementary

Karen E. Young

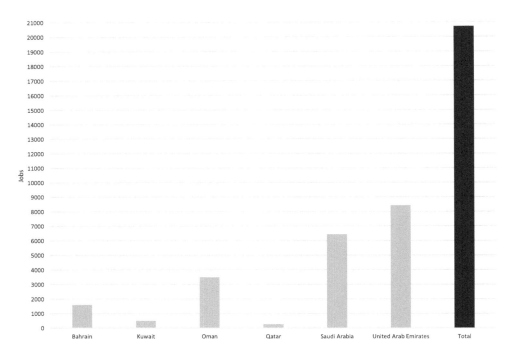

Figure 15.2 Total jobs created by Chinese companies in the GCC (2003–2020)

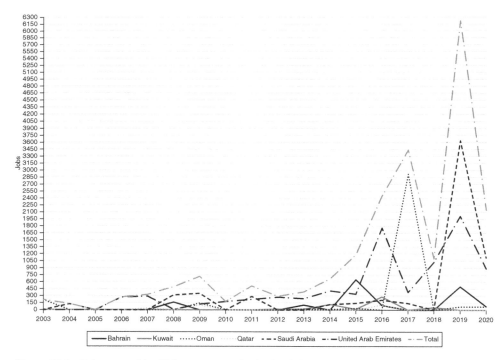

Figure 15.3 Jobs created by Chinese companies in the GCC (2003–2020)

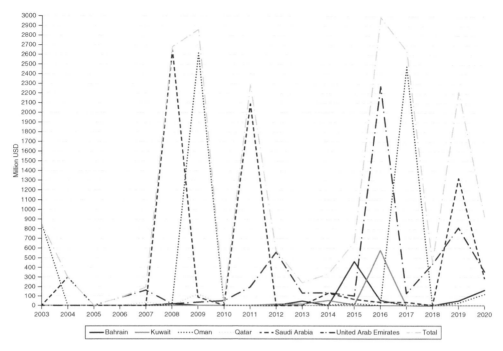

Figure 15.4 Chinese capital investments in the GCC (2003–2020)

Gulf state policy objective, as evidenced by the Dubai Silk Road strategy, which comprises 9 initiatives and 33 projects aimed at enhancing the emirate's trade and logistics capacity (Oxford Business Group, 2019).

After Saudi Crown Prince Mohamed bin Salman's state visit to China in 2019, investors signed $28 billion worth of MOUs for projects in Saudi Arabia, including construction sector agreements with China State Construction Engineering Corporation (CSCEC), including an agreement to build housing units (worth $667 million) for the Saudi National Housing Company (Yiu, 2019). The CSCEC has completed $7.8 billion worth of projects in the Middle East in the last 15 years and has $19 billion worth of contracts according to MEED Projects. In 2019, there were $520 billion worth of pre-execution phase projects in Saudi Arabia alone.

By 2021, Chinese solar firms had gained contract awards to help Saudi Arabia reach its ambitious solar electricity generation goals, in partnership with ACWA Power, a firm partly owned by the Saudi sovereign wealth fund, the Public Investment Fund (Aguinaldo, 2021). Outside of oil and gas, renewables have also been a focus of Chinese investment in the Gulf. In 2017, Abu Dhabi awarded a contract to a consortium led by Japan's Marubeni Corporation and China's Jinko Solar to develop a 1,177 MW PV solar independent power project at Sweihan, the world's largest single-site solar project (AP News, 2020).

China imported $6.7 billion (or 2.8 percent) of its total oil requirements from the UAE in 2018. But more than a key export market, China is increasingly an active investor in Gulf oil and gas infrastructure, including recent co-investments in Abu Dhabi National Oil Co (ADNOC) onshore concession and new offshore concessions. In the summer of

2020, for the first time, a dedicated Chinese offshore oil and gas company has joined ADNOC offshore concessions. ADNOC pointed out that PetroChina holds a 10 percent interest in the Lower Zakum concession as well as 10 percent of the Umm Shaif and Nasr concession. With the agreement, CNOOC will hold 4 percent interest in Lower Zakum and Umm Shaif/Nasr, with PetroChina holding the remaining 6 percent (Saadi, 2020).

Total trade between the UAE and China totaled $50 billion in 2017, and 60 percent of Chinese goods imported into the UAE are re-exported to the Middle East and Africa, making the UAE more central to China's trade ambitions and networks regionally. Chinese financial institutions are also making inroads in the Gulf finance sector. The UAE's federal government-owned development bank (Emirates Development Bank, EDB) issued its first bond in 2018 (after a decree allowing federal debt issuance), in which the $750 million five-year bond was arranged by Emirates NBD Capital, the Industrial and Commercial Bank of China, and Standard Chartered. China's largest state-owned commercial banks—the Industrial and Commercial Bank of China, the China Construction Bank, the Agricultural Bank of China, and the Bank of China—have been increasing their market share in the Middle East. Also known as the "Big Four," these are the world's top four largest banks. With their first foothold established in the Dubai International Financial Centre (DIFC), each of the Big Four has opened branches in the Middle East and North Africa (MENA) region and been operating there since 2008. From their branches in the DIFC, these banks run major regional operations and continuously are expanding their activities. According to the 2015 full-year operating review results of the DIFC, Chinese banks in the DIFC doubled their balance sheet over a period of 18 months (Dubai International Financial Centre, 2016). As of March 2019, the Big Four contributed a quarter of DIFC's collective balance sheet for banking (Xueqing, 2019).

China is quickly becoming a major contender in large project development in the Middle East. Because Chinese contractors can often bid on awards with state-backed financing, they are able to assess and win projects with higher risks in new and less-established markets. Chinese financing has played a significant role in a railway network in Iran and other projects in Iraq, Algeria, and Saudi Arabia, according to research by MEED in its "The Future of Middle East Energy" report (MEED, 2018). These four countries, along with the UAE, accounted for 75 percent of the total estimated value of projects awarded to Chinese contractors in 2000–2017. China's total share of contracts awarded across the region was almost 13 percent, and Chinese contracting is expected to grow further. The UAE was a prime destination for Chinese policy lenders in the last two years, with $2.3 billion in loans, including financing toward the expansion of both Dubai International Airport and Al Maktoum Airport. Jordan came in second, with total lending valued at $1.7 billion, followed by Saudi Arabia with $977 million and Egypt with $890 million.

Looking toward new projects, Chinese firms are aggressively bidding on MENA infrastructure (Aguinaldo, 2018). They bid to build part of a railway in the UAE, a rail network already linked to Huawei technology products (Huawei, n.d.). MENA governments have encouraged Chinese firms to bid and often award contracts because they are the most price-competitive, given their ability to rely on state banks for financing for projects that relate to the Belt and Road Initiative. The linkages of technology to infrastructure projects have created a sensitive collaborative model, in which companies like Siemens have agreed to partner with Chinese contractors in order to win participation in these large projects (Siemens, 2018).

4 Competition and Transition: The Future of Gulf-China Economic Relations

Export-oriented growth now includes the provision of finance as a service. The Chinese strategy of port development, large-scale construction services, and the provision of state-backed finance instruments is gaining traction in the Gulf, but it is also inspiring Gulf states to emulate this strategy, sometimes in the same places where China is engaged. As these forces combine, their incentives to create opportunity and development in recipient countries will differ sharply from traditional multilateral sources of development finance.

The synergy now created by both Chinese economic statecraft and Gulf states' increasing orientation eastward is a powerful force that will affect patterns of investment in emerging markets, but also practices of development finance, of post-conflict reconstruction, and ideas about appropriate governance of markets of the Middle East. Much of this relationship involves the Gulf supply of China's seemingly insatiable demand for energy, but China is also eying the Gulf for its own industries and investment. China and the Arab Gulf states are likely to use their capacities as financiers, contractors, and developers to increase ties and exert regional influence at a time when the United States is signaling a desire to be less engaged in the Middle East.

The future of growth for the Gulf states will rely on the control of ports and transit waterways (of the Red Sea corridor, the Arabian Sea, and the Indian Ocean), of export markets for energy products in Asia, and favorable access to the largest economies in the Middle East and Africa (Saudi Press Agency, 2018). Trends in urbanization and energy demand map closely to where the Arab Gulf states are now investing their political and economic resources (Reel, 2018). Chinese investment is symbiotic to Gulf security and economic objectives; though they are competing for many of the same projects, they are at times cooperative rivals.

China is a source of finance, a competitor in infrastructure projects, and a constant reminder of the power of alternative economic organization to the West. The growth in financial flows is compelling, but it requires constant feeding from its state-backed forces. Both China and the Gulf states use state-owned firms, including financial entities and banks, such that constant expansion of projects and financing serves a domestic priority to show assets on balance sheets as well (*Asian Banking and Finance Magazine*, 2019). Some scholars term the expansion of Chinese state-backed lending as "debt book diplomacy" as the expansion serves a political goal of the Belt and Road Initiative, but also gives commercial purpose to a growing financial sector (Parker and Chefitz, 2018). Lending, however, is not as substantial as the gain from contracting awards and co-investments in the energy and transport sectors.

The opening of two new ports in Oman, Sohar and Duqm, along with the new Hamad port in Qatar, are adding shipping capacity and new mechanisms of regional integration, in spite of a difficult period within the GCC because of the tension between Qatar and its Gulf neighbors (Young, 2018b). China financed the development of the Duqm port, as well as a new expansion of Khalifa Port in Abu Dhabi, and has an interest in their growth. Abu Dhabi's new Cosco Shipping Ports (CSP) container terminal at Khalifa Port serves to boost trade with China, but also competes directly with its sister port, Jebel Ali, in Dubai, which is currently the world's busiest port outside of Asia. Khalifa is set to be the largest container freight station in the Middle East, the result of a 35-year agreement between Abu Dhabi Ports and Cosco Shipping Ports Ltd, a subsidiary of Cosco Shipping Corporation Limited of China (Rahman, 2018). The port agreement comes on the heels of President Xi Jinping's 2018 official three-day visit to the United Arab Emirates, the first by a Chinese leader to the Emirates in nearly 30 years. The UAE is China's second-largest trading partner and its largest export/re-export market within the MENA region. In addition to their "comprehensive strategic partnership," the UAE and China have gone beyond shared investment and trade ties to increasing cooperation on security and counterterrorism issues (Fulton, 2018).

China clearly articulated its policy toward the Arab world and its economic interests in its 2016 Arab Policy Paper, which detailed its interests in trade agreements and technology (Ministry of Foreign Affairs of the People's Republic of China, 2016). Energy supply is a key, but not exclusive, concern; increasing bilateral trade and tourism from China to the Arab world is also a policy objective. The value of commercial activity between China and the GCC states accelerated from just under $10 billion in 2000 to nearly $115 billion in 2016 (Qian and Fulton, 2017).

This growth in bilateral trade flows continues and by 2018, according to research by First Abu Dhabi Bank, the GCC states now account for China's largest source of oil and are the second largest provider of its gas needs (Saidi, 2018). China is likely to become the GCC's largest export market within the next two years (Menon, 2014). The increase in trade ties is not one-way; by 2020, GCC imports from China were expected to double in value to around $135 billion. Flows of people are increasing as well, as a recent estimate showed a 40 percent increase in Chinese tourist arrivals between 2014 and 2017 (Forrest, 2018).

Both Saudi Arabia and the UAE are courting Chinese investment in shared energy projects, encompassing traditional oil production to renewable capacity and energy storage. State-owned enterprises Aramco and SABIC aim to partner with China's Sinopec and China North Industries Corp, creating a synergy of government firms. In the UAE, these projects include a contract worth $1.6 billion between ADNOC and the China National Petroleum Corporation (following an earlier $1.17 billion investment in Abu Dhabi's offshore fields) (*Gulf News*, 2018). In addition, there is a partnership and investment agreement between Dubai's Electricity and Water Authority (DEWA) and China's Silk Road Fund to create the world's largest solar energy plant (Halligan, 2018). In November 2018, ADNOC signed a new agreement for the sale of liquefied petroleum gas (LPG) to Wanhua Chemical Group of China, owner of the world's largest underground LPG storage facility (Bridge, 2018). According to research by Qamar Energy, there are at least ten current energy projects planned or active in the GCC with Chinese investment, from traditional and solar electricity generation, to pipeline development in the UAE, methanol production in Oman, and uranium exploration in Saudi Arabia (Mills, Ishfaq, Ibrahim, and Reese, 2017).

The recent growth in ties is based on China's demand for energy and the Gulf's ability to provide an important and growing market. China requires energy, especially to supply its infrastructure and construction boom as it builds new cities. Automobile sales in China quadrupled between 2008 and 2016, and transportation needs have also increased demand for petroleum and related products. As China seeks to shift its own energy mix away from polluting coal-fired power plants, its demand for gas has multiplied. The most important factor driving global gas consumption in 2017 was the surge in Chinese gas demand, where consumption increased by over 15 percent, accounting for nearly a third of the global increase in gas consumption (BP, 2018). It may create some leverage for Gulf major gas producers to shift China's attention their way in the first phase of a post-oil transition, as liquefied natural gas is considered a bridge fuel to more renewable sources.

The Gulf states are competing with each other to secure China as an export market for their energy products beyond just oil and gas. The proliferation of downstream energy products in petrochemicals, including the construction of new refineries and chemical plants, is both a diversification strategy and a new product arena (and profit maker) for Gulf state energy companies (Di Paola, 2018). Despite this synergy of interests, there is already conflict, as evidenced in the recent dispute over control of shares of the Doraleh Container Terminal in Djibouti between DP World, the Dubai-based port management company, and the Djibouti Ports Authority (PDSA). Djibouti forced DP World out of the site by nationalizing the terminal; notably, the government partner of the port authority, the Hong Kong-listed China Merchants Port Holdings Company Ltd, a company overseen by Beijing's State Assets Supervision and Administration Commission, holds a 23.5 percent ownership stake in the terminal (Mooney, 2018). Effectively, the government of Djibouti made a choice of prioritizing ties to China as an investor, over its commercial ties to DP World.

Yet, there is a demographic dilemma in China, and it will acutely affect the oil exporters of the Gulf. It poses the most serious threat to the political economy of the region, and that includes the legitimacy of ruling families. A report from the investment bank Natixis finds that population aging in China will be fast and furious, with a steep decline in economic growth rates, from 6 percent a year in 2010 to 2.5 percent by 2030, with real impacts on global potential growth (Cheng, 2021). Chinese imports currently account for 12 percent of global imports. Right now, Chinese consumption of global commodities (as a percent of global consumption) is about 15 percent of global oil and about 8 percent of global gas. As domestic demand falls with an aging population that is not replenished, that commodity demand will fall. Saudi Arabia may still pump the last barrel of oil, but it will most certainly also be the cheapest barrel and one that fewer consumers in China will need.

Perhaps the competition that China provides to the United States is best described as security on the fringes. As Afshin Molavi describes it, China's ability to provide technology products that the United States does not offer the Gulf Arab states has been a wedge into Gulf markets and a wedge between the GCC states and their traditional security provider in the USA (Molavi, 2020). From the sale of drones to providing 5G technology, China's niche provisions do not compare to the level of US military sales or military training exercises shared in the Gulf Arab states. But the fact that China has become more needed as a source of technology, especially for defense, is an increasing source of tension with the United States.

But the idea of a forced choice between superpowers, in a Cold War scenario between China and the United States, is not realistic for the Middle East. There are states that are more vulnerable in their need for access to finance, for which China might be a valid alternative. And there are states that are simply serving their export markets and seeking longer-term investment partners. And there are states that have few other options. The problem in pitting the USA versus China in each of these situations is ignoring a larger universe of investment sources and partners, private, multilateral, and state-supported in nature. The GCC states themselves are equally, if not more important as China in the Middle East as sources of capital investment and job creation, not to mention less formal sources of aid and bilateral government support.

When it comes to foreign direct investment (FDI), aid, capital expenditure, and job creation, China is often characterized as the investor of choice in the Middle East. It is often erroneously labeled as the region's most important source of FDI. Certainly, China is a major source of FDI in a few places, especially in the GCC. When Chinese investment does arrive, it usually targets the energy sector and large government contracts. China's investment can be volatile, with surges and then declines; in fact, globally, China's 2019 outgoing investment was the weakest since 2011 (Young, 2020).

When compared with American and European private investment efforts, China spends less and creates fewer jobs in most of the Middle East, North Africa, and West Asia (Organisation for Economic Co-operation and Development, 2018). Indeed, the GCC states have higher capital expenditure and create more employment across the Middle East and North Africa than China—and that's not counting remittance flows, aid, financial intervention such as central bank deposits, and in-kind oil and gas transfers (Young, 2018a). China is active as a regional investor and contractor where private capital doesn't want to go—places like Iran, Syria, and, to a degree, Turkey (Sahloul, 2020). One notable exception is the United Arab Emirates, where Chinese investment and contracts have surged since 2016. This skews the data and inflates China's reputation as a regional investor and source of capital. The view that China is the largest investor in the Arab region overlooks the fact that Beijing has invested inconsistently over time, and picks and chooses its engagement in the broader region, from Morocco to Pakistan. The assertion also fails to mention that the GCC is a major source of FDI in that same geography, and also in the Horn of Africa.

China and the Gulf are linked and will continue to rely on each other for trade, investment and partnerships in the years ahead. But their partnerships are in no ways cemented on any ideological basis or political or security pact. And as the energy exporters of the Gulf seek to diversify their own economies and become more engaged in the production and expertise of renewable energy, China could become less of a customer and less of an active local investor.

References

Aguinaldo, J. (2018) Chinese contractors are becoming a dominant force, MEED, December 5. Available at: www.meed.com/chinese-contractors-relentless-pursuit-bears-fruit/

Aguinaldo, J. (2021) Chinese firm appointed for Saudi solar schemes, MEED, April 14. Available at: www.meed.com/chinese-firm-appointed-for-saudi-solar-schemes

Al-Ansary, K. (2021) Iraq walks away from $2B upfront oil deal with China, *World Oil*, February 22. Available at: www.worldoil.com/news/2021/2/20/iraq-walks-away-from-2b-upfront-oil-deal-with-china

AP News (2020) JinkoSolar sells its stake in Abu Dhabi Sweihan Power Station, November 27. Available at: https://apnews.com/press-release/pr-newswire/business-brazil-corporate-news-latin-america-and-caribbean-north-america-2401d0ed5f0c5eadbb392ed7b8f71e42

Asian Banking and Finance Magazine (2019) Tighter rules targeting shadow banking put brakes on China banks' expansion. Available at: https://asianbankingandfinance.net/retail-banking/exclusive/tighter-rules-targeting-shadow-banking-put-brakes-china-banks-expansion

Bhatia, N. (2020) Chinese firm wins Etihad Rail wagons deal, MEED, August 4. Available at: www.meed.com/chinese-company-wins-etihad-rail-wagons-deal

BP (2018) BP Statistical Review of World Energy, June. Available at: www.bp.com/content/dam/bp/business-sites/en/global/corporate/pdfs/energy-economics/statistical-review/bp-stats-review-2018-full-report.pdf

Bridge, S. (2018) UAE's ADNOC signs major LNG sales deal with China's Wanhua, *Arabian Business*, November 12. Available at: www.arabianbusiness.com/energy/407837-uaes-adnoc-signs-long-term-lng-sales-deal-with-chinas-wanhua

Cheng, E. (2021) China's aging population is a bigger challenge than its 'one-child' policy, economists say, CNBC, February 28. Available at: www.cnbc.com/2021/03/01/chinas-aging-population-is-bigger-problem-than-one-child-policy-economists.html

Di Paola, A. (2018) Saudi looks to petrochemicals for its next big projects, Bloomberg, October 10. Available at: www.bloomberg.com/news/articles/2018-10-10/saudis-look-past-crude-with-100-billion-in-downstream-projects?sref=euelgVQS

Dubai International Financial Centre (2016) Growing UAE-China trade complements Dubai International Financial Centre growth strategy, February 29. Available at: www.difc.ae/newsroom/news/growing-uae-china-trade-complements-dubai-international-financial-centre-growth-strategy/

Esfandiary, D. (2021) Iran's 'new' partnership with China is just business as usual, *World Politics Review*, April 22. Available at: www.worldpoliticsreview.com/articles/29593/the-iran-china-deal-isn-t-all-that

Forrest, E. E. (2018) Chinese visitor surge set to boost UAE, *The National*, February 13. Available at: www.thenationalnews.com/business/travel-and-tourism/chinese-visitor-surge-set-to-boost-uae-1.702547/

Fulton, J. (2018) China's power in the Middle East is rising, The Washington Post, August 9. Available at: www.washingtonpost.com/news/monkey-cage/wp/2018/08/09/chinas-rise-in-the-middle-east/

Fulton, J. (2019) China's changing role in the Middle East, Atlantic Council, June. Available at: www.atlanticcouncil.org/wp-content/uploads/2019/06/Chinas_Changing_Role_in_the_Middle_East.pdf

Gordon, M. (2021) Iran oil sanctions relief expected in months if Vienna talks result in deal, *S&P Global*, May 6. Available at: www.spglobal.com/platts/en/market-insights/latest-news/oil/050621-iran-oil-sanctions-relief-expected-in-months-if-vienna-talks-result-in-deal

Gulf News (2018) Adnoc awards $1.6b contract to China's CNPC, July 19. Available at: https://gulfnews.com/business/energy/adnoc-awards-16b-contract-to-chinas-cnpc-1.2254117

Halligan, N. (2018) China's Silk Road Fund to invest in Dubai solar project, *Arabian Business*, July 22. Available at: www.arabianbusiness.com/energy/401242-chinas-silk-road-fund-to-invest-in-dubai-solar-project

Huawei (n.d.) Huawei helps Etihad Rail build GCC railway network. Available at: https://e.huawei.com/topic/leading-new-ict-en/etihad-rail-case.html

MEED (2018) Report: The future of Middle East energy, September 20. Available at: www.meed.com/future-middle-east-energy/

Menon, A. (2014) China to become GCC's biggest export market, *ME Construction News*, December 22. Available at: https://meconstructionnews.com/7458/china-to-become-gccs-biggest-export-market

Mills, R., Ishfaq, S., Ibrahim, R. and Reese, A. (2017) China's road to the Gulf: Opportunities for the GCC in the Belt and Road Initiative, *emerge85*, October. Available at: https://emerge85.io/wp-content/uploads/2017/10/Chinas-Road-to-the-Gulf.pdf

Ministry of Foreign Affairs of the People's Republic of China (2016) China's Arab Policy Paper, January 13. Available at: www.fmprc.gov.cn/mfa_eng/zxxx_662805/t1331683.shtml

Molavi, A. (2020) Enter the dragon: China's growing influence in the Middle East and North Africa, Hoover Institution, December 4. Available at: www.hoover.org/sites/default/files/research/docs/molavi_webready_revised.pdf

Mooney, T. (2018) DP World deploys legal attack on Djibouti terminal nationalization, *The Journal of Commerce online*, September 12. Available at: www.joc.com/port-news/terminal-operators/dp-world/dp-world-deploys-legal-attack-djibouti-terminal-nationalization_20180912.html

Organisation for Economic Co-operation and Development (2018) FDI in fragile and conflict affected economies in the Middle East and North Africa: trends and policies, December 4. Available at: www.oecd.org/mena/competitiveness/ERTF-Jeddah-2018-Background-note-FDI.pdf

Oxford Business Group (2019) Dubai Silk Road strategy to capitalise on logistics infrastructure and global connections. Available at: https://oxfordbusinessgroup.com/analysis/sleek-strategy-dubai-silk-road-strategy-outlined-mid-2019-aims-capitalise-emirate%E2%80%99s-trade-and

Parker, S. and Chefitz, G. (2018) China's strategic leveraging of its newfound economic influence and the consequences for U.S. foreign policy, *Harvard Kennedy School*, May. Available at: www.belfercenter.org/sites/default/files/files/publication/Debtbook%20Diplomacy%20PDF.pdf

Perlez, J. (2016) President Xi Jinping of China is all business in Middle East Visit, New York Times, January 30. Available at: www.nytimes.com/2016/01/31/world/asia/xi-jinping-visits-saudi-iran.html

Qian, X. and Fulton, J. (2017) China-Gulf economic relationship under the "Belt and Road" Initiative, *Asian Journal of Middle Eastern and Islamic Studies*, 11(3), pp. 12–21.

Rahman, F. (2018) Cosco built container terminal opens in Abu Dhabi, *Gulf News*, December 10. Available at: https://gulfnews.com/business/energy/cosco-built-container-terminal-opens-in-abu-dhabi-1.60856478

Reel, M. (2018) The irresistible urge to build cities from scratch, *Bloomberg Businessweek*, November 2. Available at: www.bloomberg.com/news/features/2018-11-02/the-irresistible-urge-to-build-cities-from-scratch?sref=euelgVQS

Saadi, D. (2020) UAE's ADNOC adds CNOOC of China as new partner in two offshore concessions, *S&P Global*, July 27. Available at: www.spglobal.com/platts/en/market-insights/latest-news/natural-gas/072720-uaes-adnoc-adds-cnooc-of-china-as-new-partner-in-two-offshore-concessions.

Sahloul, A. (2020) China's Syria policy could increase Beijing's Middle East footprint, Newlines Institute for Strategy and Policy, January 22. Available at: https://newlinesinstitute.org/china/chinas-syria-policy-could-increase-beijings-middle-east-footprint/

Saidi, N. (2018) Why the GCC should adopt the petroyuan, *The National*, January 9. Available at: www.thenationalnews.com/business/comment/why-the-gcc-should-adopt-the-petroyuan-1.694111

Saudi Press Agency (2018) Custodian of the two holy mosques receives number of Arab, African Foreign Ministers, December 21. Available at: www.spa.gov.sa/viewfullstory.php?lang=en&newsid=1852492#1852492

Siemens (2018) Siemens awarded high efficiency steam turbine modernization and upgrade project in China, March 27. Available at: https://press.siemens.com/global/en/feature/siemens-awarded-high-efficiency-steam-turbine-modernization-and-upgrade-project-china

United Nations Development Programme (2021) Brief on White Paper on China's international development cooperation in the new era, February 5. Available at: www.cn.undp.org/content/china/en/home/library/south-south-cooperation/issue-brief---brief-on-white-paper-on-china-s-international-deve.html

Xueqing, J. (2019) BOC unit to ramp up services in Middle East, *China Daily*, March 29. Available at: www.chinadaily.com.cn/a/201903/29/WS5c9d85daa3104842260b34a7.html

Yiu, K. (2019) Saudi prince's trip to China highlighted by $10 billion petrochemical deal, *ABC News*, February 22. Available at: https://abcnews.go.com/International/saudi-princes-trip-china-highlighted-10-billion-petrochemical/story?id=61233563

Young, K. E. (2018a) Game on: The new politics of Gulf financial intervention, American Enterprise Institute, December 18. Available at: www.aei.org/economics/international-economics/game-on-the-new-politics-of-gulf-financial-intervention/

Young, K. E. (2018b) Oman's investment and reform strategy: "slow and go", The Arab Gulf States Institute in Washington, January 25. Available at: https://agsiw.org/omans-investment-and-reform-strategy-slow-and-go/

Young, K. E. (2020) China is not the Middle East's HIGH ROLLER, *Bloomberg Opinion*, July 2. Available at: www.bloomberg.com/opinion/articles/2020-07-02/china-is-not-the-middle-east-s-high-roller?sref=euelgVQS

16

CHINA-MAGHREB RELATIONS

South-South Cooperation or Authoritarian Advancement?

Julia Gurol

1 Introduction

With the Chinese Belt and Road Initiative (BRI) making inroads into different regions of the world, the People's Republic of China (PRC) has become one of the most important global powers. Fostering cooperation under the frame of emerging South-South relations, it is expanding its bilateral outreach and both economic as well as political engagement abroad. The BRI, as the PRC's most ambitious foreign policy flagship project, is thought to revive the ancient Silk Road, connect different world regions, and build on China's past glory and wealth (Gurol and Rodriguez, 2022). A region of particular importance in that regard, is the Central Maghreb. Its strategic position, linking Asia, Africa and Europe via land and sea, as well as its proximity to crucial sea lines of communication in the Arabian Sea, make this geographical area in many ways interesting. Hence, it is not surprising, that in the context of its partnership diplomacy, China has also increased its engagement in this region (Chaziza, 2018). Despite their continuously close links to European countries—in particular, France which are a remnant of their colonial past, the countries from the Maghreb have developed solid economic relations with China in the past few decades. In particular, Sino-Algerian relations have flourished but also Morocco has stepped up its ties to the PRC significantly. Yet, so far, little is known about the respective motives behind both sides of the cooperation initiatives. While the Middle East and North Africa (MENA) region in general is comparably under-researched in the context of China's external relations, literature on China's relations with the Maghreb or the Mediterranean has hitherto remained extremely scarce. This is puzzling, given that China-Maghreb relations have been growing closer over the past two decades and have accelerated considerably since the official launch of the BRI in 2013.

China's growing presence in the region has raised a number of questions and concerns (Bayes, 2019). What drives the Maghreb countries' reaching out to China? Does China constitute an alternative partner to Western countries, such as France? And what role does the region play, in turn, for the BRI? How does the increasing Chinese engagement in the region affect the EU's role and what are the consequences for the countries involved? Answering these questions is at the core of this chapter. Instead of providing

DOI: 10.4324/9781003048404-18

in-depth analyses on the relationship between single Maghreb countries and China, it seeks to offer an overview of broader regional developments and China-Maghreb relations through the prism of South-South cooperation. In this context, it will also discuss whether we can observe increased Chinese authoritarian leverage in this specific region, which is often referred to as a reason for concern by Western actors. Finally, the chapter points toward possible future avenues of development of the complicated triangle between the Maghreb, China and the EU.

The remainder of this chapter is structured as follows. Section 2 begins by sketching the evolution of China's increasing presence in the Maghreb region. Subsequently it provides insight into three cases, outlining China's political and economic role. The case selection comprises Algeria (Section 2.1), Tunisia (Section 2.2) and Morocco (Section 2.3). Section 3 proceeds by discussing the divergent underlying principles of engagement of the EU and China with the region that have led to the emergence of what can be called a "crooked triangle" in the Maghreb. Over the course of this discussion, the chapter brings together literatures on authoritarianism in China's foreign policy as well as on democracy promotion of the EU. Based on this, the chapter carefully reflects on the agency of the Maghreb states within this triangle and explains how the Maghreb states have sought to counterbalance EU policy in the region by strengthening their ties to China. Finally, the chapter concludes by discussing the opportunities and challenges of the "crooked triangle" and points toward future avenues for development.

2 China-Maghreb South-South Relations

The concept of South-South cooperation, understood as the exchange of resources, technology and knowledge between developing countries has become more *en vogue* with the rise of the so-called "emerging powers" (Asante, 2018; Destradi and Gurol, 2022). Among these, China has made a name for itself as a protagonist in the context of South-South Cooperation, in particular with regards to its engagement on the African continent (Mthembu, 2018). As I have argued elsewhere, the increasing engagement of China in regions other than its own has brought to light a new debate about whether China really is striving toward transregional cooperation on eye-level in the sense of South-South cooperation (Gray and Gills, 2016), or whether it actually reproduces traditional North-South asymmetries, creating what could be criticized as "neo-colonial" structures. An often-voiced criticism is that the particular modes and mechanisms of China's engagement with other, mostly less powerful countries bears the risk of creating lop-sided realities that simply shift but ultimately reproduce existing dependencies (Destradi and Gurol, 2022). This is often discussed in the context of China's lack of hesitation in collaborating with non-democratic regimes as well as the lack of conditions attached to its loans. Through such a "no strings attached" approach, China is often believed to undermine the democratization and liberalization efforts of other cooperation partners and/or donors, such as the USA and European countries. Against this backdrop, the following sections scrutinize South-South relations between China and the Maghreb. These relations have a long history (Belhadj, Sun, and Zoubir, 2016) and mainly unfold bilaterally as well as in the institutional context of the Forum on China-Africa Cooperation (FOCAC), set up in 2001, and the China-Arab States Cooperation Forum (CASCF), set up in 2004.

Prior to the late 1990s, China's economic presence in North Africa in general and the Maghreb in particular was negligible. Economically Sino-Maghreb relations picked up speed in the context of the region's anti-colonial struggles. While in the beginning relations were primarily characterized by ideological support for national liberation movements in the context of China's expansion of bilateral economic ties and its general opening-up under Deng Xiaoping since 1978, the PRC has also turned toward the Maghreb and has by now become a top-three import origin for all North African countries (Bayes, 2019). This shift from ideologically driven relations to business-driven relations (Pairault, 2015; Calabrese, 2017) has led to a prioritization of commercial relations over political influence in the Maghreb. Until today, the economic pillar of the China's partnerships with the countries from the region is much stronger than their cooperation in other policy fields.

Over the past decades, but in particular since the official launch of the BRI in 2013, China's relations with the Maghrebian countries—Algeria, Morocco, Tunisia, Libya and Mauritania—have picked up speed (Zoubir, forthcoming). In 2018, the Maghreb accounted for 7.76 percent of China's imports from Africa, while Chinese exports to the Maghreb increased to 14.7 percent of the overall exports of the PRC to Africa (Lafargue, 2018; Zoubir, 2020), lending the region a more important place on the BRI. This is due not least to the region's strategic location as a gateway to Europe and Africa likewise. Its proximity to vital shipping routes of the Arabian Sea makes it an ideal hub to control passages between key regions. Most importantly, the Maghreb geographically connects Africa, Asia and Europe through the Suez Canal which is one of the most vital sea lines of communication for the PRC (Gurol, 2022). Although the BRI in its current form does not officially include the Maghreb, many individual countries have signed memoranda of understanding (MoUs) with China, and form part of the broader Arab-Chinese cooperation under the BRI framework (CASCF, 2018). Thereby, they are demonstrating their willingness to participate in China's large-scale infrastructure project, lending Beijing a stronger foothold in the region. However, despite the growing Chinese presence in the area in terms of investment, trade, ports, shipping, tourism and manufacturing, it does not yet match US or EU dominance (Chaziza, 2021a).

Politically and diplomatically, China's approach to the Maghreb can be understood in terms of "partnership diplomacy." Thereby, it refashions the PRC's overall tactic in the MENA region, which is commonly known as "1+2+3 cooperation." This strategic type of cooperation entails: (1) further collaboration in the energy sector; (2) infrastructure, trade and investment; and (3) technology exchange in the realm of nuclear energy, space satellites and renewable energy (MFA, 2018). Similar to other regions, China lacks a regional strategy but rather approaches the individual Maghrebian countries on a bilateral basis (Zoubir, forthcoming; Sun and He, 2015; Gurol, 2020). This facilitates adherence to its principle of non-interference, as it enables the PRC to take into account the specificities of each country.

The following sections scrutinize the economic and political relations between China and the Maghreb, thereby taking into consideration the two pillars of South-South cooperation. The analysis will focus on Algeria, Morocco and Tunisia, which make up the Central Maghreb, rather than on the five members of the Arab Maghreb Union, i.e., the Central Maghreb plus Mauritania and Libya.[1] That is because Algeria, Tunisia and Morocco have quite advanced relations with China but also remain closely connected to the EU. Hence, they constitute fruitful cases to discuss China-EU-Maghreb relations. Yet, it should not be left unmentioned that also Mauritania has increased its collaboration with China in the past few years. Libya, in turn, had quite advanced relations to the PRC before the 2011 revolution, based on the high amount of oil exports. In fact, it has been China's closest partner in the region before the protests again erupted in

2011 and Colonel Gadhafi was toppled. Ever since, China's involvement in Libya has mainly focused on economic penetration and behind-the-scenes diplomacy (Wehrey and Alkoutami, 2020) but has never since reached the pre-protest depth and height. Hence, the analysis will focus on Algeria, Tunisia and Morocco to provide an overview over China's new role in the Maghreb and how it affects the EU's position in the region.

2.1 China-Algeria Relations

Both in economic as well as in political terms, Algeria is undoubtedly the most important partner for China in the Maghreb and also its largest market. Cooperation between Algeria and China has a long history and officials from both sides frequently laud the longevity of its bilateral relationship (Zoubir, 2021; MFA, 2015). In fact, the bilateral Sino-Algerian partnership dates back to the Afro-Asian Bandung Conference in 1955, which is often referred to as the origin of South-South cooperation (Destradi and Gurol, 2022). As Strauss (2009) argues, Beijing still frames its intentions and activities in Algeria as a South-South partnership, stressing the "imagined fraternity with African anti-colonial and developmental struggles." China-Algeria relations were established in the midst of the 1954 Algerian War for Independence, when the PRC, in line with broader anti-colonial dispositions, supported the Algerian National Liberation Front (FLN) (Houlden and Zaamout, 2019). Similarly, the PRC was the first country outside the Arab world to recognize the independence of the People's Democratic Republic of Algeria (Wang and Wang, 2019). Yet, South-South cooperation in this bilateral relationship was not a one-way street. In turn, Algeria supported China politically in the aftermath of the Tiananmen Square protests in 1989, when China was faced with harsh criticism from Western countries after violently cracking down on the protesters. Moreover, Algeria helped China to mitigate the ensuing sanctions by mobilizing African countries through the African Union (Olimat, 2014).

Based on these roots, China-Algeria relations have blossomed in the past two decades. In 2004, the two sides concluded a Strategic Partnership that was elevated to a Comprehensive Strategic Partnership (CSP) in 2014, with Algeria becoming the first country from the MENA region to do so. The most important documents, accompanying this development of China-Algeria South-South relations are the Declaration for China-Algeria Strategic Partnership and Cooperation (2006) (*People's Daily*, 2006), the Five-Year Plan for China-Algeria Comprehensive Strategic Cooperation (2014) (MFA, 2014) and the MoU on cooperation under the BRI framework (2018) (Algeria Press Service, 2018).

The strength of these long-standing ties provides a fruitful basis for economic cooperation that has increased since 2000 and has turned China into Algeria's main trade partner in 2013. The overall trade volume between the two countries has reached a height of $9 billion (Ministère des Finances-Direction Générale des Douanes, 2019). While China generally imports little oil from Algeria, it is involved in the energy sector and mostly in the construction sector. Yet its engagement does not involve a lot of overseas lending. In terms of construction, China has taken part in building the new Ministry of Foreign Affairs Building, the Algiers Opera House and the Great Mosque of Algiers, among others, in the past two decades (Calabrese, 2021). According to the China Global Investment Tracker (CGIT), construction activities were focused mostly in the transport and real estate sectors and reached an amount of $23.85 billion in total over the course of 2005–2020. [2] Yet, beyond the economic realm, Algeria also plays a crucial role for China's security interests (Zoubir, 2022), as it borders the Sahel and additionally shares a border

2.2 China-Morocco Relations

In contrast to its neighbor Algeria, Morocco has until today maintained a close relationship with its former colonial power France as well as with the USA but has not yet fully embraced the potential of the new kid on the block, namely China. Yet, economic ties to China have genuinely increased in importance for Morocco over the past decades. Now China is Morocco's third largest trading partner after the EU and the USA. However, unlike in the case of Algeria, this does not automatically mean that Morocco is loosening its ties to Europe or the USA. Instead, Morocco signed a 10-year military cooperation agreement with the USA in October 2020 and has not yet pivoted fully to the East. Hence, Morocco's deeper engagement with China can rather be interpreted as a means to diversify its bilateral partnerships also with non-Western countries. This aim was already voiced explicitly during the visit of King Mohamed VI to China in 2016 (CGTN Africa, 2020).

In political terms, Morocco is still a predominantly pro-Western state. Yet, it also maintains good relations with the Gulf monarchies, which is certainly a valuable asset from the Chinese perspective. Yet, it is not surprising that Morocco's relationship with China mostly centers on trade and investment, while the political pillar of their South-South relationship is considerably less advanced. Economically speaking, trade flows between Morocco and China have increased since the launch of the BRI, first rapidly, then more modestly. According to the UN Comtrade Database, Morocco's exports to China reached $282 million in 2020, while its imports from the PRC totaled $5.18 billion. [3] During the 2018 FOCAC Summit, the Chinese president Xi Jinping flagged that Chinese enterprises would increase investments in manufacturing in Africa. This aim is reflected in the establishment of ambitious Chinese-funded free-trade zones and industrial parks, such as Mohamed VI Tangier Tech City in Morocco. Moreover, both sides signed an MoU in January 2021, in order to strengthen bilateral economic relations, particularly against the backdrop of the ravaging COVID-19 pandemic (Alouazen, 2021). Also, Morocco's strategic location as a gateway to Europe via the port of Tangier plays an important role and could even render Morocco one of the most dominant maritime hubs in the western Mediterranean (Tanchum, 2020). According to reports, China and Morocco have started to establish a major industrial zone, the so-called Mohammed VI Tangier Tech City, in September 2019 (Zoubir, 2020). This industrial zone will be connected to the rest of the country via road and rail links and is supposed to attract further foreign investors (Hatim, 2020).

The outbreak of the global corona pandemic hit Morocco the hardest in comparison to other countries from the Maghreb (Chaziza, 2021b). Reacting to the needs of the Moroccan people, the PRC took this as a window of opportunity to export its development model and model of health care, a development that can be observed in many countries of the broader MENA region and is often interpreted as a "silver platter" for autocratic regimes to export their policies (Gurol et al., 2022). Besides acquiring around 65 million doses of the Chinese-produced vaccine Sinopharm (Xinhua, 2020c), Morocco developed a clinical test center with the help of Chinese pharmaceutical companies in August 2020 (Chaziza, 2021b). Thereby, China became one of the most important players in flattening the infection curve on the African continent.

2.3 *China-Tunisia Relations*

Tunisia is rather a latecomer regarding friendly relations with China. On the contrary, ever since the early 1980s, Tunisia's view of China has been rather antagonistic and characterized by mistrust. That is despite already ongoing economic relations. As of today, China's presence in Tunisia is still on a comparatively low level (Zhang, 2020). Yet its antagonistic position toward China changed during the so-called Arab Spring and in the context of the toppling of President Ben Ali in 2011. After his fall, the Chinese government in Beijing granted Tunisia support, noting that it would be willing to "cement and develop the bilateral traditional friendship" between the two countries (Chinese Embassy in Tunis, 2011). This development might not be directly connected to the launch of the BRI that took place shortly after the Arab Spring uprisings. Yet, it is noteworthy that Tunisia occupies a strategic location as a gateway to Europe through the port of Bizerte (Souli, 2018). Despite this fact, Sino-Tunisian South-South relations are behind Sino-Algerian and Sino-Moroccan relations until today, both politically and economically.

In political as well as in economic terms, Tunisia is the country from the Maghreb region, in which China faces the greatest challenges and competition from European and US firms and investments as Tunisia's main export markets remain in Europe, with France leading the list as its most important trading partner. [4] Hence despite the strong motivation from both sides to heat up the long-standing rather lukewarm relations, Sino-Tunisian ties should not be over-exaggerated and very much remain weak in comparison to Sino-Algerian or Sino-Moroccan ties (Zhang, 2020; Zoubir, 2020). This fact notwithstanding, Tunisia has taken some small steps toward closer alignment with the PRC by adhering to the BRI and the Asian Infrastructure Investment Bank. Moreover, both sides have signed various trade agreements and Tunisia has actively tried to increase its cooperation with China, well aware of its strategic location (Zoubir, 2020). Yet, one could argue that Tunisia sees more potential in deeper alignment with China than vice versa. In particular, it considers China as both a significant investor and a market that is likely to ease Tunisia's economic struggles (Zhang, 2020). This resulted in the Tunisian foreign minister signing an MoU with his Chinese counterpart for Tunisia's adhesion to the BRI in July 2018 (Ghanmi, 2018; MFA, 2018). Through this MoU, Tunisia seeks not only to deepen its economic and political ties with China but also to position itself as a strategic player in trade and investment networks stretching between Asia, Europe and Africa.

Also, since the outbreak of the global pandemic, Sino-Tunisian relations have experienced a further boost. In the context of China's health diplomacy and newly launched Health Silk Road Initiative, Tunisia profited from Chinese aid deliveries (Chaziza, 2021b) that included sterile and antiseptic masks as well as other medical equipment. Yet again, these aid donations were comparably small in comparison to the medical equipment sent from China to its closest regional partner, Algeria.

3 China in the Maghreb: Counterbalancing the EU?

Concluding these findings, all that is left is to discuss whether the increased engagement of China provides a window of opportunity for the Maghrebian countries to counterbalance the influence of the EU, in particular, France. This question is closely connected to claims or accusations that China is actively promoting authoritarianism abroad or advancing authoritarian practices. While there is certainly evidence for authoritarian practices traveling transregionally from China to the broader MENA region (in particular, the Gulf region; see, for example, Demmelhuber et al., 2022), what we observe in the Maghreb is rather an economy-focused approach of the PRC. Yet, as this approach does not come with strings or reform requests attached, it often seems to undermine European efforts of democratization or liberalization and ultimately foster the persistence of authoritarian structure or could even be interpreted as a form of democracy prevention, albeit not necessarily an arbitrary one. Besides that, it needs to be mentioned that China is not automatically the "bad guy" among the region's external partners. Also the EU's role can be discussed critically and comes attached with a lot of colonial legacies. The Maghreb still plays a very important role for the EU. Ever since the launch of the so-called Euro-Mediterranean Partnership, North Africa has been at the core of the EU's external projection (Colombo, 2019). In addition, the Maghreb forms an important part of the EU's Neighborhood Policy. All three countries, Algeria, Tunisia and Morocco, have signed Association Agreements with the EU (European Commission 2021a, 2021b, 2021c). Moreover, the EU actively promotes the creation of Free Trade Areas (FTAs) as a part of its trade and aid relations with its former colonies in the region (Langan and Price, 2020). For instance, the EU established FTAs with Morocco, Algeria and Tunisia in the context of their Association Agreements (European Commission 1998, 2000; Council of the European Union, 2002). Hence, without any doubt, the EU still plays a very dominant, if not the most dominant, role in the region. As the trade statistics between the EU and Algeria, Tunisia and Morocco reveal very clearly, colonial patterns of trade seem to prevail. Especially Morocco and Tunisia still remain highly dependent upon exports to Europe, despite the growing Chinese presence. For both countries, the EU is still the most important trading partner, accounting for 59.4 percent (Morocco) and 64 percent (Tunisia) of their overall trade in 2017 (European Commission, 2019a, 2019b).

While for now, there is not a lot of evidence supporting the claim that China actively and intentionally seeks to confront the European countries that are partnering with Algeria, Tunisia and Morocco, the growing Chinese presence in the Maghreb indeed challenges the EU's traditional role as the main donor of the Maghrebian countries as well as its political efforts. For instance, it undermines the EU's ongoing attempts at promoting democracy in the broader Mediterranean (Haddadi, 2006; Pace, 2009; van Hüllen, 2012). This endeavor is not always welcomed by the receiving countries. Instead, very much in the spirit of South-South Cooperation, Algeria, Tunisia and Morocco have capitalized on having a non-traditional, non-Western donor to choose as an alternative at least at times. Hence, Beijing has come to view the Maghrebian countries not only as an economic partner that brings natural resources to the relationship, offers a growing market to Chinese companies and investors and constitutes a strategic location as the crossroads to the Arab world, Africa and the Mediterranean. In engaging with Algeria, Tunisia and Morocco that are striving to reduce their traditional dependence on Western donors from the EU, China also seems to see a promising opportunity to promote its particular model of development that is often contrasted with the normative model of Western democracies (Ghafar and Jacobs, 2019).

Yet, such an interpretation would be misleading and disregard the agency of Algeria, Tunisia and Morocco in actively reaching out to China, as mentioned earlier. Concluding that China as a new donor and cooperation partner in the context of South-South cooperation actively challenges the EU's dominant role would lead the observer astray. To the contrary, the European role in the region is not regarded without criticism by Algeria, Tunisia, and Morocco. For instance, regarding the establishment of Free Trade Areas, there has been criticism from all three countries about the argument of imperialist and neo-colonial domination of the region (Langan and Price, 2020: 16).

It is thus not surprising that the increased Chinese activity in the Maghreb has caused concern in Brussels. Historically, the region has had close ties with Europe, in particular France, based on its colonial past. But to what extent does China really constitute a competing actor to the EU? The answer to this question diverges if we look at economic and political components. In economic terms, FDI flows from the EU to the Maghreb are very low, with more than half coming from France. In that regard, China constituted a welcome alternative to Western donors for many of the countries from the Maghreb. Yet, when it comes to the political pillar of South-South cooperation, the Maghrebian countries, with the exception of maybe Algeria, maintain much closer ties to Europe than to China. Despite the PRC's repeated statements of endorsement in the context of the fall of Ben Ali in Tunisia in 2011, or after that, in the context of Algeria's struggle for independence, colonialism proves to have a long-lasting legacy in the region, impacting Algeria's, Morocco's and Tunisia's choice of political partners until today, at least to some extent. These traditional ties might have begun to weaken in light of a rising China that constitutes a somewhat easier and alternative partner to traditional donors, in particular in the setting of an emerging South-South cooperation. Yet, these developments still remain in their infancy, at least in Morocco and Tunisia.

4 Conclusion

All in all, this research shows that the relationship between China and the Maghreb has strengthened substantially since 2011 and in particular since 2013 and the launch of the BRI. Hence, China is gradually becoming more influential economically, diplomatically, and eventually geo-strategically in the Maghreb. Although mostly framed in terms of South-South cooperation, offering the Maghreb an alternative to Western dominance, China's engagement with the region is inherently strategic. Beijing is setting up the Maghreb to play a crucial role in its BRI strategy, fostering commercial ties. Within this framework, China is also promoting its development model that seeks to combine authoritarianism with economic growth. Yet, so far, the economic pillar of South-South cooperation dominates China's relationships with Morocco, Algeria and Tunisia, while political cooperation has remained scarce—with the exception of Algeria. All three countries play a crucial role in the context of China's BRI as they provide crucial gateways to Europe as well as to strategic sea lines of communication. From the vantage point of Algeria, Morocco and Tunisia, on the other hand, a deeper engagement with China has helped to diversify the portfolio of external cooperation partners as well as investors and decreased the dependencies on their traditional European donors. While there are no direct signs of an authoritarian advancement of China, the concrete modes and mechanisms of its engagement might definitely challenge the EU's approach to the Maghreb in terms of democracy promotion and liberalization.

Yet, the outbreak of the global pandemic was certainly a turning point for China-Maghreb ties. On the one hand, China was among the first to offer solidarity and help to Algeria, Morocco and Tunisia and provided them with medical aid and expertise. On the other hand, as Zhang pointedly argues, the pandemic has caused a massive blow to China's economy and China's investor capacities decreased significantly. This may have significant implications for China's overall approach to the BRI, but might also have an impact on its South-South relations to other countries from the Global South, including those from the Maghreb region.

Notes

1 This selection also builds on M. Arkoun (1984), who included Algeria, Tunisia and Morocco in his definition of the Maghreb. In his lectures, he also included Libya (from Benghazi westwards) into the Maghreb. Yet, Libya was excluded from the case selection based on the reasons mentioned above.
2 For concrete data, see China Global Investment Tracker, available at: www.aei.org/china-global-investment-tracker/
3 For concrete data, see UN Comtrade, available at: https://comtrade.un.org/data/
4 For concrete data, see *Trading Economics*, available at: https://tradingeconomics.com/tunisia/exports

References

Algeria Press Service (2018) "Algeria Inks MoU on Adherence to China's Belt and Road Initiative." Available at: www.aps.dz/en/economy/25756-algeria-inks-mou-on-adherence-to-china-s-belt-and-road-initiative (accessed 22 April 2021).

Alouazen, S. (2021) "Morocco, China Sign Agreement to Boost Growing Economic Ties," *Morocco World News*, 17 January. Available at: www.moroccoworldnews.com/2021/01/332411/morocco-china-sign-agreement-to-boost-growing-economic-ties/ (accessed 22 April 2021).

Arkoun, M. (1984) *Pour une critique de la raison islamique*. Paris: Maisonneuve et Larose.

Asante, R. (2018) "China and Africa: Model of South-South Cooperation?," *China Quarterly of International Strategic Studies* Vol. 4, No. 2, pp. 259–279.

Bayes, T. (2019) "China's Emerging Diplomatic and Economic Presence in North Africa," *Atlantic Community*. Available at: https://atlantic-community.org/chinas-emerging-diplomatic-and-economic-presence-in-north-africa/ (accessed 22 April 2021).

Belhadj, I., Sun, D. and Zoubir, Y. H. (2016) "China in North Africa," in Y. H. Zoubir, and G. White (Eds.), *North African Politics: Change and Continuity*. New York: Routledge, pp. 329–349.

Calabrese, J. (2017) "Sino-Algerian Relations: On a Path to Realizing Their Full Potential?" Middle East Institute. Available at: www.mei.edu/publications/sino-algerian-relations-path-realizing-their-full-potential#_ftn8 (accessed 20 April 2021).

Calabrese, J. (2021) "'The new Algeria' and China," Middle East Institute, 26 January. Available at: www.mei.edu/publications/new-algeria-and-china (accessed 2 January 2023).

CASCF (2018) "Declaration of Action on China-Arab States Cooperation under the Belt and Road Initiative," China-Arab States Cooperation Forum. Available at: www.chinaarabcf.org/chn/lthyjwx/bzjhywj/dbjbzjhy/P020180726404036530409 (accessed 22 April 2021).

CGTN Africa (2020) "A Typical Strategic Partnership Between Morocco and China." Available at: https://africa.cgtn.com/2020/09/01/a-typical-strategic-partnership-between-morocco-and-china (accessed 22 April 2021).

Chaziza, M. (2018) "The Chinese Maritime Silk Road Initiative: The Role of the Mediterranean," *Mediterranean Quarterly* Vol. 29, No. 2, pp, 54–69.

Chaziza, M. (2021a) "China's Friendly Cooperative Relations with Tunisia in the Age of the New Silk Road Initiative," *Journal of Balkan and Near Eastern Studies* Vol. 23, No. 2, pp. 1–20.

Chaziza, M. (2021b) "Chinese Health Diplomacy and the Maghreb in the COVID-19 Era," London: Middle East Institute. Available at: www.mei.edu/publications/chinese-health-diplomacy-and-maghreb-covid-19-era (accessed 26 April 2021).

Chinese Embassy in Tunis (2011) "Vice Foreign Minister Zhai Jun Meets with Beji Caid-Essebsi, Prime Minister of the Tunisian National Unity Government." Available at: www.china-embassy.org/eng/zgyw/t804639.htm (accessed 23 April 2021).

Colombo, S. (2019) "Re-conceptualising EU-North Africa Relations: 'Outside-In' and 'Inside-Out' Dynamics," in S. Giusti and I. Mirkina (Eds.), *The EU in a Trans-European Space*. Basingstoke: Palgrave Macmillan, pp. 177–196.

Council of the European Union (2002) "EU Algeria Association Agreement." Available at: https://investmentpolicy.unctad.org/international-investment-agreements/treaty-files/2643/download (accessed 3 May 2021).

Demmelhuber, T. et al. (2022). "The COVID-19 temptation? Sino-Gulf relations and autocratic linkages in times of a global pandemic," in Z. Hobaika, L. Möller and J. Völkel (Eds.), *The MENA Region and COVID-19: Impact, Implications and Prospects*, New York: Routledge, pp. 19–35.

Destradi, S. and Gurol, J. (2022) "South-South Cooperation: Between Cooperation on Eye-Level and Accusations of Neo-Colonialism," in J. Rüland, and A. Carrapatoso (Eds.), *Handbook on Regionalism and Global Governance*. Cheltenham: Edward Elgar Publishing, pp. 160–170.

European Commission (1998) "EU Tunisia Association Agreement." Available at: https://eur-lex.europa.eu/resource.html?uri=cellar:d3eef257-9b3f-4adb-a4ed-941203546998.0008.02/DOC_4&format=PDF (accessed 3 May 2021).

European Commission (2000) "EU Morocco Association Agreement." Available at: https://eur-lex.europa.eu/resource.html?uri=cellar:ecefc61a-c8d6-48ba-8070-893cc8f5e81d.0006.02/DOC_1&format=PDF (accessed 3 May 2021).

European Commission (2019a) "Morocco-Trade." Available at: https://ec.europa.eu/trade/policy/countries-and-regions/countries/morocco/ (accessed 30 April 2021).

European Commission (2019b) "Tunisia-Trade." Available at: https://ec.europa.eu/trade/policy/countries-and-regions/countries/tunisia/ (accessed 1 May 2021).

European Commission (2021a) "European Neighborhood Policy and Enlargement Negotiations – Algeria." Available at: https://ec.europa.eu/neighbourhood-enlargement/neighbourhood/countries/algeria_en (accessed 26 April 2021).

European Commission (2021b) "European Neighborhood Policy and Enlargement Negotiations – Tunisia." Available at: https://ec.europa.eu/neighbourhood-enlargement/neighbourhood/countries/tunisia_en (accessed 26 April 2021).

European Commission (2021c) "European Neighborhood Policy and Enlargement Negotiations – Morocco." Available at: https://ec.europa.eu/neighbourhood-enlargement/neighbourhood/countries/morocco_en (accessed 26 April 2021).

Ghafar, A. A. and Jacobs, A. (2019) "Beijing Calling: Assessing China's Growing Footprint in North Africa," Brookings Doha Center. Available at: www.brookings.edu/wp-content/uploads/2019/09/Beijing-Calling-Assessing-China%E2%80%99s-Growing-Footprint-in-North-Africa_English-1.pdf (accessed 22 April 2021).

Ghanmi, L. (2018) "Tunisia joins China's Belt and Road Initiative as it seeks to diversify trade, investment," *The Arab Weekly*. Available at: https://thearabweekly.com/tunisia-joins-chinas-belt-and-road-initiative-it-seeks-diversify-trade-investment (accessed 30 April 2021).

Gray, K. and Gills, B. (2016). "South–South Cooperation and the Rise of the Global South," *Third World Quarterly*, Vol. 37, No. 4, pp. 557–574.

Gurol, J. (2020) "The Role of the EU and China in the Security Architecture of the Middle East," *Asian Journal of Middle Eastern and Islamic Studies*, Vol. 14, No. 1, pp. 18–34.

Gurol, J. (2022) *The EU-China Security Paradox: Cooperation against All Odds?* Bristol: Bristol University Press.

Gurol, J., and Rodríguez, F. (2022) "'Contingent Power Extension' and Regional (Dis)integration: China's Belt and Road Initiative and its Consequences for the EU," *Asia Europe Journal*, Vol. 20, No. 4, pp. 441–456.

Gurol, J., Zumbrägel. T., and Demmelhuber, T. (2022) "Elite Networks and the Transregional Dimension of Authoritarianism: Sino-Emirati Relations in Times of a Global Pandemic," *Journal of Contemporary China*, Vol. 32, No. 139, pp. 138–151.

Haddadi, S. (2006) "Political Securitization and Democratization in the Maghreb: Ambiguous Discourses and Fine-Tuning Practices for a Security Partnership," in E. Adler, et al. (Eds.), *The Convergence of Civilizations: Constructing a Mediterranean Region*. Toronto: University of Toronto Press.

Hatim, Y. (2020) "Chinese Corporations Formalize Role in Tangier Tech City Project," *Morocco World News*. Available at: www.moroccoworldnews.com/2020/11/324730/chinese-corporations-formalize-role-in-tangier-tech-city-project/ (accessed 29 April 2021).

Houlden, G. and Zaamout, N. M. (2019) "A New Great Power Engages with the Middle East: China's Middle East Balancing Approach," China Institute, University of Alberta. Available at: https://era.library.ualberta.ca/items/1b3e3afa-8065-4d13-8dea-fa7629e2aca6 (accessed 22 April 2021).

Lafargue, F. (2018) "The Economic Presence of China in the Maghreb: Ambitions and Limits," Fondation pour la Recherche Stratégique. Available at: www.frstrategie.org/en/programs/obser vatoire-du-monde-arabo-musulman-et-du-sahel/economic-presence-china-maghreb-ambitions-and-limits-2018 (accessed 20 April 2021).

Langan, M. and Price, S. (2020) "Imperialisms Past and Present in EU Economic Relations with North Africa," *Interventions* Vol. 22, No. 6, pp. 703–721.

MFA (2014) "Wang Yi: Practical Cooperation Between China and Algeria Enters a New Stage," Available at: www.fmprc.gov.cn/mfa_eng/zxxx_662805/t1164074.shtml (accessed 22 April 2021).

MFA (2015) "Xi Jinping Meets with Prime Minister Abdelmalek Sellal of Algeria," Available at: www.fmprc.gov.cn/mfa_eng/zxxx_662805/t1260832.shtml (accessed 22 April 2021).

MFA (2018) "Xi Meets Tunisian Prime Minister," Available at: www.fmprc.gov.cn/mfa_eng/wjb_663304/zzjg_663340/xybfs_663590/gjlb_663594/2893_663786/2895_663790/t1593095.shtml (accessed 30 April 2021).

Ministère des Finances-Direction Générale des Douanes (2019) "Statistiques du Commerce Extérieur the l'Algérie-Période: onze mois de l'année 2019." Available at: www.douane.gov.dz/IMG/pdf/rapport_comext_11_mois_19_vf.pdf (accessed 22 April 2021).

Mthembu, P. (2018) *China and India's Development Cooperation in Africa: The Rise of Southern Powers.* Cham: Palgrave Macmillan.

Olimat, M. S. (2014) *China and North Africa since World War II: A Bilateral Approach.* Lexington, MD: Lexington Books.

Pace, M. (2009) "Paradoxes and Contradictions in EU Democracy Promotion in the Mediterranean: the Limits of EU Normative Power," *Democratization* Vol. 16, No. 1, 39–58.

Pairault, T. (2015) "Economic Relations between China and Maghreb Countries," in *China, the European Union and the Developing World.* Cheltenham: Edward Elgar Publishing, pp. 298–324.

People's Daily (2006) "China-Algeria Sign Statement on Strategic Cooperation." Available at: http://en.people.cn/200611/07/eng20061107_319102.html (accessed 23 April 2021).

Souli, S. (2018) "Tunisia Hopes Boost in Chinese Investment Can Ease Economic Woes." Available at: www.al-monitor.com/originals/2018/03/boost-china-investment-tunisia-europe-trade.html#ixzz6t8Dfe6DJ (accessed 26 April 2021).

Strauss, J. C. (2009) "The Past in the Present: Historical and Rhetorical Lineages in China's Relations with Africa," *The China Quarterly*, Vol. 199, pp. 777–795.

Sun, D. and He, S. (2015) "From a By-stander to a Constructor: China and the Middle East Security Governance," *Journal of Middle Eastern and Islamic Studies* Vol. 9, No. 3.

Tanchum, M. (2020) "China's Challenge in Morocco's Africa-to-Europe Commercial Corridor," *East Asia Forum.* Available at: www.eastasiaforum.org/2020/08/01/chinas-challenge-in-moroc cos-africa-to-europe-commercial-corridor/ (accessed 30 April 2021).

van Hüllen, V. (2012) "Europeanisation through Cooperation? EU Democracy Promotion in Morocco and Tunisia," *West European Politics* Vol. 35, No. 1, pp. 117–134.

Wang, X. and Wang, Z. (2019) "Is China Able to Export its Developmental Model? Upstream–Downstream Integration in Sino–African Petroleum Engagement," *Transnational Corporations Review* Vol. 12, No. 1, pp. 24–36.

Wehrey, F. and Alkoutami, S. (2020) "China's Balancing Act in Libya," Carnegie Endowment for International Peace, 10 May. Available at: https://carnegieendowment.org/2020/05/10/china-s-balancing-act-in-libya-pub-81757 (accessed 3 May 2021).

Xinhua (2020a) "China Sends Medical Aid to Algeria to Help Combat COVID-19," 28 March. Available at: www.xinhuanet.com/english/2020-03/28/c_138924278.htm (accessed 26 April 2021).

Xinhua (2020b) "China Sends 2nd Medical Donation to Help Algeria Combat COVID-19," 16 April. Available at: www.xinhuanet.com/english/africa/2020-04/16/c_138979681.htm (accessed 26 April 2021).

Xinhua (2020c) "Morocco to Buy 65 mln Doses of COVID-19 Vaccine," 25 December. Available at: www.xinhuanet.com/english/2020-12/25/c_139617652.htm (accessed 26 April 2021).

Zhang, C. (2020) "Potential to Leap Forward? Interrogating the Relations between China and Tunisia," *Asian Journal of Middle Eastern and Islamic Studies* Vol. 14, No. 4, pp. 594–606.

Zoubir, Y. H. (2020) "Expanding Sino–Maghreb Relations: Morocco and Tunisia." London: Chatham House. Available at: www.chathamhouse.org/2020/02/expanding-sino-maghreb-relations/2-china-and-maghreb (accessed 20 April 2021).

Zoubir, Y. H. (forthcoming) "China in the Southern Mediterranean: Integrating the Greater Maghreb in the New Silk Road," *Mediterranean Politics*. https://doi.org/10.1080/13629395.2022.2035137

Zoubir, Y. H. (2021) "China's Relations with Algeria: From Revolutionary Friendship to Comprehensive Strategic Partnership," in A. Abdel-Ghafar, (Ed.), *China and North Africa.* London: I.B. Tauris, pp. 126–165.

Zoubir, Y. H. (2022) "Algeria and China: Shifts in Political and Military Relations," *Global Policy.* https://doi.10.1111/1758-5899.13115

17

CHINA AND CONFLICT MANAGEMENT IN THE MIDDLE EAST

Guy Burton

Rising Powers and Conflict

Conflict entails an antagonistic interaction between two or more entities (Jeong, 2010: 10). While conflict can sometimes be positive, this chapter focuses on its more disruptive and sometimes destructive cases in which one or more actors look to satisfy their own demands and interests at the expense of others.

The reasons for conflict are varied, ranging from the individual and human nature to more diverse and complex explanations. They may include material considerations, from access to or exclusion from resources such as water, agricultural land or finance, to non-material ones, including ideas about ethnic identity, race or religion. The cause of conflict may also be found within domestic settings, within established states and societies, with some groups having or being perceived to have advantages over others. Grievances can also be found at the international level, based on the relatively greater influence that some states have, both to persuade or coerce others (Goldstein and Pevehouse, 2014; Stern, 1995).

Conflict need not lead to violence, but that is a possibility should its intensity rise. Moreover, as a conflict escalates, the parties may become trapped in a vicious cycle whereby the use of force is matched by similar combative behaviour. That situation may continue so long as the competing sides consider it worth their while to maintain that approach. Only when the difference between the perceived benefits associated with sustaining a conflict begin to be outweighed by the costs will a party revise its position and start to see the appeal of reducing the intensity of the conflict (Jeong. 2010).

What role can third parties play during these phases for conflict? They can contribute to its escalation or defuse it. They escalate conflict by exploiting underlying grievances and instigating conflict, by supporting one or more sides. As tensions rise, they can provide direct assistance (e.g. through financial aid or arms on one side to active intervention on the other) or indirect support (e.g. by providing diplomatic cover).

Alternately, a third party may want to support moves towards peace. These may range from modest involvement to more forceful and active measures (Crocker, Hampson and Aall, 2007). At the "softer" end it may be limited to making statements, encouraging

DOI: 10.4324/9781003048404-19

217

dialogue or finding points of common ground, perhaps even facilitating negotiations between conflicting parties. Such involvement may be seen as managing the conflict and containing its impact, perhaps through the use of peacekeeping where violence is absent or has ended.

At the "harder" end of the spectrum, third parties may adopt a more direct and active opportunity to frame intervention to halt violence through peace enforcement or, where violence is no longer present, active measures to tackle the causes of the conflict through peacemaking or peacebuilding (Butler, 2009). What constitutes peacemaking has evolved over time. Following the end of the Cold War, the liberal paradigm was ascendant. Peace initiatives were invariably predicated on establishing pluralist political systems with representative democratic institutions and elections and underpinned by a market economy (Oxford Research Group, 2019). This approach inspired the peace processes in Northern Ireland and the Oslo process between Israel and the Palestinians in the 1990s as well as the Bush administration in Afghanistan after 9/11 and Iraq following the 2003 invasion. While such approaches have been recently challenged in the academic and policy circles, in practice the focus remains the same (Paffenholz, 2021).

Why would a third party seek to engage in a conflict setting? This may happen if the third party had some historical association or vested interest in the conflict and its parties, if the conflict was especially violent or if it was perceived as relatively easy to resolve (Grieg and Rost, 2013). In the case of China and the Middle East, these factors are largely missing, given the historical, geographic and commercial "distance" between the two. Despite this, the "gap" between China and the Middle East has closed in the past two decades, owing to China's economic rise and status of a rising power, which has meant that its commercial interests have become more widespread and far-flung. In this respect, China's current experience echoes that of hegemonic powers in the past and present, from the Europeans and their global empires of the past to the superpower patrons of the Cold War.

China's global stature today means that whether it wants to or not, it cannot avoid conflict in the Middle East. At the same time, a rising power like China may welcome the opportunity to take a more mitigating role for reasons of status; it is important for a rising power to be perceived as such (Larson, Paul and Wohlforth, 2014). With that in mind, what forms of behaviour might a rising power take? Broadly, they can act as supporters, spoilers, shirkers or shapers of the international system (Schweller, 2014; Stuenkel, 2015). First, their economic growth and associated global rise owed much to the existing liberal order of a global market and free trade. That should therefore mark them out as "supporters" of the system.

On the other hand, rising powers' prior identities as developing countries and part of the Global South distinguished them from the Western powers who helped create the current international order. Although they had played the game and "won", they observed that the liberal order was weighted against them, especially in terms of representation on international institutions like the IMF and the World Bank. What would be their response to this state of affairs? One option was to not take a position and stand apart; to "shirk". Another, more radical option was to reject the system, by "spoiling" against it.

In each of these three possible behaviours, rising powers' choices are reactive. Alternately, a more proactive and constructive approach is also possible, to build and "shape" a new international system in its image. However, charting a new course could vary. At its narrowest it might involve a modest reform of the prevailing system, by increasing their presence and influence within existing institutions. By contrast, a more expansive approach might entail a comprehensive transformation of the system, ranging from the bodies which operate within it to the underlying norms and patterns of behaviour.

China and Conflict in the Middle East

Each of these four modes of behaviour can similarly be applied to conflict and whether to support, oppose, stand apart or reshape it into something different. With these various positions in mind, what have been the implications for China in the Middle East? Broadly, China's approach towards conflict in the Middle East can be encapsulated into three broad phases. Here, a long-term historical perspective is useful. In the first period, it was an activist and confrontational one. Its support for insurgent groups and their revolutionary aims marked it out as a "spoiler" of the status quo. By contrast, in the second period, its retreat from revolution and commitment to diplomacy and focus on economic interaction marked it out as a less disruptive force. Although it still had sharp words for its superpower rivals, it presented a more supportive force to the regional order. At the same time, it was both unwilling and unable to take a more active role in managing the system.

That unwillingness to engage fully – "shirking" – became more prominent in the third period, in the wake of China's rise. At the same time, standing apart presented problems in a context of growing regional disorder. Consequently, there may be signs in Beijing that its support for regional states and avoidance of regional conflicts may be coming to an end. An alternative course is necessary, leading to suggestions to manage and mitigate conflict that have begun to emerge through proposals for regional security and peace and the role that the Belt and Road Initiative (BRI) might play in it. Should this lead to China taking on a more substantive role as an active conflict mediator, this might point to China being viewed as a "shaper" of conflict management in the region.

Contributing Towards Conflict, 1950s–1970s

China's first contact with the Middle East began in the mid-1950s once the People's Republic of China (PRC) was consolidated both at home and in East Asia (Harris, 1994). The ceasefire which halted the fighting in Korea in 1953 provided a degree of regional security and space for Beijing to expand its diplomatic ties beyond its neighbourhood and into the wider world (Gray, 1990: 319–321).

In the Middle East, Gamal Nasser's Arab nationalist regime in Egypt was an early partner. China was a public supporter of Nasser and his wars against Israel (Yang, 2010). In 1956, China was suspected of providing behind-the-scenes support to enable Egypt to acquire Czechoslovak arms. Beyond Egypt, the Chinese found it difficult to advance relations with the wider Middle East due to regional and global constraints. Regionally, it proved hard to build relations beyond Nasser and the Baathists, given China's communism (Harris, 1994; Shichor, 1999). Beijing was viewed with suspicion by much of the regional elite who identified more with the West. Globally, China's relations with the Soviet Union became more fraught after Stalin's death. Beijing took an increasingly dim view of the new Soviet leader, Nikita Khrushchev, who was seen as insufficiently confrontational towards the West and revisionist (Gray, 1990: 321).

Given Moscow's status as the communist superpower, there was less need for regional elites to cultivate the People's Republic of China (Harris, 1994; Dillon, 2004). Perhaps as a result, China was pushed to find alternative partners to the states. They found them in insurgent nationalist movements, from Algeria in the 1950s to Palestine, the Gulf (especially Oman) and the Eritrean Liberation Front (ELF) in the second half of the 1960s. These groups' opposition to colonialism, Western imperialism and Israel chimed with similar sentiment in China and domestic political agitation and radicalism which were sweeping both the leadership and the masses in the form of the Cultural Revolution.

The Arab defeat by Israel in 1967 not only diminished Nasser's influence in the Arab world and among Arab nationalists, it also prompted a rethink in Beijing. Chinese leaders concluded that fighting a conventional war would not be successful and that instead the Arabs should focus on fighting a "people's war" which was concerned less with acquiring territory and more on winning over the population (*Peking Review*. 1967). The model for this approach came from the Chinese communists themselves, during their successful civil war against the Nationalists.

In practice, the strategy was embraced by insurgent groups like the Palestinian Liberation Organization (PLO), ELF and the nationalists in the Gulf (*Peking Review*, 1968; Behbehani, 1981; Kenyon, 2018: 398–399). Chinese financial and military assistance began to flow to them while some of the most promising fighters (among whom included Eritrea's future President Isaias Afwerki) received political and military training in China or in the region. The bulk of these Chinese training camps in the region were in South Yemen, where a Marxist regime held sway (Olimat, 2014).

Avoiding Conflict, 1970s–2000s

Although welcome, Chinese assistance to insurgent groups in the 1960s was neither sufficient nor comprehensive enough for them to achieve their goals. Moreover, it did not replace the greater importance of Soviet patronage. The failures of insurgents to break through pointed to a further re-evaluation by Chinese leaders. One was that it seemed to be becoming clear that neither the Arab nationalist regimes like Nasser's nor the insurgents were going to make the breakthrough that the Chinese hoped. Following the Arab defeat in 1967 and Sadat's succession to the presidency after Nasser's death, Egypt began a transition into the American orbit and an eventual peace settlement with Israel. Meanwhile, the nationalists in the Gulf failed to build sufficient support to sustain themselves and their struggle while tensions between the PLO and the government in Jordan led to a bloody struggle and their eviction (Behbehani, 1981). Around this time, Chinese leaders realised that support for insurgents hampered their ability to build relations with other states (Dreyer, 2012: 345). Meanwhile, the British departure from the Gulf not only introduced new independent states into the Gulf region, but also magnified Iran's influence (Olimat, 2014).

Globally, meanwhile, Beijing's fortunes were changing. In 1971, US President Richard Nixon travelled to Beijing in a bid to improve relations between the two countries and freeze out the Soviets. The visit heralded Beijing's re-entry into the international system, including its replacement of the Nationalist regime (in Taiwan) from the top table of the United Nations Security Council (Dreyer, 2012: 345). That same year, China also saw its diplomatic recognition in the region grow, with Turkey and Iran, and followed by Oman in 1978; the other Arab Gulf monarchies would follow in the 1980s.

The shift towards a more formal, state-based set of relationships in the Middle East dovetailed neatly with China's further change in foreign policy orientation after 1978. Following Mao Zedong's death and subsequent political turmoil, Deng Xiaoping eventually emerged as the paramount leader (ibid.: 116–117). He emphasised economic development at home as the principal goal and brought foreign policy in line with it.

A result of China's greater focus on commercial considerations over political ones was first felt regionally during the Iran-Iraq War. Whereas China had previously contributed to the continuation of regional conflict through assistance to Palestinian, Algerian, Dhofari and Eritrean nationalists on political solidarity and ideological grounds, in the 1980s China took advantage of its relations with both Iran and Iraq to become important arms suppliers to each. By the time the war ended in 1988, China was believed to have earned at least \$6.2 billion in total (SIPRI, n.d.; Razoux, 2015: 241). At the same time, China directed blame for the war to the American and Soviet superpowers for causing and exacerbating the Iraq-Iraq War (UN, 1980, 1988).

The prioritization of commercial interests continued into the 1990s and 2000s. In 1993, China became a net energy importer for the first time. In order to maintain its economic growth, Beijing became more concerned about ensuring regular and reliable sources of energy imports. For this reason, while it had reservations regarding the American-led invasions of Iraq in 1991 and 2003, it did not adopt a directly confrontational stance towards Washington (Sassoon, 2018: 152). Notwithstanding its public opposition to war, practical considerations won out, including an American offer of loans in 1991 and Chinese unwillingness to confront the USA directly in 2003 (Burton, 2020: 93).

Much to its advantage, Chinese ambivalence towards American hegemony was not only noted, but opened doors too. During the 1990s, Chinese state firms signed contracts to refurbish and develop the oil sectors in both Iraq and Sudan, both of whom had fewer options to turn to, given the Western sanctions they both faced at the time (Large, 2009; Al-Shafiy, 2015). Though welcome, Chinese assistance presented its own challenges, including the constraints presented by sanctions (Al-Tamimi, 2013; Al-Shafiy, 2015). In Iraq, for example, the American-led invasion and occupation created an unstable environment in which Chinese companies had to work.

As in Iraq, Chinese businesses were also exposed to the various conflicts present in Sudan, both in the vicinity of the oil fields which drew its personnel into the confrontation between Khartoum and the separatists, as well as in Darfur. Much against its will, China was drawn into the management of the Darfur crisis (Holslag, 2007; Sun and Jin, 2009; Jian, 2018). The growing crisis attracted international attention and pressure in the West to sanction the Sudanese government. For its part, the Sudanese pushed back, refusing to accept outside interference in its affairs. China sought to navigate between these two poles, owing to its status as a permanent member of the UN Security Council (UNSC) and its contact with Omar al-Bashar's government. Although it was eventually able to persuade Bashar to accept an international peacekeeping force and contributed some of the troops to it, its efforts were insufficient to resolve the conflict in Darfur (Holslag, 2007; Jian, 2018).

Managing and Defusing Conflict, 2011–Present

China's management of the Darfur crisis presaged similar wariness and reluctance by Beijing, especially after the 2011 Arab uprisings. Libya was a first test. Although Libya was not a principal site for Chinese business and investment, several Chinese firms had signed contracts and had been undertaking operations in the oil sector since the 1980s (Bearman, 1986: 259, 260; Schinn, 2005). When protests first began against his rule, Muammar Gaddafi showed little willingness to stand aside and instead resorted to repression. The uprising soon became an armed one and the country began to disintegrate. China's initial response in this period was to undertake a mass evacuation of its citizens, an exercise which was followed by removing several hundred of its own nationals and other foreigners in 2015 when the Saudi-led military campaign in Yemen began (Chan and Miles, 2011; *The Economist*, 2011; Wang, 2015).

The uprisings led to other, far-reaching consequences. One was growing international pressure, especially by the West, to remove leaders like Gaddafi. Using UNSC resolutions as justification, Europeans and Americans carried out airstrikes against Gaddafi's forces, which the Chinese saw as an attempt to change regime. That suspicion prompted China to take a more robust stance against Western demands for Assad to stand aside in Syria. Coupled with Russia's diplomatic and later military support to Assad, the prospect of UNSC consensus broke down.

Russian involvement in Syria was only one example of the increasing interference by outside actors in the region's conflicts. Alongside the role of external parties were also regional powers. In Syria, Iran and Hezbollah provided assistance to Assad while Turkey came out against the regime and the growing autonomy of the Kurdish groups in the country's north. In Yemen, the Saudis and the United Arab Emirates intervened on behalf of the internationally recognised government against the Houthis. In Libya, Europeans like the French and Italians found themselves on opposite sides, as did Russia and Turkey in later years.

The fragmentation of societies and states was felt in other ways too. In Syria, new, more militant groups emerged, like ISIS. Along with the limited outreach of the Iraqi state, ISIS expanded its territorial control over large parts of Syria and Iraq. It announced its intention to build a new caliphate while the group's leader, Abu Bakr Al-Baghdadi, condemned Chinese actions against Muslims, including in Xinjiang and urged his co-religionists to either join them in their struggle at home or in the region (Sands, 2014; Lin, 2017).

China's response to the regional unravelling after 2011 was strongly Westphalian, backing state elites and their regimes. It offered support to the Syrian and Iraqi governments and may have provided logistical support in its campaign against extremists. It also distinguished between the Russian and Western presence in Syria by pointing out the former's invitation by Damascus against the other's self-appointed presence (Tiezzi, 2015).

Beyond the uprisings, wars and proxy conflicts that occurred across the Arab world, there was also growing confrontation between the USA as the region's hegemonic power and Iran. Iran's active nuclear programme was revealed in 2002, resulting in American pressure to sanction Iran to halt its development. Although China opposed Western confrontation and was sympathetic to Iran's claim that the programme was for civilian use only, it shared Western reservations at nuclear proliferation (van Kemenade, 2010). It therefore accepted UN resolutions and sanctions insofar as they focused on the nuclear programme and did not punish Iran's leadership or people (Singh, 2010; van Kemenade, 2010). Later, the prospects for better relations between the USA and Iran emerged, when Obama was re-elected and a new, more pragmatic president was elected in Iran, replacing the more hardline and confrontational Ahmadinejad. Then, China adopted a similar role to the one it had followed in Sudan, seeking to reduce the difference between the West and Iran, resulting in the Joint Comprehensive Plan of Action (JCPOA) (Garver, 2018).

The growing turbulence across the Middle East – both within states and societies and at the international level – had coincided with China's global economic rise. It also occurred at the same time that China had begun to project itself as a global power with benign intent. Central to this image of itself is the Belt and Road Initiative, which was launched in 2013, two years after the uprisings swept the Arab world. Although the focus for the BRI was the Eurasian landmass rather than the Middle East specifically, the looseness and ambiguity inherent in the vision have meant that it can be interpreted in different ways and appeal to different audiences (Miller, 2017: 30–34; Shichor, 2018; Garlick, 2019). For Beijing, the BRI not only promised greater connectivity across the landmass, but also the development of local markets where surplus Chinese capital could be invested. For China's prospective partners that investment would be felt in the construction of infrastructure projects. As a result, there has been great interest by political elites across the region in accessing such opportunities, both from countries with substantial economic exchanges with China, such as Iran and the Arab Gulf, to conflict-affected countries, such as Syria, Libya and Yemen, which are eager for reconstruction funds (Ghiselli and Al-Sudairi, 2019; Naderi, 2019; Wehrey and Alkoutami, 2020).

Some Chinese scholars and analysts have sought to make a virtue of Beijing's behaviour. They have critiqued the predominant Western mode of conflict management and resolution and suggested that China's present approach could hold the seeds to not only containing, but also diffusing tensions. Sun and Zoubir, for instance, have suggested that China's primary concern with its business interests in the Middle East makes its political activity there more modest and risk-averse than the West's more proactive and agenda-setting approach. By adopting a less bombastic style, this Chinese "quasi-mediation" can encourage dialogue, resulting in a more participatory process that helps de-escalate conflict (Sun and Zoubir, 2018).

More recently, Sun has returned to the subject and critiqued the West's approach to peacebuilding as based on two paradigms: the first was through strength, where the USA and its allies focused on building up military capacity to deter adversaries – but which generated insecurity and an arms race; the second from a lack of democracy as the principal cause for regional instability, with democratisation as the solution – but which has also generated instability as well (Sun and Zhang, 2019; Sun and Wu, 2020). Concluding that these approaches have failed, Sun points to a lack of material wealth as the principal cause of conflict. Therefore, what is needed is to boost economic growth and opportunity to ensure greater development in society so as to remove the sources of grievance and frustration. Moreover, he sees this approach as more inclusive than the Western efforts, since they are based on cooperation between China and its regional partners rather than being imposed from outside.

This "peace through development" paradigm is one that China is both well positioned to provide and one which may receive a receptive regional audience. First, it draws on China's own past experience of development after 1978. Second, it makes use of its own current regional engagement through trade and the Belt and Road Initiative, along with Chinese humanitarian and other aid. Third, regional elites may welcome this Chinese approach, because it makes few demands on them, especially when compared to the West's demands for political reforms or in relation to human rights (Walt, 2021).

However, precisely because the peace through development model may appeal to regional elites, this may also prevent it from delivering a resolution to conflict or even its management. As the principal parties that China engages with are the regimes that control the states in the region, there is little space for the regimes' opponents in this process. Additionally, the focus on economic prosperity as the solution to all ills overlooks other non-economic sources of grievance, for example, those associated with identity or ideology or transitional justice (Galtung, 1967). To these may also be noted the distinct experience of China's development after 1978 and the absence of war which does not make it synonymous with that of conflict-affected states and societies in the Middle East like Syria, Libya, Yemen or Palestine.

Meanwhile, for the regimes who partner with China, the peace through development model may also pose potential risks. One is the finite nature of Chinese capital available in the region. Despite the great fanfare that the BRI has received, Chinese credit in the region may have already peaked (Young, 2020; American Enterprise Institute, n.d.). If that is the case, the limited availability of resources could lead to the BRI becoming a source of tension and competition rather than a means to mitigate differences and achieve cooperation. Second is regime ambivalence regarding the implications of accepting Chinese credit. Although both Chinese and regional officials are keen to emphasise these relationships as partnerships, in some cases this may lead to be an imbalance between the two. Indeed, differences have emerged within Iran's regime over how widely and deeply it should build ties with China, lest it become increasingly dependent as a result (Rafizadeh, 2021)

Conclusion

This chapter has surveyed China's response to conflict and its management in the Middle East. Since the 1950s this can be characterized into three main periods. During the first period, China's actions were motivated by political considerations and support for radical, insurgent groups. The second, from the early 1970s until the 2000s, downplayed politics and emphasised diplomatic relations alongside economic development. Generally, China's position on conflict was to avoid any involvement in its management. Conceptually, this entailed a shift from the harder and more active end of the spectrum regarding third-party involvement to the softer and less engaged end.

Since then, China has embarked on a third phase in response to regional conflict, in the wake of the Arab uprisings in 2011. In this period, the region became more fractured and unstable, alongside a decline in American hegemony and China's status as a global economic power with a substantial presence in the region. While China's preferences have been to avoid involvement in the conflicts – and maintain the status of a "shirker" – that has become harder to do. As a result, there is both growing awareness of the need for change and efforts to reverse-engineer some of China's current (economic) activities in the region, such as its Belt and Road Initiative, as a form of peacemaking.

In essence, then, China's approach to conflict in the region appears to have come full circle. In both the 1950s and today it has taken a more active approach to conflict, although in terms of content the motives for doing so could not be more different. Whereas previously, China's interest in conflict was stoking it, today it prefers to see tensions scaled back. The difference owes much to China's changed circumstances, having become a more significant economic actor in the region, with a wide range of business interests that are vulnerable to instability.

However, even if China's leaders are beginning to take a greater interest in the Middle East's various conflicts, that does not mean that its participation is substantive. Mac Ginty has highlighted the differences across the conflict response spectrum from conflict management to conflict resolution to conflict transformation (Mac Ginty, 2021). Conflict management is the most conservative and limited of responses, being focused with containing violence and ensuring state sovereignty and the wider international system. Conflict resolution is more "enlightened" than conflict management; it can accommodate change, like secession and new forms of governance, but only within certain parameters. Conflict transformation is the most comprehensive mode of peacemaking, breaking with the underlying dynamics and causes of conflict and including the whole of society, down to the level of the individual.

Viewed along this spectrum, China's recent interest and involvement towards regional conflict occupy the conflict management/conflict resolution end. The examples of the Darfur crisis, the Iranian nuclear deal or the Syrian civil war all point towards this position. Moreover, across them all, China's preference has been to follow its regional (state) partners rather than engage them and their peoples directly in measures which might resolve the principal grievances and their causes. Looking ahead, it is likely that this will be China's preferred approach in the region. Indeed, the effort being put into the design and abstraction of paradigms like quasi-mediation and peace through development provide not only a counterweight to more traditional (Western) ways of peacemaking, but also a justification and model for future action.

References

Al-Shafiy, Haider Hamood Radhi. (2015) "CNPC, CNOOC and SINOPEC in Iraq: Successful Start and Ambitious Cooperation Plan". *Journal of Middle Eastern and Islamic Studies (in Asia)*, Vol. 9, No. 1, pp. 78–98.

Al-Tamimi, Naser. (2013). "China in Iraq: Winning Without a War". *Al-Arabiya*, 16 March. Available at: http://english.alarabiya.net/en/views/2013/03/16/China-in-Iraq-Winning-Without-a-War.html (accessed 8 May 2021).

American Enterprise Institute. (n.d.). "China Global Investment Tracker". Available at: www.aei.org/china-global-investment-tracker/ (accessed 8 May 2021).

Bearman, Jonathan. (1986). *Qadhafi's Libya*. London: Zed Books.

Behbehani, Hashim. (1981). *China's Foreign Policy in the Arab World, 1955–75: Three Case Studies*. London: Kegan Paul International.

Burton, Guy. (2020). *China and Middle East Conflicts: Responding to War and Rivalry from the Cold War to the Present*. London: Routledge.

Butler, Michael. (2009). *International Conflict Management*. London: Routledge.

Chan, Royston, and Miles, Tom. (2011). "Libya Evacuation: China Evacuates 12,000 Nationals Via Naval Frigates". *Christian Science Monitor*, 25 February. Available at: www.csmonitor.com/World/Latest-News-Wires/2011/0225/Libya-evacuation-China-evacuates-12w-000-nationals-via-naval-frigate (accessed 8 May 2021).

Crocker, Chester, Hampson, Fen Osler, and Aall, Pamela. (2007). "Leashing the Dogs of War". In Chester Crocker, Fen Osler Hampson, and Pamela Aall (eds), *Leashing the Dogs of War: Conflict Management in a Divided World*. Washington, DC: United States Institute of Peace.

Dillon, Michael. (2004). "The Middle East and China". In Hannah Carter and Anoushiravan Ehteshami (eds), *The Middle East's Relations with Asia and Russia*. London: Routledge.

Dreyer, June Teufel (2012). *China's Political System: Modernization and Tradition*. 8th ed. London: Longman.

Galtung, Johan. (1967). *Theories of Peace: A Synthetic Approach to Peace Thinking*. Oslo: International Peace Research Institute.

Garlick, Jeremy. (2019). *The Impact of China's Belt and Road Initiative: From Asia to Europe*. London: Routledge.

Garver, John. (2018). "China and the Iran Nuclear Negotiations: Beijing's Mediation Effort". In James Reardon-Anderson (ed.), *The Red Star & the Crescent: China and the Middle East*. London: Hurst & Co.

Ghiselli, Andrea, and Al-Sudairi, Mohammed. (2019). "Syria's "China Dream": Between the Narratives and Realities". King Faisal Centre for Research and Islamic Studies, Commentaries, 15 September. Available at: www.kfcris.com/en/view/post/234 (accessed 8 May 2021).

Goldstein, Joshua, and Pevehouse, Jon. (2014). *International Relations*. 10th ed. Harlow: Pearson Education Limited.

Gray, Jack. (1990). *Rebellions and Revolutions: China from the 1800s to the 1980s*. Oxford: Oxford University Press.

Grieg, J. Michael, and Rost, Nicholas. (2013). "Mediation and Peacekeeping in Civil Wars". *Civil Wars*, Vol. 15, No. 2, pp. 192–218.

Harris, Lillian Craig. (1994). "Myth and Reality in China's Relationship with the Middle East". In David Shambaugh (ed.) *Chinese Foreign Policy: Theory and Practice*. Oxford: Clarendon Press.

Holslag, Jonathan. (2007). "China's Diplomatic Victory in Sudan's Darfur". *Sudan Tribune*, 2 August. Available at: https://sudantribune.com/spip.php?article23090 (accessed 8 May 2021).

Jeong, Ho-Won. (2010). *Understanding Conflict and Conflict Analysis*. London: SAGE Publications.

Jian, Junbo. (2018). "China in International Conflict Management: Darfur Issue as a Case". In Chris Alden, Abiodun Alao, Chun Zhang and Laura Barber (eds) *China and Africa: Building Peace and Security Cooperation on the Continent*. Basingstoke: Palgrave Macmillan.

Kenyon, Paul. (2018). *Dictatorland: The Men who Stole Africa*. London: Head of Zeus.

Large, Daniel. (2009). "China's Sudan Engagement: Changing Northern and Southern Political Trajectories in Peace and War". *The China Quarterly*, No. 199, pp. 610–626.

Larson, Deborah Welch, Paul, T.V., and Wohlforth, William. (2014). "Status and World Order". In T.V. Paul, Deborah Welch Larson, and William Wohlforth (eds), *Status in World Politics*. Cambridge: Cambridge University Press.

Lin, Christina. (2017). "Chinese Uyghur Colonies in Syria a Challenge for Beijing". *Asia Times*, 21 May. Available at: https://archive.transatlanticrelations.org/publication/chinese-uyghur-colonies-syria-challenge-beijing-christina-lin/ (accessed 8 May 2021).

Mac Ginty, Roger. (2021). "Conflict Disruption: Reassessing the Peace and Conflict System". *Journal of Intervention and Statebuilding*, Vol. 16, No. 1, pp. 40–58.

Miller, Tom. (2017). *China's Asian Dream*. London: Zed Books.

Naderi, Bobby. (2019). "Opinion: A Historic Chance to Marshal Yemen Reconstruction Plan", *CGTN*, 14 March. Available at: https://news.cgtn.com/news/3d3d674e78557a4d33457a6333566d54/index.html (accessed 8 May 2021).

Olimat, Muhammad. (2014). *China and the Middle East since World War II: A Bilateral Approach*. Lanham, MD: Lexington.

Oxford Research Group. (2019). "Peace Processes: An Interview with Roger Mac Ginty", 2 July. Available at: www.oxfordresearchgroup.org.uk/blog/peace-processes-an-interview-with-roger-mac-ginty (accessed 22 February 2020).

Paffenholz, Thania. (2021). "Perpetual Peacebuilding: A New Paradigm to Move Beyond the Linearity of Liberal Peacebuilding". *Journal of Intervention and Statebuilding*, Vol. 15, No. 3, pp. 367–385.

Peking Review. (1967). "Lessons of the Arab War Against Aggression". 8 September.

Peking Review. (1968). "Palestinian People Have Found the Way to Free Their Homeland". 24 May.

Rafizadeh, Majid. (2021). "Iran-China Deal a Blow for Tehran Regime". *Arab News*, 1 April. Available at: www.arabnews.com/node/1836026 (accessed 27 May 2021).

Razoux, Pierre. (2015). *The Iran-Iraq War*. Trans. Nicholas Elliott. Cambridge, MA: Belknap Press.

Sands, Gary. (2014). "China and the ISIS Threat". *The Diplomat*, 26 September. Available at: https://thediplomat.com/2014/09/china-and-the-isis-threat (accessed 8 May 2021).

Sassoon, Joseph. (2018). "China and Iraq". In James Reardon-Anderson (ed.), *The Red Star & the Crescent: China and the Middle East*. London: Hurst & Co.

Schinn, David. (2015). "China's Approach to East, North and the Horn of Africa". Testimony before the U.S.-China Economic and Security Review Commission, 21 July. Available at: web.archive.org/web/20131003072729/http://elliott.gwu.edu/news/testimony/shinn4.cfm (accessed 8 May 2021).

Schweller, Randall. (2014). *Maxwell's Demon and the Golden Apple: Global Discord in the New Millennium*. Baltimore, MD: Johns Hopkins University Press.

Shichor, Yitzhak. (1999). "The People's Republic of China and the Arab Middle East, 1948–1996: Arab Perspectives". In Jonathan Goldstein (ed.), *China and Israel, 1948–1998: A Fifty-Year Retrospective*. Westport, CT: Praeger.

Shichor, Yitzhak. (2018). "Vision, Revision and Supervision: The Politics of China's OBOR and AIIB and Their Implications for the Middle East". In Anoushiravan Ehteshami, and Niv Horesh (eds), *China's Presence in the Middle East: The Implications of the One Belt, One Road Initiative*. London: Routledge.

Singh, Jagdish. (2010). "Russian, Chinese and Indian Ambivalence Policies on Iranian Nuclear Question". *Journal of Middle Eastern and Islamic Studies (in Asia)*, Vol. 4, No. 4, pp. 64–81.

SIPRI (Stockholm International Peace Research Institute). (n.d.). "SIPRI Arms Transfers Database". Available at: www.sipri.org/databases/armstransfers (accessed 8 May 2021).

Stern, Geoffrey. (1995). *The Structure of International Society*. London: Pinter.

Stuenkel, Oliver. (2015). *The BRICS and the Future of Global Order*. Lanham, MD: Lexington.

Sun, Degang and Wu, Sike. (2020). "新时代中国参与中东安全事务：理念主张与实践探索" [China's Participation in Middle East Security Affairs in the New Era: Ideas and Practice]. *Weixin*, 23 July. Available at: https://mp.weixin.qq.com/s/Hk9gMzVOOvfrNLqj9pHeog (accessed 8 May 2021).

Sun, Degang and Zhang, Dandan. (2019). "以发展促和平：中国参与中东安全事务的理念创新与路径选择" [Promoting Peace Through Development: China's Participation in Middle East Security]. 全球评论 [*Global Review*], Vol. 11, No. 6, pp. 109–129.

Sun, Degang and Zoubir, Yahia. (2018). "China's Participation in Conflict Resolution in the Middle East and North Africa: A Case of Quasi-Mediation Diplomacy?" *Journal of Contemporary China*, Vol. 27, No. 110, pp. 224–243.

Sun, Xuefeng and Jin, Feng. (2009). "China's Major Approaches to Solving the Darfur Crisis". *Journal of Middle Eastern and Islamic Studies (in Asia)*, Vol. 3, No. 3, pp. 29–41.

The Economist. (2011). "The Libyan Dilemma". 10 September. Available at: www.economist.com/node/21528664 (accessed 8 May 2021).

Tiezzi, Shannon. (2015). "Does China Approve of Russia's Airstrikes in Syria?" *The Diplomat*, 8 October. Available at: https://thediplomat.com/2015/10/does-china-approve-of-russias-airstrikes-in-syria/ (accessed 8 May 2021).

UN (1988). "Speech of Li Luye before the Security Council", UN Document S/PV.2819. 15 July.

UN (1980). "Speech of Ling Qing before the Security Council", UN Document S/PV.2254 and Cor. 1. 29 October.

van Kemenade, Willem. (2010). "China vs. the Western Campaign for Iran Sanctions." *Washington Quarterly*, Vol. 33, No. 3, pp. 99–114.

Walt, Stephen. (2021). "The World Might Want China's Rules." *Foreign Policy*, 4 May. Available at: https://foreignpolicy.com/2021/05/04/the-world-might-want-chinas-rules/ (accessed 5 May 2021).

Wang, Kevin. (2015). "Yemen Evacuation a Strategic Step Forward for China." *The Diplomat*, 10 April. Available at: https://thediplomat.com/2015/04/yemen-evacuation-a-strategic-step-forward-for-china/ (accessed 8 May 2021).

Wehrey, Frederic, and Alkoutami, Sandy. (2020). "China's Balancing Act in Libya", Carnegie Endowment for International Peace, 10 May. Available at: https://carnegieendowment.org/2020/05/10/china-s-balancing-act-in-libya-pub-81757 (accessed 8 May 2021).

Yang, Fuchang. (2010). "China-Arab Relations in the 60 Years' Evolution". *Journal of Middle Eastern and Islamic Studies (in Asia)*, Vol. 4, No. 1, pp. 1–5.

Young, Karen. (2020). "China Is Not the Middle East's High Roller", Bloomberg, 2 July. Available at: www.bloomberg.com/opinion/articles/2020-07-02/china-is-not-the-middle-east-s-high-roller (accessed 8 May 2021).

18

THE UYGHUR ISSUE IN SINO-MENA RELATIONS

The Case of Turkey

Thierry Kellner and Vanessa Frangville

A General Overview of the Uyghur Plight in China-MENA Relations

If we exclude Turkey, the Uyghur diaspora is rather small in the Middle East and North Africa (MENA) region, with recent estimates of 15,000 individuals, mostly religious students and businessmen, spread across Iran, Saudi Arabia, the UAE and Egypt. Nevertheless, indifference to China's treatment of the Uyghurs is related to factors that go beyond the relative invisibility of this Turkic community and find their roots in recent history. Indeed, while concerns were expressed in the early 1950s when the Communist Party took over administrative and political power in the Uyghur region, the firm handling of Muslim communities in China did not attract much attention in the Mao era (Shichor, 2015), except in Turkey. As diplomatic and economic engagement with the PRC became a priority after the 1980s, criticism of Beijing's policy in the Uyghur region became even more marginalized. In the twenty-first century, the plight of the Uyghurs poses a dilemma that the MENA countries would prefer to skirt but cannot ignore anymore, as the PRC is now asking for their active support. As Beijing has solicited MENA countries to sign extradition treaties, most of them were called to exert extra pressure and control over their Uyghur communities, sometimes deporting hundreds back to China (Nader, 2020). In 2017, the Egyptian police collaborated with Chinese officials to arrest dozens of Cairo-based Uyghur students and restaurant owners presented by Beijing as radicals. Most of them were deported to China or fled to Turkey and Europe. The raid took place a couple weeks after China and Egypt signed a security memorandum against terrorism. Other cases of deportation were reported in the MENA countries including Saudi Arabia, the UAE, Morocco and even Turkey.

Beijing's interest in the MENA region mostly revolves around energy markets and its Belt and Road Initiative (BRI). China is the main destination for oil exports from Saudi Arabia, Iraq, Yemen, Iran (before 2018) and Oman, and it is also a key market for Qatar's LNG exports, while the UAE has become a major gateway for China's exports to the Middle East. Gulf countries have actively joined China's massive infrastructure projects around its new Silk Roads and have been successful in attracting Chinese companies.

228

DOI: 10.4324/9781003048404-20

China also has invested billions in infrastructure projects in Cairo since 2018, becoming one of Egypt's biggest investors. In this context, most MENA countries cannot afford to jeopardize their deep economic and financial ties with China.

In addition, Beijing is increasingly involved in maritime security operations in the region, in particular in the Arabian Sea, the Sea of Oman and the Gulf of Aden. This is partly explained by the necessity of securing the region's natural resources essential to the BRI, and partly due to efforts to displace American influence in the region. At the same time, Beijing's insistence on non-interference and non-intervention principles finds good resonance for most MENA countries, which also share China's anti-colonial and anti-imperialist narratives. This common ideological platform of Beijing and MENA authoritarian regimes is critical in understanding the absence of reaction regarding the Uyghurs: Beijing avoids criticizing human rights-related issues in the MENA countries (which use similar repressive tactics within their borders), and it expects them to reciprocate by refraining from condemning China's policies in the Uyghur region.

Besides, most MENA states share China's fear of separatism and are unlikely to sympathize with Uyghur nationalist and secessionist tendencies (Shichor, 2015). MENA countries seek to suppress Kurdish, Azeri or other minority movements and protests, and support discourses similar to the Chinese line that Uyghur separatism is a Western (or US)-orchestrated conspiracy. Moreover, political Islam is also a sensitive topic, especially after the 2011 Arab Spring, and is often associated with terrorism. Beijing's claim to fight against terrorism thus resonates with the concerns of many MENA states.

For all these reasons, the relationship between the PRC and the MENA states has been little affected by the Uyghur issue. Criticism and protests from the MENA region remain marginal and unofficial. Even after stepping back from the letter supportive of Beijing's policy, Qatar only stated that it was taking a "neutral" position without further criticism. In this general picture, though, Turkey offers a much more complex picture.

Turkey and the Uyghurs before the 1990s

Compared to other MENA countries, Turkey has the most significant historical, religious, ethnic and cultural ties to the Uyghurs, with contacts dating back to the sixteenth-century Ottoman era. These remained even after the Qing conquest of the whole region in the eighteenth century. The area, named "Xinjiang" or "new frontier" in 1756 by Qianlong Emperor, remained a peripheral march of the Empire. From 1865, as the Manchus were driven out by a large Muslim revolt, Yaqub Beg (1820–1877) imposed his authority over Eastern Turkestan (ET) – as the region was usually known by Western geographers at the time – from the oasis of Turfan to the "Little Pamir." Yaqub Beg initiated an official correspondence with the Sublime Porte and secured support from the Sultan-Caliph. The Ottoman flag was thus raised in Kashgar.

The region's diplomatic connections with the Porte were interrupted by the Russo-Ottoman war (1877–1878), the early passing of Yaqub Beg (1877) and the Manchu reconquest of the ET – which became for the first time a province of the Manchu Empire in 1884, however, these events did not end their cultural and religious ties. While the region was re-annexed to the Manchu Empire, Istanbul remained involved and concerned with the fate of the Muslims in China. Several Ottoman missions traveled extensively across the country to visit Muslim communities and promote ties with the Sublime Porte. The Sultan Abdul Hamid II (reigned 1876–1909) even tried to negotiate with the

Manchu Emperor for the recognition of "Muslim Consuls," following the example of the "Consuls" imposed on the Qing Court by Western powers, whose mission would be to "protect" and look after Muslims in China. However, pan-Islamic policies worried both the Qing Court and the Western powers. Relations between China and the Ottoman Empire eventually came to an end as a result of internal unrest in both countries in the early twentieth century.

Contact between Turkey and Chine resumed in the 1920s. Turkey welcomed Uyghur merchants and students, and some of the future Uyghur nationalist leaders, such as Masud Sabri (1886–1952), even studied in Istanbul. Nationalist, pan-Islamic and pan-Turkic ideas had indeed spread since the end of the nineteenth century among the Turkic population of the oasis-cities of the Tarim basin (Klimeš, 2015). An Islamic Republic of East Turkestan was founded in Kashgar in November 1933, its national flag modelled on the Turkish one, strongly demonstrating the extent to which Turkey was a reference for Uyghur reformers. The leaders of this Republic turned to Kemalist Turkey for support, but Mustapha Kemal had rejected the pan-Islamic ideas of Abdul Hamid II. Mustapha Kemal was also less sympathetic to pan-Turkic ideas, focused as he was on reconstructing a Turkish state after the First World War. Moreover, the state made it a top priority in its foreign policy to maintain good relations with the USSR – the most influent actor in Xinjiang at the time, and also the political master of many Turkic populations (Gökay, 2006). No tangible assistance was thus given to the Islamic Republic of East Turkestan. In February 1934, the Republic was put to an end by the military intervention of the Dungans (Chinese Hui Muslims). Turkish influence would remain minimal in subsequent years.

Another reference to Uyghur nationalism is the second Eastern Turkestan Republic (ETR), founded with Soviet assistance in October 1944 (Wang, 1999). Here too, Turkey did little to formally support the Republic. In 1949, Moscow facilitated the transfer of power from the *Guomindang* to the Chinese Communist Party (CCP) in Xinjiang. In exchange for economic concessions, Moscow later agreed to the integration of the ETR's territory into the PRC, then to the dissolution of its political structure by Beijing in January 1950. However, Ankara made a crucial contribution that would have far-reaching consequences in the relationship with Beijing, namely by welcoming Uyghur refugees fleeing the People's Liberation Army (PLA) in the early 1950s. Nationalist and pan-Turkic leaders such as Isa Yusuf Alptekin (1901–1995) or Riza Bekin (1925–2010) settled in Turkey and grew to be the spiritual fathers of the Uyghur diaspora's nationalist organizations. Other waves of Uyghur refugees would later be welcomed, contributing to the formation of a small community in the country, essentially in Istanbul and, to a lesser extent, in Kayseri (Anatolia). In the 2000s, Uyghurs arrived in numbers due to the gradual tightening of the security measures in Xinjiang. This flow dried up in early 2017 when the Xinjiang authorities made travel virtually impossible, but many Uyghurs fled from other MENA countries to Turkey. The Uyghur community in Turkey is estimated at between 35,000 and 50,000 in 2021.

The Uyghur Issue in Post-Cold War Sino-Turkish Relations

Support from the Turkish public as well as in pan-Turkic circles yielded this numerically limited community considerable influence. The Uyghur question had been an issue in Sino-Turkish relations since the 1950s but after the 1990s it became a real object of tensions. The end of the Cold War and the emergence of new independent states following the demise of the USSR marked a radical transformation of the international system and a recalibration of foreign policy for most countries in the world. This new context was conducive to the activities of Uyghur organizations seeking assistance from Turkish authorities and politicians of all persuasions (Shichor, 2009). In 1992, President Turgut Özal declared that it was East Turkestan's turn to gain its independence after the collapse of the USSR (Furtun, 2010). These comments were not well received by Beijing, which faced low-level political agitation in Xinjiang. From 1994 onwards, Turkish authorities became more careful, fearing that Beijing could retaliate by providing more active support to the Kurds. Still, the Uyghur issue continued to cause friction when the name of Uyghur nationalist leader Isa Yusuf Alptekin was attributed to parks and streets in several Turkish cities after his death in 1995. Turkish Uyghurs were also given governmental incentives to develop economic – and even marital – links with Central Asia. In 1997, the Turkish Minister of Defense criticized Chinese suppression of Uyghur demonstrations in the city of Ghulja/Yining (Northwest Xinjiang) (Millward, 2004). Beijing warned Turkey against "any interference in its internal affairs" (Shichor, 2009: 34). This rebuff was met by reinforced measures by the Turkish authorities to control Uyghur organizations to assuage the PRC.

1997 marked the end of the period of Turkey's "Uyghur First" policy (Çolakoğlu, 2021). Ankara, willing to develop its economic and political ties with Beijing, became more cautious in its treatment of the Uyghur issue. The Turkish government issued a confidential circular in 1999, forbidding any minister or civil servant from participating in meetings organized by Turkish activists of Uyghur origins (Zan, 2013). In 2000, the Turkish Minister of Internal Affairs met with China's Public Security Minister and signed an agreement on cooperation against cross-border crime (Çolakoğlu, 2015: 14). These goodwill gestures paved the way for a substantial rapprochement with Beijing. The diplomacy of that period reached its peak with Jiang Zemin's historical trip to Turkey in 2000. This was the first visit of a Chinese President to Turkey since 1984 and led to the signing of a joint communiqué and an agreement to "fight against terrorism, separatism and religious extremism" (MFA Turkey, 2000).

In the aftermath of 9/11, Beijing established a policy aimed at bringing the Uyghur diaspora's nationalist organizations into disrepute by associating them with international *jihadist* movements (IOFC, 2002). In this context, the objective of Premier Zhu Rongji's trip to Turkey in 2002 was to ensure Ankara's commitment to "fight separatism" (AFP, 2002). Later, Deputy Prime Minister Devlet Bahçeli was allowed to visit Ürümchi, the capital of Xinjiang, and Kashgar. This was, at the time, the highest-level visit of a Turkish official in the region and could be seen as a gesture from the PRC stemming from the good bilateral relations established at that time in political terms. By securing a commitment from Ankara not to interfere in the Uyghur issue, Beijing had significantly advanced its goal of drawing a security "cordon sanitaire" around its Turkic minority.

Between 2003 and 2009, bilateral political relations gradually intensified. On the occasion of the Beijing Olympics in 2008, the issue became quite concrete, as Turkey was to host the Olympic Torch Relay, a high-profile stage in China's eyes. To avoid any incident that could draw attention to the Uyghur issue during this event, the Turkish police forces held back and even arrested some Uyghur protesters (Ant, 2008). This move was greatly appreciated by Beijing, especially when compared to protests that were allowed during the passage of the Olympic Torch in London or Paris, and President Gül was invited to visit Ürümchi in 2009, making him the first Turkish President to go to Xinjiang. As a matter of fact, Ankara's strategy of cooperating with the Chinese authorities led it to establish direct ties with Xinjiang, with Beijing's blessing.

Sino-Turkish Relations in the Aftermath of the 2009 Ürümchi Riots

In July 2009, Ürümchi became the scene of inter-ethnic riots, opposing Uyghurs against the Chinese Han majority. The entire region of Xinjiang was closed off and Beijing quickly regained control. The Turkish authorities were thus confronted with a dilemma. On the one hand, they were inclined to preserve the political and economic relations set up with Beijing as well as the positive climate established in the bilateral relationship that had just reached a peak with President Gül's visit. On the other hand, they could not lose interest in the fate of Uyghurs, and this was due to three main factors: first, the events in Ürümchi stirred a great deal of emotion and impacted Turkish public opinion. Second, some of the Turkish elites did feel sympathy and affinity with the Uyghur population. Third, Muslim solidarity and the leadership of Turkey on the Islamic world were important dimensions of Ankara's diplomacy at this time (Tabak, 2017). The response of the Turkish authorities therefore echoed these conflicting interests.

Concretely, the Turkish Foreign Minister and President not only made public statements emphasizing the bonds that existed between Turks and Uyghurs; they also demanded the arrest and trial of those behind the Ürümchi events, going as far as to mention a "massacre" (Anatolia, 2009a, 2009d). There was also an international echo to Ankara's preoccupations, as Davutoglu met officials of the UK, France, the USA, Sweden – which had just taken over the presidency of the European Union – and even Iran (Anatolia, 2009c). Ankara also voiced its worries to the UN High Commissioner for Human Rights and to the political affairs committee of the Council of Europe's Assembly, and called upon the European Union to react. In addition, it expressed its concerns with the members of the Gulf Cooperation Council (GCC) during the first dialogue meeting that gathered the Foreign Ministers of the respective member nations in Istanbul (Anatolia, 2009b).

In the thrall of emotion, pressures and even criticism from the public, Premier Erdoğan used tough rhetoric with Beijing, pointing to a "sort of genocide" (Canadian Press, 2009) and announcing his intention to raise the issue before the UN Security Council. Chinese media urged Erdoğan to withdraw his "irresponsible" and "groundless" comments (AFP, 2009). China then abstained from escalating tensions, but the image of China became rather tarnished in Turkish public opinion. The climate in bilateral relations was heavily altered by these events, throwing the global spotlight on the Uyghur issue, now seen as disruptive and barely controllable in the framework of the bilateral relationship, to such an extent that some began to question its future.

However, following the events in Ürümchi, attempts to relaunch relations increased rapidly. Beijing wanted to quickly restore its image in Muslim countries, including Turkey. A real blossoming of contacts, visits and mutual exchanges between high-level officials occurred, rapidly normalizing relations. The emphasis was on economic collaboration, a traditional diplomatic strategy used by the PRC to build common ground while setting aside disagreements. A delegation of Turkish media was received in China, while the Turkish ambassador was also invited to visit Xinjiang. At the state level, the restoration of normalcy in the bilateral relationship quickly became a reality.

In 2010, Prime Minister Wen Jiabao visited Turkey. Uyghur opponents organized demonstrations in Istanbul, but these had no impact on the Turkish government's desire to make this visit a success. On this occasion, both governments signed a "joint declaration on establishing strategic relationship of cooperation" (Xinhua, 2010). An MoU on the fight against organized crime, illegal migration, cross-border crimes, cybercrime and "separatist terrorism" was also concluded during the Turkish Interior Minister's visit to Beijing (Anatolia, 2010). While responding to China's expectations, Ankara believed that good Sino-Turkish relations would encourage the Chinese authorities to soften their approach towards their Turkic minority. Some encouraging signs indeed emerged at that time, during the Xinjiang Labor Forum convened in May 2010 by Hu Jintao (Li, 2018).

Reciprocal visits in early 2012 marked a new turning point in the two countries' bilateral relations, which then entered a "honeymoon" phase (Zan, 2013). On this occasion, Erdoğan visited Xinjiang. The two parties concluded agreements on energy cooperation and technology transfer, thus moving beyond the 2009 crisis. Another symbol of reconciliation during this period was the acceptance of Turkey's application to become a dialogue partner of the Shanghai Cooperation Organization (SCO). This trend would accelerate in the context of the launch of the BRI from 2013, regardless of the Uyghur issue.

Unfortunately for the Erdoğan administration, tensions resurfaced following the "Arab Spring" and the rise of Islamic radicalism in Iraq and Syria, causing fresh turbulences in bilateral relations. Indeed, reports on the presence of Uyghur jihadist fighters in Syria and Iraq began to circulate at that time. In the autumn of 2012, Chinese government officials alleged that Chinese militants from "East Turkestan terrorist organizations" were joining anti-government rebels in Syria (Lin, 2015). After the Kunming railway station attack in 2014, attributed to Uyghur separatists by the Chinese police, the Xi administration decided to drastically increase "security" in Xinjiang by launching a "Strike Hard Campaign against Violent Terrorism" (Ramzy and Bukley, 2019). Beijing's policies were further strengthened after the appointment of a new regional CCP Secretary in 2016, Chen Quanguo who enacted drastic measures such as mass surveillance and forced internment (HRW, 2021). These severe policies led an increasing number of Uyghurs trying to leave the PRC. In this context, Turkish diplomats posted in Southeast Asia apparently issued documents for travel to Turkey to some Uyghurs fleeing China via the Yunnan province and then Southeast Asian countries (Tiezzi, 2015a). Turkish diplomatic intervention also prevented some 300 Uyghurs from being deported from Thailand to China (Solmaz, 2014). Beijing did not appreciate these moves, nor the fact that – according to Chinese media – the Turkish authorities offered transit facilities to some radicalized Uyghurs on their way to Syria through Turkish territory (Qiu, 2014). Moreover, the all-out tightening of control over Uyghurs in Xinjiang provoked growing criticism and reactions in Turkish public opinion. In the summer of 2015, protests rocked the country following reports that Uyghurs in China were banned from fasting during the holy month of Ramadan (Al-Jazeera, 2015). The demonstrations and disturbances, including attacks on Chinese restaurants and the burning of Chinese flags, continued for ten days. Turkish authorities summoned the Chinese ambassador over these reports and the Turkish Foreign Ministry issued a statement conveying the "sadness" of the Turkish public on learning that Uyghurs were not allowed to perform other religious duties in Xinjiang (Girit, 2015). In response, China stated that it fully respected freedom of religious belief for Muslims and issued travel advice to its citizens visiting Turkey, an indirect way of putting pressure on Ankara given the importance of the tourism sector for the Turkish economy.

Caught between public opinion and the need to protect relations with Beijing, in July 2015, Erdoğan declared that recent reports in the Turkish media about Chinese government oppression of Uyghurs were "exaggerated" or "fabricated" (Başaram, 2015). During his trip to China a few days later, Erdoğan then declared that Turkey would never support activities undermining China's sovereignty or territorial integrity on Turkish soil.

Over a hundred members of the Turkish Council for Foreign Economic Relations accompanied Erdoğan, reflecting the priority given to bilateral economic relations. Turkey's involvement in China's BRI was, in fact, high on Erdoğan's agenda, given his interest in attracting more Chinese investment and cementing Turkey's place as a hub connecting Asia and Europe (Atli, cited in Tiezzi, 2015b).

In late 2015, Erdoğan met Xi again in the wake of the G20 summit in Antalya. The two leaders signed an MoU to connect the BRI to Erdoğan's "Middle Corridor Initiative." a project aimed at strengthening connectivity with the heart of Eurasia and the Chinese market via Georgia, Azerbaijan, the Caspian Sea and then Central Asia, while also allowing Ankara to reach Central Asia and China by avoiding transit through Russian or Iranian territories. Erdoğan's project overlapped with the China-Central Asia-West Asia corridor promoted by Beijing, making it possible to envisage synergies. If used effectively, the corridor could help Turkey benefit from China-Europe trade and infrastructure investments and strengthen Ankara's regional weight as a trade hub for China-Europe trade with all the benefits that would accompany this position. The complementarity between the two projects was again underlined by Erdoğan on the sidelines of the First BRI summit he attended in Beijing in May 2017.

Intensification of Sino-Turkish Relations after 2016

In the face of Turkey's deteriorating relationship with its Western allies following the failed military coup in 2016 and influenced by the "Eurasianist" (*Avrasyacilik*) current of thought favoring links with Russia and China (Üngör, 2019), Erdoğan intensified his collaboration with Beijing. He saw the PRC not only as an alternative to the West in terms of trade, finance, investment, or technology, but also as a useful political partner to increase his maneuvering space in the international realm and his negotiating power vis-à-vis the USA or the EU. For Beijing, in addition to economic interests within the BRI framework, up to the present, Ankara's "independent" policy allows it to increase its geopolitical influence while reducing that of the USA in a pivotal country that is also a member of NATO. This distancing between Turkey and its Western allies contributes not only to the weakening of the US and the Atlantic alliance but also to the multipolarization of the international system favored in the Beijing foreign policy. The PRC supported Erdoğan more directly on several occasions: after the attempted coup in 2016, Beijing dispatched the Vice Foreign Minister to Turkey to offer support to the Turkish government. In July 2018, during a difficult moment for the Turkish economy, ICBC provided a loan package worth $3.6 billion for the Turkish energy and transportation sector (Anadolu, 2018). Later, under a currency swap agreement signed in 2012, Beijing conveniently transferred $1 billion worth of funds to Turkey during a critical election period for Erdoğan (Karakaya and Kandemir, 2019). Finally, in 2019, the purchase of 51 percent of the Yavuz Sultan Selim Bridge – a mega-project supported by Erdoğan – was announced by a consortium of Chinese companies (Alemdaroğlu and Tepe, 2020).

The international context and the cross-interests of the two regimes explain why the Uyghur issue remained low on the Turkish president's agenda after 2016. To boost the relationship, Erdoğan, accompanied by a very large delegation, participated in the First BRI Forum in May 2017. Both parties signed agreements on road transport and the reciprocal establishment of cultural centers, as well as a more controversial agreement on the extradition of criminals, ratified by Beijing in December 2020. Although not yet ratified by Turkey as of January 2023, human rights advocates fear that the Uyghur diaspora could become a target of this agreement (Klimeš, 2021a). On several occasions, the Turkish authorities have complied with PRC requests for detention or extradition targeting Uyghurs (Klimeš, 2019). In the same area of security, Ankara promised Beijing that it would work to eliminate anti-Chinese reports in Turkish media (Reuters, 2017). The shared interests and the close relationship established between Ankara and Beijing do not mean, however, that bilateral relations have been free of turbulences. The Turkish president cannot ignore the Uyghur issue, given the increasing support enjoyed by Uyghurs among opposition political parties in Turkey such as the Good Party (İyi) or the Felicity Party (Saadet Partisi), which began a public campaign in early 2019 to support Turkic Muslim minorities in China and put pressure on Turkey's ruling coalition ahead of local elections (Çolakoglu, 2019). The Uyghur issue can thus be used on the domestic scene to criticize Ergodan's government and weaken the ruling coalition.

The alleged death in custody in Ürümchi of a popular Uyghur poet and singer, Abdurehim Heyit, however, caused a new outcry in Turkey. Public reactions led to the Turkish Foreign Ministry denouncing the treatment of Uyghurs for the first time since 2009, accusing China of carrying out "a great shame for humanity" (MFA Turkey, 2019). In response, Beijing closed its consulate in Izmir and released a video allegedly showing that Mr. Heyit was alive and calling on Turkey to retract its "false" claims. A few days later, at the UN Human Rights Council, to Beijing's anger, Turkey expressed its concern –, albeit rather mildly – over China's mistreatment of Uyghurs and other Muslims (Nebehay, 2019). Yet there appears to have been no further movement on either side, suggesting that both sides preferred not to escalate the conflict. Turkey refrained from raising the Uyghur issue at the Organization of Islamic Cooperation summit in Abu Dhabi, and the organization praised the PRC for its policies towards Muslim citizens. However, this episode cast a shadow over the bilateral relationship at the time: unlike in 2017, the Turkish president did not participate in the 2019 Second BRI summit in Beijing.

Nevertheless, Erdoğan soon met Xi on the sidelines of the CICA summit in Dushanbe and the G20 summit in Osaka in June 2019, and visited China in July 2019, showing his desire to quickly normalize relations once again with Beijing. Prior to his visit, Erdoğan published an op-ed in the *Global Times*, highlighting the two countries' mutual economic interests and geopolitical convergence (Erdoğan, 2019), and was then quoted by Chinese state media stating that people in Xinjiang "live happily" (Reuters, 2019). Turkish officials later said Erdoğan's comments on Xinjiang had been mistranslated but Beijing had refused to correct them (Jun, 2019). Still, unlike numerous other Muslim countries, Erdoğan didn't go as far as to join the 37 states – rising to 46 in July 2020 –that signed the July 2019 letter supporting China's policy in Xinjiang during the 41st session of the Human Rights Council in Geneva. This would probably have been a step too far for Turkey to take, given the weight of the Uyghur issue on the Turkish domestic scene.

Despite the positive climate that has developed over the past few years, the Uyghur issue continues to loom large in China-Turkey relations. Beijing is systematically trying to disrupt activities in the Uyghur diaspora in Turkey by directly attacking members of the Uyghur community (Klimeš, 2020), but also by seeking to diversify contacts and relays in Turkey to increase China's influence and disseminate the Chinese narrative on the Uyghur issue. These alliances are partly organized within the framework of the "United Front" strategy led by the CCP's International Liaison Department. Beijing also uses its media and various relays in the framework of people-to-people and public diplomacies to spread this kind of propaganda and influence activities. In this context, a CCP delegation met with representatives of the ruling AKP in 2017, but also with those of other Turkish political parties deemed useful to Beijing's objectives, such as the Vatan Party, known for its Eurasianist positions and its support of China's policy in Xinjiang in its media *Aydınlık* daily (Klimeš, 2021b). These activities produce results that should not be overlooked: in 2019, 37 percent of respondents of an opinion survey had a positive image of China (Pew Research Center, 2020).

In bilateral relations, Erdoğan's party or government occasionally criticizes China. For instance, in 2020, the AKP disapproved of the PRC's repressive policy in Xinjiang. Along with recognizing China's sovereignty and territorial integrity and its right to fight terrorism, the party described China's treatment of Uyghurs as a violation of human rights and freedom of religious belief, and declared that in China's fight against terror, a distinction should be made between terrorists and non-terrorist forces (Alhas, 2020). In April 2021, the Turkish Foreign Ministry summoned the Chinese ambassador after he used his Twitter account to denounce the leader of the opposition party İyi, and the Ankara Mayor for their support of Uyghurs. The ambassador's comments were widely interpreted as a threat to the two politicians and caused an uproar on social media in Turkey (Fraser, 2021). Under these circumstances, it was difficult for the Erdoğan administration not to react; but in essence, Turkey continues to do little to address the Uyghur issue in foreign affairs and the AKP administration quickly reverted to its policy of appeasement with Beijing after the outburst.

As the gap between government policy and public opinion is growing (Yackley, 2021), the Turkish authorities have allowed advocacy organizations, public demonstrations, political lobbying, or the Uyghur diaspora media outlets to continue their activities, but at the same time the situation of Uyghurs in Turkey has deteriorated. Applications for long-term residence are often rejected. Many are labeled illegal migrants; some of them are sent to detention locations. Uyghurs who are living illegally in Turkey or those whose travel documents have expired are particularly frightened by the prospect of being arrested (Sezer, 2019). Even with valid documents, Uyghurs in Turkey remain under threat of deportation and imprisonment in China. Turkey has reportedly sent some Uyghurs back to China via third countries, like Tajikistan, which has an extradition treaty with China (Kashgary and Emet, 2019). Recent developments also show that finding support in Turkey will remain a challenge for Uyghurs: in July 2020, the AKP and the Nationalist Movement Party (MHP) voted against the İyi's proposal to investigate Beijing's abusive actions toward the Uyghurs, and in early 2021, the public channel TBMM TV suspended its broadcasting during the hearing of a young Uyghur woman invited by the İyi.

Conclusion

The contradictory treatment of the Uyghur issue by MENA leaders is not only driven by economics, but also political and ideological factors, as most MENA countries wish to avoid international scrutiny of human rights abuses within their own borders. It should be noted that there is no "Islamic solidarity" in the case of the Uyghurs. Against this general background, it appears that Turkey stands out for at least two reasons: first, Turkey is the most affected MENA country due to its historical and cultural ties to the Uyghurs;

second, Ankara's responses to the Uyghur dilemma have evolved over time, but generally are much more ambivalent than in other MENA countries. Indeed, the Uyghur issue offers Ankara a certain degree of leverage in its relations with China. Despite its cooperation with Beijing, by facilitating deportations, for instance, the Turkish government also decided to play the "Uyghur card" for its own benefit (Ramachandran, 2020), which explains its ambiguity in the Uyghur matter. But China's growing role in the Turkish economy and the Turkish regime's increasing dependence on Beijing ensure that Ankara will remain cautious on the Uyghur issue. Yet for domestic reasons, Erdoğan cannot afford to give the impression of abandoning the Uyghurs altogether. This is a dilemma in which the Turkish president has himself become trapped because of his ambitions and choices.

References

AFP. (2002). "China's premier departs on trip to Turkey, Egypt and Kenya," April 15.

AFP. (2009). "Turkey PM's genocide remarks 'irresponsible': China's state media," July 14.

Alemdaroğlu, A. and Tepe, S. (2020). "Erdogan is turning Turkey into a Chinese Client State," *Foreign Policy*, September 16.

Alhas, A.M. (2020). "Turkey: China's Uighur policy on Ankara's agenda," *Anadolu Agency*, September 29.

Al-Jazeera. (2015). "China bans Muslims from fasting Ramadan in Xinjiang," June 18.

Anadolu. (2018). "China's ICBC to loan $3.6 billion for Turkey's energy and transport, Albayrak says," July 27.

Anatolia (2009a). "Turkey urges justice over violence in China protests," via BBC SWB, July 6.

Anatolia (2009b). "Turkey, Gulf Cooperation Council concerned about China's Uighur region," via BBC SWB, July 8.

Anatolia (2009c). "Turkey calls international community to show more concern for China's Uighurs," via BBC SWB, July 9.

Anatolia (2009d). "Turkey's president urges China to prosecute perpetrators of Xinjiang 'massacre'," via BBC SWB, July 10.

Anatolia (2010). "Turkey, China agree on combating organized crime," via BBC SWB, October 29.

Ant, O.C. (2008). "Uighur protest in Turkey against China," *Associated Press Online*, April 3.

Başaram, E. (2015). "President Erdogan warns against provocations over Uighur Turks' situation," *Daily Sabah*, July 10.

Canadian Press. (2009). "Turkey's PM likens ethnic violence in China to genocide," July 10.

Çolakoğlu, S. (2015). "Dynamics of Sino-Turkish relations: A Turkish perspective," *East Asia*, 32(7): 7–23.

Çolakoğlu, S. (2019). "Why Turkey finally criticized China's Uighur internment camps," *World Politics Review*, February 19.

Çolakoğlu, S. (2021). *Turkey and China: Political, Economic, and Strategic Aspects of the Relationship*, Singapore: World Scientific.

Erdoğan , R.T. (2019). "Turkey, China share a vision for future," *Global Times*, July 1.

Fraser, S. (2021). "Turkey summons China's ambassador over Twitter posts," *Associated Press*, April 6.

Furtun, F. (2010). "Turkish-Chinese relations in the shadow of the Uyghur problem," *Today's Zaman*, March 29.

Girit, S. (2015). "China-Turkey relationship strained over Uighurs," *BBC News*, July 9.

Gökay, B. (2006). *Soviet Eastern Policy and Turkey, 1920–1991. Soviet Foreign Policy, Turkey and Communism*, New York: Routledge.

HRW (Human Rights Watch). (2021). "'Break their lineage, break their roots'. China's crimes against humanity targeting Uyghurs and other Turkic Muslims," April 19.

IOFC (Information Office of the State Council). (2002). "'East Turkistan' terrorist forces cannot get away with impunity." Available at: China.org.cn, January 21.

Jun, M. (2019). "Turkish president Recep Tayyip Erdogan's 'happy Xinjiang' comments 'mistranslated' in China," *South China Morning Post*, July 22.

Karakaya, K. and Kandemir, A. (2019). "Turkey got a $1 billion foreign cash boost from China in June," Bloomberg, August 9.

Kashgary, J. and Emet, E. (2019). "Uyghur mother, daughters deported to China from Turkey," *RFA*, August 9.

Klimeš, O. (2015). *Struggle by the Pen: The Uyghur Discourse of Nation and National Interest, c. 1900–1949*, Leiden: Brill.

Klimeš, O. (2019). "China's tactics for targeting the Uyghur Diaspora in Turkey," *China Brief*, 19(19), November 1.

Klimeš, O. (2020). "China's Xinjiang propaganda and United Front work in Turkey: Actors and content," *Monde chinois*, 62(2): 44–71.

Klimeš, O. (2021a). "The Xinjiang crisis and Sino-Turkish relations during the pandemic: Part one," *China Brief*, 21(4), February 26.

Klimeš, O. (2021b). "China's Xinjiang propaganda and United Front work in Turkey: Part Two," *China Brief*, 21(5), March 15.

Li, Y. (2018). *China's Assistance Program in Xinjiang: A Sociological Analysis*, Lanham, MD: Rowman & Littlefield.

Lin, C. (2015). "Chinese General: Anti-Chinese Uyghurs are in Syria's Anti-Assad Force," *ISPSW Strategy Series*, 353, May.

MAF Turkey. (2000). "Joint communiqué between the Republic of Turkey and The People's Republic of China," April 19.

MAF Turkey. (2019). "Statement of the Spokesperson of the Ministry of Foreign Affairs, Mr. Hami Aksoy, in response to a question regarding serious human rights violations perpetrated against Uighur Turks and the passing away of folk poet Abdurehim Heyit," February 9.

Millward, J. (2004). "Violent separatism in Xinjiang: A critical assessment," East-West Center, *Policy Studies*, 6, v–54.

Nader, E. (2020). "Middle East countries deported exiled Uighurs to China: Report," *BBC*, October 1.

Nebehay, S. (2019). "Turkey, Britain raise China's treatment of Uighurs at U.N. rights forum," *Reuters*, February 25.

Pew Research Center. (2020). "China," in *Global Indicators Database*, March.

Qiu, Y. (2014). "Turkey's ambiguous policies help terrorists join IS jihadist group: analyst," *Global Times*, December 15.

Ramachandran, S. (2020). "Has Turkey abandoned the Uighurs?" *The Caci Analyst*, November 11.

Ramzy, A. and Buckley, C. (2019). "'Absolutely no mercy': Leaked files expose how China organized mass detentions of Muslims," *New York Times*, November 16.

Reuters. (2017). "Turkey promises to eliminate anti-China media reports," August 3.

Reuters. (2019). "China says Turkey president offered support over restive Xinjiang," Reuters, July 2.

Sezer, M. (2019). "Without papers, Uighurs fear for their future in Turkey," Reuters, March 27.

Shichor, Y. (2009). "Ethno-diplomacy: The Uygur hitch in Sino-Turkish relations," East-West Center, *Policy Studies*, 53.

Shichor, Y. (2015). "See no evil, hear no evil, speak no evil: Middle Eastern reactions to rising China's Uyghur crackdown," *Griffith Asia Quarterly*, 3(1): 62–85.

Solmaz, M. (2014). "Government asks Thailand to send 300 Uighur refugees over to Turkey," *Daily Sabah*, November 27.

Tabak, H. (2017). "Manifestations of Islam in Turkey's foreign policy," in H. Tabak, O. Tufekci and A. Chiriatti (Eds.), *Domestic and Regional Uncertainties in the New Turkey*, Newcastle upon Tyne: Cambridge Scholars Publishing, pp. 85–104.

Tiezzi, S. (2015a). "Uyghur issues cast pall over Turkey-China relations," *The Diplomat*, July 28.

Tiezzi, S. (2015b). "Can China-Turkey relations move on?" *The Diplomat*, July 30.

Üngör, C. (2019). "Heading towards the East? Sino-Turkish relations after the July 15 Coup attempt," in E. Erşen and S. Köstem (Eds.), *Turkey's Pivot to Eurasia: Geopolitics and Foreign Policy in a Changing World Order*, Abingdon: Routledge. pp. 64–78.

Wang, D. (1999). *Under the Soviet Shadow: The Yining Incident: Ethnic Conflicts and International Rivalry in Xinjiang, 1944–1949*, Hong Kong: The Chinese University Press.

Xinhua. (2010). "China, Turkey issue joint declaration on establishing strategic relationship of cooperation," October 9.

Yackley, A.J. (2021). "Turkey summons Chinese ambassador in rare spat about treatment of Uyghurs," *Financial Times*, April 7.

Zan, T. (2013). "An alternative partner to the West? Turkey's growing relations with China," Middle East Institute, October 25.

19

CHINA'S "HEALTH SILK ROAD" DIPLOMACY IN THE MENA

Yahia H. Zoubir and Emilie Tran

Rough roads test a horse's stamina; high winds reveal a tree's strength; adversities try a friend's character.

(Chinese saying)

A friend is the one who lends a hand during the time of need.

(Arab proverb)

Introduction

The health diplomacy of the People's Republic of China (PRC) (Zoubir and Tran, 2022) and its more recent Health Silk Road[1] (HSR) took on a different dimension during the COVID-19 pandemic. This chapter focuses on China's medical cooperation with and aid to the Middle East and North Africa (MENA) since the emergence of COVID-19, first identified in Wuhan in Hubei Province in late 2019. The deadly virus, which caused a pandemic with disastrous consequences, occurred at a time when China-MENA relations were witnessing important developments in various sectors. Indeed, in recent years, China has paid particular attention to the MENA, not just because of its dependence on hydrocarbons from the region, from which it imports about 50 percent of its oil (Aluf, 2021). The MENA countries are an important component of the 2015 Belt and Road Initiative (BRI), which succeeded the One Belt, One Road that President Xi Jinping launched in 2013. Hitherto, 17 MENA states have signed on to the BRI (Green Finance and Development Center, 2021), while 15 have entered comprehensive strategic partnerships, strategic partnerships, or another form of strategic partnership with China (Sun, 2020). China has stressed the importance of the MENA in its foreign policy, as illustrated in the different official documents and statements. To this effect, Beijing has set up institutions whose aim is to consolidate the formal framework of interaction with the MENA states. The pandemic has served as a litmus test for the type of relations that have developed between China and the MENA. Interestingly, when the epidemic struck

240

DOI: 10.4324/9781003048404-21

in Wuhan and other cities in China, most MENA states, regardless of their level of economic development, provided aid to the PRC to fight the pandemic. China reciprocated when the MENA states were struck by the pandemic. Naturally, the MENA states were not the only states receiving aid from China during the pandemic. According to President Xi Jinping (Xinhuanet, 2021), China offered free vaccines to more than 80 developing countries and exported vaccines to 43 countries. Furthermore, Xi affirmed that China provided $2 billion in assistance for the COVID-19 response and economic and social recovery in developing countries hit by the pandemic. He added that the PRC delivered medical supplies to more than 150 countries and 13 international organizations, and delivered more than 280 billion masks, 3.4 billion protective suits, and 4 billion testing kits to the world. In addition to the material aid, China sent medical experts while Chinese doctors held video conferences with their overseas counterparts to share infection healing and control experience with more than 170 countries (Wang, 2020). China rejected Western accusations that this aid was aimed at making geopolitical and geo-economic gains. In June 2020, Beijing published a document, "Fighting Covid-19: China in Action" (State Council Information Office of the People's Republic of China, 2020), which detailed the aid that China was providing to many countries.

Most news media, political commentators, and officials suggested that China has used the pandemic to advance its soft power, leverage, and influence and that helping others during the pandemic was merely a propaganda tool that Beijing has been employing as part of its ambition to establish its world domination and supplant the United States and other rivals like the European Union (EU). Political and academic debates in Western countries concerning China's health aid revolved around how to counter China's economic and political influence (Döpfner, 2020). Because countering China had been the first of the Trump Administration's priorities before the pandemic (White House, 2017), COVID-19 further exacerbated tensions between the two strategic rivals, hostilities which have persisted under the Joe Biden administration because China poses a challenge to US hegemony (Leoni, 2021).

The questions asked in this chapter are, why were the responses to China's health diplomacy in the Global South, including the entire MENA region, quite the opposite of what they were in Western countries? Why have MENA governments and people been quite receptive to China during the pandemic? Why did they not display anti-Chinese sentiments? Why despite US warnings against developing closer ties with China (Harris, 2020), have MENA states decided to improve those relations instead? Methodologically, this chapter uses document analysis. The authors have perused dozens of official documents and speeches, as well as hundreds of media articles in China, Europe, and the MENA region. The articles are from publications in Arabic, Chinese, English, and French. For the volume of aid, we also relied on similar sources. The Appendix lists the types of medical items and vaccines that China provided to the MENA states to combat the COVID-19 at the peak of the pandemic in 2020.

Before answering those questions, it is necessary to examine China's philosophy on health assistance and learn how Chinese policy-makers conceive the PRC's role in the global community and the country's foreign policy orientations. Understanding Chinese role conceptions allows for a more analytical examination of China's deep-seated beliefs and its foreign policy motivations, regardless of whether one believes them to be true or not.

China's Health Diplomacy Contribution to the "Community of Common Destiny"

Because of the domestic changes since the early 1980s, coupled with its rise as a major power, albeit a developing one, China has sought to formulate a different attitude toward international relations, positioning itself as a nation whose relations with the outside world are unlike the power politics that has been pursued by other great powers up till now. Resembling Western Liberalists, Chinese officials cast aside the concept that the international system should inevitably be considered as a zero-sum game arena or that a rising power will unavoidably defy the entrenched incumbent hegemonic power, the so-called "Thucydides's Trap" (Allison, 2017). Through the concept of a "community of common destiny" or "community of shared future," supported by the BRI and a multitude of new initiatives, Beijing seeks to project, according to Fu Ying, chairwoman of the Foreign Affairs Committee of the National People's Congress of China, the notion that nations can exist in harmony and also reach collective prosperity (Fu, 2017). President Xi Jinping argued in 2015 that,

> To build a community of common destiny, we need to make sure that all countries respect one another and treat each other as equals. Countries may differ in size, strength or level of development, but they are all equal members of the international community with equal rights to participate in regional and international affairs. On matters that involve us all, we should discuss and look for a solution together. Being a big country means shouldering greater responsibilities for regional and world peace and development, as opposed to seeking greater monopoly over regional and world affairs.
>
> *(Xi, 2015, March 29)*

The adoption by the 55th United Nations Commission for Social Development (CSocD) of a resolution calling for support for the building of "a human community with shared destiny" (Xinhua, 2017) reflected China's claim.

Thus, China's proliferated bilateral partnerships and "win-win" cooperation agreements with countries around the world to advance its philosophy and interests. Although they argue that China does not seek to disentangle the current world system, Chinese officials do, however, emphasize that the PRC wishes to play a greater role in global governance (Poh and Li, 2017) and assist in establishing a new global, fairer order that is more even-handed and in which China would have a leadership role (Huang, 2017). Yet, this does not mean that China would not fight when it perceives that its core interests (national sovereignty, territorial integrity, etc.) are threatened, particularly in its neighborhood, as was the case during and after US House Speaker Nancy Pelosi's visit to Taiwan on August 3, 2022 (Associated Press, 2022). In other words, when its core interests are at stake, China will adopt an uncompromising position. The contention here is that the apparent inconsistency between the quest for cooperation, peaceful development, and the building of a community of common interests, on the one hand, and an unyielding nature when it comes to core interests, on the other hand, is undoubtedly what has, partly, caused misgivings toward and distrust of China, mainly in the Western world.

China's actions during the COVID-19 pandemic match China's attempts at erecting a new world order, in which the development of a "global health community" is now presumably one of the responsibilities of Beijing's diplomacy (Cao, 2020), labeled "mask diplomacy" (Wong, 2020) after China furnished truckloads of masks and medical equipment (from both the state and the private sector) to European countries when cases of COVID-19 were multiplying speedily and exponentially in 2020.

China's health cooperation with and aid to developing countries did not emerge with this pandemic; neither did it start with the 2014 Ebola epidemic when China assisted the afflicted Central and Western African countries. China's health cooperation can be traced back to the 1950s, that is, soon after the foundation of the PRC in 1949. Algerian nationalists remember all too well China's provision of medical assistance during their anti-colonial war of independence in the mid-1950s (Zoubir, 2021). The arrival of a Chinese medical team in 1963, only one year after Algeria gained its independence in July 1962, marked the first time in modern history that China had dispatched a medical team overseas (Balazovic and Li, 2013; Killeen et al., 2018). At that time, Algeria was in dire need of doctors and nurses. Since the sending of the medical team to Algeria, China has dispatched doctors and nurses abroad to run clinics, established malaria prevention and treatment centers, built hospitals and other health facilities, offered medicines and equipment, as well as trained medical staff from developing countries in China. This illustrates China's long-lasting willingness to provide medical aid to developing countries.

An examination of China's medical aid demonstrates that China's health diplomacy is an intrinsic part of China's South-South cooperation, particularly in Africa (Li, 2011). Actually, China is one of the few countries in the world that dispatch government-paid medical personnel to work and remain in Africa for prolonged periods of time. In general, other medical organizations operating in Africa are not funded by governments; they receive donations from charities or private groups (Knowledge@Wharton, 2011). China's Ambassador to Algeria, Li Lianhe disclosed that "since 1956, China has made available to Algeria 26 medical teams (81 doctors) with approximately 3,400 Chinese medical staff, who have treated Algerian patients free of charge throughout the country" and "medical teams have managed to treat 23,7 million people and participate in the birth of some 1,6 million babies" (APS, 2020). In May 2019, the 26th group of Chinese health practitioners, covering different specialties, including gynecology-obstetrics, surgery, resuscitation, as well as ophthalmology, was on its way to Algeria (APS, 2019). Another country that has received China's medical assistance is Mauritania, which, like Algeria, has a long history of health cooperation with China dating back to 1968 (Li, 2011: 10). China built two hospitals in the country, the most recent completed just prior to the COVID-19 pandemic. A keen observer of African Affairs, a former US ambassador to countries in the continent, explained that,

> Chinese teams offer an array of medical specialties in addition to traditional medicine. The most recent team of 27 to arrive in Mauritania included specialists in scanning, orthopedics, epidemiology, gynecology, surgery, ophthalmology, water chemistry, bacteriology, and virology. They often serve in rural areas, something that many African doctors do with great reluctance.
>
> *(Shinn, 2006: 2)*

Algeria and Mauritania are not the only states in the MENA or Africa to have received such comprehensive aid from China. Since the 1960s, China has sent 32 medical teams composed of more than 800 medical workers, "creating the only group of experts in disease prevention and control and public health among Chinese medical teams abroad and establishing the only center for ophthalmological cooperation with Chinese assistance in Africa" (CIDCA, 2018).

China's Evolving Relations with the MENA and Health Cooperation

Recently, China's relations with the MENA countries have flourished in all sectors, especially, trade, business, energy, technology, and economics. China has signed Comprehensive Strategic Partnerships (CSP) with Algeria, Egypt, Saudi Arabia, Iran, and the UAE, and Strategic Partnerships (SP) with Sudan, Iraq, Morocco, Qatar, Jordan, Djibouti, Kuwait, and Oman. It also signed a Strategic Cooperation Relationship with Turkey and an Innovative Comprehensive Partnership with Israel. Soon after his coming to power and launching the One Belt, One Road, President Xi indicated at the Ministerial Meeting of the CASCF in 2014 that "the establishment of the China–Arab States Cooperation Forum was a strategic step the two sides took for the long-term development of the China–Arab relations" (Xi, 2014). This was followed two years later by the publication of the Arab Policy Paper, which stressed that China would maintain its long-established friendship with the Arab states and promote cooperation at all levels, reiterating the strategic nature of those relations whose aim is to promote peace and stability (Foreign Ministry of the PRC, 2016). Beijing launched other initiatives to include the MENA (Khan, 2021) in its proclaimed South-South cooperation. Clearly, before COVID-19 struck China, Beijing had already enhanced its bonds with most MENA states. While fighting the virus on its territory, Chinese authorities clearly linked their response to the epidemic to the necessity to "remind[s] the world that, in the era of globalization, all countries' interests are closely interconnected and human society has one shared future," and global society must thus "continue building the community of common destiny." President Xi insisted that, "China hopes to step up public health cooperation with the world to interpret the true essence of building a community with a shared future for humanity ..." (Xinhua, 2020c). This was precisely the policy that he presented to the world on May 18, 2020:

> Mankind is a community with a shared future. Solidarity and cooperation is [sic] our most powerful weapon for defeating the virus. This is the key lesson the world has learned from fighting HIV/AIDS, Ebola, avian influenza, influenza A (H1N1) and other major epidemics. And solidarity and cooperation is [sic] a sure way through which we, the people of the world, can defeat this novel coronavirus.
>
> *(Foreign Ministry of the PRC, 2020, May 18)*

Therefore, China's approach to addressing COVID-19 in the MENA, as well as in the rest of the world, reflected the foreign policy and the theory of international relations and the philosophy that it has been putting in place since at least the presidency of Hu Jintao (2003–2013). As Wang Yi, Foreign Minister of the PRC, put it early during the pandemic, China would offer aid within its capability to countries in need to fight coronavirus, endorsing the concept of one human community with a shared future (Wen, 2020).

The evolution of Sino-MENA relations and their consolidation partially explain why the MENA states came to China's aid so quickly after the epidemic spread in China. Subsequently, they sent millions of masks and other medical equipment to Wuhan (Zoubir, 2020). Once China had contained the epidemic internally, China reciprocated by providing massive aid to the MENA region.

China's Bilateral Aid to the MENA Countries in Containing COVID-19

In 2020, China's "anti-epidemic diplomacy" (Zhang and Sun, n.d.)[2] in the MENA was significant, not least because of the level of trust, an important, though neglected, dimension in International Relations (Stiles, 2018) that characterized not only the ties but also othe pledge to develop and/or enhance relations in the post-COVID-19 era. In contrast to the distrust that has characterized the European narrative on China's aid (Tran and Zoubir, 2023), virtually all MENA countries showed no such doubts about China. China's bilateral aid to the MENA during the pandemic applied across the board, regardless of the importance of the states to China. Indeed, both strategic partners and non-strategic partners benefited from this aid. While the first phase consisted of medical equipment, the second phase comprised the delivery of vaccines, a promise that China had made after the COVID-19 turned into a pandemic.

Bilateral Aid to Strategic Partners

Strategic partners are those that have signed Comprehensive Strategic Partnerships (CSPs) or a Strategic Partnership (SP) with China. States with CSPs are Algeria, Egypt, Saudi Arabia, Iran, and the UAE. States with SPs are Turkey (Strategic Cooperation Relationship), Israel (Strategic Innovation Relationship), Sudan, Iraq, Morocco, Qatar, Jordan, Djibouti, Kuwait, and Oman. Although there is no evidence that China provided greater assistance to strategic partners than to nonstrategic partners, it is unmistakable that from a political/geopolitical perspective, CPS and SPs are more important to China than the latter. Most of these countries responded quickly to China's appeal to the world community when COVID-19 struck Wuhan, Hubei Province, in late 2019. They dispatched medical equipment to China (masks, medical gloves, and respirators). Poor MENA states or those in difficult economic conditions also sent aid to China. For example, Iran, under severe US sanctions and suffering from dire socio-economic woes, was among the 21 countries, including Turkey, the UAE, Algeria, and Egypt, that shipped medical aid to China in the early phase of the pandemic. The Kingdom of Saudi Arabia sent ultrasound machines, non-invasive ventilators, defibrillators, patient monitors, infusion pumps, injection pumps and continuous renal replacement therapy; other material included 1,159 medical devices, 300,000 N95-standard masks, 1,000 protective suits, etc. The international Abu Dhabi-based leading AI and Cloud Computing company, G42, initiated a humanitarian program to defend healthcare personnel in China working to contain COVID-19. The firm joined efforts with the Chinese genomics corporation BGI group to launch a new gigantic-throughput lab in the UAE to enable testing and diagnosis of COVID-19. This lab, the first in the world of this level to operate outside China, can perform tens of thousands of RT-PCR tests daily. These are just a few examples of the aid that MENA states sent to China.

Once the epidemic in China became a pandemic, affecting the MENA region in February–March 2020, it was China's turn to respond to the urgent calls from MENA states for assistance. China provided medical aid not only to the MENA region but also to the rest of the world (150 countries). In the MENA, China sent epidemiologists/virologists/doctors to numerous countries such as Algeria, Djibouti, and Sudan. The bulk of China's medical assistance consisted of regular deliveries of millions of masks, including N95 masks, goggles, temperature-screening devices, COVID-19 testing kits, protective garments, and ventilators. In Egypt, for instance, a Sino-Egyptian face mask plant in Cairo became part of the Sino-Egyptian cooperation aiming to produce 1.5 million masks daily. China also arranged for videoconferences (or face-to-face with Chinese medical staff dispatched to the region) between doctors in China with their counterparts in the region. The medical teams sent by China to the region trained local doctors in hospitals about how to contain the pandemic. During their trips to some MENA countries, Chinese doctors worked in hospitals treating COVID-19 patients and visited quarantine centers. Chinese aid did not come from the government only but it came also from Chinese corporations like Alibaba, or private citizens. Chinese companies operating in the MENA countries participated in the drive to help financially or through the supply of medical equipment. For instance, the Bank of China and the Industrial and Commercial Bank of China (ICBC) Doha Branch offered one million pairs of medical gloves and 7,000 sets of protective clothing. In Oman, for instance, Chinese citizens and businesses donated infrared thermograph thermometers to Muscat Airport, offered testing kits to the Ministry of Health, as well as money donations. Chinese companies operating in Duqm contributed medical supplies (Li, 2020). In Morocco, the China Development Bank (CDB) donated medical equipment to fight against COVID-19; the gift comprised 36 (badly needed) respirators and tens of thousands of masks (*Le Matin*, 2020). In Israel, tens of flights with tons of protective medical equipment, coronavirus testing supplies and other urgently needed supplies to fight the virus arrived from China (Chafets, 2020). Calling on the international community to cooperate with Iran and safeguard public health, China shipped several containers of medical supplies (Chloroquine Phosphate medicine, N95 masks, and disposable medical masks) to Iran (Tasnim (Tehran), 2020). Beijing also sent a team of doctors to Tehran in February to collaborate with their Iranian counterparts. In addition to financial donations, charity foundations, businesses, including Alibaba, also provided aid. Overall Chinese aid to Iran was substantial; China also donated 500 prefabricated rooms with beds, desks, and chairs, as well as tons of all kinds of medical supplies (diagnostic kits, oxygen-breathing apparatus, body temperature monitors, hospital disinfectants, ordinary and N95 masks, clothing, gloves, and protective glasses, and anti-corona drugs (Gupta and Singh, 2020). Such Chinese aid helped assuage the medical shortages due to the severe sanctions that the United States has imposed on Iran.

These are only a few examples of the aid that China offered its strategic partners in the MENA. However, non-strategic partners also benefited from China's needed assistance that MENA states desperately needed.

Bilateral Aid to Non-Strategic Partners

The MENA states with no special partnerships, such as Tunisia, Lebanon, Libya, Mauritania, Palestine, Syria, or Yemen, also responded with whatever means to COVID-19 in China; they reacted the same way as China's strategic partners did. For instance, a Tunisian factory in Sfax began producing masks to ship to Wuhan. The 30-employee factory operated nonstop in rotating shifts to fabricate masks; the factory offered 100,000 masks to China. Naturally, when the pandemic affected the nonstrategic states, China responded swiftly, delivering medical aid to all of them, including those undergoing civil wars , i.e., Libya, Syria, and Yemen, or under occupation like Palestine. With respect to Syria, China's permanent representative to the UN, Zhang Jun alerted international public opinion about conditions in the country: "We are seriously concerned about the negative impact of unilateral sanctions on countries' capacity to respond to the pandemic, especially for vulnerable countries like Syria… civilians and innocent people are suffering severely from those sanctions" (*Middle East Monitor*, 2020). The Palestinians also received aid from China. In March 2020, for instance, they secured badly needed test kits from China (*Times of Israel*, 2020).

The Delivery of Chinese COVID-19 Vaccines

China had promised to deliver vaccines to the developing and poor countries as soon as they became available (Culver and Gan, 2020). Once produced, China sent both Sinopharma and Sinovac vaccines to Middle Eastern and African countries. In December 2020, Egypt received the first doses of vaccines from China; it obtained another batch in March 2021. In September 2021, Egypt launched the production of millions of the Chinese vaccines in two factories, aiming to become the Middle East and Africa's "biggest vaccine producer" (*Africanews*, 2021). In March 2021, Djibouti received the first batch of Chinese COVID-19 vaccines made by Sinovac and another shipment of vaccines donations by China in November 2021 (CIDCA, 2021). On September 29, 2021, Algerian authorities inaugurated the production plant of the Chinese vaccine CoronaVac in Constantine in eastern Algeria. This is a joint venture between the Chinese company Sinovac with Algeria's Saidal. The production capacity of this plant is 8 million doses per month and could be doubled if needed (*Le Monde*, 2021). Algeria has begun donating vaccines produced in Algeria to its neighbors (Tunisia, Mali, and Niger) (TSA, 2022) and, like Egypt, aims to send vaccines to Sub-Saharan African countries that need it.

Reactions from the MENA States to China's Health Diplomacy

In all the MENA countries, China's aid was very well received by the people and the governments alike. Having expressed their sympathy as China was battling the coronavirus, they subsequently conveyed their gratitude for China's health programme in various ways. The most dramatic illustration was certainly in the UAE. In Burj Khalifa, ADNOC Headquarters, and other UAE iconic landmarks lit up the colors of the Chinese national flag and slogans in solidarity with China on February 2, 2020; and "many Chinese living and working here in the UAE were moved to tears." (Lin Yaduo, Chargé d'affaires at Chinese Embassy in Abu Dhabi, cited in Emirates News Agency, 2020). The only glitch was in Turkey: China's deliveries on April 9, 2020, of medical supplies with a label referring to Ararat Mountain provoked an uproar; however, the Turkish government seemed content with Beijing's clarification that the writing in English was attached to the packages after it left China (Ghazanchyan, 2020). One can surmise that the mutual aid during the pandemic, coupled with other geopolitical interests, will likely strengthen Sino-Turkish relations (Stone, 2020).

Thanks to its health diplomacy and the aid it sent to the MENA countries while most Western powers were in lockdown mode, China undoubtedly scored many points with regards to political rapprochement and economic cooperation. In pro-Western Jordan, China appeared, according to a Jordanian expert on Arab-China relations, as "a trustworthy country sharing precaution experience and offering medical equipment to the world" (Xinhua, 2020d). In Sudan, the experts' visit offered the occasion to reiterate the strong bonds of friendship and oft-repeated mottos of "strategic trust" and "mutual trust, mutual benefit, mutual help and mutual learning." Omer Gamar-Eddin, Sudan's state minister for foreign affairs, declared that, "We hope the China-Sudan ties would continue, and we hope to continue working with the People's Republic of China in its work to support Sudan in its development and in the fields of health, education, agriculture and others." (Xinhua, 2020, June 12). In Oman, according to Omani Professor Mohammad Al-Muqadam, such support "gave China a lot of appreciation as a true ally and friend of these countries [those it aided] and as a *trusted friend* in a time of trouble" (Xinhua, 2020a; emphasis added). In the Maghreb, Tunisian President Kais Saied acknowledged China's strong assistance to Tunisia's economic and social development, as well as shipping numerous batches of medical materials to Tunisia to fight COVID-19. Kais Saied also expressed his admiration for China's accomplishments and his conviction that he was optimistic about cooperation between Tunis and Beijing. He stated that bilateral relations would serve as a model of international relations (Xinhua, 2020d). The Palestinian Authority expressed its thanks to China for its support to the Palestinian cause. In Morocco, the editorial of China's Xinhua news agency pointed out that: "China and Morocco have strengthened relations through joint efforts to combat the COVID-19 pandemic. In parallel, their multilayered cooperation in public health, culture and other fields has deepened under the Belt and Road framework" (Xinhua, 2020b). However, it remains to be seen how Morocco, like other traditional US allies, will be able to balance its foreign relations in the post-COVID-19 era when Sino-US and Sino-European relations might enter a severe storm. In Syria, China's aid, and the country's geopolitical position and need for investments from China for its post-conflict reconstruction, and Damascus' weighty role in the BRI, will certainly lead to stronger relations in the post-pandemic period. Likewise, given Lebanon's participation in the BRI, its dire need for investment and infrastructure development, Sino-Lebanese relations will surely be enhanced.

Undoubtedly, the post-COVID-19 crisis and the mutual aid will contribute to the enhancement of relations, including in the health sector, between the MENA States and China.

Reactions from Western Powers to China's Health Diplomacy

While struggling with the first wave of the pandemic in Europe and the United States, Western governments observed China's deployment with great fanfare of its massive anti-COVID-19 assistance to MENA countries, thus winning the hearts and minds of the Arab world, Iran, Israel, and Turkey. In fact, European states, too, benefitted from China's health diplomacy; and they, too, appreciated the assistance, all the more when compared to the initial absence of intra-EU solidarity in the first months of the COVID-19 outbreak in Europe, in spring 2020. However, reports that some of the protective equipment and virus testing kits were of substandard quality and dysfunctional, coupled with aggressive messages from Chinese diplomatic missions that criticized European democracies in their handling of the public health crisis, and Beijing's alleged disinformation campaign (European External Action Service, 2020), exacerbated the rift between China and the EU. Although China was prompt to address drastically the issue of defective or poor-quality products (Bradsher, 2020; Stevenson and May, 2020), criticism of China continued unabated and China's image in Europe, which had already been negative before the pandemic (Silver and Devlin, 2020; Silver, Devlin and Huang, 2021), declined further since the outbreak (Krastev and Leonard, 2020; Le Corre and Brattberg, 2020).

This came at time of a trade war between China and the United States that had started in 2019. President Trump, whose "great relationship with President Xi" had initially become closer (Goodman and Schulkin, 2020), changed his rhetoric—using offensive and provocative phrases, such as "kung flu" virus, "China plague," "China virus," and "Wuhan virus" (Coleman, 2020). He also criticized the World Health Organization for being "very China-centric" and "severely mismanaging and covering up the spread of the coronavirus" (Goodman and Schulkin, 2020). Eventually, the US announced its withdrawal from the WHO. Sino-US relations reached their lowest point since the Tiananmen crackdown (Bermingham and Zhou, 2020) with a level of mutual mistrust and suspicion not seen since the 1970s, prompting scholars to debate whether this was the next Cold War (Leoni, 2021) or a rivalry for a new age (Bisley, 2019).

Against this backdrop of heightened tensions and rivalry between China and the West, the prominence of Beijing's health diplomacy and its so-called "Wolf-Warrior" narrative unnerved China's rivals and compelled them to react to China's actions in the MENA, which the Western nations consider their area of influence. Both in the USA and the EU think tanks called their respective governments to provide a robust alternative to China's Health Silk Road, in order to prevent the HSR from reaping domestic and global benefits (Hillman and Tippett, 2021; Rudolf, 2021). Therefore, once they contained the outbreak at home, the Western powers sought to counter China's health diplomacy in providing aid to MENA states. Both the EU and the USA engaged in a "battle of narratives" (Delegation of the European Union to China, 2020) with China, blaming and shaming one another.

The European Union initiated "Team Europe" and committed funding to the MENA countries, such as Jordan, Lebanon (European Union External Action, 2020), Iran, and Turkey (Osiewicz, 2020). The EU showed solidarity with its partners in the Southern Neighbourhood by marshalling a support package of over €2.3 billion, as part of its global response to the pandemic. The EU's financial support included more than €1 billion to contain the spread of coronavirus and to respond efficaciously to the health crisis. It allocated €1.3 billion to support the socio-economic recovery of the countries at the regional level for the medium to long term. The funding was undertaken through the European Neighbourhood Policy, and programs such as the EU Emergency Trust Fund for Africa–North Africa, and the EU Regional Trust Fund in Response to the Syrian Crisis. The EU also mobilised more than €133 million, channeled largely through European and international financial institutions, to help Turkey respond to the health crisis and mitigate the economic and social impact (European Commission, n.d.).

For its part, the United States announced an aid package totaling $110 million to help the MENA states (ShareAmerica, 2020). The funding was aimed at improving disease detection, prevention, and response. Although the USA had imposed sanctions against Bashar Al-Assad's regime, the USA offered more than $31 million to the Syrian government to fight COVID-19. The USA also provided nearly $30 million to Iraq, and $8.3 million in specific COVID-19-related assistance to help Jordan. The USA provided almost $12 million to Libya, $13.3 million to Lebanon, and $5.7 million to Morocco. According to the US Government, the objective of the funding was to strengthen those countries' health preparedness through improved disease detection and response. The US private sector also contributed to the aid; indeed, US companies and charities made financial donations for the acquisition of medical supplies.

It remains to be seen whether the pandemic will result in genuine international cooperation (China, the USA, the EU, and Russia) to fight pandemics in the future or will accentuate the rivalry between China and the US-EU globally and in the MENA and Sub-Saharan Africa, in particular.

Conclusion

The reactions to China's aid to fight COVID-19 in the MENA were reminiscent of those in Africa in 2014 when China provided considerable aid in fighting Ebola (Chen, 2019).

China's health diplomacy is a long-standing one. Since the 1960s, Chinese medical teams have worked in numerous African countries and elsewhere. Regarding COVID-19, most MENA governments and civil society organizations provided aid to China initially. When the pandemic affected those states, Beijing aided all of them, donating medical supplies and equipment. While it is true that the MENA, particularly the Gulf region, is important to China, evidence shows that Beijing's actions derived from an old public health tradition. Undoubtedly, this health diplomacy enhances China's soft power and image, as highlighted in the latest surveys conducted in 2020 and 2021 (Robbins, 2020, 2021). China is not the only power practicing health diplomacy. The United States has deployed this soft power for decades. Today, in the MENA alone, Turkey, the UAE, Saudi Arabia, Kuwait, and Qatar have undertaken a similar type of diplomacy (e.g., religious, sports, or cultural). However, the question is whether health diplomacy between the great powers might become an instrument that serves their rivalries or whether it will be used for the service of humankind.

Notes

1 President Xi Jinping is said to have used the phrase "Health Silk Road," during a conversation with Italian Prime Minister Giuseppe Conte in March 2020, when Italy had been hit hard by the COVID-19 epidemic. In reality, Chinese officials had begun using Health Silk Road in 2015 (National Health Commission of the People's Republic of China, 2015).
2 This phrase was coined by Chinese scholars who kindly shared their paper with the authors; see Zhang Dan and Sun Degang, "构建命运共同体：浅析中国对中东的抗疫外交" [Building a Community of Destiny: An Analysis of China's Anti-Epidemic Diplomacy in the Middle East], unpublished paper. Many thanks to Dr. Chuchu Zhang for the translation.

References

Africanews (2021) Egypt to produce 1 billion Sinovac vaccines a year. September 1. Available at: www.africanews.com/2021/09/01/egypt-to-produce-1-billion-sinovac-vaccines-a-year/
Allison, G. (2017) *Destined for War: Can America and China Escape Thucydides's Trap?* New York: Houghton Mifflin Harcourt.
Aluf, D. (2021) China's reliance on Middle East oil, gas to rise sharply, Asia Times, December 30. Available at: https://asiatimes.com/2021/12/china-to-rely-more-on-middle-east-for-oil-and-gas/
APS (2019) Santé: des équipes médicales chinoises prochainement en Algérie, May 30. Available at: www.aps.dz/sante-science-technologie/90101-sante-des-equipes-medicales-chinoises-procha inement-en-algerie
APS (2020) L'Ambassadeur de Chine: L'Algérie, 5e grand parténaire commercial africain de la Chine, February 24. Available at: www.elmoudjahid.com/fr/actualites/138308
Associated Press (2022) China halts climate and military dialogue with the U.S. over Pelosi's Taiwan visit. August 5. Available at: www.npr.org/2022/08/05/1115878668/china-taiwan-pelosi-climate-military?t=1659858488749
Balazovic, T. and Li, A. (2013) Healing agents. China Daily. August 23. Available at: www.chinada ily.com.cn/m/chinahealth/2013-08/23/content_21973033.htm
Bermingham F. and Zhou, C. (2020) Coronavirus: China and US in 'new Cold War' as relations hit lowest point in 'more than 40 years', spurred on by pandemic. South China Morning Post. May 5. Available at: www.scmp.com/economy/china-economy/article/3082968/coronavirus-china-us-new-cold-war-relations-hit-lowest-point

Bisley, N. (2019) US-China relations are certainly at a low point, but this is not the next Cold War. *The Conversation*, May 21. Available at: https://theconversation.com/us-china-relations-are-certainly-at-a-low-point-but-this-is-not-the-next-cold-war-117509

Bradsher, K. (2020) China delays mask and ventilator exports after quality complaints. New York Times, April 11. Available at: www.nytimes.com/2020/04/11/business/china-mask-exports-coro navirus.html

Cao, D. (2020) Wang: China will never let foreign forces interfere in domestic affairs. May 24. Available at: www.chinadaily.com.cn/a/202005/24/WS5eca3c5ea310a8b241157fb7.html

Chafets, Z. (2020) Israel, too, turns to China for Covid-19 help. Bloomberg. April 8. Available at: www.bloomberg.com/opinion/articles/2020-04-08/israel-too-turns-to-china-for-covid-19-help

Chen, W. (2019) China's aid to Africa's fight against Ebola. In *South-south Cooperation and Chinese Foreign Aid*. Vienna, Austria: Springer, pp. 77–93.

CIDCA (China International Development Cooperation Agency) (2018). Chinese medical staff helps in Mauritania. August 3. Available at: http://en.cidca.gov.cn/2018-08/03/c_283868.htm

CIDCA (China International Development Cooperation Agency) (2021). Djibouti receives another shipment of COVID-19 vaccine donation from China. December 3. Available at: http://en.cidca.gov.cn/2021-12/03/c_696300.htm

Coleman, J. (2020) Trump again refers to coronavirus as 'kung flu". The Hill. June 23. Available at: https://thehill.com/homenews/administration/504224-trump-again-refers-to-coronavi rus-as-kung-flu

Culver, D. and Gan, N. (2020) China has promised millions of coronavirus vaccines to countries globally. CNN, December 2. Available at: https://edition.cnn.com/2020/12/01/asia/china-coro navirus-vaccine-diplomacy-intl-hnk/index.html

Delegation of the European Union to China (2020) 'EU HRVP: Josep Borrell: The Coronavirus pandemic and the new world it is creating. March 24. Available at: https://eeas.europa.eu/delegati ons/china/76401/eu-hrvp-josep-borrell-coronavirus-pandemic-and-new-world-it-creating_en

Döpfner, M. (2020) The coronavirus pandemic makes it clear: Europe must decide between the US and China. Business Insider, May 3. Available at: www.businessinsider.com/coronavirus-pande mic-crisis-clear-europe-must-choose-us-china-2020-5?r=USandIR=T

Emirates News Agency (2020) UAE's gestures of support moved Chinese to tears: Envoy. February 6. Available at: www.wam.ae/en/details/1395302821822

European Commission (n.d.) EU response to the coronavirus pandemic. Available at: https://ec.eur opa.eu/neighbourhood-enlargement/eu-response-coronavirus-pandemic_en

European External Action Service (2020) Special Report on Disinformation on the Coronavirus: Short assessment of the information environment, May 20. Available at: https:// euvsdisinfo.eu/eeas-special-report-update-short-assessment-of-narratives-and-disinformation-around-the-covid19-pandemic-updated-23-april-18-may/ accessed July 23, 2020).

European Union External Action (2020) 'Team Europe' – Global EU response to Covid-19 supporting partner countries and fragile populations. April 11. Available at: https://eeas.europa. eu/headquarters/headquarters-homepage/77470/%E2%80%9Cteam-europe%E2%80%9D-glo bal-eu-response-covid-19-supporting-partner-countries-and-fragile-populations_en

Foreign Ministry of the PRC (2016) China's Arab Policy Paper, January 13. Available at: www. fmprc.gov.cn/mfa_eng/zxxx_662805/t1331683.shtml

Foreign Ministry of the PRC (2020) Fighting COVID-19 through solidarity and cooperation-building a global community of health for all- statement by H.E. Xi Jinping President of the People's Republic of China at virtual event of opening of the 73rd World Health Assembly, May 18. Available at: www.fmprc.gov.cn/mfa_eng/zxxx_662805/t1780221.shtml

Fu, Y (2017) China's Vision for the world: A community of shared future. *The Diplomat*, June 22. Available at: https://thediplomat.com/2017/06/chinas-vision-for-the-world-a-community-of-sha red-future/

Ghazanchyan, S. (2020) "Turkey asks China to clarify aid packages to Armenia. Public Radio of Armenia, April 12. Available at: https://en.armradio.am/2020/04/12/turkey-asks-china-to-clar ify-aid-packages-to-armenia/

Goodman, R. and Schulkin, D. (2020) Timeline of the coronavirus pandemic and U.S. response. *Just Security*, May 7. Available at: www.justsecurity.org/69650/timeline-of-the-coronavirus-pandemic-and-u-s-response/

Green Finance and Development Center (2021) Countries of the Belt and Road Initiative (BRI). Available at: https://greenfdc.org/countries-of-the-belt-and-road-initiative-bri/

Gupta, M. and Singh, M. (2020) COVID-19: China's 'Health Silk Road' diplomacy in Iran and Turkey, ORF. April 13. Available at: www.orfonline.org/expert-speak/covid-19-chinas-health-silk-road-diplomacy-in-iran-and-turkey-64533/

Harris, B. (2020) Intel: US warns Middle Eastern partners against Chinese investment. *Al-Monitor*, June 4. Available at: www.al-monitor.com/pulse/originals/2020/06/schenker-china-uae-israel-lebanon-coronavirus-covid19.html

Hillman, J. and Tippett, A. (2021) A robust U.S. response to China's health diplomacy will reap domestic and global benefits, April 15. Available at: www.thinkglobalhealth.org/article/robust-us-response-chinas-health-diplomacy-will-reap-domestic-and-global-benefits

Huang, Z. (2017) Chinese president Xi Jinping has vowed to lead the 'new world order', Quartz Daily Brief, February 22. Available at: https://qz.com/916382/chinese-president-xi-jinping-has-vowed-to-lead-the-new-world-order/

Khan, S.A. (2021) China's increasing influence in the Middle East. *E-International Relations*, September 20. Available at: www.e-ir.info/2021/09/20/chinas-increasing-influence-in-the-middle-east/

Killeen, O., Davis, A., Tucker, J.D., and Meier, B.M. (2018) Chinese global health diplomacy in Africa: Opportunities and challenges, *Global Health Governance*, 12(2): 4.

Knowledge@Wharton (2011) Health diplomacy: In Africa, China's soft power provides a healing touch, November 22. Available at: https://knowledge.wharton.upenn.edu/article/health-diplomacy-in-africa-chinas-soft-power-provides-a-healing-touch/

Krastev, I. and Leonard, M. (2020) Europe's pandemic politics: How the virus has changed the public's worldview. European Council on Foreign Relations. Available at: www.ecfr.eu/publications/summary/europes_pandemic_politics_how_the_virus_has_changed_the_publics_worldview

Le Corre, P. and Brattberg, E. (2020) How the coronavirus pandemic shattered Europe's illusions of China', Carnegie, July 9. Available at: https://carnegieendowment.org/2020/07/09/how-coronavirus-pandemic-shattered-europe-s-illusions-of-china-pub-82265

Le Matin (2020) Covid-19: China Development Bank fait don de matériel médical au Maroc, May 16. Available at: https://lematin.ma/express/2020/covid-19-china-development-bank-don-materiel-medical-maroc/337500.html

Le Monde (2021) En Algérie, lancement de la production locale du vaccin chinois CoronaVac contre le Covid-19, September 30. Available at: www.lemonde.fr/afrique/article/2021/09/30/en-algerie-lancement-de-la-production-locale-du-vaccin-chinois-coronavac-contre-le-covid-19_6096559_3212.html

Leoni, Z. (2021) *American Grand Strategy from Obama to Trump: Imperialism after Bush and China's Hegemonic Challenge*. New York: Palgrave Macmillan.

Li, A. (2011) Chinese medical cooperation in Africa with special emphasis on the medical teams and anti-malaria campaign, Discussion paper no. 52. Uppsala: Nordiska Afrikainstitute. Available at: www.diva-portal.org/smash/get/diva2:399727/FULLTEXT02.pdf

Li, L. (2020) Oman's Covid-19 cure rate among the top in the region, Oman Observer, May 5. Available at: www.omanobserver.om/omans-covid-19-cure-rate-among-the-top-in-the-region/

Middle East Monitor (2020) China calls for the lifting of sanctions against Syria to fight coronavirus, April 1. Available at: www.middleeastmonitor.com/20200401-china-calls-for-the-lifting-of-sanctions-against-syria-to-fight-coronavirus/

National Health Commission of the People's Republic of China (2015) Major health exchange and cooperation on the Belt and Road Initiative, reprinted in China Daily, December 18. Available at: www.chinadaily.com.cn/m/chinahealth/2015-12/18/content_22774412.htm (accessed July 23, 2020).

Osiewicz, P. (2020) EU-MENA relations in a time of pandemic. Middle East Institute. April 28. Available at: www.mei.edu/publications/eu-mena-relations-time-pandemic

Poh, A. and Li, M. (2017) A China in transition: The rhetoric and substance of Chinese Foreign Policy under Xi Jinping. *Asian Security* 13(2): 84–97.

Robbins, M. (2020) Is this China's moment in MENA? Arab Barometer. Available at: www.arabbarometer.org/2020/07/is-this-chinas-moment-in-mena/

Robbins, M. (2021) U.S. and China's competition extends to MENA, Arab Barometer. www.arabba rometer.org/2021/01/u-s-chinas-competition-extends-to-mena/

Rudolf, M. (2021) China's health diplomacy during Covid-19. Stiftung Wissenschaft und Politik. Available at: www.swp-berlin.org/10.18449/2021C09/

ShareAmerica (2020) U.S. helps counter COVID-19 outbreaks in Middle East and North Africa. May 4. Available at: https://usunrome.usmission.gov/u-s-helps-counter-covid-19-outbreaks-in-middle-east-and-north-africa/

Shinn, David H. (2006) Africa, China and health care. *Inside AISA*, Numbers 3 and 4 (October/December): 14–16.

Silver, L. and Devlin, K. (2020) Around the world, more see the U.S. positively than China, but little confidence in Trump or Xi. Pew Research Center, January 10. Available at: www.pewresea rch.org/fact-tank/2020/01/10/around-the-world-more-see-the-u-s-positively-than-china-but-lit tle-confidence-in-trump-or-xi/

Silver, L., Devlin, K. and Huang, C. (2021) Large majorities say China does not respect the personal freedoms of its people, June 30. Available at: www.pewresearch.org/global/2021/06/30/large-maj orities-say-china-does-not-respect-the-personal-freedoms-of-its-people/

State Council Information Office of the People's Republic of China (2020) Fighting Covid-19: China in action. Available at: http://english.scio.gov.cn/whitepapers/2020-06/07/content_7 6135269.htm

Stevenson, A. and May, T. (2020) China pushes to churn out corona gear, yet struggles to police it. The New York Times. March 27. Available at: www.nytimes.com/2020/03/27/business/china-coronavirus-masks-tests.html

Stiles, K. (2018) *Trust and Hedging in International Relations*. Ann Arbor, MI: University of Michigan Press.

Stone, R. (2020) How coronavirus pandemic could expand China's footprint in Turkey. *Middle East Eye*. May 21. Available at: www.middleeasteye.net/opinion/how-coronavirus-pandemic-could-expand-chinas-footprint-turkey

Sun, D. (2020) China's partnership diplomacy in the Middle East. *Asia Dialogue*. Available at: https://theasiadialogue.com/2020/03/24/chinas-partnership-diplomacy-in-the-middle-east/

Tasnim (Tehran) (2020) China sending Iran new aid shipment, vows support in coronavirus fight. March 25. Available at: www.tasnimnews.com/en/news/2020/03/25/2230164/china-sending-iran-new-aid-shipment-vows-support-in-coronavirus-fight

Times of Israel (2020) In recovery mode, Chinese donors shell out for Israel's coronavirus fight, April 6. Available at: www.timesofisrael.com/in-recovery-mode-chinese-donors-shell-out-for-israels-coronavirus-fight/

Tran, E and Zoubir, Y.H. (2023) China's Health Diplomacy in the "New Cold War" Era: Contrasting the Battle of Narratives in Europe and the Middle East and North Africa. In K. P. Tan (Ed.), *Asia in the Old and New Cold Wars: Ideologies, Narratives, and Lived Experience*. Basingstoke: Palgrave Macmillan.

TSA (2022) Covid-19: l'Algérie offre des vaccins à trois pays voisins, January 25. Available at: www. tsa-algerie.com/covid-19-lalgerie-offre-des-vaccins-a-trois-pays-voisins/

Wang, Q. (2020) Saving lives was China's only goal behind global aid, Wang [Yi] says. *China Daily*, May 24. Available at: www.chinadaily.com.cn/a/202005/24/WS5eca2e72a310a8b241157f73.html

Wen, Q. (2020) Shared answers for shared problems: Renewed calls for global efforts to contain COVID-19 pandemic, *Beijing Review*. March 20. Available at: www.bjreview.com/Current_Is sue/Editor_Choice/202003/t20200323_800198186.html

White House (2017) A new national security strategy for a new era, December 18. Available at: www. whitehouse.gov/articles/new-national-security-strategy-new-era/

Wong, B. (2020) China's mask diplomacy: By shipping medical supplies to European countries, China is seeking to boost its image as a responsible global leader, *The Diplomat*, March 25. Available at: https://thediplomat.com/2020/03/chinas-mask-diplomacy/

Xi, J. (2014) Promoting the Silk Road spirit and deepening China-Arab cooperation: Speech at the opening ceremony of the 6th Ministerial Meeting of the China–Arab States Cooperation Forum, June 4. Available at: www.mfa.gov.cn/ce/ceiq/eng/zygx/t1164662.htm

Xi, J. (2015) Full text of Chinese President's speech at Boao Forum for Asia. China.org. March 29. Available at: www.china.org.cn/business/2015-03/29/content_35185720.htm

Xinhua (2017) Chinese landmark concept put into UN resolution for first time, February 11. Available at: www.xinhuanet.com//english/2017-02/11/c_136049319.htm

Xinhua (2020a) Oman-China ties to prosper under BRI after COVID-19, say experts. June 9. Available at: http://en.people.cn/n3/2020/0609/c90000-9698832.html

Xinhua (2020b) How China, Morocco support each other in fight against COVID-19, June 1. Available at: www.xinhuanet.com/english/2020-06/01/c_139105827.htm

Xinhua (2020c) Commentary: In war against COVID-19, vision of community with shared future shines, March 11. Available at: www.xinhuanet.com/english/2020-03/11/c_138866546.htm

Xinhua (2020d) Roundup: Cooperation in fight against COVID-19 deepens China-Jordan relationship, June 5. Available at: http://en.brnn.com/n3/2020/0605/c416051-9697754.html

Xinhua (2020e) Tunisian president thanks China for anti-epidemic assistance, June 8. www.focac.org/eng/zfgx_4/zzjw/t1787002.htm

Xinhua (2020f) Sudanese officials praise Chinese medical team's support in fight against COVID-19, June 12, Available at: http://en.people.cn/n3/2020/0612/c90000-9699944.html

Xinhuanet (2021) China offers free vaccines to over 80 developing countries: *Xi*, May 21, Available at: www.xinhuanet.com/english/2021-05/21/c_139961369.htm

Zoubir, Y.H. (2020) China's 'Health Silk Road' diplomacy in the MENA, Konrad Adenauer Stiftung, Med Dialogue Series Research Paper No. 27, pp. 1–14, July. Available at: www.kas.de/documents/282499/282548/MDS_China+Health+Silk+Road+Diplomacy.pdf/

Zoubir, Y.H. (2021) China's relations with Algeria: From revolutionary friendship to Comprehensive Strategic Partnership, in A. Abdel-Ghafar (Ed.), *China and North Africa*. London: I.B. Tauris.

Zoubir, Y.H. and Tran, E. (2022) China's Health Silk Road in the MENA amidst COVID-19 and a shifting world order, *Journal of Contemporary China*, 31(135): 335–350.

PART II

Bilateral Relations

20

THE SINO-ALGERIAN RELATIONSHIP

Strengthening the Comprehensive Strategic Partnership

Siham Matallah

1 Introduction

China has been strategically ramping up its forward-looking engagement with Algeria and has expanded its diplomatic presence, cooperation initiatives, trade, and economic relations with this North African country, which lies at the geostrategic intersection of the Mediterranean, Africa, and the Middle East. Sino-Algerian relations date back to 1958 when China was the first non-Arab country which recognized both the Provisional Government of the Algerian Republic (GPRA) and the Algerian National Liberation Front (FLN) that embraced secular, nationalist, and socialist ideologies. Algeria views China as the new savior that can reduce its ultimate dependence on Western powers, fill the chronic gaps in infrastructure, widen trade exchange, boost foreign direct investment and joint projects, and alleviate poverty; these interests match China's approach to development and peacebuilding in the Global South. Algeria welcomed the Chinese development model which successfully combines spectacular economic growth with authoritarian political rule and has, as a result, gained considerable appeal in the authoritarian regimes in the MENA region.

Algeria views China as an increasingly important trade and investment partner and a means to enhance its own economic growth. China is committed to pursuing a win-win partnership with Algeria based on mutual respect for each other's interests and non-interference in each other's domestic affairs, which is in line with Algeria's development interests. China has demonstrated the importance it attaches to Algeria by signing several bilateral cooperation agreements, elevating the bilateral relationship to a Comprehensive Strategic Partnership in 2014, building much-needed infrastructure, aggressively increasing its investments, and expanding its trade activities there (Zoubir, 2021). But Sino-Algerian cooperation is still far from its potential as this North African partner has much to do to realize the full potential benefit of this strategic partnership. Sino-Algerian cooperation is on the right track but equally important are the delayed developments and the slow pace at which structural and economic reforms are being implemented in Algeria. Another issue is that of the underdeveloped and non-transparent business

DOI: 10.4324/9781003048404-23

environment; Algeria has yet to create a stable and predictable investment climate conducive to attracting Chinese investments into non-energy sectors. However, the lack of transparency and openness, ambiguity in government policies, and incomplete development in Algeria are leading Chinese firms to focus mainly on securing construction contracts for infrastructure projects and actively investing in energy projects that guarantee low risks and high returns. Despite the alleged good intentions of the Chinese government, China's rise and Algeria's economic landscape seem to be pretty far apart. In fact, Sino-Algerian cooperation is based upon uneven levels of development and very disparate capacities to capture tangible benefits from such a partnership. Algeria did indeed receive some returns, especially in terms of infrastructure development but it could gain much more from genuine win-win cooperation if it were to make major strides toward achieving large-scale reforms.

Algeria cannot achieve more positive outcomes and broad-based benefits from its engagement with China if it continues to maintain the inefficient status quo and delay the eventually unavoidable reforms. According to the World Bank (2021a), these reforms are:

- improving the business climate;
- promoting private sector development;
- alleviating the lengthy bureaucratic process;
- enforcing contracts;
- resolving the uncertainties;
- stabilizing the regulatory environment;
- establishing special economic zones;
- rooting out corruption;
- enhancing public sector transparency;
- strengthening accountability.

Algeria will support China's peaceful rise in Africa; for instance, China's expansion in Angola, Tanzania, Zambia, Uganda, and Ethiopia, just to name a few, is aimed at improving its own image and developing its own interests, not the interests of these African countries (Lisimba, 2020). It is true that China has now taken the lead in marketing its idealist vision of mutual cooperation and win-win benefits to the rest of the world (Abdulai, 2017), but given the completely different reality, Algeria must do its homework to strategize how it can best benefit from its cooperation with China.

This chapter aims to analyze all aspects of Sino-Algerian relations, especially in the economic realm; therefore, it is divided into six sections. After introducing the topic in Section 1, Section 2 explores the historical development of Sino-Algerian relations; Section 3 discusses the burgeoning China-Algeria trade relationship; Section 4 highlights China's foreign direct investment in Algeria; Section 5 casts a critical eye on China's engagement with Algeria; and, finally, Section 6 concludes the chapter and draws some policy implications.

2 Historical Development of Sino-Algerian Relations

China has been ramping up economic, political, cultural, and military engagement with Algeria for some time. Successive Algerian governments welcomed China's growing role and were optimistic about future cooperative exchanges and potential benefits of China–Algeria cooperation despite suspicions on the part of Western countries about China's intentions. By 2013, China has replaced France as Algeria's leading trading partner (supplier). China was always keen to establish and develop a new type of Sino-Algerian cooperative relations built on the basis of sincerity, friendship, equality, mutual respect, mutual trust, mutual support, mutual benefits, unity, cooperation, and common progress. China sees Algeria as the center of the anti-French colonial struggle and touched the most sensitive chord of a country which attempted to sustain the reconstruction of its economy after the devastating French colonization. The historical connections between the two countries date back to many decades of cooperation.

In 1958, China was the first non-Arab country which recognized both the GPRA and the FLN that embraced secular, nationalist, and socialist ideologies. Thus, the historical development of good Sino-Algerian relations has paved the way for the genesis of the modern phase of Sino-Algerian relations. From 1958 to 1962, China focused on filling some of the huge financial gaps by providing the FLN's military wing with important economic aid and military assistance without intervening militarily in Algerian security affairs (Zoubir, 2021). After Algeria gained independence from France in 1962, China continued to consolidate its alliance and friendship with Algeria, gave moral, logistical, and military support to this newly independent North African country and alleviated Algeria's financial burden by offering a low-interest loan of $50 million to bolster the 'Beijing–Algiers axis' and show solidarity with Third World African countries (Copper, 2016). In the 1970s, China took a neutral stance on the Western Sahara dispute that triggered a decade of tension between Algeria and Morocco to avoid damaging the harmonious relationship with Algeria (Zoubir, 2020a). In 1971, Algeria helped China to gain a permanent seat at the UN General Assembly and the UN Security Council, and thus consolidated Sino-Algerian ties (Belhadj et al., 2015). In the 1990s, China sold $55.4 million worth of weapons to Algeria during the bloody civil war (the "black decade"), which caused 200,000 deaths (Grimmett, 2003).

China has strengthened and enlarged the basis for economic cooperation with Algeria under the umbrella of the Forum on China–Africa Cooperation (FOCAC) and the China–Arab States Cooperation Forum (CASCF), launched in 2000 and 2004, respectively (Olimat, 2013). Since the early 2000s, Algeria's development requirements and the government's major infrastructure projects have driven the demand for China's strong comparative advantage in infrastructure projects as levels of violence fell significantly and a brisk growth followed the previous deep slump. Hence, Sino-Algerian relations have made great progress and the Chinese presence in Algeria has grown enormously, strengthening a new type of strategic partnership between Algeria and China. With security and political stability restored and oil revenues increased, public investment has risen and reached about 20 percent of non-hydrocarbon GDP on average since 2000. In the 2000s, the Algerian government allocated on average about 70 percent of public investment to the expansion of physical infrastructure (roads, ports, airports, power, railways, water, etc.) and social infrastructure (health, education, housing, etc.) (IMF, 2018). A substantial portion of the oil revenue windfall was directed to finance the 2001–2004 Economic Recovery Support Program (PSRE) and the 2004–2009 Complementary Support Program for Growth (PCSC) that featured massive public investment programs. Those programs focused on affordable housing and basic infrastructure and opened the door for China to play an increasingly important role in Algeria's key construction projects (AfDB/OECD, 2005; Castel et al., 2011). Since 2006, the pace of construction ha picked up in Algeria, and Chinese companies and contractors have fared well with larger infrastructure projects like the East-West highway, the Capital's new airport, Oran's

Olympic Stadium, the Constitutional Court, a 750-km-long water pipeline project, the country's largest prison, and the largest mosque in Africa in Algiers; furthermore, the state has increasingly awarded several contracts to Chinese companies in the energy sector (Oxford Business Group, 2014).

According to data from the China Africa Research Initiative (CARI) at the Johns Hopkins University School of Advanced International Studies (SAIS), the gross annual revenues of Chinese companies' construction projects in Algeria totaled $6.335 billion in 2019, compared with only $78.6 million, $211.6 million, and $2.34 billion in 1998, 2002, and 2007, respectively. Algeria alone accounts for 14 percent of all Chinese companies' 2019 construction projects' gross annual revenues in Africa, while these revenues did not exceed $93.7 million in Tunisia, $335.3 million in Morocco, and $3.189 billion in Egypt in 2019. Due to many large- and small-scale projects, huge numbers of Chinese laborers have flocked to Algeria. The number of Chinese workers has doubled from 44,217 in 2010 to 91,596 in 2016 (China Africa Research Initiative, Johns Hopkins University, 2021); the number markedly declined to 42,999 in 2019 (making up 25 percent of total Chinese laborers in Africa). Regardless, Chinese workers still represent the largest foreign-born population in Algeria, making this country the host to the biggest Chinese community in Africa (ibid.).

In fact, China has historically maintained a long-term relationship with Algeria and has been successful in upgrading its position from a traditional trading partner to a strategic economic partner of Algeria, which perceives China as an economic umbilical cord to offset the miseries of threats posed by Western interests, tackle the infrastructure deficit, improve transport, attract maximum foreign investment, and further expand trade. Algeria's interest in improving relations with the fire-breathing Chinese dragon coincide with the latter's pragmatic and geopolitical objectives and endeavors in Africa in particular and the Third World in general.

3 The Burgeoning China-Algeria Trade Relationship

China-Algeria bilateral trade has been increasing steadily for the past three decades. According to UN COMTRADE data, between 1992 and 2013, the value of China's imports from Algeria rose from $2.7 million to $2.16 billion, but then declined to $1.14 billion in 2019, encompassing a range of fuels, oils, distillation products, organic chemicals, raw hides and skins, and cork (see Table 20.1). China's exports to Algeria amounted to $6.94 billion in 2019 compared with $1.94 billion in 2006, $112.96 million in 1997 and $27.34 million in 1992, encompassing a range of machinery, electronics, textiles, clothing, metals, plastic products, rubber, miscellaneous manufactured products, transport equipment, footwear, articles of stone and glass, and chemicals (see Table 20.1). In fact, China faces strong competition from France, Italy, and the USA in Algeria. France's imports from Algeria reached $1.49 billion in 1994, $7.08 billion in 2008, and $4.6 billion in 2019. Italy's imports from Algeria increased from $1.62 billion in 1994 to $11.59 billion in 2012, but then decreased to $4.86 billion in 2019. The USA's imports from Algeria grew from $1.69 billion in 1992 to $16.08 billion in 2006 and $20 billion in 2008, but then decreased to $2.59 billion in 2019 (see Table 20.2). Although Algeria's exports to China jumped 44-fold between 2000 and 2019, they remain relatively smaller than Algerian exports to France, Italy, and the USA. In terms of exports, France's exports to Algeria more than tripled from $2.41 billion in 1994 to $8.17 billion in 2014, but then declined to $5.51 billion in 2019. Over the same period, Italy's exports to Algeria

The Sino-Algerian Relationship

Table 20.1 China-Algeria trade, 1992–2019 ($ million)

Year	China importing from Algeria	China exporting to Algeria
1992	2.70	27.34
1993	6.65	33.54
1994	3.77	59.80
1995	22.03	57.49
1996	0.01	54.50
1997	0.02	112.96
1998	0.12	116.79
1999	62.19	159.95
2000	25.94	172.92
2001	69.99	222.23
2002	81.90	351.90
2003	99.22	645.94
2004	259.08	980.52
2005	363.73	1404.42
2006	143.12	1947.51
2007	1160.93	2741.98
2008	849.22	3751.91
2009	946.62	4180.24
2010	1177.32	4000.00
2011	1960.89	4471.88
2012	2311.91	5416.66
2013	2164.55	6023.90
2014	1314.68	7395.24
2015	767.36	7583.35
2016	331.89	7647.85
2017	448.32	6784.75
2018	1178.82	7923.38
2019	1141.65958	6945.57125

Source: UN Comtrade, https://comtrade.un.org/data/ (accessed March 5, 2021).

rose from $934.3 million in 1994 to $5.73 billion in 2014, but then declined to $3.26 billion in 2019. US exports to Algeria amounted to $2.61 billion in 2014 compared with $676.59 million in 1992 and $1.03 billion in 2001, but then declined to $999.32 million in 2019 (see Table 20.2).

Despite decreasing from $42.38 billion in 2013 to $20.65 billion in 2019, the EU remains a major market for Algeria's exports. Similarly, although the EU's exports to Algeria declined significantly from $30.52 billion in 2014 to $19.07 billion in 2019, the EU remains Algeria's largest import supplier (see Table 20.3). But, notably, with $6.94 billion worth of Chinese exports to Algeria in 2019, China is still Algeria's largest single import supplier, overtaking France, and this reveals Algeria's attempts to diversify its strategic relations to get some bargaining power vis-à-vis its traditional partners, especially France.

Although bilateral trade between China and Algeria has accelerated noticeably since 2003, so far, however, the trade volume has not increased as expected due to a lack of institutional capacities at the national level. The Algerian government is not making

Table 20.2 Algeria's trade with France, Italy and the USA, 1992–2019 ($ million)

Year	France importing from Algeria	France exporting to Algeria	Italy importing from Algeria	Italy exporting to Algeria	USA importing from Algeria	USA exporting to Algeria
1992	n/a	n/a	n/a	n/a	1693.779	676.592
1993	n/a	n/a	n/a	n/a	1710.781	897.976
1994	1496.579	2414.036	1627.021	934.303	1664.329	1191.117
1995	1509.211	2855.567	2288.743	789.403	1807.209	774.819
1996	1720.521	2460.494	2713.152	734.479	2270.363	631.667
1997	2168.698	2290.488	2969.686	706.945	2645.617	694.949
1998	1554.548	2658.5	2559.515	875.414	1798.656	650.167
1999	1578.232	2574.417	998.206	769.252	1951.535	456.325
2000	2311.717	2656.448	1443.76	791.557	2724.27	861.813
2001	2681.256	3031.638	1038.574	924.03	2701.903	1037.799
2002	2555.412	3543.035	1117.353	1170.68	2560	984
2003	3474.207	4183.37	1614.681	1320.352	5126	487
2004	3574.409	5258.185	1866.179	1533.491	7926	972
2005	4582.169	5809.564	1910.667	1662.249	10835	1161
2006	5190.543	5057.741	2218.412	1948.012	16089	1102
2007	4627.196	5695.716	1083.62	2518.691	18432	1653
2008	7082.517	8108.166	1536.528	4402.727	20032	1243
2009	3817.858	6959.563	8418.309	3598.025	11150	1109
2010	3073.577	6933.296	10682.493	3794.07	14944	1194
2011	6112.713	8023.029	11568.209	4181.947	14913	1597
2012	5039.14	8161.643	11594.641	4864.907	10201	1363
2013	5632.882	7843.393	8327.998	5661.87	4960	1849
2014	5866.215	8175.042	5093.361	5730.037	4795	2617
2015	4320.016	6891.472	3349.722	4596.283	3537	1876
2016	3306.012	5622.727	4733.282	4107.15	3419	2191
2017	3830.531	5632.72	5601.144	3585.183	3987	1060
2018	4923.927	6225.039	6757.608	3650.128	4782	1261
2019	4665.382	5512.627	4860.706	3268.81	2593.386	999.323

Source: UN Comtrade, https://comtrade.un.org/data/ (accessed March 5, 2021).

a complete and tangible commitment to good governance, which is in effect vital to a vibrant trade economy. According to the World Bank's Worldwide Governance Indicators (WGI) database, Algeria obtained a low WGI governance average of -0.86 in 2019 on a scale of -2.5 (weak performance) to +2.5 (strong performance) (World Bank, 2021b). Doing business in Algeria is particularly difficult and challenging for import-export businesses. In fact, there is often a wide gap between written laws and actual practice in the country. Further, the fairness with which laws are implemented is often questionable. Algeria remains an aggressively unfree market economy, with several significant barriers to market access. According to the World Bank's Doing Business 2020, Algeria ranks 172 among 190 economies in terms of trading across borders with a score of 38.4/100 which is well below the regional average of (61.8/100), mainly due to lack of adequate trade-related infrastructure, the time it takes to export and import goods, and the very

Table 20.3 EU-Algeria trade, 2000–2020 ($ million)

Year	EU importing from Algeria	EU exporting to Algeria
2000	15291.012	5736.769
2001	14480.438	6933.801
2002	13619.325	7880.791
2003	16506.728	9087.135
2004	18969.952	11832.528
2005	25940.705	13037.501
2006	30344.356	12541.074
2007	28245.962	15469.814
2008	41646.009	22700.896
2009	24269.992	20693.898
2010	27685.014	20510.258
2011	38758.198	23988.334
2012	42115.957	27081.049
2013	42383.904	29635.708
2014	39078.597	30528.007
2015	23175.555	24520.061
2016	18108.235	22496.459
2017	20875.249	20998.208
2018	24662.326	22027.878
2019	20650.916	19078.49
2020	12916.446	15120.101

Source: UN Comtrade, https://comtrade.un.org/data/ (accessed March 5, 2021).

high cost of exporting and importing (World Bank, 2020). According to theHeritage Foundation's 2021 Index of Economic Freedom, Algeria's trade freedom score is 57.4/100, which is below the regional average of (70.7/100); this score has recently been on a downward trajectory due to the high trade-weighted average tariff rate (13.8 percent of GDP) and layers of nontariff barriers that substantially discourage the smoother flow of trade. Additionally, the Algerian government has largely pursued protectionism and a strategy of import-substitution and imposed strict import quotas since 2015; with such measures, Algeria has lowered its trade capacity (ibid.).

The reasons why China is not a readily accessible market for Algeria's non-oil exports are many, including the lack of industrial development, the absence of a solid foundation to develop heavy and manufacturing industries, a massively failed industrial infrastructure, the underdevelopment of light industry, the shortage of skilled workers, and the need for technological upgrading. Moreover, the relatively modest agricultural production and traditional marketing and processing structures continue to deprive Algeria of the rising demand for foreign food in China. In 2008, China and Algeria reached an agreement to establish the Jiangling Economic and Trade Cooperation Zone in a bid to boost trade exchange (Zeng, 2015), but this zone has not yet materialized. Postponing such initiatives prevents Algeria from increasing its trade volume with China and frustrates China's hopes of leveraging Algeria's location. Yet, in Beijing's eyes, Algeria is an attractive market for Chinese traders. China greatly values Algeria' strategic location at the crossroads between Africa, the Middle East, and Europe, and considers it an asset that deserves a wide-open window of opportunity. As a result, there is an unmistakable Chinese move toward fortifying cooperative trade ties with Algeria.

Although China has been strategically ramping up commercial engagement with Algeria, the latter is not officially included in the current map of the Belt and Road Initiative (BRI) launched in 2013, but it is worth noting that Algeria signed a memorandum of understanding on the China-proposed BRI to grasp the opportunity to increase trade volumes and share the fruits of the new "Silk Road" (Abdel Ghafar and Jacobs, 2020). Overall, due to Algeria's strategic location as a gateway to Africa and a junction between European, African, and Asian markets, China will continue to expand its presence in Algeria, particularly in the realm of trade.

4 China's Foreign Direct Investment in Algeria

Chinese FDI annual flows to Algeria have increased steadily since 2003; these flows have risen from $2.47 million in 2003 to $665.71 million in 2014, but then declined to $178.65 million in 2018 (China Africa Research Initiative, Johns Hopkins University, 2021) (see Table 20.4). Algeria is keen to preserve its close ties with China and attract more Chinese FDI flows to offset its dependence on Western powers, expand its manufacturing capacities, and enhance its economic development. China has been primarily interested in tapping into Algeria's construction, housing, and energy sectors (Abdel Ghafar and Jacobs, 2020). China's breakthrough in terms of FDI is also still very limited in Algeria. Despite creating some job opportunities, Chinese FDI in Algeria remains below Algerian aspirations and China's real capacities and is not yet a panacea which can remedy the

Table 20.4 Chinese FDI flows to Algeria, 2003–2019 ($ million)

Year	Chinese FDI
2003	2.47
2004	11.21
2005	84.87
2006	98.93
2007	145.92
2008	42.25
2009	228.76
2010	186
2011	114.34
2012	245.88
2013	191.3
2014	665.71
2015	210.57
2016	-99.89
2017	-140.53
2018	178.65
2019	-123.68

Source: China Africa Research Initiative, Johns Hopkins University, www.sais-cari.org/chinese-investment-in-africa (accessed March 5, 2021).

The Sino-Algerian Relationship

Table 20.5 French, Italian, and US FDI flows to Algeria, 2005–2019 ($ million)

Year	French FDI	Italian FDI	US FDI
2005	75.8	3.7	1 079,0
2006	5.0	-8.8	1 781,0
2007	-23.3	4.1	1 117,0
2008	309.9	110.1	-401
2009	598.8	308.8	578
2010	317.9	1 476,0	715
2011	229.8	1 644,2	581.0
2012	281.5	1 684,8	-649.0
2013	-146.0	2 630,7	-652.0
2014	-46.4	1 806,2	457.0
2015	245.1	1 835,6	15.0
2016	70.8	920	-673.0
2017	205.2	981	-105.0
2018	283.253	1060.045	n/a
2019	91.794	807.832	-211.0

Source: OECD stat database. https://stats.oecd.org/ (accessed March 5, 2021).

development problem, by being an integral part of the poverty reduction toolkit, increasingly contributing to skills development, providing a higher spillover potential, transferring new technologies and knowledge to local partner firms, advancing industrialization, and expanding the production and export of goods with high value added.

Table 20.4 HereThe flow of Chinese FDI to Algeria has failed to keep pace with FDI flows coming from the United States, Italy, and France, especially in the energy sector. As shown in Table 20.5, during 2005–2007, US FDI flows to Algeria exceeded those from China, France, and Italy. France surpassed the USA as the largest provider of FDI to Algeria between 2008 and 2009. Over the period 2010–2019, Italy was Algeria's biggest FDI partner, overtaking France. In 2019, the top two senders of FDI to Algeria were Italy and France with flows of $807.83 million and $91.79 million, respectively, and these flows appear mainly in the exploitation and distribution of oil and gas resources, and in other sectors like telecommunications, transportation, automobiles, machinery, and pharmaceuticals manufacturing. In the Maghreb, Algeria still receives the lion's share of Chinese FDI inflows. Between 2003 and 2018, the value of China's FDI flows to Morocco rose from $0.19 million to $90.78 million. Tunisia receives the smallest proportion of Chinese FDI inflows compared to Algeria and Morocco. By the end of 2019, China's FDI inflows to Tunisia stood at $19.96 million, representing an increase of $19.74 million since 2004 (see Table 20.6). The limited amount of Chinese FDI inflows to Morocco and Tunisia indicates that many Chinese investors generally lack investment experience and are not initially enthusiastic about establishing and maintaining a successful joint venture investment in both countries. The bilateral investment cooperation between China and these two North African countries has yet to take off from its primitive stages. It is also worth noting that language and cultural barriers still prevent not only Morocco and Tunisia but also Algeria from taking full advantage of Chinese investments (Zoubir, 2020a).

Table 20.6 Chinese FDI flows to Morocco and Tunisia, 2003–2019 ($ million)

Year	Chinese FDI flows to Morocco	Chinese FDI flows to Tunisia
2003	0.19	0.00
2004	1.80	0.22
2005	0.85	0.00
2006	1.78	1.73
2007	2.64	-0.34
2008	6.88	0.00
2009	16.42	-1.30
2010	1.75	-0.29
2011	9.11	3.76
2012	1.05	-0.65
2013	7.74	7.06
2014	11.44	0.71
2015	26.03	5.64
2016	10.16	-3.22
2017	59.86	-0.82
2018	90.78	5.96
2019	-95.16	19.96

Source: China Africa Research Initiative, Johns Hopkins University, www.sais-cari.org/chinese-inv estment-in-africa (accessed March 5, 2021).

Several sectors, including renewable energy, agribusiness, tourism, recycling, manufacturing, and services are all of great interest to Chinese investors who perceive that Algeria's investment environment is both challenging and potentially highly rewarding. Chinese firms want to benefit from investing in Algeria as this would enable them to enter European markets, but they are hesitant to do so because of the political uncertainty, insecurity, the difficult business climate, the inconsistent regulatory environment, restrictive fiscal measures, and the contradictory government policies that deter new FDI inflows and even drive away investors already operating in Algeria. According to the World Bank's Worldwide Governance Indicators (WGI) database, the overall picture is quite gloomy, Algeria obtained a low political stability score of -1 in 2019 and a very low regulatory quality score of -1.3 in 2019 on a scale of -2.5 (weak performance) to +2.5 (strong performance) (World Bank, 2021b). Thus, Chinese investors hesitate to make a key breakthrough in non-oil sectors and invest in the Algerian environment which is nebulously uncertain and unpredictable and exhibits high political risk; they are reluctant to invest in such an ambiguous, murky, and unpredictable regulatory environment. According to the World Bank's Doing Business 2020 ranking, Algeria is ranked 157 among 190 economies with a score of 48.6/100, this low score was mainly due to concerns over starting a business, regulatory and institutional barriers to entry for new businesses, stifled access to credit, inefficiency of property transfers, weak protection of minority investors, cumbersome taxation systems, and difficult trading across borders. For example, the report estimates that an average of 12 procedures have to be completed, taking a total of 18 days to complete registration for a new business in Algeria, compared to 4.9 procedures which take just 9.2 days on average in high-income OECD countries. Interestingly, this report also lists 10 procedures that cumulatively take an average of

55 days to register property in Algeria, while it takes only 5.4 procedures/26.6 days and 4.7 procedures/23.6 days on average to register a property in MENA countries and high-income OECD countries, respectively. The payment of taxes in Algeria is also a problem, resulting from 27 payments required in a year and the 265 hours per year it takes to file and pay taxes, compared to 16.5 payments/202.6 hours on average in MENA countries and 10.3 payments/158.8 hours on average in high-income OECD countries (World Bank, 2020). According to the Heritage Foundation's 2021 Index of Economic Freedom, Algeria's investment freedom score is 30/100 which is below the regional average of (50.7/100). This score shows a sharp downward path due to the deficient investment framework, non-transparent and discriminatory investment regime, and the obstructive investment policies, such as restrictions on foreign ownership, lingering bureaucracy in the regulatory environment, inconsistent enforcement of regulations, and lack of digitization of information that can plug the loopholes and streamline the bureaucratic processes; further, the Algerian government frequently changes business regulations, and this attitude seriously undermines the certainty and predictability of investment climate in Algeria (ibid.).

The Algerian government is now eager to attract FDI by offering generous tax exemptions and reductions to multinational corporations (MNCs) and foreign investors, but this is still not enough to achieve its aims. Algeria so far lacks foreign trade zones and free ports; and what makes matters worse is the inefficiency of the National Agency for Investment Development (ANDI), which is responsible for attracting, facilitating, and retaining foreign investments. In fact, US MNCs in Algeria reported that the ANDI is ineffective and grossly understaffed and does not demonstrate any interest or enthusiasm to maintain dialogue with foreign investors after they have established their investments and operated them, especially during economic hard times (US Department of State, 2019). China is an important part of Algeria's vision to attract investments and diversify the economy. Thus, Algeria needs to implement a wide range of specially tailored investment measures and harness its potential to ensure a better investment climate and become a magnet for foreign direct investment, particularly in sectors other than natural resource extraction.

5 Casting a Critical Eye on China's Engagement with Algeria

Even though Chinese success in Algeria has become visible, there are some problems and critics of China's marketing of its soft power assets. China's growing engagement in economic and infrastructure development contains some problematic aspects that require more reflection and attention. Notable among these critics is the use of cheap and semi-skilled Chinese labor forces in Chinese-funded, sponsored, and managed projects (Abdel Ghafar and Jacobs, 2020). Many questions have been raised about the extent to which Chinese projects have helped or will help ease growing unemployment in Algeria. In fact, many Chinese firms working in Algeria rely on imported Chinese labor and they have always their justifications for doing so, such as low labor costs, relatively high productivity, and linguistic and cultural familiarity (Zhang, 2010; Shinn and Eisenman, 2012), and more importantly, familiarity with the technologies used by Chinese firms; all these factors undoubtedly make it more efficient, dynamic, and appropriate for Chinese firms to use Chinese workers than to train local workers in Algeria. Thus, Chinese companies operating in Algeria employ mainly Chinese workers, whose number have increased in Algeria from 44,217 in 2010 to 91,596 in 2016, and then markedly declined to 42,999 in

2019 (making up 25 percent of total Chinese laborers in Africa) (China Africa Research Initiative, Johns Hopkins University, 2021). There is now a Chinatown in a suburb of Algiers. Even if Chinese firms offer employment opportunities for locals, there will always be concerns regarding exploitative labor practices and poor working conditions. Chinese firms operating abroad are notoriously lax about labor standards. for instance, Chinese firms working in Africa avoid following local labor laws, apply the same low labor standards common in China, repeatedly violate local minimum wage laws, and fail to pay social security and allowances, besides violations of child labor, illegal overtime, and exposure to hazardous materials and machinery (Brautigam, 2011). In fact, Chinese companies operating in Algeria offer jobs that suit unskilled and uneducated Algerian job seekers, while educated Algerians do not seem to have much opportunity to work in such companies. Strictly speaking, the employment created by Chinese firms tends to be mainly skewed toward male, less-educated workers, who can be employed as security guards, truck drivers, construction workers, janitors, and carpenters at construction sites. Hence, it can be said that the kinds of jobs that are created by Chinese companies do not match the Algerian labor market's needs to curb the persistently high unemployment among educated youths. China's contribution to the Algerian labor market lags far behind knowledge-based job creation and skills development, that are necessary for a thriving economy. It does not generate employment that promotes much-needed technology transfer and, instead, targets the lower-skilled, lower-cost, and lower value-added labor-intensive jobs (Alden and Aggad-Clerx, 2012).

One of the most prominent and notable criticisms of China's presence in Algeria is corruption, which serves to grease the wheels of Chinese business. A key point of Chinese adaptation to Algeria's business climate is China's pragmatic approach in facing local corruption. Chinese companies have been a key player in infrastructure and energy projects in Algeria and turned a blind eye to corruption and bribery, something many foreign investors and companies, including Italian ones, did in order to navigate the process of granting contracts. Corruption scandals and lack of transparency surrounding Chinese infrastructure projects and construction deals in Algeria have impaired Chinese companies' reputation (Elgebeily, 2020). Besides corruption charges made against Japanese, Italian, Swiss, Spanish, Canadian, and Portuguese companies, the East-West Highway scandal also revealed that the China Railway Construction Company (CRCC) delivered bounced checks to more than 15 small Algerian subsidiary enterprises and faced corruption allegations of withholding at least $4.2 million in wages (Alden and Aggad-Clerx, 2012). The lack of oversight and accountability by the Algerian authorities allowed Chinese companies to circumvent transparency and escape accountability (Ghanem and Benabdallah, 2016). In 2012, the Algerian business environment was shaken by the bribery scandal which clouded Huawei and ZTE that were banned from bidding for government contracts for two years after their executives allegedly paid $10 million in bribes to cut corners and win contracts (Farivar, 2019). According to Kowalczyk-Hoyer and Côté-Freemann (2019), Chinese companies are among the least transparent in a sample of 100 companies from 15 emerging markets, and they have been debarred from the World Bank and other multilateral development banks for corrupt practices, such as paying bribes and inflating costs (Hillman, 2019). Chinese companies could not really keep their hands clean in an oil-rich country like Algeria where corruption prevails everywhere; Algeria's economic mismanagement and corrupt business climate provided those companies a safer and more fertile environment to engage in improper acts and corrupt practices because institutional rules are either unclear or politically unenforceable in this climate. According to the 2020 Corruption Perception Index (CPI), released by Transparency International, Algeria is the 104th least corrupt nation out of 180 countries with a score of (36/100) which is slightly below the regional average score of (39/100) (Transparency International, 2021). Algeria remains at a standstill on the CPI due to the lack of political integrity, the existence of non-transparent, non-responsive, and unaccountable institutions, the absence of a separation of powers, dependent judiciaries that lack credibility and the potential to keep the executive branch of government in check, the embezzlement of public funds, the broken trust between the people and their government, the absence of whistleblower protection legislation, the restricted access to information, the limited public participation in decision-making processes, and the stifling of civil society (Al-Shami, 2019; Elgebeily, 2020; Heritage Foundation, 2021). As a result of the Hirak[1] protest movement in 2019, many Algerian political leaders, officials, and businessmen were imprisoned on corruption charges. To date, it seems unlikely that the stolen assets will be recovered, mainly due to the lack of international cooperation and coordination in identifying, tracing, recovering, and returning those assets to Algeria in an effective and expedited manner (Freedom House, 2020).

Regarding the fear of entering an endless cycle of excessive borrowing from China and being subject to Chinese interference, it can be claimed that Algeria is quite far from the disastrous consequences that Pakistan, Sri Lanka, and Ecuador have faced because of borrowing extensively from China under various pretexts and opaque practices (Abdel Ghafar and Jacobs, 2020). In 2002, China provided a loan worth $9 million to Algeria which is far better when compared to other North African countries like Egypt, Morocco, and Tunisia that have received Chinese loans worth $4.181 billion, $1.182 billion, and $132 million, respectively, between 2000 and 2018, and that are already struggling to reduce their external debt burdens (China Africa Research Initiative, Johns Hopkins University, 2021). In other words, the Algerian government enjoys a wider margin of safety than the Egyptian, Moroccan, and Tunisian governments that need to be more vigilant against Chinese debt-trap diplomacy.

Despite all the apprehensions and criticisms surrounding China's presence in Algeria, China expressed its solidarity and support for Algeria in the battle against COVID-19 by sending two batches of medical aid on March 27 and April 15, 2020, respectively (Xinhua, 2020a). Further, China sent medical supplies and equipment and a medical team composed of 20 Chinese medical experts to Algeria, on May 14, 2020, to assist with control efforts (Xinhua, 2020b; Zoubir, 2020b). In fact, China extended a helping hand to Algeria in its time of dire need, when no similar action was taken by the United States or other European partners, especially France. As the old saying goes, "a friend in need is a friend indeed."

6 Conclusion

China has been a trusted economic and political ally of Algeria, which was wise to methodically and gradually cultivate its bilateral ties with China from mainly economic cooperation to a comprehensive strategic cooperative partnership, perhaps as a means of strategic hedging behavior against the United States and the European countries, especially France. China covets the most important markets in the Maghreb, as entry points to European and African markets, and abundant natural resources; Algeria fulfills all these conditions. Although China has gained an impressive and important strategic foothold in Algeria, it has never matched the American and European, particularly French, dominance in the country. France still plays a much stronger role in Algeria, mainly due to its colonial past and close post-independence ties with Algeria.

China has made gigantic steps in increasing its volumes of trade and investment in Algeria; but there are many obstacles and challenges that prevent China from fully realizing its potential in the Algerian market. The acute risk of political instability and social upheavals that has been growing steadily in Algeria creates an uncertain investment climate and introduces the "wait and see" attitude toward investment decisions that China often tends to adopt when markets entail huge risks and this makes the planning and monitoring of investment projects more difficult and expensive. Since the beginning of the Hirak, China has reaffirmed its adherence to the policy of neutrality and noninterference in the internal affairs of Algeria. But if China continues to support any new regime, public mistrust and suspicion will surround China's policies and aims in Algeria.

Despite all the criticisms surrounding China's growing footprint and rise in Africa, China provides an alternative to the unhealthy economic dependency on the West and Western development cooperation; but a number of obstacles stand in the way of greater Sino-Algerian economic cooperation, such as an unfavorable business climate, unnecessarily lengthy bureaucratic procedures, poor enforcement of contracts, the slow rate of land acquisition, an uncertain regulatory environment, ongoing ambiguity, and lack of transparency. There appears to be a vicious circle that stems from the incapacity of the Algerian government to show a strong commitment to promoting a market-friendly environment, express a firm determination to adopt stringent economic reform measures, and pursue wide-ranging structural and institutional reforms. Thus, the Algerian government must develop coherent policies to create an enabling investment climate by easing the constraints on accelerating Chinese investment, particularly in the non-oil sectors. In terms of attracting export-oriented Chinese FDI, this can be done by creating an export processing zone and establishing special economic zones. Furthermore, the Algerian government must find its own path to root out corruption and make more effort to enhance public sector transparency and strengthen accountability in filtering out Chinese investors and companies that have opaque business practices and lack transparency. There is also a need to improve post-investment services to satisfy Chinese investors' needs after they come to Algeria.

Other issues which must be addressed are language barriers and cultural differences that somehow impede the development of relations between China and Algeria. China's cultural presence in Algeria is still weak; similarly, the Algerian culture in China is largely absent (Zoubir, 2021). Very little has been done until now to promote a mutual cultural understanding between China and Algeria. After more than six decades of friendship and cooperation, cultural exchanges lag far behind economic cooperation. The Algerian government needs to nurture the cultural understanding and promote awareness and understanding of Chinese culture and language among people in Algeria by seeking and allowing the establishment of a Chinese Confucius Institute and hosting Chinese cultural centers and programs as all these efforts will help create a favorable environment for intensive cooperation in all spheres.

Note

1 Hirak is an Arabic term, meaning the large-scale protest movement that broke out in February 2019 in Algeria after the ailing 82-year-old President Abdelaziz Bouteflika declared he would seek a fifth term in power. The Hirak movement successfully resulted in Bouteflika's resignation

and continued as marchers demanded the departure of the entire ruling elite, political change, and root and branch reform. However, with the pandemic and the implementation of the government's roadmap, the hirak receded and only a few of its demands have been met.

References

Abdel Ghafar, A. and Jacobs, A. (2020). China in the Mediterranean: Implications of Expanding Sino-North Africa Relations. Brookings Doha Center. Available at: www.brookings.edu/research/china-in-the-mediterranean-implications-of-expanding-sino-north-africa-relations/ (accessed August 24, 2020).

Abdulai, D. N. (2017). *Chinese Investment in Africa: How African Countries Can Position Themselves to Benefit from China's Foray into Africa*. New York: Routledge.

AfDB/OECD (2005). *African Economic Outlook 2004/2005*. Paris: OECD Development Centre.

Alden, C. and Aggad-Clerx, F. (2012). Chinese Investments and Employment Creation in Algeria and Egypt. African Development Bank, Economic Brief, pp. 1–24.

Al-Shami, S. (2019). Perceptions of Corruption on the Rise across MENA. Arab Barometer, December 12. Available at: https://blogs.worldbank.org/arabvoices/arab-barometer-report-perceptions-corruption-rise-across-mena (accessed September 7, 2020).

Belhadj, I., Sun, D. and Zoubir, Y. (2015). China in North Africa: A Strategic Partnership, in Y. H. Zoubir and G. White (Eds.), *North African Politics: Change and Continuity*. London: Routledge. pp. 329–349.

Brautigam, D. (2011). *The Dragon's Gift: The Real Story of China in Africa*. Reprint edn. Oxford: Oxford University Press.

Castel, V., Mejia, P. X. and Kolster, J. (2011). The BRICs in North Africa: Changing the Name of the Game? *North Africa Quarterly Analytical*, First Annual Quarter: 1–20.

China Africa Research Initiative, Johns Hopkins University (2021). Chinese Workers in Africa. Available at: www.sais-cari.org/data-chinese-workers-in-africa; (accessed March 5, 2021).

Copper, J. F. (2016). China's Foreign Aid and Investment Diplomacy to African Nations—I. In *China's Foreign Aid and Investment Diplomacy*, vol. III. New York: Palgrave Macmillan, pp. 1–41.

Elgebeily, S. (2020). A Comparative Analysis of Corruption and Constitutionalism in the Muslim-Majority MENA States of Algeria, Morocco, and Egypt, in C. M.Fombad and N. Steytler (Eds.), *Corruption and Constitutionalism in Africa*. Oxford: Oxford University Press, pp. 110–138.

Farivar, M. (2019). Bribery, Corruption Charges Follow Huawei around World. VoA News, February 11. Available at: www.voanews.com/east-asia-pacific/bribery-corruption-charges-follow-huawei-around-world (accessed September 6, 2020).

Freedom House (2020). Freedom in the World 2020: Algeria. Available at: https://freedomhouse.org/country/algeria/freedom-world/2020 (accessed September 7, 2020).

Ghanem, D. and Benabdallah, L. (2016). The China Syndrome. Carnegie Middle East Center, November 18. Available at: https://carnegie-mec.org/diwan/66145 (accessed September 6, 2020).

Grimmett, R. F. (2003). *Conventional Arms Transfers to Developing Nations, 1994–2001*. Hauppauge, NY: Nova Publishers.

Heritage Foundation (2021). Index of Economic Freedom 2020. Available at: www.heritage.org/index/country/algeria (accessed March 5, 2021).

Hillman, J. (2019). 1MDB Probe Shines Uncomfortable Light on China's Belt and Road. *Nikkei Asian Review*, January 18. Available at: https://asia.nikkei.com/Opinion/1MDB-probe-shines-uncomfortable-light-on-China-s-Belt-and-Road (accessed September 6, 2020).

IMF (2018). Algeria Selected Issues. IMF Country Report No. 18/169. Washington, DC: IMF.

Kowalczyk-Hoyer, B. and Côté-Freemann, S. (2013). Transparency in Corporate Reporting: Assessing Emerging Market Multinationals. Transparency International. Available at: http://issuu.com/transparencyinternational/docs/2013_trac_emergingmarketmultination?e=2496456/5251512 (accessed September 6, 2020).

Lisimba, A. F. (2020). *China's Trade and Investment in Africa: Impact on Development, Employment Generation and Transfer of Technology*. Singapore: Palgrave Macmillan.

Olimat, M. (2013). *China and the Middle East: From Silk Road to Arab Spring*. London: Routledge.

Oxford Business Group (2014). *The Report: Algeria 2014*. Oxford: Oxford Business Group.

Shinn, D. H. and Eisenman, J. (2012). *China and Africa: A Century of Engagement*. Philadelphia, PA: University of Pennsylvania Press.

Transparency International (2021). Corruption Perceptions Index. Available at: www.transparency.org/en/cpi (accessed March 5, 2021).

U.S. Department of State (2019). Investment Climate Statements: Algeria. A Report of the U.S. Department of State, U.S. Embassy in Algeria. Available at: www.state.gov/reports/2019-investment-climate-statements/algeria/; (accessed August 24, 2020).

World Bank (2020). *Doing Business 2020*. Washington, DC: World Bank.

World Bank (2021a). *Algeria Economic Monitor, Spring 2021: Accelerating Reforms to Protect the Algerian Economy*. Washington, DC: World Bank.

World Bank (2021b). *Worldwide Governance Indicators*. Available at: https://databank.worldbank.org/source/worldwide-governance-indicators (accessed March 5, 2021).

Xinhua (2020a). Algeria's COVID-19 Deaths Surpass 1,500. August 31. Available at: www.xinhua net.com/english/africa/2020-08/31/c_139329758.htm (accessed September 13, 2020).

Xinhua (2020b). Chinese Medical Team Arrives in Algeria to Help Fight Corona Virus. May 15. Available at: www.xinhuanet.com/english/2020-05/15/c_139057780.htm (accessed September 13, 2020).

Zeng, D. Z. (2015). Global Experiences with Special Economic Zones: Focus on China and Africa. World Bank Policy Research Working Paper No. 7240. Washington, DC: World Bank.

Zhang, C. (2010). China's Energy Diplomacy in Africa: The Convergence of National and Corporate Interests, in C. M. Dent (Ed.), *China and Africa Development Relations*. London: Routledge, pp. 143–162.

Zoubir, Y.H. (2020a) Expanding Sino–Maghreb Relations: Morocco and Tunisia, Chatham House Research Paper, February 2020. https://www.chathamhouse.org/publication/expanding-sino-maghreb-relations-morocco-and-tunisia

Zoubir, Y. H. (2020b) China's 'Health Silk Road' Diplomacy in the MENA, Konrad Adenauer Stiftung, Med Dialogue Series No. 27, Research Paper, pp. 1–14. Available at: www.kas.de/documents/282499/282548/MDS_China+Health+Silk+Road+Diplomacy.pdf/

Zoubir, Y. H. (2021). China's Relations with Algeria: From Revolutionary Friendship to Comprehensive Strategic Partnership, in A. Abdel-Ghafar (Ed.), *China and North Africa*. New York: I.B. Tauris, pp. 126–165.

21

CHINA-EGYPT RELATIONS

A Model for Comprehensive Strategic Partnership

Bassem Elmaghraby

1 Introduction

Among the countries of the Middle East and North Africa (MENA), Egypt is a special partner for the Chinese government, whether for cultural, geopolitical, or economic reasons; Egypt is recognized as a pivotal country with a great history and a bright future (Foreign Ministry of the PRC, 2021), an extraordinary geopolitical and international position, is a promising rising power, and a fine representative of Arab, African, and Islamic countries. Some scholars have described it as a "strategic pivot" and a "regional priority," while others have considered it as "the most important regional country" for the Chinese government (Bakhtin et al., 2013: 17–18).

Nevertheless, some politicians doubt Egypt's ability to upgrade its relations with China or to achieve significant development rates due to the huge economic, political, and security challenges, such as the rising inflation rate, the Ethiopian Renaissance Dam, and terrorism, especially after two successive revolutions in 2011 and 2013 (Saif and Ghoneim, 2013: 2–12; Marks, 2013, 2–14; Dunne, 2020, 1–2). On the other hand, some scholars have suspected the ability of Chinese mega-projects to achieve real development for the MINA countries (Horn, Reinhart, and Trebesch, 2019: 5–76; Hurley, Morris, and Portelance, 2018: 11–24; Adeniran et al., 2021: 12–16, 28–30). This chapter disputes such arguments by claiming that Egyptian-Chinese relations have evolved dramatically, despite the aforesaid challenges, thanks to their mutual understanding, common interests, and a "win-win" strategy.

Accordingly, several questions will be addressed in this chapter, including how have the relations between Egypt and China evolved? What is the current situation? How important and at what level is their cooperation? In which fields? How does the Covid-19 pandemic affect their relationship? What about the future of their relationship?

2 An Overview of Recent History

Both Egypt and China are among the most ancient and richest civilizations in the world, the two civilizations have converged commercially, politically, and culturally throughout ages; the similarity between the two countries' historical experiences and the convergence

DOI: 10.4324/9781003048404-24

of their civilizations were crucial factors in allowing their relationship to flourish (State Information Service, 2018: 6–8).

In ancient times, trade, culture, and literature attracted the two countries to each other; then, the old Silk Road linked the two nations commercially, economically, culturally, and scientifically (El-Saadany, 2014; State Information Service, 2014).

In the modern era, the establishment of the People's Republic of China (PRC) in 1949, coupled with the success of the Egyptian "23 July" revolution in 1952, have led to greater convergence between the tendencies of the two countries, especially in defending Third World issues. The establishment of diplomatic relations between the two countries in 1956 made Egypt the first Arab and African country to recognize the PRC (Rózsa, 2020: 2–3); this step was a milestone in China's international relations during the Cold War climate, where Egypt's leading role among the Arab and African countries had a major impact on the international arena, that led to the successive recognitions of the PRC.

In contemporary times, the Belt and Road Initiative (BRI), the Comprehensive Strategic Partnership agreement, and the compatibility of the strategic plans of the two countries have taken their relations to an unprecedented level.

Egypt-Sino relations have gone through many stages, which can be depicted as follows: Chinese silk was used in the textile industry in Egypt, and porcelain pots were the second-largest Chinese export to Egypt for ages; on the other hand, Egyptian cotton was an important commodity for China. The two countries have suffered from the scourge of war and colonialism, they both are seeking to rebuild their glories, and they also aim to restore their international position.

Establishing New China (PRC) in 1949 converged with establishing the first republic in Egypt in 1953. On May, 30 1956, Egypt announced the establishment of diplomatic relations with the PRC in defiance of US pressure and displeasure.

On July 26, 1956, China supported the historical decision of Egypt's president Nasser to nationalize the Suez Canal Company; then, on November 1 condemned the tripartite aggression against Egypt, coupled with huge demonstrations in China to support Egypt.

During the Indo-Chinese War, President Nasser sought to mediate by communicating with the leaders of both sides.

As a result of the cultural revolution in 1966, China withdrew its ambassador from the entire region except for Egypt (State Information Service, 2018).

On April 2, 1983, the first official visit of an Egyptian president to China was by President Mubarak, followed by the first official visit of a Chinese president to Egypt by the Chinese president Li Xiannian on March 17, 1986.

In 1999, during President Mubarak's visit to China, he called jointly with President Jiang Zemin for the establishment of "the China-Egypt relationship of strategic cooperation", to be the first Chinese strategic agreement in the region. This agreement was an excellent starting point for developing the two countries' relations in the twenty-first century.

3 Cultural Relations (Media, Tourism)

Once China is mentioned, Arabs and Muslims instantly remember the famous statement "Seek knowledge even if you have to go as far as China" (Alharbi, 2019). This well-known phrase exposes the importance of knowledge and the roots of cultural relations of the Arab world with China.

As cited above, the cultural relations between Egypt and China have developed rapidly throughout ages, during the 1930s, a group of Chinese Muslim students was dispatched to study in Cairo at Al-Azhar University "The third oldest university in history and the largest Islamic religious institution in the world, founded in 970" (Al-Azhar University, n.d.; Scimago Research Centers, n.d.) to develop Chinese relations and understanding with Egypt and other Muslim and Arab countries (Benite, 2008: 5–21; Chen, 2014: 24–51). Most of these students later became intellectual and political leaders and translators, and they provided great works and translations, such as the Confucian Analects translation into Arabic, and the translations of the Qur'an and other religious and Arabic literature into Chinese. Among them, Ma Jian served as the first professor of Arabic and Islamic studies at Peking University (PKU) from 1946 and was a translator for Chairman Mao (Chebbi, 2005: 378–383). These works and translations represent a considerable cultural legacy that helped the two sides learn more about each other and enhanced their cultural understanding (Cieciura, 2015).

In order to facilitate and enhance the cultural exchange between the two nations in a sustainable way, the Egyptian Cultural Office was inaugurated in China in November 2011. During President Xi's visit to Cairo in 2016, which marks the 60th anniversary of the official establishment of diplomatic relations between Egypt and the PRC, the two countries announced the year 2016 as the Egyptian-Chinese cultural year, "the year of Chinese culture in Egypt and the year of Egyptian culture in China." About 102 events were planned to be held during 2016, 63 events in China, and another 39 in Egypt (Anon., 2016b).

There are two Confucius Institutes in Egypt; in 2007, the first one was founded in Cairo University in collaboration with the PKU and the China National Office for Teaching Chinese as a Foreign Language, the second was founded in 2008 in Suez Canal University (SCU) in collaboration with the Beijing Language and Culture University; besides, Confucius Institutes have established branches in many other places around the country, including Benha University, Pharos University, and Fayoum University, Ain Shams University (Ain Shams University, 2019), accompanied by other branches in many high, preparatory, and elementary schools (Anon., 2016a).

The Confucius Institute in Cairo was awarded the "Model Confucius Institute" international prize in 2016; in addition, it also was awarded the prize of the best institute for HSK exams twice, in 2017 and 2020 (Cairo University, 2018).

The Egyptian Chinese University (ECU), founded in 2013, serves as the only Chinese university in the Middle East and is considered the first technological and non-traditional university which depends on productive technology (Egyptian Chinese University, 2021); in the same context, a new Chinese technological faculty at the SCU was inaugurated in 2018 (Suez Canal University, 2018).

Another important step was to include Mandarin Chinese as an elective foreign language in pre-university schools in Egypt in 2020 (*Al-Ahram Journal*, 2020).

Accordingly, in an exception to Benabdallah's argument which stated "while China–Arab state relations show robust economic exchange, they lag in terms of people-to-people exchanges and cultural diplomacy, two strong features of China–Africa relations" (Benabdallah, 2018: 10–11), the Chinese relations with Egypt show robust development in both ways.

An important part of the cultural relations between Egypt and China focuses on the religious aspect, due to the huge Muslim population within the Chinese community and the importance of Egypt and Al-Azhar for the Muslim world; on many occasions, President Xi has emphasized China's eagerness to continue "inter-civilization dialogue and roundtable on eradicating extremism to promote intercultural communication and religious discussions" (Jalal, 2014: 19), he also frequently stressed the need to reach a high level of tolerance, brotherhood, and positivity through openness to religions and modern religious interpretations during his discourse of "friendship between ancient civilizations" and the cultural links with Muslim states. The establishment of "the China–Arab Research Centre on Reform and Development" in 2017 is considered an implementation of this policy (SISU, 2017). In the same context, the Egyptian government cooperated with its Chinese counterpart in addressing the Uyghurs issue and extradited many Uyghur students to China (Batke 2017; Mahmut, 2019: 29–32).

Most of these cultural and people-to-people relations have been linked with the BRI since 2013, such as the project to cross-translate 100 Arabic and Chinese books, hundreds of educational exchange programs, workshops, mutual visits and invitations for leaders, and thousands of training opportunities, whether on the African or Arab level (Chinese Embassy, 2018).

4 Economic Cooperation

Several economic indicators that can be used to better understand the situation of Egyptian and Chinese economies and their economic cooperation level are as follows. Foreign direct investment (FDI) is an important economic indicator of capital movements; in Egypt, FDI witnessed a slow growth from $598 million in 1995 to $1.235 billion in 2000, then a swing period till 2004 ($1.253 billion) due to the adoption of five-year plans. The next five years witnessed a historical increase to reach the peak in 2007 of $11.578 billion ($10.325 billion increase in only three years), which is attributed to the structural reform plans, including the reform of the financial sector, monetary policies, the tax system, and privatization, and business legislation. But this economic reform did not last long and turned into a dramatic decrease in the following three years to $9.5 billion in 2008, $6.7 billion in 2009, $6.4 billion in 2010, and finally reached a historical decrease in 2011 of -$482.7 million due to the government's failure to share the wealth and growth benefits with the population, especially with the growing problems of unemployment and poverty; in other words, the government failed to achieve a satisfactory political reform, which in turn led to the revolution of 25 January 2011. Since then, a steady increase in FDI has been achieved, reaching $9.01 billion in 2019 due to the new political and economic reform plans in Egypt (Figure 21.1).

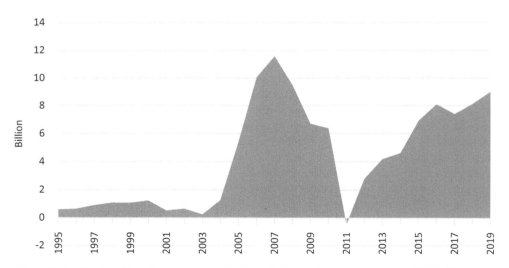

Figure 21.1 Foreign direct investment, net inflows (balance of payments, current US$): Egypt

In China, a steady slow FDI growth has been achieved from $35.85 billion in 1995 to $68.12 billion in 2004; with a faster growth reaching $171.54 billion in 2008; the biggest increase in one year was in 2010 (by $112.65 billion) reaching $243.71 billion compared to $131.06 billion in 2009; followed by a swing period of ups and downs until it reached $155.82 billion in 2019. There are two peaks: the highest in 2013 of $290.93 billion, the second in 2011 of $280.08 billion (Figures 21.2 and 21.3).

In 2020, Egypt's FDI increased by $1.6 billion in September, compared with an increase of $1.5 billion in the previous quarter. China's FDI increased by $86.2 billion in December, compared with an increase of $58.1 billion in the previous quarter. Tracking the development of GDP value is an important indicator of the economic situation in both nations; in general, both countries have achieved a steady increase in the GDP value in the last two decades, but China was faster and more stable than Egypt.

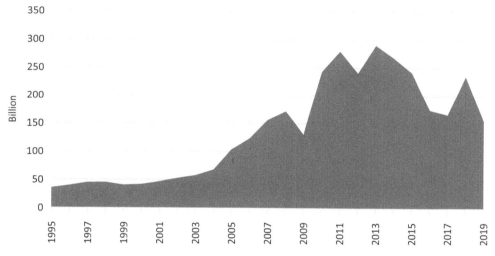

Figure 21.2 Foreign direct investment, net inflows (balance of payments, current US$): China

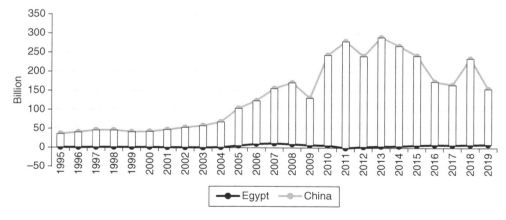

Figure 21.3 Foreign direct investment, net inflows (balance of payments, current US$): Egypt vs China, 1995–2019

Source: Based on data extracted from the Central Bank of Egypt, China's State Administration of Foreign Exchange, and the World Bank at: https://data.worldbank.org/

In Egypt, the GDP increased slowly from $60.56 billion in 1995 to $78.78 billion in 2004, then started to increase faster until it reached the peak in 2016 of $332.44 billion; in 10 years the GDP had tripled from $107.43 billion in 2006 to $332.44 billion in 2016, but 2017 witnessed a huge drop to $235.73 billion, which could be attributed to the economic reform measures, especially the floating of the exchange rate; then, resumed growing to record $249.71 billion in 2018 and a great jump in 2019 by $303.1 billion with an increase of $53.4 billion in one year (Figure 21.4).

In China, the GDP has increased constantly over time, but the current decade was faster than the previous one, where it recorded $734.55 billion in 1995 and $2.29 trillion in 2005, compared to $5.1 trillion in 2009 and $14.28 trillion in 2019 (more than $9.18 trillion increase in 10 years) (Figures 21.5 and 21.6).

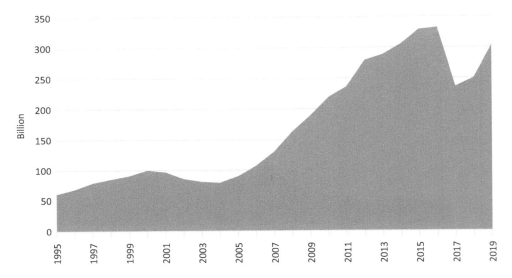

Figure 21.4 GDP (current US$): Egypt

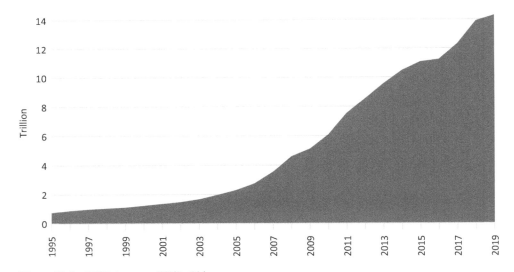

Figure 21.5 GDP (current US$): China

For a more accurate assessment of the economic development in both nations, the annual percentage growth rate of GDP should be highlighted. The GDP growth rate for Egypt increased from 4.64 percent in 1995 to 6.05 percent in 1999, in contrast, it decreased from 10.95 percent in 1995 to 7.66 percent in 1999 for China; then the growth rate began to increase in China until it reached the peak to record 14.23 percent in 2007, followed by a huge drop in 2008 to record 9.65 percent (almost 5 percent decrease in one year), then continued to decrease until it reached the lowest record in three decades of 5.95 percent in 2019. In Egypt the growth rate was fluctuating, dropping down from 6.37 percent in 2000 to 2.39 percent in 2002, then rising up to reach its peak in 2008 of 7.16 percent, then down again to record the lowest rate in two decades of 1.76 percent in 2011, due to the effect of the revolution. Most importantly to note is that the growth rate has been increasing constantly in Egypt since 2011 to reach 5.56 percent by 2019 due to the political reform policies of the new governments (Figure 21.7).

In 2020, China's GDP expanded 6.5 percent year-on-year (YoY) in December, following a growth of 4.9 percent in the previous quarter, while the record low was -6.8 percent in March 2020 due to COVID-19. On the other hand, Egypt's GDP contracted 1.7 percent YoY in June, following a growth of 5.0 percent in the previous quarter, while the record low was -4.3 percent in March 2011 due to the revolution (Circular Economy Innovation Communities, 2021).Measuring the commercial cooperation or bilateral trade between Egypt and China offers a very important perspective to evaluate the level of their economic relations; in general, both imports from and exports to China have been rising steadily with Egypt over the previous three decades, but the imports were more stable than exports. Imports increased relatively slowly from $295.9 million in 1995 to $661.3 million in 2004, then started to increase much faster over time to reach $9.7 billion in 2015 and recorded its peak in 2019 of $12 billion; in 2020, imports reached about $9.1 billion despite the outbreak of COVID-19, (Figure 21.8).

On the other hand, exports also increased relatively slowly from $6.3 million in 1995 to $129.7 million in 2007, then started to increase faster over time to reach $747.1 million in 2012 and recorded its peak in 2018 of $1 billion, but exports were more up and down as some extreme values were recorded, such as $221.4 million in 2002 and the second peak in

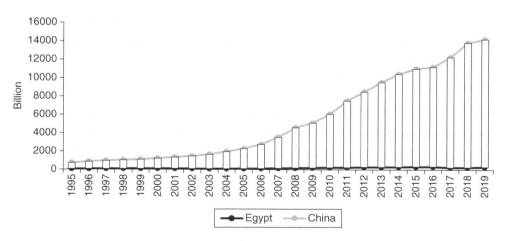

Figure 21.6 GDP (current US$): Egypt vs China, 1995–2019

Source: Based on data extracted from the IMF and the World Bank at: https://data.worldbank.org/ and: www.imf.org/

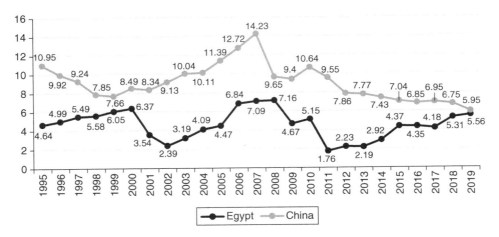

Figure 21.7 GDP (current US$): Egypt vs China, 1995–2019

Source: Based on data extracted from the IMF and the World Bank at: https://data.worldbank.org/ and www.imf.org/

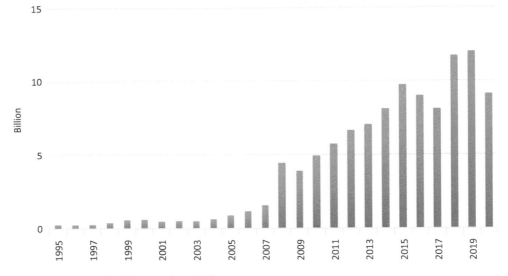

Figure 21.8 Egyptian imports from China

2009 of $975.1 million. There were some downs against the mainstream, such as in 2014 of $329.9 million and 2019 of $556.9 million; in 2020, exports reached $603.1 million, with a $46.2 million increase over the previous year (Figure 21.9).

It is very easy to spot the trade imbalance here, as shown in the gap between imports and exports, which obviously increased over time and has been expanding fast since 2005 (Figure 21.10).

In 2020, the bilateral trade was valued at $9.7 billion, the trade balance recorded was -$8.4 billion; China was the 11th largest export market for Egypt (almost 2.2 percent of Egyptian exports) and the first largest import market for Egypt (about 15 percent

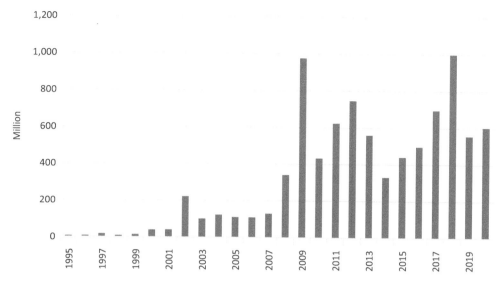

Figure 21.9 Egyptian exports to China

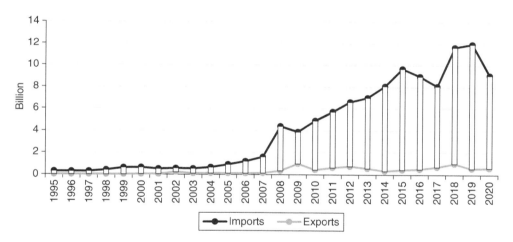

Figure 21.10 Egypt's trade in goods with China, 1995–2020

Source: Based on data extracted from the UN Comtrade database at: https://comtrade.un.org/ See also: https://tradingeconomics.com/egypt/imports/china

of Egyptian imports). Mineral fuels, oils, and other related distillation products were the most exported Egyptian goods to China in 2020, totaling $372.2 million, followed by edible fruits, nuts, peel of citrus fruit, and melons totaling $78.2 million; then in third place, stones, plaster, cement, asbestos, mica, and other related products, totaling $20.6 million; the top ten goods exported from Egypt to China can be summarized in Figure 21.11.

On the other hand, electrical goods and electronic equipment were the most imported goods from China to Egypt in 2020, totaling $2.1 billion, followed by nuclear reactors,

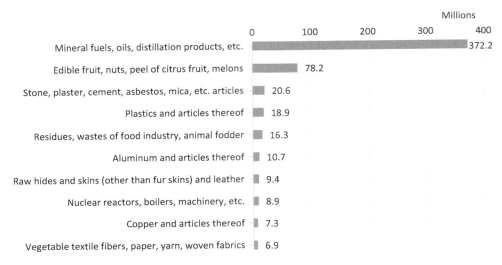

Figure 21.11 Top ten Egyptian exports of goods to China in 2020

Source: Based on data extracted from the UN Comtrade database at: https://comtrade.un.org/ See also: https://data.wto.org/

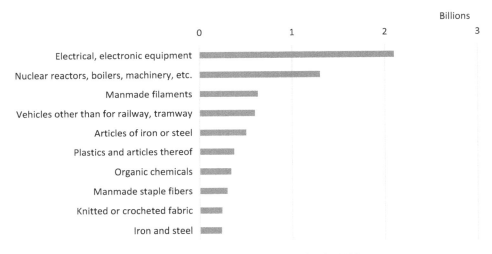

Figure 21.12 Top ten Egyptian imports of goods from China in 2020

Source: Based on data extracted from the UN Comtrade database at: https://comtrade.un.org/ See also: https://oec.world/en

boilers, and machinery, totaling $1.3 billion; then, in third place, manmade filaments, totaling $629.5 million; the top ten imported goods from China to Egypt are summarized in Figure 21.12.

The volume of bilateral trade between the two countries has witnessed a relatively steady rise during the previous three decades; it has developed from $302 million in 1995 to $679.5 million in 2000, $1.02 billion in 2005, $5.33 billion in 2010, $10.14 billion in 2015 (Al-Naggar, 2016), then $12.56 billion in 2019. It dropped to $9.7 billion, as mentioned

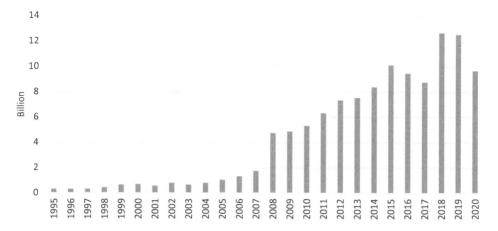

Figure 21.13 Bilateral trade between Egypt and China, 1995–2020
Source: Based on data extracted from the UN Comtrade database at: https://comtrade.un.org/

above, due to the effect of COVID-19. The highest bilateral trade volume was recorded in 2018 of $12.7 billion and the second peak was in 2019. This makes China already the largest trading partner of Egypt (Figure 21.13) (Doyon et al., 2017: 8–9).

In addition to the above-mentioned economic indicators, many other important activities display the level of economic cooperation between the two countries, for example, various agreements have been signed between the two countries to enhance their economic cooperation, including agreements in 1964, 1985, 1995, 1997, and 2006 (Abu-Hatab et al., 2012: 314–326). In May 2012, another agreement was signed, in which China extended $90 million, 700 police cars, and two containers of search instruments (State Information Service, n.d.).

In January 2012, the Jushi Egypt Business Group, in the fiberglass industry, was founded in the Suez Economic Zone, the project had a total investment of $521 million with 200k tons capacity, which was unique in Africa; the first phase accounted for $223 million investment with 80k tons annual capacity, employing about 800 Egyptian workers and using the most advanced ultra-large tank furnace production technology in the world. The project exports 95 percent of its products to Europe, the Middle East, and India (Luo et al., 2018: 8; Jushi, n.d.).

On December 30, 2013, the two parties announced the establishment of the Egyptian-Chinese Chamber of Commerce to boost bilateral trade and investment exchange.

On April 19, 2015, a joint-cooperation protocol was signed to establish a branch of the Beijing Institute of Technology in the city of Ismailia, in partnership with Misr Elkheir Foundation and SCU; the project aimed to provide qualified educated workers for the Egyptian job market (Ministry of Communications and Information Technology, 2015).

In March 2015, during the Egypt Economic Development Conference, several agreements were signed with Chinese companies in the field of electricity and power with a total investment of $1.8 billion, to develop the National Electricity Network and establish electric transformer stations. Meanwhile, the Egyptian Ministry of Transport signed two agreements with two Chinese companies to produce trains with a total investment of $500 million and to operate and manage the electric train service (Alexandria to Abu Qir).

In 2019, telecommunication companies in Egypt partnered with Huawei to build 5G networks, despite some American warnings (Lons et al., 2019).

China is one of the main contributors to the new Egyptian mega-projects, including the construction investments in the New Administrative Capital, such as the highest building in Africa and other buildings (Magdy, 2018; State Information Service, 2018: 30); also, the Chinese investment in the railway project of 10th of Ramadan city. Tens of thousands of job opportunities for Egyptians have been created by Chinese companies' investment and projects in the Suez Canal Zone (Xia and Caicen, 2016; 109–126). Therefore, probably the most important aspects of the new chapter in the Egyptian-Chinese relations are the BRI, the Suez Canal Zone (this will cover around 9.12 km^2 with around $2 trillion investments), the New Administrative Capital (170K acres, will have a population of 6.5 million people, over $11.2 billion Chinese investments) (*Egypt Independent*, 2017).

On the other hand, many scholars—especially Western ones—criticize Chinese foreign investments in the region claiming it is a pretext for the debt trap (Behuria, 2018: 77–102; Mobley, 2019: 55–68); although the same criticisms have been directed to the situation in Egypt, the statistics prove the weakness of such arguments, as in 2019 the total Egyptian external debt amounted to $109.36 billion (only 1 percent higher than the 2018 total of $108.69 billion; Abdel-Razek, 2020) and China's share of this debt is only $6.5 billion (Salem, 2020). In 2020, the total external debt hit $123.5 billion (Al-Feqi, 2021; 95) while in 2021 it reached $129.19 billion in January and $137.85 billion in July, but the Chinese share of this debt is still only about $7.7 billion, the remainder of the debt is distributed among other creditors, including Arab countries, Western countries, and multilateral institutions, such as the International Monetary Fund, the International Bank for Reconstruction and Development, and the European Investment Bank (Central Bank of Egypt, 2021; Hussein, 2021; Mounir, 2021; *Trading Economics*, 2021). The former Egyptian Prime Minister Essam Sharaf has confirmed this viewpoint in an interview with CGTN, in which he described the debt trap as a "jealous attempt by the West to slow down the success of BRI" (CGTN, 2021).

Theoretically, some scholars have compared the Egyptian current model of development with the Chinese model, arguing that the Chinese development miracle is a result of the economic reform policies of the Chinese leaders especially Deng Xiaoping's strategy (1978–1992), in which great attention was paid to the infrastructures and industries to attract foreign investments (*Al-Ahram Journal*, 2019), and have compared that with the economic reform of the El-Sisi regime—also called the "Look East" policy (Jun, 2016: 75–89)—as it also pays great attention to the infrastructure, industry, and mega-projects as well as attracting foreign investment through economic incentives and economic reform policies such as floating the exchange rate, improving the credit rating, and returning the trust of international financial organizations.

Copying the details of the development model of any other developing country is very difficult as each country faces different environments, challenges, values, and experiences; therefore, adopting an appropriate model that best fits the country usually requires merging different models and learning the lessons from the experiences of others. Consequently, the reform program in Egypt adopted since 2016 has combined some characteristics of the Chinese model, such as balancing between central control and economic openness and liberalization, creating a favorable climate to attract investments, and providing high-quality workers through training and high-level education, as well as some characteristics of the Western or decentralized model of development, such as reducing state involvement in favor of the private sector and boosting the transparency of state-owned enterprises.

In fact, promoting or praising the Chinese development model is favorable to the Egyptian regime in many ways; economically, it provides proof that adopting a patriotic model of development that suits the uniqueness of the system and the state's traditions, values, or needs is the best choice, not necessarily a Western model of development. Accordingly, it provides answers to the criticism of some governmental economic policies, such as subsidies, external debts, and fund distribution. Politically, it lends a kind of legitimacy to the government's activities and emphasizes the importance of stability, national security, production, construction, and development, at the expense of other aspects (Winter and Ella, 2019: 3–5).

In addition, China's involvement and its role in the region are growing over time, in 2009, it became the largest trading partner of Africa, with a total trade volume of $91.07 billion, surpassing the USA (China-Africa Research Initiative, 2017); in 2016, China became the largest investor in the Middle East with about $29.5 billion (Quero, 2020: 86–104), in 2017, China surpassed the USA as the top importer of crude oil worldwide, with 8.4 million barrels per day (US Energy Information Administration, 2018); in 2017, China's consumption of energy reached 4.48 billion metric tons of standard coal, its growing demand for energy resources is pushing it toward more dependence on the Arab countries' supplies (Han and Rossi, 2018).

5 Political Relations

The development of presidential visits may show the growing cooperation level between the two nations: in March 1986, President Li Xiannian conducted the first visit of a Chinese President to Egypt; in December 1989, President Yang Shangkun visited Cairo; in April 1983, former President Hosni Mubarak conducted the first visit of an Egyptian President to China (he visited it in 1976 and 1980 as Vice President), then he visited Beijing again in 1990, 1992, 1994, 1999, 2002, and 2006; former President Jiang Zemin visited Cairo twice in May 1996 and April 2000; in August 2012, former President Mohamed Morsi chose Beijing as his first destination outside the Arab world (PRC Embassy in Egypt, 2004; *The National*, 2012).

Since the new regime in Egypt came to power in 2014, presidential visits have witnessed a significant increase: in six years President Abdel-Fattah El-Sisi has visited China six times and met with President Xi eight times, including accepting the Chinese invitations to the Egyptian President to participate in international summits, such as BRICS, the G20, the China-Africa Summit, and the Belt and Road Forum for International Cooperation; while President Xi Jinping visited Egypt in 2016 (Abd-Elaleem, 2019; Elmaghraby, 2020: 145–150). Arguably, the shift in Egypt's political regime, coupled with the US unwanted interference and sharp reduction of US aid, has provided an opportunity for China to play a greater role in the region, whether at the economic and investment level or even at the security and stability level.

In the twenty-first century, Egypt-China relations began a new chapter that's based on a strategic partnership and cooperation, particularly after the 1999 Partnership Agreement which opened the way for further cooperation in various fields.

In 2000, the Forum on China-Africa Cooperation (FOCAC) was founded as a multilateral platform to coordinate China-Africa relations, it includes 53 African states plus the Commission of the African Union (US Institute of Peace, 2020: 12). Egypt hosted the Forum in 2009 and shared its presidency with China in from 2006 to 2012 (State Information Service, 2018: 44).

In 2004, the China Arab States Cooperation Forum (CASCF) was founded during President Hu Jintao's visit to Cairo, to guide China-Arab relations, it includes the 22 member countries of the Arab League. Egypt hosted the First Ministerial Meeting of CASCF (BRICS Policy Center, 2016).

Both forums have enhanced relations between China, on one side, and Egypt, the Arab states, and African nations, on the other. They also play important political and economic roles, but the economic role of CASCF is relatively more important, while the political role of FOCAC is comparatively weightier, whereas CASCF takes place "mainly" at the ministerial level rather than at the summit level of the African forum, which also provides a stage for highlighting Chinese contribution to global peace and security (Alden, 2014); China-Africa trade was valued at about $170 billion in 2017, compared with nearly $197 billion of trade between China and the Arab states and growing rapidly ($244 billion was recorded in 2018) (Cheng, 2016: 51; Ministry of Commerce of the PRC, 2018; Pepa, 2018: 21–22).

An important aspect of the political relations between China and Egypt, as well as other Arab or Muslim countries, is the Chinese interest in maintaining stability in the region due to two main concerns. First, to safeguard its interests in the BRI; second, regarding the Chinese Muslims in Xinjiang (Benabdallah, 2018: 5). These two concerns are linked to China's national and regional security and have become a driving force of the Chinese policy toward the region (Zenz, 2018: 5–23). A very clear example showing how the instability in the region may affect Chinese interests is the case of Libya, where more than 35,000 Chinese nationals were evacuated with massive investment losses, resulting from the 2011 conflict and its consequences for the Libyan regime. Consequently, after the Chinese elites learned that the lesson the hard way, they played a more active role in similar cases, such as the Syrian conflict, where China used 10 vetoes in the UN Security Council, out of only 17 vetoes throughout the history of the UNSC (about 60 percent), in favor of the Syrian regime (Elmaghraby, 2018: 27–54; UN Dag Hammarskjold Library, 2021).

China is the economic partner of most of the MENA states, rather than entering into an alliance, to avoid any political commitments and get itself out of any political skirmishes in such a complicated region. This partnership is hierarchical with five levels:

1. Friendly Cooperative Partnership;
2. Cooperative Partnership;
3. Comprehensive Cooperative Partnership;
4. Strategic Partnership;
5. Comprehensive Strategic Partnership.

China has signed a Strategic Partnership agreement with eight MENA countries (Djibouti, Iraq, Jordan, Kuwait, Morocco, Oman, Qatar, and Turkey), and a Comprehensive Strategic Partnership with five others (Egypt, Algeria, Iran, the KSA, and the UAE); Egypt was the first MENA country to sign a partnership agreement with China in 1999, then a Strategic Partnership in 2012, followed by the Comprehensive Strategic Partnership in 2014, while the rest signed their agreements after 2014, with only one exception, Turkey, that signed their agreement in 2010; which indicates that China perceives these five countries as the most important in the region, with Egypt having priority among them (Fulton, 2019: 4).

Despite the American recommendations to involve China in the security arrangements in the Middle East, China is reluctant to raise the level of security cooperation with any country in the region, to avoid being part of any conflict, which may affect its economic interests and its reputation as a peaceful friendly country, as well as allaying the US concerns regarding the Chinese military presence in the region. This policy is described by some scholars as a "wary dragon," but the Middle East is a complex region loaded with conflicts of interest, so what would China do if events escalated between two or more countries and it had to choose which party to support? This question needs further consideration and analysis, an example that may be applicable here is the Renaissance Dam crisis between Egypt and Ethiopia.

Noteworthy, the argument that "American presence to ensure security stability in the region is serving Chinese interests" is not necessarily true, where the conflict between China and the USA is primarily economic, only secondary political. The US presence in the region is not necessarily a guarantee of stability, rather it may fuel and escalate the conflicts, most clearly the disagreement between the two sides in the Syrian and Libyan crises (Scobell and Nader, 2016: 3–80).

The counter-terrorism issue has occupied a large portion of the debate between the two countries and has been mentioned in most of their discourses and meetings (Winter and Orion, 2016: 1–2). China strongly supports the Egyptian war against terrorism; In 2009, a security cooperation agreement was conducted between the Defense Ministers of the two countries; another technical security cooperation agreement was signed between the Egyptian Ministry of Interior and the Chinese Ministry of Public Security in September 2016 (Shorouk News, 2016). Chinese drones were manufactured in the KSA and deployed to Egypt for counterterrorism purposes (Lons et al., 2019).

6 Pandemic Diplomacy

Despite the negative perceptions of the COVID-19 pandemic that affected China's image in the region, as the country where the virus emerged (Ahmed, 2020), Chinese leaders worked on converting this negative image into a positive one by promoting the Health Silk Road, which had already been included in the BRI playbook since 2017, through which China can cooperate or provide health assistance in parallel to the multiple over-land Silk Road corridors and the Maritime Silk Road (Janardhan, 2020).

The two countries expressed solidarity and supported each other; Egypt was one of the first countries to send medical aid to China, in February 2020, Egypt sent 1 million medical masks to China; the Minister of Health flew to Beijing delivering 10 tons of medical equipment and conveying Egypt's solidarity with China in combating the coronavirus.

On the other hand, when the pandemic hit Egypt, China offered medical aid in three batches; the first one arrived in April, it weighed 4 tons and included "20,000 N95 masks, 10,000 protective medical suits, and 10,000 COVID-19 testing kits." The second weighed 4 tons also but was composed of "70,000 COVID-19 testing kits, 10,000 N95 masks, and 10,000 protective medical suits." The third batch contained "a million masks, 150,000 N95 masks, 70,000 COVID-19 test kits, 1,000 temperature screening devices, 70,000 protective medical suits, and 70,000 medical gloves" (*Egypt Today*, 2020).

Furthermore, China provided Egypt with successive batches of the COVID-19 vaccines, including grants of 300.000 doses of Sinopharm in March 2021 and two million doses of Sinovac in November 2021 (Magdy, 2021; RT Network, 2021).

The two sides are cooperating to produce vaccines for Covid-19, influenza, and polio for the African continent through Egypt's VACSERA and Sinovac projects; especially, to combat the new Covid-19 variant "Omicron," by establishing vaccine-storing facilities at the VACSERA factory complex with a storage capacity of 150 million doses of vaccines, making Egypt the first African country to manufacture them (Middle East New Agency, 2021; State Information Service, 2021).

Many agreements have been signed within the framework of the strategic relations between the two sides to boost their development strategies, including the Economic and Technical Cooperation agreement in November 2021; and the agreement between Egypt's New Urban Communities Authority (NUCA) and the China State Construction Engineering Corporation (CSCEC) to build five residential skyscrapers in New Alamein City in February 2021 (*Egypt Today*, 2021; Xinhua, 2021b).

The above-mentioned indicators are evidence that during the pandemic the economic, cultural, and political relations kept growing, which was confirmed also by the Chinese ambassador to Egypt Liao Liqiang during an interview with the Xinhua network (Xinhua, 2021a). In addition, almost all the indicators are leading to one conclusion that the relationship between Egypt and China can be regarded as a role model of friendly cooperation and mutual understanding; their relationship is growing rapidly and constantly; and is expected to develop into further horizons especially with Egypt's Vision 2030 and its plans to expand the railway industry, increasing local manufacturing, and climate financing.

References

Abd-Elaleem, W. (2019). "Egypt and China... 6 summits and strategic partnership in the Belt and Road." *Al-Ahram Journal*. Available at: http://gate.ahram.org.eg/News/2148263.aspx

Abdel-Razek, S. (2020). "2011–2020: Egypt: Escaping the debt trap." *Al-Ahram Journal*, December. Available at: https://english.ahram.org.eg/

Abu Hatab, A.R., Shoumann, N.A., and Xuexi H. (2012). "Exploring Egypt-China bilateral trade: Dynamics and prospects." *Journal of Economic Studies*, Vol. 39, No. 3: 314–326.

Adeniran, A., Ekeruche, M. A., Onyekwena, C., and Obiakor, T. (2021). "Sector-wide assessment of Chinese BRI investment in Africa." South African Institute of International Affairs, Special Report, June, pp. 12–16, 28–30.

Ahmed, S. (2020). "In the wake of Covid-19, Egypt's Asians fall victim to racism." *Egyptian Streets*, April. Available at: https://egyptianstreets.com/2020/04/15/in-the-wake-of-covid-19-egypts-asians-fall-victim-to-racism/

Ahram. (2020). "China, Egypt sign protocol to teach Chinese language in Egyptian schools." September 8. Available at: https://english.ahram.org.eg/NewsContent/1/64/379545/Egypt/Politics-/China,-Egypt-sign-protocol-to-teach-Chinese-langua.aspx

Ain Shams University. (2019). "Laying the foundation stone of the Confucius Institute at Ain Shams University." March 24. Available at: www.asu.edu.eg/338/news/laying-the-foundation-stone-of-the-confucius-institute-at-ain-shams-university

Al-Azhar University. (n.d.). "Report." Available at: www.azhar.edu.eg

Alden, C. (2014). "Seeking security in Africa: China's evolving approach to the African peace and security architecture." Norwegian Peacebuilding Resource Centre. March. Available at: www.saiia.org.za/

Al-Feqi, F. (2021). "The general government debt." Egyptian Cabinet Information and Decision Support Center, Contemporary Economic Prospects, 2(January): 95.

Alharbi, M. (2019). "Get to know the story of the famous phrase (Seek knowledge even if you have to go as far as China)." *Alarabiya*. Available at: www.alarabiya.net/

Al-Naggar, A. (2016). "Developing Egyptian–Chinese relations." *Al-Ahram Journal*, January 24. Available at: http://english.ahram.org.eg/NewsContentP/4/185697/Opinion/Developing-EgyptianChinese-relations.aspx

Anon. (2016a). "Confucius Institute in Egypt sees growing popularity." December 29. www.china.org.cn/world/2016--12/29/content_40004514.htm

Anon. (2016b). "China-Egypt Cultural Year 2016." November 4. Available at: http://en.chinacult ure.org/2016-04/11/content_751353.htm

Bakhtin, V., Clemesha, A., Guofu, L., Huber, D., and Kumaraswamy, P. R. (2013). "The Mediterranean region in a multipolar world, China: An emerging power in the Mediterranean." German Marshall Fund of the US, pp. 17–18.

Batke, J. (2017). "China is forcing Uighurs abroad to return home. Why aren't more countries refusing to help?" *China File*. Available at: www.chinafile.com/reporting-opinion/viewpoint/ china-forcing-uighurs-abroad-return-home-why-arent-more-countries

Behuria, A. K. (2018). "How Sri Lanka walked into a debt trap, and the way out." *Strategic Analysis*, 42(2): 77–102.

Benabdallah, L. (2018). "China's relations with Africa and the Arab world: Shared trends, different priorities." South African Institute of International Affairs, pp. 10–11.

Benite, Z. B. (2008). "Nine years in Egypt: Al-Azhar and the Arabization of Chinese Islam." *HAGAR Studies in Culture, Polity and Identities*, 8, 5–21.

BRICS Policy Center. (2016). "CASCF." Available at: https://bricspolicycenter.org/en/forum-de-cooperacao-china-paises-arabes/

Cairo University. (2018). "Confucius Institute at Cairo University wins best institute award for HSK placement exams." January 2. Available at: https://cu.edu.eg/Cairo-University-News-12151.html

Central Bank of Egypt. (2021). "Government debt." Available at: www.cbe.org.eg/ar/Pages/defa ult.aspx

CGTN. (2021). "Interview with the former Egyptian Prime minister Essam Sharaf." November 29. Available at: www.youtube.com/watch?v=ugpgXa3_tvM

Chebbi, L. (2005). "China." In K. Versteegh (Ed.), *Encyclopedia of Arabic Language and Linguistics*. Leiden: Brill, pp. 378–383.

Chen, J. T. (2014). "Re-Orientation: The Chinese Azharites between Umma and Third World." *Comparative Studies of South Asia, Africa and the Middle East*, 34(1): 24–51.

Cheng, J. (2016). "China's relations with the Gulf Cooperation Council states: Multilevel diplomacy in a divided Arab world." *The China Review*, 16(1): 51.

China-Africa Research Initiative. (2017). "Data: China-Africa trade." December. Available at: www.sais-cari.org/data-china-africa-trade/

Chinese Embassy. (2018). "Joining hands to advance Sino-Arab Strategic Partnership in the new era." July 10. Available at: http://bh.china-embassy.org/eng/xwdt/t1578660.htm

Cieciura, W. (2015). "Bringing China and Islam closer: The first Chinese Azharites." The Middle East Institute. April. Available at: www.mei.edu/content/map/bringing-china-and-islam-closer-first-chinese-azharites

Circular Economy Innovation Communities. (2021). "Data." Available at: www.ceicdata.com/

Doyon, J., Godement, F., Kratz, A., Pavlićević. D., Rudolf, M., and Vasselier, A. (2017). "China and the Mediterranean: Open for business?" European Council on Foreign Relations, 219: 8–9.

Dunne, M. (2020). "Egypt: Trends in politics, economics, and human rights." Carnegie Endowment for International Peace, September, pp. 1–2.

Egypt Independent. (2017). "China to invest $11.2 billion in projects for Egypt's New Administrative Capital," 4 September. Available at: https://egyptindependent.com/china-invest-11-2-billion-projects-egypts-new-administrative-capital/

Egypt Today. (2020). "3rd Chinese medical aid to Egypt weighing 30 tons arrives amid COVID-19 crisis." Available at: www.egypttoday.com/Article/1/86799/3rd-Chinese-medical-aid-to-Egypt-weighing-30-tons-arrives

Egypt Today. (2021). "Egypt, China sign new economic, technical cooperation agreement to enhance joint cooperation efforts." Available at: www.egypttoday.com/Article/3/109706/Egypt-China-sign-new-economic-technical-cooperation-agreement-to-enhance

Egyptian Chinese University. (2021). "About ECU." Available at: www.ecu.edu.eg/?page_id=3828

Elmaghraby, B. (2018). "Chinese veto power in the UN Security Council and dealing with the Syrian issue." *Korean Journal of Chinese Affairs*, 10: 27–54.

Elmaghraby, B. (2020). "The impact of reviving the Maritime Silk Road on Egyptian-Sino relations." *Journal of East China Normal University*, Special issue, 2: 145–150.

El-Saadany, A. (2014). "Egypt-China relations." *Civilized Dialogue (Alhewar Almutamadin)*. 4560, August. Available at: www.ahewar.org/debat/s.asp?aid=430677

Foreign Ministry of the PRC. (2021). "China and Egypt." Available at: www.fmprc.gov.cn/mfa_eng/wjb_663304/zzjg_663340/xybfs_663590/gjlb_663594/2813_663616/

Fulton, J. (2019). "China's changing role in the Middle East." Atlantic Council. Available at: www.atlanticcouncil.org/

Han, A., and Rossi, R. (2018). "What are the implications of expanded Chinese investment in the MENA region?" Atlantic Council. August 10. Available at: www.atlanticcouncil.org/

Horn, S., Reinhart, C. M., and Trebesch, C. (2019). "China's overseas lending," Washington, DC: National Bureau of Economic Research, Working Paper No. 26050, pp. 5–76. Available at: www.nber.org/papers/w26050

Hurley, J., Morris, S., and Portelance. G. (2018). "Examining the debt implications of the Belt and Road Initiative from a policy perspective." Washington, DC, Center for Global Development. Policy Paper, pp. 11–24. Available at: www.cgdev.org/publication/examining-debt-implications-belt-and-roadinitiative-policy-perspective

Hussein, I.E. (2021). "The risk of debt rising to 130 billion dollars." *Al-Shorouk News*. Available at: www.shorouknews.com/

Jalal, M. (2014). "The China-Arab States Cooperation Forum: Achievements, challenges and prospects." *Journal of Middle Eastern and Islamic Studies (in Asia)*, 8(2): 19.

Janardhan, N. (2020). "China's soft power makes hard gains." *Gulf Today*, April. Available at: www.gulftoday.ae/opinion/2020/04/07/chinas-soft-power-makes-hard-gains

Jun, Z. (2016). "Egypt development strategy and the Belt and Road Initiative." *Arab World Studies*, 3: 75–89.

Jushi. (n.d.). "Report." Available at: www.jushi.com/en/business

Lons, C., Fulton, J., Sun, D., and Al-Tamimi, N. (2019). "China's Great Game in the Middle East." European Council on Foreign Relations. Available at: https://ecfr.eu/publication/china_great_game_middle_east/

Luo, A., Luo, Y., and Wu, T. et al. (2018). "China in the Middle East and Africa." Brief No. 1: China in Egypt. Botho Emerging Markets Group, June, 8.

Magdy, M. (2018). "China to finance majority of New Egypt Capital's Tower District." Bloomberg. Available at: www.bloomberg.com/news/articles/2018-03-18/china-to-finance-majority-of-new-egypt-capital-s-tower-district

Magdy, S. (2021). "Egypt receives 2nd shipment of vaccine as gift from China." *AP News*. Available at: https://apnews.com/article/health-care-reform-cairo-coronavirus-pandemic-health-covid-19-pandemic-62e56e073391f206479d4724693d53d0

Mahmut, D. (2019). "Controlling religious knowledge and education for countering religious extremism: Case study of the Uyghur Muslims in China." *FIRE: Forum for International Research in Education*, 5(1), 29–32.

Marks, J. (2013). "No friends left to lose: Reassessing the United States' strategy in Egypt." *International Institute for Counter-Terrorism (ICT)*, August: 2–14.

Middle East News Agency. (2021) "Sisi lauds Egyptian-Chinese cooperation in producing coronavirus vaccines." Available at: www.mena.org.eg/news/dbcall/table/textnews/id/9294076

Ministry of Commerce of the PRC. (2018). "Statistics on China-Africa bilateral trade in 2017." January 26. Available at: http://english.mofcom.gov.cn/article/statistic/lanmubb/AsiaAfrica/201803/20180302719613.shtml

Ministry of Communications and Information Technology. (2015). "Press release." Available at: https://mcit.gov.eg/en/Media_Center/Press_Room/Press_Releases/3552

Mobley, T. (2019). "The Belt and Road Initiative: Insights from China's backyard," *Strategic Studies Quarterly*, 13(3): 55–68.

Mounir, H. (2021). "Egypt's external debt increases to $137.9bn in June 2021: Central Bank." *Daily News Egypt*. December 4. Available at: https://dailynewsegypt.com/2021/12/04/egypts-external-debt-increases-to-137-9bn-in-june-2021-central-bank/

Pepa, M. (2018). "What is the role of China as land grabber in Sub-Saharan Africa? Between reality and myth: A literature overview." Master's thesis. University of Padua, pp. 21–22.

PRC Embassy in Egypt. (2004). "Exchange of visits by Head of States." March 17. Available at: http://eg.china-embassy.org/eng/zaigx/zzgx/js/t76098.htm

Quero, J. (2020). "China's impact on the Middle East and North Africa's regional order: Unfolding regional effects of challenging the global order." *Contemporary Arab Affairs*, 13(1): 86–104.

Rózsa, E. N. (2020). "Deciphering China in the Middle East." European Union Institute for Security Studies, 2–3.

RT Network. (2021). "China provides Egypt with 2 million doses of Sinovac as a gift.". Available at: https://arabic.rt.com/

Saif, I., and Ghoneim, A. (2013). "The private sector in postrevolution Egypt." Carnegie Endowment for International Peace, June, 2–12.

Salama, A. M. (2019). "Chinese miracle in Egypt." Al-Ahram Institute for Strategic Studies. Available at: https://gate.ahram.org.eg/

Salem, M. (2020). "Egypt's external debts map." *Al-mal News*. Available at: https://almalnews.com/

Scimago Research Centers. (n.d.). "Institutions ranking." Available at: www.scimagoir.com/institution.php?idp=2286

Scobell, A., and Nader, A. (2016). *"China in the Middle East: The Wary Dragon."* Santa Barbara, CA: RAND Corporation.

Shorouk News (2016). "Signing of a security cooperation document between Egypt and China," September 21. Available at: www.shorouknews.com/news/view.aspx?cdate=21092016andid=215e3f2a-5381-4185-9baf-aea7fcae2f98

SISU (Shanghai International Studies University). (2017). "China-Arab research center on reform and development established at SISU." April 21. Available at: http://en.shisu.edu.cn/resources/news/china-arab-reserch-center-at-sisu

State Information Service. (2014). "Egypt-China relations: Cultural relations." Available at: www.sis.gov.eg/Story/92485/

State Information Service. (2018). "Egypt-Sino relations booklet." Available at: www.sis.gov.eg/Story/.

State Information Service. (2021). "Egypt, China discuss cooperation on vaccine production." Available at: www.sis.gov.eg/Story/161718/Egypt percent2C-China-discuss-cooperation-on-vaccine-production?lang=en-us

State Information Service. (n.d.). "Political relations." Available at: www.sis.gov.eg/section/186/2965?lang=en-us

Suez Canal University. (2018). "The ECU... a pioneer university to serve the projects of Suez Canal Zone." September 25. Available at: http://suez.edu.eg/ar/?p=33785

The National. (2012). "Egypt's Morsi visits China in investment bid." August 29. Available at: www.thenational.ae/news/world/asia-pacific/egypts-morsi-visits-china-in-investment-bid

Trading Economics. (2021). "Egypt total external debt." Available at: https://tradingeconomics.com/egypt/external-debt

UN Dag Hammarskjold Library. (2021). "Research report." Available at: https://research.un.org/en/docs/sc/quick

US Energy Information Administration. (2018). "China surpassed the United States as the largest oil importer in 2017." February. Available at: www.eia.gov/todayinenergy/detail.php?id=34812

US Institute of Peace. (2020). "China's impact on conflict dynamics in the Red Sea arena," 12. Available at: www.jstor.org/stable/resrep24926.5

Winter, O., and Ella, D. (2019). "The Chinese development model: A cure for Egyptian woes?" Institute for National Security Studies, pp. 3–5.

Winter, O., and Orion, A. (2016). "Egypt and China following Xi's visit." Institute for National Security Studies. 795, February, pp. 1–2.

Xia, M., and Caicen, S. (2016). "China-Egypt Suez Economic and Trade Cooperation Zone: New oasis on the Belt and Road." *West Asia and Africa*, 2: 109–126. Available at: https://en.cnki.com.cn/Article_en/CJFDTotal-XYFZ201602009.htm

Xinhua. (2021a). "Interview: China eyes deeper friendship with Egypt in new era: ambassador." Available at: www.xinhuanet.com/english/africa/2021-05/30/c_139979361.htm

Xinhua (2021b). "Egypt, China sign contract to build 5 skyscrapers in Egypt's Alamein city." Available at: www.xinhuanet.com/english/2021-02/09/c_139731046.htm

Zenz, A. (2018). "'Thoroughly reforming them towards a healthy heart attitude,' China's political re-education campaign in Xinjiang." *Central Asian Survey*. Special Issue, September, 5–23.

22

THE SINO-IRANIAN RELATIONSHIP

Preserving the Status Quo in the Region?

Kambiz Zare

Iran: A Linchpin State within a "Shatterbelt"

A "linchpin state" in the Cold War lexicon was defined as a State in a location of strategic value and of economic and military attraction that served to contain the spread of Soviet influence in the Third World. The term "shatterbelt" was also used to describe a strategically oriented region that is both divided internally and caught up in the competition between great powers in the geostrategic territories (Cohen, 2003). The Middle East is still a divided region internally due to many factors, such as the Sunni-Shia rivalry and the security alliances opposing one another. Iran is the second largest country in terms of size in the Persian Gulf region after Saudi Arabia, and 17th largest in the world. If we benchmark Iran against two of its neighbors, Iraq and Afghanistan, Iran is over 65 percent larger than the two combined. It is bounded to the north by the Caucasian region and the Caspian Sea which connect the region to the Persian Gulf and the Gulf of Oman, crossing the country from North to South. Iran also shares maritime borders with the Gulf Cooperation Council (GCC) countries. To the West, Iran shares borders with Turkey and Iraq, and to the East, with Pakistan and Afghanistan. Although large swathes of territory within Iran are uninhabitable and uninhabited, it is the third most populated country in the MENA region after Egypt and Turkey; it has a population density of 52 per square kilometer. With a total population of 83 million, of which 60 percent are under the age of 30, Iran represents an attractive market (World Bank, 2021a). Thus, we can safely affirm that based on Iran's geography, strategic, and economic value; as a linchpin state in Sino-Iranian relations, Iran could potentially serve China in undermining the US presence and posture in the region. Sino-Iranian relations are therefore analyzed within this framework.

The first agreement between China and Iran, the "friendship agreement," was signed in 1920 (League of Nations Treaties, 1922); however, the major impetus after Iran's recognition of the People's Republic of China (PRC) in 1971 that bolstered the bilateral relationship was the so-called Iranian 'Islamic Revolution.' Throughout the 1950s and 1970s, major powers, including the United States, became increasingly interested in Iran

292 DOI: 10.4324/9781003048404-25

because of Iran's geostrategic location and coveted resources. Although for US President Jimmy Carter, Iran, in 1977, under the late Shah was considered a beacon of stability in one of the most troubled areas of the world, the Islamist movement led by Rouhollah Khomeini, in 1979, changed the course not only of Iran's history but the region's history as well. The new Islamic regime targeted the US Embassy in Tehran which was sacked and US diplomats were held hostage. While the United States lost a major ally in the region, China, albeit gradually, gained one. China was among the few countries that recognized the new revolutionary regime in its early days. The Chinese move was aimed at achieving two goals. The first was to guarantee access to energy supplies and other natural resources, especially since this period coincided with China's modernization under Deng Xiaoping. Indeed, one year before the proclamation of Iran's Islamic Republic, China had launched its huge economic reform program and was implementing its opening-up policies. Therefore, having the USA and Western countries out of the Iranian market served China's interests and its growing economy. The situation facilitated China's efforts to penetrate a large market (in terms of population) and, above all, to procure energy and other raw materials. China's second objective was to hinder prudently both the US and Soviet influence in Iran and the wider region. In sum, China sought to fill the vacuum left by the US loss of Iran.

In 1980, due to the outbreak of the Iran-Iraq War shortly after the Iranian Revolution, outside powers became directly or indirectly involved, mainly through the provision of weapons in support of one side or the other or in favor of both. China became the biggest provider of military supplies to Iran. Based on China's foreign policy principle of "Asian people to uphold the Asian security" (Forough, 2021), the Islamic Republic's ideological foundations, particularly its antagonism toward the USA and the West in general, pushed Iran further toward China. The Iran-Iraq War, for China, was also an opportunity to foster the bilateral relationship. The war ultimately completely transformed Iran's foreign policy priorities, forcing it to seek alliances and cooperation with the East. Subsequently, Iran's trade and business relations with the West were at their lowest; in 1983, in the midst of the war with Iraq, Iran and China agreed to increase bilateral trade to $500 million. Although China had declared its neutrality in the conflict, it avoided alienating Iraq (Sun and Zoubir, 2018: 227). For instance, Deng Xiaoping expressed deep concern about the Iran–Iraq War, urging both Tehran and Baghdad to settle their dispute through peaceful dialogue and to avoid an escalation of conflict (Hua, 2010: 25). According to some estimates, China's arms sales to Iran since 1982 have been valued at $170 million/yearly (Delpech, 2006). China's military support and assistance to Iran aimed first to prevent the two countries from falling under the US or Soviet sphere of influence, in the same way the Chinese had tried with Afghanistan in the 1980s by supporting the Mujahedeen to fight Afghanistan's pro-Soviet government and the USSR (Kinsela, 1992; Starr, 2004). This can also be understood and analyzed in connection with China's controversial "March West" strategy proposal (Wang, 2012) that would undermine the influence of other major powers in the Middle East and Central Asia. Second, the Chinese sought to guarantee economic and political influence in the oil-rich region with a lucrative share of postwar reconstruction projects (Weisskopf, 1983). After the Iraq-Iran War ended in 1988, and following a series of events and factors, such as the fall and disintegration of the USSR, the growing Chinese economy, the Iraq invasion of Kuwait in 1990, the US-led coalition's invasion of Iraq, and the Syrian civil war in 2011, the way was paved for further deepening of the Sino-Iranian relationship through the conclusion of common grounds and geopolitical interests (Temiz, 2021). Throughout the 1990s, in the aftermath of the disintegration of the USSR and the end of the Iran-Iraq War, some of China's strategic objectives in the region were to reduce US influence in the Middle East, while avoiding confrontation or undermining the US security role in the Persian Gulf region, and for Shi'a Iran to affirm itself as a regional power and to undermine the influence of anti-Iranian Sunni-led countries. Indeed, since its inception in 1979, the Islamic Republic and the clerical regime considered the revolution to be an Islamic one and not only a Shiite one, and tried to offer a compelling model to the whole Muslim world by supporting and assisting like-minded Shiite groups and even Sunni ones that would fight their rulers (Byman, 2019). In the meantime the importance of Iran to China's geo-economic and political interests continued to grow. This was illustrated by the visits of Chinese leaders Jiang Zemin and Xi Jinping to Iran in 2002 and 2016, respectively. The visits of the two Chinese presidents highlighted the informal Sino-Iranian alliance. The strengthening of the bilateral relationship grew within this framework within which one can understand China's support to Iran today. China has provided a lifeline to Iran not only militarily and economically but also politically. In the UN Security Council, China has opposed measures aimed at punishing Iran. For its part, Iran has supported China's policy in Hong Kong's (national security law) and defended the Chinese treatment of the Muslim Uighur minority in Xinjiang at the United Nations (Putz, 2020).

China: Resources and Trade Routes

Iran, a linchpin state within a shatterbelt region, is also critical part of China's One Belt, One Road (OBOR) policy, launched in 2013, renamed the Belt and Road Initiative (BRI) in 2015. Although the BRI has been presented as a peaceful economic project, the military and the geopolitical dimensions underpin this global project (Russel and Berger, 2020). The BRI represents a marked shift in China's foreign policy. The BRI includes over 65 countries spanning three continents; together, they account for 62 percent of the world's population and hold 75 percent of all discovered and known energy sources and reserves. These countries will be connected to China and connect China to the other regions through a series of economic corridors (Figure 22.1). Each corridor will include several countries and choke points that are ultimately set to facilitate and guarantee China's access to other parts of the world. Pakistan is the flagship of the BRI and the only corridor made of only one country. The China-Pakistan corridor is a very important trading route for China because it gives direct access to energy suppliers from both Africa and the Middle East through the Gwadar port, situated on the shores of Arabian Sea astride the Gulf of Oman. The fact that China is the largest importer of oil and gas proves further evidence the geostrategic importance of this corridor, enabling China also to gain direct access to the Indian Ocean. Although the China-Pakistan corridor is pivotal for energy supplies to China, its importance goes beyond trade and commercial purposes since Pakistan borders both India and Iran. Contrary to the Sino-Indian relationship, which is antagonistic and fragile, the Sino-Iranian relationship rests on mutual security and commercial interests. If the Pakistan corridor is the BRI's flagship, Iran should be considered the BRI's pillar, for obvious reasons. Iran shares borders with Afghanistan, Iraq, Turkey, Armenia, Azerbaijan, Pakistan, and Turkmenistan. Adding the maritime borders with Kuwait, Qatar, Saudi Arabia, Oman, Bahrain, and the United Arab Emirates, one gets a sense of how unique Iran's strategic position is within the Middle East and North Africa (MENA) region. Thus, Iran is the only country in the Middle East that can enable

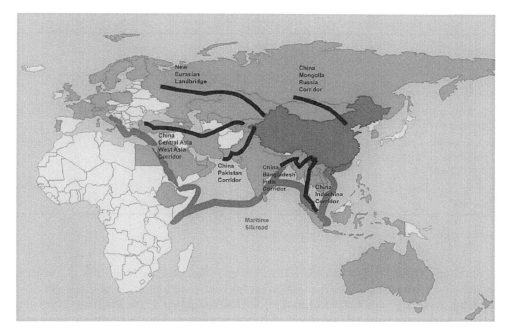

Figure 22.1 The westward direction of the BRI project emanating from China. The proposed economic corridors: in black (Land Silk Road), and in gray (Maritime Silk Road)

Source: https://en.wikipedia.org/wiki/User:Lommes / Wikimedia Commons; Additional sources: www.merics.org/en/merics-analysis/infographicchina-mapping/china-mapping/ www.cbbc.org/cbbc/media/cbbc_media/One-Belt-One-Road-main-body.pdf). This file is licensed under the Creative Commons Attribution-Share Alike 4.0 International license

China to control and secure the development and implementation of the BRI project and ultimately secure China's continued access to resources and secured and safe trade and commercial routes.

Iran is one of the most diversified economies within the MENA region. However, a decreasing GDP per capita since 2010, which today is around $13,000, shows that because of decades of economic mismanagement, systemic corruption, and crippling international sanctions, Iran's economy is declining and has not broken its high dependency on hydrocarbons resources. Iran ranks fourth in the world for proven crude oil reserves and second for proven natural gas. Iran's government revenues rely heavily on the export of hydrocarbons. Therefore, the other major industries are shaped and built around hydrocarbons. Crude oil's share was around 50 percent of Iran's total exports in 2019 and was valued at $12.3 billion of $25 billion (OEC, 2021) total exports. Not surprisingly, China is the first destination of Iranian crude oil; Chinese needs for oil from Iran were estimated to be at about 6 percent of its total need in 2019 (ibid.; Reuters, 2021). Iran also exports ethylene polymer, iron ore, and acyclic alcohol, of which China is also Iran's first export destination (Table 22.1). Iron ore and oil are the two main commodities integral to the world economy, and China is one of the main clients for these commodities.

Table 22.1 The main products exported from Iran to China in 2020

Product	Trade value (2020) ($ billion)	Financial amount	(%)
Polymers of ethylene, in primary forms	1.91	Billion	32.6
Petroleum oils and oils obtained from bituminous minerals; crude	1.15	Billion	19.7
Acyclic alcohols and their halogenated, sulphonated, nitrated or nitrosated derivatives	780	Million	13.3
Iron ore, non-alloy-steel, semi-finished product thereof	528	Million	9.3

Source: Observatory of Economic Complexity (2021).

Although China's GDP growth was down to 2.3 percent in 2020, it is the world's economic powerhouse and, as such, its thirst for energy and natural resources will continue for decades to come; Iran cannot be a reliable supplier in the longer term for the following reasons (World Bank, 2021c). On the one hand, Iran lacks the capacity and the required capabilities to further exploit its natural resources to trade more, because it does not have the financial resources to invest in the energy sector. If we also add the impact of international sanctions, which Iran tried to alleviate through measures, such as offering attractive oil prices (Faucon, 2020) or discounts on its raw materials, the trade statistics still remain low (Adesnik and Ghasseminejad, 2018). Besides, China has a well-diversified list of suppliers that provide the country with crude oil, iron ore, and the other raw materials needed for the good performance of its economy. As reported in Table 22.2, the main crude petroleum suppliers to China are Saudi Arabia, Russia, Iraq, Angola, and Brazil.

China only imported 0.77 percent of its required crude petroleum from Iran in 2020. The same can be argued for the import of iron ore. During the past two decades, Iran's official exports to China have increased at an annual rate of 18.7 percent (OEC, 2021); however, Iran's main export items in terms of natural resources today are offered by many other countries worldwide and Iran is facing severe competition. This is confirmed by looking at China's well-diversified list of suppliers and partners in the region. This is also one of the main reasons why Iran's share of China's international commerce is not significant and stays at 0.5 percent of China's total global trade and commerce. Objectively, one can conclude that at least in the current circumstances, China's interest in Iran is based on the security-related issues, that is, securing access to trade and commercial routes through Iran, with choke points, such as the Strait of Hormuz. This will enable Beijing to continue to secure access to a diversified list of energy-related suppliers.

China: A Lifesaver for Iran

In this section, we will look at the main ways Iran has tried since 1979 to shape and try to manage the Sino-Iranian relationship. China was one of the few countries that, within days after the Islamic Republic's proclamation in February 1979, recognized the

Table 22.2 Sources of China's import of crude petroleum in 2020 (total of $150 billion)

Crude petroleum imported from	Trade value (2020) ($ billion)	Percentage of total amount imported
Saudi Arabia	24.7	16.4
Russia	23.8B	15.8
Iraq	16.9	11.3
Angola	12.1	8.7
Brazil	11.4	7.56
Oman	11.3	7.53
UAE	8.6	5.72
Kuwait	7.9	5.26
Iran	1.15	0.77

Source: Observatory of Economic Complexity (2021).

theocratic regime in Iran. Despite different alternatives, the relationship with China under the auspices of the revolution's leadership received more favorable attention. Indeed, the PRC's Five Principles of foreign policy, namely, mutual respect for sovereignty and territorial integrity, mutual non-aggression, mutual non-interference in internal affairs, equality and mutual benefit, and peaceful coexistence, were appealing to the Iranian political establishment. Since then, the Sino-Iranian relationship has developed further, though slowly and quietly, reaching its apex in the twenty-first century. Although, in 2016, the two countries set the goal of increasing further their bilateral trade to $600 billion by 2026, in 2019, only less than a third of Iran's total imports ($35 billion) originated from China. Iran imported $9.61 billion of goods from China and China imported some $12 billion from Iran, and the bilateral trade in 2020 was valued at $14.9 billion, far below the set goal (Green and Roth, 2021). Iran imports a wide range of products from China, from industrial machinery and components and chemical products to textiles and foodstuffs. The top product imported in 2019 was telecommunication equipment, worth $358 million, followed by electronic devices and vehicle parts, valued at $354 million. Iran's imports from China confirm the fact that many of these are categorized under dual-use goods and technologies that would serve both civilian and military purposes. In recent years, the regulators have expanded the role that dual-use products and technologies can play to other areas, such as terrorism, cyber security, and human rights abuses. Indeed, these dual-use goods and technologies are determinants for economic development of any developing nation. However, these technologies and products can also be used to develop weapons, and military hardware for military and defense industries (Simpson, 2010). A combination of factors, such as sanctions, Iran's geopolitical ambitions, security-related concerns, and regional adventurism, that clash with those of other regional and world powers makes it difficult for Iran to procure those goods and technologies categorized as such. Therefore, China can offer what others are not legally authorized to offer or would consider as risky business. Thus, for the political establishment in Iran, vehemently opposed to and skeptical about the West, China is a trustworthy ally. Since the inception of the new regime in Iran, the two countries have identified mutual interests that would strengthen the Sino-Iranian cooperation despite their differences. Even though there is a strong asymmetry in the current economic relationship, for Iran, there are no other viable alternatives. For Iran, as George Kennan stated in 1946, regarding the USSR's stance and the fact that there cannot be a peaceful coexistence with the West (Kennan, 1946), the same can be argued for the current Iranian political establishment, for which there will not be a peaceful coexistence with the USA and the Western bloc in the long run and, therefore, the focus must be on the East and to invest on China's increasing worldwide power. This can also be better understood throughout the 25-year Cooperation Agreement signed between the two countries in March 2021.

Financial Resources

In the development of a nation, besides the need for access to natural and human resources, technology and know-how, an equally important role is also played by financial resources. All nations vie for access to international financial markets, while trying to implement the reforms required to attract foreign investors. Therefore, providing a secure and stable business environment is the first condition for attracting foreign investment. Beside the domestic business environment, political stability, and the legal framework, the international political and geopolitical context within which states interact are included as well. Undoubtedly, foreign direct investments (FDI) has had a major role in many countries' efforts to develop their economies and to improve their societal conditions. FDI can serve as an indicator to track the ins and outs of financial resources into and from a particular country. In connection with Sino-Iranian relations, FDI analysis can offer insights as to what extent the two economies are integrated and the relevant sectors of each economy.

Iran is far behind many other countries in the MENA region in paving the way for foreign investors. Based on some estimates (UNCTAD, 2020), in 2020, the FDI inflow to Iran contracted by 11 percent compared to the previous year, which was approximately around $1.508 billion in 2019 (UNCTAD STAT, 2020). Although FDI inflow to Iran experienced a negative trend from 2000 to 2008, it did have years of positive trends, too, from 2008 to 2018. In fact, during 2016–2017, there was optimism, following the signing between Iran and the 5+1 powers, of the Joint Comprehensive Plan of Action (JCPOA) on Iran's nuclear program. Consequently, in 2017, Iran had its major FDI inflow since 1979 valued at around $5.019 billion. Afterwards, a series of political and geopolitical events, such as continuous proxy wars in the region, the US withdrawal from the JCPOA, Iranian nuclear breaches, and small-scale military confrontations in the region, again reduced the inflow of foreign direct investment to Iran. The FDI inward stock, which measures the total level of investment at a given point in time, for Iran, was estimated at about $58.7 billion in 2020 (Table 22.3).

Because Iran is isolated from the rest of the world and with a nonfunctioning economy, it looks at China for FDI inflow and other types of aid or financial assistance to fuel and run its economy. Estimates between 2003 and 2014 show that Iran secured around $32 billion in loans under different development funds schemes (AidData, 2017; Green and Roth, 2021). Iran badly needs foreign capital to renovate and expand its energy and extractive sectors. China is the country at the top of the list of foreign investors and between 2003 and 2020 it invested in 21 Greenfield FDI projects. Throughout that period, the total value of Chinese FDI in Iran increased by over 500 percent. In 2019, China invested approximately $3 billion with a focus on the primary sector of Iran's economy, energy, and natural resources (Dettoni, 2020). However, in line with a global decline and

Table 22.3 Foreign direct investment, net inflows (% of GDP) in 2020 for Iran standing at 0.6% of GDP

2015	2016	2017	2018	2019	2020
0.5	0.7	1.0	0.7	0.5	0.6

Source: World Bank (2021c).

negative flow of FDI to Iran, due to regional instability and the future of the nuclear dossier, it seems that China has already started to divest its Iranian assets in accordance with the global trend. In 2017, Iran needed approximately $140 billion just to keep its energy sector breathing and eventually improve some aspects of it, whereas the total FDI inward stock stood at merely around $58.7 billion in 2020. Despite Iran's desire and push for more Chinese engagement, even major Chinese companies such as the state-owned China National Petroleum Corporation or China's Petroleum and Chemical Company (Sinopec) either exited from certain projects or are struggling to implement their projects and make them operational (Kurtenbach, 2007; Shahla and Ratcliffe, 2019). The oil industry and the primary sector are not the only ones facing difficult times. Under US sanctions and international pressure, Chinese companies involved in technology are also hesitant to remain in, invest in, or trade with Iran. Multinational companies, such as Lenovo or Huawei, have reportedly reduced their operations and businesses in Iran. From 2017 to 2019, Iran had to face a capital outflow of approximately $990 million of Chinese funds (Green and Roth, 2021).

Sino-Iranian economic relations are suffering from the crippling international sanctions but continue to provide Iran with an economic lifeline. Despite the constraints caused by the international sanctions and the prevailing geopolitical tensions in the region, in 2016, both countries agreed that China should redesign its economic relationship with Iran and make more investment in Iran's critical industrial sectors, such as oil and gas, mining, and infrastructures. Years of economic mismanagement, corruption, and sanctions have made Iran's energy sector obsolete and inefficient. Iran is lagging far behind other oil and gas producers in terms of exploration, extraction, and production. However, for China to invest in impaired assets there might be well-calculated returns in the long run. This is framed to guarantee future returns on Chinese investments in Iran, an important country situated at the confluence of East and West. Iran is desperately trying to get more investment from China by offering a large market, facilitated access to its territory being a key component within the BRI, and continuous access to oil and raw materials at a discounted rate (Alterman, 2019). Iran is considering a steady reintegration to the global economy through Chinese investments, even if the nuclear dossier and other regional issues continue to be destabilizing factors in the region. In sum, currently, in the current circumstances, not much economic integration in different sectors through trade and investment is taking place.

Military-Based Interests and Security Considerations

To understand the Sino-Iranian relationship better and the stakes that are involved, military and defense exchanges and cooperation must also be analyzed. This aspect is categorized under three main domains of interactions. The first domain concerns the transfer of knowledge and technology. China was one of the few countries that developed a considerable bilateral defense strategy with Iran after the inception of the Islamic Republic. China was one of the few that supported Iran throughout its long and devastating war with Iraq in the 1980s. Since Iran cannot obtain conventional weaponry and military hardware from the USA and the European powers, China is again one of the very few countries that can assist Iran in keeping its modern military capabilities. Iran does this also through developing its own domestic industries, based on existing technologies provided by China or others willing to do so, such as North Korea and Russia. China was also among the first countries to support Iran's nuclear program after the Islamic Revolution of 1979 (Delpech, 2006) and did not hesitate to help Iran with the technologies needed to improve its missile systems and other equipment related to military and the defense industry (Hickey, 1990). Although China in the past two decades officially stopped helping Iran with know-how and the transfer of related technologies, due to the sanction regimes and embargo schemes, some of the Chinese state-owned companies were recently sanctioned by the US Treasury Department for violating the Iran, North Korea, and Syria Nonproliferation Act (Lincy, 2021). In fact, these technologies helped and are still helping Iran to improve different aspects of its missile program and the quality of its missiles with respect to range and precision. There are reports that revealed the fact that some of the missile systems that Iran recently used to attack US forces are based on China's ballistic missile technologies that Iran was able to obtain in the past from China and that are considered highly precise, effective, and destructive (Roblin, 2020).

The other aspect somehow crucial to Iran is access to the conventional weapons market. Being cut off from the US and European arms industry, again China has helped Iran to compensate for its conventional warfare deficit in regional conflicts and proxy wars in the region. Iran's overall military expenditure, based on official statistics, stood at $16 billion in 2020, which, for a country under international sanctions, and arms embargo, is a considerable figure (World Bank, 2021b). On many occasions, Iran has expressed its interest in purchasing a wide range of military equipment and systems, from jet fighters to tanks and from submarines to unmanned aerial vehicles from China, beyond what the deal stipulates. The embargo has now expired despite US objection (Nadimi, 2016).

The other domain where Iran is looking to develop further with China is regular training and educational programs as well as joint defense R&D. In 2016, the two countries signed a military cooperation agreement that was aimed to expand military training as well as holding more joint exercises. For the Iranian authorities, these exercises are publicized and presented as countering the US influence and hegemony in the region (Brennan, 2019). The statements from Iranian officials and China's continuous support confirm the determination of the two countries to keep Iran as a regional power and at the same time to weaken the position of the USA and its allies in the region.

In any event, besides considering the Chinese military assistance as an effort to keep the USA at bay, letting Iran remain a regional power and preserving the balance of power among major regional powers, China would like to see Iran politically, economically, and militarily stable for two main reasons. First, China would like to continue to have safe and secured access to Iran's oil and natural resources and subsequently defend against any threat to the trade routes within the Persian Gulf region, most notably the Strait of Hormuz. Second, the BRI's integration can be swiftly moved forward, and the section of the BRI that passes through Iran would not face any setback. However, China has its own redlines in military cooperation and trading with Iran. The reason is to avoid jeopardizing the regional balance of power and free flow of goods and energy in and out of the Persian Gulf region and the Arabian Peninsula. China has its own bilateral security, trade, and military relations with other countries in the region, such as the United Arab Emirates and Saudi Arabia, with which it has Comprehensive Strategic Partnerships and from which it imports substantial quantities of oil, as discussed in other chapters in this volume. This constrains China from deepening its military cooperation with Iran.

The 25-Year Agreement: The BRI, and Regional Implications

In the past few years, two main official bilateral meetings have tried to provide the Sino-Iranian relations with a redesigned roadmap. In 2016, a year after the JCPOA, a Chinese delegation visited Iran. This was an important meeting that elevated the partnership level between the two countries from being a "Strategic Partnership" to a "Comprehensive Strategic Partnership." This is one of the highest levels in the Chinese multi-tier system of ranking relating to its diplomatic partnerships (Sun, 2020). Besides signing different MOUs and the pledge to further develop bilateral military cooperation, the two countries also sent signals to the USA that their robust partnership and geopolitical influence and effectiveness would equal that of the USA and its direct allies in the region. Other equally important items were on the table as well. One was to facilitate and accept Iran's full membership within the Shanghai Cooperation Organization (SCO), a China-centered security-oriented organization, and the other item was a pledge to increase bilateral trade to $600 billion by 2026. The full membership of Iran in SCO was approved in 2021 which indeed at its best allows Iranians to argue that Iran is not isolated from the rest of the world. However, considering the dynamics within the SCO itself, such as the current territorial disputes and the military issues among some of the members, and other bilateral issues, this would make it difficult for Iran to really leverage its membership through this organization. Although the negotiations to grant Iran full membership in the SCO were successful and Iran is part of the bloc, however, the pledge to increase bilateral trade to $600 billion by 2026 seems to be unrealistic as this chapter has shown.

The other event that made headlines was the signing of the 25-year Cooperation Agreement in 2021. The agreement is mainly structured around $400 billion of Chinese investments in Iran. Although the main terms of the deal are secret and not accessible, based on publicly available drafts of the agreement, the deal includes a wide range of bilateral cooperation from military and infrastructure to energy and telecommunications. Through this $400 billion deal, Iran seeks to revamp its economy. But decades of economic mismanagement, systemic corruption, malign regional behavior, and sanctions have made Iran's economy, despite its potential, a market to be avoided by businesses and investors (China Ministry of Commerce via CEIC Database Coface and GlobalEdge, 2021). In connection to the rationale behind China's investment in infrastructure development, China considers Iran as a regional hub that connects Asia to Europe and, as such, it can integrate further and deepen the BRI, mainly regionally. For China, the regional connectivity is crucial for both transporting goods and providing services, besides guaranteeing security along it economic corridors. For China, a growing economy, having access to a well-developed railroads and road transportation and infrastructure, would also guarantee future access to energy and other raw materials, and thus guarantee resource security. Therefore, China is investing with the objective of improving the connectivity with Iran not only domestically but also internationally. Iran is supposed to connect China and the whole of Central Asia to Europe. Iran is pivotal to that economic corridor. The corridor has already received billions of dollars in investments from China for the development of infrastructural works on this corridor (Reed and Trubetskoy, 2019). However, Iran's share of the BRI so far has amounted to only $12 billion, compared with the Gulf Cooperation Council (GCC) countries, which have received $69 billion; this suggests that China does not wish to upset the status quo and balance of power in the region.

Geopolitics as an approach to International Relations considers the following factors as being essential in geopolitical analysis: security, resources, and continuous access to secure and safe trade and commercial routes. As such, it confirms that both China and Iran have a neorealist view on the international system. Thus, to overcome the security dilemma and consequently the risk of large-scale conflicts, creating and keeping the balance of power in the region as an ordering mechanism are major goals.

Conclusion

The Sino-Iranian relationship was re-engineered through the elevation of the bilateral diplomatic relationship from Strategic Partnership to Comprehensive Strategic Partnership in 2016, and the signing of the 25-year Cooperation Agreement, with its economic features, made further visible the creation of a new Chinese-led geostrategic economic bloc in the Middle East. Different components of this bloc, such as the China-Pakistan corridor, the Europe-East-Central Asia corridor, as part of the BRI project, once and if further connected and integrated, would have a huge impact on the geopolitical equilibrium of the region, which is already affected by the US withdrawal from Afghanistan and China's readiness to invest billions of dollars in Afghanistan as soon as security measures are restored. The prospect of a China, Afghanistan, Pakistan, and Iran corridor would also further integrate the region to China's sphere of influence and its partners, to the detriment of other major world and regional powers, such as the United States, Russia, Saudi Arabia, and India.

The GCC countries' economic relationship with China is already much bigger and considerable compared to that of Iran with China and continues growing. For instance, the Sino-Iranian trade, as of 2020, was valued at around $14.9 billion, far behind Saudi's $67.2 billion and the UAE's $49.3 billion. The same holds true for investment. China also has comprehensive strategic partnerships with the UAE and Saudi Arabia. Thus, the same level of diplomatic principles is applied to both rivals, Saudi Arabia and Iran. Having the USA somehow disengaged from the region, China's security, the need for continuous access to the resources from the region, and guaranteeing access to secured and safe trade and commercial route will continue to be at the top of China's agenda in the Middle East. For China, the stability in the region and preserving some sort of balance of power are crucial for now. Therefore, it will seek to maintain the status quo in the coming years. In the short and medium run, China, without any direct involvement, would let the USA continue its retreat from the region. The long-term objective is, as Mao once said: 'The enemy advances, we retreat; the enemy camps, we harass; the enemy tires, we attack; the enemy retreats, we pursue.'

References

Adesnik, D. and Ghasseminejad, S. (2018). "Foreign Investment in Iran: Multinational Firms' Compliance with U.S. Sanctions, Foundation for Defense of Democracies." *SSRN Electronic Journal*, January. DOI:10.2139/ssrn.3257581

AidData (2017). "Global Chinese Official Finance Database." Available at: www.aiddata.org/data/chinese-global-official-finance-dataset

Alterman, J. (2019). "Chinese and Russian Influence in the Middle East: Written Testimony for House Foreign Affairs Subcommittee on the Middle East, North Africa, and International Terrorism." Available at: www.congress.gov/116/meeting/house/109455/witnesses/HHRG-116-FA13-Wstate-AltermanJ-20190509.pdf

Brennan, D. (2019). "Iran Warns U.S. Its Middle East Dominance Is Over after Naval Drills with Russia, China." *Newsweek*. Available at: www.newsweek.com/iran-warns-us-middle-east-dominance-over-naval-drills-russia-china-1479628

Byman, D. L. (2019). "Order from Chaos: The Iranian Revolution and its Legacy of Terrorism." Brookings. Available at: www.brookings.edu/blog/order-from-chaos/2019/01/24/the-iranian-revolution-and-its-legacy-of-terrorism/

China Ministry of Commerce via CEIC Database Coface and GlobalEdge (2021). "Iran: Risk." Available at: https://globaledge.msu.edu/countries/iran/risk

Cohen, S. (2003). *Geopolitics of the World System*. Lanham, MD: Rowman & Littlefield Publishers.

Delpech, T. (2006). *Iran and the Bomb: The Abdication of International Responsibility*. New York: Columbia University Press.

Dettoni, J. (2020). "The Biden Fix: Iran." *FDI Intelligence*. Available at: www.fdiintelligence.com/article/79077

Faucon, B. (2020). "Iranian Oil Exports Rise as Tehran Circumvents Sanctions, Finds New Buyers." *Wall Street Journal*. Available at: www.wsj.com/articles/iranian-oil-exports-rise-as-tehran-circumvents-sanctions-finds-new-buyers-11608052404

Forough, M. (2021). "Raisi's Foreign Policy: Pragmatic Revolutionism and the Iranian Pivot to Asia." GIGA Focus Nahost, 7. Hamburg: German Institute for Global and Area Studies (GIGA).

Green, W. and Roth, T. (2021). "China-Iran Relations: A Limited but an Enduring Partnership." U.S.-China Economic and Security Review Commission.

Hickey, D. (1990). *New Directions in China's Arms for Export Policy: An Analysis of China's Military Ties with Iran*. New York: Routledge, pp. 15–29.

Hua, L. [华黎明] (2010). '新中国与伊朗关系六十年' [Six Decades of the PRC–Iran Relations]. 西亚非洲 [*Journal of West Asia and Africa*], 4.

Kennan, G. (1946). *Long Telegram*. Wilson Center. Available at: https://digitalarchive.wilsoncenter.org/document/116178.pdf

Kinsella, W. (1992). *Unholy Alliances*. New York: Lester Publishing.

Kurtenbach, E. (2007). "China's Sinopec, Iran Ink Yadavaran Deal." Associated Press.

League of Nations (1922). "Treaties." Available at: www.worldlii.org/int/other/LNTSer/1922/42.html

Lincy, V. (2021). "Hearing on China's Nuclear Forces, written testimony for U.S.-China Economic and Security Review Commission." Available at: www.uscc.gov/sites/default/files/2021–06/Valerie_Lincy_Testimony.pdf

Nadimi, F. (2016). "Iran and China Are Strengthening Their Military Ties." Washington Institute. Available at: www.washingtoninstitute.org/policy-analysis/view/iran-and-china-are-strengthening-their-military-ties

OEC (Observatory of Economic Complexity) (2021). "Iran (IRN) and China (CHN) Trade." Available at: https://oec.world/en/profile/bilateral-country/irn/partner/chn

Putz, C. (2020) "Which Countries Are for or Against China's Xinjiang Policies?" *The Diplomat*, October 9. Available at: https://thediplomat.com/2020/10/2020-edition-which-countries-are-for-or-against-chinas-xinjiang-policies

Reed, T. and Trubetskoy, A. (2019). "Assessing the Value of Market Access from Belt and Road Projects." Washington, DC: World Bank Group. Available at: http://documents1.worldbank.org/curated/en/333001554988427234/pdf/Assessing-the-Value-of-Market-Access-from-Belt-and-Road-Projects.pdf

Reuters (2021). "China's Oil Purchases Rebound." Available at: www.reuters.com/business/chinas-iran-oil-purchases-rebound-lower-prices-fresh-quotas-2021-11-10/

Roblin, S. (2020). "Meet the Qiam Missile Iran Used to Blast a U.S. Airbase." *National Interest*. Available at: https://nationalinterest.org/blog/buzz/meet-qiam-missile-iran-used-blast-us-airbase-112911

Russel, D. R. and Berger, B. H. (2020). "Weaponizing the Belt and Road Initiative." The Asia Society Policy Institute. Available at: https://asiasociety.org/sites/default/files/2020-09/Weaponiz ing%20the%20Belt%20and%20Road%20Initiative_0.pdf

Shahla, A. and Ratcliffe, V. (2019). "CNPC Quits Flagship Iran Gas Project as Sanctions Bite." Bloomberg. Available at: www.bloomberg.com/news/articles/2019-10-06/iran-says-china-s-cnpc-is-no-longer-part-of-giant-gas-project

Simpson, G. (2010). "Russian and Chinese Support for Tehran: Iranian Reform and Stagnation." *Middle East Quarterly*, 17: 63–72.

Starr, F. (2004). *Xinjiang: China's Muslim Borderland*. New York: M.E. Sharpe, pp. 157–158.

Sun, D. (2020) "China's Partnership Diplomacy in the Middle East." *The Asia Dialogue*, March 24. Available at: https://theasiadialogue.com/2020/03/24/chinas-partnership-diplomacy-in-the-mid dle-east/

Sun, D. and Zoubir, Y.H. (2018) "China's Participation in Conflict Resolution in the Middle East and North Africa: A Case of Quasi-Mediation Diplomacy?" *Journal of Contemporary China*, 27(110): 224–243.

Temiz, K. (2021). *Chinese Foreign Policy toward the Middle East*. New York: Routledge.

UNCTAD (United Nations Conference on Trade and Development) (2020). "World Investment Report." Available at: https://unctad.org/webflyer/world-investment-report-2020

UNCTAD STAT (United Nations Conference on Trade and Development) (2020). "Country Profile." Available at: https://unctadstat.unctad.org/countryprofile/generalprofile/en-gb/364/index.html

Wang, J. (2012). The World in 2020 According to China. Leiden: Brill, pp. 129–136.

Weisskopf, M. (1983). "China Plays Both Sides in Persian Gulf War." *The Washington Post*, January 13. Available at: www.washingtonpost.com/archive/politics/1983/01/13/china-plays-both-sides-in-persian-gulf-war/e5f921aa-5797-467c-9d6d-293eed9911dc/

World Bank (2021a). "Population Distribution." Available at: https://data.worldbank.org/indica tor/EN.POP.DNST?locations=IR

World Bank (2021b). "Military Expenditure." Available at: https://data.worldbank.org/indicator/MS.MIL.XPND.CD?locations=IR-SA-US-CN

World Bank (2021c). "GDP Growth, Annual %." Available at: https://data.worldbank.org/indica tor/NY.GDP.MKTP.KD.ZG?end=2020&locations=CN&start=1993&view=chart

World Bank (2021d). "Foreign Direct Investment, Net Inflows (BoP, Current US$)." Available at: https://data.worldbank.org/indicator/BX.KLT.DINV.CD.WD?locations=IR

23

CHINA-ISRAEL

Trilateral Dimensions of Bilateral Relations

Yitzhak Shichor

Introduction

Ordinarily, relations between two countries, for better or for worse, are a direct and bilateral issue. This is especially true when these countries share a common border, which means that territorial conflicts may be involved, and, occasionally, ethnic identities, historical memories, cultural values, natural resources, and political attitudes. Once these problems are overcome or sidestepped—the door opens, first, for unofficial, and then, for official diplomatic relations. However, sometimes, bilateral relations are blocked, though such obstacles are absent: the two countries do not share a common border, have no territorial conflicts, and are ethnically and culturally separate. They may still have different—even contradictory—ideological beliefs, but these have never precluded official, let alone unofficial, relations between countries. Still, while bilateral constraints are missing, relations between two countries could be affected by trilateral constraints, which may delay the establishment of bilateral relations or, once official relations *are* established, continue to undermine them. This, in brief, is the history of Sino-Israeli relations.

Established in October 1949 (the People's Republic of China [PRC]), and May 1948 (Israel), these two countries are located far away from each other, on Asia's eastern and western edges. Geographic and cultural distance separated them in pre-modern times, when knowledge of the other hardly existed. There is nothing in the Chinese classics about the people of Israel, Judaism, or Jews. Although the name *Sin* (China, in Hebrew) does appear six times in the Bible, and *Sinim* (Chinese, in Hebrew), is mentioned once, they do not refer to "China" but to the Sinai Peninsula, perhaps to part of Egypt. No direct connections existed, but Jewish traders criss-crossed Central Asia spreading manuscripts as far as China's western regions (*xiyu*), and beyond.

While no Chinese ever settled in the Land of Israel, Jews did settle in China, probably in the eleventh century. Creating five communities, led by Kaifeng, they integrated into China's bureaucracy, civilian and military, but were slowly assimilated. By the early twentieth century, they had essentially disappeared. Unlike in the West, anti-Semitism was not integral to Chinese society, nor politics; Jews were never persecuted. In fact, Chinese leaders were aware of their contributions to China, and appreciated them (Shichor, 2020b). Sun Yat-sen sympathized with their wish for a homeland in Palestine and his

DOI: 10.4324/9781003048404-26

305

widow, Song Qingling, later PRC Vice-president, openly criticized Nazism for the Jewish plight in the 1930s.[1] Chinese intellectuals underlined similarities between oppressed Jews and the Chinese (Eber, 1980). In his memoirs, Chiang Kai-shek remarked: "Most of the Russian leaders holding responsible party and government positions who expressed regard for Dr. Sun and sincere desire to cooperate with China in her National Revolution, were Jews" (Chiang, 1957: 22). Aware of Zionism (Mao, 1919), Mao Zedong planned a chapter on "The Jewish National Liberation Movement" in a volume entitled *Collected Writings on the National Liberation Movement* (19 May 1926), never published (Schram, 1992: II, 382).

By that time, Baghdadi Jews had already been settled in China since the 1850s and Russian Jews later moved to Harbin, Tianjin, and other northeast China cities. They excelled in developing trade, banking, industry, medicine, energy, etc. Although the Chinese were engaged in fighting the Japanese, and themselves, they recognized the Jewish problem, underlined by the influx of some 20,000 European Jewish refugees who found haven in Shanghai (occupied by Japan) in the late 1930s and early 1940s (Kranzler, 1976). Chinese still frequently mention the friendly relationship and warm hospitality extended to Jewish refugees. Even before seizing the mainland, the communists welcomed the establishment of the State of Israel. Undoubtedly influenced by Moscow, which had preceded the USA in offering Israel *de jure* recognition, and even arms, Chinese Communist Party (CCP) leaders considered Israel an example of "national liberation" from British imperialism—thereby laying a foundation for future Sino-Israeli relations.

By 1950, the first layer of bricks had been built on this foundation. Israel displayed socialist tendencies to the point that the USA, and its intelligence agencies, were concerned that Israel would join the Soviet Bloc. Indeed, on January 9, 1950, Israel became the first Middle Eastern country to offer diplomatic recognition to the PRC—and the seventh among non-communist countries. Officially, Israel adopted a "non-alignment" policy in the Cold War (Bialer, 1990). Also, unlike most Arab nations (as well as Turkey and Iran), it never recognized the Republic of China (Taiwan), ignoring such a proposal in March 1949. In those years, most, if not all, Middle Eastern nations, allied with the West and rejected diplomatic relations with the PRC. Under these circumstances, Sino-Israeli diplomatic relations appeared only a question of time—definitely not as long as it actually took. Who was responsible for the 42 years delay, until early 1992, and for the fluctuations in Sino-Israeli relations since? To some extent, Israel; to a greater extent, China; but to the greatest extent—third parties: notably the Americans; the Soviets and the Russians, and Muslim and Arab countries. Occasionally they facilitated Sino-Israeli relations, blocked them, or disrupted them. These third parties are by no means symmetric. While the impact of Russia and the Arabs has declined over time and, to some extent has diminished, the impact of the USA on Sino-Israeli relations has persisted, less positively and mostly negatively. This chapter is about the role of third parties in Sino-Israeli relations.

The Arab Impact

Arabs affected Sino-Israeli relations in three different stages. First, in the 1950s and 1960s, they offered an alternative to China's relations with Israel and helped to block them. Second, since the late 1960s and the 1970s, they unintentionally paved the ground for unofficial Sino-Israeli relations by siding with Moscow in its conflict with Beijing, and by their poor performance in the 1967 and 1973 wars. Third, the 1979 Israel-Egypt peace treaty had launched a dramatic change in the Middle East (whose implications are still evident), thereby removing the main obstacle to official Sino-Israeli relations.

Initially, Beijing had regarded Israel favorably as a country "liberated" from British imperialism, while displaying reservations about the Arab (and many Muslim) countries, still associated with the West, and considered orthodox and backward. Responding to Israel's recognition of the PRC (100 days after its proclamation), Zhou Enlai, PRC Prime Minister and Foreign Minister, cabled Moshe Sharett, Israel's Foreign Minister. Acknowledging Israel's decision, he extended the PRC "welcome and thanks" (Zhonghua, 1957, I, 22–23). Although Zhou avoided any intention to establish diplomatic relations, there are indications that this was on the Chinese agenda, at least then (Shichor, 1979: 216, notes 46, 47). Some of the reasons why Sino-Israeli relations were not established in the early 1950s reflected the objection of Arab and Muslim countries.

By that time Beijing had realized that the international impact of Arab and Muslim countries overshadowed that of Israel—all the more so since some Middle Eastern nations had managed to defy the West, even considering switching sides. Furthermore, although others still maintained a Western orientation, all shared a common attitude: extreme hostility to Israel. Beijing decided to exploit this attitude to win friends. Published in 2005, a study using available Chinese Foreign Ministry documents showed that Beijing had decided as early as November 1953 to associate itself with the Arabs—at Israel's expense: "We do not have urgent political and economic need to establish diplomatic relations with Israel" (Xia, 2005: 76–79). Yet, a more recently accessible document reveals an even earlier decision.

In a recorded conversation with Nikolai V. Roshchin, Soviet ambassador to the PRC, on July 24, 1951, Zhou Enlai surveyed China's foreign policy toward capitalist countries—which he divided into two groups. The first, including (among others) the Arab League governments, which depended on the imperialist camp, still maintained friendly relations with the Chinese Government through their representatives in Beijing. "China tries to use them in its interest," sharpening their contradictions with the imperialist countries. Zhou then added:

> In this group *China will not establish relations only with Israel. Establishing relations with Israel will not bring anything substantial and besides, this can lead to a worsening of relations with the countries of the Arab League which, in a number of cases, have supported the PRC.*
>
> *(Roshchin, 1951, emphasis added)*

Thus, about 18 months *after* Israel's recognition of the PRC, and the exchange of cables between their foreign ministers, and five years *before* the first Arab state recognized the PRC, Beijing had already decided to reject diplomatic relations with Israel.

Over time, the Arabs, and the Palestinians, constantly reiterated their anti-Israel arguments in meetings with PRC leaders and officials. For example, Egypt's ambassador to Indonesia told Huang Zhen, China's ambassador, that Egypt was concerned about the visit of an Israeli trade delegation to China (reportedly from January 28 to February 21, 1955). He said that PRC-Israel negotiations "would leave a very negative impression on the Arab League countries and this may reflect on the relations between Arab countries and the PRC." Huang Zhen, who told the Soviet ambassador about the meeting, had responded that "the PRC maintains a policy of establishing and developing relations with all countries on the basis of equal rights, mutual benefit, and mutual respect of territorial integrity and sovereignty" (Zhukov, 1955). This standard reply, given before the Bandung Conference, possibly meant that, while Sino-Israeli relations had already been shelved, China's ambassador to Indonesia was unaware of it.

Representing a watershed in Sino-Arab relations, the Bandung Conference gave Chinese leaders the first opportunity to meet high-level Arab leaders. Zhou Enlai and his entourage became aware of the potential in using the hostility to Israel, and the Palestine problem, to win the goodwill of the Arab governments (none of which, at that time, had recognized the PRC). Zhou was quick to exploit Egypt's concerns about Israel's military power to mediate an arms deal offered by Moscow. On May 21, 1955 (four weeks after the conference), the Soviet ambassador in Cairo was told that

> during the conference President Nasser met with Zhou Enlai, who was willing to assist Egypt in its struggle against Israel. Zhou Enlai was willing to supply the Egyptian army with weapons from China, Moscow, or Czechoslovakia—we believe that Zhou Enlai contacted Moscow and reached an agreement on this with officials there.
>
> *(Anon., 1955; Tuhami, 1955; Heikal, 1973: 54–55, 226–277)*

It did not take long for Beijing, which had initially praised Israel's liberation, to associate Israel with imperialism, an about-turn prompted by the Arabs. In his reported meeting with China's ambassador Chen Zhihfang in February 1957, Syria's Foreign Minister Salah al-Bitar referred to Israel not only as a "tool of imperialism" but also as the "essence of imperialism," planning to invade Arab lands. "Israeli occupation of Palestine," he said "can be compared to a hypothetical occupation of your Shanghai by imperialists, this is not tolerable" (Chinese Embassy in Syria, 1957). While the Chinese were not intimately familiar with the intricate Palestine situation, they did understand Shanghai—and Taiwan.

One way to drive a wedge between China and Israel was to underline the "connection" between Israel and Taiwan. Meeting Zhou Enlai in late 1963, Nasser said that Middle East disarmament problem "is not an issue of Israel itself but one of those who support Israel, just as Taiwan is not an issue of Chiang Kai-shek but one of those who support him." Zhou replied: "Only after resolution of the issues of Israel and Taiwan will it be possible to consider disarmament" (Zhou, 1963). Meeting the first PLO delegation to China in March 1965, Mao said: "Israel and Formosa are bases of imperialism in Asia. You are the front gate of the great continent, and we are the rear. They created Israel for you and Formosa for us" (quoted by Cooley, 1973: 176). This "connection" made Sino-Israeli relations more improbable, although Israel *has never recognized Taiwan*—unlike some Arab countries.

The Russian Impact

Russians affected Sino-Israeli relations in four different stages. First, by facilitating Israel's independence in 1948, they had also legitimized Israel's recognition of the PRC, and Beijing's initial interest in Israel. Second, as their relations with Israel had soured and the Arab gates opened, Moscow now legitimized China's exclusion of Israel. Third, in the 1970s, the Soviet military threat to China, and its invasion of Afghanistan, had unintentionally triggered Beijing's quest for Israel arms and military technology. These *unofficial* exchanges had laid the foundations for *official* Sino-Israeli diplomatic relations in 1992.

Fourth, since the 1990s, the resumption of Sino-Russian relations also enabled Beijing's turn to Moscow for arms and military supply, at the expense of Israel, whose arms sales to China have anyway been blocked by Washington (see below).

Initially, Moscow had played an important role in promoting Sino-Israeli relations (Gorodetsky, 2003; Kramer, 2017). This by no means reflected any sudden friendliness toward Israel, Zionism, or Jews—nor even China. On the contrary, the Soviets often displayed hostility toward Jews and Zionism, and reservations about Maoist communism. Moscow's (short-lived) support for Israel was grounded in self-interests, primarily terminating the British presence in the Middle East. Moscow even sustained Israel's Liberation War by indirect arms supply. Articulated in the United Nations and expressed by Moscow's swift recognition *de jure* of the new State of Israel (while the USA extended only *de facto* recognition), this attitude gave Beijing a green light to consider official relations with Israel. In fact, some of the early Sino-Israeli diplomatic talks were held in Moscow. However, in 1953, Israel's relations with the Soviets deteriorated following an explosion near the Soviet legation in Tel Aviv on February 9, triggered by Moscow's abuse of Soviet Jews. Suspended diplomatic relations were restored in July after Stalin's death. By then, Beijing had already shelved relations with Israel.[2]

In 1967, following Israel's defeat of four Arab countries, armed by Soviet and Eastern Bloc weapons, Moscow cut off diplomatic relations with Israel yet again. Apparently, this act had nothing to do with China but, retrospectively and ultimately, it paved the way for Sino-Israeli diplomatic relations. China's decision to buy Israeli arms and military technology in the 1980s reflected Israel's experience in challenging and upgrading Soviet arms and technology—all beneficial to China's military capability. One reason why Israel could have done it was that, unlike the USA and Western countries, Israel was relatively immune to Soviet pressures. Without the presence of diplomats and agents, Moscow could hardly have gathered intelligence, and its ability to threaten Israel not to sell arms to China was crippled. If Moscow, primarily KGB Chairman Yuri Andropov, had overcome their anti-Zionist and anti-Semitic urge to cease relations with Israel—later regretted (Andrew and Mitrokhin, 2006: 152, 230)—Israel's arms sales to China would have been unlikely to happen. These arms supplies could be seen as a kind of retaliation for Moscow's huge quantities of arms delivered to Israel's enemies over the years.

Moscow's last impact on Sino-Israeli relations emerged in the early 1990s, following post-Soviet Russia's reconciliation with China. One outcome has been the resumption of Beijing's acquisition of Russian (in fact, Soviet-made) weapons. Given that most of its military equipment had been based on Soviet models, China's policy has been logical—but detrimental to Israel. In an uncoordinated pincer movement, third parties, Moscow and Washington, terminated Israel's bilateral military relations with China.

The American Impact

Americans affected Sino-Israeli relations in three different stages. First, in the 1950s and 1960s, they applied pressure on Israel to prevent official relations with the PRC, already recognized by Israel. Second, in the 1970s and 1980s, Washington encouraged Israel to sell arms and military technology to China, as a deterrent against Soviet threats along the borders. Third, following the deterioration of Sino-US relations, since the 1990s, Washington has applied pressure on Israel to abort military and technology transfers to China, and to limit Chinese infrastructure investments in Israel, considered detrimental to US interests.

Israel recognized the PRC in January 1950, without the knowledge, let alone the approval, not only of Washington, but also of Israel's diplomats there. At that time, Israel's relations with the USA were not as close as they later became. It had taken Washington nearly *nine months* to recognize Israel *de jure* (on US reservations and opposition to the establishment of Israel, see Herf, 2022). Moreover, through 1950, and even after the outbreak of the Korean War, Jerusalem still defended its China policy, including a UN vote for Beijing's admission, contrary to US policy (more details in Shichor, 2010). China's military intervention in Korea in October, and Israel's growing dependence on the USA, had forced Jerusalem to change its attitude. However, although Jerusalem began to have doubts about relations with China, it never lost hope.

Yet since early 1951, Washington had warned Israel that its China policy contradicted US intentions to impose sanctions on Beijing, it should reject its admission to the UN, and oppose Sino-Israeli relations. On November 21, 1951, Acting US Secretary of State James E. Webb notified Israel that such a step "would be most inappropriate," when the "Chinese Communists" are still engaged in hostilities against the UN in Korea. "*Establishing [a] Legation in Peiping by Israel this time might be considered as moral support for [the] Communist regime and as such could be construed as assistance*" (Anon., 1951b, emphasis added). Following a November 29 meeting with another US official, Moshe Sharett, Israeli Foreign Minister, confessed: "Perhaps it is to be regretted that we had not established diplomatic relations with China immediately after we recognized it" (Anon., 1951a). Some Israeli diplomats still toyed with the idea of relations with China (also to ensure better treatment of Soviet Jews), but the leadership realized that such relations would be inconceivable before the end of the war, probably even after. Henceforth, while Israel still favored diplomatic relations with China, any progress had to conform to Washington's policy. Israel's senior diplomats in the USA consistently promoted this approach, faithfully adopting US hostility to China.

Not all Israeli diplomats accepted this attitude. David Hacohen, Israel's Minister to Burma, who had maintained friendly relations with China's ambassador there, and in early 1955 led a commercial delegation to China, was furious. He called the US China policy "foolish" as well as "pointless," and condemned Israel's "total submission to the US State Department's real or imagined dictates and sacrificing the global needs of the State of Israel," whose diplomats bowed to this demand.

> I've become more and more convinced that my colleagues in Washington are hit by blindness, lack objective political sense and exaggerate giving such high priority to the United States' mood while giving up our essential needs ... I was firm in my view that we have to ignore America's heated animosity toward China and act in accordance to our needs.

Most of the Americans he had met, he added, deplored the lack of logic and political wisdom in the US alienation from China "because of some irrational mental complex that has nothing to do with wise policy." He said that "the fear of America's reactions" was not merely "exaggerated, inflated and imaginary," but provided the Arabs with an advantage over Israel regarding China (Hacohen, 1954, 1974: 254–256). His words are as right today as they were then.

In February 1954, General Walter Bedell Smith, Under-Secretary of State and former CIA Director, expressed his views on China to Reuven Shiloah, political minister in Israel's embassy and former Mossad Director:

> As a friend of Israel I advise you, delay the [China] issue for the time being. Who but you know that I personally would like, based on important reasons, to see an Israeli mission in Pekin. [But], in view of the existing situation in public opinion and the Congress, I am ready to sacrifice certain interests and recommend to you not to take any step that could be interpreted as encouraging the process of China's admission to the UN family. You cannot imagine the difficulties facing [Secretary of State] Dulles. ... *You have to understand that there is no question of political logic here. The issue is a mental complex that drives people insane.* You could not have chosen a less suitable time. My advice to you, delay the issue to a more appropriate moment.
>
> *(Shiloah, 1954, emphasis added)*

Bedell Smith's doubts about the wisdom of US-China policy were shared by several prominent Americans (such as Vice-president Richard Nixon and US ambassador to the UN, Henry Cabot Lodge), who believed that this policy should change (Lewin, 1954). In Jerusalem, Israel's Foreign Ministry retreated from its intention to establish relations with China, but only one step. Instructing all of Israel's missions abroad to cultivate good relations with the Chinese and to show good will, the Director-general warned them not to "take any official or public measure that could lead to revenge in our relations with the West and especially with the United States." He added: "Be careful not to say a word that could be interpreted as a commitment, or even as just a hint, that the question of diplomatic relations was discussed by us" (Eytan, 1954a; Sharett, 1978: II, 515).

Israeli officials, especially in the USA, reiterated that accommodating China would not only harm US-Israeli relations, but also the Jewish community's efforts to enlist US political and material support for Israel, and the United Jewish Appeal's ability to raise money remittances for Israel. Israel's Foreign Ministry's Director-General indicated that the UK (and other Western countries) had formed official relations with China notwithstanding US opposition: Israel is discriminated against,

> [because of] the Americans' feeling that we are 'in their pocket' anyway. An act that reveals independence, such as the establishment of relations with China, may show the Americans that we are not so much 'in their pocket' as they believe.
>
> *(Eytan, 1954b)*

By the end of 1954, after China shelled Taiwan's offshore island of Quemoy, the US rejection of any relations with Beijing increased. Reporting on a meeting with US officials on China's UN representation, Abba Eban, Israel's ambassador to the USA and the UN, said: "The US would fight forcefully against the admission of People's China. They will do their best to defeat this issue by proposing a procedural postponement like last year and they solemnly request our support" (Eban, 1954). On September 21, 1954, after the Korean armistice, Israel voted, for the first time, *for* the US proposal (presumably against Beijing). Whatever the excuses, Israel's UN mission yielded to Washington's pressure.

Having forced Israel to comply with its demands against China, the USA turned to block the visit of Israel's forthcoming trade delegation to China. They threatened that under US regulations, all US assets of the delegation's members were liable to be frozen, also banning all their financial and commercial transactions. Later hinting that sanctions would be avoided, they still added that, given the anti-Chinese climate in the USA, such a mission might damage Israel's public image and could blemish Israel's compliance with the UN embargo on China (Anon., 1954). They warned that the visit "cannot but have negative effect on U.S.-Israel relations" (US Division, 1954). Disregarding US objections, the delegation visited China from January 28 to February 23, 1955. Though practically it achieved nothing, least of all political, David Hacohen, who headed the delegation, concluded that the visit "should not become an isolated episode because of complacency and neglect on our side and perhaps also [because] of the influence of an external party [i.e. the US]" (Hacohen, 1955a). Foreshadowing the future, he said:

> There is one and united China ... and there is no reason to doubt its sovereign existence. The entire world knows it, and America will have to confess its mistake and reform. Any state, Israel included, that would consolidate its relations with China would help deliver America from its mental crisis and extricate it from the distress it had found itself in.
>
> *(Hacohen, 1955b)*

As mentioned above, it was Beijing that blocked relations with Israel, but neither Jerusalem nor Washington were aware of it. Still, if Washington had not sabotaged them, Sino-Israeli relations might have been established earlier, perhaps even before the Korean War. As David Hacohen had predicted, Washington began to change its mind about Beijing in the late 1960s, which shortly led to China's admission to the UN and to a dramatic expansion in China's diplomatic network. One of the main US incentives to collaborate with China was to make it militarily stronger against the Soviet Union. Cut off from Soviet military supplies since 1960, the PRC desperately needed arms which, however, neither the USA nor Western Europe could provide. For one reason, Moscow threatened the West, and primarily the USA, not to play the "China Card." For another, Western arms were incompatible with China's, which did not have the funds to buy them anyway. Israel was not only a *better* option; it was the *only* option (Shichor, 2020b). First, Israel could provide the Chinese with upgraded Soviet weapons, as well as with the experience it had accumulated in fighting them. Also, unlike the West, Israel was much less exposed to Soviet pressure since Moscow had broken off diplomatic relations with Israel following the 1967 War. Finally, unlike Western suppliers, Israel was ready to sell China the technology to produce the weapons at a lower cost, and do it as secretly as possible, unlike the Western hullabaloo that accompanied its arms sales explorations with China.

Despite Israel's potential advantages as an arms supplier to China, military relations between the two appeared inconceivable, not only because of the huge difference in size, and because the two countries did not have diplomatic (or any other) relations, but also because the Chinese provided Israel's enemies with revolutionary rhetoric and arms. So, whose idea was it to engage China and Israel in military relations? Most circumstantial and documentary evidence point to the USA. As early as 1971, Henry Kissinger, then National Security Adviser to President Nixon, may have suggested to China's leaders that Israel could help them withstand Soviet military threats along the border, following a series of armed clashes. Other US leaders who visited China in the next years reiterated this option. They included James Schlesinger, Secretary of Defense and former CIA Director, who visited China in September 1976; Zbigniew Brzezinski, President Jimmy Carter's National Security Advisor, who arrived in China in May 1978; and Secretary of Defense, Harold Brown, who visited China in December 1979 (after an Israeli military delegation had already visited China). This issue was also raised by Dr. Edward Luttwak, at that time Research and Visiting Professor at Johns Hopkins and at Georgetown universities who accompanied Schlesinger (Shichor, 2020b: 14–28).

Classified in those years, details about Washington prompting Israel's arms sales to China were revealed later, primarily in a number of briefings at the US Senate committees, which confirm that Washington had not only known about these transfers but also approved—if not facilitated—them, and not just implicitly. A testimony before the US-China Security Review Commission in 2001 confirmed that Israel's arms sales to China *had been a U.S.-sponsored activity* (U.S. China Security Review Commission, 2001). In a statement, Richard D. Fisher, Jr., China expert and Senior Fellow at the Jamestown Foundation's Center for Security Policy, said: "During the late 1970s and early 1980s, the United States *encouraged* Israel to develop military technical ties with the PRC, to aid PRC military modernization against the former Soviet Union" (Anon., 2004: 80, emphasis added). At that Hearing, C. Richard D'Amato, Vice-chairman, and former Chairman, of the Senate U.S.-China Economic and Security Review Commission, also said: "Obviously, *we encouraged the Israelis to get involved with the Chinese during the Cold War*. They obliged us" (ibid.,: 109, emphasis added). In a 2006 Senate hearing, D'Amato raised again the issue of Israel's arms sales to China, "some of which may have American technologies": "Of course, we let ourselves into this during the Cold War, *encouraging the Israelis to provide a counterweight to the Russians via China*. So, we're not entirely blameless here" (Anon., 2006: 158, emphasis added). Thus, by pushing Israel's arms sales to China, the USA had helped pave the way for Sino-Israel diplomatic ties, established on January 24, 1992. By that time, however, US relations with China had begun to deteriorate in the wake of the Tiananmen massacre and the resumption of Sino-Russian relations after the collapse of the Soviet Union.

Washington, which had earlier promoted Israel's arms sales to China, now began blocking them, also criticizing Israeli civilian technology transfers to China and Chinese investments in Israeli companies and infrastructures, considered a "security threat." US pressure forced Israel to cancel the sale of a Phalcon Airborne Warning and Control System, for which China had already paid some $250 million, and to stop upgrading the Harpy UAVs, sold to the Chinese (Shichor, 2005: 7–9). Israel's experienced security companies faced US objections to offering their services in Beijing's 2008 Olympic Games. These American obstacles were applied to Chinese investments in Israeli ports, railways, light trains, tunnels, power stations, Dead Sea minerals, desalination projects, food industries, and more. Israel has also been accused of allowing high-tech Chinese companies, such as Huawei, to set up branches in Israel, enlisting its qualified workforce. Although Beijing understood Israel's dependence on the USA (interpreted in traditional Chinese terms as the required obedience of a younger brother to an elder brother), Sino-Israeli relations have been damaged. One of Israel's ambassadors was denied access to high-ranking officials in Beijing throughout his service.

Conclusion

Trilateral intervention in Sino-Israeli bilateral relations is not unique or exceptional. India-Israel diplomatic relations were also delayed because of Delhi's sensitivity to the reactions not only of its huge Muslim population, but also of the Arab and Muslim countries. Singapore's attempts to conceal its relations with Israel, especially in the military field (Ho, 2020), were also intended to avoid irritating Muslims and Arabs, especially in nearby hostile countries (Malaysia, Indonesia, Brunei, and Bangladesh). Japan, the first Asian country to establish diplomatic relations with Israel, maintained a low-key presence in Israel for years, fearing reprisals by its Middle Eastern oil suppliers. Most African countries cut off diplomatic relations with Israel either in June 1967 or in October 1973, identifying with the Arabs. Cyprus postponed official relations with Israel because of Arab pressure. Poland and Hungary cut off diplomatic relations with Israel in 1967, parroting the Soviet Union. Common to all these examples is that only *one* third party was involved, either (in most cases) the Arabs, or (in fewer cases) the Soviets.

What is special in the case of China-Israel relations is that *three* kinds of third parties intervened in their bilateral relations, often simultaneously. Of these third parties, the role of the Soviets and the Arabs appeared, in retrospect, provisional. US involvement, however, has been the most consistent, most damaging, and only partly helpful. Its counterproductive obsession with China is still evident today, among others, in its occasionally brutal pressure on Israel.

Notes

1 Well before the inauguration of the PRC, and Israel, Song Qingling had been sympathetic to Zionism and the Jewish people. She was one of the founders and leaders of the China League for Civil Rights. On May 13, 1933, she published "A Denunciation of the Persecution of German Progressives and the Jewish People," where she said: "Another sign of human and cultural retrogression to the Middle Ages and the darkest days of Czarist Russia, is the persecution of the Jews and the anti-Semitic pogroms, systematically organized by the German Government and the Fascist Party" (Soong, 1953: 57–60). Later she expressed sympathy to right-winger Zionists, the ancestors of Begin's Party. In late 1948, she attended a farewell party for a group of Shanghai Revisionist Jews who were about to leave for Israel. Reportedly, she said: "Your revolution will spark a chain of revolutions that will shatter British imperialism throughout the world" (Ben-Eliezer, 1985: 379).

2 In his meeting with the Director of the Asia Department in China's Foreign Ministry as a member of the Israeli delegation to China in early 1955, Dr. Daniel Lewin, Head of the Asia Division in the Israeli Foreign Ministry, elaborated Israel's attitude to the forthcoming Bandung Conference. He got the impression that the Chinese delegation would act along these lines "unless they receive a negative opinion from the USSR government" (Anon., 1955).

References

Andrew, C. and Mitrokhin, V. (2006). *The KGB and the West: The Mitrokhin Archive II.* London: Penguin.

Anon. (1951a). "Report 130.02/2455/1," *Documents on the Foreign Policy of the State of Israel, 1951,* 7 December, no. 519, pp. 354–355.

Anon. (1951b). "Secret Telegram 601.84A93/11–2151," November 21, 1951, Foreign Relations of the United States (FRUS), (The China Area), 7: 1853–1854.

Anon. (1954). "Telegrams W203 and W214, 92.01/2211/12," *Documents on the Foreign Policy of the State of Israel 1954,* December 7–8, pp. 533–534.

Anon. (1955). "Actions of the [Israeli] Foreign Ministry toward the Bandung Conference" (Secret), No. 9541/a, 458/9. April 14: 2. Appeared in *Al-Ahram,* January 22, 1958.

Anon. (2004). "Hearing on Military Modernization and Cross-Strait Balance, before the U.S. China Economic and Security Review Commission," February 6. Washington, DC: U.S. Government Printing Office.

Anon. (2006). "China's Military Modernization and U.S. Export Controls, Hearing before the U.S.-China Economic and Security Review Commission," March 16–17. Washington, DC: U.S. Government Printing Office.

Ben-Eliezer, J. (1985). *Shanghai Lost, Jerusalem Regained.* Tel Aviv: Steimatzky.

Bialer, U. (1990). *Between East and West: Israel's Foreign Policy Orientation, 1948–1956.* Cambridge: Cambridge University Press.

Chiang, K.S. (1957). *Soviet Russia in China: A Summing-Up at Seventy.* New York: Farrar, Straus and Cudahy.

Chinese Embassy in Syria (1957). "The Situation of Ambassador Chen's Visit to the Syrian Foreign Minister." cable, February 11. History and Public Policy Program Digital Archive, PRC FMA 107-00250-06: 51-2. Available at: http://digitalarchive.wilsoncenter.org/document/114822

Cooley, J.K. (1973). *Green March, Black September: The Story of the Palestinian Arabs.* London: Frank Cass.

Eban, A. (1954). "Note from Eban to Gideon Rafael (Counselor for Middle Eastern and UN Affairs in the Foreign Ministry)," August 7. Israel State Archive, 748/232.

Eber, I. (1980). *Voices from Afar: Modern Chinese Writers on Oppressed Peoples and Their Literature.* Ann Arbor, MI: Michigan Monographs in Chinese Studies.

Eytan, W. (1954a). "Note from Eytan to Israel's Missions Abroad," 130.02/2414/3. May 31, *Documents on the Foreign Policy of the State of Israel (DFPSI) 1954,* no. 231, pp. 355–356.

Eytan, W. (1954b). "Note from Eytan to Sharett," 93.04/42/8. July 20, *Documents on the Foreign Policy of the State of Israel (DFPSI) 1954,* no. 293, pp. 470–471.

Gorodetsky, G. (2003). "The Soviet Union's Role in the Creation of the State of Israel," *Journal of Israeli History,* no. 22(1), pp. 4–20.

Hacohen, D. (1954). "Note from Hacohen to Levavi," 130.02/2413/30. February 17, *Documents on the Foreign Policy of the State of Israel (DFPSI) 1954,* no. 71, pp. 104–105.

Hacohen, D. (1955a). "Note from Hacohen to Eytan," 1877/950:71, 226/3II. March 2. Israel State Archive.

Hacohen, D. (1955b). "Note from Hacohen to Sharett (Secret-Personal)," 2010/950:71. April 21, David Hacohen Archives, Section 16, File 238.

Hacohen, D. (1974). *Et Lesaper [My Way].* Tel Aviv: Am Oved (in Hebrew).

Heikal, M. (1973). *Nasser: The Cairo Documents.* London: New English Library.

Herf, J. (2022). *Israel's Moment: International Support for and Opposition to Establishing the Jewish State, 1945–1949.* Cambridge: Cambridge University Press.

Ho, P. (2020). "A Mexican Fandango with a Poisonous Shrimp," in M. Tomba (Ed.), *Beating the Odds Together: 50 Years of Singapore-Israel Ties.* Singapore: World Scientific Publishing, pp. 35–47.

Kramer, M. (2017). "Who Saved Israel in 1947?" *Mosaic: Advancing Jewish Thought,* November 6. Available at: https://scholar.harvard.edu/files/matinkramer/files/who_saved_israel_1947.pdf

Kranzler, D. (1976). *Japanese, Nazis and Jews: The Jewish Refugee Community in Shanghai, 1938–1945.* New York: Yeshiva University Press.

Lewin, D. (1954). "Director of the Asia Division Daniel Lewin in Israel's Foreign Ministry to Sharett," 130.02/2414/3, May 14, *Documents on the Foreign Policy of the State of Israel 1954,* no. 212, pp. 320–323.

Mao, Z.D. (1992 [1919]). "So Much for National Self-Determination (14 July)," in S.R. Schram (Ed.), *Mao's Road to Power: Revolutionary Writings 1912–1949,* vol. I: *The Pre-Marxist Period, 1912–1920.* Armonk, NY: M.E. Sharpe, p. 337.

Roschin, N.V. (1951). "From the Diary of N. V. Roshchin: Memorandum of Conversation with Chinese Premier Zhou Enlai on 24 July 1951," July 27. History and Public Policy Program Digital Archive, AVPRF. Available at: http://digitalarchive.wilsoncenter.org/document/118735

Schram, S. (1992). *Mao's Road to Power,* vol. II: *National Revolution and Social Revolution, December 1920–June 1927.* Armonk, NY: M.E. Sharpe, p. 382.

Sharett, M. (1978). *Personal Diary,* vol. II. Tel Aviv: Ma'ariv Library, p. 515 (in Hebrew).

Shichor, Y. (1979). *The Middle East in China's Foreign Policy, 1949–1977.* Cambridge: Cambridge University Press.

Shichor, Y. (2005). "The U.S. Factor in Israel's Military Relations with China," *China Brief,* 5(12).

Shichor, Y. (2010). "The US Role in Delaying Sino-Israeli Relations: Two's Company, Three's a Crowd," *Jewish Political Studies Review,* 22(1–2): 7–32.

Shichor, Y. (2020a). "Combining Contradictions: Jewish Contributions to the Chinese Revolution," *International Journal of China Studies,* 11(2): 183–212.

Shichor, Y. (2020b). "Proxy: Unlocking the Origins of Israel's Military Sales to China," *The Asia Papers,* 3. Washington, DC: Center for International and Regional Studies, Georgetown University.

Shiloah, R. (1954). "Note from Reuven Shiloah to Foreign Minister Sharett," File 75/140, 24 February 1954, Israeli State Archive.

Soong, C.L. (1953). *The Struggle for New China*. Peking: Foreign Languages Press.

Tuhami, H. (1955). "Intelligence Brief Submitted by Hassan Tuhami, Head of the Intelligence Branch at the President's Office, to Gamal Abd al-Nasser," June 15. History and Public Policy Program Digital Archive, Muhammad al-Tawil, Lubat al-Amm wa-Gamal Abd al-Nasser (Cairo: 1986), pp. 165–169. Available at: http://digitalarchive.wilsoncenter.org/document/112262

U.S. China Security Review Commission (2001). "Briefing: Proliferation Issues." October 12: 551. Available at: www.uscc.gov/sites/default/files/transcripts/10.12.01HT.pdf

US Division (1954). "Coded Telegram, to Israel Embassy in Washington," 182, 130.09/2310/8, December 17, *Documents on the Foreign Policy of the State of Israel 1954*, no. 551, p. 896.

Xia, L.P. (2005). "Cong waijiaobu kaifang dangan kan 20 shiji 50 niandai zhongyi jiechu shimo" [Contacts between China and Israel in the 1950s as Seen from Declassified Files of the Chinese Ministry of Foreign Affairs], *Dangdai zhongguo shi yanjiu* [*Contemporary China History Studies*], 12(3).

Zhonghua (1957). *Zhonghua Renmin Gongheguo duiwai guanxi wenjianji* [*Collected Documents on the Foreign Relations of the People's Republic of China*], vol. 1. Beijing: Shijie Zhishi Chubanshe.

Zhou, E.L. (1963). "Record of Premier Zhou Enlai's Calling on President Nasser," December 20, 1963, History and Public Policy Program Digital Archive, PRC FMA 107-01027-08: 63-80. Available at: http://digitalarchive.wilsoncenter.org/document/165432

Zhukov, D.A. (1955). "Journal Entry of Ambassador Zhukov: Visit of the PRC Ambassador to Indonesia, Huang Zhen," March 23. History and Public Policy Program Digital Archive, AVPRF. Available at: http://digitalarchive.wilsoncenter.org/document/110254

24

UNOFFICIAL DIPLOMACY

The Paradox of Israel-Taiwan Relations

Yitzhak Shichor

Introduction

There are relatively few studies of Israel-Taiwan "relations." Some go back to the attitudes of the Republic of China (ROC) since its establishment in January 1912, toward Jews, Judaism, and Zionism, given that Israel did not exist at that time. Thus, while these attitudes are interesting in themselves, and while the role played by the ROC in international organizations—first in the League of Nations and later in the United Nations—is important, they are theoretical and irrelevant to the questions raised above. Existing studies, some only in Hebrew and some in English fail to address these questions in any systematic way.

Some of the ROC leaders, including Sun Yat-sen, his widow Soong Ch'ing-ling (Song Qingling), and his son Sun Fo, had shown sympathy toward the Jews and even Zionism (Goldstein, 2004). Song Qingling, who joined the communists and later assumed senior positions in the PRC hierarchy, had been sympathetic to Zionism and the Jewish people. She was one of the founders and leaders of the China League for Civil Rights. On May 13, 1933, she published "A Denunciation of the Persecution of German Progressives and the Jewish People," where she said: "Another sign of human and cultural retrogression to the Middle Ages and the darkest days of Czarist Russia, is the persecution of the Jews and the anti-Semitic pogroms, systematically organized by the German Government and the Fascist Party" (Soong, 1953: 57–60). Later she expressed sympathy to right-winger Zionists, the ancestors of Begin's party. In late 1948, she attended a farewell party for a group of Shanghai Revisionist Jews who were about to leave for Israel. Reportedly, she said: "Your revolution will spark a chain of revolutions that will shatter British imperialism throughout the world." ROC officials offered weapons to Jewish right-wingers in Shanghai (Ben-Eliezer, 1985: 379).

Yet, the ROC's initial attitude toward the State of Israel was reserved, if not suspicious--well before the establishment of the PRC, and its competition over the Middle Eastern and Muslim votes in the UN. Thus, on November 29, 1947, after much Jewish efforts, the ROC abstained on the UN Palestine Partition Plan (Resolution 181). A year later, on November 29, 1948, after the foundation of the State of Israel, the ROC abstained on Israel's first application to join the UN. On December 17, 1948, the ROC abstained on

DOI: 10.4324/9781003048404-27

Israel's second application to join the UN at the Security Council, together with the UK, Belgium, Canada, and France. On March 2, 1949, the ROC offered Israel diplomatic recognition and two days later voted for Israel's admission to the UN (Resolution 273). However, this was a desperate step taken when its survival was doubtful, and just half a year before its final defeat by the communists. Had Israel agreed to the establishment of diplomatic relations with the ROC in March 1949, it would have undoubtedly pleased the USA, but created a problem for both the ROC (concerning the Muslim and Arab countries) and Israel (concerning the PRC and the Soviet bloc, which had backed its own establishment) (Gorodetsky, 2003).

This chapter is divided into two sections. The first deals with Israel-Taiwan unofficial relations from about 1950 to around 1990. Heavily dependent on Middle Eastern oil, and on Arab votes in the UN, Taiwan rejected any official relations with Israel despite many similarities and association with the USA. At the same time, and secretly, Taiwan allowed unofficial relations, particularly in conventional and non-conventional military fields, and intelligence. These unofficial relations continued even after the PRC has displaced the ROC in the UN and its Security Council in October 1971. Israel and most of the Arab countries voted for the exclusion of Taiwan. The second section reflects "pseudo diplomatic relations" governed by the mutual establishment of economic and cultural offices in Taipei and Tel Aviv. In fact, these are "embassies" for all intents and purposes, except for official diplomacy. They enable, since the early 1990s, a wide range of economic, technological, cultural, and security relations, though not military.

Given this reality, the conclusion will sum up the reasons why in the first period, and despite the convenient conditions, Israel and Taiwan failed to establish diplomatic relations, and why, in the second period, Israel and Taiwan, despite inconvenient conditions, the two countries established quasi-diplomatic relations. A related conclusion is that, occasionally, unofficial quasi-diplomatic relations offer better opportunities for exchanges between countries, by sidestepping obstacles blocking official diplomacy. Taiwan is a special case to underline the advantages of unofficial and quasi-diplomatic relations over no relations at all. But Taiwan is by no means the only case—nor is Israel.

Official and Unofficial Relations: Mutual Incentives

From the very beginning, Israel and Taiwan shared several features. Both were established in the late 1940s, Israel in 1948 and Taiwan (the Republic of China) in 1949, following years of conflicts and armed confrontations. Both have been constantly threatened by external enemies, Taiwan by the People's Republic of China, and Israel by a score of Arab countries and "national liberation movements," which claimed their territories. Both have been associated with the United States, and represented advanced and modernized societies and economies. Facing constant threats, the survival of both has depended on strong armed forces and high military budgets, among the highest in the world (per capita). Given these similarities, it would have been expected that Taipei and Jerusalem maintain official diplomatic relations. This, however, has never happened.

Theoretically, Israel and Taiwan could have established diplomatic relations in that period, very much like many other countries. When the State of Israel was established in May 1948, about 53 states had maintained diplomatic relations with the Republic of China. In March 1949, the ROC offered to establish diplomatic ties with Israel. However, at that time, the ROC was on the verge of collapse, defeated by the communists, and its offer was not reciprocated. Instead, soon after the proclamation of the People's Republic of China on October 1, 1949, Israel officially recognized it. Apparently, this recognition, on January 9, 1950, signaled the end of optional official relations with the ROC (heretofore Taiwan), because diplomatic ties with both would have been inconceivable. It should be stressed that China continued to maintain diplomatic relations with countries engaged in anti-Chinese armed "aggression" (like India, in 1962; the Soviet Union, in 1969; and Vietnam, in 1979). However, Beijing has never accepted the "two China" policy, and immediately severed official relations with those countries that preferred diplomatic relations with the Taiwan (such as the Central African Republic, in 1991, and Dahomei, in 1966). Moreover, the Chinese instantly downgraded diplomatic relations with governments (e.g. Lithuania, in December 2021) once they agreed to the opening of an *unofficial* "Taiwan" (using this name) representation office, followed by extensive economic sanctions.

> Any country seeking to establish diplomatic relations with China must show its readiness to sever all diplomatic relations with the Taiwan authorities and recognize the government of the PRC as the sole legal government of China. The Chinese government will never tolerate any country scheming to create "two Chinas" or "one China, one Taiwan"; nor will it tolerate any moves on the part of countries having formal diplomatic relations with China to establish any form of official relations with the Taiwan authorities.
>
> *(Ministry of Foreign Affairs of the PRC, n.d.)*

This, however, did not apply to Israel. Eventually, Israel and the PRC did not establish diplomatic relations until January 24, 1992. Soviet documents show that Beijing rejected such relations as early as July 27, 1951, when its Prime Minister and Foreign Minister Zhou Enlai told N.V. Roshchin, the Soviet ambassador to the PRC:

> China will not establish relations … with Israel. Establishing relations with Israel will not bring anything substantial and besides, this can lead to a worsening of relations with the countries of the Arab League, who in a number of cases have supported the PRC.
>
> *(Roshchin, 1951)*

China's growing association with the Arabs and the Palestinians, providing them with arms, military training, and ideological-revolutionary indoctrination, and condemning Israel in the harshest words to the point of denying its right to exist—potentially paved the way for relations with Taiwan.

As mentioned above, over the years, both relatively small countries have become dependent on US protection against external threats. Both were established by a large-scale migration that in a few years practically transformed the ethnic-demographic balance of their countries and turned the indigenous population into a second-rate minority.[1] Both have created sophisticated military systems, among the largest in the world on a *per capita* basis, as well as advanced technological economies. Yet, there was no real attempt, by either side, to form official relations. Publicly, even unofficial relations appeared marginal. The question is why and whose fault was it that diplomatic relations between Israel and Taiwan have never been established, and why unofficial relations— of whatever kind—were largely kept secret. As it happened, both sides were reluctant to form ties, primarily official but also unofficial, each for its own reasons.

Beijing's rejection of relations with Israel did not prompt Taipei to offer relations with Israel, and, thereby, win another country into its primarily Western-oriented diplomatic network. Typical of the dynamics of Israel's relations with Asia, Taipei's rejection of relations with Israel was based on trilateral considerations. Except for Israel's early recognition of the PRC—which the Chinese had practically ignored—there was nothing to prevent Taiwan-Israel bilateral relations. However, there were third-party considerations that Taipei felt obliged to take into account.

In late 1954 and early 1955, Israel and Taiwan (and the PRC) found themselves associated from outside, without any bilateral (let alone trilateral) coordination or initiative. As preparations were made for the forthcoming African-Asian Conference in Bandung, the question of who should be invited was discussed among the organizers, especially at the preparatory Bogor Conference. Initially, China was not supposed to participate and Israel was not either (Chinese Embassy in Indonesia, 1954; Chinese Foreign Ministry, 1954). China was concerned that Taiwan would be invited instead. In the list the Chinese prepared of Asian-African countries attitudes toward Taiwan, they said: "Israel … does not have diplomatic relations with Jiang [Kai-shek] bandits [*fei*]" (Chinese Foreign Ministry, 1955). Ultimately, a compromise was reach whereby the PRC was invited, but Israel and Taiwan were not. Although the first Asian-African conference associated Israel and Taiwan, Taiwan still rejected official relations with Israel. For one reason, a number of Middle Eastern countries still maintained diplomatic relations with the ROC, including Turkey, Iran, Iraq, Egypt, and Saudi Arabia. Until the early 1970s, most of these countries—and other Muslim countries, all associated with, and relying on, the USA—represented a powerful bloc in international organizations, especially in the United Nations General Assembly, in favor of Taipei and against Beijing. Taiwan leadership believed that relations with Israel would have undermined this support (Wang, 1993; Yamada, 2015). Yet, UN votes tell a different story.

The UN votes on China's representation covered three different options: postponement to the next session; designating the issue an "important" question that requires a two-thirds majority; and seating the PRC at the expense of the ROC (Wang, 1977). Most pro-Soviet Middle Eastern countries voted for the PRC, and consistently against the ROC—whatever its relations with Israel. Four countries associated with the West consistently voted for the ROC and against the PRC—but Taiwan's dependence on them was minimal. Relations with Israel could cost Taiwan little more than their votes, a rather marginal damage. Saudi Arabia, associated with the USA and Taiwan's main oil supplier, was inconsistent in its votes. It abstained on all the votes of "postponement," on more votes on the admission of the PRC, and on few votes on the "important question" issue. Israel, another country closely associated with the USA, was also inconsistent in its Taiwan votes, not to mention its early diplomatic recognition of the PRC. Israel consistently voted for Taiwan on the "important question" issue, and abstained on a number of votes on the "postponement" and the representation issues. Put differently, Israel failed to create a real incentive for Taiwan to offer diplomatic ties, to overcome the expected damage to its relations with the pro-Western Middle Eastern countries. In 1961, Israel voted *for* the ROC proposed resolution to consider the PRC admission to the UN as "an important question," which requires a two-thirds majority of the UN General Assembly members (adopted on December 15, 1961). Yet Taiwan showed no interest in official relations with Israel.

Usually, reluctance or refusal of Asian nations to establish official--or even unofficial--relations with Israel, originated in two main considerations. One has been the existence of a large Muslim population. This is still the case with Pakistan, Bangladesh, Afghanistan, Malaysia, and Indonesia, for example. *But this is not the case of Taiwan.* Muslim populations in Taiwan are not only tiny, some 60,000 today out of some 24 million, or 0.3 percent, but many are not indigenous migrants. In 2009, they numbered only 23,000. Taiwan's Muslims have never been an issue, which affected government policy—unlike in the PRC (with nearly 23 million) where Islam has become a serious issue whose implications are not only domestic but also international. The other consideration, which has affected Taiwan's attitude toward Israel for many years, has been its dependence on Persian Gulf crude oil.

Taiwan does not have traditional energy resources of its own. Since its "relocation" to Taiwan in 1949, the ROC has become heavily dependent on oil imports. Although the share of oil in Taiwan's energy mix is only around 50 percent (around 30 percent is coal; 15 percent gas; and 5 percent nuclear), nearly all the oil it needs has to be imported. Most of it (around 83 percent) comes from the Persian Gulf, including one-third from Saudi Arabia—to this very day. No major oil-producing country in the Persian Gulf, i.e. Saudi Arabia, Iran, Kuwait, Oman, and the United Arab Emirates, had maintained diplomatic relations with Beijing before 1971. Therefore, until that time, politics converged with economics. Those countries that opposed the PRC were also the countries which sided with the ROC and also were the ROC oil suppliers. Notwithstanding occasional fluctuations in the amount of crude oil imported by Taiwan over time, the fact of its nearly total dependence on the Persian Gulf has been permanent. Taipei has always taken this factor into account, which determined and underlined its reservations toward Israel. Taipei could not afford to upset the Arab oil-producers by forming visible relations—certainly official but even unofficial—with Israel. Yet all these reservations had not deterred Taipei from maintaining invisible relations with Israel, primarily in getting conventional and non-conventional military technology and weapons, and providing intelligence.

Non-Institutional Unofficial Relations: Missed Opportunities

Taipei's interest in Israel's non-conventional weapons development had begun by the late-1950s, when its leaders became aware of three parallel processes. One, the progress of the PRC nuclear program (intelligence of which was collected, among others, by regular U2 flights from Taiwan); two, the US refusal to help Taiwan create its indigenous non-conventional power; and three, in a retrospective view, the US implicit agreement that other US allies would help Taiwan reach nuclear capability against China. Washington (through the CIA) had known almost from the very beginning that Israel was helping Taiwan's military nuclear program. It could have blocked it at any time, but did it only as late as 1988. [2]

Initial meetings on this issue began during the International Atomic Energy Agency (IAEA) annual sessions in Vienna between Professor Ernst David Bergmann, first Chairman of the Israel Atomic Energy Commission, and the Head of the Taiwanese delegation. He first visited Taiwan in 1961 at the invitation of Chiang Kai-shek, and drafted a comprehensive science and technology program for Taiwan, which included the building of a nuclear reactor along the lines of the Israeli reactor in Dimona. This cooperation, that continued at least until 1975, when Bergmann died, was hardly known about, let alone approved, by the Israeli Government (though the Ministry of Defense was, at least partially, involved).

While rejecting political relations with Israel, Taiwan saw no problem in sending its scientists for training in Israel, since the mid-1960s, in secret. They visited the Soreq Nuclear Research Reactor, Institutes of Science and Technology, and industrial facilities. Following the visit, Taipei requested permission to send a dozen graduate students to complete their PhD course in Israel instead of the USA, where they preferred to stay, and this was approved by Israel's Foreign Minister Abba Eban. Yet, while he harshly criticized the PRC, Eban may have been reconsidering relations with Taiwan, "but the nuclear area seems to me too delicate for cooperation" (Eban, 1966). Beijing's hostility notwithstanding, Israeli Foreign Ministry officials still believed in eventual relations with the PRC. Exploring ways to cement bilateral relations, a Taiwanese official allegedly affiliated with the ROC Government Information Office, but probably involved in intelligence, visited Israel in September 1967, and met with Israeli Foreign Ministry Asia Division officials. His visit paved the way for another secret visit the next month. Defined as an "economic" delegation, it met with officials of the defense complex.

From February 25 to March 12, 1968, yet another delegation visited Israel, led by General T'ang Chün-po, Taiwan's Ministry of Defense Chief of R&D, and head of the newly formed Institute of Nuclear Energy Research (INER). They visited the Soreq nuclear reactor, defense industries and research institutes, universities, and military units, as well as meeting high-ranking officers, and Defense Minister Moshe Dayan. Non-conventional and conventional, their military interests were wide-ranging, hinting that Taipei wanted to extricate itself from its scientific and military dependence on the United States, and that Israel could be a possible, albeit partial, substitute. It seems that by that time, Taipei had already been aware of Washington's plan to improve relations with the PRC.

Yet the Israeli Foreign Ministry was much more cautious and concerned about Beijing's possible reaction to Israel's expanding relations with Taiwan, notably in "delicate [nuclear] matters." An additional example of the tension between the Foreign Ministry and the Ministry of Defense, it reflected not just bureaucratic competition over policy-making procedures but also Jerusalem's frustration at Taipei's attempts to acquire advanced Israeli conventional and non-conventional military technologies, while Taiwan was at the same time identifying with the Arabs and rejecting economic and other relations with Israel. In the spring of 1967, Israel was supposed to launch confidential negotiations with Taipei regarding the possibility of establishing diplomatic relations between the two countries. Anticipating Arab reprisals, Taipei suddenly canceled the meeting using an excuse that the time was "inconvenient" (Yegar, 2004: 289, 463 notes. 4, 5). Israel's attempts to hold meetings with Taiwan's Foreign Ministry officials were rejected, and Taipei blocked business transactions with Israel—despite initial signs of Sino-US rapprochement, expected to lead Taiwan to greater diplomatic isolation. Yet, for Taiwan, unofficial and invisible military cooperation with Israel was top priority and continued.

In 1970, Chaim Herzog, then a retired Major General, formerly Chief of Military Intelligence, and later ambassador to the United Nations (1975–1978), and President of Israel (1983–1993), visited Taiwan on a private basis but as a guest of Chiang Ching-kuo, China Kai-shek's son and ROC Vice-premier who was supervising Taiwan's military nuclear program. By then, Israel and Taiwan had already exchanged unofficial non-diplomatic representatives. Taiwan's Intelligence Bureau envoy arrived in Israel in early 1969 (allegedly on behalf of Taiwan's Information Office), to work directly with the Mossad. Sidestepped yet again, the Foreign Ministry had "to keep in touch with the

Mossad in order to influence the contents of the relations with the man" (Israel Foreign Ministry Director-General, 1969). Although the Mossad was also represented in Taiwan, it was reportedly "lean and aimless" (Israel's Ambassador in Manila, 1974). In two separate visits to Israel in 1973, Taiwanese "professors," probably on a collecting political intelligence mission inspired by Taipei, said that the government wanted to establish a consulate and a commercial office in Tel Aviv, and asked whether El Al (Israel Airlines) would be interested in starting flights to Taiwan. Israel agreed (for political rather than economic reasons), and there was no opposition from Washington—but nothing happened (US Embassy in Tel Aviv, 1973; Washington, 1973).

While Israel's Foreign Ministry deplored Taiwan's "identification in most cases with the Arabs in its UN votes" (Erell, 1968), Bergmann continued his personal foreign policy in support of Taiwan's nuclear program, including the acquisition of technologies and machinery from other countries, organizing the science and technology complex, and importing Israeli conventional weapons. In 1961, Taiwan began to buy considerable quantities of Israeli Uzi submachine guns, indirectly from Belgium where they had been produced by license, because of Taipei's refusal to provide visas for Israelis. Taipei's attitude softened a bit after Israel's 1965 UN vote against the PRC admission. It was now ready to enable scientific cooperation, leading Israeli Foreign Ministry officials to claim "that it was about time to establish diplomatic relations" (Director of the Asia Division, 1966). Diplomatic relations were not established but, unofficially, the Mossad helped facilitate visits and other exchanges, also through Taiwan's intelligence representative in Israel.

By the late 1960s, Taiwan's interest in Israeli arms had increased, especially in naval firepower—a major military weakness. To develop anti-ship missiles, Taiwan decided, based on Bergmann's suggestion, to use the Israeli Gabriel type, produced by Israel Aviation Industries (IAI). Following negotiations, the Israel Government finally agreed to sell three sets of Gabriel missiles to Taiwan, renamed Hsiung Feng (Brave Wind). Defense and naval teams were sent to Israel, and returned in late August 1969 after signing the contract. Chiang Kai-shek was personally involved.

Rumors about Israel's activities in Taiwan triggered a debate at the Parliament (Knesset) on July 15, 1970. Foreign Minister Abba Eban admitted that Israel did maintain "practical relations with Taiwan, in a variety of fields, between civilians and institutions on a non-governmental level. On a governmental level," he said, "there are occasional and restricted contacts, mainly at the UN." He reiterated that Israel had recognized the PRC in 1950, and added that, although the issue of forming diplomatic relations with Taiwan "is not on the agenda at this stage, nothing prevents the constant development of practical relations" (Eban, 1970). As far as they knew about arms sales to Taiwan, the Israeli Foreign Ministry turned a blind eye.

Still anticipating relations with the PRC, in 1971, Director-General Gideon Rafael, opposed the missile and other relations with Taiwan as "a serious provocation." His, and Foreign Minister Eban's attempts to convince Prime-Minister Golda Meir and Defense Minister Moshe Dayan to delay the sales failed (Rafael, 1971). In October 1971, Yaakov Shimoni, Deputy Director-General for Asian and African Affairs, briefed Yitzhak Rabin, ambassador to the USA, that despite Taipei's hostile policy toward Israel, "over the last years Israel responded in a quite far-reaching way to Taiwan's wish to set up unofficial relations." He informed Rabin that a semi-official representative of Taipei's "information system, who was probably connected to its intelligence system," was in Israel. He also admitted to "sales in the defense field" (Shimoni, 1971). Less than two weeks later, the PRC joined the United Nations, at the ROC's expense. Israel's eventual vote for the admission (and consequently against Taiwan), failed to entail any progress with Beijing and there was no need to stop exchanges with Taiwan, still coordinated by Bergmann, who died in April 1975. Others continued his mission.

One of them was Brigadier-General Yitzhak Yaakov (Yatza), former Head of the IDF weapons R&D program. Invited to Taiwan in the mid-1970s, he took over Bergmann's "scientific assistance," and later became a special World Bank advisor to Taiwan and South Korea when they underwent their rapid high-technology industrialization (Eilam, 2009: 169; Yatza, 2011: 252–254, 299). Several visits followed, from both sides. In 1975, INER appointed Dr. Alvin Radkowsky a high-level consultant. He visited Taiwan almost every summer, possibly until the late 1980s, and was using Thorium to fuel reactors for generating energy while blocking the possibility of producing nuclear weapons. Since 1978, he also had explored the feasibility of building nuclear powered submarines and destroyers in Taiwan, but these studies soon ended since Taiwan lacked the capability to construct submarines and warships.[3] Allegedly, Israel-Taiwan nuclear cooperation continued. A CIA report discussed a mysterious explosion, probably nuclear, off the coast of eastern Africa on September 22, 1979. The report—like several others—could not determine definitely who had been involve in the test, but mentioned Israel, Taiwan, and South Africa—that provided both with uranium shipments (CIA, 1980).

In 1977, a contract was signed with Taiwan for the licensed production of Gabriel-2 missile (Yegar, 2004: 290). With an additional 200 missiles bought in 1979 (Hau, 2000: 68), licensed production began in 1980. By 1992, 523 Gabriel-2 missiles (Hsiung Feng) and 77 launchers had been produced (Shichor, 1998: 72–73). This was the first modern weapon system to be developed in Taiwan, leading not only to an "extraordinarily significant" (*feifan yiyi*) upgrade of Taiwan's defense industries, but also to reducing—partly and temporarily—Taiwan's reliance on US arms. Displayed for the first time in the National Day (October 10) 1978 parade, these Hsiung Fengs had still been made in Israel. However, the technological cooperation related to the missile opened the door for further visits of Taiwanese scientists in Israel, some very senior.[4] Taipei has been concerned that the US turn to Beijing would limit its commitment to defend the island, and allegedly welcomed alternative sources of arms and military technology. In a sense, Israel's arms transfers to Taiwan also helped Washington to smooth its relations with the PRC further.

Taiwan was also interested in the Shafrir-2 air-to-air missile, developed and built since the early 1970s by Israel's RAFAEL Armament Development Authority, later renamed Advanced Defense Systems. By 1977, some 450 Shafrir-2 missiles had been delivered to Taiwan to arm its US-made F-100 and F-105 jets, facilitated by Washington's refusal to sell Taiwan Harpoon and air-intercept 9L Sidewinder missiles. Unwilling to irritate Beijing while they were about to establish diplomatic relations, US policy-makers let Israel, whose missile technology had been genuine, to penetrate Taiwan's military market. In fact, they may have tacitly welcomed Israel's military transactions with Taiwan. Taiwan's T'ien Chien (Sky Sword, *Tianjian*) air-to-air missiles are probably based on the Shafrir-2.

Parallel to the Hsiung Feng missiles deal, in 1979, Israel delivered to Taiwan two Dvora-class fast patrol boats, manufactured by Israel Aviation Industries (IAI). Used as prototypes, in 1980–1986, Taiwan produced its own version, the Hai Ou (Seagull), which are almost identical to the Dvora and armed with two Hsiung Feng missiles. Fifty Hai Ou boats had been built before they began to be phased out by the late 1990s, after over 20 years of service although, reportedly, in 2010, 47 were still operational. Taiwan also acquired other Israeli arms, such as LAR-160 127mm multiple rocket launchers; Galil rifles; ammunition; and a variety of electronic equipment. Much of this was acquired through the services of Shaul Eisenberg, a Jewish World War II refugee who became engaged in postwar business in East Asia. Born in Harbin in 1923, in 1975, Yaacov (Yana) Liberman had become the Managing Director of the Eisenberg's Taipei Yi Nien Trading Company that represented some of Israel's leading arms producers, including Israel Aviation Industry, Elbit, Tadiran, Israel Shipyards, and RAFAEL (Goldstein, 2015: 84–87). By 1985, when he left, these companies had sold Taiwan communication equipment; facilities for a battery plant; know-how; and command and control electronics, worth $560 million (SIPRI, 1983: 275, 340). Summing up his experience in Taiwan, Liberman admitted:

> Selling this equipment was not easy and the general political climate in Taiwan was not at all pro-Israeli. There were some exceptions and certainly, Israel had some friends, especially in the science-oriented community. But the majority of highly placed Government officials, including the army and air force, were dealing with Israel strictly because of necessity rather than choice.
>
> *(Liberman, personal letter, August 7, 1998, quoted in Goldstein, 1999)*

Indeed, Israel's attempts to sell weapons to Taiwan occasionally failed. Taipei, that wanted to diversify its arms suppliers, frowned at Israel's attempts to penetrate Taiwan's arms market at the expense of other potential suppliers. Hau Pei-tsun, Taiwan's army chief of the General Staff (1981–1989) grumbled about Israel's "secret attempts" to force him to buy Israel's outdated US M48A5 tanks instead of the US-made M-60 tanks, and Israeli-made naval torpedoes instead of the Netherlands Navy's M-37 torpedo. In his diary, Hau wrote, in a slightly anti-Semitic tone, that Israel had been mainly interested in profit, and that, whereas Taiwan wanted the most advanced military technology, Israel had treated Taiwan as a backward market for downstream obsolete military equipment through which it could eliminate its competitors (Hau, 2000: 254, 1152, 367). Nevertheless, Israel's arms sales to Taiwan continued and even deepened.

These sales were given a boost after Washington decided, in August 1982, to phase out its arms sales to Taiwan. This led Taipei to upgrade its indigenous defense fighter Ching-Kuo, and its 300 F-5 fighters, by installing Israeli El-Op Head Up Display (HUD), made in Taiwan under license. In addition to arming the ROC Navy's Yang destroyers with Gabriel missiles, Israel also sold Taiwan IAI Reshet fire-control and command systems, and retrofitted old Taiwan's navy vessels (Friedman, 2006: 75). Reportedly using Israeli models, underground systems for sheltering Taiwan's fuel reserves, armaments, and aircraft, were planned (Shichor, 1998: 73). But the most promising deal concerned aircraft.

Eventually aborted, the possibility of Israeli aircraft sale to Taiwan had emerged after the mid-1970s. IAI Kfir—an all-weather, multirole combat aircraft based on a modified French Mirage 5, with Israeli avionics and a General Electric J79 turbojet engine—became operational in Israel in 1975. Taiwan's initial interest in the Kfir is indirectly reflected in the US approval of the sale. Soon after US Vice-president Mondale ended his visit to Israel in July 1978, a US State Department spokesman said that the USA would "look favorably upon Israel's sale of its Kfir warplanes to Taiwan should those two governments agree on a contract." While Washington had considered selling its F-4 Phantom jets to Taiwan, it now, in a change of mind and given its forthcoming diplomatic relations with

Beijing, let Israel make the sale (Jewish Telegraphic Agency, 1978). Israel did not have any relations with Beijing at that time, and could act as a proxy. While Taiwan began to diversify its military suppliers and to experiment with self-sufficiency in view of the US rapprochement with China, Washington needed a reliable, indirect, and dependent supplier of arms to Taiwan. Israel, a long-standing US military experienced ally—consistently rejected by Beijing—was the perfect choice. West European countries, which had already maintained diplomatic relations with China, could hardly play this role.

Yet Taiwan, presumably interested in an explicit and direct US commitment, refused to play the game and the deal was off, temporarily. Unhappy with the proposed deal, Beijing found a way to deliver the message to Israel. At a reception in New York, Chaim Herzog, Israel's ambassador to the UN, was introduced to visiting PLA officers, offering then to start a dialogue with Israel based on "common interests," The representative of the PLA Air Force replied that the [Israeli] intention to supply the Kfir to Taiwan ("about which he had read") was "not helpful" (Israel's UN Mission, 1978). Actually the proposed deal (and Israel's earlier arms sales to Taiwan), may have been *very* helpful in facilitating Israel's arms sales to the PRC, which were launched just a few months later and paved the way for diplomatic relations. Richard Holbrooke, US Assistant Secretary for East Asia, warned Israel's ambassador to the US, Ephraim Evron, in May 1979 that Israel's sale of the Kfir would reinforce Taiwan's military power and "would create a huge problem for the Chinese," who "would undoubtedly regard it as a provocation," Off the record, he said that "if he were an Israeli he would have avoided selling weapons to Taiwan so as not to irritate China. History is on China's side, not Taiwan's" (Evron, 1979).

In 1991, Taipei tested yet again the US decision to phase out military supplies by reiterating its interest in acquiring advanced fighter jets for its ageing Air Force. Potential choices were French Dassault's Mirage-2000; US General Dynamics' F-16D; and 40 Israeli IAI's Kfir C7 fighter-bomber jets. Apparently, the Israeli offer should have been the most attractive to Taipei since the unit's price was about one quarter of the competitors' offers, with the entire deal estimated at $800 million. The Israeli planes were available for immediate delivery (the French Mirage would have been available only in 1995) and the sale received US approval (Lee, 1993: 148). Washington was still careful not to upset Beijing and preferred to use Israel as a convenient proxy. But that was not what Taiwan wanted, nor what the Israeli Foreign Ministry wanted.

In retrospect, it appears that Taipei considered the Israeli Kfir option merely as leverage against France, and particularly against the USA, to overcome their reluctance to upset China, and supply Taiwan with advanced aircraft. But, if the Mirages were unavailable, the Kfirs would "help plug Taiwan's air defense gap at least on a temporary basis," provided the Israeli aircraft were fitted with upgraded radar and weapons systems (Richardson, 1992). Yet, while outwardly interested in the Kfirs, what Taipei really wanted (and still wants) was a clear reaffirmation of Washington's commitment to Taiwan's defense—something that Israel could by no means provide. Ultimately, its gamble did pay off and Taiwan was assured *both* French and US aircraft. In March 1992, two months after the establishment of diplomatic relations between Jerusalem and Beijing, Taipei notified Israel that it did not intend to purchase the Kfir (Associated Press, 1992). Taipei's refusal, whether reflecting retaliation against Israel, or concerns about future Arab oil supply, was not a serious blow for Israel. On the contrary.

Taiwan's message took Israel off the hook. It now faced the same dilemma that the USA has been facing: arms sales to the ROC were incompatible with maintaining diplomatic relations with the PRC. On August 3, 1992, Prime Minister Rabin discussed with senior Israeli staff the implications of the deal (already rejected by Taiwan) but also the future of Israel's military relations with the ROC. Given Beijing's threats to downgrade the recently established relations (conveyed to Israel by its first ambassador to Beijing, Zev Sufott), the discussion's conclusion must have been that Israel's military relations with Taiwan had no future. In fact, in 1991, during the Sino-Israeli dialogue on diplomatic relations, Beijing raised the issue of Israel's contacts with Taiwan. "We assured our hosts that the only contacts between Israel and Taiwan were of a commercial and non-governmental nature" (Jewish Telegraphic Agency, 1992; Sufott, 1997: 18). The Chinese were undoubtedly aware that this was far from the truth, but they insisted that it should be. To be sure, when PRC Foreign Minister Qian Qichen visited Israel in September 1992, Rabin told him that "*Israel had decided* not to sell Kfir aircraft to Taiwan. He asked that China would not sell weapons to Arab states" (emphasis added). Thanking Rabin for this decision, Qian replied that "China will not sell any weapons to the region" (Israel Ministry of Foreign Affairs, 1992). Yet, Chinese arms sales to the "region" (which Qian never defined) have continued. Some later trickled to Syria, to Hizbullah in Lebanon, and the Hamas in Gaza—and were fired at Israel.

Institutional Unofficial Relations: Mixed Opportunities

Taipei, which had definitely been aware of the forthcoming rapprochement between the USA and the PRC in the late 1960s, had also been aware of the approaching diplomatic relations between Israel and the PRC since the late 1980s. This had finally caused Taipei to change its mind and to seek relations with Israel. In early December 1990, a relatively low-level official was sent by Taiwan to offer a variety of relations. Meeting a senior Israeli diplomat *privately*, he suggested one of three options: full diplomatic relations at an embassy level; a consulate general; or a trade office—all based on reciprocity. He also admitted that in the past his government's refusal to maintain official relations with Israel had been a mistake, which could now be corrected. [5] Israel, in the final stages of stitching its diplomatic relations with Beijing, and following the precedents of other countries, agreed to the third option. Negotiations on this option, a trade office, continued for three years.

On January 24, 1992, China and Israel established diplomatic relations, which forced Israel to stop whatever military relations Israel had with Taiwan. Israel did not have to cut off *official* or *political* relations with Taiwan that other countries had to, let alone economic and cultural relations. After avoiding any institutional relations with Israel since the early 1950s, Taipei has now tried to add a political shade to its relations with Israel. On November 8, 1992, ten months after Israel and the PRC had established diplomatic relations, and two months after China's Foreign Minister Qian Qichen visited Israel, Taiwan's Vice Foreign Minister arrived in Israel in an attempt to open a trade office. The Israeli Foreign Ministry did not invite him, nor offer him a visa, but opposed his visit and considered him a guest of the Israeli Export Institute, a non-governmental organization. Initially named Taipei Economic and Trade Office, it opened in May 1993 in Tel Aviv. In August 1993, Israel opened a similar office in Taipei. This was the first time that the two countries had exchanged official and visible institutes. In September 1995, the names of these were changed to Economic and Cultural Office, to cover a wider ranges of activities. Officially, similarly unofficial, their functions are not exactly the same: there are more restrictions on Taiwan's office in Israel than on Israel's office in Taiwan.

Although both offices are mostly headed, with rare exceptions, by seasoned diplomats, these are called "representatives," not "ambassadors," and as such do not give accreditation letters to the respective presidents. While in government circles, especially in Israel, they are strictly referred to as "representatives," in Taiwan, they are more often referred to as "ambassadors," notably by the media. Still, they operate along the lines of an official embassy; appear to enjoy diplomatic privileges, immunity, and security, as well as the use of diplomatic mail and diplomatic vehicles' registration plates. Scores of bilateral agreements have been signed, yet between ministries and other organization—and not the "states." Mutual visits and meetings are held *below* ministerial levels, between director-generals and other officials. National state signs, like using letterheads or raising flags are not allowed. This is especially true about TECO (Taiwan Economic and Cultural Office). National Days are celebrated but government officials, nor ministers, do not participate. Also, Israeli diplomats abroad are regularly reminded not to attend Taiwan's national receptions in other countries. However, Members of Parliament (Knesset) attend Taiwan's receptions and Knesset delegations visit Taiwan occasionally (Bender, 2016). At the current 24th Knesset (since May 2021), Member May Golan is Responsible for Israel-Taiwan Inter-Parliamentary Relations. Because it is above the Government, the Knesset has its own Taiwan policy, though the PRC Embassy is watching it closely. Thus, in 2009, the Deputy Speaker had to cancel his participation in a Knesset delegation visit to Taiwan following a protest by the PRC Embassy, which claimed that it would have become an official visit. Two years later, while no longer Deputy Speaker (but still Chairman of the Economics Committee), he visited Taiwan. For its part, in April 1995, Israel rejected a private visit (defined as "pilgrimage") by Taiwan's president, Lee Teng-hui. In February 1996, it rejected a "private" visit by Taiwan's Vice Foreign Minister.

Finally, the highest cost that both have had to pay for Israel's diplomatic relations with China was the abrogation of Israel's military relations, conventional and non-conventional, with Taiwan, and, consequently, their mutual military representation. Yet this has been accomplished only partially and gradually. In addition to its civilian diplomatic stuff (first and second secretaries, counsellors, and various divisions such as Information, Economic, Consular, and Science and Technology), the Taiwanese mission in Tel Aviv (TECO) also has *unofficially*, military attachés, and a representative of the Chung-Shan Institute of Science and Technology, which belongs to Taiwan's Ministry of National Defense. Until August 1999, Israel maintained a Ministry of Defense representation, in addition to the Mossad extension (which had existed in Taiwan probably since the early 1970s), separately from Israel's diplomatic representation (personal information).

Despite Rabin's commitment not to export arms and military technology to Taiwan, and China's objections, there were attempts to sidestep these understandings. Still classified, one attempt involved Shimon Sheves, Director-General of the Prime Minster Office (1992–1995). Reportedly, representatives of a "foreign Far Eastern country" (Taiwan, whose implication in the affair Israel censored), approached Israeli businessmen aiming at a large-scale defense acquisition. Estimated at $2 billion, the deal was aimed at manufacturing Israeli military equipment in Taiwan. In return, Taiwan insisted that its President (Lee Teng-hui) pay an official visit to Israel. Sheves, who was supposed to smooth the visit (and the deal, allegedly for a bribe), met with these representatives in 1994 in Taiwan and in London. Initially unaware of the deal's implications, Rabin was informed about it (on September 11, 1994) by Foreign Ministry officials. They objected to Lee's visit and warned Rabin about the potential damage to Sino-Israeli relations. Consequently, the visit was postponed several times and finally canceled—together with the deal (*Taipei Times*, 2000; *7 Days*, 2004: 20–26).

This was the end of Israel's arms *sales* to Taiwan. From 1975 to 1992, these sales were valued at a little over $850 million, with the majority delivered in the first half of the 1980s. In those years, Israel was Taiwan's second-ranking arms supplier, but its share was 7.6 percent (compared with the USA, over 77 percent). Taiwan was Israel's second-ranking arms customer, at 23 percent, just behind South Africa, at 26 percent (SIPRI, 2022). Nonetheless, while outright Israeli arms sales to Taiwan stopped, other defense relations may have continued. These probably included upgrades and maintenance based on earlier contracts; exchange of military intelligence and visits by high-ranking delegations and officers; and regular meetings between military and defense ministry personnel in Israel and Taiwan. Military industries were also involved (personal information).

While Israel complied with Beijing's conditions with regard to Taiwan, primarily in terms of arms sales, the Chinese have continued to sell arms, including missiles, to Middle Eastern countries, in breach of their earlier promise. This led Israel, in 1993, to try again to penetrate Taiwan's defense market by taking part in a number of military exhibitions and by offering its Ofeq-3 spy satellite services. However, these overtures failed not only because of US objections and obstructions, but also because of China's protests and warnings—which in turn forced Jerusalem to downgrade its defense relations with Taiwan (Anon, Flight International, 1993; Kogan, 1995: 34–35). Still, Taiwan later became a major customer of Israel's satellites EROS A and B (Earth Remote Observation System), launched in December 2000 and June 2006. Designated commercial satellites, they flew over China's territory four times a day, offering accurate surveillance and reconnaissance, which Taiwan contracted since 2001 (*World Tribune*, 2001). Israel may have turned down Taiwan's request for promoting cooperation in developing space research programs. According to *Defense News*, a Taiwanese delegation that arrived in Israel on June 18, 2001, to pursue this cooperation and obtain "high resolution satellite photography equipment for our future space programs," met a dead end—at least publicly (Dagony, 2001).

While Israel's military relations with Taiwan reached a dead end, cultural and economic relations prospered. Avoiding ministerial levels, these have been promoted by director-generals and lower rank officials, as well as by parliamentary delegations and friendship associations. Mutual fields of interest included academic and scientific exchanges and agreements in telecommunications, biotechnology, aviation, and chemicals (Yegar, 2004: 292). Bilateral cooperation includes arts, festivals, exhibitions, music, sports, theaters, dance, cinema, opera, conferences, scholarships, lectures, medicine, youth, tourism (including an agreement on visa exemption signed in August 2011), and religion (more details in Navon, 2016: 252–273). Finally, one of the most impressive and visible aspects of Israel-Taiwan cooperation is economics. In 2021, Israel's exports to Taiwan reached $1.06 billion, an increase of over 44 percent over 2020–more than Israel's exports to Japan, yet about a quarter of exports to China. Imports from Taiwan in 2021 reached $1.11 billion, compared to $938 billion in 2020, well below imports from South Korea, Singapore, and India, and about 10 percent of imports from China. In 2021, Taiwan ranked 15–16 in Israel's foreign trade; Israel's share in Taiwan's foreign trade was 0.3–0.4 percent (Israel Central Bureau of Statistics, 2022).

Conclusion

Apparently, Israel-Taiwan relations represent a bilateral paradox. As soon as Taiwan realized that, despite Israel's recognition of the PRC in January 1950, attempts at establishing diplomatic relations with Beijing had failed—because of internal (political) or external (American) opposition—Taipei should have been interested in forming relations, official or at least unofficial, with Israel, as it had done with many other countries. This alleged paradox deepened as China became more and more hostile to Israel, to the point of denying its right to exist. Similarly, as soon as Israel realized that, despite its being one of the first in the world to recognize the PRC in January 1950, Beijing rejected the establishment of diplomatic relations, Jerusalem should been interested in forming relations with the ROC, official or unofficial. In fact, neither Taiwan nor Israel chose to institutionalize unofficial, let alone official, relations. Each had its own reasons. Heavily dependent on Arab oil and, at least until 1971, on votes in the UN to retain its seat, Taiwan, despite its association with the USA, feared that relations with Israel would undermine its interests. Rejected and opposed by the Chinese, Israel has never doubted that the PRC is part of the international community, and that the time would come when diplomatic relations between the two would be established. Given these considerations, Taiwan-Israel relations reflect not a paradox but optimal and rational policy choices, right rather than wrong.

Notes

1 By 1949, Taiwan's population had increased by 2.2 million (from 6.1 million in 1946), most of them mainlanders. By 1953, Israel's population had nearly doubled by 723,000 (from 806,000 in 1948).
2 This paragraph is based mostly on Shichor (2016).
3 Alvin Radkowsky, who gained a PhD in nuclear physics in the USA in 1947. From 1938 to 1972, he served as Chief Scientist in the US Navy Bureau of Ships' Nuclear Propulsion Division, collaborating with Admiral Hyman G. Rickover. From 1950 to 1972, he was also Chief Scientist in the US Atomic Energy Commission's Office of Naval Reactors. In 1972, he moved to Israel, taught Nuclear Engineering at Tel Aviv University (1972–1994) and at Ben-Gurion University (1994–2002). He died in early 2002, aged 86 (Levenson, 2007: 260–264; Chang, 2002; He, 2015: 142–143).
4 One of them was Yen Chen-hsing (Yan Zhenxing, 閻振興), who had been President of the Chungshan Institute until 1965. Born in 1912, he was Minister of Education (1965–1969) and President of the National Taiwan University (1970–1981).
5 This section draws on Yegar (2004: 288–292).

References

7 Days (2004). "Money Has No Smell," *Yediot Aharonot*, Weekly Supplement, May 28 (in Hebrew).
Anon. (1993). "Israel Drops Out of Taiwan Market." Flight International, December 8.
Associated Press (1992). "Israel Gets U.S. Consent to Offer Jet Fighters to Taiwan." *Los Angeles Times*, April 17.
Bender, A. (2016). "'Thirsty for Cooperation': Members of Knesset Delegation Is Visiting Taiwan." August 10 (in Hebrew). Available at: www.maariv.co.il/politics/Article-552878
Ben-Eliezer, J. (1985). *Shanghai Lost, Jerusalem Regained*. Tel Aviv: Steimatzky.
Chang, K. (2002). "Alvin Radkowsky, 86, Developer of a Safer Nuclear Reactor Fuel." The New York Times, March 5.
Chinese Embassy in Indonesia (1954). "Report on the Situation of the Bogor Conference." Cable, December 4. Available at: http://digintalarchive.wilsoncenter.org/document/112441 (accessed October 9, 2020).

Chinese Foreign Ministry (1954). "On the Asian-African Conference." The Asia Section, December 15. Available at: http://digintalarchive.wilsoncenter.org/document/112442 (accessed October 9, 2020).

Chinese Foreign Ministry (1955). "Existence of Diplomatic Relations Between Afro-Asian Conference Participant Countries and Jiang Bandits' [fei]." February 1. Available at: http://digintalarchive.wilsoncenter.org/document/113244 (accessed October 9, 2020).

CIA (1980). "The 22 September 1979 Event," Interagency Intelligence Memorandum, MORI DocID 1108246 (20 January 1980), Director of Central Intelligence, Secret, approved for release June 2004, very heavily sanitized.

Dagony, R. (2001). "Israel Refused Defense Cooperation Initiatives with Taiwan, for Fear of Harming Relations with China," *Globes*, August 30.

Director of the Asia Division (1966). "Cable from Director of the Asia Division to Heads of Missions." February 11, classified, Israeli State Archive, 4047/47.

Eban, A. (1966). "Note from Eban to Bergmann." September 7, personal-classified. Israel State Archive ISA 4047/47,

Eban, A. (1970). "Diveri HaKnesset," [Knesset Records], 59 (November 2, 1970–February 10, 1971), 279 (in Hebrew).

Eilam, U. (2009). *Eilam's Bow*. Tel Aviv: Miskal (in Hebrew).

Erell, M. (1968). "Israel UN Delegation to the Asia and Oceania Division, Foreign Ministry, 'Formosa.'" December 4, Classified, Israeli State Archive, 4219/16.

Evron, E. (1979). "Conversation with Richard Holbrooke." Israel Embassy in Washington to the Foreign Minister, Director-General (Top Secret). May 1, Israeli State Archive, 8358.

Friedman, N. (2006). *The Naval Institute Guide to World Naval Weapon Systems*, 5th ed. Annapolis, MD: Naval Institute Press.

Goldstein, J. (1999). "The Republic of China and Israel," in J. Goldstein (Ed.), *China and Israel. 1948–1998: A Fifty-Year Retrospective*. Westport, CT: Praeger.

Goldstein, J. (2004). "The Republic of China and Israel, 1911–2003." *Israel Affairs*, 10(1–2): 224–239.

Goldstein, J. (2015). *Jewish Identities in East and Southeast Asia: Singapore, Manila, Taipei, Harbin, Shanghai, Rangoon and Surabaya*. Berlin: De Gruyter.

Gorodetsky, G.(2003). "The Soviet Union's Role in the Creation of the State of Israel." *The Journal of Israeli History*, 22(1): 4–20.

Hau, P.T. (2000). *Banian canmouzong zhang riji* [*Diary of Eight Years as Chief of the General Staff*]. Taipei: Tianxia wenhua.

He, L. (2015). *Hedan MIT: Yige shangwei jieshu de gushi* [*"A" Bomb Made in Taiwan: the Story Is Not Over*]. Taipei: Women Chubanshe.

Israel Central Bureau of Statistics (2022). "Press Release." Available at: www.cbs.gov.il/he/media release/doclib/2022/028/16_22_028-L1.pdf (accessed June 10, 2022).

Israel Foreign Ministry Director-General (1969). "Memorandum from Israel Foreign Ministry Director-General to Director of the Asia and Oceania Division." February 2. Israeli State Archive, 4219/16.

Israel Ministry of Foreign Affairs (1992). "Summary of a Meeting between Prime Minister Rabin and Foreign Minister Qian Qichen of China – 17 September 1992," Document 15, Yearbook *(1992–1994)*, pp. 13–14.

Israel's Ambassador in Manila (1974). "Confidential Dispatch from Israel's Ambassador to Manila to the Director of the Foreign Ministry's Asia and Oceania Division." April 19. Israeli State Archives (personal copy).

Israel's UN Mission (1978). "Confidential Cable from Israel's UN Mission New York, to the Foreign Ministry." April 28. Israeli State Archive, 792.

Jewish Telegraphic Agency (1978). "U.S. Favors Israel's Sale of Kfir Warplanes to Taiwan," July 6.

Jewish Telegraphic Agency (1992). "Chinese Put Pressure on Israel to Cancel Jet Sales to Taiwan." August 4.

Kogan, E. (1995). "The Israeli Defence Industry Presence in the East Asian Market." *Asian Defence Journal*, April 4.

Lee, W.C. (1993). "Desperately Seeking Fighters: Taiwan's Military Aircraft Deals." *Pacific Focus*, 8(2).

Levenson, M. (2007). "Alvin Radkowsky 1915–2002: Memorial Tributes." National Academy of Engineering, 11. Washington, DC: The National Academies Press.

Ministry of Foreign Affairs of the PRC (n.d.). "White Paper–The One-China Principle and the Taiwan Issue." Available at: www.mfa.gov.cn/ce/celt/eng/zt/zgtw/t125229.htm (accessed May 23, 2022).

Navon, E. (2016). "Taiwan-Israel Relations," In J. Goldstein and Y. Jerusalem (Eds.), *China and Israel: From Discord to Concord*. Tel Aviv: The Magnes Press.

Rafael, G. (1971). "Director General to the Foreign Minister, 'Gabriel' Sale to Taiwan." August 2. Abba Eban Center for Israeli Diplomacy, the Harry S. Truman Research Institute for the Advancement of Peace, the Hebrew University of Jerusalem, container C-20, File F-187.

Richardson, M. (1992). "Taiwan May Turn to Israel for Warplanes." The New York Times, May 18.

Roshchin, N.V. (1951). "From the Diary of N.V. Roshchin: Memorandum of Conversation with Chinese Premier Zhou Enlai on 24 July 1951." July 27. Available at: http://digintalarchive.wilso ncenter.org/document/118735 (accessed October 9, 2020).

Shichor, Y. (1998). "Israel's Military Transfers to China and Taiwan." *Survival*, 40(1).

Shichor, Y. (2016). "The Importance of Being Ernst: Ernst David Bergmann and Israel's Role in Taiwan's Defense." *The Asia Papers*, 2. Center for International and Regional Studies, Georgetown University.

Shimoni, Y. (1971). "Note from Shimoni to Rabin, 'Relations with Taiwan.'" October 12. Israeli State Archive, 4219/4.

SIPRI (1983). *Yearbook*. London: Taylor & Francis.

SIPRI (2022). "Arms Trade." Available at: https://armstrade.sipri.org/armstrade/html/export_val ues.php (accessed June 6, 2022).

Soong, C.L. (1953). *The Struggle for New China*. Peking: Foreign Languages Press.

Sufott, E.Z. (1997). *A China Diary: Towards the Establishment of China-Israel Diplomatic Relations*. London: Frank Cass.

Taipei Times (2000). "Taiwan Named in Israeli Weapons Sale Bribery Case." October 24, 3.

US Embassy in Tel Aviv (1973). "Confidential Cable from US Embassy in Tel Aviv to Washington." September 14. Available at: http://wikileaks.org/plusd/cables/1973TELAV07243_b.html (accessed May 25, 2022).

Wang, J.K.C. (1977). "United Nations Voting on Chinese Representation: an Analysis of General Assembly Roll Calls, 1950–1971." PhD dissertation, University of Oklahoma. Available at: https://shareok.org/bitstream/handle/11244/4401/7815387.PDF?sequence=1

Wang, T.Y. (1993). "Competing for Friendship: The Two Chinas and Saudi Arabia." *Arab Studies Quarterly*, 15(3), 63–82.

Washington (1973). "Confidential Cable from Washington to US Embassy Tel Aviv." September 17. Available at: http://wikileaks.org/plusd/cables/1973STATE184706_b.html (accessed May 25, 2022).

World Tribune (2001). "Taiwan Granted Use of Israel's Spy Satellite." *World Tribune*, August 15. Available at: www.worldtribune.com/worldtribune/WTARC/2001/ea_china_08_15.html (accessed June 7, 2022).

Yamada, M. (2015). "Islam, Energy, and Development: Taiwan and China in Saudi Arabia, 1949–2013." *American Journal of Chinese Studies*, 22(1), 77–98.

Yatza, Y.I. (2011). *The Memoirs of Mr. Zero Squared*. Tel Aviv: Yedioth Ahronoth (in Hebrew).

Yegar, M. (2004). *The Long Journey to Asia: A Chapter in the Diplomatic History of Israel*. Haifa: Haifa University Press (in Hebrew).

25

SAUDI ARABIA'S RELATIONS WITH CHINA

Sean Foley

Introduction

For decades, Jamil Baroody, Saudi Arabia's long-time representative to the United Nations (UN), passionately defended his nation's diplomatic interests and that of its allies, especially the United States. At no point was this clearer than in 1971 when the international organization debated two questions: (1) whether the government of the People's Republic of China (PRC) should enter the international institution; and (2) whether the PRC should serve as the sole representative of China at the UN—replacing the government of the island of Taiwan, which had represented all of China there for decades.

Throughout the debate, Baroody not only tabled a resolution based on the US draft resolution on the matter, but his nation was the only one in the Arab world or the Middle East to join the United States in voting against the PRC entering the international body as the sole representative of China (Lipscy, 2017: 255). That vote in part reflected Riyadh's close ties to Washington along with its ties to Taipei, also a close ally of Washington. The Kingdom was the island's chief source of petroleum, while RSEA, a Taipei-based construction and engineering firm, was then working on several major construction projects in Saudi Arabia (Wang, 1993: 63). Indeed, Baroody proposed allowing the Taiwanese to determine whether they wished to remain part of China, a measure opposed by the PRC and many other UN delegates.

Although Riyadh and Washington failed to keep Beijing out of the UN as the sole representative of China, Baroody earned effusive praise for his work from American media and politicians. "The oratorical skill of the distinguished delegate is almost overpowering," Congressman and later Cabinet Secretary Ed Derwinski told *Time* in late 1971, adding: "I am convinced that if Mr. Winston Churchill in his heyday had debated Mr. Baroody, he would have come across second best" (Burke, 2010: 132).

Half a century later Baroody and Derwinski have long left the scene, while much has changed about Saudi Arabia's relationship with both the United States and China. The shift, which began under King Abdullah (2006–2015) and accelerated under the current monarch King Salman (2015–), coincided with the fracking boom and the decline of US oil imports from Saudi Arabia, along with the increase in demand for energy in

DOI: 10.4324/9781003048404-28

China. Although Saudi Arabia and the United States maintain a close strategic partnership, Riyadh backs Beijing's positions on Taiwan and other critical international questions, especially in Asia. China is the Kingdom's largest trading partner, while Saudi Arabia is China's largest supplier of oil (Xu and Aizhu, 2021b). Nor is there any indication that Riyadh believes the situation will change in coming decades. In March 2021, Amin Nasser, CEO of ARAMCO, Saudi Arabia's state oil company, told the China Development Forum: "Ensuring the continuing security of China's energy needs remains our highest priority—not just for the next five years but for the next 50 and beyond" (Xu and Tan, 2021).

A crucial driver of this shift in policy was Vision 2030—the plan of King Salman's son, Crown Prince Muhammad bin Salman (MBS), to reform the Saudi society by reducing dependence on oil exports and expatriate labor. In its place, the plan aims to promote a variety of industries where Chinese investment and participation are seen as critical: E-commerce, tourism, increasing foreign participants in the Hajj and Umrah pilgrimages, and providing logistical services to the fast-growing trade in the Middle East that is tied to Asia. Since the late 2000s, that trade and the need to secure it have prompted China and many of Asia's other leading governments to increase their diplomatic and military presence in the Persian Gulf and the Red Sea, potentially bringing Asia's fiercest conflicts to the country's shores. These geostrategic changes have prompted Saudi Arabia to further recalibrate its relations with the United States, Asia, and its neighbors in Africa and the Middle East.

Recent events, however, suggest that Saudi foreign policy, including its burgeoning ties with China, retains elements that Baroody would have recognized from the 1970s. That was an era in which Riyadh was willing to part ways with its closest allies—such as in the 1973 Arab Israeli War—when it believed it was necessary. Here it is worth noting that the Kingdom did not follow Bahrain and the United Arab Emirates (UAE), neighboring states with deep ties to China, in deploying Chinese Covid-19 vaccines to combat the global pandemic. Instead, Riyadh has firmly aligned the country's response to the virus with those of the European Union (EU) and the United States. Not only has Riyadh used Euro-US developed vaccines, but it has also, in concert with several Western countries, prohibited all travelers, which have received a Chinese Covid-19 vaccine, from entering the country (*TRT World*, 2021). The latter decision will influence the Kingdom's economy and the lives of Muslims around the world, especially those in Asian nations which have used the Chinese vaccines. Equally importantly, MBS has signaled that he expects energy to be key to the Kingdom's future, noting on Saudi TV in March 2021: "There is a wrong perception among many analysts that Saudi Arabia wants to get rid of oil." He continued: "This is not true, We want to benefit from everything in Saudi Arabia, whether oil or any other sector" (Saadi, 2021).

New Economic Ties

Saudi Arabia's economic ties with China strengthened substantially during the three decades after the end of the Cold War. During that period, declining US imports of Saudi oil coincided with exponential growth in oil imports in Asia's largest countries, especially China, reoriented oil markets and Riyadh's global outlook (Al-Tamimi, 2013: 112–113). While the United States imported more than 2 million barrels a day of Saudi petroleum in spring 1991 and again in spring 2003, it imported 111,000 barrels of

Saudi oil in December 2020—thanks in part to the revitalization of the American oil industry after the introduction of shale oil drilling techniques, a surge in Canadian oil exports to the USA, and a decision by Western nations to pull their investments from oil companies (US Energy Information Administration, 2021b, 2021c; Wald and Ferziger, 2021). By contrast, in 1993, three years after Riyadh and Beijing first formalized diplomatic ties, China became, for the first time, a net importer of oil, transforming it into one of Saudi Arabia's top trading partners. In 1999, China and Saudi Arabia signed a strategic energy cooperation agreement, opening the door to a significant increase in bilateral trade (Olimat, 2013: 226). By 2021, Chinese investors were reportedly interested in buying a portion of ARAMCO, a company owned by Americans in the 1970s (Wu, Lawler, and Arnold, 2021).

That interest reflected the fact that Saudi-China trade rose from $1.8 billion in the late 1990s annually to $59.4 billion by the 2020s (International Monetary Fund, 2021), fueled by China's economic growth and a steep rise in China's daily oil imports (Al-Tamimi, 2018: 256). The rise in oil imports had, by 2017, propelled China into the role the United States had held for many decades—the largest oil importer in the world, making access to China's oil market an economic imperative for Saudi Arabia (US Energy Information Administration, 2018a). By 2019, China's oil imports had risen to almost 10 million barrels of oil a day, the largest share of which, or 1.7 million barrels a day, was Saudi (Turak, 2019b; US Energy Information Administration, 2020). After the economic dislocation caused by Covid-19 and a "war" with Russia over world oil prices in April and May 2020, Saudi Arabia, through deep discounts on its oil, increased its supplies to China to 2.2 million barrels a day—the most it had ever sold to the country and nearly a third of its total crude oil exports in May 2020 (DiPaola, Wingfield, and Lee, 2020a, 2020b). By the end of 2020, Saudi Arabia had retained its top position, exporting, on average, about 1.69 million bpd, beating out Russia again for the top spot (Xu and Aizhu, 2021b). Overall, Chinese petroleum imports surged by 7 percent in 2020, reaching 10.85 million barrels per day, maintaining its position as the largest importer of oil in the world (Xu and Aizhu, 2021a).

China's emergence in global energy markets has helped to convince Riyadh that it needed to form close ties with China's energy companies, its refining industry, as well as its oil distribution and retail sales companies. Consequently, ARAMCO signed a series of partnerships with Zhejiang Petrochemical, an energy company, and Sinopec—the world's largest oil, refining, gas, and petrochemical conglomerate (Aizhu, El Gamal, and Meng, 2019). ARAMCO is also administering joint ventures in China with Sinopec and ExxonMobil (LaFond, 2007). Since 2015, the company and Sinopec have run an oil refinery in Yanbu, a Saudi port city on the Red Sea coast (Reuters, 2015). The Yanbu refinery was Sinopec's first project outside of China, paving the way for it to build other facilities, including the largest refinery in the Middle East: A state-of-the-art facility in Al-Zour in Kuwait near the country's border with Saudi Arabia (*Oil Review of the Middle East*, 2019).

These types of massive investments have reinforced Riyadh's confidence that its oil supplies will play a central role in the global economy for many decades to come—despite attempts by the Chinese, the Europeans, the Biden Administration, and others to accelerate the use of renewable fuels at the expense of oil and other fossil fuels (MacIntyre and French, 2021; Wald and Ferziger, 2021). MBS made this point clearly in a March 2021 TV interview in which he predicted that global demand for oil will continue to grow through 2030 or 2040 but that production would decline rapidly in several key oil-producing nations:

> The United States of America will not be an oil-producing country after ten years. Today, it produces approximately 11 million barrels. After ten years, it will hardly produce two million barrels. China today produces 4 million barrels, and it will produce zero barrels in 2030 or something marginal. Russia today produces approximately 11 million barrels; after 19 or 20 years, it will produce one million or less or more barrels, as the supply decreases much more than the decrease in oil demand.
>
> *(Saadi, 2021)*

He is not alone in his confidence. In June 2021, Saudi Arabia's Energy Minister Prince Abdulaziz bin Salman was asked about a recent International Energy Agency report that concluded that alternative energies would replace the need for investment in oil and in other fossil fuel production. His response was simple and to the point: "I believe it is a sequel to the *La Land* movie" (Wald and Ferziger, 2021).

Under Prince Abdulaziz's leadership, ARAMCO has invested billions in its facilities to increase the company's maximum sustained production to 13 million barrels of oil a day (El Gamal and Rashad, 2020). That decision was seemingly validated by booming demand for oil in China (Slav, 2021), which powered a strong rebound in global oil prices in 2021. By June 2021, it was estimated that prices could reach $75 a barrel by the end of the year (Ajrash, 2021). If it reaches that level, it would be the highest since 2014 and be above the $66 a barrel price for oil that the International Monetary Fund has predicted would be the breakeven price for the Kingdom's national budget in 2021 (Omar and Martin, 2020).

The profits from higher oil prices could, in turn, be reinvested in other sectors of the Saudi economy beyond oil—showing the synergy that MBS referenced in March 2021 while also helping to reinforce the maturation of Saudi-Sino economic ties beyond energy. Two of the industries involved in this growing commercial relationship are transportation and infrastructure. Starting in March 2011, Saudia (formerly Saudi Arabian Airlines), the Saudi flag carrier, began direct service from Jeddah and Riyadh to Guangzhou. Today it has seven non-stop flights to China: four from Riyadh and three from Jeddah (ENP Newswire, 2021). Those increased services reflect the success of Saudi companies in China and Huawei, one of China's most recognizable brands, in the Kingdom. It was the first Chinese company to receive a 100 percent commercial license to invest in Saudi Arabia, a major achievement in a country where most foreign firms have to work with a local partner (Al-Tamimi, 2018: 254).

Huawei's success in the Kingdom rested on its ability to bridge deep cultural divisions while meeting the technical needs of its customers. In particular, the company has educated its Chinese staff about Arab culture and Islam while also devising work plans to address the needs of its local employees (Li, Chang, and Guo, 2020: 256–257, 287). Huawei also built a prayer hall for Muslims in the lobby of its corporate headquarters—a decision which greatly impressed a visiting delegation of Saudi business officials in 1999 (Shaolong, 2016: 195). In the 2000s, the company proved that its equipment was able to provide cell phone service (1) to the remote mountainous regions of Saudi Arabia, and, (2) to the Hajj pilgrimage, where cell phone traffic grew to 19 times more than normal in Mecca because of the presence of millions of pilgrims (Huawei, 2007).

In 2009, the Saudi and Chinese governments, agreed, for the first time, to cooperate on a joint economic project: A $1.8 billion special Mecca railway to facilitate the Hajj (Moore, 2009). In 2010, after China Railway Engineering Corporation successfully finished the project in Mecca, the Saudi government asked Chinese firms to build the Haramain High-Speed Railroad, the Mecca Metro, an expansion of King Khalid University, and multiple other industrial facilities (Al-Tamimi, 2013: 132–134).

While these projects enhanced bilateral ties, they served a bigger strategic purpose for Beijing analogous to what the Yanbu oil refinery had meant for Sinopec—namely, they showed Saudi Arabia's neighbors in Africa and the Middle East that Chinese companies could build the types of infrastructure projects that were essential to their economies along with the BRI. The Mecca railway was in fact the first railway China had ever built in the Middle East (Bhaya, 2018).

More than a decade after the completion of that project, Chinese firms are building infrastructure projects in many of the Kingdom's neighbors in Africa and the Middle East (*Economist*, 2019). New projects are already in the planning stage. In 2019, Zain KSA, the Saudi affiliate of the Kuwaiti-Middle East telecom giant Zain, announced that it had partnered with Huawei to provide 5G, Video Streaming, and other services to its customers (Zain KSA, 2019). A year later, the Saudi Authority for Data and Artificial Intelligence and Huawei announced a memorandum of understanding where the company's researchers and Saudi researchers would create systems for recognizing Arabic characters through artificial intelligence technology (Reuters, 2021a). That same year, Batic, a leading Saudi investment and logistics firm, "cemented a deal with Huawei to work on 'smart city' projects in the kingdom, where it is already a main partner in the Yanbu Smart Industrial City project" (El Massassi, 2021).

The deals in 2020 are remarkable given the US government's extensive legal and public relations campaign against Huawei. The Trump Administration not only imposed sanctions on Huawei but also argued relentlessly that the company has "close ties to China's military and that Beijing could use its equipment for espionage" (ibid.). Still, "by gaining the trust of our partners in the Middle East," Charles Yang, Huawei's Middle East Chief, noted to Agence France-Presse (AFP) in early 2021 "we have been able to mitigate external political pressures like those pursued by the US" (ibid.).

These words were seemingly borne out by the company's announcement, in January 2021, that Riyadh would soon be the site of the company's largest flagship consumer store outside of China (Reuters, 2021a). Reuters reported that the company hoped that the new store, which will be built in cooperation with Saudi real estate developer Kaden Investment, will provide "direct access to consumers amid rising demand for digital products and services in the kingdom" (ibid.).

That emerging market could be extremely lucrative for Huawei and other large telecommunications companies. In 2021, the Ministry of Investment announced that it expects 82.6 percent of the country to have access to the internet by 2022, up from 73.2 percent in 2017 (ibid.). By May 2021, Huawei, along with Xiaomi and OPPO, two Chinese electronics and smartphone brands, accounted for nearly a quarter of all smartphones phone sales in Saudi Arabia (Wang, 2021).

Digital products and services delivered on smartphones are essential to Vision 2030, the Crown Prince's plan to reform Saudi Arabia's economy and its society while reducing its traditional dependence on exporting oil. In remarks introducing Vision 2030 in 2016, he addressed the cyclical nature of state spending under the current system and the danger it poses to the country: "We have developed a case of oil addiction in Saudi

Arabia" (Nakhoul, 2016). In the future, the Crown Prince continued, "we will not allow our country ever to be at the mercy of commodity price volatility or external markets" (ibid.). Though measures linked to women driving, the opening of movie theaters, integrating more Saudis into the private workforce, and the ARAMCO initial public offering have made headlines worldwide, other parts of the plan, which specifically look to China, have garnered less attention.

When Saudi officials unveiled Vision 2030, they hoped that it would benefit from China's bold diplomatic and economic plan: the One Belt and Road Initiative (OBOR). Now known as the Belt and Road Initiative (BRI), the initiative is widely seen as Chinese President Xi Jinping's signature initiative. It aims to use development and infrastructure investments to connect China to Saudi Arabia and dozens of countries across Asia, Africa, Europe, and the Middle East. Saudi policy-makers expect that China, as part of the BRI, will invest in two key parts of Vision 2030—namely, new Saudi E-commerce companies, many of which will use Huawei equipment, and logistical and transportation hubs modeled on the success of Dubai (Saudi Arabia Ministry of Transport, 2020).

Saudi planners in particular hope that the new hubs will be able to take advantage of the country's eight international land borders along with its 1,640-mile (2,640 km) coastline, both of which provide access to a vast geographic area: more than 15 countries in Africa and the Middle East, along with a series of waterways essential to world trade from the Red Sea to the Arabian Sea to the Persian Gulf. While the African and Middle Eastern countries have already benefited from loans and significant investments from China, these waterways are perhaps even more significant, for they are the central arteries of twenty-first-century global trade connecting China with its energy suppliers in the Middle East and principal markets in Europe.

A New Diplomatic Framework

Taking advantage of the new strategic opportunities created by China's rise and of Vision 2030 has compelled Riyadh to reconceptualize many of its strategic and diplomatic relationships, especially since Beijing does not support the Saudi-led intervention in Yemen, the Qatar blockade, and Riyadh's intense hostility toward Tehran. In fact, Chinese leaders have long seen Tehran as essential geographically and politically to the success of the BRI (Vatanka, 2017).

Saudi leaders have navigated this dynamic by building on 15 years of diplomacy dedicated to expanding their nation's ties to Asia, especially China. When King Abdullah ascended to the throne in 2005, he signaled his commitment to a new "look east policy" by making his first trip outside of the Middle East as monarch to four Asian nations, including China (Panda, 2015). On the trip, which took place in 2006, the King became the first Saudi leader ever to visit China. A decade later, after Donald Trump entered the White House in 2017, King Salman, Abdullah's successor, visited Xi in China *before* traveling to meet Trump in the United States (Kane, 2017).

When Salman made that trip, he and other Saudi officials had already long signaled their commitment to deepening diplomatic ties with China, even if those ties conflicted with Washington's core goals. In 2014, Saudi Arabia became a founding member of the Beijing-backed Asian Infrastructure Investment Bank (AIIB), an institution which is seen as crucial to the success of the BRI, which Washington opposes as a threat to its global interests and to the work of existing global institutions, such as the World Bank (Huang, 2015). The Islamic Development Bank (IsDB)—a multilateral development institution in Jeddah whose largest shareholder is the Saudi government—forged a new partnership with the AIIB to provide loans throughout IsDB member states (Rakhmat, 2019). The loans, which built on the IsDB's investments in China dating back to the late 1980s, led to joint ventures in business innovation, knowledge transfers, laboratories, and student scholarships in IsDB member states throughout the Muslim World (Saudi Press Agency, 2021b; Zhang, 2021).

Even more striking, as the US Navy challenged China's claims to the South China Sea and Washington pushed Indonesia and other Southeast Asian nations closely linked to Saudi Arabia to resist Beijing's actions in Asian waterways, Saudi diplomats, in May 2016, welcomed what they characterized as "China's adherence to peaceful means in settling disputes concerning the South China Sea" (ECNS, 2016). In August 2016, MBS made his government's view of US policies in Asian waterways even more explicit during a press conference in the Chinese capital. There, he "condemned the actions of the United States of America in the South China Sea," describing them as "contrary to the interests of China and the Kingdom" (*El Watan News*, 2016).

Three years later, following intense US criticism of China's treatment of the Uighur Muslims in Xinjiang, MBS, during a state visit to Beijing, refused to touch the matter, stating that "China has the right to take anti-terrorism and de-extremism measures to safeguard national security" (Aljazeera, 2019). In global disputes involving Beijing and Washington, MBS has shown a willingness to defer to Beijing's positions—acknowledging China's position in Asia along with its "multifaceted and dynamic material footprint" across the Middle East (Al-Sudairi, 2020: 7).

Riyadh's decision to defer to Beijing's positions, however, does not mean that there are not fundamental tensions within the bilateral relationship, especially in the Middle East. On the one hand, Beijing desires warm ties with Saudi Arabia and has shown deference to Riyadh at sensitive moments. In January 2016, for instance, President Xi Jinping visited Saudi Arabia shortly after the Kingdom's execution of a prominent cleric had set off a fierce diplomatic conflict between Riyadh and Tehran (BBC World, 2016). In March 2021, Beijing condemned the attacks on Saudi territory originating in Yemen, including those targeting sensitive oil facilities (Saudi Press Agency, 2021a).

On the other hand, Beijing's vision of the Middle East is more expansive than those of Saudi leaders. While Saudi Arabia views Iran as the central source of conflicts in Iraq, Lebanon, Syria, and Yemen, China has remained officially neutral in these conflicts. As the Chinese have courted Riyadh, Beijing has deepened it military ties with Tehran, with Beijing, in March 2021, reaching a 25-year $400 billion economic and security partnership with Tehran (Fassihi and Myers, 2021). China has also joined other major powers in backing the Iranian nuclear deal, the Joint Comprehensive Plan of Action (JCPOA), an agreement which Riyadh views as a fundamental threat to regional peace. For instance, when a US airstrike killed Qasem Soleimani in January 2020, Beijing praised Tehran for its restraint while pledging "relentless" diplomacy to salvage the JCPOA—"an important pillar," in Beijing's eyes, "for global nuclear non-proliferation and peace and stability for the Middle East" (Wu, 2020). In addition, Beijing has retained links with Doha after Riyadh launched a regional boycott of its neighbor in 2017 (Blanchard, 2019; Siyech, 2019).

Although China, like Saudi Arabia, publicly supports the Palestinians and strongly condemned the Israeli bombing of Gaza in May 2021 (Matthews, 2021), it has, in recent years, intensified ties with Israel, a country which has no diplomatic relations with Saudi Arabia. Beijing has growing investments in high-tech industries ($16 billion) (Liu, 2017) and construction ($4 billion) in Israel (Efron, Schwindt, and Haskel, 2020: xvi). In fact, Beijing views Israel as central to the BRI, and Chinese companies have signed lengthy contracts worth billions of dollars to invest in the Port of Ashdod, one of Israel's two main cargo ports, and Haifa, the country's largest port (ibid.: 38–39, 70). Israel agreed to the port deals over the vehement objections of Washington—which annually provides Jerusalem over $3.8 billion in military assistance and had just brokered historic diplomatic agreements between Israel and four Arab states: Bahrain, Morocco, Sudan, and the UAE (Shesgreen, 2021).

Saudi Arabia has responded to this changing regional dynamic in much the same way that Israel has: It has sought to retain its traditional diplomatic positions, including its military ties with Washington, while taking small but significant steps to accommodate the interests of other powers, especially China. As Hesham Al-Ghannam, a Senior Fellow at the Gulf Research Centre, has noted, Riyadh does not wish to replace one "ally with another"—instead, it seeks to balance the great powers through new diplomatic frameworks (Al-Ghannam, 2020a).

This type of strategy is of course not new. Although Riyadh aligned its policies with Washington on China and other key issues when Jamil Baroody was the Kingdom's UN ambassador, it still found ways to collaborate with Arab states hostile to US interests. Five decades later, we can see a strategy analogous to the ones employed in the mid-1970s and laid out by Alghannam.

While Riyadh did not join its neighbors in the Abraham Accords, which Beijing and Washington strongly supported (Cafiero and Wagner, 2020), it nonetheless agreed to allow overflight rights for all planes traveling to or from Israel. Previously the Kingdom had only allowed Air India to use its territory to travel to Israel (Kershner, 2018). Riyadh's decision to expand access to all aircraft, including Israeli airlines, was a small but critical part of the Abraham Accords. After all, the only viable flight path between Tel Aviv and Dubai was via the Kingdom's territory and a key part of Israel's strategy to further link itself to China and to other Asian nations (Holland, 2020). Notably, the flights continued without interruption throughout the May 2021 Israel-Gaza conflict—despite Saudi rhetoric that criticized Israel, an approach that mirrored China's (Ibish, 2021).

A year earlier, after the assassination of Iran's Qasem Soleimani, Riyadh worked to ease regional tensions, stressing support for Washington but adding that it had not been consulted on the strike (Zilber, 2020). That cautious approach continued in the multilateral response, including working with the United Nations, as Beijing advised, that Riyadh employed after the drone attack on the massive oil refineries at Abqaiq and Khurais in September 2019 (Yeranian, 2019).

To date, Riyadh's cautious approach has paid dividends with China, as evidenced by the late March 2021 visit of China's Foreign Minister and State Counselor Wang Yi to Riyadh. While he signaled Beijing's appreciation for Riyadh's "support for China on the issues related to Xinjiang, Hong Kong, and Taiwan" (*Foreign Affairs*, 2021; Xinhua, 2021), Wang also stressed his government's support of the Kingdom's role in Middle East politics as well as its right to "pursue a path of development that fits its own conditions" (Xinhua, 2021). The latter comment was an indirect reference to US criticisms of Saudi human rights practices, including President Biden mentioning prominent human rights cases by name and his administration's release, in February 2021, of an intelligence report that stated that MBS ordered the murder of Jamal Khashoggi. Wang, in fact, reinforced this point when he stressed that Beijing opposed any interference in Saudi Arabia's "internal affairs under any pretext" (ibid.). For his part, MBS hailed China's rise as a global power, stressing his country's willingness to enhance existing partnerships in fields from energy to telecommunication, including nuclear power and 5G (ibid.).

Beijing's support for Saudi regional diplomacy could prove to be increasingly important, as Riyadh faces an ever more complicated regional military balance—one where conflicts in the Gulf, the Levant, and Yemen must be considered alongside those in East Africa and the Red Sea. There, Beijing's growing presence in East Africa and the Red Sea has created a new zone of potential conflict adjacent to Saudi Arabia's 1,100-mile (1,760 km) western border.

China's opening of a naval facility in 2017, in Djibouti, an East African country just 370 nautical miles (684 km) from the coast of Saudi Arabia, sparked particular concern among world powers, compelling many to increase deployments in the Red Sea. In 2020, France, Italy, Japan, and the United States operated military forces in the Red Sea region alongside those of a host of other nations: China, Egypt, European Union states, India, Iran, Israel, Russia, South Korea, Turkey, and the United Arab Emirates (Melvin, 2019: 2). In the eyes of India and Japan, their deployments in the Red Sea and the surrounding region are key elements of their geopolitical strategies to check China's rising naval power in the Indo-Pacific.

In response to this changing regional and international dynamic, Riyadh has sought to build a base in Djibouti to supplement the UAE base there (set up for the war in Yemen) and its existing bases in the Western regions of the Kingdom. Saudi officials, in January 2020, also spearheaded the formation of the Council of Arab and African Coastal States of the Red Sea and the Gulf of Aden (CAACSRA). In a report for Riyadh's King Feisal Center, Saudi Arabia's leading research center, Muhammad Alsudairi stressed that the Kingdom's policy-makers needed to use CAACSRA to create a regional dialogue among the region's key stakeholders, especially China. In particular, he argued that CAACSRA should promote a set of maritime protocols for the navies operating in the region. These protocols, he explained, could reduce "the risk of confrontations" while protecting the "vital maritime passageway from being impacted by other … external conflicts happening elsewhere in the globe" (Al-Sudairi, 2020: 46). By making this argument, Al-Sudairi was also making a larger point: The presence of many rival navies in the Red Sea risked involving Saudi Arabia in conflicts that had little or nothing to do with the Kingdom's interests.

The dangers of great power competition in the Red Sea that Al-Sudairi highlighted help us see how China casts a shadow over the Kingdom's military ties in the region and its ties with other powers, especially the United States. For years, the United States has been one of Saudi Arabia's principal suppliers of advanced weapons, with the Kingdom becoming the top market in the world for US weapons between 2013 and 2017 (Ivanova, 2018). The Royal Saudi Air Force maintains the third largest fleet of the US-made F15 fighter aircraft in the world after the United States and Japan (Cone, 2019). Even after Riyadh implemented unprecedented budget cuts in May 2020 in response to a drop in oil prices and the Covid-19 economic crisis (Turak, 2020), it continued to buy US-made weapons (England and Warrell, 2020)—a decision that helped to maintain the long-standing ties between the two countries, whose interests and institutions align very well. The US military sees Iran as a central threat to the Middle East and has a strong foothold in the waterways surrounding the Kingdom and those connecting it to Asia.

But the Sino-US rivalry in Asia over the last decade presents serious challenges to the military alliance, which has been the cornerstone of Saudi security policy for decades. First, the Sino-US rivalry, which intensified during the Covid-19 epidemic (Tan, 2020), risks drawing Riyadh into a dangerous global conflict, where Beijing could, in a crisis, replace Saudi oil imports with Iranian or other oil imports. Second, the Sino-US rivalry has refocused US politics and national priorities away from Saudi Arabia and the Middle East to Asia. The last three presidents—Barack Obama, Donald Trump, and Joseph Biden—have pledged to reduce the nation's military commitments in the Middle East while refocusing priorities to Asia. While Obama publicly broke with Riyadh over the Arab Spring and the Iranian nuclear deal, Trump used harsh language toward the Saudis, accusing the Kingdom's leaders of abusing the American military umbrella (Keith, 2017; Hubbard, 2019). He even threatened to withdraw US protection (Gardner et al., 2020). During his campaign for the presidency in 2020, Biden threatened that he would make Saudi Arabia a "pariah state" for the murder of Khashoggi (Knickmeyer, 2021). Since becoming president, Biden has authorized the release of a damning intelligence report on Khashoggi along with sanctions on many people allegedly involved in murdering him (ibid.).

Even more importantly, many of Biden's allies in the Democratic Party in Congress have pushed him to go further, proposing using military aid and other tools to increasingly distance Washington and Riyadh (Wilkins, 2021). Soaring US budget deficits because of the costs associated with the Covid-19 crisis and deterring China militarily have compelled both Trump and Biden to propose cuts to Pentagon budgets along with major reallocations as to what is funded (Werner, 2020). The Biden Administration has already announced that it would pull US forces out of Afghanistan, with other withdrawals possible (Macias, 2021). In remarks given to Congressional hearings in June 2021 about the Biden Administration's proposed 2022 defense budget, Chairman of the Joint Chiefs of Staff General Mark Milley stated that "deterring China takes precedence" over all other considerations (Gould, 2021). While members of Congress and the Administration may have disagreed on what weapon systems should be funded or how much should be spent, all agreed on the basic principle guiding US strategy: the nation's chief military threat was in the Pacific, not in Europe or the Middle East (ibid.).

Should Washington withdraw some of its military commitments to Riyadh, could China provide Saudi Arabia the security guarantees that the United States now does? The People Liberation Army Navy of China (PLAN) already operates naval forces in many of the same strategic waterways that the US Navy does and could complement the Kingdom's military capabilities and strategic objectives. The PLAN is already the largest navy in the world, and Beijing has begun to put in place the assets it would need to build a fleet in the Indian Ocean (Colley, 2021). The PLAN and the Saudi navy conducted joint drills in 2019 (Saudi Press Agency, 2019). Beijing has sold Riyadh weapons, such as missiles and armed drones, which Washington has refused to provide to the Saudi military (Turak, 2019a). The Chinese and Saudi militaries also have long-standing ties to the Pakistani army, which has deployed its forces to the Kingdom and uses US-made weapons. As Al-Ghannam noted, many Saudis assume that it is "inevitable" that their nation's robust economic ties with Beijing will expand to include a strong military component (Al-Ghannam, 2020b).

Deeper military ties with Beijing, however, could still present challenges to Riyadh. They risk dragging Riyadh into the complicated politics of Asia and into a set of strategic partnerships where Tehran has sway. In December 2019, China, Iran, and Russia conducted a joint naval drill in the Indian Ocean (Westcott and Al-Khshali, 2019). The three nations also took part in joint drills in 2020 (AP News, 2020) and 2021 (Reuters, 2021b). Beijing remains focused on its traditional military interests in East Asia instead of the Middle East. There, in the words of two Chinese military experts, China "has become an economic heavyweight" but "remains a diplomatic lightweight and is likely to remain a military featherweight" for decades to come (Xu and Sun, 2019). Even if that situation were to change and Riyadh were to upgrade ties to China's military, Washington would also likely limit Riyadh's access to the spare parts needed to operate its US-made weapons. In June 2020, US Central Command General Kenneth McKenzie warned that China's presence in the Middle East was a "significant factor that we need to confront" (Williams, 2020). Since Khashoggi's murder, there have been repeated bipartisan calls in the US Congress to curb military sales to Riyadh, calls that would grow louder should Riyadh ally with Beijing (Gould, 2019).

Cultural Ties and Covid-19

While it may take decades for a Sino-Saudi military alliance to emergence, closer cultural and people-to-people ties are already taking shape. In 2010, King Saud University (KSU), one of Saudi Arabia's top universities, began teaching Mandarin (Curry, 2020). Following MBS' trip to Beijing in February 2019, the Chinese government funded a special program to teach Mandarin in Saudi Arabia (Abumaria, 2020). That program began modestly, limited to just eight secondary schools in Dammam, Jeddah, and Riyadh (ibid.). Another initiative is a collaboration between the Arab Open University and Nabegh Educational Center to teach more than 3,000 teachers and employees Mandarin in 12 cities around the Kingdom (Obaid, 2020). In 2019, the Confucius Institute and the Beijing Language and Culture University signed an agreement with KSU as part of a process to establish a Chinese language department at the Saudi university (Aiqing, 2019). In 2020, the University of Jeddah agreed to establish the first Confucius Institute in the Kingdom (*Saudi Gazette*, 2019). Together, these programs are expected to facilitate Vision 2030 by creating a long-term process where 50,000 Saudi citizens get new positions (Abumaria, 2020).

Few have followed this process more closely than Chen Weiqing, China's Ambassador to Saudi Arabia and its first representative to the Organization of Islamic Cooperation—a multilateral Muslim organization based in Jeddah (Weiqing, 2021) He thanked MBS, on social media, for introducing Mandarin into Saudi schools. He has over 66,000 followers on Twitter alone, and frequently posts comments there in Arabic (Obaid, 2020). He not only tweets about China and his official business but also about his trips to the desert, eating Saudi food, and visiting Abha and different parts of the Kingdom. He also has participated in the Saudi forestation program (Saudi Press Agency, 2021c), a key part of the Sino-Saudi partnership on the environment and climate change (*Arab News*, 2021). In addition, he has marked key cultural events. In November 2020, he hailed a concert, held in Beijing, to mark the thirtieth anniversary of Sino-Saudi ties, where Aghla Balad, a famous Saudi musician, performed with a philharmonic orchestra based in the Chinese capital (*Arab News*, 2020). Three years earlier, in 2017, Kamal al-Mualem, a Saudi sculptor, was one of the artists selected to be one of the nearly 200 individuals to participate in the Silk Road International Art Exhibition in Xian, China. That event is sponsored by the Chinese government (Hassan, 2017).

For their part, Saudi officials have similarly promoted Sino-Saudi ties. In 2016, MBS had Ahmed Mater, one of the Kingdom's most accomplished visual artists, accompany him on a trip to Beijing. There, Mater presented President Xi with "Silk Road"—a large twin silkscreen piece he had painted in the style of Chinese miniatures, with one side depicting the history of China and the other the history of Saudi Arabia (Musakkis, 2016). A year later, in 2017, King Salman received an honorary doctorate from Beijing University, one of China's most prestigious universities, and presided over the opening of the King Abdulaziz Library at the same university (*Arab News*, 2017). During that trip to Beijing, the King also oversaw the unveiling of the Arab-Chinese Digital Library, a joint project of the Arab League, Riyadh's King Abdul Aziz Public Library, and the National Library of China in Beijing (*Arab News*, 2019).

During MBS' visit to Beijing in 2019, Prince Badr bin Abdullah bin Farhan, the Saudi Culture Minister, announced the "Prince Mohammed bin Salman Award for Cultural Cooperation between the Kingdom of Saudi Arabia and the People's Republic of China" (*Al-Arabiya*, 2019). The award, the Prince noted, demonstrated his government's commitment "to building cultural bridges between the two countries, developing cultural exchanges, and enhancing artistic and academic opportunities" for Chinese and Saudi citizens (ibid.). Later that same year, Saudi officials met with their Chinese counterparts to enhance the Arab-Chinese Digital Library through a new five-year program to increase the number of texts in "Arabic and Chinese and enhancing mutual knowledge through the promotion of common cultural programs" (*Arab News*, 2019).

Growing Chinese-Saudi cultural ties have also extended beyond official channels to the Hajj, one of the five pillars of Islam and one of the oldest institutions linking Saudi Arabia with China. In recent years, up to 10,000 Chinese travel individually or in groups on Hajj, many with the state-backed China Islamic Association (Jia, 2020). Many of the other countries that contribute to the Hajj, such as Pakistan, are also in Asia and have deep ties with China (Khan, 2012). According to Saudi official statistics, 75 percent of the 2.49 million pilgrims who participated in the 2019 Hajj traveled from overseas (Saudi Arabian General Authority for Statistics, n.d.: 10) while about 40 percent of the 19 million Umrah pilgrims in 2019 were from overseas (Nineteen million pilgrims, 2020).

And those numbers are set to grow substantially. Vision 2030 identified opening Saudi Arabia to tourism and increasing Mecca and Medina's capacity for the Hajj and Umrah as two critical objectives. These plans recognized that there is pent-up demand among tourists to visit the Kingdom, which is widely seen as an exotic locale, and even higher demand among the world's nearly 2 million Muslims to undertake the Hajj pilgrimage. In China and other Asian nations there are long waiting lists for a coveted spot to go on Hajj (Jia, 2020), with some having to wait 20–40 years for an opportunity to travel (Renaldi and Ibrahim, 2021). By 2030, Riyadh aims to host at least 30 million Hajj and Umrah visitors, an expansion that is expected to increase Hajj and Umrah revenues to at least $13.2 billion annually (El Yaakoubi and Rashad, 2020). Saudi economists hope that tourism and expanded Hajj and Umrah pilgrimages will contribute $150 billion to the Kingdom, potentially enough to fund "the entire national economy" (Bensaid, 2019).

Beijing and Riyadh have seen Chinese tourists as essential to these plans. In 2018, shortly before the tourist visa was introduced, Li Huaxin, China's then Ambassador to Saudi Arabia, predicted that the Kingdom would be a major tourist destination and that Chinese tourists would become a major factor in Saudi tourism (*Arab News*, 2018). After all, he noted, 140 million Chinese had traveled overseas as tourists over the previous year (ibid.). After the introduction of Saudi Arabia's visa for tourists, the ambassador was proven correct: A third of the first wave of tourists visiting the Kingdom were Chinese (Al-Sherbini, 2019). Equally importantly, those visitors spent, on average, $1,582 each (Chinese visitors, 2019). In December 2019, it was predicted that a million Chinese would visit the Kingdom in 2020 (*Saudi Gazette*, 2019).

Most of those visitors, however, never made it to the Kingdom because of the Covid-19 pandemic. In the opening days of the pandemic, the Kingdom sent medical aid and supplies directly to Wuhan (Serrieh, 2020). When the virus arrived in Saudi Arabia, it quickly spread, compelling the government to impose a lockdown in late March 2021. During this moment of crisis, Riyadh cooperated with Washington on containing global energy markets while turning to Beijing for essential medical assistance. Not only were Chinese doctors welcomed into Saudi Arabia to fight Covid-19 (*Ashraq Al-Awsat*, 2020; Laskar, 2020), but, in May 2020, Riyadh also bought $265 million worth of Covid-19 testing kits from BGI, a Chinese company that US officials have negatively compared to Huawei (Westall and Levingston, 2020).

Following the deal, which was finalized during a telephone call between Salman and Xi, a spokesperson for the Saudi Royal Court told Bloomberg that the large purchase "confirms the strength of long-standing Saudi-Chinese ties" (ibid.). These comments were echoed by the Saudi media, which, as Yahia H. Zoubir has noted, was "laudatory towards China's handling of the fight against Covid-19" (Zoubir, 2020: 8). In particular, he notes, Saudi commentators praised China "as the only country that has acted competently in handling the crisis and, surprisingly, criticized the United States for blaming China, seen as a helpful US electoral scheme but an unproductive foreign policy, with huge drawbacks" (ibid.: 8). Indeed, these commentators concluded that "maybe it [the virus] started in a country before China, but its origin does not concern us as much as overcoming it and returning to 'normal' life" (ibid.: 8).

A year later, Chinese officials worked to promote this image of China and the close collaboration between the Kingdom and China. In an interview with *Al-Arabiya* during his March 2021 trip to Saudi Arabia, Chinese Foreign Minister Wang Yi spoke at length about the close cooperation between China and the Kingdom during the early days of the pandemic:

> When COVID-19 struck last year, the two countries came to each other's help. The government and people of all sectors of Saudi Arabia extended generous assistance to China … China provided Saudi Arabia with emergency supplies and sent its medical experts to help boost Saudi Arabia's testing ability. Our joint response is a new chapter of solidarity and cooperation at trying times.
>
> *(Al-Arabiya, 2021)*

That aid had been especially needed in spring and summer 2020 in the large labor camps and immigrant neighborhoods in the Kingdom's western region—especially Jeddah, Mecca, and Medina (Nereim, 2020). By May 2021, foreign workers, including those expanding Mecca's Grand Mosque, made up as much as 70 percent of Saudi Arabia's Covid-19 cases (Sherlock, 2020). As Eman Al-Hussein noted, few regions of the Kingdom were more devastated by the virus than Al-Nakkasah (Al-Hussein, 2020)—a densely populated and very poor area of 200,000 Burmese and Bangladeshis in the center of Mecca, a short distance from the Kaaba (Al-Kanani, 2020). Due to the rapid spread of the virus in Mecca, other parts of the Kingdom, and around the world, Saudi Arabia, in summer 2020, limited the annual Hajj to just 1,000 pilgrims. All of the Hajj pilgrims were based in the Kingdom and had to adhere to strict Covid-19 safety protocols (Hubbard and Walsh, 2020).

After the announcement, multiple countries, including China, announced that they would suspend all Hajj and Umrah trips indefinitely (Jia, 2020). Shortly after that announcement, China also introduced a series of new relations regarding Hajj pilgrims. Henceforth Chinese Muslims could only go on the Hajj pilgrimage with tours organized by the state-backed Chinese Islamic Association, had to obey all Chinese and local laws while they were on Hajj, and had to oppose religious extremism (Varma, 2020).

While no public reason was given for the change in Hajj policy, it is worth noting that it coincided with the introduction of the Saudi tourist visa. That visa allows Chinese Muslims, for the first time, to enter the Kingdom as ordinarily vacationers but then go on Umrah or Hajj. As anyone who has lived in Saudi Arabia knows well, Mecca and Medina are well integrated into the country's modern transportation system and there are also few internal checks on domestic travelers. Visiting Chinese Muslims could travel to the two holy cities, both of which are large metropolises that expand to vast seas of humanity during Hajj, without notifying either Chinese or Saudi authorities. In fact, before the Covid-19 pandemic, it was not uncommon for domestic pilgrims to go on Hajj annually—with many of them staying in tents pitched alongside highways to escape official scrutiny, flaunting regulations that limit them to going on Hajj once every five years.

Vaccines

Whatever the reasons for the new Chinese Hajj policy, six months after it was enacted, many people assumed that Chinese and other pilgrims would be allowed to go on Hajj in 2021. Some Umrah visitors had already been allowed to go from Indonesia (Rayda, 2021). Pakistan's Religious Affairs Minister, Noorul Haq Qadri, predicted in early spring 2021 that up to 50,000 Pakistanis in good health could perform Hajj that year (*Express Tribune*, 2021). And vaccines were widely seen as part of making Hajj possible in 2021, with Muslim Tanzanians pushing their government to accelerate its vaccination program so they could go on pilgrimage (Kombe, 2021). Saudi clerics had even joined colleagues from the around the world in signing a fatwa (Islamic legal opinion) in early 2021 urging the world's Muslims to take Covid-19 vaccines (Organization of Islamic Cooperation's International Fiqh Academy, 2021). Since no specifics were given on which vaccines were acceptable, presumably Chinese vaccines were as acceptable as a vaccine developed in India, Europe, or the United States.

In late May 2021, however, Saudi Arabia, following the lead of the EU, banned all travelers from entering the Kingdom who had not received one of the vaccines approved by the country's medical authorities: AstraZeneca, Moderna, Pfizer, and Johnson & Johnson (*TRT World*, 2021). All four of these vaccines had been developed by Western companies. Absent from the list were Sinopharm and Sinovac, two vaccines produced by China that had been widely used in Bahrain and the UAE (Gambrell, 2021)—the latter of which plans to produce Sinopharm in cooperation with China (El Sherif, 2021).

Although Saudi Arabia provided an exemption to allow travelers from the UAE to enter the country (Serrieh, 2021), it did not initially make a similar exception for travelers from most Asian nations. That decision seemingly put it at odds with China, its largest trading partner, and a host of other nations in Asia, especially after the World Health Organization authorized the two Chinese vaccines for emergency use (Regan and Langmaid, 2021). Millions of people in Asia and the wider world faced the real possibility of not being able to travel to the Kingdom for Hajj or Umrah or for work. Leaders in Africa, the Middle East, and from the Indus River Valley to the South China Sea Asia loudly complained about the decision to not include Chinese vaccines, reflecting their citizens' anger (Daim, 2021). The stakes were high. Not only did many Muslims travel to the Kingdom for education, Hajj, or Umrah but also millions of Muslims and non-Muslims have worked in Saudi Arabia. For decades, remittances from those workers have helped drive Asia's economies from the Arabian Sea to the South China Sea.

The Pakistani Foreign Office, for instance, in a note to its Saudi counterpart, argued that: (1) Chinese vaccines were the only vaccines Pakistan could readily acquire; (2) many Pakistanis had already received a Chinese Covid-19 vaccine; and (3) doctors did not recommend giving these Pakistanis another jab (*Express Tribune*, 2021). Prime Minister Ahmed Khan of Pakistan and Chief Minister of Sindh, Murad Ali Shah, reacted with alarm to the Saudi decision to exclude the Chinese vaccines, with Shah expressing his feelings directly in a June 2021 meeting with Nawaf Saeed Al-Maliki, Saudi Arabia's Ambassador to Pakistan (News Desk, 2021). Shah specifically told Al-Maliki, "Our people are quite upset that they would not be allowed to visit Saudi Arabia, as they have vaccination certificates for Chinese vaccines" (Siddiqui, 2021). Al-Malaki assured the Chief Minister that he would communicate his concerns to Riyadh (ibid.).

Others were no less stunned by the Saudi decision to exclude Chinese vaccines. Khairy bin Jamaluddin (widely known as KJ), the public face of Malaysia's vaccine program, had been the first in the Southeast Asian nation to receive the Sinovac vaccine. Following his vaccination, he assured Malaysians that they should not be hesitant to take Sinovac. "It has been proven to be safe and effective in preventing Covid-19," he stated, "and it has been used in 27 countries such as China, the UAE, Indonesia, Turkey and Brazil" (*Straits Times*, 2021). He even joked that the vaccine had given him the ability to speak Mandarin fluently (Syahrul, 2021). But once it was clear that Riyadh would not accept Sinovac for Hajj travelers, KJ and his colleagues rushed to assure worried Malaysians that those going on Hajj would be vaccinated with the Pfizer vaccine—even if they had already been vaccinated with a Chinese vaccine (Daim, 2021).

KJ's colleagues in Indonesia initially lobbied Saudi Arabia to accept Indonesian pilgrims who had received the Sinovac vaccine (Rayda, 2021). "Indonesia's COVID-19 mitigation efforts," Indonesian Religious Minister, Yaqut Cholil Qoumas stated publicly "have been relatively good," adding "I don't know why Indonesians are still denied entry into Saudi" (ibid.). But when that argument did not convince Saudi officials, Qoumas and others avoided all the questions that accompanied Riyadh's failure to recognize Chinese vaccines. In June, they canceled their nation's official Hajj two months early, citing health concerns linked to the Covid-19 epidemic. Abdul Kadir Jaelani, the Director-General for Asia Pacific and African Regions at Indonesia's Foreign Ministry, dismissed "rumors that the cancelation was due to the coronavirus vaccine that the country is mostly relying on its immunization drive" (Tisnadibrata, 2021). "There is no problem with the [Chinese] vaccine, since the WHO has validated it for emergency use," he added (ibid.). "This cancelation," he continued "is purely out of concern to protect ourselves from the outbreak" (ibid.).

For their part, Saudi officials resisted the pressure to accept the Chinese vaccines from Asian governments while also searching for a face-saving way out of what had become a public relations crisis. On June 12, 2021, the Saudi Ministry of Hajj and Umrah presented a solution to the crisis: the Hajj would be small (60,000) and, most importantly, closed to pilgrims outside of the Kingdom (*Al-Sharq al-Awsat Online*, 2021). In explaining the decision, Saudi officials cited the rise of Covid-19 variants along with the low numbers who had been vaccinated worldwide (ibid.). That same day the Saudi Ministry of Health released a statement that said that four Covid-19 vaccines had been authorized for use in the country but that it was still "possible that other vaccines may be approved in the future" (*Al-Mowaten*, 2021). Eventually that happened. On August 25, 2021, Saudi Arabia's government permitted travelers vaccinated with the Chinese vaccines to enter the country—provided they had received a booster with one of the four vaccines (Al-Kudair, 2021). By March 2022, travelers were no longer required to show proof of vaccination status to enter the Kingdom (*Arab News*, 2022).

Those changes, however, did not answer the larger question: Why did Saudi Arabia refuse to accept vaccines produced by China, its largest trading partner, while jeopardizing cultural and commercial ties built over decades across Asia? After all, the UAE had wholeheartedly accepted the Chinese vaccines. Public health considerations likely provide part of the explanation—reinforced by the fact that 350 doctors and medical workers, most of whom were vaccinated with Sinovac, were infected in late June 2021 by Covid-19 in Indonesia. There positivity rates exceeding 23 percent (Widianto and Lamb, 2021). Well-publicized outbreaks of Covid-19 in nations that used Sinopharm along with the decision of Bahrain and the UAE to offer those who had received Sinopharm a third shot of Sinopharm or a Pfizer booster shot would further reinforce these concerns (Taylor and Schemm, 2021). Saudi health officials had also only vaccinated about a quarter of the country's population by June 2021—a number that reflects, in part, skepticism among some Saudis about the vaccines (Chopra, 2021). Furthermore, maintaining public health has often been challenging for anyone administering the Hajj—even under the best of circumstances. That event brings together people from around the world to carry out a series of holy rituals, some of which take place in confined spaces. One of the cities where those events take place, Mecca, often led Saudi Arabia in new cases in summer 2021 (Al-Jindi, 2021).

Refusing to recognize Sinovac and Sinopharm had the added benefit of helping the Kingdom meet goals outside of public health, including a central objective of Vision 2030: encouraging Saudi private businesses to hire more citizens. If Pakistanis and others could not enter the Kingdom nor work there because they had been vaccinated with a Chinese vaccine, Saudi employers would have a strong incentive to hire more Saudis. Prominent voices had already pressed the government to use the pandemic as an opportunity to end foreign domination of the workforce (Barbuscia and Rashad, 2020). Most of those workers are from Africa, South Asia, and Southeast Asia, with few from China. That is very different from the UAE, where there are 270,000 Chinese nationals (Wang, 2020: 8).

Strikingly, neither President Xi nor his counterparts in the Chinese government commented publicly on Riyadh's vaccine policy or even encouraged Saudis to use Chinese vaccines. There has been no discussion of penalizing Riyadh or even defending the vaccine with Beijing's considerable publicity apparatus, both in Saudi Arabia and globally. This is surprising, given how closely Beijing and Riyadh's economic and political interests had seemingly aligned in China's favor in recent years, resembling the relationship between Riyadh and Washington in the 1970s. Chinese officials also recognize Saudi Arabia's cultural and political influence in the Middle East and the wider Muslim world—including in countries where China's influence is strong. Indeed, Riyadh effectively acts as a domestic political force in nations as different as Indonesia and Pakistan.

One example of Chinese behavior was especially telling in this context. In late March 2021, Chinese embassies in Israel, Pakistan, the Philippines, the United States, and a number of other countries around the world posted a statement on their websites stating that all visa applicants to China would receive preferential treatment if they had received a Chinese vaccine (Ng, 2021). A number of experts saw the statement as an attempt by

Beijing to leverage its economic power, compelling nations around the world to use its Covid-19 vaccines if they wanted to do business with China (Woertz and Yellinek, 2021). Whether that is the case or not remains to be seen, but no similar statement was posted by China's diplomats in Riyadh. There, applicants are asked to provide proof that they had received a Covid-19 vaccination.

The inclination of Chinese leaders to ignore Riyadh's decision on vaccines may reflect, in part, their desire to lessen any negative publicity associated with Sinopharm or Sinovac or to simply adhere to their past promises to defend Saudi Arabia's internal affairs. Equally importantly, they may have assumed, rightly, that the Saudi policy on Chinese vaccines is only temporary—at least until the Kingdom is fully vaccinated. Most nations in Asia, Africa, and the Middle East, where most Muslims live today, have no realistic option for Covid-19 vaccines *other* than the Chinese ones. A good example is this Philippines, which provided Chinese Covid-19 vaccines to many of its overseas workers—a larger percentage of whom work in Saudi Arabia (Garcia, 2021). They and others throughout Africa and Asia are unlikely to get any of the four vaccines that are currently authorized in Saudi Arabia (Taylor and Schemm, 2021).

The changes in Saudi policy in late 2021 and early 2022 showed, either economically and politically, that it was not viable for Riyadh to ban Chinese businesspeople or tourists, no less the millions of Egyptians, Indonesians, Pakistanis, and others who have taken part in the Hajj for years, from entering Saudi Arabia. Even with higher oil prices and pressure to reduce foreign laborers in the Kingdom's workforce, it would have been difficult for Saudi Arabia to achieve any of the goals of Vision 2030 without millions of individuals from Asia, Africa, or the Middle East visiting the Kingdom.

Finally, as Saudi Arabia seeks to address the bilateral and multilateral challenges of Chinese vaccines, it will want to closely examine the experience of Israel. There, public health authorities achieved impressive gains against Covid-19 by using Western vaccines. But Israeli health authorities refused to recognize the Chinese vaccines, signaling in particular that they didn't trust Sinopharm (Lappin, 2021). That hampered Israeli efforts to deepen ties with China while complicating efforts to re-start cross-border trade in the Levant and to take advantage of the commercial potential of the Abraham Accords (ibid.). Here it is worth noting that Sinopharm has not only been extensively used by Israel's neighbors—Egypt, Jordan, and the Palestinians Territories—but also by Bahrain, Morocco, Sudan, and the UAE. Turkey has also depended on Chinese vaccines. Initially, Israel only reached a vaccine passport mutual recognition deal with Bahrain (Estrin, 2021) and had difficulty reaching a similar deal with either China or other Arab states, including the UAE. "We are trying to create a test," Israel's then Foreign Minister Gabi Ashkenazi noted in June 2021, "that will address the concerns of the [Israeli] Health Ministry while taking into account the professionalism with which the UAE authorities have handled the COVID-19 pandemic" (Berman, 2021). Eventually, Israeli officials resolved the dilemma by allowing all visitors—regardless of their vaccine status—to enter Israel (Reuters, 2022).

Conclusion

In her 2012 book, *On Saudi Arabia*, Karen Elliot House argues that Saudi Arabia had "clearly shifted from a singular dependence on the United States to a multipolar foreign policy"—a framework in which US-Saudi relations, were, in the words of former Saudi Foreign Minister Prince Saud al-Faisal "a Muslim marriage, not a Catholic marriage"

(House, 2012: 238). According to House, this sentence was a very clever way of saying that Riyadh could enjoy multiple spouses, as is permitted for men under Islamic law. Still, she concludes, "the United States remains Saudi Arabia's first and paramount wife" (ibid.: 238). For House, little had really changed since Baroody's day in the early 1970s.

A decade after House wrote those words, Beijing is Riyadh's "first and paramount wife." As Chinese and Saudi leaders have made clear on multiple occasions, they agree on all major international issues, including contentious ones, such as the status of Hong Kong or Taiwan, where Chinese and Western leaders now vehemently disagree. Beijing and Riyadh see Chinese investments in energy, telecommunications, and tourism as essential to Vision 2030, while Riyadh has positioned itself as China's chief source of oil for decades to come.

Although Washington maintains a strategic relationship with Riyadh in public health and military and regional affairs, the United States imports substantially less Saudi oil than it did in the past—helping to erode a bilateral relationship damaged by the murder of Jamal Khashoggi and other disagreements over events in the region and elsewhere in the world (US Energy Information Administration, 2021a). In this era of transition and emerging new global powers, the bilateral relationship with Beijing is more important than ever for Saudi leaders. But they nonetheless must balance it against its ties to Washington and the EU. Again, the Kingdom has used US and European vaccines to combat Covid-19.

As the Kingdom seeks to chart this new path, it will undoubtedly benefit from a key diplomatic principle it shares with China. For many years, Beijing has pursued "of both this and that," where it hedges risk in foreign policy and avoids "either or choices" whenever it can (Guzansky and Lavi, 2021). This approach can produce seemingly contradictory policies but can be extremely successful. China, for instance, has developed cordial ties with both Israel and with Iran, a nation which many Israelis view as an existential military threat. In the case of Covid-19 and Saudi Arabia, Beijing has focused on the areas of agreement with Riyadh while effectively ignoring the refusal of Saudi public health authorities to authorize Sinopharm or Sinovac.

One sees similar frameworks in Saudi government policy, both today and in the past. While Saudi Arabia did not join the Abraham Accords in 2020, it nonetheless provided critical overflight rights for Israeli airlines and those of other nations traveling from the Gulf and Asia to Israeli airports. And those flights continued throughout the recent Israel-Gaza War.

Forty years before that agreement, we saw Riyadh apply a similar approach when it bought all of ARAMCO. At the time, an American journalist met with Ahmed Yamani, Saudi Arabia's then Minister of Petroleum and Mineral Resources. The journalist asked Yamani about buying ARAMCO, which he likened to nationalization—a term then associated in the West with decolonization, hostility to the West, and high oil prices. "If nationalization means divorce," Yamani responded, "then this will not be nationalization" (Sheehan, 1974: 58). Instead, he explained, "it will be another form of marriage that we are attempting to define" (ibid.: 58).

Yamani's approach proved successful for the Kingdom and the global community. Not only did Saudi Arabia establish a 100 percent control of ARAMCO, but it also did so while keeping much of its foreign staff in place and retaining its commercial links to the outside world (Cordesman, 2003: 472). Over the next five decades, ARAMCO continued to develop, produce oil for growing global markets, and hire more Saudis to join its workforce.

Yamani and Riyadh's success in achieving "another form of marriage that we are attempting to define" suggests that the Kingdom has the tools to build a richer relationship with China—one that will be beneficial for Beijing and Riyadh but will, at the same time, not compel Saudi Arabia to "divorce" its earlier relationships entirely to Washington and other Western powers. Were Riyadh able to achieve that goal, it would be a "win-win" for all involved.

References

Abumaria, D. (2020, January 21). Saudi Arabia to Teach Chinese as Third Language. *The Media Line*. Available at: www.jpost.com/international/saudi-arabia-to-teach-chinese-as-third-language-614768

Aiqing, F. (2019, June 13). Learn Chinese in Riyadh. *China Daily*. Available at: www.chinadaily.com.cn/a/201906/13/WS5d019ee2a310176577230e1e_1.html

Aizhu, C., El-Gamal, R., and Meng, M. (2019, February 21). Saudi Aramco to Sign China Refinery Deals as Crown Prince Visits: Sources. Reuters. Available at: www.reuters.com/article/us-asia-saudi-china-xi/saudi-aramco-to-sign-china-refinery-deals-as-crown-prince-visits-sources-idUSKCN1QA0OE

Ajrash, K. (2021, June 12). Iraq Sees Oil Prices at $68 to $75 a Barrel in 2nd Half. Bloomberg. Available at: https://finance.yahoo.com/news/iraq-sees-oil-prices-68-180327524.html

Al-Arabiyya. (2019, February 21). Saudi Arabia Announces Cultural Cooperation Award with China. Available at: https://english.alarabiya.net/life-style/art-and-culture/2019/02/21/Saudi-Arabia-announces-a-cultural-cooperation-award-with-China

Al-Arabiya. (2021, March 26). Transcript of State Councilor and Foreign Minister Wang Yi's Exclusive Interview with Al Arabiya. Available at: http://us.china-embassy.gov.cn/eng/zgyw/202103/t20210326_9014478.htm

Al-Ghannam, H. (2020a, July 8). Ana la ʻatahadath huna ʻan aistibdal halif biakhar ʻaw alaintiqal min muʻaskar limuʻaskar mukhtalif bal ʻan *alqudrat ealaa almuazanat bayn alduwal aleuzmaa* waʼijad muʻadalat jadidat liltaeamul mʻa hadhih alduwali, takhtalif ʻan altartibat walmuazanat alsaabiqati by Hesham Alghannam. Twitter. [@HeshamAlghannam]. Available at: https://twitter.com/HeshamAlghannam/status/1280931801431760896

Al-Ghannam, H. (2020b, July 8). fan altawajuh nahw ʻalaqat ʻakthar ʻumqana watarabutana mae alsin tataʻadaa almajal alaiqtisadiu yabdu hatmaya. Wasatushajiʻ alsiyn dhalik watahafizuh wasatʻamal bihamas ʻalaa ʼiideaf alhaymanat al ʻamrikiat alati kanat mutlaqatan liʻuqud ʻalaa almintaqat waealaa aistighlal alshiqaq fi alnizam alduwalii walainqisamat bayn dualih khasatan bialkhaliji, litahqiq hadha alhadafi by Hesham Alghannam. Twitter. [@HeshamAlghannam] Available at: https://twitter.com/HeshamAlghannam/status/1280939757598629888

Al-Hussein, E. (2020, April 24). Migrant Workers at the Epicenter of Public Health Crisis in the Gulf. *AGSIW Blog Post*. Available at: https://agsiw.org/migrant-workers-at-the-epicenter-of-public-health-crisis-in-the-gulf/

Aljazeera. (2019, February 23). Saudi Crown Prince Defends China's Right to Fight 'Terrorism.' Available at: www.aljazeera.com/news/2019/2/23/saudi-crown-prince-defends-chinas-right-to-fight-terrorism

Al-Jindi, M. (2021, June 7). Fayrus Kuruna <<Kufid-19>> fi Alsuʻudiat alyawm aliathnayn 7 yunyu 2021. *Arabia*.

Al-Kanani, J. (2020, March 31). Ijraʻat Iḥtiraziya liʻaḥyaʼ tarikiya biMakka. *Al-Riyadh*. Available at: www.alriyadh.com/1813410

al-Khudair, D. (2021, August 25). Saudi Arabia Approves Sinovac and Sinopharm Vaccines, *Arab News*. Available at: www.arabnews.com/node/1916756/saudi-arabia

Al-Mowaten. (2021, June 12). Wazir alsihati: aʻitimad allaqahat yatimu min qibal alghidhaʼ waldawaʼ. Available at: https://bit.ly/35jZYLz

Al-Sharq al-Awsat. (2020, April 16). Eight Chinese Medical Experts Arrive in Saudi Arabia. Available at: https://english.aawsat.com//home/article/2237086/8-chinese-medical-experts-arrive-saudi-arabia

Al-Sharq al-Awsat. (2021, June 12). Alsʻaudiat tʻulin qasr haji hadha alʻam ʻalaa almuatinin walmuqimin biʼijmalii 60 ʻalf hajin. Available at: https://bit.ly/3whO68x

Al-Sherbini, R. (2019, October 8). Saudi Arabia Says 24,000 Tourists Visited in First Ten Days. *Gulf News*. Available at: https://gulfnews.com/world/gulf/saudi/saudi-arabia-says-24000-touri sts-visited-in-10-days-1.66990138

Al-Sudairi, M. (2020). The People's Republic in the Red Sea: A Holistic Analysis of China's Discursive and Material Footprint in the Region. *Dirasat* 52. Available at: https://kfcris.com/ en/view/post/259

Al-Tamimi, N. M. (2013). *China-Saudi Arabian Relations, 1990–2012: Marriage of Convenience or New Strategic Partnership?* London: Routledge.

Al-Tamimi, N. M. (2018). China's 'Rise' in the Gulf: A Saudi Perspective. In M. Al-Rasheed (Ed.). *Salman's Legacy: The Dilemmas of a New Era in Saudi Arabia*. Oxford: Oxford University Press, pp. 251–271.

AP News. (2020, September 10). China, Others to Join Military Exercises in Russia. Available at: https://apnews.com/article/pakistan-belarus-iran-myanmar-russia-0d2f7ebbf673fccf3f2c6 43cc495a177

Arab News. (2017, March 17). King Salman Launches Library at Peking University. Available at: www.arabnews.com/node/1069746/saudi-arabia

Arab News. (2018, July 10). Chinese Envoy sees KSA as a Major Tourist Destination. Available at: www.arabnews.com/node/1336756/saudi-arabia

Arab News. (2019, January 1). Saudi Arabia, China to Enhance Cultural Bridges. Available at: www. arabnews.com/node/1429541/saudi-arabia

Arab News. (2020, November 26). Diplomatic Quarter: A Cultural Concert Marks Strong Saudi-China Diplomatic Ties. Available at: www.arabnews.com/node/1768471/saudi-arabia

Arab News. (2021, April 20). Saudi Arabia's Crown Prince and China's President Discuss Climate Change. Available at: www.arabnews.com/node/1845876/saudi-arabia

Arab News. (2022, March 23). Unvaccinated Travelers Can Enter Saudi Arabia After Health Ministry Updates COVID-19 Requirements. Available at: www.arabnews.com/node/2048416/ saudi-arabia

Barbuscia, D. and Rashad, M. (2020, May 7). 'What's the Point of Staying?': Gulf Faces Expatriate Exodus. Reuters. Available at: www.reuters.com/article/us-health-coronavirus-gulf-jobs-idUSKBN22J1WL

BBC World. (2016, January 19). China's President Xi Visits Saudi Arabia to Improve Ties. Available at: www.bbc.com/news/world-middle-east-35351391

Bensaid, A. (2019, August 9). Is Saudi Arabia Unfairly Profiting from its Holy Sites? *TRT World*. Available at: www.trtworld.com/magazine/is-saudi-arabia-unfairly-profiting-from-its-holy-sites-28899

Berman, L. (2021, June 8). Israel Working on Arrangement to Allow Vaccinated Emiratis to Visit Israel. *Times of Israel*, Liveblog. Available at: www.timesofisrael.com/liveblog_entry/israel-work ing-on-arrangement-to-allow-vaccinated-emiratis-to-visit-israel/

Bhaya, A. G. (2018, August 30). Chinese-Built Light Railway Praised by Pilgrims. CGTN. Available at: https://news.cgtn.com/news/3d3d514f7a55444f79457a6333566d54/share_p.html

Blanchard, B. (2019, January 31). China Calls for Harmony as It Welcomes Qatar Emir Amid Gulf Disputes. Reuters. Available at: www.reuters.com/article/us-china-qatar/china-calls-for-harm ony-as-it-welcomes-qatar-emir-amid-gulf-dispute-idUSKCN1PP1EV

Burke, R. (2010). *Decolonization and the Evolution of International Human Rights*. Pennsylvania, PA: University of Pennsylvania Press.

Cafiero, G. and Wagner, D. (2020, September 22). China and the Abraham Accords Peace Agreement. MEI. Available at: www.mei.edu/publications/china-and-abraham-accords-peace-agreement

Chopra, A. (2021, May 23). Saudi Ups Pressure on Anti-Vaxxers as it eyes Economic Recovery. AFP. Available at: https://news.yahoo.com/saudi-ups-pressure-anti-vaxxers-034344545.html

Colley, C. (2021, April 2). A Future Chinese Indian Ocean Fleet. *War on the Rocks*. Available at: warontherocks.com/2021/04/a-future-chinese-indian-ocean-fleet/

Cone, A. (2019, May 13). Boeing Nets $11.2M for F-15 Engineering Services in Saudi Arabia, Israel. UPI. Available at: www.upi.com/Defense-News/2019/05/13/Boeing-nets-112M-for-F-15-engineering-services-in-Saudi-Arabia-Israel/9481557751557/

Cordesman, A. (2003). *Saudi Arabia Enters the 21st Century*. Westport, Ct: Greenwood Publishing Group.

Curry, E. (2020, February 6). Saudi Introduces Chinese in Schools to Boost Diversity. *The Pie News*. Available at: https://thepienews.com/news/saudi-introduces-chinese-schools-diversify-kingdom/

Daim, N. (2021, May 30). Malaysia to Discuss With Saudi To Allow Entry For Pilgrims Who Received Sinovac Vaccine. *New Straits Times*. Available at: www.nst.com.my/news/nation/2021/05/694398/malaysia-discuss-saudi-allow-entry-pilgrims-who-received-sinovac-vaccine

DiPaola, A., Wingfield, B., and Lee, J. (2020a, May 6). Saudi Arabia Gains an Edge in Oil Market After Prices Plunge. Bloomberg. Available at: www.bloomberg.com/news/articles/2020-05-06/saudis-gain-edge-in-global-oil-sales-contest-by-whacking-prices

DiPaola, A., Wingfield, B., and Lee, J. (2020b, June 3). China Is Getting Its Hooks Deeper into Middle East Oil Supplies. Bloomberg. Available at: www.bloomberg.com/news/articles/2020-06-03/china-is-getting-its-hooks-deeper-into-middle-east-oil-supplies

ECNS. (2016, May 12). Riyadh Hails Beijing's Stance on South China Sea. Available at: www.ecns.cn/2016/05-13/210322.shtml

Economist. (2019, April 20). Chinese Money Is Behind Some of the Arab World's Biggest Projects. Available at: www.economist.com/middle-east-and-africa/2019/04/20/chinese-money-is-behind-some-of-the-arab-worlds-biggest-projects

Efron, S., Schwindt, K., and Haskel, E. (2020). Chinese Investment in Israeli Technology and Infrastructure: Security Implications for Israel and the United States. Santa Monica, CA: Rand Corporation. Available at: www.rand.org/pubs/research_reports/RR3176.html

El Gamal, R. and Rashad, M. (2020, August 10). Saudi Aramco to Press Ahead with Plan to Boost Output Capacity, CEO Says. Reuters. Available at: www.reuters.com/article/us-saudi-aramco-results-capacity/saudi-aramco-to-press-ahead-with-plan-to-boost-output-capacity-ceo-says-idUSKCN2561U9

El Massassi, A. (2021, February 24). Huawei, Controversial in the West, Is Going Strong in the Gulf. AFP. Available at: https://au.finance.yahoo.com/news/huawei-controversial-west-going-strong-024244842.html

El Sherif, A. (2021, April 1). UAE First Country in Arab World to Begin Manufacturing COVID-19 Vaccine. *Mobi Health News*. Available at: www.mobihealthnews.com/news/emea/uae-first-country-arab-world-begin-manufacturing-covid-19-vaccine

El Watan News. (2016, August 28). Asrihat Khatirat lil'amir Muhamad Bin Salman qabl Tawajuhih 'iilaa al-Sin. Available at: www.elwatannews.com/news/details/1365543?t=push

El Yaakoubi, A. and Rashad, M. (2020, June 8). Saudi Arabia Considers Limiting Haj Pilgrims Amid COVID-19 Fears. Reuters. Available at: www.reuters.com/article/us-health-coronavirus-saudi-haj/saudi-arabia-considers-limiting-haj-pilgrims-amid-covid-19-fears-idUSKBN23F1VJ

England, A. and Warrell, H. (2020, June 6). Saudi Arabia To Keep Buying Arms Despite Austerity. *Financial Times*. Available at: www.ft.com/content/062a1fa4-2892-4b84-8518-0a1a35d78bf1

ENP Newswire. (2021, March 30). Saudia Marks 10 Years of Operations to China; Saudia Operates 7 Weekly Flights between Saudi Arabia and Guangzhou. Gale OneFile. Available at: news, link.gale.com/apps/doc/A656760846/STND?u=tel_middleten&sid=bookmark-STND&xid=827038f3 (accessed June 2, 2021).

Estrin, D. (2021, April 22). Vaccine Passports: Israel, Bahrain Reach Landmark Agreement. NPR. Available at: www.npr.org/sections/coronavirus-live-updates/2021/04/22/989891650/vaccine-passports-israel-bahrain-reach-landmark-agreement

Express Tribune. (2021, May 22). FO Takes Up Vaccine Issue with Saudi Govt. *Express Tribune*. Available at: https://tribune.com.pk/story/2301113/fo-takes-up-vaccine-issue-with-saudi-govt

Fassihi, F. and Myers, S. L. (2021, March 27). China, with $400 Billion Iran Deal, Could Deepen Influence in Mideast. *New York Times*. Available at: www.nytimes.com/2021/03/27/world/middleeast/china-iran-deal.html

Foreign Affairs. (2021, March 26). MIL-OSI China: China, Saudi Arabia Vow to Oppose Interference in Other Countries' Internal Affairs. Gale OneFile: News. Available at: link.gale.com/apps/doc/A656261373/STND?u=tel_middleten&sid=bookmark-STND&xid=65bd1a8b (accessed June 2, 2021).

Gambrell, J. (2021, June 3). Bahrain Offers Pfizer Booster for Some Who Got Chinese Shots. AP News. https://apnews.com/article/bahrain-middle-east-coronavirus-vaccine-coronavirus-pandemic-health-2d4b5c26b1480f1fd0d7e3a9e9a62d0e

Garcia. B. (2021, June 21). Sinovac, Covishield Vaccine Takers Await Their Fate On Return to Kuwait. *Kuwait Times*. Available at: https://news.kuwaittimes.net/website/sinovac-covishield-vaccine-takers-await-their-fate-on-return-to-kuwait/

Gardner, T., Holland, S., Zhdannikov, D., and El-Gamal, R. (2020, April 30). Special Report: Trump Told Saudi: Cut Oil Supply Or Lose U.S. Military Support – Sources. Reuters. Available at: www.reuters.com/article/us-global-oil-trump-saudi-specialreport/special-report-trump-told-saudi-cut-oil-supply-or-lose-u-s-military-support-sources-idUSKBN22C1V4

Gould, J. (2019, June 29). US Senate Allows Arms Sales to Saudi Arabia, Sustaining Trump Vetoes. *Defense News*. Available at: www.defensenews.com/congress/2019/07/29/us-senate-allows-arms-sales-to-saudi-arabia-sustaining-trump-vetoes/

Gould, J. (2021, June 10). Austin, Milley Defend Weapons Cuts In Biden's Defense Budget *Defense News*. Available at: www.defensenews.com/congress/2021/06/10/austin-milley-defend-biden-defense-budgets-weapon-cuts-to-wary-lawmakers/

Guzansky, Y. and Lavi, G. (2021, June 13). Relations between China and the Gulf States: Opportunities and Risks for Israel. The Institute for National Security Studies. Available at: www.inss.org.il/publication/china-gulf-states/

Hassan, R. (2017, August 11). Saudi Artist to Showcase Work at Silk Road Exhibition. *Arab News*. Available at: www.arabnews.com/node/1142931/saudi-arabia

Holland, S. (2020, November 30). Saudi Arabia Agrees to Allow Israeli Commercial Planes to Cross Its Airspace - Senior Trump Official. *Reuters*. Available at: www.reuters.com/article/mideast-usa-kushner-int/saudi-arabia-agrees-to-allow-israeli-commercial-planes-to-cross-its-airspace-senior-trump-official-idUSKBN28A2TF

House. K. E. (2012). *On Saudi Arabia*. New York: Alfred A Knopf.

Huang, C. (2015, April 15). 57 Nations Approved As Founders of China-Led AIIB. *South China Morning Post*. Available at: www.scmp.com/news/china/diplomacy-defence/article/1766970/57-nations-approved-founder-members-china-led-aiib

Huawei. (2007, January 11). Huawei Helps Saudi Telecom Support Enormous Peak Traffic During Hajj Season for Second Consecutive Year. *RealWire*. Available at: www.realwire.com/releases/huawei-helps-saudi-telecom-support-enormous-peak-traffic-during-hajj-season-for-second-consecutive-y

Hubbard, B. (2019, April 28). Trump Accuses Saudis of Giving U.S. a Bad Deal. Is That True? *New York Times*. Available at: www.nytimes.com/2019/04/28/world/middleeast/trump-saudi-arabia-military.html

Hubbard, B. and Walsh, D. (2020, June 23). The Hajj Pilgrimage Is Canceled, and Grief Rocks the Muslim World. *New York Times*. Available at: www.nytimes.com/2020/06/23/world/middleeast/hajj-pilgrimage-canceled.html

Ibish. H. (2021, May 27). Gaza War Spoils Israel's Arab Outreach. Amid a Renewed Focus on the Plight of Palestinians, Friendship with Israel Is an Awkward Prospect. Bloomberg. Available at: www.bloomberg.com/opinion/articles/2021-05-27/abraham-accords-gaza-war-queers-israel-s-arab-outreach

International Monetary Fund. (2014). Direction of Trade Statistics: Saudi Arabia 2013. Available at: https://data.imf.org/?sk=9D6028D4-F14A-464C-A2F2-59B2CD424B85

International Monetary Fund. (2021). Direction of Trade Statistics: Saudi Arabia 2020. Available at: https://data.imf.org/?sk=9D6028D4-F14A-464C-A2F2-59B2CD424B85

Ivanova, I. (2018, October 12). Saudi Arabia is America's No. 1 Weapons Consumer. CBS News. Available at: www.cbsnews.com/news/saudi-arabia-is-the-top-buyer-of-u-s-weapons/

Jia, C. (2020, June 25). Annual Pilgrimage Trips for Chinese Muslims Suspended Due to Virus. *China Daily*. Available at: https://global.chinadaily.com.cn/a/202006/25/WS5ef43f6da31083481 72554c6.html

Kane, F. (2017, February 26). Saudi Delegation to Asia an Opportunity to Be Part of New World Order in Trade. *Arab News*. Available at: www.arabnews.com/node/1060326

Keith, T. (2017, May 20). Trump Arrives in Saudi Arabia to a Warm Welcome, Despite Troubles at Home. *NPR News*, Weekend Edition, Saturday. Available at: www.npr.org/2017/05/20/529136712/trumps-troubles-at-home-likely-wont-hold-him-down-in-saudi-arabia

Kershner, I. (2018, March 28). El Al Sues Israel After Air India Flies Through Saudi Airspace. *New York Times*. Available at: www.nytimes.com/2018/03/28/world/middleeast/el-al-air-india-israel-saudi-arabia.html

Khan, F. (2012, October 10). Largest Ever Number of Chinese Pilgrims Coming for Haj This Year. *Arab News*. Available at: www.arabnews.com/largest-ever-number-chinese-pilgrims-coming-haj-year

Knickmeyer, E. (2021, March 1). Analysis: Biden Retreats From Vow to Make Pariah of Saudis. *AP News*. Available at: https://apnews.com/article/biden-retreats-saudi-arabia-sanctions-khashoggi-killing-d91d31edece5db07112d1c2d4dd3be33

Kombe, C. (2021, May 30). Tanzanian Muslims Fear Missing Hajj Due to Vaccination Delay. *VOA News*. Available at: www.voanews.com/covid-19-pandemic/tanzanian-muslims-fear-missing-hajj-due-vaccination-delay

LaFond, A. (2007, March 29). ExxonMobil, Saudi and Chinese Oil Companies in Joint Ventures For Chinese Petroleum Projects. *Manufacturing.Net*. Available at: www.manufacturing.net/home/news/13061300/exxonmobil-saudi-and-chinese-oil-companies-in-joint-ventures-for-chinese-petroleum-projects

Lappin. Y. (2021, April 19). How China and Russia Are Using 'Vaccine Diplomacy' to Enhance Influence in the Middle East. *Jewish News Syndicate*. Available at: www.jns.org/how-china-and-russia-are-using-vaccine-diplomacy-to-enhance-influence-in-the-middle-east/

Laskar, R. H. (2020, May 14). India Permits 835 Healthcare Professionals to Travel to Saudi Arabia for Fight Against Covid-19. *Hindustan Times*. Available at: www.hindustantimes.com/india-news/india-permits-835-healthcare-professionals-to-travel-to-saudi-arabia-for-fight-against-covid-19/story-nOCLSNcZNqBUsIbrOY4EWO.html

Lawler, D. (2020, July 3). The 53 Countries Supporting China's Crackdown on Hong Kong. *Axios*. Available at: www.axios.com/countries-supporting-china-hong-kong-law-0ec9bc6c-3aeb-4af0-8031-aa0f01a46a7c.html

Li, W.H., Chang, X., and Guo, B. (2020). Huawei's Internationalization Journey. In X. Wu and X. P. Murmann (Eds.), *The Management Transformation of Huawei: From Humble Beginnings to Global Leadership*. Cambridge: Cambridge University Press, pp. 244–291.

Lipscy, P. Y. (2017). *Renegotiating the World Order: Institutional Change in International Relations*. Cambridge: Cambridge University Press.

Liu, C. (2017, November 26). Why Israel Is The New Promised Land for Chinese Investors. *South China Morning Post*. Available at: www.scmp.com/week-asia/business/article/2121498/why-israel-new-promised-land-chinese-investors

Macias, A. (2021, May 6). U.S. Sends More Firepower to Middle East as Troops Withdraw from Afghanistan. *CNBC*. Available at: www.cnbc.com/2021/05/06/us-sends-more-firepower-to-middle-east-as-troops-withdraw-from-afghanistan.html

MacIntyre, S. and French, M. (2021, February 17). U.S. Will Import 62 Percent More Crude by 2022 Due to Domestic Production Declines, Says EIA. *World Oil*. Available at: www.worldoil.com/news/2021/2/17/us-will-import-62-more-crude-by-2022-due-to-domestic-production-declines-says-eia

Mann, Y. and Yellinek, R. (2021). The New Chinese Oil Benchmark: Implications for the Middle East. *Middle East Policy* 27(4): 143–156.

Matthews, S. (2021, June 7). China's Ties with Israel Are Tested by Gaza, But Not Sorely. Al-Jazeera. Available at: www.aljazeera.com/economy/2021/6/7/chinas-ties-with-israel-are-tested-by-gaza-but-not-sorely

Melvin, N. (2019, April). The Foreign Military Presence in the Horn of Africa Region. SIPRI Background Paper. Available at: https://sipri.org/sites/default/files/2019-04/sipribp1904.pdf

Moore, M. (2009, February 11). China Will Build Special Railway for Muslim Pilgrims in Saudi Arabia. *The Telegraph*. Available at: www.telegraph.co.uk/news/worldnews/middleeast/saudiarabia/4587544/China-will-build-special-railway-for-Muslim-pilgrims-in-Saudi-Arabia.html

Musakkis, A. (2016). Hadiya al-Mamlaka al-'Arabiya As-Sa'udiya li-Daula As-Sin 'Unwan At-Thaqafa wa Al-Fann. *Al-Sharq al-Awsat*. Available at: http://bit.ly/2cjvn4A

Nakhoul, S., Maclean, W., and Rashad, M. (2016, April 25). Saudi Prince Unveils Sweeping Plans to End 'Addiction' to Oil. *Reuters*. Available at: www.reuters.com/article/us-saudi-economy/saudi-prince-unveils-sweeping-plans-to-end-addiction-to-oil-idUSKCN0XM1CD

Nereim, V. (2020, April 14). Saudi Arabia Races to Contain Epidemic in Islam's Holiest City. *Bloomberg*. Available at: www.bloomberg.com/news/articles/2020-04-14/saudi-arabia-races-to-contain-epidemic-in-islam-s-holiest-city

News Desk. (2021, June 4). Saudi Arabia Has Assured of Approving Chinese Vaccines for Hajj Pilgrims: Sindh CM. *Express Tribune*. Available at: https://tribune.com.pk/story/2303498/saudi-arabia-has-assured-of-approving-chinese-vaccines-for-hajj-pilgrims-sindh-cm

Ng, A.. (2021, March 17). Entering China Is Now Easier for People Who Have a Vaccine— But Only If It's Made in China. CNBC. Available at: www.cnbc.com/2021/03/17/china-relaxes-border-restrictions-for-those-who-received-china-made-vaccines.html

Obaid, R. (2020, January 19). Students Begin Studying Chinese In Public Schools in Saudi Arabia. *Arab News*. Available at: www.arabnews.com/node/1615436/saudi-arabia

Oil Review of the Middle East. (2019, December 17). Sinopec Completes Main Unit of Al-Zour Refinery Project in Kuwait. Available at: www.oilreviewmiddleeast.com/petrochemicals/sinopec-completes-main-unit-of-al-zour-refinery-project-in-kuwait

Olimat, M. S. (2013). *China and the Middle East Since World War II: A Bilateral Approach*. New York: Routledge.

Omar, A. A., and Martin, M. (2020, October 5). Saudi Arabia's Budget Based on $50 Oil, Goldman Sachs Estimates. *World Oil*. Available at: www.worldoil.com/news/2020/10/5/saudi-arabia-s-budget-based-on-50-oil-goldman-sachs-estimates

Organization of Islamic Cooperation's International Fiqh Academy. (2021, February 21). Final Statement and Recommendations of the Medical Fiqh Symposium: Shariah Rulings regarding the Use of Covid-19 Vaccines, Their Purchase and the Financing of their Distribution with Zakat Funds. Available at: www.iifa-aifi.org/wp-content/uploads/2021/03/IIFA-Symposium-on-Anti-Covid-19-Vaccines-Feb-2021-3.pdf

Panda, A. (2015, January 23). King Abdullah's Legacy in Asia. *The Diplomat*. Available at: https://thediplomat.com/2015/01/king-abdullahs-legacy-in-asia/

Rakhmat, M.Z. (2019, February 15). The Rise of Islamic Finance on China's Belt and Road. The BRI in the Gulf Has Given Rise to Chinese Investment in Developing the Islamic Financial Sector. *The Diplomat*. Available at: https://thediplomat.com/2019/02/the-rise-of-islamic-finance-on-chinas-belt-and-road/

Rayda, N. (2021, June 8). Indonesian Travel Businesses Are Reeling As COVID-19 Halts Pilgrimages to Saudi Arabia. *Channel News Asia*. Available at: www.channelnewsasia.com/news/asia/indonesia-covid19-businesses-losses-haj-umrah-saudi-arabia-mecca-14939282

Regan, H. and Langmaid, V. (2021, June 2). World Health Organization Authorizes China's Sinovac Covid-19 Vaccine for Emergency Use. *CNN*. Available at: www.cnn.com/2021/06/01/health/who-approves-sinovac-covid-vaccine-intl-hnk/index.html

Renaldi, E. and Ibrahim, F. M. (2021, June 10). Indonesia Cancels Islamic Hajj Pilgrimage to Mecca for Second Year Over COVID-19 Concerns. *ABC News*. Available at: www.abc.net.au/news/2021-06-11/indonesia-cancels-hajj-two-years-in-a-row-mecca-saudi-arabia/100204150

Reuters. (2015, April 15). Saudi's Yasref Refinery Gets $4.7 Bln International Loan. *Reuters*. Available at: www.reuters.com/article/saudi-aramco-loans/saudis-yasref-refinery-gets-4-7-bln-international-loan-idUSL5N17I2M6

Reuters. (2021a, January 15). Huawei to Open Its Biggest Flagship Store Outside China in Riyadh. *Reuters*. Available at: www.reuters.com/article/saudi-huawei-tech-int/huawei-to-open-its-biggest-flagship-store-outside-china-in-riyadh-idUSKBN29K1RW

Reuters. (2021b, February 8). Russia, China, and Iran to Hold Joint Naval Drills in Indian Ocean Soon–RIA. *Reuters*. Available at: www.reuters.com/article/russia-military-iran-china/russia-china-and-iran-to-hold-joint-naval-drills-in-indian-ocean-soon-ria-idUSKBN2A81Q8

Reuters. (2022, February 20). Israel to Allow in All Tourists Regardless of COVID Vaccination Status. Available at: www.reuters.com/world/middle-east/israel-allow-all-tourists-regardless-covid-vaccination-status-2022-02-20/

Saadi, D. (2021, April 28). Saudi Sees Future Demand for Its Oil Amid Aramco Share Sales Plan: Crown Prince. *S&P Global Platts*. Available at: www.spglobal.com/platts/en/market-insights/latest-news/oil/042821-saudi-sees-future-demand-for-its-oil-amid-aramco-share-sales-plan-crown-prince

Saudi Arabia Ministry of Transport. (2020, December 13). KSA Logistics Hub. Available at: www.mot.gov.sa/en/AboutUs/Pages/Logisticsplatform.aspx

Saudi Arabian General Authority for Statistics. (n.d.). Hajj Statistics 2019 - 1440H. Available at: www.stats.gov.sa/sites/default/files/haj_40_en.pdf

Saudi Gazette. (2019, December 18). Chinese Visitors to GCC to Balloon 54 Percent by 2023. Available at: https://saudigazette.com.sa/article/585249

Saudi Gazette. (2020, July 25). University of Jeddah to Teach Chinese Language. Available at: https://saudigazette.com.sa/article/595937

Saudi Press Agency. (2019, November 17). Saudi Arabia, China Conduct Drill To Improve Combat Readiness. *Arab News*. Available at: www.arabnews.com/node/1585431/saudi-arabia

Saudi Press Agency. (2021a, March 22). China Condemns Attacks Targeting Civilians, Oil Facilities in Saudi Arabia. Right Vision Media. Premium Official News,. Gale OneFile: News. Available at: link.gale.com/apps/doc/A656003967/STND?u=tel_middleten&sid=bookmark-STND&xid=c4edab81

Saudi Press Agency. (2021b, April 9). President of IsDB Meets with Chinese Ambassador to Saudi Arabia. Right Vision Media. Premium Official News, Gale OneFile: News. Available at: link.gale.com/apps/doc/A658052654/STND?u=tel_middleten&sid=bookmark-STND&xid=c2ff60ef (accessed June 2, 2021).

Saudi Press Agency. (2021c, May 28). Chinese Ambassador Takes Part in Saudi Forestation Campaign. Arab News. Available at: www.arabnews.com/node/1866171/saudi-arabia

Serrieh, J. (2020, March 11). Coronavirus: Saudi Arabia Sends Assistance to China. *Al Arabiya*. Available at: https://english.alarabiya.net/News/gulf/2020/03/11/Coronavirus-Saudi-Arabia-sends-assistance-to-China

Serrieh, J. (2021, May 29). Saudi Arabia Allows Entry of Travelers from Countries Including UAE, US. *Al Arabiya*. Available at: https://english.alarabiya.net/coronavirus/2021/05/29/Saudi-Arabia-allows-entry-of-travelers-from-countries-including-UAE-US

Shaolong, T. (2016). *The Huawei Way: Lessons from an International Tech Giant on Driving Growth*. New York: McGraw Hill Education.

Sheehan, E. R. F. (1974, March 24). Unradical Sheiks Who Shake the World. *New York Times*, pp. 13–14, 50–54, 58–60, 66–68. Available at: ProQuest Historical Newspapers: The New York Times (1851–2009).

Sherlock, R. (2020, May 5). Migrants Among Those Worse Hit by Covid-19 in Saudi Arabia, Gulf Countries. *NPR*. Available at: www.npr.org/sections/coronavirus-live-updates/2020/05/05/850542938/migrants-are-among-the-worst-hit-by-covid-19-in-saudi-arabia-and-gulf-countries

Shesgreen, D. (2021, May 31). US aid to Israel Was Always a Given. Will Growing Support for Palestinians Change That? *USA Today*. Available at: www.usatoday.com/in-depth/news/politics/2021/05/31/us-aid-israel-palestinian-support-change-arms-deals-biden-democrats/7438217002/

Siddiqui, T. (2021, June 5). Saudi Envoy to Take Up Chinese Vaccines Issue with Authorities. *Dawn*. Available at: www.dawn.com/news/1627609

Siyech, M. S. (2019, April 9). India-Qatar Relations: Navigating Turbulent Seas. MEI. Available at: www.mei.edu/publications/india-qatar-relations-navigating-turbulent-seas

Slav, I. (2021, June 15). Chinese Gasoline Demand Is Driving Oil Prices Higher. *Oil Price*. Available at: https://oilprice.com/Latest-Energy-News/World-News/Chinese-Gasoline-Demand-Is-Driving-Oil-Prices-Higher.html

Straits Times. (2021, March 18). Minister Khairy Jamaluddin first in Malaysia to get Sinovac jab against Covid-19. Available at: www.straitstimes.com/asia/se-asia/coronavirus-minister-khairy-jamaluddin-first-in-malaysia-to-get-sinovac-jab

Syahrul. (2021, March 19). Khairy Jamaluddin Jokes About Speaking Mandarin Fluently After Getting Sinovac Vaccine. *Hype*. Available at: https://hype.my/2021/220344/khairy-jamaluddin-jokes-about-speaking-mandarin-fluently-after-getting-sinovac-vaccine/

Tan, W. (2020, May 7). As US-China Rivalry Heightens, The Pandemic Could Tilt Global Power in Beijing's Favor. *CNBC*. Available at: www.cnbc.com/2020/05/08/coronavirus-us-china-tensions-increase-beijing-seeks-more-influence.html

Taylor, A. and Schemm, P. (2021, June 3). China's Great Vaccine Hope, Sinopharm, Sees Reputation Darkened Amid COVID Spikes In Countries Using It. *Washington Post*. Available at: www.washingtonpost.com/world/2021/06/03/bahrain-seychelles-sinopharm-vaccine/

Tisnadibrata, I. L. (2021, June 4). Indonesia to Skip This Year's Hajj Over Coronavirus Fears. *Arab News*. Available at: www.arabnews.com/node/1869981/world

TRT World. (2021, May 31). Saudi Arabia and EU Bars Travelers Who Received Chinese-Made Jabs. Available at: www.trtworld.com/magazine/saudi-arabia-and-eu-bars-travelers-who-received-chinese-made-jabs-47142

Turak, N. (2019a, February 21). Pentagon Is Scrambling as China 'Sells the Hell Out of' Armed Drones to US Allies. *CNBC*. Available at: www.cnbc.com/2019/02/21/pentagon-is-scrambling-as-china-sells-the-hell-out-of-armed-drones-to-americas-allies.html

Turak, N. (2019b, August 15). Saudi Arabia Dramatically Changing Its Oil Exports to China and the US. *CNBC*. Available at: www.cnbc.com/2019/08/15/saudi-arabia-dramatically-changing-its-oil-exports-to-china-and-the-us.html

Turak, N. (2020, May 11). Saudi Arabia's Austerity Drive Seen as 'Decisive and Necessary,' But Could Delay a Consumer Recovery. *CNBC*. Available at: www.cnbc.com/2020/05/11/saudi-arab ias-austerity-drive-decisive-and-necessary-but-could-delay-a-consumer-recovery.html

US Energy Information Administration. (2018a, February 5). China Surpassed the United States as the World's Largest Crude Oil Importer in 2017. Available at: www.eia.gov/todayinenergy/det ail.php?id=34812

US Energy Information Administration. (2018b, December 31). China Surpassed the United States as the World's Largest Energy Importer in 2017. Available at: www.eia.gov/todayinenergy/det ail.php?id=37821

US Energy Information Administration. (2020, March 23). China's Crude Oil Surpassed 10 Million Barrels a Day in 2019. Available at: www.eia.gov/todayinenergy/detail.php?id=43216

US Energy Information Administration. (2021a, April 13). Oil and Petroleum Products Explained. Oil Imports and Exports. Available at: www.eia.gov/energyexplained/oil-and-petroleum-produ cts/imports-and-exports.php

US Energy Information Administration. (2021b, May 28). US Imports from Saudi Arabia of Crude Oil and Petroleum Products. Available at: www.eia.gov/dnav/pet/hist/LeafHandler.ashx?n= PET&s=MCRIMUSSA2&f=M

US Energy Information Administration. (2021c, May 28). US Imports from Canada of Crude Oil and Petroleum Products. Available at: www.eia.gov/dnav/pet/hist/LeafHandler.ashx?n= PET&s=MTTIMUSCA1&f=M

Varma, K. J. M. (2020, October 12). China Announces New Rules for Muslims Visiting Saudi Arabia for Haj. *PTI*. Available at: https://in.news.yahoo.com/china-announces-rules-muslims-visiting-130355330.html

Vatanka, A. (2017, November 1). China Courts Iran. Why One Belt, One Road Will Run Through Tehran. *Foreign Affairs*. Available at: www.foreignaffairs.com/articles/china/2017-11-01/china-courts-iran

Wald, E. R. and Ferziger, J. F. (2021, June 16). Climate Policies Could Hand Power and Profits Back to OPEC. *Foreign Policy*. Available at: https://foreignpolicy.com/2021/06/16/climate-goals-opec-oil-prices-energy-crisis-shortages-fossil-fuels/

Wang, T. Y. (1993). Competing for Friendship: The Two Chinas and Saudi Arabia. *Arab Studies Quarterly* 15(3), 63–82.

Wang, Y. (2020). *Chinese in Dubai: Money, Pride, and Soul-Searching*. Leiden: Brill.

Wang, Y. (2021, January 15). Middle East Smartphone Market Sees Light at the End of 2020 Tunnel. Counterpoint. Available at: www.counterpointresearch.com/middle-east-smartphone-market-end-tunnel/

Weiqing, C. (2021, June 15). China's Relations with Islamic World Reach Historic Point. *Arab News*. Available at: www.arabnews.com/node/1877311

Werner, B. (2020, May 4). SECDEF Esper Preparing for Future Defense Spending Cuts. *USNI News*. Available at: https://news.usni.org/2020/05/04/secdef-esper-preparing-for-future-defense-spending-cuts

Westall, S. and Levingston, I. (2020, May 20). Chinese Genetics Firm's Testing in Middle East Raises New U.S. Tensions. *Bloomberg*. Available at: www.bnnbloomberg.ca/chinese-genetics-firm-s-testing-in-middle-east-raises-new-u-s-tensions-1.1438631

Westcott, B. and Al-Khshali, H. (2019, December 27). China, Iran, and Russia Hold Joint Naval Drills in the Gulf of Oman. *CNN*. Available at: www.cnn.com/2019/12/27/asia/china-russia-iran-military-drills-intl-hnk/index.html

Widianto, S. and Lamb, K. (2021, June 17). Hundreds of Vaccinated Indonesian Health Workers Get COVID-19, Dozens in Hospital. *Reuters*. Available at: www.reuters.com/world/asia-pacific/hundreds-indonesian-doctors-contract-covid-19-despite-vaccination-dozens-2021-06-17/?utm _source=Facebook&utm_medium=Social&fbclid=IwAR1fltKAeYxtM_WeBMIilwG-FWVJ k0py0rzfr4fMSPAPIvL2kJlHqiI-YtY

Wilkins, B. (2021, January 28). Ilhan Omar: Arms Sale Freeze Is "First Step" to End US Support for War on Yemen. *Truthout*. Available at: https://truthout.org/articles/ilhan-omar-arms-sale-freeze-is-first-step-to-end-us-support-for-war-on-yemen/

Williams, K. B. (2020, June 10). Top US General in Mideast: 'I Do Worry About China Quite a Bit.' *Defense One*. Available at: www.defenseone.com/threats/2020/06/top-us-general-mideast-i-do-worry-about-china-quite-bit/166047/?oref=d-previouspost

Woertz, E. and Yellinek, R. (2021, April 14). Vaccine Diplomacy in the MENA Region. *MEI*. Available at: www.mei.edu/publications/vaccine-diplomacy-mena-region

Wu, K., Lawler, A., and Arnold, T. (2021, April 28). EXCLUSIVE Major Chinese Investors in Talks to Take Aramco Stake-Sources. *Reuters*. Available at: www.reuters.com/world/middle-east/exclusive-major-chinese-investors-talks-take-aramco-stake-sources-2021-04-28/

Wu, W. (2020, January 6). China Promises 'Relentless Efforts' to Save Iran Nuclear Deal After US Drone Strike on Qasem Soleimani. *South China Morning Post*. Available at: www.scmp.com/news/china/diplomacy/article/3044886/china-promises-relentless-efforts-save-iran-nuclear-deal-after

Xinhua. (2021, March 25). China, Saudi Arabia Vow to Oppose Interference in Other Countries' Internal Affairs. Available at: www.xinhuanet.com/english/2021-03/25/c_139835478.htm

Xu, M. and Aizhu, C. (2021a, January 13). UPDATE 1 China's 2020 Crude Oil Imports Hit Record on Stockpiling, New Refineries. *Reuters*. Available at: www.reuters.com/article/china-economy-trade-crude/update-1-chinas-2020-crude-oil-imports-hit-record-on-stockpiling-new-refineries-idUSL1N2JP07X

Xu, M. and Aizhu, C. (2021b, January 20). Saudi Arabia Pips Russia to Be China's Biggest Oil Supplier in 2020. *Reuters*. Available at: www.reuters.com/article/china-economy-trade-oil-int/saudi-arabia-pips-russia-to-be-chinas-biggest-oil-supplier-in-2020-idUSKBN29P0ZG

Xu, M. and Tan, E.. (2021, March 21). Saudi Aramco to Prioritise Energy Supply to China for 50 Years, Says CEO. *Reuters*. Available at: www.reuters.com/article/us-china-forum-saudiaramco/saudi-aramco-to-prioritise-energy-supply-to-china-for-50-years-says-ceo-idUSKBN2BD0GK

Xu, R. and Sun, D. (2019). Sino-American Relations in the Middle East: Towards A Complementary Partnership? *Asian Journal of Middle Eastern and Islamic Studies*, 13(2): 143–161. https://doi.org/10.1080/25765949.2019.1605563

Yellinek, R., Mann, R., and Lebel, U. (2020). Chinese Soft-Power in the Arab World–China's Confucius Institutes as a Central Tool of Influence. *Comparative Strategy* 39(6): 517–534. https://doi.org/10.1080/01495933.2020.1826843

Yeranian, E. (2019, October 2). Iran, Saudi Arabia Reportedly in Contact, Despite Official Saudi Denial. *VOA News*. Available at: www.voanews.com/middle-east/iran-saudi-arabia-reportedly-contact-despite-official-saudi-denial

Zain KSA. (2019, February 27). Zain KSA and Huawei Sign Agreements for 5G, IoT and Video Streaming Service. Available at: https://sa.zain.com/en/all-news/zain-ksa-and-huawei-sign-agreements-5g-iot-and-video-streaming-service

Zhang, R. (2021, June 15). China, Middle East, Ramp Up Public Health Cooperation against Coronavirus Pandemic. *South China Morning Post*. Available at: www.scmp.com/news/china/diplomacy/article/3137395/china-middle-east-ramp-public-health-cooperation-against

Zilber, A. (2020, January 5). Iraqi Prime Minister Says Qasem Soleimani Was in Iraq to 'Discuss De-Escalating Tensions Between Iran and Saudis' When He Was Killed - and Claims Trump Had Asked for Help Mediating Talks After Embassy Attack. *Daily Mail*. Available at: www.dailymail.co.uk/news/article-7854971/Soleimani-Iraq-discuss-escalating-tensions-Saudis-killed-PM-says.html

Zoubir, Y. H. (2020, July). China's 'Health Silk Road' Diplomacy in the MENA. Konrad Adenauer Stiftung, *Med Dialogue Series* 27, 1–14. Available at: www.kas.de/documents/282499/282548/MDS_China+Health+Silk+Road+Diplomacy.pdf/

26

CHINA AND SUDAN

Daniel Large

Introduction

In December 2019, commemorating 60 years of diplomatic ties between China and Sudan, the Chinese ambassador in Khartoum presented ten "significant milestones" in relations: China began to train Sudanese acrobats and send medical teams to Sudan (1971); China helped build Khartoum's Friendship Hall (1972); oil cooperation (1995) and pharmaceutical cooperation (1998) began; China contracted to build three dams, notably Merowe (2003); an agricultural cooperation development zone was established (2012); a Strategic Partnership was created (2015); a Belt and Road Initiative (BRI) agreement was signed (2018); and, in November 2019, China launched Sudan's first ever satellite (Ma, 2019a). The Chinese ambassador's list highlighted important connections, but it was conspicuously at odds with more fundamental political changes at the end of a momentous year in Sudanese politics. President Omar Bashir was deposed in April 2019 and there was no 30th anniversary of the June 1989 military coup that had brought him to power. Instead, a new government was undertaking a challenging transition in which the role of China, Sudan's most important external partner for many years under Bashir, was evolving in a context of the ending of the country's international isolation.

This overview of China's relations with Sudan is organised into three sections. The first outlines the historical context. The second considers relations between 2011, when South Sudan became independent, and the fall of President Bashir in April 2019. After 2011, and facing a precarious economic situation compounded by ongoing conflict, Sudan became less important for China in economic terms. For the government of Sudan, however, Chinese military, economic and political assistance remained important in the ruling National Congress party's (NCP) pursuit of regime maintenance. The fall of President Bashir precipitated changes in China's position by enabling, crucially, improved ties with the USA. The third section examines how the political upheaval of the Sudanese revolution has affected relations with China. In the face of the ongoing uncertainty attending Sudan's political transition, the Chinese government's preference for stability and cautious approach to engaging post-Bashir military and civilian politics continues.

360

DOI: 10.4324/9781003048404-29

Historical Ties

The framing and legitimating use of historical narratives, which have been integral to China's statecraft and relations with Sudan, provide a revealing window on the changing state of relations. The historical reference points commonly cited in official exchanges have changed since 2012 to reflect China's global role as a self-declared "major power" under Xi Jinping. The legend of "Chinese Gordon", a symbol of violent imperialism and heroic anti-colonial resistance, had previously been a prominent shared reference point.[1] When Chinese Premier Zhou Enlai visited Khartoum in 1964, for example, the fact that the Sudanese people had "finally punished" Gordon was a rare case of a genuine historical political connection between the Chinese government and Africa. It formed a common reference point in China-Sudan relations after 1989. Today, however, the port of Sawakin is standardly cited as a historical reference point to highlight ancient trade links "connecting the destinies of Sudan and the Chinese people" (Ma, 2020). Highlighting historic trade as foundational to present relations fits the narrative of China's global strategy under the BRI and is also central to the Chinese government's vision of a "community of common destiny" and the future centrality of China in world affairs.

China-Sudan relations featured notable historical connections before and after Sudan's independence in 1956, but the context for relations today was influenced most by the June 1989 military coup that brought the National Islamic Front (NIF), which became the NCP nearly a decade later, to power. Notable strands of relations, such as medical or military links, have continued for some five decades since China adroitly forged good relations with Sudan under Jaffar Nimeiri in 1971. The 1989 NIF coup, however, was a major turning point. Amid economic dire straits, civil war with the Sudan People's Liberation Army/Movement (SPLA/M) and a dormant oil industry, the new NIF regime under the influence of its leading ideologue, Hassan Turabi, pursued an Islamist project within and outside Sudan, leading to a June 1995 assassination attempt on the Egyptian President in Addis Ababa. This triggered international condemnation, catalysed efforts by regional powers and the USA against the more radical elements under Hassan Turabi's banner. The USA had designated Sudan a state sponsor of terrorism in 1993 but the attempted assassination led to UN sanctions in 1996, further US sanctions in 1997, and an American missile attack on a pharmaceutical factory in Khartoum in 1998.

In this context, the NIF's turn to China became more important and consequential. Bashir's visit to Beijing in September 1995 facilitated China's entry into Sudan's oil sector and a conjunction of interests was converted into practical cooperation. The NIF was desperate to develop its domestic oil sector. China was interested in Sudan for strategic reasons and, in its own terms, successfully exploited an economic opportunity shaped by political circumstances. In the process, it benefited from the unintended consequences of US-led attempts to sanction and isolate Sudan. Not under the control of major Western oil companies, Sudan represented a strong opportunity and played a significant role in a formative phase of China's overseas energy strategy. China became a net oil importer in 1993. Sudan was targeted as a friendly long-term overseas oil supply base and an arena for the global development of Chinese corporations. The Chinese National Petroleum Corporation (CNPC) promised the rapid completion of an oil export pipeline and offered to build an oil refinery, which won the Chinese a leading role in Sudan's oil sector (Patey, 2014). For China, Sudan became a model site of its engagement in Africa: an outpost demonstrating the technical accomplishment of Chinese oil companies, China's first overseas refinery and China's largest overseas dam construction project at Merowe.

Pragmatic opportunism and the prospect of elite win-win benefits forged a partnership initially based on oil but characterised by shared political interests. China's principle of non-interference in internal affairs was welcome to Khartoum.

In contrast to official, valorised Chinese and Sudanese depictions, the actual development of Sudan's oil sector was militarised and violent. Oil development, exacerbating existing conflicts, inflicted great civilian suffering in Southern Sudan's oil-bearing regions. An indirect result of Sudan becoming an oil exporter in 1999 was to change the incentives and calculus concerning the conflict between the SPLA/M and the government of Sudan. Oil was one contributing factor to the signing of the Comprehensive Peace Agreement (CPA) between the government of Sudan and the SPLA/M in January 2005, which ended the conflict and would lead to the creation of South Sudan in July 2011 (see Large, 2020). For China, Sudan proved to be a pioneering engagement not just in overseas oil investment or the security practices deriving from this, but also in other, more political senses as three subsequent and related transitions paving the way for current relations illustrate: (1) Darfur and CPA; (2) the secession of South Sudan; and (3) Sudan's April 2019 "revolution".

First, conflict in Darfur underscored the complexity of China's engagement with Sudan. One aspect involved arms exports and Chinese assistance in developing Sudan's arms manufacturing capability, which helped China develop links with the NIF regime and military-industrial complex in the 1990s. China accounted for around 58 percent of self-reported Sudan government arms imports between 2001 and 2012. Violating the UN arms embargo on Darfur, the government retransferred some imported Chinese weapons and ammunition to allied groups in Darfur and rebel groups in South Sudan (Leff and LeBrun, 2014). Following the escalation of armed rebellion in Darfur in 2004, China's support for the government of Sudan resulted in Beijing being accused of complicity in genocide and highlighted the risks of global reputational damage before the 2008 Beijing Olympics. Facing international pressure to expand its engagement beyond economics, and threats to Chinese citizens and oil assets within Sudan, the Chinese government's approach changed. In 2007, Beijing used its influence in Khartoum to facilitate the deployment of a joint UN–AU peacekeeping force to Darfur. By seeking Sudanese government consent to admitting UN blue helmets, despite staunch opposition led by President Bashir, Beijing was negotiating the boundaries of its non-interference principle by innovating its political practice. As well as addressing international concerns, however, Beijing continued to support President Bashir's government. Nonetheless, there were tensions, notably over China's abstention in UN Security Council (UNSC) Resolution 1593 (31 March 2005), which made a Chapter VII referral of Darfur to the International Criminal Court (ICC) and led to an ICC arrest warrants being issued in March 2009, including for President Bashir. Even though Beijing subsequently called for a suspension of the ICC process, the lack of a Chinese veto, which indicated limits to actual solidarity, remained a sore point in Khartoum.

Darfur exposed the question of what leverage Beijing might have over the government of Sudan, and the tensions over China's traditional foreign policy principles in the face of new circumstances and investment protection challenges, but in important respects Sudanese political-military actors successfully deployed "China cards" for their own purposes. In northern Sudan, the NCP shared a belief in authoritarian single party rule and the power of transformative big infrastructure like dams. Outwardly proclaiming the virtues of a "Sino-Sudanese model of development", in practice, it incorporated China into its domestic regime maintenance agenda. Beijing acted as a friendly shield for Khartoum in the international arena. Marking the 50th anniversary of China-Sudan relations, in November 2009, the former CNPC General Manager and Party Secretary and powerful member of the Standing Committee of China's Politburo, Zhou Yongkang, spoke in Khartoum about how 2009 also marked the 20th anniversary of Sudan's "National Salvation Revolution" and how, under Bashir's leadership, Sudan had become one of the fastest-growing African economies. In Southern Sudan, the SPLA/M, which had targeted Chinese oil infrastructure to pressure Khartoum, sought to use China to advance their political ambitions of secession (Large, 2011).

The second key change concerned the secession of Southern Sudan to become an independent sovereign state in July 2011. This happened under the terms of the 2005 CPA, which established a government of national unity in Khartoum and a semi-autonomous government of Southern Sudan in Juba under SPLA/M control. The Chinese government continued relations with the NCP but developed new links with the SPLA/M, catalysed by the visit to Beijing by Southern Sudan's president, Salva Kiir Mayardit, in July 2007. That Beijing was compelled to develop relations with Juba was clear: the main Chinese oil concessions were mostly located in Southern Sudan and in Sudan's contested north-south border areas. The necessity for the SPLA/M to develop relations with China was also clear: China's support for its independence ambition was crucial. In northern Sudan, China's apparent diplomatic realism, evident in a hedging strategy of formally supporting a united Sudan but in practice preparing for Southern secession, smacked of betrayal for some in the NCP ruling circles. For others, it was unsurprising: supporting political stability, and seeking to protect its interests, Beijing's bottom line was a peaceful transition.

Although Sudan stood out for China's role in its oil sector, there were other, related reasons why Sudan became a notable case of China's engagement in Africa. First, Sudan stood out as a site of innovation in Chinese security engagement: it was a testing ground in the challenges of protecting Chinese citizens and investments some years before these became integral to China's official foreign policy. The CNPC pioneered corporate security through its experience of operating during conflict, and coordination with Chinese state and military bodies (Patey, 2014). Second, Sudan also showed how China's rise in Africa was accompanied by increasing expectations and pressure on Beijing to contribute more to security, thereby balancing its emphasis on business. One avenue through which this was pursued was UN peacekeeping. Sudan was a notable site of Chinese UN peacekeeping: the first Chinese contingents serving in the UN Mission in Sudan were deployed in Southern Sudan in 2005, and Chinese peacekeepers subsequently contributed to the AU-UN Hybrid Mission for Darfur (UNAMID) after it was created in July 2007. Third, another more challenging avenue involved delicate political balancing in Chinese diplomacy, as seen with the independence of South Sudan.

Before 2011, the fundamental basis of government of Sudan relations with China developed around oil cooperation from 1995 onward. One essential point of continuity was Bashir's leadership: he was the principal interlocutor for three Chinese leaders: Jiang Zemin, Hu Jintao and, from 2012, Xi Jinping. These phases saw pronounced changes in China's politics and foreign policy, defined by Xi Jinping's reassertion of Chinese Communist Party (CCP) control within China that, among other things, saw Zhou Yongkang sentenced to life imprisonment in 2015. These changes in Sudanese and Chinese politics combined to ensure that the 60th anniversary of relations in 2019 was markedly different from the 2009 anniversary. To understand this, the next sections first consider how relations evolved between 2011 and the overthrow of Bashir in 2019, and then the main contours of relations in post-Bashir Sudanese politics.

China-Sudan Relations, 2011–2019

Much attention was directed to China's relations with the new Republic of South Sudan from July 2011, and following renewed conflict in December 2013, but the Chinese government's engagement with Sudan continued and evolved. Beijing had to engage the interconnected entities of Sudan and South Sudan, which had separated without agreement on many vital issues, including oil. China's then Foreign Minister, Yang Jiechi, who later became a member of the CCP Central Committee Political Bureau and Head of the Office of the Commission of Foreign Affairs, visited Khartoum in August 2011, in the context of a dispute between South Sudan and Sudan about oil revenue, which exposed China to unfinished CPA business concerning wealth-sharing. Much of Beijing-Khartoum engagement after July 2011 concerned efforts to reset economic ties, while China embarked on a major push to engage with South Sudan.

Following South Sudan's secession, political ties between Beijing and Khartoum became more important in the context of a changed economic partnership. In the new circumstances, where the bulk of China's oil investment was now in South Sudan (albeit relying on transit through Sudan for export), the functional downgrading of economic ties meant politics became more prominent as the Sudan government sought to pursue economic cooperation in a new context. In this, a ministerial-level Sudan-China political consultations committee was prominent, but CCP-NCP political party cooperation continued to underpin relations. Political party connections resumed in January 2012, when the CPC and the NCP held what was touted as the first high-level dialogue. The CCP's International Department met frequently with the NCP. Indeed, the NCP ranked 7th of the CCP's 20 most important partners between 2002 and 2017 in terms of total number of contacts (Hackenesch and Bader, 2020: 727). Political party connections had always been significant, given the power and role of both ruling parties, but became even more so after 2011. Such connections also testified to the significance of non-material links, notably the NCP's genuine and more instrumental interest in China's political experience.

China and Sudan declared a new Strategic Partnership in 2015, an official upgrade in relations that provided renewed impetus and formed the formal basis for strengthening relations. Foreign Minister Wang Yi's January 2015 visit to Khartoum started an eventful year, which saw President Bashir's attendance at the June AU summit in Johannesburg spark a major controversy concerning his ICC indictment. Bashir did not return to South Africa for the December 2015 Johannesburg Forum on China-Africa Cooperation (FOCAC) summit but by then he had already achieved a breakthrough in relations after visiting Beijing in September 2015. As well as celebrating the 70th anniversary of China's victory over Japan in the Second World War, Bashir's meeting with Xi Jinping during this visit marked the genesis of a formal Strategic Partnership. This signalled official intent to deepen relations and saw agreements signed across a range of areas, in which economic cooperation was central.

Underneath such public markers of official progress, economic relations had changed significantly after 2011. Simply put, Sudan became far less important for China in economic terms and, facing a precarious economic situation compounded by ongoing conflict, struggled to meaningfully advance economic relations. The government of Sudan actively courted Chinese business and investment, such as in agriculture, and attempted to market itself as business-friendly. Despite all official presentations to the contrary, China's approach was cautious in the context of the fractious relations between Sudan and South Sudan and the ongoing conflict within Sudan. Indeed, Khartoum received more significant financial support from Qatar as it tried to cope with the loss of oil revenue. There were also tensions, such as over debt (including but not only regarding the Khartoum refinery). However, Sudan's reduced economic importance for China was evident. Due to oil, Sudan had been a leading economic partner of China in Africa. In 2011, Sudan was China's seventh leading supplier of oil but by 2018, due to conflict and much reduced production in South Sudan, 'had fallen out of the top forty' (Barber, 2020: 4). In this context, China-Sudan trade declined significantly. After 2011, China also lent markedly less to Sudan and Chinese FDI flows to Sudan contracted (Table 26.1).

The 2015 Strategic Partnership offered a focal point for the Sudan government efforts to pursue new economic cooperation with China, which in practice mostly meant formalising and continuing much of what had been happening or discussed before. Sudan government ministries endeavoured to attract Chinese investment but Awad Ahmed al-Jaz, a Bashir loyalist, former Oil Minister and long-time instrumental Sudanese interlocutor with China, played a crucial role. For instance, al-Jaz visited China in 2016 with a delegation composed of the Ministers of Finance, Petroleum, and Foreign Affairs as well as the Governor of Sudan's central bank; the delegation presented 170 projects to Chinese investors.

The economic cooperation agenda was evident in oil, agriculture, mining, and energy. First, in September 2015, there was an agreement for Chinese companies to explore for oil and gas in the Red Sea, Sinnar, and West Kordofan. Oil cooperation continued but in a very different phase. Second, having long been considered as an area of future economic relations amid efforts to diversify Sudan's economy beyond oil, agriculture became

Table 26.1 Chinese FDI flows to Sudan, South Sudan and African countries, 2003–2019 (US$ million, unadjusted)

Year	Sudan	South Sudan	Africa total
2003	0.00	–	74.81
2004	146.70	–	317.43
2005	91.13	–	391.68
2006	50.79	–	519.86
2007	65.40	–	1574.31
2008	-63.14	–	5490.56
2009	19.30	–	1438.87
2010	30.96	–	2111.99
2011	911.86	0.05	3173.14
2012	-1.69	7.80	2516.66
2013	140.91	11.49	3370.64
2014	174.07	-6.82	3201.92
2015	31.71	13.08	2977.92
2016	-689.94	2.03	2398.73
2017	254.87	12.21	4104.98
2018	57.12	-13.12	5389.11
2019	-70.78	5.49	2704.39 (2.70bn)

Source: China–Africa Research Initiative, Johns Hopkins University School of Advanced International Studies.

a priority. There had been limited Chinese engagement in agriculture before the 2015 Strategic Partnership, but this subsequently expanded. In August 2016, the speaker of Gezira State Legislative Council said an MOU had been signed by the Sudan government allowing Chinese companies to cultivate one million feddans of cotton. In September 2016, China's Minister of Agriculture, Han Changfu, visited Sudan with a delegation of Chinese investors and agricultural experts. Some six agreements were signed, including using technology in irrigation and rainfall projects, and a $60 million grant was advanced to Sudan, framed as boosting the agricultural part of the China-Sudan Strategic Partnership. Over 27 Chinese institutions were investing in Sudan's agricultural sector (*Sudan Now*, 2016). Third, mining was a further area of new investment, having been much hyped to mitigate the loss of oil revenue. Efforts were made to expand the previous engagement. In January 2017, China's then ambassador to Sudan cited 'about 20 Chinese companies operating in about 30 mining fields in Sudan' while speaking at a Sudan-China Mining Communication Forum in Khartoum (Xinhua, 2017a). Finally, energy remained an area of cooperation that evolved to be framed in terms of Sudan's role in the BRI. In May 2016, a framework agreement to allow the China National Nuclear Corporation to build Sudan's first atomic reactor was signed in Khartoum by the visiting Director of China's National Energy Administration. This was touted by some Chinese analysts as progress in what was then called One Belt, One Road and became the BRI as part of a reorientation of China's foreign policy.

Sudan's government continued to faithfully support Beijing in foreign policy terms. Khartoum offered staunch support for the Chinese government's "core interests", such as its territorial claims in the South China Sea. Sudan also supported China's new institutions, joining the Asian Infrastructure Investment Bank in March 2017, for instance. China was only one part of Sudan's post-2011 foreign relations; Khartoum sought to navigate regional relations and solicit economic support, supporting Saudi Araba's intervention in Yemen, for instance, or attempting to court Indian investment. However, China remained Khartoum's main international friend and, with a UNSC seat, its patron. Belonging to both FOCAC and the China-Arab States Cooperation Forum, Sudan positioned itself to maximise the benefits of two of China's regional engagements.

The instrumental rationale behind the government of Sudan's support for China was, at a basic level, pursuing military and economic diplomacy via political means to secure resources to assist NCP regime maintenance. Rendered more important because of the state of Sudan's economy after 2011, this was seen in military cooperation and in terms of Sudan's efforts to join the BRI, which encompassed security as well as economic and political dimensions. First, military connections continued after 2011 and evolved in the context of China's changing regional and global security engagement. Arms imports from China accounted for 41 per cent of Sudan's total arms imports between 2014 and 2019 and topped the list of Sudan's most important supplying countries (Munyi, 2020). High-level military exchanges between the People's Liberation Army (PLA) and the Sudan Armed Forces (SAF) continued. In August 2015, a PLA Navy escort taskforce visited Port Sudan for the first time, signalling the expanding role of the PLA. UNAMID was wound down from December 2020, but China's first UN peacekeeping helicopter unit had been operational in Darfur from August 2017. Second, one of the most notable aspects of this strategy was Sudan joining the BRI in 2018. In May 2017, against the backdrop of the first BRI Forum in Beijing, Al-Jaz stressed Khartoum's commitment to the BRI and marketed Sudan as an attractive "linking ring between the Arab world and Africa" (Xinhua, 2017b). Efforts by the Sudan government to reorient relations around the BRI represented a familiar pattern of efforts to attract Chinese investment but in a different context where Sudan no longer had the privileged attention its role in China's overseas oil expansion had once accorded it. The BRI became a focal point in Sino-Sudanese relations. For example, during his August 2017 visit to Khartoum, Vice-Premier Zhang Gaoli promoted BRI cooperation while meeting President Bashir.

BRI cooperation proceeded in a changing global context, in which evolving US policy on Sudan was pivotal. In October 2017, the Trump administration lifted economic sanctions imposed on Sudan two decades previously. This move had long been anticipated. China's business engagement amid the relative lack of competition induced by international sanctions had been a sore point for some Sudanese. As one analyst commented in January 2011, China was Sudan's "only friend" and "saviour" at that time but this was unlikely to be indefinite (interview with Ali Abdalla Ali, Khartoum, 17 January 2011). Facing the prospect of business competition following the lifting of sanctions, Chinese press coverage went to great lengths to talk up China's contribution to economic development in Sudan. One article, for example, argued that "China has been offering a unique 'China plan' and a new development model to help industrialize Sudan amid the decades-long US sanctions" (Song, 2017). What transpired in terms of politics, however, saw dramatic change in Sudan.

China and Sudan's 2019 "Revolution"

In September 2018, the Chinese government hosted President Bashir in Beijing for FOCAC VII. There was much talk at this FOCAC of future China-Sudan cooperation prospects but, despite an agreement for China to write off a portion of Sudan's debt, hopes Bashir entertained about securing substantial Chinese financial assistance did not materialise. In the context of a deep, multifaceted crisis in Sudan, economic dynamics contributed to the outbreak and spread of anti-government demonstrations from December 2018, when protests in Atbara against food price increases spread to Khartoum and other cities as part of what became a mobilisation for political reform, culminating in Bashir's overthrow in April.

Much was made of the Chinese government's lack of meaningful actual support for Bashir, seemingly at odds with its more robust public statements backing him. In September 2018, for example, a Chinese Ministry of Foreign Affairs (MFA) spokeswoman said that Xi Jinping had informed Bashir "that 'foreign forces' should not interfere in Sudan's internal affairs" and that "China has always had reservations" about the ICC indictment and arrest order against Bashir (CGTN, 2018). With a proven track record of being pragmatic, the Chinese government appeared unwilling to risk jeopardising its longer-term engagement with Sudan by going against the domestic political tide. Although no significant Chinese interests in Sudan were threatened by protesters, the Chinese government also had little choice and could readily invoke non-interference. Beijing adopted a cautious attitude to the unfolding crisis and political upheaval in Sudan from January 2019. Nonetheless, Beijing maintained its engagement against this backdrop of economic distress and mounting opposition to Bashir and the NCP state. High-level political exchanges continued, such as the visit by a Supreme People's Court of China delegation to Khartoum in December 2018. Following calls earlier in January by some 22 political groups in Sudan for a "new regime", the visit by Presidential Envoy Faysal Hassan Ibrahim Ali to Beijing in late January 2019 continued high-level connections. On 4 February 2019, Presidents Xi and Bashir exchanged congratulations on the 60th anniversary of China-Sudan diplomatic relations but the situation within Sudan continued to deteriorate.

The Chinese government continued its non-interference and sovereignty rhetoric in response to the removal of Bashir but rapidly moved to engage the new military-political reality and continue bilateral relations. On 12 April, the day after Bashir was ousted, a Chinese MFA spokesman, invoking non-interference, asserted: "We believe that Sudan has the ability to handle internal affairs and safeguard the peace and stability of the country" (CGTN, 2019). In private, amid a purge of Islamist figures in the old NCP regime, Chinese diplomats quietly moved to sever ties with the NCP and meet General Abdel Fattah Abdelrahman al-Burhan, Head of Sudan's Transitional Military Council (TMC), and Mohamed Hamdan Daglo (or Hemetti), the TMC's Deputy Head (Barber, 2020). China did not engage to any meaningful extent in the transitional political process following Bashir's removal but did attempt to secure its own engagement. In early May, the Special Representative of the Chinese Government on African Affairs, Xu Jinghu, visited Sudan and met key protagonists, including al-Burhan and Hemetti. Outside Sudan, China indirectly engaged through its UNSC position. In June, following the violent military crackdown in Khartoum by security forces and RSF, the UNSC failed to agree a common position in response. Eight European countries issued a joint condemnation of "the violent attacks in Sudan by Sudanese security services against civilians" but China insisted this was an internal affair. Not long after, a UNSC press statement condemned the violence in Sudan while also noting its "strong commitment to the unity, sovereignty, independence and territorial integrity" of Sudan (UNSC, 2019). Pressure on the TMC to agree to a transitional government with the Forces of Freedom and Change (FFC), an opposition coalition, grew and that exerted by Riyadh and Abu Dhabi, influential backers of Hemetti, was influential in helping advance negotiations. China's special envoy did not appear to have played any role in the subsequent AU-convened talks in July 2019. The lack of an involved Chinese role in the political transition following April and the events of June 2019 contrasted with its more engaged diplomacy over Darfur and South Sudan.

Relations after Bashir

In the face of the uncertainty attending Sudan's political transition, the Chinese government favoured stability, but this goal remained challenging amid turbulent politics. In August 2019, the TMC signed a power-sharing deal with the civilian FFC, leading to a hybrid civilian-military government being formed. In September 2019, at the UN General Assembly in New York, Foreign Minister Wang Yi congratulated Sudan's new Prime Minister Abdalla Hamdok on assuming power and, together with familiar language about time-honoured friendship, predictably stressed the importance of stability. This, however, remained challenging in the face of political divisions and conflict. Following an initial Juba Peace Agreement (JPA) of August 2020, after talks between the Sudan government and insurgents to end decades of conflict, an accord was officially signed on 3 October 2020, setting out principles on a range of issues, including power- and wealth-sharing, transitional justice, and security, as well as a new timetable for Sudan's post-Bashir transitional period that targets 2024 for elections.

The new transitional government after the JPA involved representatives of Sudan's conflict-affected regions being incorporated into key government positions. However, two of the biggest rebel groups on the ground did not join the talks, resulting in a precarious combination of military, armed movement, and civilian elements. In February 2021, a new cabinet continued to pursue economic reform but in challenging circumstances. One example concerned transitional justice. With popular frustration at the lack of progress over the enquiry into the 3 June 2019 atrocities in Khartoum, the Sovereign Council "general amnesty" decree of November 2020 appeared to provide a reprieve for the government security forces and provoked further concern. After ICC prosecutor Fatou Bensouda visited Khartoum in February 2021, the government signed an MOU of cooperation with the ICC.

As the prominence of such issues amidst economic difficulty illustrated, China's relations with Sudan had undergone a change entailing a de facto downgrading of economics in relations and advance of a more important role for politics. In December 2020, an agreement to build a slaughterhouse in Omdurman, Khartoum, with a Chinese government grant of over 458 million yuan ($70 million) was given prominent attention. This paled in comparison to the scale and impact of multi-billion oil investment from 1995 until around 2005, when the CNCP alone was responsible for some $10 billion of investment (Barber 2020). The politics of debt became a major challenge. Facing nearly $60 billion of debt, Sudan sought debt relief from international creditors; in June 2021, it was announced Sudan was eligible for debt relief under the enhanced Heavily Indebted Poor Countries Initiative. How much Sudan owes China remained unknown; it appeared that Sudan still owed China more than $2 billion and had failed to honour an agreement that delayed repayments for five years (ibid.). Going forward, long-mooted plans were to diversify Sudan's economy and China's engagement in the face of myriad challenges in the aftermath of the NCP regime. Sudan plans for rehabilitating infrastructure (such as railways and roads) and pursuing economic reform meant, however, Chinese companies were well positioned for future involvement.

Beyond inter-state connections, the complexity of China within Sudan was hard to ascertain but was important. In terms of deeper Sudanese society, and in a context of wide economic hardship, the Chinese engagement faced diverse reactions against long years of perceived China dominance, inextricably linked to the NCP. A wide swath of Sudanese civil society has been critical of China's role, from long-standing grievances with Beijing's close support for the corrupt, violent NCP regime to complaints about the environmental practices of Chinese companies. Such grievances underscored the importance of Sudanese and Chinese relations outside official channels. In terms of official links, however, state-sponsored education exchanges continued, such as the Confucius Institute at the University of Khartoum established in 2010, illustrating how far China has become an established partner. In 2020, there were over 3,000 Sudanese students studying in China and some 500 Chinese students studying in Sudan (Ma, 2019a).

In contrast to such discontent among civil society, there were signs of pragmatic outreach to the CCP by Sudanese political parties in the emerging landscape of post-NCP politics. Political party exchanges were evolving. The NCP had dominated exchanges with the CCP, but by 2021 other political parties in Sudan, such as the National Umma Party, now sought to cultivate links with the CCP. The major question, however, was how Sudanese security power brokers and forces would proceed.

In foreign policy, Sudan's post-Bashir government continued to support Beijing in its "core interests", such as Xinjiang and Hong Kong, but the BRI had become the most important topic. China sought to use Sudan government support in its hardline policy in Xinjiang. In July 2019, for instance, following a letter signed by 22 states to the UN Human Rights Council criticizing China's repression in Xinjiang, Sudan was one of 37 states that signed a letter defending China's policies and praising its "contribution to the international human rights cause". In early 2021, Sudan's ambassador to China, Gafar Karar Ahmed, told a Chinese Academy of Social Sciences forum that "Xinjiang is a safe place that is developing well, and the region's religious freedom is fully guaranteed" (Zhou and Zhao, 2021). Khartoum also supported China over Hong Kong and, notably, its June 2020 Security Law. The continuity of such support by Khartoum was unsurprising: it offered a straightforward means to manage and enhance relations with Beijing. It came in a very different context for Sudan's foreign relations, however, when its transitional government was endeavouring not just to maintain good relations with China but also enhance relations with other powers, most notably the USA. Following Sudan's signing of the Abraham Accords with the USA in January 2021, paving the way for normalizing ties with Israel, the prospect of Khartoum-Tel Aviv relations added a new dimension in China's engagement. By 2021, China's relations with Sudan were to a significant degree framed in terms of the BRI but the context had importantly changed. Khartoum continued to position itself as having current and future strategic value under the BRI. Emerging from sanctioned isolation, however, Khartoum's options were more diverse. Conversely, the Chinese government now confronted the scenario of competition within Sudan, which had long been speculated about in the context of anticipating a post-Bashir era, but how far this would involve the return of US business in particular was difficult to ascertain.

Conclusion

China's relations with Sudan stand at a very different juncture of Chinese and Sudanese politics. As the 100th anniversary celebrations in July 2021 of the founding of the CCP showed, China under Xi Jinping is pursuing more ambitious global goals. Sudan is one part of these. While continuing to be important, and even before Bashir's NCP regime fell, Sudan no longer has the previous outsized significance it had for China during the oil boom era. Sudan is still widely referred to as "a pioneer and model of China-Africa cooperation" and for good reasons: China's oil companies, for example, went global in Sudan from 1995 before "going global" became the declared strategy. Relations changed following South Sudan's secession, however, and Sudan now has a less distinctive and significant position in China's engagement. Where once Sudan helped pioneer security and investment protection practices by the CNPC and Chinese companies, now such challenges are familiar and protecting overseas interests are, according to China's 2019 defence White Paper, "a crucial part of China's national interests". With efforts to pursue a revised economic partnership, in which agriculture is more central, the Chinese government and other investors seemed to be cautiously engaging at a very uncertain phase in Sudanese politics.

By the summer of 2021, it was clear that the most important factor influencing relations continued to be Sudanese politics. Relations faced the uncertainty characterising Sudan's fragile transition. As well as providing new directions in Sudanese politics and external relations, post-Bashir Sudan-China relations remain locked in an established political economy in which the role and power of military and security forces remain significant. The future of civil-military relations hangs in the balance. Important challenges, such as the formation of a Transitional Legislative Council, or the scheduled transfer of the Sovereignty Council to a civilian chair, lay ahead in a context where the military appeared reluctant to meaningfully relinquish power. How the Chinese government would engage Sudanese politics going forward, beyond its formal declarations about non-interference, is an open question. As well as its public support for political transition in Sudan, however, Beijing has cultivated links with influential military and security powerbrokers and thus appears to be attempting to position itself for different political scenarios going forward. The government of Sudan's external relations has changed markedly, while Khartoum continues to use foreign policy as a necessary means of pursuing domestic objectives. In this, a major question is whether the USA will engage meaningfully, including in economic terms. Khartoum has new external choices, in theory, but it remains to be seen what configuration of governing power will emerge and what it will do with these choices.

Note

1 In China, General Gordon commanded a militia fighting Taiping rebels on behalf of the Qing government from March 1863 and went on to become Governor General of Egyptian-governed Sudan before eventually, in 1885, being killed in Khartoum in the Mahdi uprising.

References

Barber, L (2020) "China's Response to Sudan's Political Transition", USIP Special Report No. 466.

CGTN (2018) "No Strings Attached with Africa deal – China's Xi Jinping", 3 September. Available at: https://africa.cgtn.com/2018/09/03/no-strings-attached-with-africa-deal-chinas-xi-jinping/

CGTN (2019) "China Closely Watching Development of Sudan Situation: FM Spokesman", 12 April.

Hackenesch, C. and Bader, J. (2020) "The Struggle for Minds and Influence: The Chinese Communist Party's Global Outreach", *International Studies Quarterly* 64(3): 723–733.

ICG (2021) "The Rebels Come to Khartoum: How to Implement Sudan's New Peace Agreement", Africa Briefing No. 168, 23 February.

Large, D. (2011) "South Sudan and China: Turning Enemies into Friends?", in D. Large and L. Patey (Eds.), *Sudan Looks East: China, India and the Politics of Asian Alternatives*, Oxford: James Currey, pp. 157–175.

Large, D. (2020) "China and the Comprehensive Peace Agreement: Developing Peace in Sudan?", in S. Nouwen, et al. (Eds.), *Making and Breaking Peace in Sudan and South Sudan: The Comprehensive Peace Agreement and Beyond*, Oxford: Oxford University Press, pp. 172–190.

Leff, J. and LeBrun, E. (2014) "Following the Thread: Arms and Ammunition Tracing in Sudan and South Sudan", HSBA Working Paper No. 32. Geneva: Small Arms Survey.

Ma, X. (2019a) "Remarks Made by Ambassador Ma Xinmin at the Inaugural Ceremony for the 'Chinese Teahouse' Salon and Also Its Debut Event", 10 December. Available at: http://sd.chineseembassy.org/eng/dshd/t1723409.htm

Ma, X. (2019b) "Everlasting China-Sudan Friendship: Work Together for a Shared Future", 24 October. Available at: http://sd.china-embassy.org/eng/dshd/t1710619.htm

Ma, X. (2020) "China, Sudan Expect Greater Opportunities for Reciprocal Growth", *Global Times*, 2 November. Available at: www.globaltimes.cn/content/1205416.shtml

Munyi, E. (2020) "The Growing Preference for Chinese Arms in Africa: A Case Study of Uganda and Kenya", CARI Policy Brief No. 49.

Patey, L. (2014) *The New Kings of Crude: China, India, and the Global Struggle for Oil in Sudan and South Sudan*. London: Hurst.

Shengxia, S (2017) "China's Ties with Sudan Offer Promising New Model", Global Times, 5 October. Available at: www.globaltimes.cn/content/1069063.shtml

Sudan Now (2016) "Sudan: China Extends U.S.$60 Million to Support Agricultural Sector", 22 September.

UNSC (2019) "Security Council Press Statement on Sudan", Press Release SC/13836, 11 June.

Xinhua (2017a), "Sudan Vows to Provide 'Appropriate Climate' for Chinese Investments", 4 January.

Xinhua (2017b), "Interview: Sudan Presidential Aide Reiterates Importance of Belt and Road Initiative", 15 May. Available at: http://news.xinhuanet.com/english/2017-05/15/c_136283 033.htm

Zhou, J. and Zhao, J. (2021) "African Diplomats Blast Meddling Over Xinjiang", *China Daily*, 16 March. Available at: www.chinadaily.com.cn/a/202103/16/WS604feb50a31024ad0baaf57d.html

27

RAILWAY COOPERATION BETWEEN TÜRKİYE AND CHINA WITHIN THE BELT AND ROAD INITIATIVE

Umut Ergunsü

1 Introduction

Perhaps the most challenging conundrum some developing countries face is how to boost their economic growth and thus improve the well-being of their people. That is why the developing world wants a larger share of the proverbial pie of economic development. Unfortunately, however, global optimism at the turn of the century has been replaced by the fear of long-term stagnation (IMF, 2017).

Some of the countries and regions around Türkiye, the majority of which are developing countries, are beset by a plethora of challenges, and there are many different approaches as to how best to overcome those challenges. Recent Chinese history provides us with an example that could work in tandem with the Western approach: economic growth as a means of reaching stability.

The combination of the Western approach and the Eastern approach may help in handling the draconian challenges in the regions around Türkiye, especially the Middle East and North Africa (MENA). Indeed, sustained European focus on institutional reform and governance support would constitute a meaningful stabilization effort (Aydıntaşbaş et al., 2021). This kind of support by international communities would be complete, should the Chinese experience of development be incorporated into efforts to stabilize the region, because one of the biggest problems in those countries and regions is the lack of economic development.

China's history is 'the land power nation's growth, development, decline and re-rise history' (Ye, 2007). China is located at the easternmost part of the Eurasian continent and China's foreign partners in successive dynasties were also in Eurasia. As a proverbial bridge between the partners, the ancient Silk Road was the main channel linking China with Asia, Africa and Europe. To some extent, the Belt and Road Initiative (BRI) marks the return of China's geo-spatial orientation towards Eurasia (State Council Information Office, People's Republic of China, 2015). According to a policy research Working Paper published by the World Bank, the BRI could contribute to lifting 7.6 million people

DOI: 10.4324/9781003048404-30

worldwide from extreme poverty, and 32 million from moderate poverty (Maliszewska and Mensbrugghe, 2019).

According to the White Paper recently issued by China's State Council Information Office, entitled 'China's International Development Cooperation in the New Era', China entered a new era after the 18th National Congress of the Communist Party of China in 2012, and proposed the vision of a global community of shared futures and the BRI, stating that the BRI is a powerful platform for international development, which entails five types of cooperation: policy, infrastructure, trade, financial and people-to-people connectivity. The White Paper also emphasizes that helping other developing countries to pursue the UN 2030 Agenda for Sustainable Development is a key goal which has much in common with the BRI (State Council, People's Republic of China, 2021a).

With the BRI was launched in 2013, China increasingly has participated in economic cooperation abroad; development financing for infrastructure is now a vital instrument for engaging with the world. China has become the second-largest exporter of foreign direct investment (FDI), and the largest source of official development finance (Carrai, 2021).

As is the case in China domestically, strengthening infrastructure connectivity may also be an effective way to facilitate sustainable economic development of the countries en route to the BRI. According to the Chinese experience, increasing infrastructure connectivity is very important for regional development; thus, China officially states that infrastructure connectivity is key to BRI cooperation. That is why China is willing to support participating countries in building trunk lines, including highways, railways, ports, bridges and telecommunications cable networks (State Council, People's Republic of China, 2021a).

Infrastructure connectivity is key to BRI cooperation, and since one of the largest problems facing the economic development of most countries willing to participate in the BRI is the lack of connectivity, it is crucial to do more research on this topic.

This chapter will focus on railway connectivity in Eurasia within the BRI framework, mainly because railways could provide an efficient long-range network. China's domestic experience with railway connectivity has reached a level to support this claim, as will be explained in this chapter.

2 Contribution of Railroads to Economic Development

Transportation infrastructure projects can improve social welfare significantly because they allow regions to exploit gains from trade (Donaldson, 2018). One of the most important aspects of the BRI in infrastructure connectivity is improving the railway network in Eurasia, the lack of which seems to contribute to the development conundrum of many developing and developed economies.

Freight transport to facilitate trade is one of the most critical aspects of increased rail connectivity within Eurasia. The abundance of funds allocated to transport infrastructure connectivity by the World Bank also indicates that this field is perceived as a development bottleneck. In 2019, for instance, 18 per cent of total World Bank lending was allocated to transportation infrastructure projects, a larger share than any other World Bank loan item in 2019 (World Bank, 2019).

During the coronavirus pandemic, the China-Europe Railway Express set a record in transporting goods by an expansion in the types of goods and their increased volume. A total of 336,500 TEUs were transported in the first half of 2021, which shows an increase of about 50 per cent over the same period in 2020, according to the chief executive officer of the United Transport and Logistics Company-Eurasian Rail Alliance (Xinhua, 2021a). Given the reasons above, it is of utmost importance to analyse the BRI through the lens of transportation infrastructure, especially railway connectivity.

2.1 Railway Connectivity in China and Beyond

A growing body of scholarly work indicates that railway connectivity has played an essential role in the economic development of countries and regions. One of the most striking examples relates to China's economic development over the past two decades when China accounted for one-third of gains in global net worth (McKinsey Global Institute, 2021). As one of the important modes of transportation in China, railway development has created favourable conditions for the sustainable development of the economy and the steady improvement of people's living standards (Zhang and Gao, 2021).

Increasing railway connectivity could increase the real income of the population by driving economic growth, promoting the flow of products, and strengthening industrial agglomeration. Railway development in China can significantly promote local incomes and increase the income of residents in neighbouring regions through the spatial spillover effect, and thus contribute to increasing household incomes (ibid.).

In China, the construction and operation of railway infrastructure played a positive role in provincial and regional economies, but it is worth mentioning that railway connectivity between provinces and regions is quite different (Fang and Wang, 2021). Since there is a general imbalance in the development of the regions on the BRI route, the influence of railway development on the income levels of residents will also have regional differences (Zhang and Gao, 2021).

The construction and operation of a high-speed railway (HSR) have become an important policy for China to achieve efficiency and fairness and promote high-quality economic growth. The HSR promotes the flow of production factors such as labour and capital and affects economic growth, and may further affect urban land use efficiency (Lu et al., 2021). The construction of large-scale transportation infrastructure, such as the HSR, must be adaptive and consistent with economic development needs. Local government should take the economic development level, resources and environmental constraints into full consideration in the HSR's construction plan. It is harmful to blindly seek speed and extend construction far beyond the regional capital and environmental carrying capacity (Ma, 2021).

China's first high-speed railway line between Beijing and Tianjin was inaugurated in 2008. Over the past ten years, China has put over 35,000 km of dedicated HSR lines into operation, far more than in the rest of the world (CGTN, 2020). By the end of 2022, the total length of HSR lines in China was 42,000 km, high-speed rail has fully covered 31 provinces, autonomous regions and municipalities, and more than 70% of passengers choose to travel by high-speed rail (State Council, People's Republic of China, 2023a). To put this into perspective, by the end of 2022,China's high-speed railway accounts for two thirds of the total mileage of high- speed rail in the world and covers over three times the distance of that of the European Union (Statista, 2021). By 2030, the length of HSR network will reach about 56,000 km. (State Council, People's Republic of China, 2023b).

By 2021, the Chinese high-speed network covered more than 95 per cent of cities with a population of more than 1 million (People's Daily, 2021). According to the latest data of the International Union of Railways, China's high-speed trains carry over two billion passengers a year, more than three-quarters of the annual volume of high-speed traffic globally and it has a further 15,000 km of HSR lines under construction (Davenne, 2021).

Since the inauguration of the first HSR line in China in 2008, the total rail passenger volume has grown at 8.5 per cent per year. It also changed people's travel patterns, i.e., conventional rail traffic has grown at an annual rate of 0.5 per cent, compared to 81 per cent for the HSR (Zhao, 2019). According to a report published by the World Bank, the benefits of increasing the high-speed rail network in China could be 'very substantial' (Lawrence et al., 2019).

Furthermore, according to Martin Raiser, World Bank Country Director for China, Mongolia and Korea, 'China has built the largest high-speed rail network in the world. The impacts go well beyond the railway sector and include changed patterns of urban development, increases in tourism, and promotion of regional economic growth.' So, if we take the Chinese experience as an example, we can assume that increased infrastructure will facilitate economic growth in different parts of the world (Ergunsü, 2020).

In stark contrast to China, economic growth has been depressed in many BRI countries due to shortfalls in infrastructure investment, and the people are deprived of essential needs. Europe is an exception, but the railway network length in the remaining BRI countries is meagre compared to the global average value which is 8.48 km/1000 km^2 (Wang et al., 2020).

Some countries in the MENA, such as Oman, Kuwait, Qatar, Lebanon, Bahrain, and Yemen, do not have railway infrastructures due to geographical or historical circumstances. The railways in Central Asia were built during the Soviet period (ibid.). The continuous civil war in Afghanistan, the India-Pakistan conflict in Kashmir, frozen conflicts in the Southern Caucasus, and Iran's long-lasting economic and political isolation all hinder governments from focusing on the construction of transport infrastructure (Batsaikhan and Dabrowski, 2017).

Therefore, given the recent Chinese experience on improving railway connectivity especially within the MENA region and the low level of railway connectivity, the BRI could constitute a sea change to increase railway connectivity should the BRI be more about economic development and less about great power competition.

As of January 2021, the BRI has already contributed to connecting over 100 cities across more than 20 countries in Europe and Asia through the China Railway Express to Europe (State Council, People's Republic of China, 2021a). Since the China-Europe freight train service was launched in 2013, 15 routes have been opened from Xi'an, the capital of northwest China's Shaanxi Province, linking Xi'an with cities in 44 countries and regions. In August 2021 Xi'an handled the 10,000th China-Europe freight train trip (Xinhua, 2021b).

3 BRI Railway Corridors Involving Türkiye

This chapter focuses mainly on those parts of the two corridors involving Türkiye and the regions around Türkiye, such as MENA, South Caucasus and Central Asia. Turkish-Chinese collaboration on the high-speed railways is used as a case study for further rail connectivity collaborations in Eurasia.

The region around Türkiye, including Central and Eastern Europe, MENA, South Caucasus and Central Asia, constitutes one of the critical elements of the Eurasian rail connectivity. Two corridors in the Silk Road Economic Belt, namely, the China-Central Asia-West Asia Economic Corridor and the Middle Corridor, pass through this region.

For some products, rail transport is more attractive than sea freight. Shipping time for cargo at ports in China and Western Europe has increased from 28 to 35 days (United Nations Economic Commission for Europe, 2016). Within the framework of the BRI, infrastructure projects such as railway lines, highways and ports have increased in Central and Eastern Europe (Ergunsü, 2018). According to experts, since it is the shortest land route between China and Europe, railway freight transport over the Middle Corridor could take less than ten days after its completion.

3.1 China-Central Asia-West Asia Economic Corridor and Railway Connectivity

The China-Central Asia-West Asia Economic Corridor is one of the six economic corridors under the BRI (Ministry of Foreign Affairs, People's Republic of China, 2015). This corridor has important symbolic significance because it follows the ancient Silk Road, and it is the shortest route between China and Europe after the Middle Corridor.

Although the China-Central Asia-West Asia Economic Corridor overlaps with some of the routes of the ancient Silk Road, its specific route may be uncertain. Of the six economic corridors of the BRI, one of the most difficult to construct is the China-Central Asia-West Asia Economic Corridor. This corridor involves many countries that are geographically far apart, have widely different systems of state administration, different levels of economic development as well as different cultural backgrounds and various religions, making its construction difficult. Therefore, some experts in China believe that the key to the success of the Silk Road Economic Belt lies in the construction of this economic corridor (He, 2017).

The China-Central Asia-West Asia Economic Corridor starts from the Xinjiang Autonomous Region and crosses Central Asia to reach West Asia. From West Asia through Türkiye, this corridor will be linked to the Trans-European Transport Network (TEN-T) railway line, which connects Türkiye to Europe.

Many countries are involved in the construction of this corridor, some of which have historically complicated relations that make it challenging to promote and coordinate at the same level (Huang and Qin, 2018). Nevertheless, countries along the China-Central Asia-West Asia Economic Corridor could be willing to participate in building the corridor should they believe that their economies might receive an impetus for development because of increased connectivity.

3.2 Türkiye's Middle Corridor Initiative and Railway Connectivity

The territories of modern Türkiye, including Anatolia in West Asia and Thrace in Southeast Europe, were important parts of the ancient Silk Road. Since ancient times and due to its geographic location, Anatolia has been a bridge between the East and the West while also being one of the most important turning points of the Silk Road. During the Middle Ages, the Silk Road covered multiple routes from Central Asia to Anatolia and then from Thrace to Europe. In order to keep the commercial activities in Anatolia alive, Seljuks took measures to provide security by building caravanserais on these roads (UNESCO, n.d.).

After the independence of Central Asian countries in the early 1990s with which Türkiye has linguistic, cultural and historical ties, Turkish leaders stressed the importance of rejuvenating the ancient Silk Road. During his tenure as the president of the Republic of Türkiye, Süleyman Demirel stated in 1999 that 'Türkiye will reform the communication and transportation sector to reach contemporary levels and the Silk Road will be reactivated so Asia will once again meet with Europe through Türkiye' (Demirel, 1999).

Furthermore, Türkiye developed the Caravanserai Project in 2008, officially igniting the dream of rebuilding the modern Silk Road in coordination with Azerbaijan, Iran, Georgia, Kazakhstan and Kyrgyzstan. The project's primary purpose was to facilitate trade at border crossings along the Silk Road by simplifying and coordinating customs procedures and forming a commercial route to attract foreign business people.

A couple of years later, the Middle Corridor Initiative (MCI), the most important component of Türkiye's plans to revive the ancient Silk Road, was announced. The MCI routes begin at the western end of Türkiye on the border with Bulgaria, and cross Türkiye on the east-west axis to reach Georgia and Azerbaijan. From the port of Baku on the Caspian Sea in Azerbaijan, the MCI divides into two routes. The first route reaches the Aktau port at Kazakhstan; after crossing Kazakhstan, it enters China through Khorgos dry port. The second route traverses the Caspian Sea from the port of Baku to Turkmenbashi port in Turkmenistan, then to Uzbekistan and Kyrgyzstan and lastly to China.

Trains along the Middle Corridor will cross the Caspian Sea by boat after passing through Central Asia, and then travel to Türkiye via the Baku-Tbilisi-Kars railway, which is planned to intersect with the railway through the China-Central Asia-West Asia Economic Corridor. Compared with the routes to its north, the Middle Corridor route has more favourable weather conditions, faster and more cost-effective transport, and a shorter distance of around 2,000 kilometres (Ministry of Foreign Affairs, Republic of Türkiye, n.d.).

The first trial run of the Middle Corridor route took place on 28 July 2015. The train from western China, named the Nomad Express, arrived in Baku from the port of Aktau after six days. After the Baku-Tbilisi-Kars railway line between Azerbaijan, Georgia and Türkiye was inaugurated in November 2017, freight trains reached Europe via Türkiye (Shirinov, 2016).

According to the President of the General Directorate of Turkish State Railways (TCDD) Hasan Pezük, the block container train services started in 2019 on the China-Türkiye-Europe line from the Middle Corridor are gradually increasing. As of 15 September 2021, 165,306 tons of cargo have been transported from China to Türkiye in 7,204 TEU containers, while 10,693 tons of cargo have been transported from Türkiye to China in 514 TEU containers. As freight trains started to pass through the Marmaray Bosphorus Rail Tube Crossing at the beginning of 2020, a step towards uninterrupted rail freight transportation between the Asian and European continents was taken (General Directorate of Turkish State Railways, 2021).

In addition to constituting the main framework of the economic corridor between Türkiye, Georgia and Azerbaijan, the Baku-Tbilisi-Kars railway will enhance connectivity in Eurasia and has the potential to provide an economic impetus for the South Caucasus economic development within the framework of the BRI (Ergunsü, 2017a).

The operation of the Baku-Tbilisi-Kars railway is encouraging other countries to invest in railway infrastructure projects to connect to the railway line, paving the way for a more efficient transport network in the region. In an interview with the author, in January 2020, Onur Uysal, a Turkish railway transport expert, said:

> Kazakhstan has just completed the western rail link and may enhance connectivity between Türkiye and China through the Caspian Sea. Iran is willing to

establish a new rail line to Azerbaijan, the Georgian government has indicated that it may reopen the Sukhumi-Tbilisi railway, and Afghanistan has declared interest in the project.

More and more Chinese companies are likely to ship their products to Europe using the Baku-Tbilisi-Kars railway line. Moreover, the Baku-Tbilisi-Kars railway may also become a new driving force for Türkiye and China to cooperate in constructing the Sivas-Kars railway line. The railway can be connected directly from Kars to Istanbul and into the broader European railway network when completed (ibid.).

A Chinese-Turkish consortium built the 158 km-long line of the second phase of the İstanbul-Ankara high-speed railway line (Xinhua, 2017a). In addition, a joint venture formed by a subsidiary of China Railway, and local Turkish companies won the bid for the first phase of the railway project from Ankara to Sivas (Reuters, 2008). The first phase of the Ankara-Sivas railway project is the 242 km-long Yerköy-Sivas line.

4 Türkiye-China Cooperation within the BRI

With complementary strengths, both China and Türkiye have their own strategies regarding the creation of the modern Silk Road in which they share converging interests (Wang et al., 2015). Should the railway transport corridors around Türkiye be actively used, the current annual trade volume between Europe and China could provide economic opportunities for the countries en route, especially if logistics centres and free trade zones are set up. Transport would be more efficient and would bring the value chains of multiple countries closer together. However, the establishment of logistics centres and free trade zones requires the completion of the necessary railway infrastructure investments.

The BRI can be a solid foundation for the further development of relations between Türkiye and China as Türkiye hopes to become one of the key countries in the BRI. During his speech at the Belt and Road Initiative International Cooperation Forum in Beijing, Turkish President Erdoğan said that Türkiye, with its special location, is one of the leading countries in the Silk Road geography: 'Türkiye is on the way to realize the Middle Corridor, which is aimed to be one of the main and complementary elements of the BRI, with various projects carried out in our country and in our region' (Presidency, Republic of Türkiye, 2017). Chinese President Xi also stressed at the opening ceremony of the Belt and Road Initiative International Cooperation Forum that China will strengthen coordination with relevant national policies and initiatives, including Türkiye's Middle Corridor Initiative (Xinhua, 2017b).

Türkiye expects to obtain a loan from China for the Edirne-Kars high-speed train project (Ergunsü, 2017b). To this end, the 'Agreement on Cooperation between Türkiye and China in the Field of Railways' was signed on 14 November 2015 (Official Gazette, Republic of Türkiye, 2017).

An essential part of the MCI, the second phase of the HSR line between the Turkish capital Ankara and Türkiye's largest city, Istanbul, was built by a Turkish-Chinese consortium. This was completed in 2014 with loans from the European Investment Bank and the Exim Bank of China (Schindler et al., 2021). The significance of this railway line is that it is China's first overseas project of this kind (State-owned Assets Supervision and Administration Commission, State Council, People's Republic of China, 2020). Turkish and Chinese companies cooperated to build the second phase of the high-speed rail line. This created favourable conditions for future cooperation between Turkish and Chinese companies within the BRI framework. An area of such cooperation could be upgrading the railway between Türkiye's westernmost Sivas and Kars, which would then become the backbone of the MCI.

Large-scale infrastructure projects on the MCI route will help build the shortest route from China to Europe, remove obstacles at major crossing points, and improve the management of logistics corridors. The large-scale infrastructure project of the MCI route will also further improve railway connectivity in Türkiye, Azerbaijan, and Georgia, greatly increasing travel speed and shortening transportation time.

The South Caucasus is likely to become one of the main channels connecting China and Europe within the BRI through the Middle Corridor. Countries in the region are more active in attracting transit logistics and are interested in reducing costs and improving efficiency.

It is fair to state that since the interests of not only Türkiye and China but also the regions and countries around Türkiye (the Central and Eastern European countries, the MENA, the South Caucasus countries, and the Central Asian countries) are aligned. All countries can cooperate to jointly build the China-Central Asia-West Asia Economic Corridor and the Middle Corridor within the BRI framework, and link these routes with the EU's Trans-European Transportation Network Orient/East-Med Corridor.

5 Challenges Facing Railway Connectivity

The leaders of both Türkiye and China emphasized their intention to revive the ancient Silk Road. Cooperation between Türkiye and China within the BRI would have an impact on the countries and regions around Türkiye. Some of the main challenges in increasing the railway connectivity of the BRI relate to lack of political trust, the possibility of economic crisis, instability, corruption, social conflict, inadequate laws, and ethnic and religious conflicts.

Enhancing mutual political trust is the precondition for constructing cooperation within the BRI (Huang and Qin, 2018) so it will be of the utmost importance to adopt suitable strategies or mechanisms to resolve or at least handle the lack of trust between countries such as Türkiye and China (DW, 2015). Achieving the interconnection of economic corridor infrastructure, and improving logistics efficiency and socio-economic development will be a lengthy process (Huang and Qin, 2018). Moreover, Chinese companies must comply with local laws and accept the social environment in which they operate (Lezak et al., 2019).

The massive infrastructure projects within the BRI framework are risky, full of difficulties that are often further complicated by weak institutional and legal regimes in the developing world. While China has leading railway expertise and high technological standards, infrastructure investments are challenging, and it is difficult to estimate their societal benefits (Carrai, 2021).

The China-Central Asia-West Asia Economic Corridor and the Middle Corridor also face significant challenges, such as the lack of cross-border investment coordination, different construction and technical standards, different administrative procedures, and colossal investment demand for transport infrastructure. Unifying and standardizing the track gauge is also a major challenge. The former Soviet Union countries use a 1,520-mm gauge, while Türkiye, the European Union and China use a 1,435-mm gauge. When trains arrive at the border town of Georgia, they need to change gauge, which may create bottlenecks. This problem is not the only challenge of the Middle Corridor and the China-Central Asia-West Asia Economic Corridor. All the Silk Road Economic Belt corridors have the same problem, which may create a bottleneck for railway transport through these routes.

To ensure the smooth implementation of the China-Central Asia-West Asia Economic Corridor, risk assessments and early warning and response mechanisms must be established (Wang and Bai, 2016). Thus, detailed research is of the utmost importance, and the lack of such research could lead to the failure of these projects.

6 Conclusion

One of the most difficult conundrums developing countries are trying to solve is how to find sustainable ways to increase their levels of economic development. As the largest developing country in terms of GDP, China's recent experience can aid developing countries.

Research shows that the increase in railway connectivity has played a significant role in promoting economic development in China. The BRI can provide a useful means to shed light on the recent Chinese experience in increasing economic development, especially for developing nations. As is the case in China, increased railway transport connectivity could help many economies to increase their respective development levels.

Türkiye is located in a region where there are many countries facing economic development problems. At the same time, it is an important crossing point between Western Europe and East Asia as the China-Central Asia-West Asia Economic Corridor and Middle Corridor pass through Türkiye. The collaboration between Türkiye and China on railway connectivity can be used as a case study for further collaborations in Eurasia.

Related countries can cooperate to jointly build the China-Central Asia-West Asia Economic Corridor and the Middle Corridor within the BRI framework, and link these routes with the EU's Trans-European Transportation Network Orient/ East- Med Corridor which would provide seamless railway connectivity across Eurasia.

This kind of multilateral cooperation undoubtedly faces some challenges. The way to overcome those challenges is to harness the channels and mechanisms of dialogue between the countries along the Belt and Road Initiative route.

References

Aydıntaşbaş, A., Barnes-Dacey, J., Bianco, C., Lovatt, H. and Megerisi, T. (2021). Cooling-Off: How Europe Can Help Stabilise the Middle East. European Council on Foreign Relations, 18 June. Available at: https://ecfr.eu/article/cooling-off-how-europe-can-help-stabilise-the-middle-east/ (accessed 21 June 2021).

Batsaikhan, U. and Dabrowski, M. (2017). Central Asia-Twenty-Five Years after the Breakup of the USSR. *Russian Journal of Economics*, vol. 3, no. 3, pp. 296–320.

Carrai, M. A. (2021). Adaptive Governance Along Chinese-Financed BRI Railroad Megaprojects in East Africa. *World Development*, vol. 141, no.105388, pp. 1–21.

CGTN (2020). From Nobody to Somebody: China's High-Speed Rail in Numbers, 1 October. Available at: https://news.cgtn.com/news/2020-10-01/From-nobody-to-somebody-China-s-high-speed-rail-in-numbers-Udm6mE3qqA/index.html (accessed 25 May 2021).

Davenne, F. (2021). *High-Speed Rail Atlas*, 3rd edn. Available at: https://uic.org/IMG/pdf/uic-atlas-high-speed-2021.pdf (accessed 25 May 2021).

Demirel, S. (1999). Turkey at the Beginning of the New Millennium: Developments in the Year 1999 and Objectives During the Year 2000. Presidency of the Republic of Turkey, 25 December.

Available at: https://tccb.gov.tr/konusmalari-suleyman-demirel/1718/4110/turkey-at-the-beginning-of-the-new-millennium-developments-in-the-year-1999-and-objectives-during-the-year-2000 (accessed 11 August 2021).

Donaldson, D. (2018). Railroads of the Raj: Estimating the Impact of Transportation Infrastructure. *American Economic Review*, vol. 108, no. 4–5, pp. 899–934.

DW (2015). Lack of Trust between Turkey and China, 28 July. Available at: www.dw.com/en/lack-of-trust-between-turkey-and-china/a-18611874 (accessed 15 August 2021).

Ergunsü, U. (2017a). Baku-Tbilisi-Kars Railway Will Enhance Connectivity in Eurasia. *China Daily*, 2 November. Available at: www.chinadaily.com.cn/a/201711/02/WS5a0d1118a31061a7384083de.html (accessed 22 August 2021).

Ergunsü, U. (2017b). Reviving the Silk Road and Its Effects on Turkey–People's Republic of China Cooperation [İpek Yolu'nun Yeniden Canlandırılması ve Türkiye - Çin Halk Cumhuriyeti İşbirliğine Etkileri]. *TYB Akademi*, vol. 20, pp. 97–124.

Ergunsü, U. (2018). European Union and the "16+1 Cooperation": Is Cooperation under the "Belt and Road" Initiative Feasible? China-CEE Institute Working Paper, 2018, No. 8.

Ergunsü, U. (2020). RCEP, CAI, BRI Can Boost Global Trade Together. *China Daily*, 9 December. Available at: www.chinadaily.com.cn/a/202012/09/WS5fd068fba31024ad0ba9ad1d.html (accessed 25 July 2021).

Fang, L. and Wang, B. (2021). Tielu jichu sheshi waiyi xiaoying de quyu bijiao yanjiu - laizi zhongguo sheng yu mianban shuju de zhengju [Regional Comparative Study of Railway Infrastructure Spillover Effects: Evidence from Chinese Provincial Panel Data]. *Zhejiang shehui kexue*, vol. 2, pp. 21–30.

General Directorate of Turkish State Railways (2021). Middle Corridor Countries Meet In Baku [Orta koridor ülkeleri Bakü'de Toplandı], 24 September. Available at: www.tcddtasimacilik.gov.tr/haber/652/ (accessed 12 October 2021).

He, W. (2017). "Zhongguo- zhongya-xiya jingji zoulang" jianshe tuijin zhong de jichu yu zhang'ai [Foundation and Obstacles in the Construction of the "China-Central Asia-West Asia Economic Corridor"]. *Jingji tizhi gaige*, vol. 3, pp. 59–67.

Huang, X. and Qin, F. (2018). Zhongguo-zhongya-xiya jingji zoulang jianshe: jichu, tiaozhan yu lujing [Building the China-Central Asia-West Asia Economic Corridor: Foundation, Challenges and Paths]. *Gaige yu zhanlüe*, vol. 2, pp. 68–73.

IMF (2017), Growth Conundrum. *Finance and Development*, vol. 54, no. 1, pp.1–57. Available at: www.imf.org/external/pubs/ft/fandd/2017/03/pdf/fd0317.pdf (accessed 15 June 2021).

Lawrence, M., Bullock, R. and Liu, Z. (2019). *China's High-Speed Rail Development: International Development in Focus*, Washington, DC: World Bank, pp.1–83.

Lezak, S., Ahearn, A., McConnell, F. and Sternberg, T. (2019). Frameworks for Conflict Mediation in International Infrastructure Development: A Comparative Overview and Critical Appraisal. *Journal of Cleaner Production*, vol. 239, no. 118099, pp. 1–14.

Lu, X., Tang, Y., and Ke, S. (2021). Does the Construction and Operation of High-Speed Rail Improve Urban Land Use Efficiency? Evidence from China. *Land*, vol. 10, no. 3, pp. 1–15.

Ma, Y. (2021). The Effect of Beijing-Shanghai High-Speed Railway on the Economic Development of Prefecture-Level Cities Along the Line Based on DID Model. *E3S Web of Conferences 235, 2020 International Conference on New Energy Technology and Industrial Development (NETID 2020)*, vol. 235, no. 01016, pp. 1–7.

Maliszewska, M. and Mensbrugghe, D. (2019). The Belt and Road Initiative: Economic, Poverty and Environmental Impacts. World Bank Group Macroeconomics, Trade and Investment Global Practice, Policy Research Working Paper No. 8814, April, pp. 1–67. Available at: https://openknowledge.worldbank.org/handle/10986/31543 (accessed 12 May 2021).

McKinsey Global Institute (2021). The Rise and Rise of the Global Balance Sheet: How Productively Are We Using Our Wealth?, November. Available at: www.mckinsey.com/industries/financial-services/our-insights/the-rise-and-rise-of-the-global-balance-sheet-how-productively-are-we-using-our-wealth

Ministry of Foreign Affairs, People's Republic of China (2015). Vision and Actions for Jointly Building the Silk Road Economic Belt and the 21st Century Maritime Silk Road, 28 March. Available at: www.fmprc.gov.cn/mfa_eng/zxxx_662805/t1249618.shtml (accessed 12 May 2021).

Ministry of Foreign Affairs, Republic of Turkey Turkey's Multilateral Transportation Policy, Available at: www.mfa.gov.tr/turkey_s-multilateral-transportation-policy.en.mfa (accessed 20 September 2021).

Official Gazette, Republic of Turkey (2017). The Law on Approval of the Agreement on Cooperation in the Field of Railways between the Government of the Republic of Turkey and the Government of the People's Republic of China [Türkiye Cumhuriyeti Hükümeti İle Çin Halk Cumhuriyeti Hükümeti Arasında Demiryolları Alanında İşbirliğine İlişkin Anlaşmanın Onaylanmasının Uygun Bulunduğuna Dair Kanun], 8 March. Available at: www.resmigazete. gov.tr/eskiler/2017/03/20170308-27.htm (accessed 15 May 2021).

Presidency, Republic of Turkey (2017). The Doors of a New Era Based on Stability and Prosperity in Our Region Will Be Opened [Bölgemizde İstikrar ve Refah Temelli Yeni Bir Dönemin Kapıları Aralanacak], 14 May. Available at: www.tccb.gov.tr/haberler/410/75192/bolgemizde-istikrar-ve-refah-temelli-yeni-bir-donemin-kapilari-aralanacak (accessed 18 September 2021).

Reuters (2008). China Railway Group Won the Bid for Several Major Domestic Projects with a Total Value of Approximately 2.86 Billion Yuan [Zhongguo zhongtie zhongbiao shu xiang guonei zhongda gongcheng, zong'e yue 28.6 yi yuan], 7 October, www.reuters.com/article/idCNChina-2474920081007 (accessed 12 November 2021).

Schindler, S., Bayırbağ, M. K., and Gao, B. (2021). Incorporating the Istanbul-Ankara High-Speed Railway into the Belt and Road Initiative: Negotiation, Institutional Alignment and Regional Development. *Journal of Geographical Sciences*, vol. 31, pp. 747–762.

Shirinov, R. (2016). Over 50 Trains Will Pass Azerbaijan Via TITR Project in 2016, *Azernews*, 3 June. Available at: www.azernews.az/business/97543.html (accessed 28 March 2021).

State Council, People's Republic of China (2021a). Woguo gaotie yunying licheng dadao 4.2 wan gongli [China's high-speed rail operation mileage reaches 42,000 kilometers], 13 January. Available at: http://english.www.gov.cn/archive/whitepaper/202101/10/content_WS5ffa6bbbc6d0f72576943922.html (accessed 8 July 2021).

State Council, People's Republic of China (2023a). China's High-Speed Rail Lines Top 37,900 Km at End of 2020, Xinhua, 10 January. Available at: http://www.gov.cn/xinwen/2023-01/13/content_5736816.htm (accessed 11 Feb 2023).

State Council, People's Republic of China (2023b). Transportation sector growth picks up speed, 16 January. Available at: https://english.www.gov.cn/statecouncil/ministries/202301/16/content_WS63c4b67fc6d0a757729e5885.html (accessed 11 Feb 2023).

State Council Information Office, People's Republic of China (2015). "Yidai yilu"changyi de zhongguo chuantong sixiang yaosu chutan [A Preliminary Study on the Elements of Chinese Traditional Thought in the Belt and Road Initiative], 10 December. Available at: www.scio.gov. cn/ztk/wh/slxy/31215/Document/1458842/1458842.htm (accessed 2 June 2021).

State-owned Assets Supervision and Administration Commission, State Council, People's Republic of China (2020). Ankara-Istanbul High-speed Railway, China's First Overseas Project of Its Kind, Is Completed and Opens on July 25, 2014, 25 July. Available at: http://en.sasac.gov.cn/2020/07/25/c_1942.htm (accessed 24 September 2021).

Statista (2021). High-Speed Railway in China: Statistics and Facts, 17 June. Available at: www.statista.com/topics/7534/high-speed-rail-in-china/ (accessed 18 September 2021).

UNESCO (n.d.). Countries along the Silk Road Route: Turkey. Available at: https://en.unesco.org/silkroad/countries-alongside-silk-road-routes/turkey

United Nations Economic Commission for Europe (2016). Identification of Cargo Flows on the Euro-Asian Transport Links, 15 November. Available at: https://unece.org/DAM/trans/doc/2016/sc2/ECE-TRANS-SC2-2016-id02e.pdf (accessed 10 June 2021).

Wang, C., Lim M. K., Zhang, X., Zhao, L. and Lee, P. T. W. (2020). Railway and Road Infrastructure in the Belt and Road Initiative Countries: Estimating the Impact of Transport Infrastructure on Economic Growth. *Transportation Research Part A: Policy and Practice*, vol. 134, pp. 288–307.

Wang, S. and Bai, Y. (2016). Zhongguo-zhongya-xiya jingji zoulang jianshe: jinzhan, wenti yu duice [Construction of China-Central Asia-West Asia Economic Corridor: Progress, Problems and Countermeasures]. *Guizhou shehui kexue*, vol. 8, pp. 126–133.

Wang, Y., Ergunsü, U. and Luo, Y. (2015). "Yidai yilu" changyi xia zhongguo yu tu'erqi de zhanlüe hezuo [China-Turkey Strategic Cooperation through the "Belt and Road" Inititative]. *Xiya Feizhou*, vol. 6, pp. 70–86.

World Bank (2019). Annual Lending Report 2019: Lending Data, Available at: https://thedocs.worldbank.org/en/doc/724041569960954210-0090022019/original/WBAR19LendingData.pdf (accessed 5 December 2020).

Xinhua (2017a). Turkey Builds Massive High-Speed Railway to Mark Centennial Anniversary, 14 May. Available at: www.xinhuanet.com/english/2017-05/14/c_136282781.htm (accessed 20 May 2021).

Xinhua (2017b). Full Text of President Xi's Speech at Opening of Belt and Road Forum, 14 May. Available at: www.xinhuanet.com/english/2017-05/14/c_136282982.htm (accessed 25 September 2021).

Xinhua (2021a). China-Europe Railway Express Sets Record in Transportation of Goods, Says Eurasian Rail Alliance CEO, 11 August. Available at: www.xinhuanet.com/english/2021-08/11/c_1310120587.htm (accessed 22 August 2021).

Xinhua (2021b). 10,000th China-Europe Freight Train Departs from Xi'an, 12 August. Available at: www.xinhuanet.com/english/2021-08/12/c_1310123911.htm (accessed 15 August 2021).

Ye, Z. (2007). Zhongguo de heping fazhan: Luquan de huigui yu fazhan [China's Peaceful Development: The Return and Development of the Continental Powers]. *Shijie jingji yu zhengzhi*, vol. 2, pp. 23–31.

Zhang, M. and Gao, H. (2021). Tielu fazhan yingxiang xia de jumin shouru kongjian yichu xiaoying [Spatial Spill-Over Effect of Residents' Income under the Influence of Railway Development]. *Jishu jingji yu guanli yanjiu*, vol. 2, pp. 95–100.

Zhao, H. (2019). Full Speed Ahead for China's Railway Development, CGTN, 20 September. Available at: https://news.cgtn.com/news/2019-09-20/Full-speed-ahead-for-China-s-railway-development-K6P2WT6w6c/index.html (accessed 25 June 2021).

28

PRAGMATIC PARTNERS
China-UAE Relations

Zhen Yu

The United Arab Emirates (UAE) is located in the eastern part of the Arabian Peninsula, bordering the Persian Gulf in the north, Saudi Arabia in the west and south, and adjacent to Oman in the east and northeast. Its geographical location happens to be the intersection of the land and sea routes of the Belt and Road Initiative (BRI). The UAE became independent in 1971, and officially became a federal state composed of seven emirates in 1972 with Ras Al Khaimah joining the Federation. China and the UAE officially established diplomatic relations in 1984. The UAE became the first Gulf Arab country to establish a Strategic Partnership with China in 2012. Then the two countries upgraded their relationship to a Comprehensive Strategic Partnership in 2018 (Xinhua, 2019a). The UAE is considered one of the Middle Eastern countries whose cooperation with China is the deepest, widest, and most profitable. Since the start of the second decade of the twenty-first century, the cooperation between China and the UAE in political, economic, and cultural aspects has continued to show a comprehensive and rapid development trend.

1 The Development of Relations between China and the UAE (1984–2018)

On December 2, 1971, after the establishment of the UAE, the first president, President Zayed bin Sultan Al Nahyan called the then-Chinese Prime Minister Zhou Enlai, expressing his willingness to develop relations with China in all aspects. On December 8, Zhou Enlai replied by announcing that the Chinese government had decided to recognize the UAE (Lan, 1989). Before China and the UAE officially established diplomatic relations, the two countries had already launched economic and trade cooperation and cultural exchanges. China held China Economic and Trade Fairs in both Abu Dhabi and Dubai, and established a China Trade Representative Office in Dubai. In 1980, China built a route to Western Europe via Dubai; the China Construction Engineering Corporation started a construction contracting business in Abu Dhabi. In 1983, China undertook a $1.58 million contracted project in the UAE (China Business Yearbook Editorial Committee, 1985: 1179–1181). In November 1980, the Chinese Muslim Hajj delegation visited the UAE for the first time. This was also the first cultural exchange

DOI: 10.4324/9781003048404-31

385

between the two countries. In July 1981, China sent the first foreign medical team to Sharjah. In 1983, the China Oriental Song and Dance Troupe was invited to participate in the UAE National Day and performed a week of visiting performances. The above-mentioned activities are believed to promote mutual understanding and trust between the two peoples and create conditions for the formal establishment of diplomatic relations between the two countries (Foreign Cultural Liaison Bureau of the Ministry of Culture of the People's Republic of China, 1993: 131; Chen and Zhang, 2011: 53).

1.1 Relations between China and the UAE (1984–2011)

On November 1, 1984, the Chinese and UAE governments issued a joint communiqué, deciding to establish diplomatic relations at the ambassadorial level, commencing the same day. In 1985, the then Vice Premier of China, Yao Yilin, and State Councilor and Minister of Foreign Affairs, Wu Xueqian, successively visited the UAE. In 1987, when the then UAE Minister of Foreign Affairs and Defense Rashid visited China, the exchanges between the two governments became increasingly close. In December 1989, the then Chinese President, Yang Shangkun, visited the UAE when Western countries were collectively sanctioning China, but UAE President Zayed still received Yang Shangkun grandly and warmly. And the UAE President Zayed visited China in May of the following year. The high-level exchange visits mentioned above have strengthened political and economic cooperation between the two countries. In 1985, the China Council for the Promotion of International Trades established a representative office in the Gulf region in Abu Dhabi, which was also the first foreign representative office established by the committee (Representative Office of the Gulf Area, China Council for the Promotion of International Trades, 2007). In the 1990s, the bilateral merchandise trade volume between the two countries, especially China's exports to the UAE, continued to increase. In 1998, the UAE became China's largest export destination country among the 13 West Asian countries,[1] with an export value of $1.29 billion, accounting for 37.8 percent of China's total exports to the aforementioned 13 countries, which was significantly higher than China's exports to Saudi Arabia ($890 million, and the total portion is 26.3 percent), which ranked the second (China Foreign Economic Relations and Trade Yearbook Editorial Committee, 1999: 396).

During this period, the relationship between China and the UAE also experienced ups and downs due to the issue of Taiwan. In March 1995, Lee Teng-hui, then Chairman of the Taiwan Nationalist Party, visited Jordan and the UAE in a so-called "personal name" visit, i.e. unofficially. Following the advance negotiations stipulated by the Chinese Ministry of Foreign Affairs, neither the UAE President nor any government officials met with Lee Teng-hui, and none of the UAE newspapers reported the visit. However, this visit broke through the Middle Eastern countries' restrictions on the level of acceptance of Taiwan's upcoming visits (Xiao, 2017: 231). After this visit, relations between China and the UAE entered a low period. It was not until Chi Haotian, then Vice-chairman of the Central Military Commission, visited the UAE in 1997 that relations began to warm up (Liu, 2019: 218). As shown in Figure 28.1, from 1997 to 2011, the bilateral trade volume between China and the UAE continued to increase. In 2005, the bilateral trade volume between the two countries was about $10.8 billion, exceeding $10 billion for the first time; in 2006, China's exports to the UAE exceeded $11.4 billion. From 2003 to 2008, the UAE's merchandise exports to China continued to increase rapidly, reaching an average annual growth rate of 73.93 percent in 2003.

Pragmatic Partners: China-UAE Relations

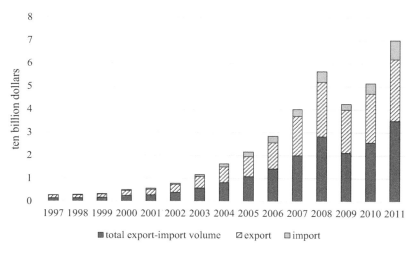

Figure 28.1 China and UAE customs import and export of goods (1997–2011)
Source: National Bureau of Statistics of China (1999–2011).

1.2 The Establishment and Upgrading of the China-UAE Strategic Partnership (2012–2018)

In January 2012, the then-Chinese Premier, Wen Jiabao, visited the UAE and the two countries established a Strategic Partnership. The UAE became the first Gulf country to establish a Strategic Partnership with China. On April 3, 2015, the UAE officially became an intentional founding member of the Asian Infrastructure Investment Bank. In December of that year, during the visit of the Crown Prince of Abu Dhabi (Mohammed Bin Zayed Al-Nahyan) to China, the two countries signed the "Memorandum of Understanding on Establishing China-UAE Investment Cooperation Fund (Limited Partnership)," so as to set up a major investment cooperation fund, which was reportedly worth $10 billion (The Cabinet, United Arab Emirates, 2015). The UAE-China Joint Investment Cooperation Fund is managed and operated by the Mubadala Development Corporation, the Abu Dhabi-based Investment Development Corporation, the China Development Bank Capital Corporation, and the State Administration of Foreign Exchange of China. In July 2018, Xi Jinping visited the UAE for the first time, which upgraded the relationship of the two countries from Strategic Partnership to a Comprehensive Strategic Partnership and they agreed to strengthen cooperation in nine areas (Emirates News Agency, 2018):

1. political, economic and financial education;
2. science and technology;
3. renewable energy and water;
4. oil and gas sector;
5. military and law enforcement and security;
6. cultural and humanitarian;
7. consular cooperation;
8. the facilitation of personnel exchanges;
9. strategic partnership implementation mechanism.

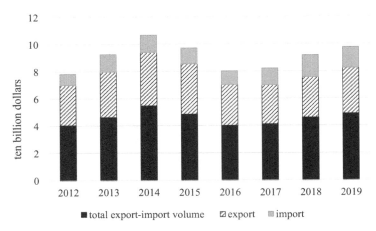

Figure 28.2 China and UAE customs import and export of goods (2012–2019)
Source: National Bureau of Statistics of China (2012–2020).

From the early twenty-first century, the UAE has long been China's largest export market in the Arab world and the second-largest trading partner, after Saudi Arabia. As shown in Figure 28.2, in 2014, the bilateral merchandise trade between China and the UAE exceeded $54.7 billion, of which China's exports to the UAE exceeded $39 billion. Affected by the continued decline in international oil prices in 2014, the volume of commodity trade between the two countries declined continuously from 2015 to 2016, but gradually recovered from 2017.

In addition to commodity trade, China's direct investment in the UAE is also steadily increasing. For example, in 2015, Chinese companies made direct investments in 50 countries along the BRI. That year, China's outward direct investment flow to the UAE was $1.27 billion, ranking it 4th in the stock of China's direct investment in countries along the BRI. At the end of 2015, China's stock of direct investment in the UAE was $4.6 billion, accounting for 6th place in China's stock of direct investment in countries along the BRI. It is the only Middle Eastern country to rank among the top 10 (Ministry of Commerce of the People's Republic of China, 2016: 93).[2] As of the end of 2018, China's direct investment stock in the UAE was $6.44 billion, accounting for the 7th place in China's direct investment stock in countries along the BRI (Ministry of Commerce of the People's Republic of China, 2020: 103).

2 Political Cooperation between China and the UAE (2019–2021)

2019 marks the 35th anniversary of the official establishment of diplomatic relations between China and the UAE. Following Xi Jinping's visit to the UAE in July 2018, during which the two countries announced the establishment of a Comprehensive Strategic Partnership, the exchange of high-level visits between the two countries and exchanges at all levels have been further developed.

On July 21–23, 2019, at the invitation of Xi Jinping, Crown Prince Mohammed bin Zayed Al Nahyan of Abu Dhabi visited China. Both leaders continued to exchange in-depth views on bilateral relations and international and regional issues of common concern, and issued the "Joint Statement of the People's Republic of China and the United

Arab Emirates on Strengthening the Comprehensive Strategic Partnership." During this visit, both sides signed a number of agreements and memorandums of understanding in the fields of trade and economy, investment, technology transfer, artificial intelligence, environmental protection, food security, culture and education, aimed at strengthening bilateral relations (People's Republic of China Ministry of Foreign Affairs, 2019b; Xinhua, 2019b).

Other high-level exchange visits include: On January 14, 2019, Yang Jiechi, Special Representative of President Xi Jinping, Member of the Political Bureau of the CPC Central Committee, and Director of the Office of the Central Foreign Affairs Commission attended the opening ceremony of the 12th Abu Dhabi Sustainable Development Week and the Zayed Sustainability Award Presentation Ceremony, and delivered a speech. He also met with Crown Prince Mohammed of Abu Dhabi on the same day. On February 10, 2019, at the invitation of the UAE government, Chinese President Xi Jinping's special envoy and Minister of Science and Technology, Wang Zhigang, attended the 7th World Government Summit held in the UAE (Xinhua, 2019a). Crown Prince Mohammed of Abu Dhabi met with the Chinese State Councilor and Minister of Defense, Wei Fenghe, in Abu Dhabi on March 21, 2019. Wei Fenghe then held talks with Mohammed Al Bawardi, Minister of State for Defense of the UAE (Central Government of the People's Republic of China, 2019a). On May 22–23, 2019, the China-Arab Cooperation Forum Affairs Ambassador, Li Chengwen, visited the UAE and met with Khalifa Shaheen Al-Marar, the Assistant Minister of Foreign Affairs and International Cooperation of the UAE. Both sides exchanged their views on China-UAE relations and China-Arab cooperation in the forum's 16th Senior Officials Meeting and the 5th Senior Officials-level Strategic Political Dialogue Preparatory Work and Regional Situation (Ministry of Foreign Affairs, People's Republic of China, 2019a).

China and the UAE also cooperated in the fight against the 2020 Covid-19 pandemic. On January 26, 2020, Crown Prince Mohammed of Abu Dhabi posted a message on social media, promising to work with the Chinese government to fight against the virus and be ready to provide various assistance to China. During the pandemic, the UAE provided medical supplies to China many times. On February 25, 2020, Xi Jinping and Crown Prince Mohammed of Abu Dhabi had a telephone conversation on anti-pandemic cooperation and the development of bilateral relations (Xinhua, 2020). After China had basically controlled the pandemic at the end of March, the two countries began to cooperate to help the world to fight the virus. On April 17, 2020, Emirates Airlines delivered 20 tons of protective equipment donated by China to the World Health Organization's regional logistics center in Dubai's International Humanitarian City (China-Arab Cooperation Forum, 2020b). As an important step in vaccine cooperation, China-based pharmaceutical company Sinopharm initiated a Phase III clinical trial to assess its Covid-19 vaccine candidate in Abu Dhabi in July 2020 (Clinical Trials, 2020). Then, the UAE authorized the emergency use of the Sinopharm vaccine for frontline workers in September 2020 (The United Arab Emirates' Government Portal, 2021).

3 Progress in Economic Cooperation between China and the UAE (2019–2021)

In 2019, the total value of China and the UAE's merchandise trade was approximately $48.6689.93 million, a year-on-year increase of 6.1 percent. In the same year, China imported $15.255.16 million worth of goods from the UAE, a year-on-year decrease of

6.1 percent; China's exports to the UAE were worth approximately $33,413.77 million, a year-on-year increase of 12.7 percent. The UAE is still China's largest export market in the Middle East (General Administration of Customs of the People's Republic of China, 2020). In 2018, China's direct investment in the UAE was approximately $1.08 billion, accounting for 90 percent of China's total $1.2 billion direct investment in Arab countries and ranking 6th in China's direct investment in countries along the BRI that year (Ministry of Commerce of the People's Republic of China, 2020: 17).

From 2018 to 2019, China and the UAE have conducted all-round cooperation in labor contracting, traditional energy and new energy security cooperation, and capacity cooperation. In 2018, the UAE was the largest market for Chinese companies in West Asia. Chinese companies signed 90 new contracts in the country with a value of $7.64 billion, a year-on-year increase of 53 percent. The value of related newly signed contracts ranks 7th in China's global market. In the same year, China completed a turnover of $3.61 billion in the UAE, a year-on-year increase of 44.8 percent; related businesses were concentrated in power engineering construction, general construction, transportation construction, petrochemicals and other fields, respectively accounting for 41.7 percent, 27.1 percent, 7.6 percent, and 7.6 percent (ibid.: 16). The oil and gas energy sector is still an important part of the economic cooperation between the two countries. In 2019, the UAE Abu Dhabi project of the China National Petroleum Corporation, or PetroChina, achieved the goal of over 10 million tons of crude oil equity production one year ahead of schedule; the UAE land and sea 3-D seismic project started; the major projects along the BRI, such as the upgrade and reconstruction of the Abu Dhabi Barbu Oilfield's comprehensive facilities are progressing smoothly. PetroChina has established technical support sub-centers and Middle East Engineering Technology Centers in Dubai and Abu Dhabi, to provide technical support for the realization of high-quality oil and gas development in the Middle East (China National Petroleum Corporation, 2020: 46, 52, 53).

China and the UAE have also strengthened cooperation in the construction of the UAE section of the Gulf Rail network and the provision of clean energy. On July 23, 2020, CRRC Yangtze Group and the Emirates Railway Company held an online signing ceremony. CRRC Yangtze Group won the contract for more than 1,600 complete railway freight cars and long-term maintenance service orders for the second phase of the UAE Railway Project, with a total value of $350 million. The project is planned to be divided into three phases, with a total length of 1,200 kilometers, and is an important part of the Gulf Railway network. The second-phase line operating vehicles currently under construction will provide rail logistics transportation equipment support to connect the trade center, the industrial center, the manufacturing center, the production center, the logistics center, the population center, and the import and export points of the region (Economic and Commercial Office of the Embassy of the People's Republic of China in the United Arab Emirates, 2020a). In addition, the Dubai Solar Power Park Phase IV 700 MW CSP project was undertaken by Hai Electric Group Co. Ltd. and key infrastructure cooperation projects such as the Dubai Hassyan clean coal-fired power station are promoted smoothly (Ministry of Commerce of the People's Republic of China and China Chamber of Commerce for Foreign Contractors, 2020: 6, 29).

New progress has also been made in the cooperation between China and the UAE in the field of clean energy. In 2020, China Jinko Power Technology Co. Ltd., or China Jinko, cooperated with EDF to obtain the Al Dhafra photovoltaic project in Abu Dhabi. The project will develop and build the world's largest solar power plant in Abu Dhabi, with a total installed capacity of 2GW. The project will be fully completed in the second half of 2022. Abu Dhabi National Energy Corporation and Masdar will account for 60 percent of the project's equity, the EDF and China Jinko will hold a total of 40 percent of the equity. After the project is completed and in operation, it will be able to meet the electricity demands of approximately 160,000 UAE households, increase the total installed photovoltaic capacity of Abu Dhabi to 3.2GW, and reduce carbon emissions by more than 3.6 million tons per year (Economic and Commercial Office of the Embassy of the People's Republic of China in the United Arab Emirates, 2020b). It is worth noting that high-growth industries, including clean energy, are the main investment directions of the China-UAE Joint Investment Cooperation Fund established in 2015 (National Development and Reform Commission, People's Republic of China, 2015).

In November 2019, Energy China Gezhouba International Corporation and French SIDEM formed a joint venture, and signed a contract with Saudi International Power and Water Group to build a desalination plant in Abu Dhabi, the capital of the UAE, on November 14. This project is ranked among the top five desalination projects in the world and an important livelihood project in the UAE (Central Government of the People's Republic of China, 2019b).

China and the UAE have also carried out cooperative investment projects in third countries. Egypt is building a new administrative capital about 50 kilometers east of its current capital Cairo, covering an area of 700 square kilometers, which will accommodate 6.5 million people. In December 2019, DP World Sokhna, the China State Construction Engineering Corporation and the China Ocean Shipping Company signed an agreement to establish a tripartite partnership. According to the agreement, Dubai Global Ports will become the import center for the building materials needed for the construction of the new administrative capital of Egypt, and the China State Construction Corporation is responsible for developing the commercial and financial center of the new administrative capital (Economic and Commercial Office of the Embassy of the People's Republic of China in the United Arab Emirates, 2019).

4 Cultural and Technological Cooperation between China and the UAE (2019–2021)

The cultural exchanges between China and the UAE can be traced back to the "Maritime Silk Road" that opened during the Western Han Dynasty. The cultural exchanges between the two countries have become closer after the formal establishment of diplomatic relations. As of the end of 2018, nearly 300,000 Chinese people worked and lived in the UAE. After Xi Jinping's visit to the UAE in July 2018, the two countries established a mechanism for normalized people-to-people and cultural exchanges and cooperation. The two governments signed a memorandum of understanding on the joint construction of the BRI and reached an agreement on the establishment of mutual cultural centers.

Before the Covid-19 pandemic, China had become the largest tourist source market for GCC countries.[3] In 2018, the GCC countries received 1.4 million Chinese tourists. At present, Chinese tourists are the second and fourth-largest source markets of Abu Dhabi and Dubai, respectively. In 2019, Dubai received 989,000 Chinese tourists, an increase of 15.5 percent year-on-year. China was Dubai's fastest-growing source of tourism that year (Arabian Business, 2019; Reuters, 2020). The UAE will continue to be the first GCC tourist destination for Chinese tourists, and it is expected to receive 1.9 million Chinese tourists by 2023.

The two countries continue to cooperate to strengthen cultural exchanges and promote people-to-people bonds. On July 20–24, 2019, to celebrate the 35th anniversary of the establishment of diplomatic relations between the two countries and the visit of Abu Dhabi Crown Prince Mohammed to China, the Ministry of Culture and Knowledge Development of the UAE organized the "UAE-China Week" series of activities in Beijing. During the event, UAE artists performed traditional folklore performances listed as intangible cultural heritage by UNESCO, introducing UAE culture to Chinese audiences (Emirates News Agency, 2019). On September 13, the "UAE National Day" was celebrated in the UAE Pavilion of the 2019 Beijing World Horticultural Exposition event park in China. The UAE Pavilion covers an area of approximately 1,850 square meters, focusing on the UAE's achievements in desert greening through technology, and in the cultural area, it showcases the UAE's historical traditions and cultural heritage (China News Network, 2019).

On February 2, 2020, the Burj Khalifa in Dubai turned on its lights three times at 19:45, 20:45, and 20:52, forming the words "Wuhan, go on" in Chinese and Pinyin. That night, Dubai's city pedestrian streets and Abu Dhabi National Oil Company also expressed their concerns about China's fight against the pandemic by lighting up their lights. In the evening of March 12, the Burj Khalifa and the Abu Dhabi National Petroleum Corporation Headquarters once again lit up the Chinese flag, and slogans "Long distance separates no bosom friends. China will win!," expressing their support for China's fight against the Covid-19 pandemic (Xinhua, 2020). The UAE's support for China's fight against the pandemic aroused a positive response in China too.

Despite the impact of the pandemic, the two countries still held various online activities in 2020. On July 5–9, 2020, the UAE Ministry of Foreign Affairs and International Cooperation held the "UAE-China Culture Week" via an online live broadcast. The activities included a series of online cultural exchange activities, such as cultural forums, art workshops, and music performances (Ministry of Foreign Affairs, People's Republic of China, 2020). On July 16, the Ministry of Culture and Tourism of China and the Ministry of Economy of the UAE jointly hosted the China-UAE Tourism Cooperation Forum through a video connection. This forum is the core section of the first China-UAE Economic and Trade Digital Expo, held from July 15–21, 2020. The forum invited the cultural and tourism authorities, related enterprises and institutes on both sides to participate, and introduced the leading cultural and tourism projects of both sides exhibited at this digital expo (Ministry of Culture and Tourism of the People's Republic of China, 2020). And during the "Expo 2020 Dubai" exhibition, officially opened on September 30, 2021, the China Pavilion combined the sub-theme of "Opportunity, Flow, and Sustainability" with the theme of "Build a Community with a Shared Future for Mankind – Innovation & Opportunity" (The China Pavilion, Expo 2020 Dubai, 2019). Xi Jinping delivered a speech for the China Pavilion on October 1 (The State Council, The People's Republic of China, 2021).

In addition to cultural exchanges, China and the UAE are also deepening scientific and technological cooperation. On July 22, 2019, during the visit of Crown Prince Mohammed of Abu Dhabi of the UAE to China, the Chinese Minister of Science and Technology, Wang Zhigang, and the UAE Minister of Foreign Affairs and International Cooperation, Abdullah Bin Zayed Al Nahyan, exchanged the "Memorandum of Understanding on Artificial Intelligence Science and Technology Cooperation between the Ministry of Science and Technology of the People's Republic of China and the Office of Artificial Intelligence of the Office of the Prime Minister of the United Arab Emirates." According to the memorandum, both sides will continue the important consensus reached by the leaders of the two countries, to promote scientific and technological cooperation between the two countries in the field of artificial intelligence, and jointly explore new models of scientific and technological cooperation between the two countries under the framework of the BRI scientific and technological innovation action plan (Ministry of Science and Technology of the People's Republic of China, 2019). China and the UAE have also established closer cooperative relations between universities and research institutes, for instance, Tsinghua University and Khalifa University of Science and Technology established a joint research partnership; the Mohamed bin Zayed University of Artificial Intelligence, established in October 2019, has also cooperated with Chinese research institutes (Al Dhaheri, 2020).

Scientific and technological cooperation between the two countries in COVID-19 has aroused the attention of the world. In March 2021, Sinopharm signed an agreement with Julphar of the UAE to start production of the Sinopharm vaccine registered as "Hayat-Vax" in the UAE from April (*The National*, 2021). The UAE became the first Arab country to produce the Covid-19 vaccine and was also the first Arab country to produce a new crown vaccine. Thanks largely to the production and sales of the Hayat-Vax vaccine, Julphar's sales in the second quarter of 2021 were 221.3 million Emirati Dirham (AEDs), an increase of 30 percent over the same period in 2020. This is also the company's first return to profitability in the past three years (Julphar, 2021). On July 12, 2021, Sinopharm and UAE G42 Group once again cooperated and signed the "Memorandum of Understanding on COVID-19 Vaccine Production" with the Serbian government online. The three parties will jointly promote Serbia's Sinopharm vaccine production plant project (Reuters, 2021).

5 Conclusion

From the formal establishment of diplomatic relations in 1984 to the first 20 years of the twenty-first century, the political and economic cooperation and cultural exchanges between China and the UAE have experienced a period of rapid growth. In particular, economic cooperation between the two countries has surpassed traditional energy cooperation, and has cultivated new cooperation growth points in third-party markets, in innovation, in finance, aerospace and other fields. Moreover, cooperation between the two countries is characterized by a clear "pragmatic cooperation." [4] That is to say, the cooperation between the two countries is based on their respective strategic needs. While continuously improving political mutual trust, they gradually have expanded cooperation topics and fields, and continue to deepen strategic mutual trust through a series of practical cooperation projects. The cooperation between China and the UAE is of strategic importance to both countries, but neither has an exclusive nature of cooperation. For China, the UAE is an important "fulcrum country" in China's Middle East diplomacy and an important strategic partner. However, Saudi Arabia and Iran, in the Gulf region too, are also "fulcrum countries" in China's Middle East diplomacy, and Saudi is China's largest trading partner in the Middle East (Sun, 2019: 118–120).

While, for the UAE, cooperation with the United States and Europe has always been a priority in its diplomacy. China, Russia, and India are all new partners for its expansion of global influence. Because of the pragmatic and compatible nature of the relationship between China and the UAE under the premise that both sides are committed to taking care of each other's core interests, the relationship between the two countries will continue to develop steadily in the foreseeable future, and there will be a certain degree of flexibility in reconciling differences in cooperation.

Notes

1 The 13 West Asian countries here include the 6 GCC countries, and Iraq, Yemen, Jordan, Syria, Lebanon, Palestine, and Israel.
2 The stock of foreign direct investment refers to the total cumulative value of foreign assets owned at a certain time. The flow of foreign direct investment refers to the amount of foreign direct investment that occurs in a given period, usually a year.
3 The Gulf Arab countries have abundant tourism resources. However, based on the security situation in Iraq and Yemen, the Chinese Ministry of Foreign Affairs and the embassies in Iraq and Yemen have issued multiple security reminders to Chinese citizens not to travel to Iraq (the latest reminder is valid until May 1, 2020) and Yemen (the latest reminder is valid until October 31, 2021).
4 In 2012, Xi Jinping, at the opening ceremony of the China-ASEAN Free Trade Area Forum, stated:

> In the second decade of the 21st century, China will further develop an open economy in an all-round way, continue to consolidate economic and trade cooperation with developed countries, and continue to strengthen common development. China's mutually beneficial cooperation will deepen and expand pragmatic cooperation with neighboring countries.
>
> Since then, Xi Jinping has advocated "pragmatic cooperation" on occasions such as expounding the cooperation between China and Russia, Central and Eastern European countries, and the BRICS, as well as the 16th G20 Leaders' Summit in November 2021. We can understand "pragmatic cooperation" as a feature of action-oriented cooperation that is different from "talking shop."

References

Al Dhaheri, A. (2020). "The UAE and China have built a hundred years of prosperity (says the ambassador)." *People's Daily (Overseas Edition)*. June 29 (in Chinese).

Arabian Business. (2019). "Revealed: The growing importance of Chinese tourists to the Gulf," December 18. Available at: www.arabianbusiness.com/travel-hospitality/435662-revealed-the-growing-importance-of-chinese-tourists-to-the-gulf (accessed October 13, 2021).

Central Government of the People's Republic of China. (2019a). "Crown Prince Mohammed of Abu Dhabi of the United Arab Emirates meets with Wei Fenghe," March 22 (in Chinese). Available at: www.gov.cn/guowuyuan/2019-03/22/content_5375857.htm (accessed October 9, 2021).

Central Government of the People's Republic of China. (2019b). "Chinese companies sign a contract to build a large-scale seawater desalination project in the UAE," November 15 (in Chinese). Available at: www.gov.cn/xinwen/2019-11/15/content_5452576.htm (accessed October 13, 2021).

Chen, H. and Zhang S. (Eds.). (2011). *Civilian Diplomacy and the Rise of Great Powers* (in Chinese). Nanjing: Phoenix Press.

China-Arab Cooperation Forum. (2020a). "China will win! UAE landmarks once again light up the Chinese flag," March 13 (in Chinese). Available at: www.chinaarabcf.org/chn/zagx/zajw/t1755 559.htm (accessed October 19, 2021).

China-Arab Cooperation Forum. (2020b). "Scholar of Shanghai International Studies University, Wang Yu: China and the UAE have cooperated and helped each other in fighting the pandemic," May 25 (in Chinese). Available at: www.chinaarabcf.org/chn/zagx/ltdt/t1782476.htm (accessed October 9, 2021).

China Business Yearbook Editorial Committee. (Ed.) (1985). *China Business Yearbook 1984*. Beijing: China Business Press.

China Foreign Economic Relations and Trade Yearbook Editorial Committee. (Ed.) (1999). *China Foreign Economic and Trade Yearbook (1999–2000)* (in Chinese). Beijing: China Foreign Economic Relations and Trade Press.

China National Petroleum Corporation. (2020). "2019 annual report" (in Chinese). Available at: www.cnpc.com.cn/cnpc/lncbw/202006/bbdaaf7f18a047bbb83fece7056143e3/files/7031d6f93df344cda72190caea57fdd2.pdf (accessed October 11, 2021).

China News Network. (2019). "Beijing World Horticultural Exposition welcomes 'UAE National Day' of 2019," September 14 (in Chinese). Available at: www.chinanews.com/gn/2019/09-14/8956166.shtml (accessed October 19, 2021).

Clinical Trials. (2020). "China's Sinopharm launches Phase III trial of COVID-19 vaccine in UAE," July 17. Available at: www.clinicaltrialsarena.com/news/sinopharm-covid-vaccine-uae-trial/ (accessed October 12, 2021).

Economic and Commercial Office of the Embassy of the People's Republic of China in the United Arab Emirates. (2019). "DP World Cooperates with Chinese Companies to develop Egypt's new administrative capital," December 18 (in Chinese). Available at: http://ae.mofcom.gov.cn/article/jmxw/201912/20191202923326.shtml (accessed October 13, 2021).

Economic and Commercial Office of the Embassy of the People's Republic of China in the United Arab Emirates. (2020a). "The 'Cloud Signing' ceremony between CRRC Yangtze River Group and UAE Railway Company was successfully held," July 27 (in Chinese). Available at: http://ae.mofcom.gov.cn/article/jmxw/202007/20200702986752.shtml (accessed October 14, 2021).

Economic and Commercial Office of the Embassy of the People's Republic of China in the United Arab Emirates. (2020b). "China Jinko and UAE Hydro Corporation sign a power purchase agreement for the Al Dhafra project," July 29 (in Chinese). Available at: http://ae.mofcom.gov.cn/article/xmzs/202007/20200702987588.shtml (accessed October 11, 2021).

Embassy of the People's Republic of China in the United Arab Emirates. (2020). "Ambassador Ni Jian attended the opening ceremony of 'China-UAE Cultural Week'" July 6 (in Chinese). Available at: www.fmprc.gov.cn/ce/ceae/chn/xwdt/t1795166.htm (accessed October 19, 2021).

Emirates News Agency. (2018). "UAE, China issue joint statement, agree to establish Comprehensive Strategic Partnership," July 21.Available at: www.wam.ae/en/details/1395302699891 (accessed October 4, 2020).

Emirates News Agency. (2019). "The Ministry of Culture and Knowledge Development is organizing the UAE-China Week in Beijing," July 22 (in Chinese). Available at: wam.ae/zh-CN/details/1395302775868 (accessed October 10, 2021).

Foreign Cultural Liaison Bureau of the Ministry of Culture of the People's Republic of China. (Ed.) (1993). *Overview of China's foreign cultural exchanges (1949–1991)* (in Chinese). Beijing: Guangming Daily Press.

General Administration of Customs of the People's Republic of China. (2020). "Table of total value of import and export commodities by country/region in December 2019 (USD value)," January 23 (in Chinese). Available at: http://jinan.customs.gov.cn/customs/302249/zfxxgk/2799825/302274/302277/302276/2851396/index.html (accessed January 19, 2023).

Julphar. (2021). "Gulf pharmaceutical industries Julphar reports financial results for Q2 2021," August 15. Available at: www.julphar.net/en/gulf-pharmaceutical-industries-julphar-reports-financial-results-for-q2-2021 (accessed October 22. 2021).

Lan, B. (1989). "The United Arab Emirates," *People's Daily*, December 24 (in Chinese).

Liu, B. (2019). *The Pearl of the Bay Inlaid with Seven Treasures* (in Chinese). Hangzhou: Zhejiang Gongshang University Press.

Ministry of Commerce of the People's Republic of China. (2016). "Report on development of China's outward investment and economic cooperation 2016." Available at: http://fec.mofcom.gov.cn/article/tzhzcj/tzhz/upload/zgdwtzhzfzbg2016.pdf (accessed October 12, 2021).

Ministry of Commerce of the People's Republic of China. (2020). "Report on development of China's outward investment and economic cooperation 2019." Available at: http://images.mofcom.gov.cn/fec/202106/20210630083446194.pdf (accessed October 12, 2021).

Ministry of Commerce of the People's Republic of China and China Chamber of Commerce for Foreign Contractors. (2020). "China's foreign contracted project development report 2018–2019" (in Chinese). Available at: http://images.mofcom.gov.cn/fec/202005/20200509174729295.pdf (accessed October 11, 2021).

Ministry of Culture and Tourism of the People's Republic of China. (2020). "China-UAE Tourism Cooperation Forum was successfully held," July 17 (in Chinese). Available at: www.mct.gov.cn/whzx/whyw/202007/t20200717_873573.htm (accessed October 17, 2021).

Ministry of Foreign Affairs, People's Republic of China. (2019a). "Ambassador for China-Arab Cooperation Forum Affairs of the Ministry of Foreign Affairs Li Chengwen visits the UAE," May 24 (in Chinese). Available at: www.fmprc.gov.cn/wjbxw_673019/201905/t20190524_388 437.shtml (accessed January 19, 2023).

Ministry of Foreign Affairs, People's Republic of China. (2019). "Xi Jinping meets again with Crown Prince Mohammed of Abu Dhabi of the United Arab Emirates," July 22 (in Chinese). Available at: www.mfa.gov.cn/web/zyxw/201907/t20190722_346935.shtml, (accessed on January 12, 2023).

Ministry of Foreign Affairs, People's Republic of China. (2020). "Ambassador Ni Jian attended the opening ceremony of 'China-UAE Cultural Week'" July 6 (in Chinese). Available at: www.fmprc.gov.cn/zwbd_673032/gzhd_673042/202007/t20200706_7421216.shtml (accessed January 19, 2023

Ministry of Science and Technology of the People's Republic of China. (2019). "The Ministry of Science and Technology and the Office of Artificial Intelligence in the Office of the Prime Minister of the United Arab Emirates signed a memorandum of Understanding on Artificial Intelligence Technology Cooperation," July 29 (in Chinese). Available at: www.most.gov.cn/zzjg/bld/wzg/wzbzxc/202004/t20200424_153426.html (accessed January 19, 2023).

National Bureau of Statistics of China. (1999–2011). "China's Foreign Trade with Related Countries and Territories (Customs Statistics)," in *China Statistical Yearbook*, Beijing: National Bureau of Statistics of China.

National Bureau of Statistics of China. (2012–2020). "China's Foreign Trade with Related Countries and Territories (Customs Statistics)," in *China Statistical Yearbook*. Beijing: National Bureau of Statistics of China.

National Development and Reform Commission, People's Republic of China. (2015). "China-UAE Joint Investment Fund was formally established," December 15 (in Chinese). Available at: www.ndrc.gov.cn/fzggw/jgsj/wzs/sjjdt/201512/t20151215_1037212.html (accessed October 16, 2021).

Representative Office of the Gulf Area, China Council for the Promotion of International Trades. (2017). "Introduction," May 14. Available at: www.ccpit.org/Contents/Channel_3916/2007/0514/507194/content_507194.htm (accessed October 4, 2021).

Reuters. (2020) "Dubai registers 16.7 million tourists in 2019, Chinese visitors rise," January 22. Available at: www.reuters.com/article/us-emirates-dubai-tourism/dubai-registers-16-7-million-tourists-in-2019-chinese-visitors-rise-idUSKBN1ZK2L5 (accessed October 13, 2021).

Reuters. (2021). "Abu Dhabi launches new COVID-19 vaccine plant with China's Sinopharm," March 28. Available at: www.reuters.com/article/us-health-coronavirus-emirates-china-idUSKB N2BL0DS (accessed October 22, 2021).

Sun, D. (2019) "On China's partnership diplomacy towards the Middle East countries in the 21st century." *World Economics and Politics*, 9: 118–120.

The Cabinet, United Arab Emirates. (2015). "UAE and China create US $10 billion strategic investment." Available at: www.uaecabinet.ae/en/details/news/uae-and-china-create-us10-bill ion-strategic-investment (accessed October 7, 2021).

The China Pavilion, Expo 2020 Dubai. (2019). "Design of the China Pavilion," August 22. Available at: www.expochina2020.org/2019-08/22/content_40919552.html (accessed October 9, 2021).

The National. (2021). "Hayat-Vax: UAE drug firm already making Sinopharm vaccine under new name," March 29. Available at: www.thenationalnews.com/uae/health/hayat-vax-uae-drug-firm-already-making-sinopharm-vaccine-under-new-name-1.1192883 (accessed October 24, 2021).

The State Council, The People's Republic of China. (2021). "Speech by Xi Jinping at the China Pavilion at the Dubai World Expo (full text)," October 1 (in Chinese). Available at: www.gov.cn/xinwen/2021-10/01/content_5640688.htm (accessed October 19, 2021).

The United Arab Emirates' Government Portal. (2021). "Vaccines against COVID-19 in the UAE." Available at: https://u.ae/en/information-and-services/justice-safety-and-the-law/handling-the-covid-19-outbreak/vaccines-against-covid-19-in-the-uae (accessed October 23, 2021).

Xiao, X. (2017). *Contemporary China-Middle East Relations 1949–2014* (in Chinese). Beijing: Chinese Book Company.

Xinhua. (2019a). "President Xi Jinping's Special Envoy and Minister of Science and Technology Wang Zhigang meets with UAE Vice President and Prime Minister and Chief of Dubai Mohamed," February 12 (in Chinese). Available at: www.xinhuanet.com/world/2019-02/12/c_1124101655.htm (accessed October 8, 2021).

Xinhua. (2019b). "Joint Statement of the People's Republic of China and the United Arab Emirates on strengthening the Comprehensive Strategic Partnership (full text)," July 23. Available at: www.gov.cn/xinwen/2019-07/23/content_5413857.htm (accessed October 4, 2021).

Xinhua. (2020). "UAE landmarks once again light up the Chinese flag," March 13 (in Chinese). Available at: http://m.xinhuanet.com/2020-03/13/c_1125706072_5.htm (accessed January 19, 2023)

Xinhua. (2020). "Xi Jinping speaks on the phone with Crown Prince Mohammed of Abu Dhabi, UAE," February 25 (in Chinese). Available at: www.xinhuanet.com/politics/leaders/2020-02/25/c_1125625216.htm (accessed October 9, 2021).

PART III

China-MENA People-to-People Interactions

29

OVERSEAS CHINESE IN THE MIDDLE EAST AND NORTH AFRICA

Proposing a Research Agenda

Yuting Wang

Introduction

China's increasing involvement in the Middle East and North Africa (MENA) for its energy needs, economic growth goals, and national security interests after the end of the Cold War means that there are many more Chinese companies operating in the region, more Chinese commodities in the market, and a growing Chinese population working and living in a predominately Arab Islamic civilizational zone. By 2016, it is estimated that the size of the Chinese population in the MENA, inclusive of earlier generations of ethnic minority emigrants from China, has exceeded 500,000 (Zhang, 2017). Despite the rapid growth, numbers of overseas Chinese in the MENA account for less than 1 percent of the entire Chinese diasporic population and are scattered in a vast region encompassing some 24 countries that vary significantly in economic and social development. Thus, there has been little systematic research on them. Overseas Chinese in the MENA are largely absent in two bodies of literature: one on the Chinese emigration and diasporic community and the other on China-MENA relations.[1]

However, with the expansion of the Belt and Road Initiative to include most of the MENA countries, there has been a growing effort from the Chinese state to integrate overseas Chinese in the region under a single powerful nationalistic rhetoric and encourage them to play a larger role in the revitalization of Chinese civilization. While the United States encourages its citizens to engage with the rest of the world through any form of scientific and cultural exchange—a concept known as citizen diplomacy (Mueller, 2008), China's Belt and Road Initiative draws from ancient Chinese wisdom that teaches "amity between people holds the key to sound relations between states" and seeks to increase interconnectivity between countries by connecting people's hearts.[2] The emphasis on people-to-people exchanges has elevated the importance of overseas Chinese in the Chinese Communist Party's (CCP) United Front work in the MENA region, especially among ethnic minority emigrants from Mainland China.[3]

DOI: 10.4324/9781003048404-33

As will be elaborated on in this chapter, studying overseas Chinese communities in the MENA region broadens the scope of overseas Chinese studies, informs China-MENA studies, and contributes to the analysis of transnationalism in a global economy, among many other topics. It sheds light on the CCP's policies on overseas Chinese, especially the management of ethnic and religious affairs in the diaspora. It enables a deeper understanding of the multidimensional and multidirectional flows of commodity, capital, technology, and people along the Belt and Road. It facilitates an assessment of the impact of China's shifting foreign policies and global strategy. It also exposes challenges generated by illicit transnational flows through porous borders in the developing world. Instead of providing a detailed account of the history and current state of overseas Chinese in the MENA countries, this chapter is intended to be a call for research. It identifies the key areas in research and suggests the need to develop multidisciplinary collaboration in studying overseas Chinese in the MENA.

Locating the Middle East and North Africa in Overseas Chinese Studies

Chinese emigration dates back to the Han dynasty as trade and commerce flourished along the Maritime Silk Road. Today, overseas Chinese make up one of the largest diasporic populations in the world, with more than 60 million living outside Mainland China, Hong Kong, Macau, and Taiwan (Jia et al., 2020). Loosely connected to China, a civilizational zone, overseas Chinese vary significantly by geographic origin, ethnicity, religion, and ideology, among other social attributes. The heterogeneity of overseas Chinese is further increased because of the historical periods of their migration, the pull and push factors, and the diverse social and political systems of their host countries.

The history of Chinese emigration since the mid-nineteenth century may be divided into three phases. First, between 1850 and the early 1950s, Chinese emigration mostly comprised male workers from the Southeast coastal region who left their homeland to escape war and famine and seek better economic opportunities. These emigrants settled down primarily in Southeast Asia, where their descendants have gained impressive economic success and sparked political tension. Around 1850, the Gold Rush in North America and Australia generated an outflow of indentured or bonded laborers from Southern China to California, Australia, British Columbia, and New Zealand. In the late nineteenth century and before WWII, there was also a growing Chinese presence in Latin America and the Caribbean and South Africa. Largely confined within racially segregated Chinatowns, upward mobility was remote to most Chinese at the time.

The second phase of Chinese emigration is characterized by a hiatus of outflow from Mainland China from the founding of the People's Republic of China (PRC) in 1949 till the reform began in the early 1980s. The Communist government implemented a household registration system, strictly controlled domestic population movement, and prohibited emigration. However, outside Mainland China, Chinese migration continued. Due to the social instability in Southeast Asia, the preferred destinations of migration shifted to more industrialized regions, such as Japan, Australia, North America, and Europe. Following the passing of the Immigration and Naturalization Act of 1965 in the United States that abolished the immigration quota system based on national origin, Chinese migration to the USA grew steadily. The country soon became the top destination for Chinese migrants.

The economic reform in Mainland China in the early 1980s set off the third phase of Chinese emigration. During this period, especially after 2000, the outflow of migrants from Mainland China not only substantially expanded the existing Chinese communities in Southeast Asia, North America, Oceania, and Europe, but also reached non-conventional destinations in Africa, South Asia, and West Asia, albeit in much smaller numbers. More importantly, these post-1980 migrants, also known as the new Chinese migrants, are notable for their multi-class and multi-skilled characteristics. Among them, there are low-skilled laborers and smaller traders, as well as well-funded entrepreneurs and highly skilled professionals. While this wave of Chinese emigration is primarily composed of voluntary economic migrants, there is also a small stream of asylum seekers after the Tiananmen Square Incident in 1989 and as the result of the East Turkestan separatist movement in Xinjiang. Thus, the political heterogeneity within the Chinese diaspora increased visibly (Miles, 2020).

With the acceleration of globalization and China's economic rise, studies on overseas Chinese have grown exponentially since the 1990s. There is little doubt that the overseas Chinese population is highly diverse. Yet, given the historical patterns of Chinese emigration, academic studies on Chinese diasporic communities gravitate toward Southeast Asia and North America and rarely make any distinction between the Han majority and ethnic minorities. Literature on the multiethnic characteristics of the overseas Chinese population in the MENA is scarce.

The enormous heterogeneity and political volatility within the MENA region pose further challenges to scholarly research on overseas Chinese there. The region contains a vast landmass and many waterways stretching from Morocco in the West to Iran in the East. The term "Middle East" was coined in the nineteenth century by the British, reflecting a Eurocentric view of the world. Flexible and contentious, the term was popularized by academics and international organizations throughout the twentieth century. Depending on the era and the user, the geographic area associated with the "Middle East" may extend as widely as to include Turkey in the North, the Arabian Peninsula in the South, Egypt in the West, and Iran in the East. By including countries north of the Sahara on the continent of Africa, the more inclusive designation—the MENA—enables scholars, journalists, politicians, and other stakeholders to delineate a civilizational zone dominated by the Arabic language and Islam.

When defined more narrowly, the MENA region encompasses some 19 countries, including Morocco, Algeria, Tunisia, Libya, Egypt, Israel, Palestine, Lebanon, Syria, Jordan, Iraq, Iran, Saudi Arabia, Kuwait, Bahrain, Qatar, United Arab Emirates, Oman, and Yemen. By other definitions, the list may include Afghanistan, Turkey, Sudan, Somalia, and Djibouti. The MENA contains only about 6 percent of the world population and 4.5 percent of the global GDP. But it produces 60 percent of the world's oil and 45 percent of the natural gas.[4] Standing at the crossroads between three continents and two oceans, the MENA holds strategic importance in international trade and transportation. It is a region of remarkable religious and ethnic diversities and complex geopolitical alliances. The Abrahamic traditions, Judaism, Christianity, Islam, and many sectarian movements within each tradition provide spiritual support for people, but also trigger violent confrontations. Muslim Empires, colonialism, and imperialism have left deep imprints on the landscape and continue to shape the social, cultural, economic, and political conditions in the region.

The Chinese migration to the MENA states roughly matches the general timeline of Chinese emigration worldwide. However, the pre-1980 outflows to the MENA countries were composed of Muslim people of different ethnic backgrounds from the northwestern region and Yunnan province in the southwest. The pull and push factors were more political and religious than economic compared to those factors that motivated the population movement in South China toward conventional destinations, such as those in Southeast Asia, North America, and Oceania. During the imperial period, the few contacts between China and the MENA were maintained by Muslims who made pilgrimages to Mecca in large numbers in the eighteenth century. Between the end of the nineteenth century and the early twentieth century, each year, tens of thousands of Muslims from Northwest and Southwest China—Uyghurs, Hui, Kazaks, and others—participated in the annual Hajj pilgrimage. Many of them eventually settled down in Saudi Arabia, Egypt, or other countries in the Middle East (Ji, 2015). From the late Qing dynasty till the 1970s, multiple waves of Turkic-speaking people from Xinjiang, self-identified as "Turkestanis," found their ways into Saudi Arabia and Turkey. These population movements were triggered by the Qing court's and the Nationalist Party's suppression of the East Turkestan independence movement in Xinjiang (1865–1877, 1933–1934, 1944–1949), the consolidation of Communist rule in 1949–1951, political upheaval in the late 1950s and 1960s, and Sino-Soviet border struggles in the 1960s and 1970s (Al-Sudairi, 2018). During the republican era between 1928 and 1935, a small stream of Sinophone Muslims or Hui students from Yunnan Province went to study at Al Azhar University in Cairo. The Chinese Islamic Association sent eight more students in 1955 and ten in 1982. These Chinese Al Azharians formed a small, tightly-knit community (Ji, 2015). A significant influx of Sinophone Muslims to the MENA states, particularly Saudi Arabia resulted from the exodus of the Hui Muslim warlord, Ma Bufang, and his associates in the early 1950s.

To the average Chinese, the MENA is interchangeable with "the Islamic world." Until recently, except for the Muslim minorities who hold embryonic ties with the region, there was hardly any incentive for Han Chinese to settle in a region troubled by political instability and offering dim economic prospects. Consequently, before the 1980s, the emigrants from China to the MENA region were predominantly Muslims—mostly Uyghurs, Uzbeks, Kazaks, and Hui. The tiny non-Muslim Chinese presence in the 1960s and 1970s was associated with Taiwan's economic contact with the region and Chinese businesspeople from Southeast Asia. The end of the Mao era and the onset of economic reform at the end of the 1970s ushered in a new phase China-MENA bilateral relations. While China remained distant from the contest between the USSR and the USA in the Middle East, it sought to form diplomatic relations and build economic ties with states across the region. By 1992, Beijing had established diplomatic ties with all the states in the MENA region.[5] As China's economy enjoyed a double-digit growth rate in the following two decades, the MENA became increasingly important to China's foreign policies. The region not only has the capacity to meet China's enormous energy needs, but also offers promising markets for Chinese commodities, laborers, and capital. As a result, the size of the overseas Chinese population in the MENA has grown rapidly over the last three decades, especially after 2000, propelled by the "going out" strategy that encouraged both state-owned enterprises and private companies to invest overseas (Nash, 2012). The rolling-out of the Belt and Road Initiative in 2013 further accelerated the trend. It is estimated that the region now hosts more than 500,000 overseas Chinese (Zhang, 2017, unevenly distributed across the region and concentrated in the UAE (2700,000–300,000), Saudi Arabia (150,000–180,000), Turkey (60,000–80,000), and Algeria (40,000) (Table 29.1). Uyghurs, Kazaks, and Hui people constitute a majority of the overseas Chinese population in Saudi Arabia and Turkey. According to Li Anshan, the preeminent scholar of ethnic minority emigration at Peking University, by early 2000, there were 150,000 Uyghurs and 20,000 Hui people in Saudi Arabia, and 50,000 Uyghurs and 25,000 Kazaks in Turkey (Li, 2003). However, overseas Chinese in other MENA countries are predominantly non-Muslim Han people.

The rapid economic development and construction boom in the oil-rich Gulf region fueled by the rising oil price and the shifting regional alliances after the Cold War gave rise to new nodes in transnational economic networks. Especially, Dubai took off as the new regional center of trade, commerce, transportation, and finance. Dubai's rise coincided with China's golden era of economic growth since its joining the World Trade Organization (WTO) in 2001. Dubai is now a key entrepôt of Chinese commodity, capital, technology, and people to Africa and a convenient hub of transportation linking China to Africa, Europe, and parts of Central Asia. Through Dubai's connections to Hong Kong, Singapore, Paris, and Southern Europe, the MENA is brought into the vast transnational networks of Chinese capitalism. The region can no longer be ignored in overseas Chinese studies.

Proposing a Research Agenda: Bridging the Micro and Macro Perspectives

Given these characteristics, the study of overseas Chinese in the MENA states is a multi-layered task that necessitates the consideration of both local and global contexts and the convergence of macro-level and micro-level analyses. At least five key areas in research could contribute to overseas Chinese studies and generate greater scholarly interest in the topic.

First, research on overseas Chinese in the MENA is a study of the complex relationship between China's Muslim minorities with the Chinese state during different periods—essentially a discussion of the changing shape of Chinese identity in response to regime change. Some Chinese historians go as far back as the eighth century in their studies of Chinese emigration to the MENA, while most would begin with the departure of Turkic-speaking minorities and Sinophone Muslims since the late Qing dynasty (Wang, 1986, cited in Ji, 2015). To be able to define the scope of research, it is necessary to examine the argument that China is a civilizational state rather than a Westphalian nation-state and conduct a thorough review of the Chinese Communist Party's *Minzu* or nationality policies. Redefining the terms *Huaren* and *Huaqiao*—commonly translated as "overseas Chinese" in English—is essential for developing a conceptual framework to guide the study of overseas Chinese in the MENA.

The term "overseas Chinese" implies the existence of "a single community with a considerable solidarity," despite the spatial and temporal distance created in the process of migration (Wang, 1991). Studies show that, historically, diasporic Chinese have generally internalized the view of overseas Chinese as forever sojourners rather than immigrants. Their connections with China are described as an embryonic one carved into their DNA and passed down from generation to generation. The understanding that China is "home," whether imagined or real, produces a sense of belonging. However, these conclusions are largely based on the experiences of Han Chinese, not the ethnic minorities. Therefore, in the study of overseas Chinese in the MENA, developing a set of criteria to determine whether a person is part of the overseas Chinese community is essential to address some key questions: Who are the overseas Chinese in the MENA? How to define "Chineseness" in the case of ethnic minority emigrants?

Table 29.1 Chinese population in major countries in the MENA region

Subregion	Country	Population (est.)	Year	Major cities of concentration
Maghreb	Morocco	2,000*	2020	Casablanca Dar El Beïda
	Algeria	40,000*	2020	Algiers Oran Constantine
	Tunisia	1,000*	2020	Tunis
	Libya	N/A		
Mashriq	Egypt	< 20,000***	2020	Cairo Alexandria Ain Sokhna
	Sudan	N/A		Khartoum
Levant	Lebanon	N/A		
	Jordan	300***	2020	Aman Aqaba
	Syria	N/A		
	Israel	10,000-25,000**	2010	Tel Aviv Haifa
GCC	Saudi Arabia	150,000-180,000**	2010	Riyadh Jeddah
	UAE	270,000-300,000	2016	Abu Dhabi Dubai
	Qatar	3000***	2020	Doha
	Bahrain	4000***	2020	Manama
	Kuwait	4000**	2010	Kuwait City
	Oman	6000***	2020	Muscat
	Yemen	N/A		
Other	Turkey	60,000-80,000**	2010	Istanbul
	Iraq	N/A		
	Iran	3000-4000**	2010	Tehran

* Source: Jia (2020).
** Source: Zhang (2010).
*** Source: Ministry of Commerce, People's Republic of China (n.d.).

These questions are not only central in the study of diasporic identity. They are also critical to the Chinese state's policies on the Chinese diaspora and may even influence China-MENA relations. In 2018, the Chinese government restructured the Overseas Chinese Affairs Office (OCAO) and merged it into the United Front Work Department to better manage the affairs of overseas Chinese. Supported by the Ministry of Foreign Affairs, the Ministry of Human Resources and Social Security, and the State Administration of Foreign Experts Affairs, the mission of OCAO is to protect the legitimate rights and interests of overseas Chinese, whether they retain Chinese nationality or not. In Saudi Arabia, for example, it is reported that long-term Turkestanis residents in Saudi Arabia were encouraged to seek assistance from the PRC embassy to resolve passport issues (Al-Sudairi, 2018: 36–37).

Second, it is beneficial to conduct a political-economic analysis of the human dimension of China-MENA relations. Overseas Chinese in the MENA are primarily made up of the staff of large Chinese enterprises and voluntary economic migrants of all kinds. By and large, the post-1980 migrants, especially the Han people, see themselves as sojourners, or more accurately expatriates.[6] The MENA region is a geopolitical hotspot and the ground for great power competition. It is also marked by uneven development, with the oil-rich Gulf states boasting some of the highest GDP per capita in the world (e.g., Qatar and the UAE) and others considered low-income countries (e.g., Sudan and Somali). The experiences of overseas Chinese have been strongly shaped and continue to be shaped by constantly shifting political and economic factors at the national, regional, and global levels. The growth and shrinking of overseas Chinese communities and population movement within the region can be quite unpredictable. Since the 1990s, the region has witnessed a long list of military confrontations, political upheavals, social movements, and diplomatic crises, such as the First Gulf War (1991), the Algerian Civil War (1991–2002), the Second Gulf War (2003–2011), the Arab Spring (2010–2013), the subsequent civil wars in Libya (2014–2020) and Syria (2011–), Saudi's military intervention in Yemen (2016–), and more recently, Qatar's diplomatic crisis (2017–2020).

During the First Gulf War, companies operating in Kuwait and Iraq were relocated to Dubai, diverting Chinese capital into the UAE. The overseas Chinese population in Libya has decreased dramatically since 2011. More than 35,000 Chinese nationals were evacuated during the 2011 civil war (Zerba, 2014). At present, there are only two Chinese state-owned companies that operate normally in Libya.[7] In Algeria, "China's oldest and closest Maghreb partner" (Calabrese, 2021), the Chinese population has also dwindled in the years after the Arab Spring. Although there is hope that China's new approach to the MENA as outlined in the 2016 Arab Policy Paper[8] will increase Chinese investment in infrastructural projects and trade and thus attract more Chinese businesses into the country, the overseas Chinese community in Algeria is unlikely to grow, given the economic crisis and social discontent deepened by the COVID-19 pandemic. Even in the Gulf countries that offer greater incentives to immigrants, the rigid immigration policies and the absence of the naturalization process instill a sense of uncertainty and transience among overseas Chinese, although some have lived in the region for decades.

These uncertainties force the overseas Chinese not only to maintain strong transnational ties with their places of origin but also to think proactively and actively cultivate good relationships with Chinese diplomatic missions and various state agencies at home. China's growing economic and security involvement in the MENA and the opportunities provided by the Belt and Road Initiative are also important factors that drive overseas Chinese closer to the Chinese state apparatus. This peculiar situation makes the position of ethnic minorities even more sensitive.

The third key area in the studies of overseas Chinese in the MENA focuses on the spatial characteristics of Chinese diasporic communities in a rapidly urbanizing region. Chinese migration to the MENA is largely motivated by China's reorientation of its foreign policies and economic development strategies since 1992. Unlike other major destinations of Chinese emigration, a large proportion of the overseas Chinese population in the MENA are staff of Chinese state-owned enterprises concentrated in the fields of energy, construction, and communication technology. This phenomenon is especially evident in volatile regions and countries with low GDP. Large Chinese state-owned enterprises were the first major Chinese players to enter the MENA. To protect their staff from potential danger due to language barriers and unfamiliar cultural environments and alleviate the challenges of living in economically less developed regions, these companies generally adopt a collective way of work and life. Some build residential compounds if their projects are far away from urban centers. Companies that operate in major cities tend to rent villas to house the staff and their families. In addition, many companies bring chefs and housemaids from China to run community cafeterias and maintain the staff accommodation, which reminds one of the socialist work units that existed in the pre-reform era. Consequently, this arrangement produces exclusive social clubs that separate Chinese staff from the host society and from other overseas Chinese who are either self-employed or work for non-Chinese entities. Although it seems that there are tens of thousands of overseas Chinese in some MENA countries, they are mostly invisible to the local population.

The UAE is one of the few MENA countries that hosts thousands of small to medium-sized Chinese-owned private businesses. In addition, there are also sizable highly skilled Chinese professionals working for foreign companies or the UAE government. The country boasts a resilient economy, a mature infrastructure, a friendly business environment, a tolerant society, and a multicultural/multiethnic foreign population. The interactions between Chinese, Emiratis, and other foreign residents are frequent and multi-faceted. The Chinese community in the UAE has also become more enduring with the coming of age of the second-generation, UAE-born/grown, young professionals, whose identities are more globally oriented than tied to the local context. The overseas Chinese in the UAE vary widely in socio-economic status, and so are their spatial distributions in cities. Although de facto ethnic enclaves have emerged as the Chinese population grew dramatically from around 2,000 in the early 1990s to somewhere between 270,000 and 300,000 by 2020, the Chinatown model is insufficient to understand these ethnic enclaves formed in a new era (Wang, 2020a).

The fourth promising research area relates to the transnationality of Chinese migrants in the MENA anchored by key regional hubs—notably Dubai, and a multitude of flows through dynamic social networks connected by these nodes. Transnationalism is central to the study of overseas Chinese. The most important dimension of transnationality is cross-border business connections. Immigration is rarely a one-way street. With their feet in two or more countries, overseas Chinese have played vital roles in brokering business deals and mediating business disputes. Kinship ties maintained by various hometown associations and trade guilds are the key to the flourishing Chinese ethnic business networks stretching on multiple continents. Chain migration ensures the vitality and continuity of these connections. The Chinese transnational business networks have grown substantially following the economic boom in Taiwan, Hong Kong, and Singapore, and later Mainland China. While family and clan are the cornerstones of historic Chinese diasporic communities, the rise of Chinese multinational corporations—both the state-owned enterprises and privately funded companies in Mainland China—has consolidated the transnational trade networks and broadened the scope of economic activities. State-owned enterprises and province- or city-based trade associations constitute one of the three pillars of the Chinese diasporic community in the MENA—the other two being Chinese language media and Chinese schools.[9]

Owing to its strategic location and reliable services, Dubai made itself the connecting point between the MENA, Mainland China, Hong Kong, South Asia, Africa, and some parts of Europe. Paralleling the high-end globalization—formal and legit economy, low-end globalization—the informal or shadow economy—connects China to the vast market in low-income countries that are thirsty for cheap but versatile consumer goods made in China (Matthews et al., 2017). The Dragon Mart and the absence of foreign exchange control in Dubai are the two most essential ingredients in making Dubai an ideal location for traders from the MENA and sub-Saharan Africa. In the last several years, the added cost of business transactions through Dubai and the relaxed policies on visas to Mainland China have encouraged more businesspeople to deal directly with Chinese sellers and factories in Yiwu and Guangzhou. However, most businesspeople still trade through Dubai to avoid dealing with the strict Chinese banking regulations. It is worth noting that many transactions between Chinese businesspeople and their customers are conducted in cash. The sources of funds are sometimes highly suspicious. Some of the money flows into the real estate market, while other money changes hands in Chinese-operated underground banks. Despite being illicit, such services have long existed in Chinese diasporic communities and constitute an important type of trans-national connection. In Dubai, these agencies handle transactions as high as several million dirhams daily through intricate business networks inside China. Since the shift to online banking, these transactions have become much more convenient and reliable. The underground banking service is not just used by businesspeople in the Dragon Mart, but also benefits other Chinese migrants who need to remit a large sum of money back home or transfer money out of China. Regulations on the transfer and withdrawal of foreign remittances to China are so strict that many would prefer to go through this informal channel to avoid the hassle. Recently, however, the Dubai government has stepped up the banking regulations and placed more restrictions on property payment methods to stop money laundering. These changes will surely have a significant impact on the trans-national business network of overseas Chinese in the broader MENA region.

Transnational connections go beyond business transactions. Despite its small size and a relatively short history of overseas Chinese in the MENA and the political and economic contexts of the MENA countries, social and cultural transnationality in the form of chain migration, transnational religious networks, and the flow of educational resources have grown rapidly over the last three decades. The most evident aspect of cultural transnationality is sustained by the Muslim minorities. Each year, more than 10,000 Chinese Muslim pilgrims holding officially approved Hajj visas travel to Saudi Arabia to perform the annual religious ritual, one of the five pillars of the Islamic faith. Each year, some Chinese Muslims who are unable to receive official permits for Hajj enter Mecca with business visas issued in a third country. The Sinophone Muslim communities in Saudi Arabia have frequently aided these Chinese pilgrims to enter the Grand Mosque of Mecca. In addition, Sinophone Muslim clergies, scholars, journalists, teachers, and artists have also played important roles in bridging the gap between Chinese society and the Arab Islamic world through research, teaching, and art exhibition. Well connected to transnational religious organizations, the Christians and Buddhists have also contributed to this cultural transnationality (Wang, 2020c).

Education is highly valued and prioritized in Chinese societies. Chinese international students have become an important component in sustaining cultural and social transnationality. Unlike the OECD countries, the MENA region lacks world-class educational institutions that would attract a large influx of Chinese students. Just a decade ago, most Chinese university or post-graduate students in the MENA were either Muslims who were pursuing Islamic studies, or university students or academics who came to learn the Arabic language and conduct research on the MENA region. Before the Arab Spring, Egypt and Syria were the key educational destinations in the MENA for Chinese students. The pattern has begun to change as the Gulf states accelerated their investment in higher education around 2000. Some universities in the UAE, Qatar, and Saudi Arabia are now competing globally to attract talented students worldwide. For example, King Abdullah University of Science and Technology (KAUST), NYU-Abu Dhabi, Khalifa University, the American University of Sharjah, the University of Sharjah, and the University of Wollongong in Dubai, among others, all have enrolled sizable numbers of Chinese students—some are locally based while others are international students from China. Currently, around 50 Chinese Muslim students are enrolled at Al Qasimia University in Sharjah, a state-of-the-art Islamic higher learning institution. Israel has also been keen on promoting social and cultural exchanges with China through various educational exchange programs and generous scholarships (Witte, 2011). Although the number of Chinese students in the MENA is still small, they play an increasingly important role in strengthening the transnational ties between the MENA and China through their daily activities and their participation on social media. They may well become opinion leaders in the future.

Chinese language education for children born or raised in the MENA is another vital dimension of transnationality. Using Chinese school textbooks in language lessons and participating in various educational events organized in collaboration with organizations inside China are two examples of transnational flows of ideas. Chinese children growing up in the MENA countries will inevitably become key bridge makers. Interracial/interreligious marriages also foster cultural transnationality. With the rapid growth of social media and virtual networks, such marriages are likely to increase in number. Recently, some Chinese women married to Arabs or Muslims have started sharing their daily lives and observations of Arab Muslim societies on Chinese-language social media. As these bloggers garner more followers, they may help to dispel misunderstandings in Arab culture and Muslim society. In these cases, the flow of population leads to the flow of ideas between China and the MENA. Yet, there has been no scholarly research that probes the virtual transnationality sustained by overseas Chinese communities in the MENA at the grassroots level.

Finally, whether state-sponsored initiatives, commercial activities or events for educational purposes, cultural and social exchanges have gained prominence in Sino-MENA relations. This area of research is central to the study of China's soft power in the MENA. It also closely relates to the status of ethnic and religious minorities among the overseas Chinese communities. While China's soft power project is largely associated with exchanges fostered by governmental institutions, such as Confucius Institutes, the CCTV Arabic channel, the *People's Daily* Arabic edition, and government-sponsored educational exchange programs, grass-root activities by overseas Chinese communities may be more effective in increasing interconnectivity between countries by connecting people's hearts.

Conclusion

Studying overseas Chinese in the MENA is a challenging task. First, the Chinese population in the MENA is small and scattered across a vast region containing some 24 countries that vary widely in economic and human development. The global and local political, social, and economic conditions limit researchers' accessibility to the field. Second, the concept of "overseas Chinese" is not yet clearly defined in the context of emigration from China to the MENA. The history of early migration to the MENA states is poorly documented. A study of ethnic and religious minorities in the Chinese diaspora is politically sensitive. Third, to probe the transnational connections of overseas Chinese in the

MENA, researchers need to overcome multiple language barriers, be relatively free to move across borders, and gain access to the virtual network. The transient lifestyle that characterizes overseas Chinese in the MENA and the volatile market conditions increase the difficulty for researchers in maintaining contact with their interlocutors. Despite these challenges, as elaborated throughout this chapter, overseas Chinese in the MENA deserve much more scholarly attention than they receive now. Collaborations across disciplines—history, political science, sociology, anthropology, and economics—are the bedrock of studying overseas Chinese in the MENA.

Notes

1 For a review of studies by Chinese scholars on overseas Chinese in the Middle East, see Ji, (2015) and Zhang (2017). For English publications on Chinese populations in the Middle East, see Armijo (2013); Jeong (2016); Al-Sudairi (2018: 16–18); and Wang (2020b).
2 "BRI: A Bridge of Friendship among Civilizations," CGTN, April 26, 2019. Available at: https://tinyurl.com/5d3nv5jr
3 The United Front is a long-standing Leninist method of building coalitions with non-Communist groups to consolidate the "leadership authority" of the Communist Party. In the last decade, the administration of Xi Jinping has restructured the United Front Work Department, considerably expanding its power to reach out to non-Party politicians, scholars, religious groups, and businesses, among others, in overseas Chinese communities. For more discussion of the CCP's United Front work in the Middle East, see Al-Sudairi (2018).
4 Statistics were compiled based on the *World Factbook* (CIA, n.d.).
5 For more detailed discussions of China-Middle East relations, see Olimat (2012). For China-Maghreb relations, see Zoubir (2019).
6 Expatriates are more commonly associated with professionals and skilled workers who reside outside their native countries, while sojourners usually connote low-skilled workers.
7 Ministry of Commerce, People's Republic of China (n.d.).
8 The full text of China's Arab Policy Paper is available at www.china.org.cn/world/2016-01/14/content_37573547.htm
9 For a detailed discussion of community institutions in Chinese diasporic communities, see Zhou and Lee (2013).

References

Al-Sudairi, M. (2018). *The Communist Party of China's United Front Work in the Gulf: The "Ethnic Minority Overseas Chinese" of Saudi Arabia as a Case Study*. Riyadh: King Faisal Center for Research and Islamic Studies, pp. 16–18.
Armijo, J. (2013). "China and the Gulf: The Social and Cultural Implications of Their Rapidly Developing Economic Ties," in T. Niblock (Ed.). *Asia-Gulf Economic Relations in the 21st Century*. Berlin: Gerlach Press, pp. 225–240.
Calabrese, J. (2021). "'The New Algeria' and China," Middle East Institute, January 26. Available at: www.mei.edu/publications/new-algeria-and-china
CIA. (n.d.). *The World Factbook: Middle East*. Available at: www.cia.gov/the-world-factbook/middle-east/
Jeong, H. (2016). *A Song of the Red Sea: Communities and Networks of Chinese Muslims in the Hijaz*. Riyadh: King Faisal Center for Research and Islamic Studies.
Ji, K. [冀开运]. (2015). "Research on Overseas Chinese Affairs in the Middle East" [中东华侨华人若干问题研究], *Middle East Studies* [中东问题研究], 1.
Jia, Y. et al. [贾益民等]. (2020). *Annual Report on Overseas Chinese Study (2020)* [华侨华人研究报告2020]. Beijing: Social Science Literature Press [社会科学文献出版社].
Li, A. [李安山]. (2003). "Ethnic Minority Overseas Chinese: Migration Characteristics, Standards for Identification, and Demographic Statistics" [少数民族华侨华人: 迁徙特点、辨识标准及人数统计], *Journal of Overseas Chinese History* [华人华侨历史研究], 3. Available at: https://caspu.pku.edu.cn/docs/20171204132339987390.pdf

Matthews, G., Lin, D., and Yang, Y. (2017). *The World in Guangzhou: Africans and Other Foreigners in South China's Global Marketplace*. Chicago: University of Chicago Press.

Miles, S. B. (2020). *Chinese Diaspora: A Social History of Global Migration*. New York: Cambridge University Press.

Ministry of Commerce, People's Republic of China. (n.d.) "Guide to Overseas Investment by Countries (Area)." Available at: www.mofcom.gov.cn/dl/gbdqzn/upload/libiya.pdf

Mueller, S. (2008). "The Nexus of U.S. Public Diplomacy and Citizen Diplomacy," in N. Snow and P. M. Taylor (Eds.), *Routledge Handbook of Public Diplomacy*, New York: Routledge, pp. 101–109.

Nash, P. (2012). "China's 'Going Out' Strategy," *Diplomatic Courier*, May 10. Available at: www.diplomaticourier.com/posts/china-s-going-out-strategy

Olimat, M. (2012). *China and the Middle East: From Silk Road to Arab Spring*. London: Routledge.

Wang, G. (1991). *China and the Chinese Overseas*. Singapore: Times Academic Press.

Wang, Q. [王庆丰]. (1986). "A Brief History of Uyghur's Migration to West Asia" [维吾尔族华侨移居西亚史探], *Overseas Chinese History* [华人华侨历史], 3.

Wang, Y. (2020a). "Making Chinese Spaces in Dubai: A Spatial Consideration of Chinese Transnational Communities in the Arabian Gulf," *Journal of Arabian Studies*, 2(2): 269–287.

Wang, Y. (2020b). *Chinese in Dubai: Money, Pride and Soul-Searching*. Leiden: Brill.

Wang, Y. (2020c). "Diverse Religious Experiences among Overseas Chinese in the United Arab Emirates," in N. Cao, G. Giordan and F. Yang (Eds.), *Chinese Religions Going Global*. Leiden: Brill, pp. 236–254.

Witte, C. (2011). "A Vision of China-Israel Academic Interchange," *Asian Jewish Life*, 6. Available at: http://asianjewishlife.org/images/issues/spring2011/PDFs/Viewpoint_Vision-of-China.pdf

Zerba, S. H. (2014). "China's Libya Evacuation Operation: A New Diplomatic Imperative—Overseas Citizen Protection," *Journal of Contemporary China*, 23(90): 1093–1112.

Zhang, G. (2010). "Distribution Patterns and Growth Trends of Overseas Chinese," *Overseas Chinese Affairs Study*, 4. Available at: http://qwgzyj.gqb.gov.cn/yjytt/155/1830.shtml

Zhang, X. [张秀明]. (2017). "Overseas Chinese in the Middle East and the Construction of 'One Belt and One Road'" [中东地区华侨华人与 '一带一路' 建设], in *Annual Report on Overseas Chinese Study (2016)* [华侨华人研究报告]. Beijing: Social Science Literature Press [社会科学文献出版社].

Zhou, M. and Lee, R. (2013). "Transnationalism and Community Building: Chinese Immigrant Organizations in the United States," *The Annals of the American Academy of Political and Social Sciences*, 647: 22–49.

Zoubir, Y. H. (2019). "Chinese Relations with the Maghreb: The Leading Role of Algeria," *Confluences Méditerranées*, 109(2): 91–103.

30
CHINA'S TOURISM IN THE MIDDLE EAST AND NORTH AFRICA
Trends and Outlook

April A. Herlevi

Introduction

The People's Republic of China (PRC) uses economic statecraft to achieve its development and foreign policy goals (Reilly, 2013; Zhang, 2014; Norris, 2016; Lim, Ferguson, and Bishop, 2020). China's economic statecraft has many components, including trade, aid, investment, and engagement with international organizations. Tourism, as a form of trade-in-services, has been an understudied component of the economic statecraft literature despite the tourism industry's contributions to economic growth. Many countries in the Middle East and North Africa (MENA) region have included strategies to attract tourism from China in their long-term growth plans. However, in 2020, the novel coronavirus disease (COVID-19) spread and halted global tourism. Both outbound tourism and the countries depending on inbound tourism for economic growth and employment were heavily impacted. Given these factors, this chapter makes two substantive contributions. First, we outline the descriptive trends related to China's outbound tourism to the MENA region over the past 25 years. Second, we examine those trends considering the COVID-19 pandemic and assess prospects for future tourism flows from China.

China's Belt and Road Initiative (BRI) has generated much debate. Blanchard (2020: 159) describes how debates about the BRI range from predicting "earthshattering effects" at one extreme to complete failure or stagnation at the other extreme. The reality lies somewhere between these extremes and these wide-ranging assertions have also been seen in the tourism sector with some countries predicting a massive influx of tourists from China (*Times of Oman*, 2019; Lin, Liu, and Song, 2015) or making overly optimistic predictions about what the BRI can bring to a country's economy (Hillman, 2020). While tourism remained modest in the MENA region as compared to China's tourism within Asia (Lin, Liu, and Song, 2015), the tourism industry had been an increasing component of trade between China and the MENA countries. We are now at an inflection point that will allow scholars to study tourism patterns before and after the pandemic and assess whether those trends will return or evolve differently. To predict future outcomes, we

DOI: 10.4324/9781003048404-34

must first examine prior patterns and put China's outbound tourism into context as a form of international cooperation and tool of economic statecraft.

Tourism policies serve as a carrot, providing financial incentives to countries interested in expanding their own tourism sectors, and as a stick, when tourists are discouraged from traveling to a particular destination to punish that state's behavior. To examine these dimensions of tourism, we address several key questions. First, what are the trends in China's outbound tourism to the MENA region? To address this question, we examine regional trends and select cases to provide context to those regional trends. Second, how does the PRC guide and manage tourism as one aspect of its overall economic statecraft? Inherent in the second question is the need to examine both PRC policy objectives and those of the recipient country. Many countries want to promote tourism as a component of their economic development. Some countries have a longer history with the tourism sector whereas others are new to the market or uniquely seeking to attract Chinese tourists. Third, given the dramatic effects of the COVID-19 pandemic on the tourism sector, we must ask: what will the impacts of the pandemic be on China's outbound tourism to the MENA region? After the pandemic, will tourism rebound? Will Chinese tourists resume travel abroad and, if so, will they remain in Asia or return to destinations in the MENA region? Which destinations will re-emerge as potential locations of choice? While we recognize that answers to the final set of questions cannot yet be answered, we pose them because the abrupt halt to global tourism has created a potential natural experiment that may offer unique insights into tourism as a tool of economic statecraft.

In the next section, we survey the academic literature on tourism and economic statecraft to synthesize the evolution of China's outbound tourism. This theoretical section addresses the first two research questions. The next section shifts from the theoretical to the demonstrable, exploring descriptive trends and highlighting the limitations of the current tourism data. The conclusion focuses on the third research question, positing whether past precedents are the best guide for the post-COVID-19 resumption of tourism. The expectation, however, is that once the pandemic is resolved and tourism flows resume, the forthcoming data will provide unique ways to compare pre- and post-COVID-19 trends in a sector that requires the physical movement of people to create economic growth.

Theoretical Foundations: Tourism as Economic Statecraft

In this section, we merge the theoretical literatures on tourism flows and economic statecraft. James Reilly (2013: 2) defines economic statecraft as "the use of economic resources by political leaders to exert influence in pursuit of foreign policy objectives." The tools of economic statecraft may include investment, preferential trade agreements, favorable monetary policies, or the threat of taking away any of those positive benefits through sanctions (Baldwin, 1985; Drezner, 1999). China's main strategies include providing capital (aid and investment) and encouraging trade. At its core, tourism is a form of trade in services (Mendez-Parra, 2017; Jensen and Zhang, 2013). However, for the tourism industry to flourish, it is often necessary to build a foundation for that industry to grow, which can include providing foreign aid to build infrastructure and foreign direct investment (FDI) to facilitate tourism flows into that country. Tourism and, more broadly, trade in services are facets of economic statecraft that have only been studied minimally in the literature as tools of foreign influence (Baldwin, 1985; Zhang, 2014; Blackwill and Harris, 2016; Norris, 2016).

During the reform era, China primarily used "economics to support political goals" [以经促政] and has employed coercive measures in addition to providing aid and FDI (Rosenberg, Harrell, and Feng, 2020). Zhang (2014) explores China's economic statecraft in the Cold War period but, given the severe restrictions on travel for PRC citizens during that time, tourism was essentially non-existent. Norris (2016) advances our understanding of the conditions "under which China is more or less successful in its pursuit of economic statecraft" objectives by providing a framework for examining commercial actors. While Norris addresses tourism flows between China and Taiwan, he does not address tourism as statecraft in other locations. Initially, the size and scope of Chinese tourism to the MENA region were small; the sector grew as China's policy controls for outbound tourism changed. PRC domestic policy encouraged the development of the tourism sector. For example, revisions to China's Tourism Law (2016) state that the regulatory rules for tourism are meant to "protect the lawful rights and interests of tourists and tourism operators, regulate the tourism market ... and *promote sustainable tourism development*" both at home and abroad.

Lim, Ferguson, and Bishop (2020: 4) analyze how individual choices and government policy affect tourism flows and bilateral relations, noting that studies of economic sanctions and interdependence have focused on trade, but their emphasis has almost entirely been on *merchandise trade*. Different market and regulatory factors shape trade in services, and thus the tourism sector must be examined in this context. For tourism, the trade pattern "requires the 'importing' consumer to be physically present in the 'exporting' country" (ibid.: 4). Moreover, China can impose sanctions by simply not allowing its residents to travel to particular countries, which is more subtle than traditional sanctions policy. Similarly, the PRC can remove a positive inducement to outbound tourism flows to a particular country by simply altering domestic policy regulations that may not be transparent to external observers.

In terms of positive economic inducements, China encourages the tourism industry and attempts to increase outbound tourism to specific locations through its "Approved Destination Status" (ADS) list (PRC State Council, 2009; Tourism Law of the People's Republic of China (2016 Revision), 2016; PRC Ministry of Culture and Tourism, 2019; Lim, Ferguson, and Bishop, 2020).[1] China has also limited tourism to particular destinations through negative sanctions by removing countries from the ADS list for violating the "one China policy" (Harrell, Rosenberg, and Saravelle, 2018; Vavra, 2018).[2] In general, China has not used the promotion of tourism flows nor restrictions on tourists to the Middle East and Africa in the same way it has in the Asia-Pacific, but tourism as a tool of negative sanctions, could serve as one source of "latent power" (Sun and Zoubir, 2020: 15) should the tourism sector rebound after the resolution of the COVID-19 pandemic.

In terms of scope, the MENA region examined in this chapter includes 25 countries or territories: Algeria, Bahrain, Comoros, Djibouti, Egypt, Iran, Iraq, Israel, Jordan, Kuwait, Lebanon, Libya, Malta, Mauritania, Morocco, Oman, Qatar, Saudi Arabia, Somalia, Sudan, Syria, Tunisia, the United Arab Emirates (UAE), the West Bank and Gaza, and Yemen.[3] Thus, this region includes Arab and non-Arab states, large African countries, and small Gulf states; within this region, data availability varies widely.[4] We describe overall trends with official international statistics, but note that no tourism data was available from our main source, the United Nations World Tourism Organization (UNWTO, 2020a) for Comoros, Djibouti, Mauritania, Iran, Somalia, the West Bank and Gaza, and Yemen. In some cases, such as Qatar and the UAE, tourist arrivals have only been reported in recent years (2017–2018), even though tourism had been open to China prior to that time. In short, there are serious gaps in the empirical data that hamper our ability to generalize to all countries in the MENA region.

How Does China Control Outbound Tourism?

China has included the expansion of tourism as an element of its economic and foreign policy for several decades. China's 12th Five-Year Plan (FYP), which covered 2011 to 2015, specifically laid out measures to enhance domestic and international tourism. The 12th FYP (Chapter 16, Section 2) primarily focused on building the domestic tourist industry stating that the PRC, "will comprehensively develop domestic tourism, actively develop inbound tourism, and encourage the orderly development of outbound tourism." The outline for the 14th FYP, released by the PRC State Council (2021), reiterated tourism as an important component within the larger services sector, describing the need for digitalization but also "strict market supervision" [严格市场监管]. In 1995, "the China National Tourism Administration (CNTA) formalized the Approved Destination Status (ADS) program," which allowed Chinese travel agencies to market and sell leisure group tours for Chinese citizens and provided a means for travel agencies to obtain visas in bulk, streamlining procedures for travelers (Arita et al., 2011: 983–4). Up until 2018, all regulations guiding outbound tourism were handled under the CNTA, which has been subsumed under the Ministry of Culture and Tourism (CCP Central Committee, 2018). Egypt was the first MENA country to sign an ADS, which opened pathways for increased tourism (Arita et al., 2011). The PRC government continues to manage tourism through the ADS. As of 2018, the ADS list included 130 countries, which is a drop from the 140 ADS agreements in 2010 (Lanteigne, 2013: 42). Of that total, 13 MENA countries have ADS agreements with the PRC, as shown in Table 30.1, which lists the year that the agreement was approved. [5]

Table 30.1 MENA countries with Approved Destination Status agreements with China

Country	Year ADS agreement signed
Egypt	2002
Malta	2002
Jordan	2004
Tunisia	2004
Morocco	2007
Syria	2007
Oman	2007
Israel	2008
UAE	2009
Lebanon	2010
Iran	2011
Sudan	2017
Qatar	2018

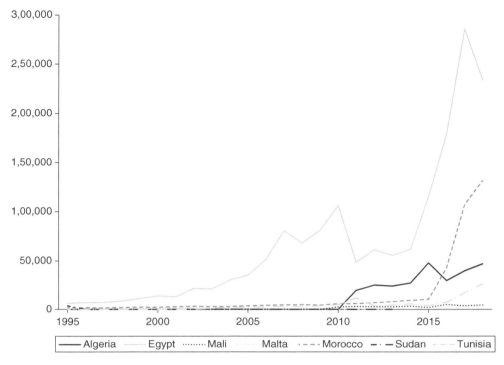

Figure 30.1 North Africa, Chinese tourist arrivals, 1995–2018
Source: Data from UNWTO (2020a).

Empirical Realities: Trends, Locations, and Prospects

During the 1990s and 2000s, China's outbound tourism grew by roughly 17 percent per year, resulting in an increase from 2.9 million travelers early in the 1990s to over 70 million by 2011 (Lin, Liu, and Song, 2015). China had millions of tourists abroad, but only a small fraction traveled to the MENA region.[6] Figures 30.1 and 30.2 show tourism arrivals in the region, which both remained modest until after 2010. Figure 30.1 depicts destinations in North Africa, whereas Figure 30.2 depicts destinations in the Middle East and Gulf States. We show the two sub-regions separately, in part, because Egypt dominates arrivals across both regions. As Figure 30.1 shows, Egypt's tourism arrivals began increasing after 2005, declined slightly after 2010, then grew again, reaching a peak in 2017 at 287,260 arrivals (UNWTO, 2020a). Tourism arrivals are much more varied among Middle East and Gulf States, and rarely exceeded 25,000 tourists per year until the 2010s (ibid.). The top three countries for China's tourist arrivals have been Egypt, Morocco, and Israel (ibid.). Like Egypt, Morocco's and Israel's tourist arrivals peaked in 2017 as well, with 132,081 and 114,068 Chinese tourists respectively.[7]

A key indicator of tourism flows from China is an ADS agreement. According to econometric analysis using a gravity model of tourism, having an ADS increases Chinese arrivals, on average, by approximately 52 percent in the three years following the signing of an agreement (Arita et al., 2011). This pattern holds in some MENA countries (Egypt, Iran, Israel) but not in others (Lebanon, Tunisia). For example, Egypt and China

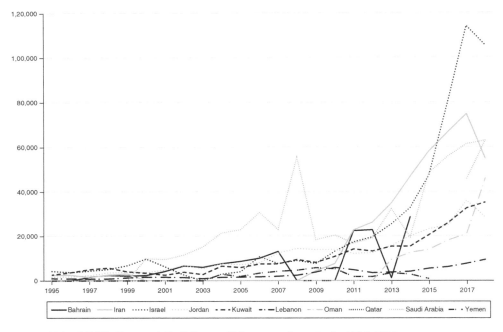

Figure 30.2 Middle East and Gulf States, Chinese tourist arrivals, 1995–2018
Source: Data from UNWTO (2020a).

formally agreed to increase tourism ties between the two countries in late 2001. At that time, "Egyptian Tourism Minister Mamdouh Beltagui … stressed that Egypt will try its best to satisfy the need of Chinese tourists" (PRC Embassy, 2002). The ADS went into effect in 2002 and tourism arrivals increased from 21,381 in 2003 to nearly 35,300 by 2005 (UNWTO, 2020a), resulting in an approximately 62 percent rise over that three-year period.

Between 2013 and 2018, two main trends in larger China-MENA relations generated interest in expanding tourism. The first was the expansion of China's signature foreign policy program, the BRI, and the second was a set of initiatives launched under the purview of China's "Arab Policy." According to official Chinese media, from 2016 onwards, "Beijing planned to send 150 million travelers to countries along the Belt and Road … with expected expenditures of $200 billion" (Chaziza, 2019). Also in 2016, Xi Jinping visited "three of the region's most powerful capitals: Riyadh, Tehran, and Cairo" and launched several key initiatives (Molavi, 2020). According to the PRC Ministry of Foreign Affairs' "Arab Policy Paper," the Chinese government would encourage tourism ties by welcoming "Arab states' application for the Approved Destination Status for outbound group tours by Chinese tourists" (PRC MFA, 2016). Qatar took advantage of this, and in 2017 negotiated an ADS agreement (PRC Ministry of Culture and Tourism, 2019).

Comparing Gulf States: Oman and the United Arab Emirates

Oman and the UAE are each an example of MENA countries actively courting Chinese tourism. In 2018, outbound tourism from the PRC to the UAE reached approximately

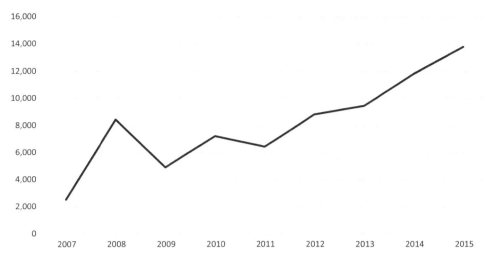

Figure 30.3 Chinese tourist arrivals to Oman, 2007–2015
Source: Data from the Oman National Centre for Statistics and Information (2018).

1,481,040, as measured in "arrivals of non-resident tourists in hotels and similar establishments, by nationality" (UNWTO, 2020a). For the MENA region, this meant that the UAE had, at least in 2018, overtaken Egypt as the main destination for Chinese tourists. According to the Chinese Outbound Travel Research Institute, "high net-worth individuals" were a key demographic for the UAE, with the Emirates "ranked as the 9th most popular destination" for Chinese tourists in this category (*Times of Oman*, 2019).

For Oman, Chinese tourist arrivals increased after the approval of an ADS in 2007, as shown in Figure 30.3. According to the Oman National Centre for Statistics and Information (2018), arrivals from China grew to 8,427 in 2008, up from 2,510 in 2007. Yet, those totals remained small with only 5,000–10,000 arrivals from 2009 until 2013. Chinese tourism arrivals increased again between 2013 and 2015, rising from 9,460 to over 13,829 travelers. Chinese tourist arrivals then skyrocketed to 64,000 in the first half of 2019, which represented nearly a 40 percent increase over arrivals in 2018 (*Oman Observer*, 2019). According to Oman's Ministry of Tourism, as reported in the *Oman Observer*, one reason for targeting China was to develop "key non-oil sectors" by "promoting Oman as a niche market." Oman was set to expand tourism from China further with media reporting that it hoped to attract 75,000 Chinese tourists by 2023, and over "11 million visitors by 2040" (Castelier, 2020).

What Can We Expect After the COVID-19 Pandemic?

Despite the hopes of the MENA governments to increase tourism, the COVID-19 pandemic disrupted those plans. Until the pandemic, tourism was set to grow. The UNWTO (2020c) notes that, "according to 2019 data, tourism generated 7 percent of global trade" and was the "third largest export sector of the global economy." In the MENA region, several countries were heavily reliant on tourism. Tourism receipts, measured as a percentage of exports (World Bank, 2021b), were high for Lebanon (48 percent), Egypt (26.6 percent), Jordan (42 percent), Morocco (22 percent), and Qatar (17 percent).

Table 30.2 Tourism receipts as a percentage of exports, select MENA countries

Country name	2000	2019
Algeria	.	0.37
Bahrain	11.90	.
Djibouti	4.19	.
Egypt	27.62	26.64
Iran	2.28	.
Iraq	.	4.04
Israel	9.90	7.30
Jordan	26.42	42.14
Kuwait	1.85	1.61
Lebanon	.	47.97
Libya	0.69	.
Malta	20.43	.
Morocco	25.76	22.74
Oman	3.20	7.31
Qatar	.	17.00
Saudi Arabia	.	6.94
Syria	.	.
Tunisia	23.10	13.99
West Bank and Gaza	10.62	.

Source: World Bank (2021b).

Table 30.2 shows these estimates for MENA countries with available data on tourism receipts in both 2000 and 2019. Countries such as Egypt and Morocco have remained reliant on tourism receipts in both time periods, whereas some countries, such as Jordan, saw an increase in reliance on tourism prior to the pandemic in 2019. Tourism receipts for the UAE were not available, but Dubai's tourism receipts contributed approximately "18 percent to Dubai's GDP directly and 29 percent indirectly," according to earlier estimates by Balakrishnan (2008: 72). The UNWTO (2020c: 5) estimates that COVID-19 has likely resulted in the "loss of $910 billion to $1.2 trillion in exports from tourism," and thus a "loss of 1.5 percent to 2.8 percent of global GDP." The effects of the pandemic on tourism-related economic development have been staggering, but also present an opportunity for many countries in the region to re-think how tourism is promoted, managed, and re-built.

Conclusion

China's tourism growth to the MENA region in the 2010s appeared to be on a continual upward trajectory. A wide range of economic, trade, and security ties were emerging between the PRC and key countries in the Middle East, and relations between China and North Africa were also on an upward trajectory as development finance under the BRI continued. With China's growing middle class, the prospects for the tourism industry seemed limitless. Then the COVID-19 pandemic emerged. Outbound tourism halted and global travel was replaced with quarantines and travel bans. For nearly two decades, outbound tourist arrivals from China had increased, and there was an expectation that those tourism numbers would only continue to rise. While we are still evaluating the impacts of the pandemic, the dramatic changes to the tourism sector will present scholars with a unique natural experiment. To preview these opportunities, we first summarize the chapter's findings and then discuss three trends to watch as the world emerges from the COVID-19 pandemic.

Two observations provide the foundation for future research, one focused on PRC policies and the other on tourism development policies of the host nation. First, the PRC is not monolithic; tourism policy practices, including programs such as ADS agreements, are created by bureaucratic actors that have their own unique goals. Prior to the pandemic, those goals were primarily to enhance China's economic development, and foreign policy goals, such as the BRI, were meant to enhance the PRC government's connectivity with other countries (Xinhua, 2017). At times though, domestic concerns conflicted with those connectivity goals. In 2018, the Chinese government explicitly discussed encouraging control over the tourism market as part of its restructuring of its regulatory bureaucracy (CCP, 2018) and the necessity for monitoring and control has only increased with the pandemic. International travel is now intertwined with health, safety, and the potential risks of spreading contagious diseases. Thus, protecting the health of PRC citizens abroad will become a critical component of outbound tourism policies.

Second, the future of tourism in the MENA region will depend on how these countries emerge from the pandemic. Egypt was the long-time leader in tourism arrivals from China, but in the years before the pandemic, the Gulf states had been actively courting tourism inflows. Oman, the UAE, and recently, Qatar, became "approved destinations" under the PRC tourism regulations. China has also been working with some MENA countries on COVID-19 testing and vaccination. For example, China has been working with the national governments in the Gulf; in December 2020, the UAE and Bahrain approved use of the Sinopharm vaccine (Cyranoski, 2020). The Sinopharm vaccine "is also undergoing phase III testing in Egypt, Jordan" so those countries may be on the path to approving the vaccine as well (ibid.). Should those efforts to increase the safety of travel be successful, these locations could see an influx of Chinese tourists hoping to travel abroad, while simultaneously limiting the risks of spreading COVID-19. On the demand-side of tourism flows, we must acknowledge the data limitations (Pratt and Tolkach, 2018; UNWTO, 2020b). The UNWTO (2020a) data does not include countries such as Comoros, Djibouti, Iraq, Libya, Mauritania, Oman, Somalia, Syria, or Yemen so it is difficult to assess past trends or future prospects. Some major destinations, such as the UAE, have only limited data, often only for one or two years. Thus, this chapter captures only a general, but not complete, picture of the region's past tourism trends.

Trends to Watch in China-MENA Tourism

The first trend to watch is simply whether or not tourism arrivals return, and if so, what the characteristics associated with those locations are. There are significant problems with the data gathering related to tourism statistics, but the pause due to COVID-19 presents an opportunity to re-think tourism promotion policies. Governments, investment and tourism promotion agencies, and international organizations should evaluate how they gather data, which programs are worth investing in, and how tourism can be done safely and sustainably in a vastly different global market. As many government budgets have been strained by the pandemic response, politicians and government officials will need to evaluate whether tourism promotion is a good use of resources and how tourism has helped and could help their economic recovery.

The second trend to watch is how the relationship between domestic and international tourism evolves in China. In the 1990s and 2000s, much of China's "outbound" tourists were actually traveling to Hong Kong, Macao, and Taiwan, which could all be considered part of "greater China" (Pratt and Tolkach, 2018). In the early 2010s, one aspect of efforts to keep Hong Kong and Macau tightly woven with the "Chinese nation" was supporting the two Special Administrative Region's status as "global tourism and leisure center[s]" (Delegation of the European Union in China, 2011: Chapter 57). Given the challenges of COVID-19 travel, there may be a renewed emphasis on keeping tourists closer to home. Similarly, COVID-19-induced restrictions, testing, and vaccine requirements may prompt tourists to travel to locations already approved by the PRC government. China's early coordination with the UAE on COVID-19 testing kits (*Global Times*. 2020) could encourage a return to tourism between these countries, but other destinations, such as Egypt and Morocco, may not see a return to pre-pandemic levels of tourism. Thus, one area of China's economic statecraft may no longer be as influential as it was pre-pandemic but could become an opportunity to cultivate tourism ties with a select set of national partners.

The third trend to watch is China's official government action encouraging (or discouraging) tourism, and whether that follows pre-pandemic patterns. Tourism is not an explicit part of China's BRI, but "unimpeded trade, financial integration and people-to-people bonds" (Xinhua, 2017) have all been touted as elements of Xi Jinping's signature foreign policy effort and China's strategic partnerships (Strüver, 2017) . If China is intent on continuing its BRI connections with countries in the MENA region, then increasing tourism post-COVID may help meet that objective. However, these trends will not be fully evaluated until the pandemic is resolved and future outbreaks of this type will not strain the health care systems of the host nations.

In closing, this chapter has shown how tourism from China to the MENA region increased from the mid-1990s to 2018, especially in the 2010s. These international interactions supported PRC foreign policy goals and the economic and development goals of the destination countries. Prior to the pandemic, there were ample opportunities for air travel companies, travel-associated companies, and investment promotion agencies to benefit from increasing interlinks between China and the MENA countries. However, the COVID-19 pandemic halted that interconnectivity and the question now is whether that halt is temporary or permanent. As the future unfolds, we will learn whether this element of China's economic statecraft has the potential to shape future relations in the Middle East and North Africa, or whether China-MENA tourism ties were simply a short-lived experiment, limited in time, scope, and duration.

Notes

1 In PRC policy documents, ADS is typically referenced as "Outbound Travel Destination Countries and Region" [出境旅游目的地国家和地区]. In the academic literature, the ADS acronym is regularly used so that convention has been adopted here.
2 As one example, China removed the Republic of Palau from its ADS list because Palau would not end its diplomatic recognition of Taiwan (Vavra, 2018).
3 This includes all countries listed as in the MENA region by the World Bank (2021a), and any countries included as a member of the League of Arab States.

4 Of the 25 countries in this analysis, quantitative tourism data was obtained from the UNWTO for 17 countries. For Oman, Sudan, and the UAE, UNWTO data was only available for a limited number of years.

5 Author dataset based on PRC Ministry of Culture and Tourism (2019) travel regulations.

6 The bulk of Chinese tourists remained in "greater China" (Taiwan, Hong Kong, or Macao) or other destinations in Asia.

7 According to the UNWTO (2020a), the UAE had over 1.4 million tourists arrivals from China in 2018. However, no data sources were found to verify this data or obtain a longer time series in order to include the UAE in the trend analysis.

References

Arita, S., Edmonds, C., La Croix, S. and Mak, J. (2011). "Impact of Approved Destination Status on Chinese Travel Abroad: An Econometric Analysis." *Tourism Economics* 17(5): 983–996. https://doi.org/10.5367/te.2011.0076

Balakrishnan, M.S. (2008). "Dubai - A Star in the East: A Case Study in Strategic Destination Branding." *Journal of Place Management and Development* 1(1): 62–91.. https://doi.org/10.1108/17538330810865345

Baldwin, D. (1985). *Economic Statecraft*. Princeton, NJ: Princeton University Press.

Blackwill, R., and Harris, J. (2016). *War by Other Means: Geoeconomics and Statecraft*. Cambridge, MA: Harvard University Press.

Blanchard, J. F. (2020). "Problematic Prognostications about China's Maritime Silk Road Initiative (MSRI): Lessons from Africa and the Middle East." *Journal of Contemporary China* 29(122): 159–174. https://doi.org/10.1080.10670564.2019.1637565

Castelier, S. (2020). "Coronavirus: Oman's Tourism Sector Takes a Hit." *The New Arab*, March 12. Available at: https://english.alaraby.co.uk/english/indepth/2020/3/12/coronavirus-omans-tourism-sector-takes-a-hit

CCP (Chinese Communist Party) Central Committee. (2018). "Deepening Party and National Reform Mechanisms Program" [深化党和国家机构改革方案]. March 21. Available at: www.gov.cn/zhengce/2018-03/21/content_5276191.htm#1

Chaziza, M. (2019). "Tourism as a Stealth Weapon." *Middle East Quarterly* 26(4): 1–8.

Cyranoski, D. (2020). "Arab Nations First to Approve Chinese COVID Vaccine — Despite Lack of Public Data." *Nature*, December 14. Available at: www.nature.com/articles/d41586-020-03563-z

Delegation of the European Union in China. (2011). "China's 12th Five-Year Plan (2011–2015)." Translation. May 11. Available at: http://cbi.typepad.com/china_direct/2011/05/chinas-twelfth-five-new-plan-the-full-english-version.html#sthash.LdNR8hQ1.dpuf

Drezner, D. (1999). *The Sanctions Paradox: Economic Statecraft and International Relations*. New York: Cambridge University Press.

Global Times. (2020). "China, UAE Launch Lab to Speed up Coronavirus Testing, Diagnosis." April 2. Available at: www.globaltimes.cn/content/1184566.shtml

Harrell, P., Rosenberg, E., and Saravelle, E. (2018). "China's Use of Coercive Economic Measures." Washington, DC: Center for New American Security. Available at: www.cnas.org/publications/reports/chinas-use-of-coercive-economic-measures

Hillman, J. (2020). *The Emperor's New Road: China and the Project of the Century*. New Haven, CT: Yale University Press.

Jensen, C. and Zhang, J. (2013). "Trade in Tourism Services: Explaining Tourism Trade and the Impact of the General Agreement on Trade in Services on the Gains from Trade." *The Journal of International Trade & Economic Development*, 22(3): 398–429. https://doi.org/10.1080/09638199.2011.574723

Lanteigne, M. (2013). *Chinese Foreign Policy: An Introduction*. London: Routledge.

Lim, D., Ferguson, V., and Bishop, R. (2020). "Chinese Outbound Tourism as an Instrument of Economic Statecraft." *Journal of Contemporary China*, 29(126): 916–933. https://doi.org/10.1080/10670564.2020.1744390

Lin, V. S., Liu, A. and Song, H. (2015). "Modeling and Forecasting Chinese Outbound Tourism: An Econometric Approach." *Journal of Travel & Tourism Marketing*, 32(1–2): 34–49. https://doi.org/10.1080/10548408.2014.986011

Mendez-Parra, M. (2017). "Policy Dimensions of Trade in Services and Economic Transformation." Paper presented at Trade, Services and Development UNCTAD Multi-year Expert Meeting, Geneva, July.

Molavi, A. (2020). "Enter the Dragon: China's Growing Influence in the Middle East and North Africa." Stanford, CA: Hoover Institution, Stanford University.

Norris, W. (2016). *Chinese Economic Statecraft: Commercial Actors, Grand Strategy, and State Control*. Ithaca, NY: Cornell University Press. Kindle edition.

Oman National Centre for Statistics and Information. (2018). "Number of Visitors, China, Inbound Tourism." Sultanate of Oman Data Portal. December. Available at: https://data.gov.om/dedblxg/tourism?regions=1000000-oman&nationality=1000230-china#

Oman Observer. (2019). "42% Rise in Chinese Tourists to Oman." September 18. Available at: www.omanobserver.om/42-rise-in-chinese-tourists-to-oman/

Pratt, S. and Tolkach, D. (2018). "The Politics of Tourism Statistics." *International Journal of Tourism Research*, 20: 299–307. Available at: https://doi.org/10.1002/jtr.2181

PRC Embassy (2002). "Egypt to Satisfy Need of Chinese Tourists: Egyptian Tourism Minister." Cairo, Egypt: Embassy of the People's Republic of China in the Arab Republic of Egypt. May 7. Available at: http://eg.china-embassy.org/eng/zaigx/dfymj/2002/t76241.htm

PRC Ministry of Culture and Tourism [文化和旅游部]. (2019). "Notice on the Prohibition of Organizing Tourist Travel to Countries (Regions) That Are Not Open to National Tourism," [关于禁止组织游客赴境外未开放旅游目的地国家(地区)旅游 的通告]. March 28. Available at: www.gylxs.com/Mobile/News/Info-3507.html

PRC MFA (Ministry of Foreign Affairs). (2016). "China's Arab Policy Paper." January 13. Available at: www.fmprc.gov.cn/mfa_eng/zxxx_662805/t1331683.shtml

PRC State Council. (2009). "旅游社条列" [Travel Agency Regulations]. Pub. L. No. Order No. 550 (2009). Available at: www.gov.cn/gongbao/content/2017/content_5219153.htm

PRC State Council. (2021). "第十四个五年规划和2035年远景目标纲要" [Outline of the Fourteenth Five-Year Plan and the 2035 Long-Term Goals]. Xinhua, March 13. Available at: www.gov.cn/xinwen/2021-03/13/content_5592681.htm

Reilly, J. (2013). "China's Economic Statecraft: Turning Wealth into Power." Lowy Institute for International Policy. Available at: www.lowyinstitute.org/publications/chinas-economic-statecraft-turning-wealth-power

Rosenberg, E., Harrell, P. and Feng, A. (2020). "A New Arsenal for Competition: Coercive Economic Measures in the US-China Relationship." Washington, DC: Center for New American Security. April. Available at: www.cnas.org/publications/reports/a-new-arsenal-for-competition

Strüver, G. (2017). "China's Partnership Diplomacy: International Alignment Based on Interests or Ideology." *The Chinese Journal of International Politics*, 10(1): 31–65. https://doi.org/10.1093/cjip/pow015

Sun, D. and Zoubir, Y. (2020). "Securing China's 'Latent Power': The Dragon's Anchorage in Djibouti." *Journal of Contemporary China*, 30(130): 677–692. https://doi.org/10.1080/10670564.2020.1852734

Times of Oman. (2019). "More than 75,000 Chinese Visitors Expected to Visit Oman by 2023: Report." December 18. Available at: https://timesofoman.com/article/more-than-75000-chinese-visitors-expected-to-visit-oman-by-2023-report

Tourism Law of the People's Republic of China. (2016 Revision) [中华人民共和国旅游法] (2016) Pub. L. No. Order No. 57 (2016). Available at: http://en.pkulaw.cn/display.aspx?cgid=f3b41d467e2d2e8dbdfb&lib=law

UNWTO (United Nations World Tourism Organization). (2020a). "China: Country-Specific Outbound Tourism, 1995–2018," January. Available at: www.e-unwto.org

UNWTO (United Nations World Tourism Organization). (2020b). "Outbound Tourism: Trips Abroad by Resident Visitors to Countries of Destination (Basis: Arrivals in Destination Countries) Methodological Notes." Available at: www.e-unwto.org

UNWTO (United Nations World Tourism Organization). (2020c). "Policy Brief: COVID-19 and Transforming Tourism," August. Available at: webunwto.s3.eu-west-1.amazonaws.com/s3fs-public/2020-08/SG-Policy-Brief-on-COVID-and-Tourism.pdf

Vavra, S. (2018). "Weaponized Tourism: China Uses Citizens as Diplomatic Pressure Points." Axios, August 25. Available at: www.axios.com/weaponized-tourism-china-uses-citizens-as-diplomatic-pressure-points-1535064926-e4995bd4-bf80-4e83-b032-17ec2f610bde.html

World Bank. (2021a). "World Bank Country and Lending Groups." In *World Bank Country and Lending Groups: World Development Indicators*. Washington, DC: World Bank. Available at: https://datahelpdesk.worldbank.org/knowledgebase/articles/906519-world-bank-country-and-lending-groups

World Bank. (2021b). "International Tourism, Receipts (% of Total Exports), World Development Indicators, ST.INT.RCPT.XP.ZS," May. Available at: https://datacatalog.worldbank.org/public-licenses#cc-by

Xinhua. 2017. "Full Text: Vision for Maritime Cooperation under the Belt and Road Initiative," June 20. Available at: www.xinhuanet.com/english/2017-06/20/c_136380414.htm

Zhang, S. G. 2014. *Beijing's Economic Statecraft during the Cold War, 1949–1991*. Baltimore, MD: Johns Hopkins University Press.

31

MIDDLE EASTERN STUDENTS IN CHINA

Motivations and Implications

Roie Yellinek

Introduction

As China's role in the international arena has grown, Middle Eastern people's attitudes to this rising power have changed. This change could be seen in economics, as most of the Middle Eastern countries have increased their trade and business with China; In politics, when high-level officials see China as a rival to US dominance in the region and favor more than once the Chinese side. And also, in many aspects of social life, from culture to high and elementary education, for example, as shown by the continued increase in the number of people who choose to learn Chinese.

This chapter looks at a relatively new phenomenon, whereby young Middle Eastern students choose to go to China to acquire their academic education and even sometimes to take their first career steps there. This relatively new phenomenon is significant, due to the fact that it shows the local attitudes toward China as a global power. This chapter describes a movement among the Middle Eastern youth that sees China as the right place "to be," i.e., that being in China can expand their chances in life, and it asks, why is that so? In addition, the chapter discusses the implications of this movement on the relationship between the China and the Middle Eastern countries.

The chapter is divided into two parts, the first broadly analyzes the role of the universities in shaping the future leadership and elites and describes the educational relationship between China and the Middle Eastern countries. The second describes the new phenomenon, seen from the perspective of a few young Middle Easterners who studied in China. Featuring broad analysis and the views of the students, given in interviews, the chapter provides a broad, unique view of the relations between the two sides, with a focus on how the Middle Eastern students view China.

The educational relations between the two parties go back to the eighteenth century when Chinese-Muslims went to study Islam and religious studies in Muslim countries in the Middle East. Al-Azhar University in Egypt was the center of the Sino-Muslim quest for authentic Arab Islam, when Ma Dexin (1794–1874), the famous Islamic scholar from Yunnan, visited the university and briefly studied there (Chen, 2014). He was the first person to translate the entire Qur'an into Chinese. Imam Wang Jingzhai also studied at Al-Azhar University along with several other Chinese Muslim students (Kurzman,

426

DOI: 10.4324/9781003048404-35

2002). Wang (1879–1949) was a well-known Muslim scholar during the Republic of China period. He was the second person to translate the entire Qur'an into Chinese (Bennett, 2013). In the 1930s, several groups of Muslim students from China arrived in order to study at Al-Azhar University in Cairo. They were destined to play an important role in the history of modern Chinese Islam (Zvi, 2008).

However, the other way around, i.e. Arabs going to China, is a relatively new phenomenon, and truly worthy of attention. The average annual growth rate of Arab students studying in Chinese universities and Chinese students at Arab universities has increased by 26 percent and 21 percent respectively in the 12 years from 2004 to 2016 (Sawahel, 2018). In 2011, China became a major destination for studying abroad, with around 265,090 foreign students studying there, according to China's Ministry of Education (*People's Daily*, 2011). In 2016, China was the third largest receiver of international students globally, with 442,773 international students and, by 2018, the numbers had grown to 492,185 with means 10.5 percent growth in a year (UNESCO Institute for Statistics, 2021). In 2013, the Middle East as a whole region sent 437,857 students abroad, in 2015, the number grew to 524,527 and in 2017, it rose to 567,486 students (ibid.). The growth in the number of Middle Eastern students in China is part of an international phenomenon, as reflected from the above numbers. Indeed, in recent years, more and more young people are choosing to leave their home country and move to acquire higher education in another country. The main reason for this development is globalization, which makes moving to a new place easier and quite a normal part of many people's lives. However, there is a uniqueness to each region and country, and this chapter specifically analyzes why Middle Eastern students choose to go to China to acquire their higher education, and not to traditional places, such as the USA, the UK, and France.

The USA hosts some of the best universities in the world and many other excellent institutes. The UK and France used to be the colonialist rulers of some of the Middle Eastern countries and there is a traditional connection between the locals and their higher education system. Therefore, what could China offer to young people in the Middle East? The chapter offers an answer which is divided into two sections: the first is based on geopolitical analyses and the second is based on interviews and conversations with relevant students.

After the end of the Cold War, the USA stood out as the one and only super-power. Therefore, the prestige of the USA attracts many to go there for academic studies and professional experience. From the early 2000s when China's economics and geopolitics were rising in parallel to the establishment of more and more academic and professional projects for foreigners at Chinese universities, an increasing number of young people went to China to study or start their career. Specifically, people from the Middle East chose to go to China, and not to the USA, and other Western countries after the massive terror attack of 9/11. For the Middle East, the reason for choosing China over the USA and the other Western countries, lies in the following: After the massive terror attack of 9/11, the US Immigration Authorities made the entry options for citizens from the Middle East very difficult, while China opened its borders to them and welcomed them for educational aspects and for other aspects, such as trade, and with the support of international organizations.

In addition, the fact that China offers a new model of success, which is not based on an open market, liberal thoughts, and democracy, makes it easier for people from non-democratic countries to find themselves and to adjust quickly to the new society. In addition, due to the fact that China was considered a developing country until recently, the curricula and the research focus all aimed to fill the gaps, while the USA and other Western countries focused on other things. This does not mean that the USA and other Western institutes cannot support Middle Eastern countries' attempts to prosper, however, China, in some sense, can do it better, at least from the student's perspective.

This attitudinal shift is reflected in China's increasing appeal to young people who are at the beginning of their professional lives. In the past, boarding a flight to China was perceived as "reaching the end of the world for nothing," as described by the father of one of the interviewees in this chapter. These days, however, it is not uncommon for students to pursue academic degrees, or for young professionals to travel to China for business.

Financial support, according to some of the interviewees, played a major role in their decision to choose to go to China to purchase an academic education. This support, that can come from the state and the municipal level, is crucial for many of the students, especially the ones from economically weak countries. The fact that the Middle East is part of the Belt and Road Initiative expands the possibilities for the local students. For example, "The Belt and Road Initiative Scholarship," a program that aims to provide financial support for students (undergraduate, Master's and doctoral) was included in the initiative (*China Scholar*, 2020). At the Second Belt and Road Forum for International Cooperation, the Chinese government announced that: "The Chinese government continues to implement the 'Silk Road' Chinese Government Scholarship Program and increases scholarships for candidates pursuing Master's and PhD degrees at Chinese institutes of higher learning" (*Global Times*, 2019).

Yemen, as an example of a weak country, has been developing an internal program in the local education system to help the students learn the Chinese language already in elementary school, in order to support their success in China as university students. The teacher in one of the classes said: "It is the language of the future and it is necessary for all generations to benefit from the tremendous scientific, industrial and economic development in China" (*China Daily*, 2020). This statement fits well with the conclusion of the article "Chinese soft power in the Arab world: China's Confucius Institutes as a central tool of influence," which argues that, by using Confucius Institutes and other soft power tools, the Chinese are trying to push the local society to adopt the view that learning the Chinese language will bring clear financial benefits (Yellinek et al., 2020).

Yemen is not the only Middle Eastern country that does so, and even an economically strong country like Saudi Arabia started at the beginning of 2020 to teach the Chinese language at eight public secondary schools, as the first stage of the local Ministry of Education's plan to include it in public education (Obaid, 2020). In an agreement signed between the Crown Prince of Saudi Arabia, Mohammad bin Salman and high-ranking Chinese officials on February 22, 2019, during his visit to Beijing, it was agreed that the Saudi administration would incorporate Chinese language studies into school curricula at all levels (Mahmoud, 2019). This declaration, even regardless of its ultimate implementation, attests to the nature of the Saudi response to the Chinese efforts mentioned above. Moreover, the strengthening of the Chinese language in this case will necessarily come at the expense of the English language currently being studied as a second language in Saudi schools (*Arab News*, 2019).

This chapter, based on personal interviews and conversations conducted in China with 14 men and women in their twenties and thirties from across the Middle East,[1] aims to shed light on a phenomenon that I observed while living in China, namely the increasing number of young Middle Easterners who relocate to China in order to obtain academic and professional credentials and experience.

Destination China

E., A., K., T., and G. are master's degree students. Four of them arrived from Turkey, and one arrived from Saudi Arabia (though is originally from Lebanon). Whereas two of these individuals chose to pursue their studies in China because they had been awarded special scholarships to do so, a third individual was on an exchange program administered by a university in Paris. The others regarded studying in China as a natural extension of their having already spent time in the country. In addition to their subject-specific substantive curriculum, all five are studying Chinese, and have become reasonably proficient at speaking the language. Importantly, all five stressed that they regard studying in China as an investment, and hope that their academic training will unlock valuable career opportunities.

Furthermore, these students are planning to pursue careers that will connect them to China: four of them by doing business between Turkey and China or joining a consultancy; and the fifth is seeking to enter the field of diplomacy and public policy and they calculate that first-hand knowledge of China will serve as a professional advantage.

Snapshots of Departure and Arrival

The five student interviewees characterized Chinese attitudes toward them as ranging from indifferent to congenial. They attributed the indifference to Chinese people's lack of knowledge or familiarity with other cultures, on the one hand, and simple disinterest, on the other. They noted that they also had to deal with some linguistic challenges: for example, "Lebanon" and "Albania" sound quite similar in Chinese, and therefore are often confused with one another. The respondents pointed out that, from the perspective of an average Chinese person, the differences between Turks, Arabs, and Iranians are imperceptible—or at any rate, irrelevant.

According to all five student interviewees, they faced neither more nor less discrimination on the basis of their national or cultural origins than did their peers from elsewhere in the world. All five also agreed that they felt physically safe while in China. This is not to suggest that the students encountered no difficulties or inconveniences in their daily lives. E. related the unnerving experience of temporarily being unable to access personal funds, as the Bank of China does not accept wire transfers from some Middle Eastern financial institutions. Nor is obtaining permission to enter China for purposes other than studying necessarily a simple matter for anyone from the Middle East.

For example, T., who is from Syria, stated that although it was relatively easy for him to secure a student visa, his fellow countrymen would find it quite difficult to arrange a tourist visa. P., a female from Iran, noted that Iranian nationals must undergo difficult interviews and deposit 100,000 yuan for three months in order to obtain a visa; they cannot convert US dollars to Chinese Yuan; and they need a local partner in order to open a bank account, whether for personal or business purposes.

E. A. is an Egyptian student who grew up in Doha, Qatar, and traveled to China to study because she discovered that there were convenient scholarship options. Her family was surprised by her choice to relocate to China for an extended period of time. However, with the help and encouragement of her brother, who had made a similar move, the family became convinced that her decision was well-informed and sensible. Prior to her arrival in China, E. A. had had a shallow knowledge of the country and was pleasantly surprised by the quality of life she encountered there.

E. A. wears the *hijab*, which made her rather conspicuous in China. However, she claims never to have met hostile glances or offensive remarks—adding, "as I could have encountered if I had gone to study in Europe." Despite the level of personal comfort that she enjoyed in China, E. A. nonetheless wishes to relocate to Europe following the completion of her studies, in order to pursue a career in international relations and diplomacy. Thus, in E. A.'s case, specific career aims, rather than disillusionment or discomfort will cause her eventually to leave China.

Y., originally from Syria, cited intellectual curiosity as his primary reason for relocating to China to study: "We, in the Middle East, know very little about China, and it is very important to study this issue." His studies were funded through scholarship donations made by "Chinese businesspeople, who wish to see China opening up to the world." Y. made a point of emphasizing the welcoming atmosphere he and his friends experienced through their interactions with members of Chinese society. Y. also noted that his Chinese counterparts evinced little interest in learning about the long-running conflict in Syria. He, like other interviewees, stated that he would advise his friends to study in China. At the same time, however, he would not encourage them to settle there, as, in his words, "it's tough for immigrants from the Middle East"—lacking a community of their own, facing a wide cultural gulf, and having to come to terms with living so far from home.

M. is a Saudi PhD student who has been living in Shanghai for the past eight years. M. chose China because his brother encouraged him to take a different path, "unlike all Saudis, who go to study in the US." Like his friends, M. speaks appreciatively about the amiability of the people he has met, exclaiming that "the Chinese are the friendliest people I've ever seen." M. plans to remain in China for the long term, probably because of the warm feelings he has for the country and its people.

A., who is originally from Yemen, is studying Engineering and Chinese. He chose to study in China on the recommendation of some of his friends, and with the support of a scholarship he obtained with the help of a family friend. A. recounted the negative reactions of some Chinese peers due to his Muslim religion. He initially found those reactions dismaying but subsequently managed to overcome them, thanks especially to having made Chinese friends. As previously mentioned, students from Yemen tend to remain in China, where opportunities for study and employment are more plentiful than in their home country. Accordingly, A. says that he "plans to stay in China as long as possible," and dreams of his parents and the rest of his family joining him.

T., the Syrian student mentioned earlier, was met with reactions from Chinese that ranged from surprise—"We didn't know there are students from there [exotic places]"—to open-minded acceptance. As with A.'s experience, the only tension he felt appeared to stem from the fact that he is a Muslim. He indicated that these sentiments were likely attributable to the problems between the Chinese government and the Muslim-Uighur minority in Xinjiang. T. also noted that, while some of his dark-skinned friends have encountered racist remarks, he has generally been warmly welcomed.

Meetings with two Iranian subjects, P. and R., took place separately in order to allow each of them to speak freely. R., a master's degree student, is one of the Iranian regime's avid supporters. Therefore, for him to return to Iran upon graduation would be natural; only an exceptionally good employment opportunity could potentially keep him in China, which he says would in any case not be for too long. Given these plans and other personal reasons, R. did not really mix with his Chinese peers. Most of his friends, including his roommates, are either Iranian or Pakistani. Nevertheless, he asserted, those Chinese with whom he came into contact were accepting of him. He further stated that he would advise friends to follow his example, which could improve their status in Iran's tough job market. Throughout the conversation, R. continually referred to the positive bilateral relationship between China and Iran, praising the Chinese for their capacity to accept people from different countries and manage diplomatic and economic relations with Iran and "even with Saudi Arabia."

P. is a female of Iranian origin whose personal background, current circumstances, and plans differ markedly from those of R. She works for a business owned by her family that operates in China, and she chose to live in Shanghai because "it is cool here and there are unlimited social and business opportunities in this city." Thus, P's decision to relocate to China appears to have been greatly influenced by her family's desire to expand their business to China and establish a stake there. Unlike R.'s view of China-Iran relations, P. stressed that there is a wide gap between how the media portrays the bilateral relationship and its actual status. She characterized the attitudes of Chinese officials and procedures governing the entry of Iranian nationals to China as hostile. She plans to stay in China for as long as she feels comfortable with the people who surround her.

A. is the brother of E. A. from Egypt. He lives in Yunnan province, where he is employed as a dentist. A. chose to study and work in China because it is "one of the most beautiful places I've ever seen, and it is a well-developed country." A. says that he and his friends were warmly accepted, and that many of his patients know about Egypt and its long, important history. E. A. commented that her brother mixed well with the locals; and that there are many Chinese patients who prefer that he treats them, as opposed to the local dentists.

A. M. relocated from Aleppo in Syria to Yiwu, China's commercial capital, in order to expand the family business. He indicated that the Chinese people with whom he has been involved, whether for business or friendship, warmly accept him. On the other hand, he says that some perceive his presence as solely for business purposes and regard him as posing an economic threat. Although A. M. would some day like to return to Syria to live, he expects to remain in China until the conflict in his home country wanes.

Middle Eastern Students' View of China

A video describing the attitude of Middle Eastern students, who are studying in their own country, to China, gives another angle to the motivation of their peers to come to China. The video filmed students from the University of Jordan, the American University in Beirut and in Dubai, the Sharif University of Technology, the University of Istanbul and the University of Tehran. Even if this video is completely staged, it can be noted how the director wants these students and their peers to imagine China.

The main themes that appear again and again in the video are the following: Defining China as a great civilization, describing China as a great power and the most populated country on Earth. China also is identified in the words of the one of students as "a well-developed industry, with links to the whole world." Another student claims that China produces: "many high-quality products for us," and another said that China is "leading in advanced technologies" and the Chinese people are smart at math, know how to invent things, and are hard workers. In addition, they talked about the Chinese food and if they like it or not, and the last student in the video, from the University of Istanbul, spoke one sentence about the Xingjian and the Uyghurs people (Liu, 2016).

All these ideas, as expressed by the Middle Eastern students, reflect well the public image that China aims to create for itself and use many tools in order to have a regional and an international impact. Of course, this match between the Middle Eastern students' views and the way the Chinese seek to market themselves may raise the possibility of all the video being staged, even more, but this does not detract from the need and ability to understand the image that emerges from this video. The reuse of the word civilization, and not a state or country, while speaking about China is not only due to showing respect, it is also adopting the separation between the Chinese civilization and Western/American civilization, and the fact that the Chinese one is defined as one of the old civilizations in the world. If it is an old civilization, it has the right to feel superiority and advantage over the other young nations.

One other aspect that emerges from the students' answers is that China is connected to almost everywhere and touches everyone's lives. This means that, not only the life of the students who choose to study in China are connected to this place, but also many other lives are affected by China. The effect is very wide and extends from Chinese cuisine to the fact that many of the goods we all use are manufactured in China, or part of them comes from there. The important emphasis that emerges from the students' views is that China is not only the source of simple goods, but also of technologically advanced goods, that are the result of China "leading in advanced technologies." In 2014, a year after being appointed, President Xi said: "China must rely on innovation to achieve sustained and healthy economic growth" (Xinhua, 2014). In September 2020, he urged his people to speed up technological innovations and step up financial support for basic scientific research (Cao, 2020). If so, it seems that the Middle Eastern students consciously or unconsciously, have internalized the messages conveyed from the direction of China and some of them seek to come and study there because of those messages.

Conclusion

The reasons why young people from the Middle East are drawn to China vary in nature, and, as mentioned above, it is part of a world-wide phenomenon. As this limited sample of interviewees indicates, students and young professionals from the Middle East region find China appealing for all sorts of personal reasons. Yet, at the same time, it is possible to draw some broad, tentative conclusions about why they chose to relocate to China. For some, whose native home is plagued by conflict, as is the case in Syria and Yemen, for example, China offers an improvement in their personal security and economic standard of living. For others, such as those from Egypt and Iran, for example, where the employment market is discouraging, students and young professionals view China as a possible gateway to economic opportunities that are otherwise not available to them, and in a more welcoming environment then in the USA and other Western countries.

Similarly, though each respondent's experiences in China are unique, there nonetheless appears to be a general agreement regarding how they have been treated by their Chinese hosts. Overall, the interviewees reported that citizens originating from the Middle East are well received by ordinary Chinese people. Though some provided accounts of less than positive experiences in obtaining visas or conducting banking transactions, at a

Middle Eastern Students in China

personal level—with few, if any exceptions—they found the Chinese with whom they interacted to be hospitable, respectful, and open. Based on these anecdotal accounts, it therefore seems as though China will continue to be an attractive destination for many young people from the Middle East for the foreseeable future. In the long run, this phenomenon could help buttress the increasingly extensive relationship between China and the Middle East.

China-Middle East higher educational cooperation is the cornerstone of these relationships, and this chapter discusses only one aspect of this cooperation. It is a cornerstone because it can help cultivate young talented people in various sectors, such as economics, management, and technology from both sides. Higher educational cooperation can support social and economic development as well as helping Chinese and Middle Eastern young people better understand the culture and values of each other and motivate the cooperation to a deeper and wider level.

The Chinese effort to bring Middle Eastern students can be considered one of the approaches that relates to the Chinese Soft Power Pipelines Diffusion (SPPD) toward the Middle East, with the tool of people-to-people strategy (Yellinek et al., 2020). [2] The Chinese President Xi Jinping even talked about this strategy extensively in one of his first speeches when he took office in 2013. This approach is advantageous due to the relatively minor investment it requires, since it involves individuals and activities within China itself, while the potential return is relatively high. The Chinese are expecting these students to return after their studies to their home countries and to play the role of "Goodwill Ambassadors" [3] for China among their own people and community. In doing so, the Chinese hope to gain widespread influence, by directing only very limited resources at just one key individual.

The implication of this development at the educational level on the relationship between China and the Middle Eastern countries is clear. The more students and young people from the Middle East who have been studying in China and have close relations with Chinese colleagues, the stronger the relations between the countries will be. Such interpersonal relationships (which can be understood also as part of the "*guanxi*"), [4] especially when it occurs at such a young age, are found to be one of the key things that connect on a practical level between countries. Since these young people will have a long time to spread their influence on their environment because of their young age, this constitutes a particularly worthwhile Chinese investment, even if those young people do not yet have considerable status and influence. This kind of interpersonal relationship can heavily support the struggle to fill the gap between the Middle East countries and China that occurs due to the major cultural differences between the two.

Notes

1 The interviews and conversations dealt primarily with those young people's choice to spend time in China, the reactions this choice elicited among those from their country of origin, and the extent to which they felt accepted by Chinese society. The interviewees are identified by pseudonyms (i.e., by the first letter of their name, and in some cases by the first letter of their surname, in order to differentiate between them and maintain their anonymity). The interviewees have not been chosen as a representative scientific sample, but rather on the basis of word of mouth introductions, with an eye toward forming a diverse group.

2 More about SPPD can be found in Yellinek et al. (2020).

3 "Goodwill ambassador" is a name for figures who generally deliver goodwill by promoting ideas from one society to another, or to a population.

4 *"Guanxi"* is defined as the fundamental dynamic in personalized social networks of power and is a crucial system of beliefs in Chinese culture.

Acknowledgments

The author wants to express his gratitude to Doron Shapir and Alex Leopold for their wonderful help in writing this chapter.

References

Arab News (2019) "Saudi Arabia Plans to Introduce Chinese into the Curriculum at all Education Levels." Available at: www.arabnews.com/node/1456466/saudi-arabia

Bennett, C. (2013) *The Bloomsbury Companion to Islamic Studies.* New York: Bloomsbury Press.

Cao, D. (2020) "Xi Calls for High-Quality Development." *China Daily.* Available at: www.chinadaily.com.cn/a/202009/19/WS5f64985da31024ad0ba7a7f0.html

Chen, J. (2014) "Re-Orientation: The Chinese Azharites between Umma and Third World, 1938–55," *Comparative Studies of South Asia, Africa and the Middle East,* 34(1): 24–51.

China Daily (2020) "More Young Yemenis Learn Chinese for Better Future." Available at: www.chinadaily.com.cn/a/202002/14/WS5e45f620a3101282172777bd_2.html

China Ministry of Education (2019) "Inbound Internationally Mobile Students by Continent of Origin." Available at: www. en.moe.gov.cn

China Scholar (2020) "China Belt and Road Scholarship." Available at: www.china-scholar.com/scholarships/belt-and-road-initiative-scholarships-bri/

Global Times (2019) "List of Deliverables of the Second Belt and Road Forum for International Cooperation." Available at: www.globaltimes.cn/content/1147744.shtml

Kurzman, C. (2002) *Modernist Islam, 1840–1940.* Oxford: Oxford University Press.

Liu, Z. (2016) "Middle Eastern Students on China," YouTube. Available at: www.youtube.com/watch?v=xhG_9TZgSg4&ab_channel=ZhaoningLiu

Mahmoud, S. (2019) "Qatari Emir Boycotts First Arab-European Summit due to Egypt's 'Unprofessional' Behavior." *Arab Post.* Available at: https://bit.ly/2Tj2YDu

Obaid, R. (2020) "Students Begin Studying Chinese in Public Schools in Saudi Arabia," *Arab News.* Available at: www.arabnews.com/node/1615436/saudi-arabia

People's Daily (2011) "China Sends More Students Abroad, Absorbs Record High." Available at: http://english.peopledaily.com.cn/90001/90776/90882/7307378.html

Sawahel, W. (2018) "Arab-Chinese HE Cooperation on the Rise," *University World News.* Available at: www.universityworldnews.com/post.php?story=2018090806594431

UNESCO Institute for Statistics (2021) "Inbound Internationally Mobile Students by Continent of Origin." Available at: www.uis.uneso.org

Xinhua (2014) "President Xi Stresses Role of Innovation in Economy." Available at: www.chinadaily.com.cn/china/2014-12/14/content_19083596.htm

Yellinek, R. et al. (2020) "Chinese Soft Power in the Arab World: China's Confucius Institutes as a Central Tool of Influence," *Comparative Strategy,* 39(6): 517–534.

Zvi, B. (2008) "Nine Years in Egypt: Al-Azhar University and the Arabization of Chinese Islam," *HAGAR Studies in Culture, Polity & Identities,* 8(1): 1–21.

32

CHINA'S SOFT POWER AND CULTURAL DIPLOMACY IN THE MENA

Sophie Zinser, Dhahi Li, and Adel Hamaizia

Introduction

China has spent decades committed to attracting the rest of the world using soft power, solidifying its relationships with its diplomatic allies and economic partners across the MENA region. American political scientist Joseph Nye originally popularized the term "soft power" in 1990 (Nye, 1990) now defined in the *Cambridge English Dictionary* as "the use of a country's cultural and economic influence to persuade other countries to do something, rather than the use of military power" (*Cambridge English Dictionary*, n.d.). Chinese scholars have expanded upon Nye's original theory as it has become intertwined in China's foreign policy strategy and now is a vital aspect of a narrative abroad increasingly influenced by domestic Chinese practice.

In contrast to Nye's definition of soft power compared to US "hard" power and diplomatic supremacy, it was Hu Jintao in 2007 who first used the term at the 17th Congress of the Chinese Communist Party to link "the rejuvenation of the Chinese nation to the ability of China to deploy cultural soft power (文化软实力)" (Hu, 2007). Subsequently in 2009, Hu Jintao emphasized that "[China] should strengthen public diplomacy and humanities diplomacy and commence various kinds of cultural exchange activities in order to disseminate China's great culture" (Hu, 2009). While the phrase "soft power" often echoes Nye's original vision, the idea's central premise—that power is wielded through institutions to shape values—is very much in line with the Confucian idea of leadership by moral elites (德治天下); a philosophy that applies in the same way in both domestic and international contexts. Hu Jintao perceived the Chinese government's influence on its own people as the primary determinant of China's influence abroad. That ethos has carried over across China's political and economic arenas.

The application of soft power in the Middle East and North Africa (MENA) can be characterized as both ethno- and geo-centric. Parts of the MENA region began exercising soft power via pan-Arab solidarity movements during the late nineteenth and early twentieth centuries and after the founding of the Arab League in 1945. Driven by upper- and middle-class urban actors, these movements were multi-faceted and centered around promoting pan-Arab soft power tools—such as culture and the Arabic language—as a departure from the region's history of Western colonialism. While religious and

DOI: 10.4324/9781003048404-36

nationalist ideologies have since eclipsed pan-Arabism's regional prominence, soft power remains a key tool for MENA diplomacy, particularly in the Gulf countries touting strong and wealthy state institutions. Saudi Arabia has seized soft power as a diplomatic tool through successfully branding its Vision 2030 strategy as a policy for opening the nation up to the rest of the world. Similarly, the Emirates' own Vision 2030 agenda and Dubai's hosting of Expo 2020 have become a symbol of the Emirates' economic vitality and resource diversification beyond oil. Qatar's hosting of the FIFA World Cup 2022 is widely viewed as the zenith of mega-events in the MENA region, having put the city state firmly on the map. Religious tourism—including the Hajj pilgrimage in Saudi Arabia, the Shia pilgrimage in Iraq, and visiting biblical sites in both Jordan and Palestine—is another tool by which MENA governments exercise soft power and attract foreigners from abroad.

China has been identified as leaning more heavily into soft power styles of diplomacy in the region, constructed in implicit opposition to the hard power of the US multi-faceted security framework. Given the terms of the US origin, soft power is often theoretically defined in comparison to the West. In stark contrast to an interventionist and security-focused American government, experts in the West have described China's soft power brand under Xi Jinping as a "charm offensive" (Kurlantzick, 2020). While China has invested in numerous diplomatic projects targeting individuals in the MENA region, there is not sufficient evidence that China's brand in the MENA assumes the same trope traditionally associated with America's more grassroots soft power attempts in the region. In other words, China does not seem to want other nations to do or think as is does (Zinser and Wei, 2021).

Therefore, while ultimately a critical part of its foreign policy strategy, China's interpretation of soft power has always been rooted in the nation's ability to win over local perspectives at home. This applies in the multiple contexts in which China exerts influence, including its own soft power in the MENA region. While China's influence has been most acutely carved out in Southeast Asia—where the nation has an incentive to maintain a peaceful and stable periphery—its forays into public consciousness in the Middle East extend beyond the energy-based investments with which it is often accredited. In recent years, the Chinese expatriate community has grown in the region, offering a new kind of people-to-people exchanges among the local populations (Lyall, 2019), As a kind of second-tier security priority for China, the MENA offers the opportunity for Chinese policy-makers to experiment with various diplomatic and economic techniques to expand its soft power influence, including via media outreach, education, and joint infrastructure projects. Building from analysis, public policy documents, and public opinion surveys of China in the MENA, this chapter will discuss the dimensions and extent of influence of China's soft power in the MENA and offer thoughts on how those soft power relations might evolve in the future.

Defining the China Brand in the MENA

China has built its brand in the Middle East on three interrelated ideological narratives: (1) the nation's impressive economic rise; (2) China's interest in becoming an economic rather than a security partner to nations in the region; and (3) China's continued and evolving status as a developing nation, as a peer—rather than a superior—to Middle Eastern nations. China's brand in the MENA is therefore fundamentally different from that of traditional American soft power. In the latter, a country's government and population are implicitly expected to behave and become over time like America. In contrast, China wields a narrative attempting to inspire peer countries and promote equal cooperative partnerships. While efforts have been made to teach the Chinese language or promote Chinese culture abroad (as described in the Education section), there is ultimately no indication that China wishes other countries to become like itself on a cultural level. Instead, China's government hopes to inspire elite economic exchanges and high-profile diplomatic efforts in the MENA to promote local acceptance of the growing Chinese commercial, diplomatic, and expatriate presence in the region.

China's impressive economic rise since the Reform and Opening period of 1978 has lifted more than 800 million Chinese citizens out of poverty. Ever since, China's economic growth has stood at almost 10% per year, with 2020 being the global exception (Robbins, 2021). The premise that China itself has successfully elevated its status from a developing to a developed country gives the nation a sense of credibility to its exchanges and predicates its trustworthiness as a reliable economic partner when dealing with country governments in the MENA. Given the tensions across the region wrought by decades of war and instability—in large part due to influence and intervention from foreign powers—Beijing's developing country status narrative presents an attractive alternative to the American presence in the region.

Additionally, China has carefully kept to a "non-interference" policy when faced with numerous security and foreign policy-related challenges in the region. Indeed, many elites inside the MENA governments consider China's development path to be more closely linked to their own conditions than the patterns shown in Western countries. This general idea led to the formation of a "Beijing Consensus" narrative as an alternative to the so-called "Washington Consensus" of the West, suggesting that economic modernization can occur without explicit Westernization (Sildo et al., 2021). This promise is epitomized in the English translation of China's January 2021 development White Paper: "China's International Development Cooperation in the New Era," which begins with the phrase "China is the largest developing country in the world," asserting that while China remains a peer to the MENA governments in its developing status, it undoubtedly boasts a larger economic and diplomatic presence than other developing nations (Ministry of Foreign Affairs of the People's Republic of China, 2021).

Well-educated elites tend to welcome Chinese investment. Indeed, those boasting university degrees are on average more supportive of closer economic relations with China (Robbins, 2021). China has continued to perpetuate elite-level engagement with other nations in the region via its brand of top-level economic and diplomatic exchanges. While no states have explicitly said that their foreign policy is designed to follow Beijing's model, admiration for China's rise is often alluded to in speeches from prominent Middle Eastern leaders. On the public front, the MENA governments have nothing but warm words for Chinese leadership. For example, under President Sisi of Egypt's rule, economic exchanges with China have blossomed. The Egyptian ruler is a far more frequent visitor to China than his predecessor Hosni Mubarak (Sim and Greer, 2021). China's diplomatic engagement will likely continue to attract high-level decision-makers across non-democratic states, particularly corporations and politicians.

From the highest level of its policy documents, China's interest in the MENA incorporates the shared histories of the two regions in implicit contrast to the comparatively new global presence of Western powers. Released in January 2016 by the Ministry of Foreign Affairs, China's "Arab Policy Paper" was the first policy blueprint from Beijing for China-Middle East relations (Ministry of Foreign Affairs of the People's Republic of

China, 2021). On the soft power side, the document grounds Chinese engagement with the MENA in its shared history with China as a peer ancient civilization. The Foreword of China's Arab Policy paper reminds the reader that "Friendship between China and Arab States dates back to ancient times," and remains rooted in "History, peace, and cooperation." Linking the regions to China via shared historical events is most clearly epitomized in the "New Silk Road" policy announced in September 2013 (Ministry of Foreign Affairs, People's Republic of China, 2013) and codified as the Belt and Road Initiative (BRI) and part of China's constitution in October 2017 (Xinhua, 2017). Both policies cite the historical links between China, South, and Central Asia as the basis for a new development model. Since the policy was launched, China's "Silk Road" branding has proliferated to intersect multiple initiatives, including the "Digital Silk Road" (数字丝绸之路) (Xinhua, 2019), the "Space Silk Road" (太空丝绸之路) (Xinhua, 2018), and, most recently, the "Health Silk Road" (健康丝绸之路), through which China hopes to exert its influence by supporting MENA states afflicted by COVID-19 beyond initial PPE donations and by increasing its foreign aid, particularly in the twin realms of pharmaceutical and technology investments (see Chapter 19 in this volume; Zoubir and Tran, 2021). These phrases are each adaptations from the so-called end goal of the Belt and Road Initiative; a "community of common human destiny" (人类命运共同体), which epitomizes the positive relations that Beijing aspires to develop with Middle Eastern and other developing powers (Mardel, 2020). Grounding Chinese soft power advances in shared common histories is likely to endure as a rhetorical method of distinguishing China's soft power influence from that of the United States and other Western powers in the MENA.

Economic and Media-Based Factors Influencing China's Soft Power Abroad

Economic relations between China and the Middle East have increased since the launch of the Belt and Road Initiative in 2013. Trade relationships between China and the Middle East have been built on symbiotic state interests; and are grounded in nations with either large population counts, such as Egypt, supply chain and logistics networks, such as Morocco and the UAE, and states with large amounts of oil, including the Gulf nations. In return, many Gulf states, for example, look to China as a promising hydrocarbons export destination, technology development leader, site of diversified exports, and entry point into a growing middle-class consumer market (Young, 2020). In fact, the origins of many partnerships between the two regions likely stem primarily from symbiotic economic interests, and, second, from shared geopolitical goals.

As the global market has become increasingly saturated with less traditional investment outlets—most notably Middle Eastern sovereign funds and family offices—that tend to be more risk-averse, Chinese companies in the region are expanding influential investments across sectors most likely to remain resilient in the face of changing market and geopolitical tides, including infrastructure, e-commerce, food delivery, biotechnology, software, and healthcare (Zinser and Wei, 2021). As many of these sectors are central to China's long-term goals in the region, it is safe to predict that Chinese investments in technology will likely increase over time. Given the tumultuous US-China relationship, it is likely that these tensions will impact the location and duration of these investments.

A persistent issue for Chinese brands has been building customer loyalty abroad and maintaining brand identity; the significance of which the nation has historically underestimated in its dealings with the MENA. To maintain market power in the Middle

East exports will need a level of loyalty—not just a low price—to maintain economic interests in products. As such, China has made attempts to indigenize its products in the Middle East, omitting the product's national affiliation and potential soft power in favor of increasing market returns. For example, in addition to its globally popular app TikTok, China has invested in Dubai-based social networking app Yalla that has boasted growing popularity in the Middle East with extensions across time (Kerr, 2021). This trend suggests that over time, China is likely to favor the commercial reputation of its goods and investments rather than use nationalized branding to push its soft power influence.

Additionally, China's global media have evolved and expanded their presence in the MENA in recent years. Historically, the media has come to define the efficacy and success of national branding efforts abroad, and the potential of the media to influence public perceptions across the world continues to rise (Albert, 2018). State-sponsored media outlets, including Xinhua, *China Daily*, and China.org are major news sources for populations in the MENA. The nation spends over $10 billion annually on various projects projecting soft power images (Hsieh, n.d.), including through funding of public diplomacy programs via the Publicity Department of the Central Committee (中宣部), which has grown significantly under Xi. To experts abroad, China intends to project an image of both leading by example and peer-to-peer diplomacy. More broadly, Beijing now spends over $10 billion annually on image-building content as part of its initiatives, each promoting China's brand abroad of win-win diplomacy, cultural values, and cooperation.

Limitations on China's Soft Power in the MENA

In terms of the Communist Party's history and China's cultural traditions, religion has not been a defining factor of Chinese society and has rarely been associated with political power. China has been a secularized country for thousands of years. According to Chinese experts, most of the Chinese population has a utilitarian attitude toward religion rather than a devout faith. Therefore, it is difficult for China to gain religious resonance with the MENA society. The positive side is that China does not have the same "religion and history burden" with the Islamic world as the West does, while the negative side is that China has always been wary of outside religious forces meddling in its domestic affairs (including integrating religions beyond Islam). At the same time, China's atheistic stance is also hardly accepted by the MENA countries. However, with the growing economic and trade ties between China and the MENA countries, this situation has changed. The economic concepts of the "China Road" or the "China Model," free from religious and ideological confinement, have successfully attracted the attention of the MENA countries. For example, in 2019, the 70th anniversary of the PRC's founding, Saudi Arabia held an exhibition on China's development achievements and seminars to discuss the "Chinese model" and demonstrate the rapid development of China's influence in the region.

Since 2020, however, the spread of the COVID-19 pandemic has severely bruised China's image in the MENA. Wuhan, the city that first reported the COVID-19, has been haunted by theories and allegations regarding the virus's origin, including the emerging "lab leak" theory. At the beginning, the MENA society had shown support for China, from both officialdom and the private sector. More importantly, this support has not only come from the same "geopolitical camp," but with similar support seen from Tehran to

Tel Aviv, from Dubai to Istanbul. However, with the lasting effects of the epidemic on the economies and the public, and the continued speculation regarding the virus's origin, public opinion in the MENA region has taken a negative turn against China on the issue of COVID-19. Chinese attempts to provide vaccine donations abroad have been labeled "vaccine diplomacy" and an "intent to rewrite the narrative," resulting in a clear setback to China's soft power in the MENA.

Another case that has seriously affected China's national image is the "Xinjiang issue." China's northwest Xinjiang province—called the Xinjiang Uyghur Autonomous Region—is the lead cotton producer in China and one of the major sites for the product's distribution across the world. Its northwest region is home to 11 million Uyghurs, who comprise a Turkic-speaking ethnic group and are mostly Muslim. The Xinjiang region has been home to varying separatist ideologies and has been controlled by multiple regimes for the past 2500 years (Hsieh, n.d.). After the establishment of the PRC, efforts were made to integrate the local minority populations and economies into the greater Chinese state as the region's Han population has increased (Lew, 2021). Clashes between the government and minority citizens have made local headlines in China—notably in 2006 and 2009—giving Xinjiang a local reputation as a site and origin of terrorist attacks against the Chinese government. Since 2017, the Chinese government in the region has identified individuals whom it asserts to be under the potential influence of the "Three Forces" known as terrorism, separatism, and religious extremism, and sent those individuals to centers called "Xinjiang Vocational Education and Training Centers." Western reporting has covered family separation, state surveillance, and physical and emotional abuse of Uyghur minorities at the hands of the local Chinese authorities.

The Xinjiang issue has deepened the Western-Chinese rift, specifically between the United States and China. Many in the Chinese public see Western press coverage of the issue as an attempt to contain China's growing global influence and undermine China's image in the Islamic world. This issue may persist in a relatively assertive posture for a long period of time.

Education from China in the MENA

Since the beginning of the twenty-first century, education cooperation between China and the MENA countries has been developing rapidly. Under the BRI, China has proposed the "Education Initiative," which hopes to promote humanistic exchanges with the MENA states through education cooperation and achieve closer people-to-people ties (郭晶、吴应辉, 2019). Compared with other regions along the BRI, China's international education cooperation in the MENA is not outstanding. The cooperation mainly includes two-way academic visits, regular institutional exchanges, cooperative research, teacher exchange, joint talent training, curriculum sharing, mutual recognition of academic qualifications, and joint schooling. While there is autonomous private cooperation at the low and medium level of exchange, at the higher level, however, the exchanges are often characterized by more official engagements.

The role of China in international education cooperation should be viewed objectively. On the positive side, given the Chinese systemic factors, educational exchanges in official contexts tend to have higher academic standards, more abundant financial support, and reliable policy guarantees. On the negative side, official cooperation inevitably includes a certain amount of "content screening," partly at the request of the Chinese Government, and partly due to the self-screening of Chinese scholars, according to Chinese "political correctness."

China promotes international education cooperation not only to enhance bilateral academic exchanges, but to improve China's soft power in the region. China's policy goal in educational cooperation is to focus on the "identification" rather than political coercion, and China does not expect to force the MENA countries to make political concessions by promoting educational cooperation.

Confucius Institutes, the quintessential example of China's official model of international education, have been suppressed in Western countries in recent years. It is also crucial to note that the MENA is not the focus of the global presence of the Confucius Institutes. At present, in the MENA, China has established Confucius Institutes in the UAE, Saudi Arabia, Lebanon, Jordan, Egypt, Tunisia, Morocco, Turkey, Israel, and Iran, nearly one-third of which were established in recent years. With the promotion of the BRI and the closer economic, trade, scientific and technological ties between China and the MENA countries, there have been more endogenous demands for educational cooperation with China from the MENA countries in the past five years than ever before, including the establishment of Confucius Institutes, which have been shown to promote political and economic cooperation.

However, the development of Confucius Institutes in the MENA is also constrained by factors, such as value identity, mind-set, and religious beliefs. In 2018, Chinese scholars proposed the concept of "Density of Confucius Institutes" to "examine the density of Confucius Institutes in a given region or country," which is calculated as "the ratio of the number of people in a region or country to the number of Confucius Institutes, to indicate the number of people covered by each Confucius Institute." According to this concept, Iran, Saudi Arabia, and Egypt are all "regions with insufficient density," but these three countries are the pivot countries of China's MENA policy and most closely connected to China in various fields (郭晶、吴应辉, 2019).

Given the evidence described above, it is reasonable to expect that China's educational cooperation with the MENA countries will probably move from a steady epoch to a period of rapid development, while the MENA countries may still have doubts about developing deeper educational cooperation with China. As China's economic and political presence in the region grows, bilateral education cooperation will also grow significantly and eventually serve China's growing soft power in MENA.

Public Opinion Polling on Soft Power in China and the MENA and Relations Going Forward

Public opinion polling assessing geopolitical dynamics is far from an exact science. This is especially true in the MENA, where social and political taboos, gender, educational status, and the racial/ethnic background of interviewees historically limit the types and accuracy of responses that can be collected. However, recent polling from both the Pew Research Center and the Arab Barometer suggest that China is viewed increasingly favorably in the MENA region. While globally, younger people tend to have a more positive view of China's power and influence, this discrepancy is especially pronounced in the MENA region (Silver et al., 2020). Further, according to the latest Arab Barometer survey, China's influence in the MENA has steadily increased over the past few years, with MENA citizens more open to engagement with China than with the United States or Russia (Robbins, 2021).

To nuance this conversation, this chapter's authors conducted a survey, collecting insights from 980 individuals across Algeria, Egypt, and the United Arab Emirates that highlight nuanced views and perceptions of China's economic and cultural influence in the region. These three countries were selected for this study because of their deep ties to China, as each are signatories of Comprehensive Strategic Partnerships with Beijing. Saudi Arabia and Iran are the only other two countries which have signed Comprehensive Strategic Partnerships with China. Given the difficult nature of collecting reliable survey results from both countries, we limited our survey sampling to the three nations selected. This modest study was conducted over a period from April–October 2021, and involved 323 respondents from Algeria, 346 from Egypt, and 311 nationals and non-nationals from the UAE. Our research interview and collection methodology took the form of phone calls and snowball sampling. We did not aim to seek a representative sample but rather gain a general overview of trends in each of the three selected countries that might deepen our analysis of China's soft power in the MENA region for the purposes of this chapter. Three of the survey's critical findings are detailed below.

Finding 1: About One-Third of Respondents Believe that China Contributes Positively to Their Country's Economy

Of the three countries surveyed, more respondents in the UAE than any other nation agreed that China contributes positively to that country's economy (Figure 32.1). This is consistent with each nation's stated economic policies toward China, as China boasts closer trade ties with the UAE than with either Egypt or Algeria. Both Egypt and the UAE also host large numbers of Chinese tourists annually at 250,000 and nearly 1 million, respectively, which may also account for public assumptions that a Chinese presence in their country may have a positive impact on their livelihoods (Reuters, 2020).

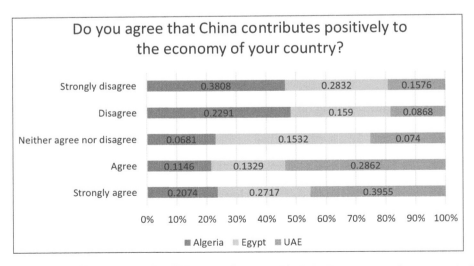

Figure 32.1 Do you agree that China contributes positively to the economy of your country?
Source: Based on poll by the authors.

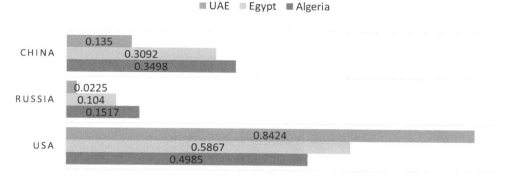

Figure 32.2 Which of the following countries would you like your country to have the strongest ties with?

Source: Based on poll by the authors.

Finding 2: While China May Be Perceived as Making a Positive Economic Contribution in the MENA Region, American Soft Power Remains More Effective in the MENA Region Than That of China

When asked, most individuals in all three countries preferred stronger ties with the United States when compared to Russia or China (Figure 32.2). Despite many individuals in the UAE crediting China with positive economic contributions to their country, 84.24 percent of respondents in the UAE preferred their country to have the strongest ties with America of any of the three countries presented, with just 13.5 percent preferring China. Despite the close diplomatic and economic relationship between China and the countries with which it signs Comprehensive Strategic Partnerships, it was clear from our study that Western nations remained the critical soft power player for individuals living in the MENA region. Few individuals surveyed stated that they would send their children to a Chinese university, perhaps due to a reliance on the traditional destinations of Europe and the United States for education and the ubiquity of the English language in global business, diplomacy, and trade (Figure 32.3).

Finding 3: Despite Acknowledging Recent Improvements in Chinese Technology, Trust Issues Remain Regarding Using Chinese Technology in the MENA Region

Most respondents agreed that Chinese technology has improved significantly over the past ten years (Figure 32.4). This could be influenced by the popularity of Chinese technology products—particularly Huawei phones, which have touted a strong presence in the Gulf since the 1990s—and the integration of Chinese technology companies into free-trade zones and government policy, such as the SETC-Zone in Egypt and recent surveillance technology deployment in Algeria (Parkinson et al., 2019). While the

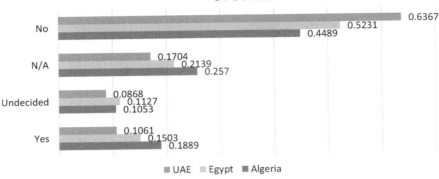

Figure 32.3 Would you consider sending your child(ren) to a Chinese university for their studies?
Source: Based on poll by the authors.

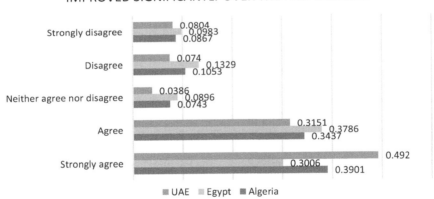

Figure 32.4 Do you agree that Chinese technology has improved significantly over the past decade?

improvements in technology itself are clear, evidence persists that individuals in the MENA may not trust Chinese technology (Figure 32.5). This could be a result of widespread public awareness of corruption charges leveled against Chinese business leaders implicated in illegal practices, including bribery related to technology sales and deployment (Cave et al., 2019), or a result of a negative "made in China" stereotype associating Chinese-made products with low-quality, cheap goods. While relevant when evaluating the extent of China's soft power in the region, it is unlikely that public perceptions of Chinese technology will feed directly into policy-making, given the elite-to-elite nature of Chinese diplomacy with its Comprehensive Strategic Partners.

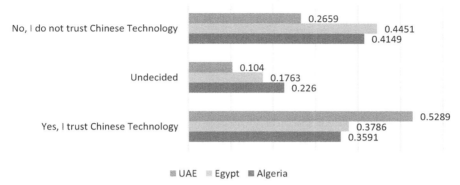

Figure 32.5 Do you trust Chinese technology (from mobile phones to 5G and critical national infrastructure)?

Source: Based on poll by the authors.

Conclusion

In today's international political reality, Sino-US competition continues to be the underlying framework guiding analysis of China's soft power achievements and difficulties abroad, particularly in the MENA region. As both China and the USA become more comfortable with a mutually antagonistic relationship, the ongoing war in Russia-Ukraine is setting the backdrop for a charged future for China-Taiwan relations. China's President Xi is leveraging Chinese nationalism—rather than a healthy Chinese economy—to legitimize his Party's governance over its people (Haas, 2022). Soft power abroad will have an increasingly divisive role in the state of relations between China and it neighboring countries as China attempts to bring other nations on board with its nationalism in implicit opposition to US influence. But in terms of hard power, the USA has the largest military presence, the largest amount of investment, and the deepest people-to-people connections in the MENA. Although China has promoted the BRI through increased tourism and education in the MENA, it will be difficult to shake the dominant position of the US there in the near future. Despite remaining in the shadow of US influence, China's footprint in the MENA is growing rapidly. The USA believes that China has the "ability" and "will" to challenge its traditional sphere of influence in the MENA. Going forward, China and the USA will inevitably engage in intense soft power competition in the region; a paradigm that is likely to be closely tracked by the MENA leaders seeking to avoid regional conflict.

References

Albert, E. (2018) "China's Big Bet on Soft Power." Council on Foreign Relations, February 9. Available at: www.cfr.org/backgrounder/chinas-big-bet-soft-power

Cambridge English Dictionary (n.d.) "Soft Power." Cambridge: Cambridge University Press. Available at: https://dictionary.cambridge.org/us/dictionary/english/softpower (accessed April 8, 2021).

Cave, D. et al. (2019) "Mapping China's Technology Giants." Australian Strategic Policy Institute. Available at: https://s3-ap-southeast-2.amazonaws.com/ad-aspi/2019-05/Mapping%20China%27s%20technology%20giants.pdf?EINwiNpste_FojtgOPriHtlFSD2OD2tL

Haas, R. (2022) "Xi Jinping's Guns of August." Project Syndicate, August 11. Available at: www.project-syndicate.org/commentary/explainning-xi-harsh-response-to-pelosi-taiwan-visit-by-richard-haass-2022-08

Hsieh, C. (n.d.) "Xinjiang, China." In *Encyclopedia Britannica*. Available at: www.britannica.com/place/Xinjiang

Hu, J. (2007) "Section 7: Promoting Vigorous Development and Prosperity of Socialist Culture." Report at 17th Party Congress, Beijing. Available at: http://en.people.cn/90001/90776/90785/6290144.html

Hu, J. (2009) Public speech given at the 11th Conference of Chinese Diplomatic Envoys Stationed Abroad, Beijing. Available at: china-un.ch/eng/tpxw/t156047.htm

Kerr, S. (2021) "Chinese-Founded Social Network Yalla Is Rising Star in Middle East." *Financial Times*, April 26. Available at: www.ft.com/content/e15a16c1-f25b-4b03-8692-ab1feb88cc3a

Kurlantzick, J. (2020) *Charm Offensive: How China's Soft Power Is Transforming the World*. New Haven, CT: Yale University Press, pp. 6–10.

Lew, L. (2021) "China Census: Migration Drives Han Population Growth in Xinjiang." *South China Morning Post*, June 15. Available at: www.scmp.com/news/china/politics/article/3137252/china-census-migration-drives-han-population-growth-xinjiang

Lyall, N. (2019) "China's Rise in the Middle East: Beyond Economics." *The Diplomat*, February 26. Available at: thediplomat.com/2019/02/chinas-rise-in-the-middle-east-beyond-economics/

Mardel, J. (2020) "China's 'Health Silk Road': Adapting the BRI to a Pandemic-Era World Metrics." November 25. Available at: merics.org/en/short-analysis/chinas-health-silk-road-adapting-bri-pandemic-era-world

Ministry of Foreign Affairs, People's Republic of China (2013) "President Xi Jinping Delivers Important Speech and Proposes to Build a Silk Road Economic Belt with Central Asian Countries." September 7. Available at: www.fmprc.gov.cn/mfa_eng/topics_665678/xjpfwzysiesgjtfhshzzfh_665686/t1076334.shtml.

Ministry of Foreign Affairs of the People's Republic of China (2016) "China's Arab Policy Paper." January 13. Available at: www.fmprc.gov.cn/mfa_eng/zxxx_662805/t1331683.shtml.

Ministry of Foreign Affairs of the People's Republic of China (2021) "China's International Development Cooperation in the New Era." January 10. Available at: www.scio.gov.cn/m/zfbps/32832/Document/1696686/1696686.htm

Nye, J. (1990) *Bound to Lead: The Changing Nature of American Power*. New York: Basic Books.

Parkinson, J., Bariyo, N. and Chin, J. (2019) "Huawei Technicians Helped African Governments Spy on Political Opponents." *Wall Street Journal*, August 14. Available at: www.wsj.com/articles/huawei-technicians-helped-african-governments-spy-on-political-opponents-11565793017

Reuters (2020) "Dubai Registers 16.7 Million Tourists in 2019, Chinese Visitors Rise." January 22. Available at: www.reuters.com/article/us-emirates-dubai-tourism-idUSKBN1ZK2L5

Robbins, M. (2021) "Is This China's Moment in MENA?" Arab Barometer, July 24. Available at: www.arabbarometer.org/2020/07/is-this-chinas-moment-in-mena/

Sidlo, K. et al. (2021) "The Role of China in the Middle East and North Africa. Beyond Economic Interests." EuroMeSCo, July 1. Available at: www.euromesco.net/publication/the-role-of-china-in-the-middle-east-and-north-africa-beyond-economic-interests/

Silver, L. et al. (2020) "People around the Globe Are Divided in Their Opinions of China." Pew Research Center, May 31. Available at: www.pewresearch.org/fact-tank/2019/12/05/people-around-the-globe-are-divided-in-their-opinions-of-china/

Sim, L. and Greer, L. (2021) "What Does the Arab Street Think of China and Russia? The Answers May Surprise You." Atlantic Council, June 17. Available at: www.atlanticcouncil.org/blogs/menasource/wha@'bn t-does-the-arab-street-think-of-china-and-russia-the-answers-may-surprise-you/

Xinhua (2017) "Belt and Road Incorporated into CPC Constitution." October 24. Available at: www.xinhuanet.com/english/2017-10/24/c_136702025.htm

Xinhua (2018) "优商业航天产业 打造太空丝绸之路-新华网." Available at: www.xinhuanet.com/money/2018-10/31/c_129983147.htm

Xinhua (2019) "人民日报:数字丝绸之路建设成为新亮点." Available at: www.xinhuanet.com/zgjx/2019-04/22/c_137997345.htm

Young, K. (2020) "China Is Not the Middle East's High Roller." Bloomberg, July 2. Available at: www.bloomberg.com/opinion/articles/2020-07-02/china-is-not-the-middle-east-s-high-roller

Zinser, S. (2020) "The Global Reach of China's Venture Capital." *The Diplomat*, January 25. Available at: thediplomat.com/2021/01/the-global-reach-of-chinas-venturecapital/

Zinser, S. and Wei, W. (2021) "China's Development Aims: More Nuanced than Soft Power." *Asia Global Online Journal*, April 15. Available at: www.asiaglobalonline.hku.hk/chinas-development-aims-more-nuanced-soft-power

郭晶、吴应辉 (2019) "孔子学院发展量化研究（2015~2017），*汉语国际教育发展报告（2015~2016），社会科学文献出版社.*" Beijing: Social Sciences Academic Press.

Zoubir, Y.H. and Tran, E. (2021) "China's Health Silk Road in the Middle East and North Africa Amidst COVID-19 and a Contested World Order." *Journal of Contemporary China*, 31(135): 335–350.

APPENDIX

China Medical Aid to the MENA States in the First Months of 2020

Compiled in Spring 2021 by Mr. N.G. Tin-chun (Chris), data analyst at the Comparative Governance and Policy Research Centre, Department of Government and International Studies, Faculty of Social Sciences, Hong Kong Baptist University, Hong Kong, with sincere thanks from the authors.

Appendix

MENA country	Health aid from China (2020-2021)	Chinese vaccines	Chinese vaccine testing on the population	Chinese vaccines production
Algeria	• First batch (worth $450,000) • 500,000 medical surgical masks • 50,000 N95 masks • 2,000 units of medical protective clothing, medical face masks, and respirators for intensive care • Announced to build a coronavirus protection hospital	• **Sinopharm** Donation: 200,000 doses		
Bahrain		• **Sinopharm** 300,000 doses purchased by Bahrain • **Sinovac** First batch	• **Sinopharm** Phase III clinical trial: 6,000 volunteers over the age of 18	
Djibouti	• Batches of medical supplies			

Egypt	• First batch (4 tons)
	• 20,000 N95 face masks
	• 10,000 articles of protective clothing
	• 10,000 coronavirus detectors (testing kit for COVID-19)
	• Second batch (440 boxes weighing 4.7 tons)
	• 10,000 N95 face masks
	• 10,000 protective suits
	• 70,000 nucleic acid detection reagents
	• Third batch (over 35 tons)
	• 1,000,000 medical surgical face masks
	• 180,000 N95 masks
	• 90,000 sets of medical protective clothing (Xinhuanet) // 70,000 sets of protective medical gowns (Zawya)
	• 80,000 testing reagents (Xinhuanet) // 70,000 coronavirus test kits (Zawya)
	• 70,000 pairs of disposable surgical gloves
	• 1,000 sets of thermometers
		• **Sinopharm**
		• First shipment
		• 350,000 doses in two batches (first batch of 50,000 doses from the UAE where were tested)
		• Second shipment as a donation from China: 300,000 doses
			• **Sinopharm/Sinovac**
			Phase III clinical trials of two Chinese vaccines: Some 6,000 people to participate
				• Sinovac Holding Company for Biological Products and Vaccines (VACSERA)

(continued)

MENA country	Health aid from China (2020-2021)	Chinese vaccines	Chinese vaccine testing on the population	Chinese vaccines production

Iran	• 250,000 masks
	• 5,000 kits to diagnose coronavirus
	• Announced sending of 20,000 laboratory kits to diagnose coronavirus cases
	• First batch along with the arrival of Chinese Red Cross delegation
	  • 50,000 test and diagnostic kits
	  • 13 respiratory machines
	• Medical materials donated to the Iranian armed forces
	  • Test kits
	  • Protective suits
	  • Medical masks
		• **Sinopharm**
		• [2021, February 28] First batch
		• 250,000 doses
		• [2021, April 15] Donation from Red Cross Society of China
		• 400,000 doses		

Iraq	• 50,000 COVID-19 test kits
	• "1,400,000 masks, protective clothing, and other pandemic protective materials"
		• **Sinopharm**: 50,000 doses
		  • First batch (donated by China): 50,000 doses
		  • Second batch: 200,000 doses		

Israel	• Donation by Jack Ma Foundation (numbers unspecified)
	  • Face masks
	  • Face shields
	  • Test kits
	  • Protective gears
	• First of 11 flights carrying donation of 20 tons of medical equipment from China (alongside goods purchased by Israel)
	  • 900,000 surgical masks
	  • 500,000 protective suits
		Pfizer-BioNTech		

	• 60 tons of medical gear produced by the Israeli firm Medical Sion in China
	  • 12,000,000 masks
	  • 1,300,000 N95 surgical masks
	  • 1,200,000 lab coats
	• Full charter by air with medical supplies from a large Chinese supplier via QUALITAIR&SEA, Germany
	  • 5,000,000 masks
	  • 2,000 thermometers
	  • 15,000 face shields		

Jordan	• [2020, June 1] $750,000 worth of medical supplies • 10,000 protective overalls • 60,000 masks • 10,000 protective glasses • 10,000 pairs of gloves • 200 infrared thermometers • 20,000 test strips	• **Sinopharm** • First batch: 196,000 doses	• **Sinopharm** • Phase III clinical trial: 500 volunteers

Kuwait	• [2020, April 8] Kuwaiti Army aircraft returned from China
	• 55 tons of medical supplies
	• [2020, May 4] Arrival of first of three shipments of medical supplies purchased from China
	  • 170 respirators
	  • Large amount of medical protective gears
		• **Pfizer-BioNTech**
		• **AstraZeneca**	

Lebanon	• 2 human temperature measuring instruments (placed at Beirut airport) • 600 medical protective goggles (to Lebanon's Health Ministry) • 3,000 PCR (polymerase chain reaction) testing kits • 200 manual thermometers	• **Sinopharm** • Two batches: 90,000 doses in total (50,000 to the Health Ministry; 40,000 earmarked for the military)	

(*continued*)

MENA country	Health aid from China (2020-2021)	Chinese vaccines	Chinese vaccine testing on the population	Chinese vaccines production

	• China's People's Liberation Army donation to the Lebanese army
	  • Surgical face masks
	  • Goggles
	  • Protective clothing
	  • Other medical supplies
	• New batch of donation
	  • 17,500 masks
	  • 1,500 protective gears
	  • 1,320 goggles
	  • 1,000 shoe covers			

Libya	• Medical shipment to Tripoli, the Government of National Accord (GNA)
	  • Medical supplies
	  • Protective equipment
	  • 834 nucleic acid diagnostic kits
	  • 5,000 medical protective suits
	  • 15,000 N95 masks
	  • 100,000 surgical masks
	  • 5,000 goggles
	  • 5,000 pairs of medical gloves
		• **Sinovac**
		• Batch from Turkey within the framework of mutual cooperation between two states: 150,000 doses		

Mauritania	• First batch of medical donation from the Jack Ma and Alibaba Foundations
	• A two-floor centre for treatment of infectious diseases built by China, several pavilions with:
	  • capacity of 30 beds
	  • large and medium-sized laboratories
	  • radiology equipment
		• **Sinopharm**
		First delivery donated by Chinese government: 50,000 doses		

Appendix

	Medical aid	Vaccines
	• Renovation of China-Mauritania Friendship Hospital, rehabilitation involving: • administrative buildings • a central pharmacy • multifunctional rooms • a personnel department • Medical equipment • Second batch of medical donation from Jack Ma and Alibaba Foundations • Respirators • Tests • Other medical equipment • Donation from the government of northwest China's Ningxia Hui Autonomous Region • 30,000 disposable medical masks • Donation along with the Chinese vaccine delivery and medical ventilators	
Morocco	• 15,000 pairs of medical gloves • 20,000 N95 masks • 2,000 medical protective suits • Chinese medical supplies • 4 flights carrying COVID-19 medical supplies from China • Donation from China Development Bank • 36 respirators • 98,000 masks	**Sinopharm** • First shipment: 500,000 doses • Second batch: 500,000 doses • Third batch: 500,000 doses • Fourth batch: 500,000 doses • Fifth shipment: 500,000 doses **Sinopharm** Phase III clinical trials (in Casablanca and Rabat): 600 volunteers to participate
Oman	• Personal protective items • Lab screening tests • Other medical devices • 100,000 masks • Testing kits • Masks • Protective clothing	**Pfizer-BioNTech** **AstraZeneca**

(continued)

Appendix

MENA country	Health aid from China (2020-2021)	Chinese vaccines	Chinese vaccine testing on the population	Chinese vaccines production
Qatar	• Ventilators • Emergency beds • Donation from the Bank of China QFC Branch to Qatar Charity • 90,000 pairs of medical gloves • 7,500 protective suits • 300 infrared thermometers	• **Pfizer-BioNTech** • **Moderna**		
Saudi Arabia	• Supplies donated by Ningxia Hui Autonomous regional government, along with a team of eight medical experts • Surgical masks • N95 masks • Protective clothing • Nucleic acid testing kits • Infrared thermometers • 9,000,000 COVID-19 test kits • To help build six large laboratories, including a mobile lab that can conduct 10,000 tests per day	• **Pfizer-BioNTech** • **AstraZeneca**		
Sudan	• Donation from Jack Ma and Alibaba Foundations • 2,000 laboratory diagnostic test kits • 100,000 medical masks • 1,000 protective suits • Donation from Chinese Embassy in Sudan to the Sudanese government • Over 400,000 surgical masks • New batch of medical supplies	• **Sinopharm** • First shipment of 250,000 doses		

Syria	• A deal signed with China's BGI • 2,016 COVID-19 test kits	**Sinopharm** • 150,000 doses
Tunisia	• N95 masks • Nucleic acid testing kits • Medical goggles • New shipment of medical supplies • Donation from the Chinese Ministry of Defence to the National Defence Department • Surgical and protective masks • Gloves • Protective visors • Protective clothing for health personnel • Resuscitation equipment • Infrared thermometers for remote temperature measurement • New batch of medical aid: 100,000 medical masks	**Chinese vaccine (Brand unspecified)**: 100,000 doses

Turkey	• 50,000 rapid detection kits
	• 300,000 rapid detection kits
	• Donation from Chinese companies and people
	  • 5,200 masks
	  • 5,000 surgical gowns
	  • 10,000 surgical hoods
	• First batch of donation from the Turkish branch of the Industrial and Commercial Bank of China (ICBC)
	  • Cash worth about US$100,000
	  • 1,200 sets of protective clothing
	  • 100 pairs of goggles
	  • 3,000 masks
		CoronaVac (Sinovac)
		• First batch: An initial consignment of 3,000,000 doses
		• First shipment of second batch: 6,500,000 doses
		• Second shipment of second batch: 3,500,000 doses
		• New batch: Number not disclosed
			Sinovac
			• Phase III clinical trials
			• First stage: 1,300 healthcare workers
			• Second stage: 10,216 participants of general population
			
			Sinovac
			• Provided licence to manufacturing the jabs

(continued)

MENA country	Health aid from China (2020-2021)	Chinese vaccines	Chinese vaccine testing on the population	Chinese vaccines production
United Arab Emirates	*UAE, like China, has been acting seemingly as one of the regional supplies of medical aid, rather than one of the recipients of Chinese donations*	**Sinopharm** • One of the three vaccine brands available	**Sinopharm** • Phase III clinical trials • 15,000 volunteers authorized to participate • 31,000 volunteers across 125 nationalities	• **Sinopharm (Hayat-Vax)** • Gulf Pharmaceutical Industries PSG (Julphar)
West Bank and Gaza	• Multiple batches of emergency medical supplies from China (numbers unspecified) • COVID-19 nucleic acid testing kits • Disposable medical protective gear • Protective goggles • Ventilators • N95 face masks	**Sinopharm** **Sinovac** was the brand donated by China • Donation by Chinese government to the Palestinian Authority o 100,000 doses		
Yemen	• [2020, July 15] Donation of a batch of medical supplies • [2021, January 17] Donation of medical equipment	**AstraZeneca**		

INDEX

Note: Figures are indicated by *italics*. Tables are indicated by **bold**. Endnotes are indicated by the page number followed by 'n' and the endnote number e.g., 176n2 refers to endnote 2 on page 176.

'1+2+3' cooperation model 1–2, 27, 58, 82, 93, 107, 117–118, 127, 179
5G network in Middle East 96

Abdullah bin Abdulaziz al-Saud, King 29
Afghanistan 12
Africa: health cooperation 243–244; *see also* individual countries
aging population in China 201
agriculture cooperation in Sudan 366
Alexander, Danny 141–143
Algeria: Belt and Road Initiative (BRI) 263; business governance in 262–263; corruption, Chinese companies and 268–269; debt trap, concerns over 269; employment practices 267–268; foreign direct investment (FDI) **264**, 264–267, **265**; French FDI in 265, **265**; health diplomacy to 243, 269; historical development of relations 258–260; increased engagement with 257; infrastructure construction 259–260; investment in 84; Italian FDI in 265, **265**; loans from China 269; Maritime Silk Route (MSR) 161; medical aid to **449**; nuclear cooperation 119; oil supply 259; problematic aspects of China's engagement with 267–269; public opinion on China's soft power 441–444, *442*, *443*, *444*, *445*; reforms needed to fulfill potential relations 257–258; relations with 208–209; security relations 259; trade relations 70, 83, 260–264, **261**, **262**, **263**; US FDI in 265, **265**; vaccine cooperation 247; view of China 257

Al Jaber, Ahmed, Sultan 143
al-Jaz, Awad Ahmed 365, 366
alternative energy technology 58–59; *see also* renewable energy
Amer, Magdy 70
Amman Declaration 35
anti-piracy missions 171–172
Arab Policy Paper (2016) 2, 27, 82, 93, 107, 127, 200, 244, 418, 437–438
Arab Spring 185
arms sales: increased 85; Iran 293, 300; Israel's, to China 312–313; to the Middle East 133; to Sudan 362, 366; Taiwan-Israel relations 328–329
Art, R.J. 176n2
artificial intelligence (AI) exports 133
Asian Infrastructure Investment Bank (AIIB) 47, 67; Beijing Consensus and 141; China's interests and 147–151; criticism of 147; development of 141–142; Egypt **145**; energy needs, China's 149; 'equality and mutual benefit' principle 150; financing of projects 142; inauguration of 141; infrastructure lending 146, 148–149; Islamic Development (IsDB) 144; Jordan 144, **145**; Middle Eastern members **143**; non-conditionality 150; non-resident directors 146; Oman 144–145, **145**, 146–147; overproduction in China 149; as platform for Middle Eastern countries 144, 146; projects in Middle East 142–147, **145**; United Arab Emirates (UAE) 142–143; US and Japan views on 142; votes distribution 141, 144
automobile manufacturing 56–57

Index

Bab al-Mandeb 161
Bahrain: medical aid to **449**; vaccine diplomacy 28
Baroody, Jamil 333
Bedell Smith, W. 310–311
Beidou Navigation Satellite System: aerospace institutions of Arab world 187–188; Arab Information and Communication Technology Organization (AICTO), ties with 180; Arab world, proposal for cooperation with 179; Belt and Road Initiative (BRI) 185–186; economic advantage 187; enrichment of 188; improvement of 189; international certification 189–190; introduction of Beidou to Arab world 188–190; laws and regulations 188; opportunities to enter Arab world 186–188; people-people relations 189; political advantages 186–187; promotion of overseas 190; Saudi Arabia 180; services to Arab states 180; strategic opportunities for 183–186; technical advantage 187
Beijing Consensus 140, 437
Beijing Su Power Technology Co. Ltd. 46
Belt and Road Initiative (BRI): Algeria 263; Beidou Navigation Satellite System 185–186; as boost for trade relations 15–16; China-Central Asia-West Asia Economic Corridor 377; "China's International Development Cooperation in the New Era" White Paper 374; conflict management in the Middle East 223; cultural relations and 275; currencies for trade 77; current projects 67; development, Chinese approach to 127, 129–130; energy diplomacy towards 33–35; expansion of global power, China's 66; extent of 65–66; factors behind 66; financial institutions 67; inauguration of 81; Iran 33–35, 294–295, *295*, 302; MENA countries' importance in 240; new markets as motivation for 66; nuclear cooperation 115; oil supply to China 26; Pakistan 294; Persian Gulf, China and US and 109; production capacity cooperation 52; railway infrastructure 373–381; routes 67; Saudi Arabia 29–32, 338; size of 294; Sudan 366–367, 368, 370; tourism and 413, 418; trade relations in West Asia and North Africa (WANA) region 68–73; Turkey 234, 373–381; US containment policy and 66; WANA region 68–78
Biden, Joe 92, 107–108
Bishop, R. 415
Blackwill, R. 156
Blanchard, J.F. 413
BRICS group 66
Bull, H. 171

Burton, Guy 95
business environment of Middle East 60
Buzan, B. 169

Calabrese, John 96
car manufacturing 56–57
Carter, Jimmy 105
China-Arab States Cooperation Forum (CASCF) 1, 118, 188, 286
China-Central Asia-West Asia Economic Corridor 377, 380–381
China Global Investment Tracker database 41
China Harbor (Egypt) Engineering Co. Ltd. 58
China National Offshore Oil Corporation (CNOOC) 33, 55
China National Petroleum Corp. (CNPC) 33, 35, 54–55
China Nuclear Engineering Group Corp. (CNEC) 30
China Petroleum & Chemical Corporation (Sinopec) 14, 33
China Railway Construction 57
"China's International Development Cooperation in the New Era" White Paper 193, 374, 437
China Vehicle Group 57
Chu Enlai *see* Zhou Enlai
cloud computing infrastructure 31
community of common destiny 242–243, 244
competition, US-China: arms sales 95–96; China's attitude towards region 92–93; geostrategic picture 94–95; global 89; New Cold War 90–91; or cooperation, dilemmas of 98; security-military 94–97; unchallenged, US as 94–95; unevenness in different regions 91; US attitude towards region 91–92
conflict management in the Middle East: 1950s-1970s 219–220; 1970s-2000s 220–221; 2011-onwards 221–224; American hegemony, ambivalence towards 221; avoidance of conflict by China 220–221; Belt and Road Initiative (BRI) 223; commercial interests 221; contribution to conflict by China 219–220; Darfur conflict, Sudan 221; defusing conflict 221–224; economic development and 223–224; insurgent groups, support for 219, 220; Iran-Iraq War 221; ISIS 222; Libya 221–222; mediation 85; peace through development paradigm 223–224; phases of China's approach 219–224; quasi-mediation 223; reasons for conflict 217; regional conflicts in MENA, neutrality of China in 2–3; rising powers and 218–219; Syria 222; third parties, role and motives of 217–218; US-Iran confrontation 222–223; vicious cycle of conflict 217
Confucius Institutes (CI) 20, **21**, 275, 441

Index

construction: Algeria 259–260; Egypt 283–284; *see also* infrastructure construction

corona pandemic *see* COVID-19 pandemic

corruption, Chinese companies in Algeria 268–269

counter-terrorism, Egypt 287

COVID-19 pandemic: aid provided to MENA states 241; aid sent to China from MENA states 245, 246; bilateral aid to contain 245–247; Egypt 287; EU aid for MENA states 249; evolution of MENA relations and 244; great power rivalry 134; impact on economic relations 84; medical aid to MENA countries **448–456**; MENA states' reactions to aid 247–248; Morocco 209–210; new world order and 242–243; non-strategic partners, aid to 246–247; propaganda tool, aid seen as 241; Saudi Arabia and 334, 345–349; Sinopharm vaccine 22; soft power, impact on 439–440; strategic partners, aid to 245–246; tourism and 419–420, 422; Tunisia 210; UAE and China 389; United Arab Emirates (UAE) 392, 393; vaccine diplomacy 28, 247, **448–456**; Western powers' reaction to health cooperation 248–249; *see also* health cooperation

Cressey, Laura 96

Cui, S. 169

cultural relations: Confucius Institute (CI) 20, **21**; economic/political interests as drivers 20; education 20, **21**, 22; Egypt 274–276; as foreign policy instrument 20; language education 20; Olympic Games 2008 22; overseas Chinese 410; people-people relations 20; Saudi Arabia 343–344; Shanghai Exhibition 2010 22; tourism 22; United Arab Emirates (UAE) 391–392

currencies for BRI trade 77

D'Amato, R. 313

Darfur conflict, Sudan 170–171, 221, 362–363

debt: Algeria 269; Egypt 283; Sudan 369

decentered globalism 169

defense industry *see* military presence/ cooperation

descriptive statistical analysis 42

development, Chinese approach to 126–130, 193

diasporic Chinese in MENA region *see* overseas Chinese

Digital Silk Road (DSR) 69

Dinarto, D. 141

Djibouti, medical aid to **449**

domestic goals as motivation for foreign policy 172

drones 85, 95–96

Eban, Abba 311

economic growth in China 140

economic relations: COVID-19 pandemic and 84; Egypt *276, 277, 278, 279, 280, 281, 282, 283*; Gulf states, China and 199–202; Iran 192–193; Iraq 192; Saudi Arabia 334–338; Sudan 364–366; tourism as economic statecraft 414–416, **416**; United Arab Emirates (UAE) 389–391; variance in economic linkages 192–193, 194–198, *195, 196*; *see also* trade relations

economic statecraft, tourism as 414–416, **416**

education: attitudes of Middle Eastern students in China 431–432; Chinese language, in Yemen and Saudi Arabia 428; Confucius Institutes (CI) 20, **21**, 275, 441; cultural relations and 20, **21**, 22, 275; development, Chinese approach to 128; Egypt 275; experiences of Middle Eastern students in China 429–431; financial support for in China 428; Middle Eastern students in China 20, 22, 426–433; military 300; overseas Chinese 409–410; preparation for China-based 428; Saudi Arabia 343–344; soft power and 440–441; Taiwan-Israel relations 322

Egypt: Asian Infrastructure Investment Bank (AIIB) **145**; conflict in the Middle East 219; construction 284; counter-terrorism 287; COVID-19 pandemic 245–246, 287–288; cultural relations with 274–276; debt trap, concerns over 284; development, Chinese approach to 128; development model, compared to China 284; doubt over relations with China 273; economic cooperation *276, 277, 278, 279, 280, 281, 282, 283*; education 276; employment 283; energy 285; exports to 70; foreign direct investment (FDI) *276*, 276–277, *277*; gross domestic product (GDP) 277–280, *278, 279*; health cooperation 287; history of relations with 273–274; as important partner 273; investment in 83–84, 162–163; Jushi Egypt Business Group 283; medical aid to **449**; nuclear cooperation 119; Persian Gulf 107, 108–109; political relations 285–287; presidential visits 285–286; public opinion on China's soft power 441–444, *442, 443, 444, 445*; stability, China's concern for 286; Suez Canal 162; trade relations 83, 173, 279–283, *280, 281, 282*; UAE-China cooperative project in 391; vaccine cooperation 247

electric vehicle manufacturing 57

emerging space-time hot spot analysis 42

employment: Algeria 267–268; Egypt 283; *see also* overseas Chinese

encirclement, fear of 11

Index

energy sector: Algeria 208; Asian Infrastructure Investment Bank (AIIB) 149; changes in approach 25; discovery of oil in Saudi Arabia 147; Egypt 283; Gulf states, China and 200–201; imports 13–14, *16*, *17*, 64–65; Iran 25, 32–35, **34**, *297*, 299; Mediterranean Sea 158; new energy industry 58–59; nuclear energy, Saudi Arabia and 31; oil supply, 1990s to BRI era 26–28, *27*, *28*; Oman 27; Persian Gulf, China and US and 106, *107*; petroleum engineering technology services 56; production capacity cooperation 54–56; production/consumption *13*, **15**; reliance on Greater Middle East 14; Saudi Arabia 25, 27, 28–32, 334–338; security 157, 161; significance of MENA region for 81–82; Sudan 361–362, 365, 366; Taiwan 321; United Arab Emirates (UAE) 390–391; *see also* nuclear cooperation

'equality and mutual benefit' principle 150

equipment manufacturing 57–58

Ethiopia: Chinese workers in 173; gas sector 173

Europe: Algeria, trade relations with 260–261, **262**, **263**; counterbalance to in Maghreb region, China as 210–212; COVID-19 aid for MENA states 249; FDI in Algeria 265, **265**; Morocco, China's ties with 209; reaction to COVID-19 health cooperation 248, 249; satellite navigation systems 186; view of China's increased security role 87

Ferguson, V. 415

Fisher, Jr., R.D. 313

5G network in Middle East 96

Five Principles of Peaceful Coexistence 2, 82

foreign direct investment (FDI): Algeria **264**, 264–267, **265**; China and 202; Egypt *276*, 276–277, *277*, 277–279; growth of 83–84; Iran 298–299, **299**; Jordan 198; Morocco **266**; Saudi Arabia 195; Sudan 365, **365**; Tunisia **266**; United Arab Emirates (UAE) 195, 197–198, 388, 390

foreign policy, China's: accusations against 126; development, approach to 126–130; historic aspects of 125

Forum on China Africa Cooperation (FOCAC) 1, 285

Fulton, J. 107

Fung, C. 131

Gamar-Eddin, Omer 247–248

Garlick, J. 25

gas sector: Ethiopia 173; Gulf states, China and 192, 200–201; production capacity cooperation 54–56; United Arab Emirates (UAE) 390; *see also* energy sector

Gaza, medical aid to **456**

geo-economic actor, China as 158, 159–160

geoeconomics: Algeria 161; defined 156; energy security 157; global maritime trade and investment 156–157; instruments of 156; Maghreb region 160–161; Mediterranean Sea 158–161; Morocco 160–161; Turkey 158–159

Ghana, nuclear cooperation and 120

Goldstein, Lyle 98

Greater Middle East relations: Economic Reform Era 12; education 20, **21**, 22; energy cooperation 14; growth in trade relations 15, **18**–**19**; Gulf War 12; Islam, advent and rise of 9–11; Islam and 9; national liberation movements, support of 11; Silk Road 9, 10; status quo orientation 11–12, 13; tourism 22; World War II and post-WWII 11

Greater Nile Petroleum Operating Company (GNPOC) 55

great power: China's ambition for 155–156; rivalry 133–134; status 168–169

gross domestic product (GDP) of Egypt and China 277–279, *278*, *279*

Gulf states, China and: finance provision 199; future for economic relations 199–202; oil and gas exporters 192; partnership agreements 193–194; US and 201; variance in economic linkages 192–193, 194–198, *195*, *196*; *see also* Persian Gulf, China and US and; individual countries

Gulf War 12

Hacohen, D. 310, 312

Hajj-related travel to Saudi Arabia 344–346, 409

Hamzelou, Reza 71

Hariri, Majid-Reza 71

Harris, J. 156

Havlová, R. 25

health cooperation: Africa 243–244; Algeria 243, 269; bilateral aid to contain COVID-19 245–247; community of common destiny 242–243, 244; Egypt 286–287; evolution of MENA relations and 244; great power rivalry 134; history 243; Mauritania 243; MENA states' reactions to 247–248; non-strategic partners, COVID-19 health aid to 246–247; as part of Belt and Road Initiative (BRI) 2; as propaganda tool 241; Saudi Arabia 345–349; South-South cooperation 243–244; strategic partners, COVID-19 health aid to 245–246; UAE and China 389; vaccine diplomacy 28, 209–210, 247, 346–349, **448**–**456**; Western powers' reaction to 248–249; *see also* COVID-19 pandemic

hegemony theory 150

Hieran-Nia, J. 35
higher education: cultural relations and 20, **21**, 22; Egypt 275; Middle Eastern students in China 20, 22, 426–433; overseas Chinese 409–410
Horesh, N. 133
Huajin Aramco Petrochemical Co. 30–31
Huawei 337
Huawei's 5G network in Middle East 96
Hu Jintao 29, 435
hydroelectric power 59

Ikenberry, J.G. 169, 172
India 66, 110, 186
Indian Ocean 157, 161
industrialization in the Middle East 53–54
industrial park-port interconnection 108
infrastructure construction: 2005-2009 phase *43*, 43–45, *44*; 2010-2012 45; 2013-2016 45–46; 2017-2019 46–47; achievements of 47–48; Algeria 259–260; Asian Infrastructure Investment Bank (AIIB) 146; bodies involved 44, 45, 46, 47; challenges of 48–50; cooperation agreements 48; data sources for research on 41–42; financing 45, 46, 47; global 40–41; history of, China's 40; hot spot areas 44, 45, 47; instability of Middle Eastern countries 49; Iran 301; legal risks 49; Middle East 41–50, *43*, *44*; new projects 198; Oman 148–149; political risks 49; private enterprises' involvement 46, 47; public opinion and 49–50; research methods used 42–43; Saudi Arabia 336–337; security risks 49; spatial distribution 43–44, 45–46, 47; state-owned enterprises (SOEs) 44, 45; types of 42, 44, 45, 46, 47; *see also* railway infrastructure
Infrastructure Investment Bank (IIB) 66
Inpex 33
instability of Middle Eastern countries: infrastructure construction 49; production capacity cooperation 59–60; *see also* stability
insurgent groups, support for 219
international business environment, understanding of 60
international government organizations (OGOs) 170
investment in MENA region: growth of 83–84; *see also* foreign direct investment (FDI)
Iran: 25-year Cooperation Agreement 301; agreement with, 2021 102; Belt and Road Initiative (BRI) 294–295, *295*, 302; bilateral trade with 69–71; connectivity 301–302; COVID-19 health aid to 246; delegation from China 2016 301; development, Chinese approach to 128; development of relations with China 297; economic linkages 192–193;

energy 25, 32–35, **34**, 295–296, *297*, 299; exports 295–296; financial resources 298–299, **299**; foreign direct investment (FDI) 298–299, **299**; infrastructure construction 301; Iran-Iraq War 221, 293; Islamic Revolution, China and 292–293; knowledge/technology transfer to 300; as linchpin state 292; medical aid to **450**; membership of SCO 301; military supplies to 293; monitoring of relationship 94–95; nuclear cooperation 32–33, 118–119; oil and gas supply 33, 295–296; Persian Gulf, China and US and 106–107, 110–111; population 292; relations with China 148; security relations 73, 300–301; size and borders of 292; steel manufacturing equipment 58; strategic partnership with 194; strategy towards 293–294; tensions with Saudi Arabia 30; trade relations 83, 297; trustworthy ally, China as 297–298
Iraq: development, Chinese approach to 129; economic linkages 192; Iran-Iraq War 221, 293; medical aid to **450**; oil exports to China 70; Persian Gulf, China and 106–107; trade relations 83
ISIS 222
Islam: advent and rise of 9–11; Hajj-related travel to Saudi Arabia 344–346, 409; Taiwan 321; Uyghur-Muslim minority, treatment of 22
Islamic Development (IsDB) 144
Israel: Americans, impact on relation with China 309–313; Arabs, impact on relation with China 306–308; arms sales to China 312–313; Biden's visit, 2022 107–108; COVID-19 health aid to 246; development, Chinese approach to 128; distance separating from China 305; infrastructure cooperation agreement 48; investment in 83, 95; Jews in China, history of 305–306; Maritime Silk Route (MSR) 158, 159–160; medical aid to **450–451**; Persian Gulf, China and 107; PRC, relations with 306; recognition of by China 306; relations with China 148; Russians, impact on relation with China 308–309; security of, US and 105; security ties with 74; trilateral constraints on relations 305; *see also* Taiwan-Israel relations

Japan: Asian Infrastructure Investment Bank (AIIB) 142; satellite navigation systems 186
Jews in China, history of 305–306
JinkoSolar 59
Jin Liqun 141, 144, 151–152
Joint Comprehensive Plan of Action (JCPOA) 33–34

Index

Jordan: Asian Infrastructure Investment Bank (AIIB) 144, **145**; foreign direct investment (FDI) in 198; medical aid to **451**; nuclear cooperation 120; reactions to COVID-19 aid 247
Jushi Egypt Business Group 283

Kamrava, M. 129
Kawai, M. 142
Kennan, G. 104–105
Kenya, nuclear cooperation and 120
Khanna, P. 149
Kuwait: Belt and Road Initiative (BRI) 16; infrastructure cooperation agreement 48; medical aid to **451**
Kwan, G. 30

labor resources and costs 54
Lake, D.A. 169, 172
language education 20
latent power, China as 111–112, 132
Lebanon: medical aid to **451–452**; reactions to COVID-19 aid 248
legal risks in infrastructure construction 49
Leverett, F. 33
Leverett, H.M. 33
liberal world order 103–104
Libya: conflict management in the Middle East 221–222; engagement with 207–208; medical aid to **452**; security relations 172–175; stability, China's concern for 285–286
Lieberthal, Kenneth 91
Lim, D. 415
Lim, K. 133

Maçães, B. 158
Mackinder, Halford 105
Maghreb region: Algeria, relations with 208–209; as counterbalance to EU 210–212; FDI to 265; growth of engagement with 207–208; increased engagement with 205; Maritime Silk Route and 160–161; Morocco, relations with 209–210; motives for cooperation 205; no-strings attached approach 206; reactions to COVID-19 aid 248; South-South relations 206–208, 209, 210; Tunisia, relations with 210; *see also* individual countries
Mali 173
Malloy, James 97
Maritime Silk Route (MSR): Algeria 161; energy security 157; geoeconomics 156–157; Israel 158, 159–160; Maghreb region 160–161; Mediterranean Sea 158–161; Morocco 160–161; security and trade as interwoven 155; Southwest Asia 161–163; Tunisia 160; Turkey 158–159

Mastanduno, M. 169, 172
Mauritania: engagement with 207; health cooperation in 243; medical aid to **452–453**
McKenzie, K. 97, 133
mediation of conflicts 85; *see also* conflict management in the Middle East
medical aid to MENA countries **448–456**; *see also* health cooperation
Mediterranean Sea 158–161
MENA region: growth in relations with 1–4; *see also* individual countries
Middle Corridor Initiative 377–379, 380–381
Middle East: early phase of relations with 81; infrastructure construction 41–50, *43*, *44*; oil supply to China 26–28, *27*, *28*; production capacity cooperation 52–62; *see also* individual countries
Milan, F.F. 96
military presence/cooperation 20; anti-piracy missions 171–172; education and training 300; exports to West Asia and North Africa 73–74; increased sales 85; Iran 293; Israel's arms sales to China 312–313; overseas facilities 174; peacekeeping operations 173–175; recognition game, China's 169–172; Sudan, exports to 362, 366; Taiwan-Israel relations 321–327, 328–329; troops, deployment of 3; West Asia and North Africa 65
mining in Sudan 366
Modelski, G. 156
Monshipouri, M. 35
Morocco: COVID-19 health aid to 246; FDI to 265, **266**; foreign direct investment (FDI) **266**; Maritime Silk Route (MSR) 160–161; medical aid to **453**; Nouao Power Station project 59; reactions to COVID-19 aid 248; relations with 209–210; trade relations 209
Moyer, J.D. 75
multipolarity in the Middle East 186

Nathan, A.J. 168
national liberation movements, support of 11
navies, blue-water 156
navigation satellite system *see* Beidou Navigation Satellite System
New Development Bank 67
new energy industry 58–59
New Silk Road and the new Maritime Silk Road *see* Belt and Road Initiative (BRI)
new world order 103–104
Nigeria, nuclear cooperation in 120
Nixon, Richard, visit in 1971 220
non-conditionality 150
non-intervention in internal affairs 72, 104, 125, 130–133, 368, 437
non-polarity, dawn of 76

Index

Norris, W. 415
North Africa region: Belt and Road Initiative (BRI) 64–78; early phase of relations with 81; *see also* individual countries
Nouao Power Station project, Morocco 59
nuclear cooperation: Algeria 119; Belt and Road Initiative (BRI) 115; China's nuclear technology 116–117; civil exports to MENA region 117–122; Egypt 119; Ghana 120; interest in 20; Iran 32–33, 118–119; Jordan 120; Kenya 120; Nigeria 120; One Belt, One Road (OBOR) 117; proliferation 133; Saudi Arabia 31, 119; Sudan 119–120, 366; Taiwan-Israel relations 321–324; Uganda 120; USA 115; US civil nuclear policy towards MENA 120–122
Nye, J. 435

Obama, Barack 91
oil sector: 1990s to BRI era 26–28, *27, 28*; Algeria 208, 259; dependence on, reduction of 148; development of 147; Gulf states, China and 192; Iran 32, 33, 295–296; Mediterranean Sea 158; Oman 27; production capacity cooperation 54–56; Saudi Arabia 27, 28–32, 334–338; Sudan 361–362, 365; Taiwan 321; transport routes 157; United Arab Emirates (UAE) 390; *see also* energy sector
Olympic Games 2008 22
Oman: Asian Infrastructure Investment Bank (AIIB) 144–145, **145**, 146–147; Belt and Road Initiative (BRI) 16; COVID-19 health aid to 246; development, Chinese approach to 129; infrastructure construction 148–149; medical aid to **453**; oil supply to China 27; reactions to COVID-19 aid 248; tourism 418–419, *419*
'1+2+3' cooperation model 1–2, 27, 58, 82, 93, 107, 117–118, 127, 179
One Belt, One Road (OBOR): nuclear cooperation 117; *see also* Belt and Road Initiative (BRI)
overseas business environment, understanding of 60
overseas Chinese: China's state policies regarding 406; cultural relations 410; education 409–410; heterogeneity of 402; history of Chinese emigration 402–403; identity, Chinese 405; in MENA region 402–405, **406**; political-economic analysis of 407; research agenda 405–410; role of for Chinese state 401; size of population 401, 402; spatial characteristics 407; studying, benefits of 402; transnationality of 408–409; United Arab Emirates (UAE) 407

Pakistan: Belt and Road Initiative (BRI) 294; development, Chinese approach to 128
Palestine: COVID-19 health aid to 246; reactions to COVID-19 aid 248
Pandian, D.J. 143
Pang Sen 30
partnership agreements 82, 93, 107, 193–194
peacekeeping operations, growth of engagement in 173–175
peace with development 129
people-people relations 20; Beidou Navigation Satellite System 189; Saudi Arabia 343–344; *see also* education; overseas Chinese; tourism
People's Republic of China (PRC), Arab and Islamic countries and 10–11
Persian Gulf, China and US and: Belt and Road Initiative (BRI) 109; China 106–108; connectivity ambitions of China 108–109; containment of Russia 104–105, 106; Egypt 108–109; energy 107; increased engagement by China 103; Iran 102, 110–111; latent power of China 111–112; partnership agreements with China 107; Saudi Arabia 105–106, 108; seaports, investment in 109; security measures 109; speculation about US role 102–103; UAE 108; USA 104–106, 112; *see also* Gulf states, China and; individual countries
petroleum engineering technology services 56
polarity, non-, dawn of 76
political relations: Egypt 285–287; Sudan 364; United Arab Emirates (UAE) 388–389
political risks: infrastructure construction 49; production capacity cooperation 59–60; West Asia and North Africa 75
politics in West Asia and North Africa 77
population aging in China 201
production capacity cooperation: aims of 52; automobile manufacturing 56–57; Belt and Road Initiative (BRI) 52; business environment 60; challenges of 59–61; characteristics of 54–59; commitment to 53; energy industry 54–56; equipment manufacturing 57–58; facilitation of 61; financial risks 60; industrialization in the Middle East 53–54; instability of Middle Eastern countries 59–60; labor resources and costs 54; Middle East 52–62; motivation for with Middle East 53–54; new energy industry 58–59; political risks 59–60; security relations 59
public opinion on China's soft power 441–444, *442, 443, 444, 445*

Qatar: bilateral trade with 68; legal risks of infrastructure construction 49; LNG exports to China 64–65; medical aid to **454**; soft power 436

railway infrastructure: challenges faced by 380–381; in China 375–376; China-Central Asia-West Asia Economic Corridor 377, 380–381; economic development and 374–376; equipment 57–58; high-speed railways (HSR) 375–376; infrastructure connectivity 374; in MENA region 376; Middle Corridor Initiative 377–379; Saudi Arabia 337; Turkey 376–381; United Arab Emirates (UAE) 390

Raiser, M. 376

recognition game, China's 169–172

Red Sea 162, 163

regional conflicts in MENA, neutrality of China in 2–3

Reilly, J. 414

religion: cultural relations with Egypt and 275–276; soft power and 439; *see also* Islam

renewable energy 129; Saudi Arabia 70; solar power 390–391; technology 58–59; United Arab Emirates (UAE) 390–391

'rentier state' model 103–104

Republic of China (ROC) *see* Taiwan-Israel relations

Responsibility to Protect (R2P) 131

rivalry, US-China: arms sales 95–96; China's attitude towards region 92–93; geostrategic picture 94–95; global 89; New Cold War 90–91; or cooperation, dilemmas of 97; security-military 94–97; unchallenged, US as 94–95; unevenness in different regions 91; US's attitude towards region 91–92

Russia: containment of 104–105, 106; impact on China-Israel relations 308–309; satellite navigation systems 186; world order and 104

Saied, Kais 248

Salman bin Abdulaziz Al Saud, King 29–30

satellite navigation system *see* Beidou Navigation Satellite System

Saudi Arabia: Beidou Navigation Satellite System 180; Belt and Road Initiative (BRI) 16, 338; Biden's visit, 2022 107–108; bilateral trade with 68–69; changes in relations with China 333–334; Chinese language education 428; cloud computing infrastructure 31; COVID-19 pandemic 334, 345–349; cultural ties 343–344; dependence on oil, reduction of 148; development, Chinese approach to 127–128; digital products and services 337–338; Digital Silk Road (DSR) 69; discovery of oil in 147; economic ties 334–338; energy 334–338; energy diplomacy towards 25, 28–32; fiscal deficit 60; foreign direct investment (FDI) in 195; Hajj-related travel 344–346, 409; health cooperation 345–349; infrastructure construction 336–337; investment in 83; medical aid to **454**; new diplomatic framework 338–343; nuclear cooperation 119; nuclear energy plan 31; oil supply 334–338; Persian Gulf, China and US and 108; privatization program 31; relations with China 148; renewable energy technology 59, 70; security ties with 73; soft power 436; stability of, US and 105–106; tensions with ran 30; tourism 344; trade relations 83; transportation sector 336–337; UN, China's membership of 333; vaccines from China, refusal of 346–349; Vision 2030 334, 337

Saudi Basic Industries Corp (SABIC) 29

science and technology, China's image and 184

Scobell, A. 168

seaports, investment in 109

security relations: active role taken in 18–19; Algeria 259; anti-piracy missions on coast of Somalia 171–172; arms sales, increased 85; Darfur conflict, Sudan 170–171; education and training 300; growing role of China 80; importance of 17–20; increased role, China's 84–85, 86; influence of China on security 133; infrastructure construction 49; Iran 300–301; level of, China and 286; Libya 172–175; mediation of conflicts 85; military industry 20; nuclear cooperation 20; peacekeeping operations 173–175; Persian Gulf, China and US and 109, 110–111; production capacity cooperation 59; recognition game, China's 169–172; rivalry, US-China 94–97; and trade as interwoven 155; US and 80–81; West Asia and North Africa 65, 73–74; *see also* military presence/cooperation

Shambaugh, D. 168

Shanghai Cooperation Organization (SCO) 301

Shanghai Exhibition 2010 22

She, G. 94

Shinn, D.H. 243

Silk Road: Islam, advent and rise of 10; origins of 9; security relations 17

Silk Road Fund 47, 70

Sinopharm vaccine 22

Sinosteel Equipment 58

'soft military footprints' 97

soft power: brand, China's in the MENA 436–438; China's interpretation of 435–436; COVID-19 pandemic, impact of 439–440; defined 435; economic factors influencing 438–439; education and 440–441; limitations on 439–440; media-related factors 439; public opinion on 441–444, *442*, *443*, *444*, *445*; religion and 439; use of 3–4; Xinjiang region in China 440

solar power 58–59, 390–391

Index

Somalia, anti-piracy missions on coast of 171–172
Southern Sudan 363
South-South relations: health diplomacy 243–244; Maghreb region 206–208
Southwest Asia, Maritime Silk Route (MSR) and 161–163
sovereignty, respect for 72, 104, 368
Soviet Union, invasion of Afghanistan 12
SP11 project 35
space cooperation: aerospace institutions of Arab world 187–188; documents and projects 170–180; timeline for **181–183**; *see also* Beidou Navigation Satellite System
space-time cube analysis 42
stability: China's concern for 285–286; in the Middle East, China and 126
status quo orientation 11–12
steel manufacturing equipment 58
Strait of Gibraltar 160
Strait of Hormuz 161
Strauss, J.C. 208
Sudan: 2011-2019 364–367, **365**; agriculture cooperation 366; arms imports from China 362, 366; Bashir as point of continuity 363; Belt and Road Initiative (BRI) 366–367, 368, 370; complexity of relations with 369–370; Darfur conflict 170–171, 221, 362–363; debt, politics of 369; economic relations 364–366; energy cooperation 365, 366; foreign direct investment (FDI) 365, **365**; foreign policy, China's, support for 366; historical context for relations with 361–363; lifting of sanctions on, China and 367; medical aid to **454**; milestones in relations with 360; mining 366; National Islamic Front (NIF) coup 361; non-intervention in internal affairs 131; nuclear cooperation 119–120, 366; number of Chinese workers and companies in 171; oil sector 361–362; political ties 364; post-Bashir transition 368–370; rail transportation equipment 57–58; reactions to COVID-19 aid 247–248; recognition game, China's 169–172; revolution of 2019 367–368; secession of Southern Sudan 363; Strategic Partnership 2015 364, 365
Suez Canal 161, 162, 163
Sun, D. 2–3, 107, 111–112, 223
Suzuki, S. 168–169
swaggering 172, 176n2
Syria: conflict management in the Middle East 222; COVID-19 health aid to 245–246; medical aid to **455**; non-intervention in internal affairs 131–132; reactions to COVID-19 aid 248

Tabrizi, A.B. 96
Taiwan and UAE-China relations 386

Taiwan-Israel relations: arms sales 321–327, 328–329; as bilateral paradox 330; education 322; institutional unofficial relations 327–329; leaders of ROC, attitudes of 317; limitations of studies of 317; military presence/cooperation 321–327, 328–329; non-institutional unofficial relations 321–327; nuclear cooperation 321–324; recognition of Taiwan by Israel 319; reserved, ROC attitudes as 317–318; similarities between 318; unofficial relations 319–321
Tammen, R.L. 75
technology, China's image and 184; *see also* Beidou Navigation Satellite System
Thompson, W.R. 156
Tiananmen Square Massacre 12
Total 35
tourism: Approved Destination Status (ADS) list 415, **416**, 417; Arab Policy Paper 2016 418; Belt and Road Initiative (BRI) 413, 418; control of outbound, from China 416, **416**, 422; COVID-19 pandemic and 419–420, 422; cultural relations and 22; data gathering related to 421–422; development, Chinese approach to 128; domestic/international 422; as economic statecraft 414–416, **416**; Egypt 417–418; future of, research and 421; Greater Middle East relations 22; Hajj-related travel 344–346, 409; as % of exports 420, **420**; Oman 418–419, *419*; religious 344–346, 409, 436; Saudi Arabia 344; trends *417*, 417–418, *418*, 421–422; United Arab Emirates (UAE) 391, 418–419
trade relations: Algeria 208, 260–264, **261**, **262**, **263**; Beidou Navigation Satellite System 187; China as welcomed 82; currencies for BRI trade 77; development, approach to 127; Egypt 173, 279–283, *281*, *282*, *283*; global maritime trade and investment 156–157; growth in **18–19**, 83; Morocco 209; railway cooperation and 374–376; and security as interwoven 155; United Arab Emirates (UAE) 386, *387*, *388*, 389–391; value of bilateral trade 65; West Asia and North Africa 68–73; *see also* energy sector; tourism
transnationality of overseas Chinese 408–409
transportation sector: Saudi Arabia 336–337; *see also* railway infrastructure
Trump, Donald 92, 134, 248–249
Tunisia: FDI to 265, **266**; foreign direct investment (FDI) **266**; Maritime Silk Route (MSR) 160; medical aid to **455**; reactions to COVID-19 aid 248; relations with 210
Turkey: Belt and Road Initiative (BRI) 234; China-Central Asia-West Asia Economic Corridor 377; development, Chinese approach to 128–129; historical

465

ties with Uyghurs 229–230; infrastructure cooperation agreement 48; Maritime Silk Route (MSR) 158–159; medical aid to **455**; Middle Corridor Initiative 377–379; overseas employees 60; rail transportation equipment 57; railway cooperation 373–381; reactions to COVID-19 aid 247; security ties with 73–74; steel manufacturing equipment 58; Uyghur-Muslim minority in China, treatment of 229–237

Uganda, nuclear cooperation and 120
Ukraine, Russian invasion of 108
United Arab Emirates (UAE): Asian Infrastructure Investment Bank (AIIB) 142–143; Belt and Road Initiative (BRI) 16; bilateral trade with 64, 68; cooperation fund 387; COVID-19 pandemic 389, 392, 393; cultural relations 391–392; development, Chinese approach to 128; development of relations with 385–388, *387, 388*; economic cooperation 2019-2021 389–391; energy sector 390–391; foreign direct investment (FDI) 195, 197–198, 388, 390; Huawei's investment in 96; investment in 83; medical aid to **456**; online cooperative activities 392; overseas Chinese 407; Persian Gulf, China and US and 108; political cooperation 2019-2021 388–389; proposed naval facility 95; public opinion on China's soft power 441–444, *442, 443, 444, 445*; railway infrastructure 390; reactions to COVID-19 aid 247; renewable energy 58–59, 390–391; scientific/technological cooperation 392–393; security ties with 73; soft power 436; Strategic Partnership (2012-2018) 387–388; third countries, cooperative projects in 391; tourism 391, 418–419; trade relations 83, 386, *387*, 388, *388*, 389–391; transnationality of overseas Chinese 408–409; vaccine diplomacy 28
United Nations, membership of Security Council 11–12
United States: Algeria, trade relations with 260, 261, **262**; Asian Infrastructure Investment Bank (AIIB) 142; civil nuclear policy towards MENA 120–122; containment policy, BRI as response to 66; COVID-19 aid for MENA states 249; FDI in Algeria 265, **265**; GPS in the Middle East 185; Gulf states, China and 201; hegemony of, China's ambivalence towards 221; hegemony theory 150; impact on China-Israel relations 309–313; nuclear cooperation 115; Persian Gulf 104–106; reaction to COVID-19 health cooperation 248–249; rivalry in MENA region 4, 89–98;

role in MENA, China's view on 86; satellite navigation systems 186; security relations in MENA region 80–81; threat, China as 194; view of China's increased security role 87; *see also* Persian Gulf, China and US and
Unmanned Aerial Vehicles (UAVs) 85, 95–96
Uyghur-Muslim minority in China 440; Arab/ Muslim states and 112; China-MENA relations and 228–229; historical ties with Turkey 229–230; intensification of Sino-Turkish relations 234–236; post-Cold War, Turkey and 230–231; responses to treatment of 22; Turkey and 229–237; Ürümchi riots, aftermath of, Turkey and 232–234

vaccine diplomacy 28, 209–210, 247, **448–456**; Saudi Arabia 346–349; tourism and 421; UAE 389; United Arab Emirates (UAE) 393
vehicle manufacturing 56–57

Wang Yi 48, 244
Wang Zemin 149–150
Washington Consensus 140
West Asia and North Africa (WANA) region: assets, China's 74–75; Belt and Road Initiative (BRI) 68–78; challenges for China 75; decreased exports to US 76–77; history of China's involvement with 76; interest in, China's 76; politics and 75, 77; security ties with 73–74; trade relations 68–73; *see also* individual countries
West Bank, medical aid to **456**
Womack, B. 133
world order, new 103–104
World War II/post-WWII: foreign policy and 11; security relations 18–19

Xi Jingping 1, 27, 30, 40–41, 58, 68, 117, 127, 140, 141, 150, 242, 244, 394n4
Xinjiang region in China 440; *see also* Uyghur-Muslim minority in China

Yanbu Aramco Sinopec Refinery (YASREF) 29, 30
Yemen: Chinese language education 428; integration of aid and development 132; medical aid to **456**
Yingli Solar 46
Yuliantoro, N.R. 141

'zero-enemy policy' 2–3
Zhang, S.G. 415
Zhang Jun 246
Zhang Xiaodong 29
Zhang Zhexin 109
Zhou Enlai 11, 18, 20, 319
Zoubir, Y. H. 111–112, 223